TABLE OF CONTENTS

Chapter 5 - Logarithms

Chapter 6 - Trigonometry, Part I

Chapter 7 - Trigonometry, Part II

Chapter 8 - Conics (Enriched Option)

THEORY AND PROBLEMS

FOR

PRE-CALCULUS 12

SECOND EDITION

CRESCENT BEACH PUBLISHING

R. J. MICKELSON

Author: R. J. Mickelson

Editors: Ken Borrie, Surrey School District #36, Surrey BC (Retired)
Gretchen McConnell, Math Tutorial Services, Surrey BC
Harbhajan Sangha, M.Sc. Mathematics, Surrey BC

Design: Vince Vachon, Carpe Diem New Publishing, Victoria BC

Photography: Mel Yap, http://eastvanguard.com

Publisher: Crescent Beach Publishing
12675 Beckett Road
Surrey, BC Canada V4A 2W9

Phone: 604 538-5494
Fax: 604 538-5454
E-mail: rjmickelson@telus.net
Website: crescentbeachpublishing.ca

Theory and Problems for Pre-Calculus 12 - 2nd Edition

ISBN 978-0-9878444-3-9
Copyright Registration Number 1072409

Other Publications:

Theory and Problems for Mathematics 8 - 3rd Edition	ISBN 978-0-9878444-4-6
Theory and Problems for Mathematics 9 - 3rd Edition	ISBN 978-0-9878444-5-3
Theory and Problems for Foundations of Math/Pre-Calculus 10 - 3rd Edition	ISBN 978-0-9878444-6-0
Theory and Problems for Foundations of Mathematics 11 - 2nd Edition	ISBN 978-0-9878444-0-8
Theory and Problems for Pre-Calculus 11 - 2nd Edition	ISBN 978-0-9878444-1-5

WNCP editions are available for all books.

Printed in Canada, June 2019.

For Ann. We could not have done this without you.

1.1 Arithmetic Sequences

A **sequence** is simply a list of numbers. In a sequence each number is called a **term** of the sequence. There is a first term, second term, third term, and so on. A sequence can be **finite**, in which it is possible to count the number of terms, or **infinite**, in which the terms continue forever.

For example: 1, 3, 6, 10 is a finite sequence
1, 3, 6, 10, ... is an infinite sequence

A sequence is a function whose domain is a set of positive integers. However, a sequence is written using subscript notation rather than function notation.

For example: $a_1, a_2, a_3, ..., a_n$

The subscript identifies the term of the sequence. For instance a_3 is the third term, and a_n is the nth term of the sequence. The entire sequence is usually denoted by $\{a_n\}$.

Sequence

A **finite sequence** is a function for which the domain is the subset of natural numbers: $\{1, 2, 3, ..., n\}$ for some finite number n.

An **infinite sequence** is a function for which the domain is the set of natural numbers: $\{1, 2, 3, ...\}$.

Example 1 Write the first four terms of the sequence.

a) $a_n = \dfrac{n+1}{n}$

b) $b_n = 2n - 3$

c) $t_n = 2^n$

► *Solution*: **a)** $a_1 = \dfrac{1+1}{1} = 2,\ a_2 = \dfrac{2+1}{2} = \dfrac{3}{2},\ a_3 = \dfrac{3+1}{3} = \dfrac{4}{3},\ a_4 = \dfrac{4+1}{4} = \dfrac{5}{4}$

b) $b_1 = 2(1) - 3 = -1,\ b_2 = 2(2) - 3 = 1,\ b_3 = 2(3) - 3 = 3,\ b_4 = 2(4) - 3 = 5$

c) $t_1 = 2^1 = 2,\ t_2 = 2^2 = 4,\ t_3 = 2^3 = 8,\ t_4 = 2^4 = 16$

Another way of defining a sequence is to define the first term, or the first few terms, and specify the nth term by a formula involving the preceding term(s). Sequences defined in this manner are called **recursive**.

Example 2 Write the first four terms of the recursive formula: $a_1 = 3,\ a_n = \dfrac{a_{n-1}}{n}$.

► *Solution*: $a_1 = 3,\ a_2 = \dfrac{a_{2-1}}{2} = \dfrac{a_1}{2} = \dfrac{3}{2},\ a_3 = \dfrac{a_{3-1}}{3} = \dfrac{a_2}{3} = \dfrac{1}{2},\ a_4 = \dfrac{a_{4-1}}{4} = \dfrac{a_3}{4} = \dfrac{1}{8}$

Sigma Notation

It is often important to find the sum of a sequence, $\{t_n\} = a_1 + a_2 + a_3 + \cdots + a_n$. The expanded notation $a_1 + a_2 + a_3 + \cdots + a_n$ can be written more compactly using **sigma notation**. The Greek letter Σ (sigma) is used as the summation symbol in sigma notation.

$$\underbrace{a_1 + a_2 + a_3 + \cdots + a_n}_{\text{expanded notation}} = \underbrace{\sum_{k=1}^{n} a_k}_{\text{sigma notation}}$$

The integer k is called the index of the sum, which shows where the summation starts. The integer n shows where the summation ends.

The summation $\sum_{k=1}^{n} a_k$ has $n - k + 1$ terms.

Example 3 Find the sum of each sequence.

a) $\sum_{k=1}^{4}(2k+1)$

b) $\sum_{k=1}^{5}(k^2+1)$

c) $\sum_{k=1}^{3}(k^3-k)$

► *Solution*:

a) $2(1)+1=3,\quad 2(2)+1=5,\quad 2(3)+1=7,\quad 2(4)+1=9$

$3+5+7+9=24$

b) $1^2+1=2,\quad 2^2+1=5,\quad 3^2+1=10,\quad 4^2+1=17,\quad 5^2+1=26$

$2+5+10+17+26=60$

c) $1^3-1=0,\quad 2^3-2=6,\quad 3^3-3=24$

$0+6+24=30$

Example 4 Write the sum using sigma notation.

a) $\frac{1}{2}+\frac{2}{3}+\frac{3}{4}+\cdots+\frac{12}{12+1}$

b) $\frac{2}{3}+\frac{4}{9}+\frac{8}{27}+\cdots+\left(\frac{2}{3}\right)^n$

► *Solution*:

a) $\sum_{k=1}^{12}\frac{k}{k+1}$

b) $\sum_{k=1}^{n}\left(\frac{2}{3}\right)^k$

Arithmetic Sequence

When the difference between successive terms of a sequence is always the same number, the sequence is called **arithmetic**. For example the sequence 3, 7, 11, 15, ... is arithmetic because adding 4 to any term produces the next term. The **common difference**, d, of this sequence is 4.

To develop a formula to find the general term of an arithmetic sequence, the first few terms need to be expanded.

1st term: $a_1 = a_1$
2nd term: $a_2 = a_1 + d$
3rd term: $a_3 = a_2 + d = (a_1 + d) + d = a_1 + 2d$
4th term: $a_4 = a_3 + d = (a_1 + 2d) + d = a_1 + 3d$

Notice that the coefficient of d is one less than the subscript of the term.

The *n*th Term of an Arithmetic Sequence

For an arithmetic sequence $\{t_n\}$ whose first term is a, with common difference d:

$$t_n = a + (n - 1)d \text{ for any integer } n \geq 1$$

Example 5 For each arithmetic sequence, identify the common difference.

a) 3, 5, 7, 9, ...

b) 11, 8, 5, 2, ...

► *Solution:* **a)** $5 - 3 = 2,\ \ 7 - 5 = 2,\ \ 9 - 7 = 2$
Therefore $d = 2$.

b) $8 - 11 = -3,\ \ 5 - 8 = -3,\ \ 2 - 5 = -3$
Therefore $d = -3$.

Example 6 Determine if the sequence $\{t_n\} = \{3 - 2n\}$ is arithmetic.

► *Solution:* $t_1 = a = 3 - 2(1) = 1$
$t_2 = a_2 = 3 - 2(2) = -1$
$t_3 = a_3 = 3 - 2(3) = -3$

$1, -1, -3, \ldots$ has a common difference of -2, therefore the sequence is arithmetic.

Example 7 Find the 12th term of the arithmetic sequence 2, 5, 8, ...

► *Solution*:

$a_1 = a = 2$

$d = a_2 - a_1 = 5 - 2 = 3$

$$t_n = a + (n-1)d$$
$$t_{12} = 2 + (12-1)\cdot 3$$
$$= 35$$

The 12th term is 35.

Example 8 Which term in the arithmetic sequence 4, 7, 10, ... has a value of 439?

► *Solution*:

$d = 7 - 4 = 3$

$$t_n = a + (n-1)d$$
$$439 = 4 + (n-1)\cdot 3$$
$$435 = 3(n-1)$$
$$145 = n - 1$$
$$n = 146$$

The 146th term is 439.

Example 9 The 7th term of an arithmetic sequence is 78, and the 18th term is 45. Find the first term.

► *Solution*: $t_n = a + (n-1)d$

$$t_7 = a + 6d = 78$$
$$t_{18} = a + 17d = 45$$
$$-11d = 33$$
$$d = -3$$

$$t_7 = a + 6d = 78$$
$$= a + 6(-3) = 78$$
$$a = 78 + 18$$
$$= 96$$

The first term is 96.

Example 10 Find x so that $3x + 2$, $2x - 3$, and $2 - 4x$ are consecutive terms of an arithmetic sequence.

► *Solution*: If a, b, and c are three consecutive terms of an arithmetic sequence, then $\frac{a+c}{2} = b$.

$$\frac{(3x+2)+(2-4x)}{2} = 2x - 3$$
$$-x + 4 = 4x - 6$$
$$-5x = -10$$
$$x = 2$$

Check: $3(2) + 2 = 8$, $2(2) - 3 = 1$, and $2 - 4(2) = -6$

$8, 1, -6$ is an arithmetic sequence with $d = -7$

1.1 Exercise Set

1. Fill in the blanks.

a) The domain of a sequence is the set of consecutive ____________ numbers.

b) A sequence with a last term is a(n) ____________ sequence.

c) A sequence with no last term is a(n) ____________ sequence.

d) The sequence $a_1 = 2,\ a_n = 2a_{n-1}$ is a ____________ sequence.

e) The formula for the nth term of an arithmetic sequence is $t_n =$ ______________ .

2. Write the first four terms of each sequence.

a) $\{n^2 - 2\}$

b) $\left\{\frac{n+2}{n+1}\right\}$

c) $\{(-1)^{n+1}n^2\}$

d) $\left\{\frac{3^n}{2^n+1}\right\}$

e) $\left\{\frac{2^n}{n^2}\right\}$

f) $\left\{\left(\frac{2}{3}\right)^n\right\}$

3. Write the nth term of the suggested pattern.

a) $1, \frac{1}{2}, \frac{1}{3}, \frac{1}{4}, \ldots$

b) $1, \frac{1}{2}, \frac{1}{4}, \frac{1}{8}, \ldots$

c) $\frac{2}{3}, \frac{4}{9}, \frac{8}{27}, \frac{16}{81}, \ldots$

d) $2, -4, 6, -8, \ldots$

4. Write the first four terms of the recursive sequence.

a) $a = 4,\ t_n = 2 + t_{n-1}$

b) $a = 3,\ t_n = n - t_{n-1}$

c) $a = 2,\ a_2 = 3,\ a_n = a_{n-1} + a_{n-2}$

d) $a_1 = -1,\ a_2 = 1,\ a_n = na_{n-1} + a_{n-2}$

5. Find the sum of each sequence.

a) $\sum_{k=1}^{5} 4$

b) $\sum_{k=1}^{4} (k^2 - 2)$

c) $\sum_{k=2}^{5} (k^2 - 1)$

d) $\sum_{k=0}^{3} (k^3 - 1)$

e) $\sum_{k=1}^{4} \frac{k^2}{2}$

f) $\sum_{k=6}^{8} (k+1)^2$

6. Express each sum using summation notation with index $k = 1$.

a) $1 + 3 + 5 + 7$

b) $1^2 + 2^2 + 3^2 + 4^2 + 5^2$

c) $\frac{1}{2} + \frac{2}{3} + \frac{3}{4} + \cdots + \frac{n}{n+1}$

d) $5 + \frac{5^2}{2} + \frac{5^3}{3} + \cdots + \frac{5^n}{n}$

7. Write the first five terms of each arithmetic sequence.

a) $7, 11, 15,$ ____ , ____

b) $15, 12, 9,$ ____ , ____

c) $a = 4,\ d = 2$

d) $a = -1,\ d = -3$

e) $a = -5,\ d = -\frac{3}{4}$

f) $a = -\frac{2}{3},\ d = \frac{1}{5}$

8. Find the indicated arithmetic term.

a) $a = 5,\ d = 3;$ find t_{12}

b) $a = \frac{2}{3},\ d = -\frac{1}{4};$ find t_9

c) $a = -\frac{3}{4},\ d = \frac{1}{2};$ find t_{10}

d) $a = 2.5,\ d = -1.25;$ find t_{20}

e) $a = -0.75,\ d = 0.05;$ find t_{40}

f) $a = -1\frac{3}{4},\ d = -\frac{2}{3};$ find t_{37}

9. Find the number of terms in each arithmetic sequence.

a) $a = 6,\ t_n = -30,\ d = -3$

b) $a = -3,\ t_n = 82,\ d = 5$

c) $a = 0.6,\ t_n = 9.2,\ d = 0.2$

d) $a = -0.3,\ t_n = -39.4,\ d = -2.3$

e) $-1, 4, 9, \ldots, 159$

f) $23, 20, 17, \ldots, -100$

10. Find the first term in the arithmetic sequence.

a) 6th term is 10; 18th term is 46

b) 4th term is 2; 18th term is 30

c) 9th term is 23; 17th term is -1

d) 5th term is 3; 25th term is -57

e) 13th term is -3; 20th term is -17

f) 11th term is 37; 26th term is 32

11. Find x so that the values given are consecutive terms of an arithmetic sequence.

a) $x + 3,\ 2x + 1$, and $5x + 2$

b) $2x,\ 3x + 2$, and $5x + 3$

c) $x - 1,\ \frac{1}{2}x + 4$, and $1 - 2x$

d) $2x - 1,\ x + 1$, and $3x + 9$

e) $x + 4,\ x^2 + 5$, and $x + 30$

f) $8x + 7,\ 2x + 5$, and $2x^2 + x$

12. If t_n is a term of an arithmetic sequence, what is $t_n - t_{n-1}$ equal to?

13. List the first seven numbers of the Fibonacci sequence $a_1 = 1,\ a_2 = 1,\ a_n = a_{n-1} + a_{n-2},\ n > 2$.

14. The starting salary of an employee is $23 750. If each year a $1250 raise is given, in how many years will the employee's salary be $50 000?

15. An auditorium has 8 seats in the first row. Each subsequent row has 4 more seats than the previous row. What row has 140 seats?

16. A well drilling company charges $8.00 for the first meter, then $8.75 for the second meter, and so on in an arithmetic sequence. At this rate, what would be the cost to drill the last meter of a well 120 meters deep?

17. It is said that during the last weeks of his life Abraham deMoivre needed 15 minutes more sleep each night, and when he needed 24 hours sleep he would die. If he needed 8 hours sleep on September 1, what day did he die?

18. The first three terms of an arithmetic sequence are $x - 3,\ \frac{x^2}{25} + 9$, and $3x - 11$. Determine the fourth term.

19. The first, third, and fifth terms of an arithmetic sequence are $2x - 1,\ x^2 - 3$, and $11 - x^2$ respectively. Determine the second term.

1.2 Arithmetic Series

The indicated sum of the terms of a sequence is called a **series**. For example $3 + 7 + 11 + 15$ is a series. Just as a sequence may be finite or infinite, a series can also be finite or infinite. However, this section will only discuss finite series.

Deriving the Sum Formula for Finite Arithmetic Series

If $a_1, a_2, a_3, \ldots, a_n$ is a finite arithmetic sequence, then $a_1 + a_2 + a_3 + \cdots + a_n$ is a finite arithmetic series.

Let $d =$ the common difference, $S_n =$ the sum of the series.

$$\begin{aligned} S_n &= a_1 + a_2 + a_3 + \cdots + a_n \\ &= a + (a + d) + (a + 2d) + (a + 3d) + \cdots + (a + (n-1)d) \quad \text{(equation 1)} \end{aligned}$$

Let $l = a + (n-1)d$ *(the last term)*

Writing the sum in reverse order: $S_n = l + (l - d) + (l - 2d) + \cdots + a$ (equation 2)

Adding equations 1 and 2: $$\begin{aligned} 2S_n &= (a + l) + (a + d + l - d) + (a + 2d + l - 2d) + \cdots + (a + l) \\ &= (a + l) + (a + l) + (a + l) + \cdots + (a + l) \end{aligned}$$

But $(a + l)$ appears n times. Therefore $2S_n = n(a + l) \rightarrow S_n = \frac{n}{2}(a + l)$.

Also, $S_n = \frac{n}{2}(a + l) \rightarrow S_n = \frac{n}{2}(a + a + (n-1)d) \rightarrow S_n = \frac{n}{2}(2a + (n-1)d)$.

> **Sum of an Arithmetic Series**
>
> The sum of the first n terms of an arithmetic series is given by:
>
> $$S_n = \frac{n}{2}(a + l) = \frac{n}{2}(2a + (n-1)d)$$
>
> where $a =$ the first term, $l =$ the last term, and $d =$ the common difference

Example 1 Find the sum of the positive integers from 1 to 50 inclusive.

▶ *Solution*: $a = 1$, $d = 1$, and $l = 50$

$$\begin{aligned} S_n &= \frac{n}{2}(a + l) \\ S_{50} &= \frac{50}{2}(1 + 50) \\ &= 1275 \end{aligned}$$

Example 2 Find the sum of the first 25 terms of the series $11 + 15 + 19 + \cdots$

► *Solution*: This series is arithmetic with $a = 11$, $d = 4$, and $n = 25$

$$\begin{aligned} S_n &= \frac{n}{2}(2a + (n-1)d) \\ S_{25} &= \frac{25}{2}(2 \cdot 11 + (25-1)(4)) \\ &= \frac{25}{2}(22 + 96) \\ &= 1475 \end{aligned}$$

Example 3 Find the sum of the series $7 + 10 + 13 + \cdots + 100$.

► *Solution*: $a = 7$, $d = 3$, and $l = 100$

To find n:

$$\begin{aligned} l &= a + (n-1)d \\ 100 &= 7 + (n-1)(3) \\ 93 &= (n-1)(3) \\ 31 &= n - 1 \\ n &= 32 \end{aligned}$$

$$\begin{aligned} S_n &= \frac{n}{2}(a + l) \\ S_{32} &= \frac{32}{2}(7 + 100) \\ &= 1712 \end{aligned}$$

Summation

If the summation expression is a linear function, then the summation is an arithmetic series.

For example: $\sum_{k=1}^{10}(2k + 1)$ is an arithmetic series since $f(x) = 2x + 1$ is linear.

$\sum_{k=1}^{10}(k^2 + 1)$ is not an arithmetic series since $f(x) = x^2 + 1$ is not linear.

Example 4 Evaluate $\sum_{k=1}^{100}(2k + 1)$.

► *Solution*: $a = 2(1) + 1 = 3$, $l = 2(100) + 1 = 201$, $d = 2$, $n = 100$

$$\begin{aligned} S_n &= \frac{n}{2}(a + l) \\ S_{100} &= \frac{100}{2}(3 + 201) \\ &= 10\,200 \end{aligned}$$

Example 5 Write $5 + 9 + 13 + \cdots + 137$ in summation notation.

► *Solution*:

$$\begin{aligned} l &= a + (n-1)d \\ 137 &= 5 + (n-1)(4) \\ 132 &= (n-1)(4) \\ 33 &= n-1 \\ n &= 34 \end{aligned}$$

The linear expression must be in the form $ax + b$, with a common difference of $d = 4$. Therefore the linear expression is $4k + b$.

When $k = 1$, $4(1) + b = 5 \rightarrow b = 1$

Then the expression is $4k + 1$, and the summation is $\sum_{k=1}^{34}(4k + 1)$.

Example 6 The sum of the first n terms of an arithmetic sequence is $S_n = 5n^2 - 3n$. Find the common difference d.

► *Solution*:

$$\begin{aligned} S_n &= 5n^2 - 3n \\ S_1 = a_1 &= 5(1)^2 - 3(1) = 2 \\ S_2 &= 5(2)^2 - 3(2) = 14 \\ S_2 &= a_1 + a_2 = 14 \\ 2 + a_2 &= 14 \\ a_2 &= 12 \end{aligned}$$

If $a_1 = 2$, $a_2 = 12$, then $d = 12 - 2 = 10$

Example 7 Find the sum of all multiples of 6 between 100 and 1000.

► *Solution*: The first multiple of 6 is 102. The last multiple of 6 is 996.

$$\begin{aligned} t_n &= a + (n-1)d \\ 996 &= 102 + (n-1)\cdot 6 \\ n &= 150 \end{aligned}$$

$$\begin{aligned} S_{150} &= \frac{150}{2}(102 + 996) \\ &= 82\,350 \end{aligned}$$

Example 8 Find two arithmetic means between 8 and 29.

► *Solution*: $a_1 = 8, \quad a_2 = 8 + d, \quad a_3 = 8 + 2d, \quad a_4 = 8 + 3d = 29$

$8 + 3d = 29 \rightarrow d = 7$

Therefore the two arithmetic means are 15 and 22.

1.2 Exercise Set

1. Find the sum of the arithmetic series.

a) $3 + 5 + 7 + \cdots + (2n + 1)$

b) $-1 + 2 + 5 + \cdots + (3n - 4)$

c) $2 + 5 + 8 + \cdots + 77$

d) $5 + 9 + 13 + \cdots + 97$

e) $(-41) + (-35) + (-29) + \cdots + 541$

f) $2\sqrt{5} + 6\sqrt{5} + 10\sqrt{5} + \cdots + 50\sqrt{5}$

g) $39 + 33 + 27 + \cdots + (-15)$

h) $23 + 19 + 15 + \cdots + (-305)$

i) $\frac{1}{2} + \frac{7}{8} + \frac{5}{4} + \cdots + \frac{55}{8}$

j) $\frac{16}{3} + \frac{13}{3} + \frac{10}{3} + \cdots + \left(-\frac{65}{3}\right)$

k) $3.7 + 9 + 14.3 + \cdots + 30.2$

l) $2.84 + 5.3 + 7.76 + \cdots + 79.1$

2. Find the indicated value using the information given.

a) S_{20}, if $a_1 = 8,\ a_{20} = 65$

b) S_{21}, if $a_1 = 8,\ a_{20} = 65$

c) S_{56}, if $a_{56} = 13,\ d = -9$

d) n, if $S_n = 180,\ a_1 = 4,\ a_n = 16$

e) d, if $S_{40} = 680,\ a_1 = 11$

f) S_{62}, if $a_1 = 10,\ d = 3$

g) S_{19}, if $d = 4,\ a_{19} = 17$

h) S_{40}, if $d = -3,\ a_{40} = 65$

i) S_{40}, if $a_5 = 42,\ a_{15} = -18$

j) S_{20}, if $a_8 = 17,\ a_{15} = 38$

3. Find the indicated sum.

a) $\sum_{n=1}^{100} n$

b) $\sum_{k=100}^{200} k$

c) $\sum_{j=0}^{72} (3j-4)$

d) $\sum_{x=7}^{24} (2x+5)$

e) $\sum_{y=11}^{48} \left(\frac{y+4}{2}\right)$

f) $\sum_{z=51}^{100} (200-z) - \sum_{z=1}^{50} (200-z)$

4. Insert k arithmetic means between the given pair of numbers.

a) $5,\ 10,\ k=2$

b) $3,\ 6,\ k=3$

c) $a,\ b,\ k=2$

d) $a,\ b,\ k=3$

5. Solve for b: $\sum_{x=2}^{b} (23-2x) = 91$

6. Find the sum: $\sum_{x=a}^{b} 5$

7. What is the last element in the 20th row?

```
      1
    2   3
  4   5   6
7   8   9   10
```

8. How many terms of the arithmetic series $1491 + 1484 + 1477 + \cdots$ are needed to give a sum of zero?

9. An auditorium has eight seats in the first row. Each subsequent row has four more seats than the previous row. How many seats are there in the 50th row of the auditorium?

10. If \$1000 is deposited into the bank the day a child is born, and \$100 more than the previous deposit is made each year until the child's 18th birthday, how much will be in the account, excluding interest?

11. Find the sum of all multiples of 6 between 50 and 500.

12. The sum of three consecutive terms of an arithmetic sequence is 3. The sum of their squares is 75. Find the three numbers.

13. If 20 people in a class shake hands with each other exactly once, how many handshakes will take place?

14. If the sum of the terms of an arithmetic series is 234, and the middle term is 26, find the number of terms in the series.

1.3 Geometric Sequences

In an arithmetic sequence, a constant number is added to each term to get the next term. In a geometric sequence, each term is multiplied by a constant number to get the next term.

Consider the sequence $3, 6, 12, 24, \ldots$ Multiplying each term by 2 results in the next term. This number is called the **common ratio**, because the ratio value is found by dividing any term by the preceding term.

In the sequence $3, 6, 12, 24, \ldots,\ \ 6 \div 3 = 2,\ 12 \div 6 = 2,\ 24 \div 12 = 2, \ldots$

Geometric Sequence

A sequence is geometric if the ratio of consecutive terms is constant.

$a_1, a_2, a_3, \ldots, a_n$ is geometric if there is a number r, $r \neq 0$ such that $\frac{a_2}{a_1} = r,\ \frac{a_3}{a_2} = r, \ldots, \frac{a_n}{a_{n-1}} = r$

The number r is called the **common ratio** of the geometric sequence.

Example 1 For each geometric sequence, find the common ratio.

a) $2,\ 6,\ 18,\ 54, \ldots$

b) $3,\ -6,\ 12,\ -24, \ldots$

c) $-8,\ -4,\ -2,\ -1, \ldots$

► *Solution*:

a) $\frac{6}{2} = \frac{18}{6} = \frac{54}{18} = 3 \rightarrow r = 3$

b) $\frac{-6}{3} = \frac{12}{-6} = \frac{-24}{12} = -2 \rightarrow r = -2$

c) $\frac{-4}{-8} = \frac{-2}{-4} = \frac{-1}{-2} = \frac{1}{2} \rightarrow r = \frac{1}{2}$

Deriving the Formula for the *n*th Term of a Geometric Sequence

let $a =$ the first term, $r =$ the common ratio

a_1
$a_2 = a_1 \cdot r$
$a_3 = a_2 \cdot r = (a_1 \cdot r) \cdot r = a_1 \cdot r^2$
$a_4 = a_3 \cdot r = (a_1 \cdot r^2) = a_1 \cdot r^3$
⋮
$a_n = a_1 \cdot r^{n-1}$

Note: The exponent in each term is one less than the subscript of the term. In general $a_m = a_n r^{(m-n)}$.

The *n*th Term of a Geometric Sequence

The nth term of a geometric sequence with common ratio r has the form $t_n = ar^{n-1}$, for any integer $n \geq 1$

Example 2 Find the 8th term of the geometric sequence $3,\ 12,\ 48,\ 192, \ldots$

► *Solution:* The common ratio is $\frac{12}{3} = 4$, with $a = 3$

$$\begin{aligned} t_n &= ar^{n-1} \\ t_8 &= 3(4)^{8-1} \\ &= 3(4)^7 \\ &= 49152 \end{aligned}$$

Example 3 The 4th term of a geometric sequence is 125, and the 9th term is $\frac{125}{32}$. Find the 13th term.

► *Solution:* The 4th term $t_4 = ar^3 = 125$. The 9th term $t_9 = ar^8 = \frac{125}{32}$

$$\begin{aligned} ar^8 = (ar^3) \cdot r^5 &= \frac{125}{32} \\ 125 \cdot r^5 &= \frac{125}{32} \\ r^5 &= \frac{1}{32} \\ r &= \frac{1}{2} \end{aligned}$$

$$\begin{aligned} ar^3 &= 125 \\ a\left(\frac{1}{2}\right)^3 &= 125 \\ a &= 1000 \end{aligned}$$

The 13th term is $t_{13} = 1000\left(\frac{1}{2}\right)^{12} = \frac{125}{512}$

Example 4 What value of x in $x,\ 2x + 2,\ 3x + 3$ will form a geometric sequence?

► *Solution:* $r = \frac{2x + 2}{x} = \frac{3x + 3}{2x + 2}$

$$\begin{aligned} 4x^2 + 8x + 4 &= 3x^2 + 3x \\ x^2 + 5x + 4 &= 0 \\ (x + 4)(x + 1) &= 0 \\ x &= -1,\ -4 \end{aligned}$$

1.3 Exercise Set

1. Determine if the sequence is geometric. If it is, find the common ratio.

a) $4,\ 12,\ 36,\ 72,\ldots$ ________

b) $3,\ 12,\ 48,\ 142,\ldots$ ________

c) $1,\ -\frac{1}{2},\ \frac{1}{4},\ -\frac{1}{8},\ldots$ ________

d) $1,\ -1,\ 1,\ -1,\ldots$ ________

e) $3,\ -6,\ -12,\ 24,\ldots$ ________

f) $1,\ \frac{1}{2},\ \frac{1}{3},\ \frac{1}{4},\ldots$ ________

g) $\frac{1}{4},\ \frac{1}{6},\ \frac{1}{9},\ \frac{2}{27},\ldots$ ________

h) $\frac{2}{5},\ -\frac{2}{3},\ \frac{10}{9},\ -\frac{50}{27},\ldots$ ________

i) $3x^2,\ 12x^4y^3,\ 48x^6y^6,\ldots$ ________

j) $\sqrt{2},\ \sqrt{6},\ 3\sqrt{2},\ 3\sqrt{6},\ldots$ ________

2. Write the first five terms of the geometric sequence.

a) 1, 4, ____, ____, ____

b) 1, ____, 4, ____, ____

c) $\frac{1}{2}$, ____, ____, $\frac{1}{16}$, ____

d) 4, ____, ____, − 13.5, ____

e) ____, 54, 18, ____, ____

f) 1, ____, 3, ____, ____

g) 3, ____, 3^{2x+1}, ____, ____

h) 1, ____, x^4, ____, ____

i) 5, 5^{2x-1}, ____, ____, ____

j) 1, $-\frac{x}{3}$, ____, ____, ____

3. Find all possible values of r for a geometric sequence with the two given terms.

a) $a_5 = 5,\ a_7 = 25$

b) $a_2 = 4,\ a_6 = \frac{1}{4}$

c) $a_4 = 2\sqrt{2},\ a_7 = 8$

d) $a_3 = 1,\ a_6 = \sqrt{2}$

4. Find the indicated value using the information given.

a) a_{11}, if $a_1 = \frac{1}{128}$, $r = 2$

b) a_9, if $a_1 = 3$, $a_2 = \sqrt{3}$

c) a_{42}, if $a_{40} = 9$, $a_{41} = 36$

d) a_9, if $a_4 = 5$, $a_6 = 20$

e) n, if $a_1 = 729$, $a_2 = 243$, $l = \frac{1}{9}$

f) n, if $a_1 = 2048$, $a_2 = 1024$, $l = 1$

g) a_1, if $a_5 = 27$, $r = 3$

h) a_1, if $a_7 = 128$, $r = 4$

i) r, if $a_{10} = 25$, $a_{12} = 225$

j) r, if $a_{25} = 12$, $a_{31} = 96$

k) a_8, if $a_n = 3a_{n-1}$, $a_1 = \frac{1}{27}$

l) a_6, if $a_n = 0.1a_{n-1}$, $a_1 = 1000$

5. Insert two geometric means between a and b.

6. Given the geometric sequence $a,\ \frac{a}{b},\ \frac{a}{b^2},\ldots$ determine an expression for $t_n - t_{n-1},\ n > 2$.

7. Find x so that $x - 1,\ x,$ and $x + 2$ are consecutive terms of a geometric sequence.

8. Find the common ratio r for the geometric sequence $x - 2,\ 5 - x,\ 5x - 7,\ldots$

9. What number must be added to $-2,\ 4,\ 19$ so that the resulting numbers are three terms of a geometric sequence?

10. If the first two terms of a geometric sequence are $\sqrt{2}$, and $\sqrt[3]{2}$, what is the fourth term?

11. If the product of the first three terms of a geometric is -8, and the sum is $\frac{14}{3}$, what is the common ratio of the sequence?

12. In the sequence $3,\ x,\ y,\ 25$, the first three terms form an arithmetic sequence, and the last three terms form a geometric sequence. Find x and y.

13. The enrolment at Earl Marriott Secondary in Surrey, BC, was 400 in 1973. If the school's population has increased by 5% a year, how many students will be going to the school in 2010?

14. If a starting salary is \$28 000, and one expects to receive an annual increase of 6%, what is the salary at the beginning of the eighth year of work?

15. With each cycle, a vacuum pump removes 25% of the air in a glass container. What percent of the air has been removed after 10 cycles?

16. A car costs a company \$40 000. Each year, the car depreciates 16% of its value. What is the value of the car after five years?

17. Initially, a pendulum swings through an arc of 45 cm. On each successive swing, the length of the arc decreases by 2% of the previous length. What is the length of the arc after 12 swings?

18. A ball is dropped from a height of 10 metres. Each time it strikes the ground it bounces up 75% of its previous height. How many bounces does the ball need before the bounce is less than 20 cm high?

19. Here is a diagram of the steps taken to get strawberries from the farmer to the consumer: *Farmer → Trucker → Regional Market → Trucker → Wholesaler → Trucker → Retailer → Consumer.* If the farmer gets 75 cents per kilogram, and if each person in the chain makes a 20% profit, how much does the consumer pay?

20. A truck radiator contains fifty litres of water. Five litres of water is removed and replaced with pure antifreeze; then five litres of the mixture is removed and replaced. How much antifreeze is in the radiator after this process is repeated five times?

1.4 Geometric Series

The sum of a geometric sequence is called a geometric series.

Deriving the Sum Formula for Finite Geometric Series

If $S_n = a + ar + ar^2 + \cdots + ar^{n-1}$ is a geometric series with common ratio r, the sum can be found by multiplying S_n by $-r$ and adding the new equation to S_n.

$$\begin{array}{rl} S_n = & a + ar + ar^2 + \cdots + ar^{n-1} \\ -rS_n = & \quad - ar - ar^2 - \cdots \qquad - ar^n \\ \hline S_n - rS_n = & a \qquad\qquad\qquad\quad - ar^n \end{array}$$

Therefore $(1-r)S_n = a - ar^n \rightarrow S_n = \dfrac{a - ar^n}{1-r} = \dfrac{a(1-r^n)}{1-r}$ or $S_n = \dfrac{a-ar^n}{1-r} = \dfrac{a - ar^{n-1}\cdot r}{1-r}$, since $t_n = ar^{n-1} = l$ $= \dfrac{a - rl}{1-r}$

Sum of a Geometric Series

The sum of the first n terms of a geometric series with first term a and last term l is given by:

$$S_n = \frac{a(1-r^n)}{1-r} = \frac{a-ar^n}{1-r}, \text{ or } S_n = \frac{a-rl}{1-r}, \text{ for } r \neq 1$$

Example 1 Find the sum of the geometric series $2 + 6 + 18 + 54 + \cdots + 1458$

► *Solution*: $a = 2,\ r = 3,\ l = 1458$

$$S_n = \frac{a-rl}{1-r} = \frac{2-3(1458)}{1-3} = 2186$$

Example 2 Find the sum of the first eight terms of the geometric series $3 + 6 + 12 + \cdots$

► *Solution*: $a = 3,\ r = 2,\ n = 8$

$$\begin{aligned} S_n &= \frac{a(1 - r^n)}{1 - r} \\ &= \frac{3(1 - 2^8)}{1 - 2} \\ &= \frac{3(1 - 256)}{-1} \\ &= 765 \end{aligned}$$

Example 3 Find the sum of the geometric series $\sum_{k=1}^{10} 3(-2)^{k-1}$

► *Solution*: $k = 1,\ a = 3(-2)^{1-1} = 3,\ l = 3(-2)^{10-1} = -1536,\ n = 10,\ r = -2$

$$\begin{aligned} S_n &= \frac{a - ar^n}{1 - r} \\ &= \frac{3 - 3(-2)^{10}}{1 - (-2)} \\ &= \frac{3 - 3(1024)}{3} \\ &= -1023 \end{aligned}$$

or

$$\begin{aligned} S_n &= \frac{a - rl}{1 - r} \\ &= \frac{3 - (-2)(-1536)}{1 - (-2)} \\ &= \frac{3 - 2(1536)}{3} \\ &= -1023 \end{aligned}$$

Note: In summation notation, an arithmetic series has its variable in the base. A geometric series has its variable in the exponent.

$\sum_{i=1}^{5} (2i - 3)$ is an arithmetic series

$\sum_{i=1}^{5} 2 \cdot 3^i$ is a geometric series

$\sum_{i=1}^{5} (2 + 3^i)$ is neither an arithmetic or geometric series

Example 4 Write the geometric series, $6 + 18 + 54 + 162 + 486$, using sigma notation with the index $k = 1$.

► *Solution*: $n = 5,\ r = 3$

The r value is written to the variable exponent. $r = 3 \rightarrow \sum_{k=1}^{5} 3^k$

To get the initial value of 6, the r value must be multiplied by 2. Therefore $\sum_{k=1}^{5} 2 \cdot 3^k$.

1.4 Exercise Set

1. Find the indicated value using the information given.

a) S_{10}, if $a = 8,\ r = \frac{1}{2}$

b) S_9, if $a = -6,\ r = 2$

c) a, if $S_8 = 765,\ r = 2$

d) S_6, if $a = -8,\ t_4 = 27$

e) S_5, if $t_3 = 3,\ r = \frac{1}{2}$

f) S_8, if $a = 12,\ t_5 = 192$

g) t_3, if $S_5 = 93,\ r = 2$

h) r, if $S_3 = 39,\ a = 3$

i) S_{100}, if $t_1 = -1,\ t_2 = 1,\ t_3 = -1,\ t_4 = 1$

j) S_{101}, if $t_1 = -1,\ t_2 = 1,\ t_3 = -1,\ t_4 = 1$

2. Find the number of terms in each finite series.

a) $\sum_{k=8}^{35}(2^k - 5)$

b) $\sum_{i=8}^{b}(2^i - 5)$

c) $\sum_{k=a}^{9}(2^k - 5)$

d) $\sum_{i=a}^{b}(2^i - 5)$

3. Find the sum of each geometric series.

a) $\sum_{i=1}^{8} 3(2)^{k-1}$

b) $\sum_{k=1}^{12} 2(-3)^{k-1}$

c) $\sum_{x=0}^{10} 5\left(\frac{1}{2}\right)^{x}$

d) $\sum_{k=0}^{9} \frac{3}{5^{k+1}}$

e) $\sum_{b=2}^{9} 18(0.1)^{b}$

f) $\sum_{i=3}^{11} \frac{2^{i}}{3^{i-1}}$

g) $\sum_{k=1}^{n} \left(\frac{2}{3}\right)^{k}$

h) $\sum_{k=1}^{n} 4 \cdot 3^{k-1}$

4. Write the geometric series using sigma notation with $k = 1$ as the index of the first term.

a) $3 + 6 + 12 + 24 + 48$

b) $2 - 6 + 18 - 54 + \cdots + 13122$

c) $\frac{3}{16} - \frac{3}{8} + \frac{3}{4} - \cdots - 384$

d) $8 + 4 + 2 + 1 + \cdots + \frac{1}{1024}$

5. Solve for a: $\sum_{i=0}^{2} a^i = 31$.

6. Which is larger, and by what amount?
$2^0 + 2^1 + 2^2 + \cdots + 2^{n-1}$, or 2^n

7. If 64 students enter a singles tennis tournament, where the winner of each match advances to the next round, how many matches must be played before a winner is determined?

8. If the sum of a geometric series is 101.01, and the first term is 100, and the last term is 0.01, find:
i) the number of terms *ii*) the common ratio.

9. If you invest $1000 at the beginning of each year at 10% interest compounded annually, what is the value of the annuity at the end of 30 years? How much of this is accumulated interest?

10. Simplify $(1 - r)(1 + r + r^2 + r^3 + \cdots + r^{n-1})$

11. You are offered two pay packages: $40 000 with increases of 5% for 5 years, or $43 000 with increases of 3% for 5 years. Which offer is better, and by how much, if:
i) Your goal is to have the largest pay after 5 years?
ii) Your goal is to have the largest total amount of money after 5 years?

12. If a person received a 10% salary increase each year and earned a total of $155 680.05 by the end of the 5th year, determine the starting salary.

13. An equilateral triangle has sides of length 10. If the midpoints of each side are joined to form another triangle, and this process is continued, what is:
i) The perimeter of the 5th triangle?
ii) The total perimeter of the first 5 triangles?

14. Terry Fox decided to walk 120 km by walking 40% of the distance remaining each day. How far does he have remaining to walk after six days of walking?

15. Which is larger? By what amount?
A: $1000 + 999 + 998 + \cdots;\ n = 1000$
B: $1 + 2 + 4 + \cdots\ ;n = 19$

16. The sum of the first and second term of a geometric progression is 4 and the sum of the third and fourth term is 36. What is the first term?

17. Determine the second term of a geometric sequence if $a_4 + a_5 = -3$ and $a_3 + a_4 = -6$.

18. If the sum of n terms of a geometric series is $S_n = 2(3^n - 1)$, determine the fifth term of the series.

19. A ball bounces up three-quarters the distance from which it falls. How far does the ball travel in total after hitting the floor the fourth time, if it dropped from 36 ft?

20. A nursery rhyme to end this section:

As I was going to St. Ives
I met a man with 7 wives
Every wife had 7 sacks
Every sack had 7 cats
Every cat had 7 kits
Kits, cats, sacks, and wives,
How many were going to St. Ives?

1.5 Infinite Geometric Series

Consider the infinite geometric sequence: $1, \frac{1}{2}, \frac{1}{4}, \frac{1}{8}, \frac{1}{16}, \ldots, \left(\frac{1}{2}\right)^{n-1}$.

As the terms of the infinite geometric get closer and closer to some real number, the sequence is said to be **convergent** and will **converge** to a real number.

$\left(\frac{1}{2}\right)^{50} = 8.8 \times 10^{-16}$, $\left(\frac{1}{2}\right)^{100} = 7.88 \times 10^{-31}$, $\left(\frac{1}{2}\right)^{200} = 6.22 \times 10^{-61}$. As n gets larger, $\left(\frac{1}{2}\right)^{n}$ gets closer to 0.

That is $\lim_{n \to \infty}\left(\frac{1}{2}\right)^{n} = 0$. This is read: as n approaches an infinitely large number, $\left(\frac{1}{2}\right)^{n}$ approaches zero.

Consider the infinite geometric sequence: $1, 2, 4, 8, 16, \ldots, 2^{n-1}$.

This sequence does not converge to some number. A sequence that does not converge is said to be **divergent**.

Geometric sequences that have r values between $-1 < r < 1$ will converge, and ones that have r values $r > 1$ or $r < -1$ will diverge.

Deriving the Sum Formula for Infinite Geometric Series

In a geometric series with first term a, and common ratio r: $S_n = \frac{a - ar^n}{1 - r} = \frac{a(1 - r^n)}{1 - r}$.

If $-1 < r < 1$, usually written $|r| < 1$, it follows $|r^n|$ approaches zero as $n \to \infty$.

Therefore $S_n = \frac{a(1 - r^n)}{1 - r} = \frac{a(1 - 0)}{1 - r} = \frac{a}{1 - r}$.

The Sum of an Infinite Geometric Sequence

The sum of the terms of an infinite geometric sequence is given by:

$$S_\infty = \frac{a}{1 - r}, \quad |r| < 1 \quad \text{or} \quad -1 < r < 1$$

Example 1 Find the sum of the infinite geometric series $\frac{2}{5} - \frac{4}{25} + \frac{8}{125} - \cdots$

► *Solution:* $r = \frac{\frac{-4}{25}}{\frac{2}{5}} = -\frac{2}{5}, \left|-\frac{2}{5}\right| < 1$, therefore it is a finite sum.

$$S_\infty = \frac{a}{1 - r} = \frac{\frac{2}{5}}{1 - (-\frac{2}{5})} = \frac{\frac{2}{5}}{\frac{7}{5}} = \frac{2}{7}$$

A good way of understanding the importance of the condition $-1 < r < 1$ for an infinite geometric sequence to have a finite sum is to look at the following two examples:

i) $S = 1 + \frac{1}{2} + \frac{1}{4} + \cdots = 1 + \frac{1}{2}\overbrace{(1 + \frac{1}{2} + \frac{1}{4} + \cdots)}^{S} \rightarrow S = 1 + \frac{1}{2}S \rightarrow S - \frac{1}{2}S = 1 \rightarrow S = 2$

This is correct because $-1 < r < 1$.

ii) $S = 1 + 2 + 4 + 8 + \cdots = 1 + 2\overbrace{(1 + 2 + 4 + \cdots)}^{S} \rightarrow S = 1 + 2S \rightarrow S - 2S = 1 \rightarrow S = -1$

This answer makes no sense because $r = 2$, which does not satisfy the condition $-1 < r < 1$.

Summation Form of an Infinite Geometric Series

An infinite geometric series with first term a and common ratio r, $|r| < 1$, is denoted by $\sum_{i=1}^{\infty} ar^{i-1}$

Example 2 Find the sum of $\sum_{k=2}^{\infty} 8\left(-\frac{1}{2}\right)^{k-1}$

▶ *Solution*: $a = 8\left(-\frac{1}{2}\right)^{2-1} = -4, \quad r = -\frac{1}{2}$

$$S_\infty = \frac{a}{1-r} = \frac{-4}{1-(-\frac{1}{2})} = -\frac{8}{3}$$

Example 3 Initially a pendulum swings through an arc of 25 cm. On each successive swing friction lessens the length of the pendulum swing by 5%. When the pendulum stops, what total length will the pendulum have swung?

▶ *Solution*: If the length of the swing is lessened by 5%, then the swing is 95% of the original arc.

$$S_\infty = \frac{a}{1-r} = \frac{25}{1-0.95} = \frac{25}{0.05} = 500 \text{ cm}$$

Example 4 A ball is dropped from 12 ft and rebounds two-thirds the distance from which it fell. Find the total distance the ball travelled.

► *Solution*: This problem can be solved starting from S_1, S_2, or S_3.

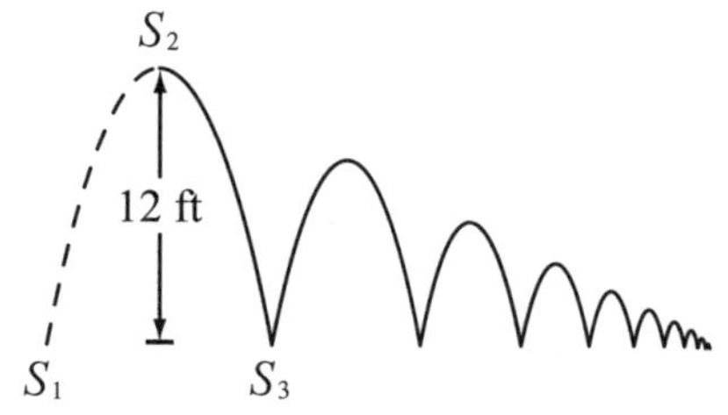

If choosing S_1 as the starting point, the first up and down motion is 24 ft. But since the 12 ft travelled from S_1 to S_2 is not part of the total distance travelled, it must be subtracted.

$$S_1 = \frac{a}{1-r} = \frac{24}{1-\frac{2}{3}} - 12 = 60 \text{ ft}$$

$$S_2 = \frac{a}{1-r} = \frac{12+8}{1-\frac{2}{3}} = 60 \text{ ft}$$

$$S_3 = \frac{a}{1-r} = \frac{16}{1-\frac{2}{3}} + 12 = 60 \text{ ft}$$

Note: *The horizontal distance travelled in the diagram is only shown to illustrate the upward and downward paths of the ball. In the problem, the ball only travels vertically.*

Example 5 Write the repeating decimal $0.2\overline{4}$ as a fraction.

► *Solution*: $0.2\overline{4} = \frac{2}{10} + \underbrace{\frac{4}{100} + \frac{4}{1000} + \frac{4}{10\,000} + \cdots}_{r=\frac{1}{10}}$

$$S_\infty = \frac{a}{1-r} = \frac{2}{10} + \frac{\frac{4}{100}}{1-\frac{1}{10}} = \frac{11}{45}$$

Example 6 Solve for x: $\sum_{k=1}^{\infty}(\tan x)^{k-1} = 1, \quad 0° \le x < 45°$

► *Solution*: $(\tan x)^0 + (\tan x)^1 + (\tan x)^2 + \cdots = 1 \quad \rightarrow \quad a = 1,\ r = \tan x$

Since $\tan x < 1$ for $0° \le x < 45°$

$$S_\infty = \frac{a}{1-r}$$

$$1 = \frac{1}{1-\tan x}$$

$$\tan x = 0$$

$$x = 0°, \ \cancel{180°} \quad (\textit{Reject } 180°)$$

1.5 Exercise Set

1. Determine if the infinite geometric series converges or diverges. State the common ratio.

a) $16 + 4 + 1 + \cdots$

b) $\frac{3}{16} + \frac{3}{8} + \frac{3}{4} + \cdots$

c) $1 + \frac{1}{1.01} + \frac{1}{(1.01)^2} + \cdots$

d) $3 - \frac{3}{2} + \frac{3}{4} - \cdots$

e) $\frac{1}{2} + \frac{1}{4} + \frac{1}{8} + \cdots$

f) $1 + 1 + 1 + \cdots$

2. Find the sum of the infinite geometric series, if it exists.

a) $1 - \frac{1}{2} + \frac{1}{4} - \frac{1}{8} + \cdots$

b) $3 + 1 + \frac{1}{3} + \frac{1}{9} + \cdots$

c) $1.2 + 0.012 + 0.00012 + \cdots$

d) $1 + \frac{3}{2} + \frac{9}{4} + \frac{27}{8} + \cdots$

e) $\frac{27}{2} - 9 + 6 - 4 + \cdots$

f) $-6 + 3 - \frac{3}{2} + \frac{3}{4} - \cdots$

g) $\sqrt{2} - 2 + 2\sqrt{2} - 4 + \cdots$

h) $(1.05)^{-1} + (1.05)^{-2} + (1.05)^{-3} + \cdots$

3. Find the sum of each infinite geometric series.

a) $\sum_{i=1}^{\infty} 3\left(\frac{1}{2}\right)^{i}$

b) $\sum_{k=1}^{\infty} 4\left(-\frac{1}{3}\right)^{k-1}$

c) $\sum_{x=2}^{\infty} 3 \cdot 4^{1-x}$

d) $\sum_{k=2}^{\infty} 5 \cdot 2^{-k}$

e) $\sum_{i=1}^{\infty} (-1)^{i}\left(\frac{2}{3}\right)^{i+1}$

f) $\sum_{k=3}^{\infty} \left(\frac{4}{3}\right)^{1-k}$

g) $\sum_{n=1}^{\infty} 5\left(-\frac{3}{5}\right)^{n-1}$

h) $\sum_{n=3}^{\infty} \frac{6}{3^{n-1}}$

i) $\sum_{k=0}^{\infty} 5\left(\frac{1}{8}\right)^{k}$

j) $\sum_{k=3}^{\infty} 10\left(-\frac{2}{5}\right)^{k-1}$

4. Find the rational number represented by the repeating decimal.

a) $0.\overline{38}$

b) $0.3\overline{8}$

c) $1.\overline{432}$

d) $1.4\overline{32}$

5. Solve for x.

a) $\sum_{k=1}^{\infty} x^k = \frac{2}{5}$

b) $\sum_{i=1}^{\infty} (2x)^{i-1} = \frac{2}{5}$

c) $\sum_{j=0}^{\infty} (\cos x)^j = 2, \quad 0^\circ \le x < 360^\circ$

d) $\sum_{n=1}^{\infty} 15x(x^2)^{n-1} = 4$

6. Rewrite each series using the new index.

a) $\sum_{n=2}^{\infty} 5^n 2^{-n} = \sum_{j=5}$ ________

b) $\sum_{i=0}^{\infty} 2^{3i-1} = \sum_{j=4}$ ________

c) $\sum_{k=1}^{\infty} 3^{1-k} = \sum_{k=3}$ ________

d) $\sum_{x=5}^{\infty} 4^{2-3x} = \sum_{x=1}$ ________

7. For what value will the infinite geometric series, $1+(1+x)+(1+x)^2+\cdots$, $x \neq 1$, have a finite sum?

8. Determine the value of x, $x \neq 0$, so that the infinite geometric series, $1+\frac{1}{3}x+\frac{1}{9}x^2+\cdots$, has a finite sum.

9. Why is it impossible to have an infinite geometric series with the first term 9 and a sum of 4?

10. The first term in an infinite geometric series is 3. Find all possible values of the common ratio r, which will give a sum greater than 4.

11. Find the sum of an infinite geometric series if the first term is 2, and each term is 4 times the sum of all the terms that follow it.

12. A weather balloon rises 100 m the first minute, and each minute after the first it rises 4% less than the previous minute. What is the maximum height reached by the balloon?

13. If a rectangle has dimensions 2×4, and each side is halved endlessly, what is the total area of all the rectangles formed if the process is continued without end?

14. A 6.25 cm nail is driven 2 cm into a board on the first hit, and $\frac{2}{3}$ of the preceding distance on each of the next hits. How many hits are required to hammer the nail into the board?

15. A clock pendulum swings through an arc of 30 cm. Each successive swing is 10% less. How far will the pendulum swing altogether before coming to a complete stop?

16. Seventy two grams of fertilizer is given to a dogwood tree the first year, 60 grams the second year, 50 grams the third year, and so on. Find the total amount of fertilizer received by the dogwood tree.

17. The side of a square is 16 cm. The midpoint of the sides of the square are joined to form another inscribed square. This process is continued forever. Find the sum of the perimeters of all the squares.

18. A side of an equilateral triangle is 10 cm. The midpoints of the side are joined to form a second inscribed equilateral triangle inside the first triangle, and the process is continued forever. Find the sum of the perimeter of the original triangle and all of the subsequent inscribed triangles that are formed.

19. A ball dropped from 10 m above ground rebounds $\frac{3}{4}$ of the distance from where it fell.

a) Find the total vertical distance the ball travels before coming to a rest.

b) Find the total vertical distance the ball travels after 10 bounces.

c) What is the total distance traveled after the 10th bounce?

20. A ball dropped from a height of 120 m rebounds 80% of the distance of the height it previously fell.

a) Determine the total vertical distance traveled when the ball hits the ground the 8th time.

b) Determine the maximum height reached after hitting the ground the 8th time.

c) Determine the total vertical distance that the ball travels before coming to a rest.

1.6 Chapter Review

1. Which is a geometric sequence?

   a) $8, -7, 6, \ldots$

   b) $0, -4, -8, \ldots$

   c) $-10, -8, -6, \ldots$

   d) $-4, -2, -1, \ldots$

2. Determine the 25th term of the arithmetic sequence $-2, -8, -14, -20, \ldots$

   a) -152

   b) -146

   c) -138

   d) -132

3. Determine the common ratio r, of the geometric sequence $2, -1, \frac{1}{2}, -\frac{1}{4}, \ldots$

   a) -2

   b) $-\frac{1}{2}$

   c) 1

   d) 2

4. Which sequence is arithmetic for all values of x?

   a) x^8, x^4, x^2, x

   b) x, x^2, x^3, x^4

   c) $x, 2x, 3x, 4x$

   d) $x, 2x, 4x, 8x$

5. When inserting two geometric means between a and b, what is the common ratio?

   a) $\sqrt{ab}$

   b) $\sqrt{\frac{b}{a}}$

   c) $\sqrt[3]{ab}$

   d) $\sqrt[3]{\frac{b}{a}}$

6. Determine the number of terms in the arithmetic sequence $5, 1, -3, \ldots, -111$

   a) 27

   b) 28

   c) 29

   d) 30

7. Determine the sum of the first 15 terms of the geometric series $16+(-12)+9+(-6.75)+\cdots$

a) 9.02

b) 9.27

c) 15.16

d) 21.05

8. Determine the number of terms in the geometric sequence $\frac{a^3}{b},\ a^2,\ ab, \ldots, \frac{b^{15}}{a^{13}}$

a) 15

b) 16

c) 17

d) 18

9. Determine the sum of the arithmetic series $5+1+(-3)+\cdots+(-111)$

a) -1594

b) -1590

c) -1586

d) -1582

10. Which is equivalent to $S_n - S_{n-1}$?

a) t_{n-1}

b) t_n

c) t_{n+1}

d) S_{n-2}

11. Determine the sum of $S = 0.3 + \frac{2}{100} + \frac{2}{1000} + \frac{2}{10000} + \cdots$

a) $\frac{29}{90}$

b) $\frac{29}{99}$

c) $\frac{32}{90}$

d) $\frac{32}{99}$

12. Determine the fourth term in the expansion of $\sum_{n=2}^{25}(3n-1)$

a) 8

b) 11

c) 14

d) 17

13. The sum of the first 8 terms of a geometric series is 6560, with a common ratio of 3. Determine the first term.

a) -3

b) -2

c) 2

d) 3

14. Determine the fifth term of an infinite geometric series with $S_\infty = 18$ and $r = \frac{2}{3}$

a) $1\frac{5}{27}$

b) $1\frac{13}{27}$

c) $1\frac{7}{9}$

d) $2\frac{1}{9}$

15. $\sum_{k=n+3}^{5n-1} 2^k$ has 45 terms. What is the value of n?

a) 11

b) 12

c) 13

d) 14

16. The general term of a geometric series is $t_n = 16\left(-\frac{3}{2}\right)^{n-1}$. Determine the sum of the first 10 terms of the series.

a) -615.09

b) -362.66

c) 375.46

d) 7813.28

17. Determine the fourth term of the geometric sequence $x, \frac{x+1}{x}, \cdots \quad x \neq 0, -1$

a) $x^2(x+1)^3$

b) $\frac{(x+1)^3}{x^3}$

c) $\frac{(x+1)^3}{x^4}$

d) $\frac{(x+1)^3}{x^5}$

18. Find $f(1) + f(2) + \cdots + f(9)$ if $f(x) = 2^x$

a) 512

b) 1022

c) 1024

d) 2046

19. Evaluate $\sum_{j=1}^{30} \frac{2}{3} j$

a) 2

b) 20

c) 310

d) 315

20. Given a geometric series with a first term of 12 and a common ratio of -1.2, determine the sum of the first 20 terms.

a) -203.66

b) -172.33

c) 1120.13

d) 2240.26

21. For what value will the infinite geometric series, $1+(1-x)+(1-x)^2+\cdots,\ x \neq 1$, have a finite sum?

a) $-2 < x < 2$

b) $-1 < x < 1$

c) $0 < x < 1$

d) $0 < x < 2$

22. Determine the value of $x,\ x \neq 0$, such that the infinite geometric series $1+\frac{1}{3}x+\frac{1}{9}x^2+\cdots$ has a finite sum.

a) $0 < x < 1$

b) $-\frac{1}{3} < x < \frac{1}{3}$

c) $-1 < x < 1$

d) $-3 < x < 3$

23. If x and $2\sqrt{2}\,x^4$ are the first and fourth terms of a geometric sequence, determine the seventh term.

a) $4x^6$

b) $4\sqrt{2}\,x^6$

c) $8x^7$

d) $8\sqrt{2}\,x^7$

24. If a student receives a 4% salary increase at the end of each year of summer work, and earned a total of \$39 020 during 3 years of work, determine the starting salary.

a) \$12 019

b) \$12 500

c) \$13 520

d) \$14 061

25. If $y-3,\ y$, and $3y+4$ are consecutive terms in a geometric sequence, determine the value(s) of y.

a) $\frac{3}{2}$

b) 4

c) $\frac{3}{2},\ -4$

d) $-\frac{3}{2},\ 4$

26. Solve for x: $\sum_{k=1}^{3} x^{k-1} = 7$

a) $-2, -3$

b) $-2, 3$

c) $2, -3$

d) $2, 3$

27. An auditorium has 8 seats in the first row. Each subsequent row has 4 more seats than the previous row. How many seats are in the 28th row?

a) 112

b) 116

c) 1680

d) 1736

28. Evaluate: $\sum_{k=3}^{\infty} 10\left(-\frac{2}{5}\right)^{k-1}$

a) $\frac{8}{7}$

b) $\frac{8}{3}$

c) $\frac{50}{7}$

d) $\frac{50}{3}$

29. What number must be added to each of 11, 15, 21 so that the resulting numbers are 3 terms of a geometric sequence?

a) -3

b) 3

c) 7

d) 9

30. If the sum of an infinite geometric series is 1, and the common ratio is $-\frac{2}{3}$, determine the 2nd term.

a) $-\frac{10}{9}$

b) $-\frac{2}{5}$

c) $\frac{2}{5}$

d) $\frac{10}{9}$

31. Evaluate: $\sum_{k=3}^{7} 2(-3)^{k-1}$

a) 41

b) 122

c) 369

d) 1098

32. A new car costs $42 000 and depreciates 20% the first year, then 15% every year after. What is the car worth in 10 years?

a) $6615

b) $7782

c) $8269

d) $9156

33. Determine S_n of the series $3 + 7 + 11 + 15 + \cdots + (4n - 1)$.

a) $4n - 1$

b) $2n^2 + n$

c) $2n^2 + 2n$

d) $4(3)^{n-1} - 1$

34. Determine the 1st term in a geometric progression whose common ratio is -3, and whose 5th term is 162.

a) -3

b) -2

c) 2

d) 3

35. Solve for x: $\sum_{k=2}^{4}(10 - k)x = 168$

a) 8

b) 21

c) 24

d) 28

36. A jogger wants to run 100 km in six days. The first day she runs 10 km, and increases the distance she runs by 20% each day for the next four days of jogging. What distance must she run on the sixth day to complete the run of 100 km?

a) 24.9 km

b) 25.6 km

c) 34.0 km

d) 79.3 km

37. If $-2x,\ -4,\ x^2$ are three consecutive terms in a geometric sequence, determine the value of x.

a) -2

b) ± 2

c) ± 4

d) $\varnothing$

38. If $t_1 = 27$ and $t_4 = -8$, determine the sum of the infinite geometric series.

a) -81

b) -16.2

c) 16.2

d) 81

39. The sum of terms in a geometric series is -910. If the first term is 5, and the last term is -1215, determine the common ratio r.

a) -6

b) -5

c) -4

d) -3

40. The first three terms of an arithmetic sequence are $x+4$, x^2+5, and $x+30$. Determine the values of x.

a) $-3,\ -4$

b) $-3,\ 4$

c) $3,\ -4$

d) $3,\ 4$

41. If the 6th term of a geometric progression is -160 and the 9th term is 1280, determine the 1st term.

a) -5

b) -2

c) 2

d) 5

42. In a geometric sequence, $t_4 = 40.5$, and $t_7 = 136.6875$. Determine the first term.

a) 12

b) 14

c) 16

d) 18

43. Determine an expression which represents: $\sum_{k=1}^{n} 6(-2)^{1-k}$

a) $4 - 4(-\frac{1}{2})^n$

b) $4 - 4(-2)^n$

c) $12 - 12(-\frac{1}{2})^n$

d) $12 - 12(-2)^n$

44. Which expression represents the sum of the series given by: $\sum_{k=3}^{12} 6(3)^{k-1}$

a) $27(3^9 - 1)$

b) $27(3^{10} - 1)$

c) $108(3^9 - 1)$

d) $108(3^{10} - 1)$

45. For a certain geometric series, $S_n = 2 - 2(-3)^n$. Determine t_3.

a) 48

b) 60

c) 72

d) 84

46. If the sum of n terms of a geometric series is $S_n = 2(3^n - 1)$, determine the 5th term of this series.

a) -628

b) -324

c) 324

d) 628

47. Evaluate: $\sum_{n=0}^{99} \sin(90° \cdot n)$.

a) 0

b) 25

c) 50

d) 100

48. The sum of the first n terms of an arithmetic sequence is given by $S_n = 3n^2 - 2n$. Determine the common difference.

a) 6

b) 7

c) 31

d) 32

49. The 5th term of a geometric series is 2, and the 10th term is $-\frac{1}{16}$. Determine the sum of the first 8 terms.

a) 21.25

b) 21.42

c) 23.91

d) 47.81

50. If $-64,\ a,\ b,\ 27$ are four consecutive terms in a geometric sequence, determine the value of b.

a) -48

b) -36

c) 36

d) 48

51. If a geometric sequence has $t_5 = 3x + 2$ and $t_7 = 7x - 22$ with common ratio $r = -3$, determine t_6.

a) -36

b) -12

c) 12

d) 36

52. Determine the second term of a geometric sequence if $t_4 + t_5 = -3$ and $t_3 + t_4 = -6$.

a) -16

b) -8

c) -4

d) -2

53. The sum of the 1st and 2nd term of a geometric progression is 4, and the sum of the 3rd and 4th terms is 36. Determine the 1st term.

a) -2 or 1

b) -1 or 2

c) -3 or 2

d) -2 or 3

2.1 Functions and Relations (Review)

In Mathematics, determining the relationship between two variables is a very important concept. This chapter will show how to visualize relations and functions by means of a graph. Graphs will become central to each aspect of this chapter, for both theoretical understanding and problem solving.

Relations

A relation is a set of ordered pairs, in other words, just a number of points in a coordinate plane.

a)

b)

c)

d)

Presented above are examples of relations. The set of x-values of all the points is called the **domain** of the relation, and the set of y-values is called the **range**. In example a) above, the domain is –1, 1, 2, and the range is –1, 0, 2.

If you are allowed to use any set of numbers you want for the domain or range, then "all real numbers" is the answer. (See Example 1 below.)

Example 1 $x = y^2$

The domain is $x \geq 0$

The range is "all real numbers."

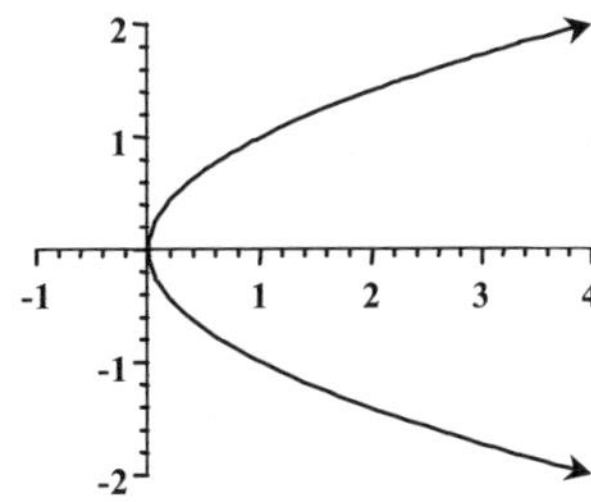

The domain and range become harder to identify when there is no graph. Remember, the domain is the set of x numbers, and the range is the set of y numbers used in the equation. There are two main concerns when working with domain and range in any equation:

- **not having a negative number inside an even root, and**
- **not having zero in the denominator.**

Example 2

$y = 2 - \sqrt{3-x}$

In this example, the domain is $x \le 3$ because an even root must be ≥ 0, so $3 - x \ge 0 \rightarrow x \le 3$. The range is $y \le 2$ because it is 2 minus the positive value of $\sqrt{3-x}$.

Functions

The next concern is to find out what kind of relations are functions. The following is a definition of a function.

> **Definition of a Function**
>
> For every value of the domain (x-value), there is one and only one value for the range (y-value), or, each element in the domain corresponds to exactly one element in the range.

What does this mean? It says any x-value can only have one y-value.

a) (1, 3), (2, 4), (3, –1) is a function because each x-value 1, 2, 3 has only one value for y.

b) (1, 3), (1, –3), (2, 4) is not a function.

c) (1, 3), (1, 2), (4, 5) is not a function because $x = 1$ gives $y = 2$ and $y = 3$, i.e., two values. If y is to an even power, then it can't be a function, e.g., $x^2 + y^2 = 9 \rightarrow y = \pm\sqrt{9 - x^2}$ (two values of y for each x-value).

One-to-One Functions

If any x-value (input) matches with exactly one y-value (output), then the function is one-to-one.

> **Definition of a one-to-one function**:
>
> A function in which every one value of the domain (x-value), is associated with one value of the range (y-value), and vice versa.
>
> This means that if f is a one-to-one function, then for each x in the domain of f, there is one and only one y in the range, and no y in the range is the image of more than one x in the domain.

Hierarchy of Relations, of Functions, and of One-to-One Functions

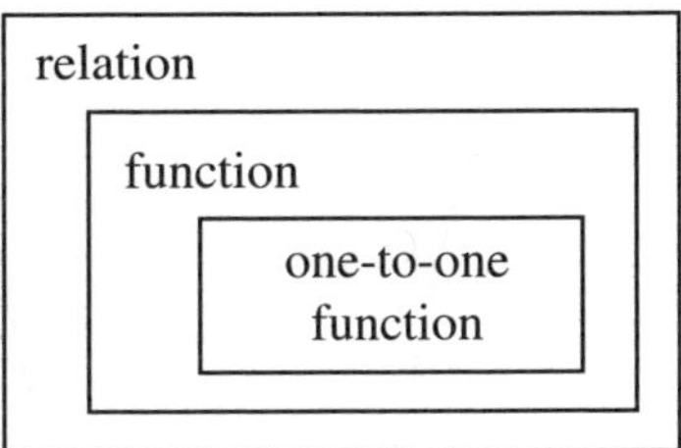

Example 4

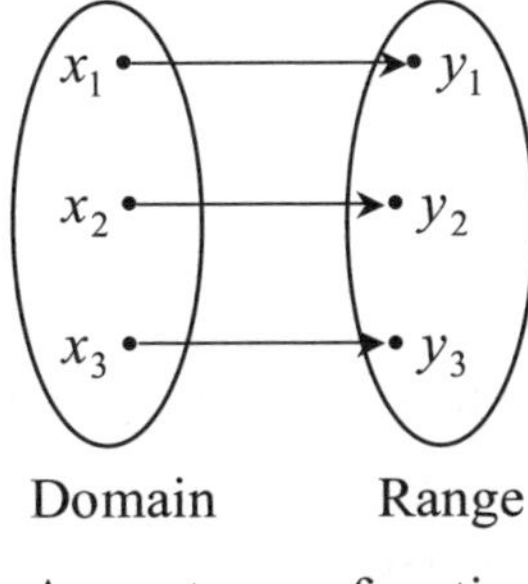

A one-to-one function

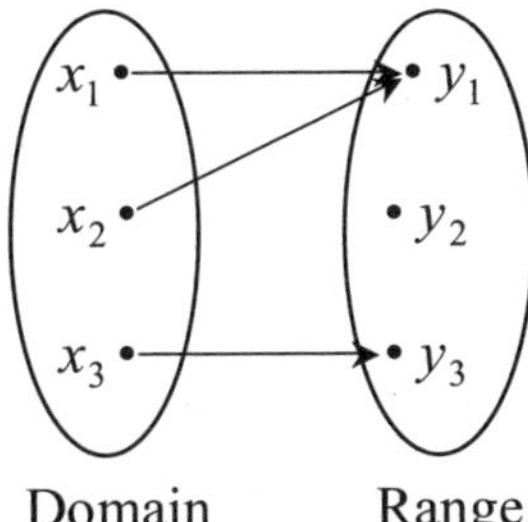

A function but **not** one-to-one. Both x_1 *and* x_2 go to y_1.

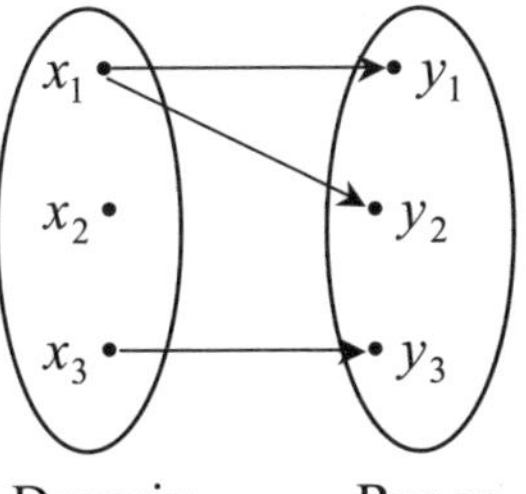

Not a function, just a relation. x_1 goes to both y_1 *and* y_2.

Line Tests for Functions

It is very easy to tell if a relation is

- just a relation
- a function
- a one-to-one function

by looking at its graph.

Vertical line test for functions:

An equation defines y as a **function** of x if and only if every vertical line in the coordinate plane intersects the graph of the equation only once.

Horizontal line test for one-to-one functions:

A function, y, is a **one-to-one function** of x if and only if every horizontal line in the coordinate plane interesects the function at most only once.

Example 5 State whether each of the following relations is a function, a one-to-one function, or neither.

a)

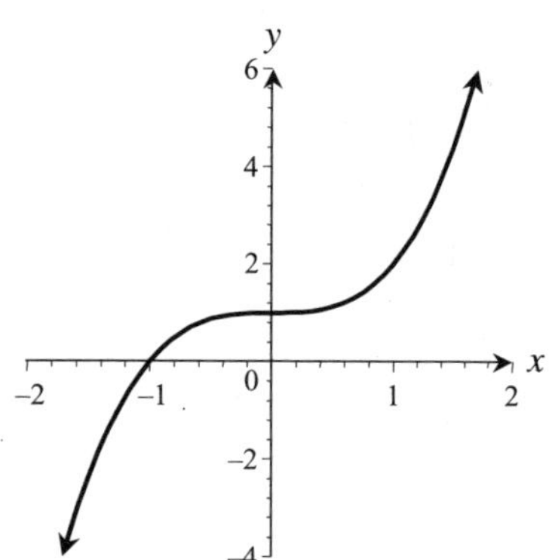

b)

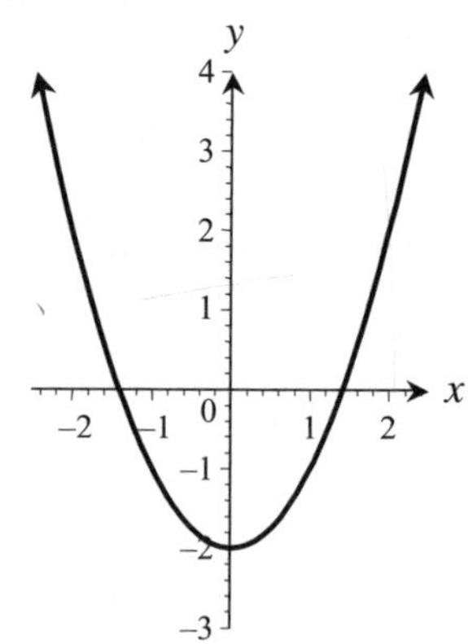

c)

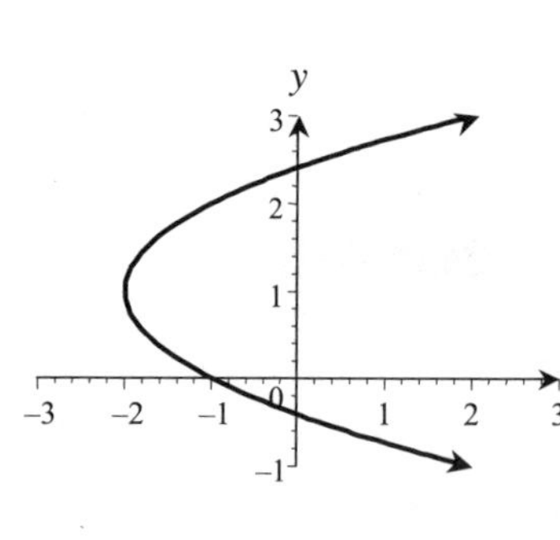

▶ *Solution:*

a) A vertical line intersects the graph once, a horizontal line intersects the graph once, therefore, graph is a one-to-one function.

b) A vertical line intersects the graph once, a horizontal line intersects the graph more than once, therefore, graph is just a function.

c) A vertical line intersects the graph more than once, so this is not a function.

Example 6 Determine the domain and range of the following relations:

a)

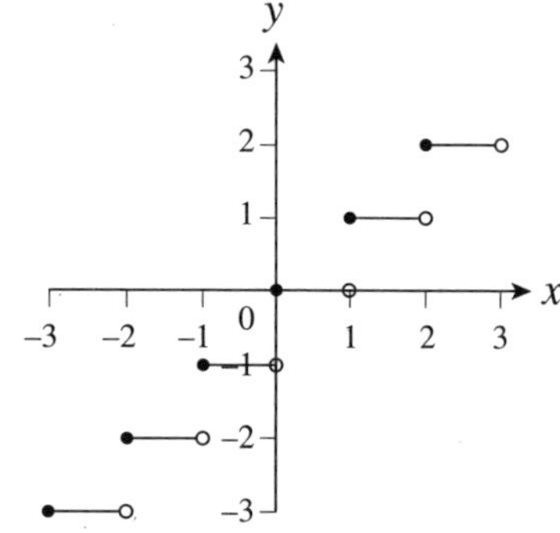

b)

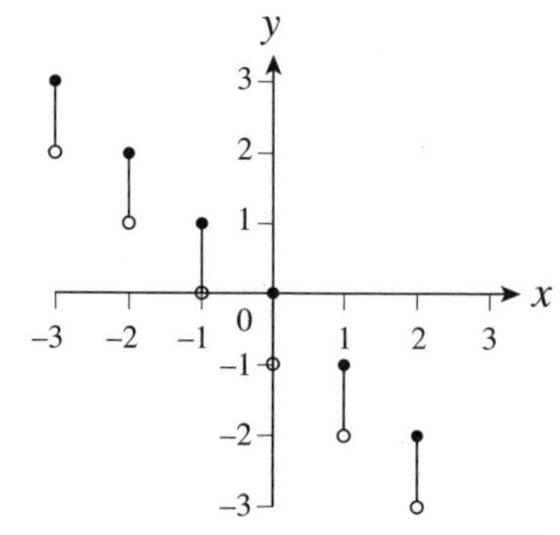

c)

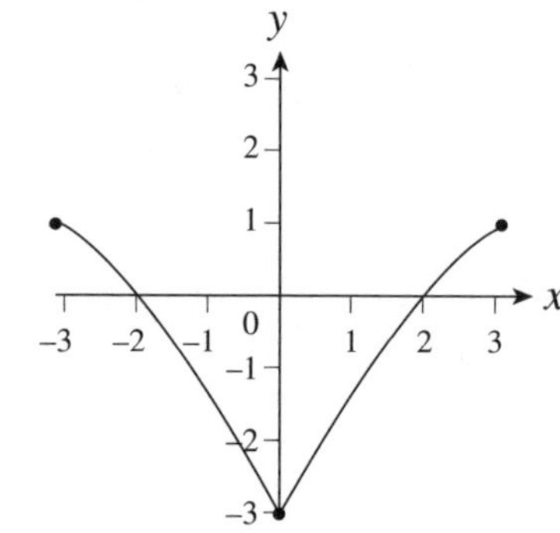

▶ *Solution:*

a) Domain: $-3 \le x < 3$

Range: $\{-3, -2, -1, 0, 1, 2\}$

b) Domain: $\{-3, -2, -1, 0, 1, 2\}$

Range: $-3 < y \le 3$

c) Domain: $-3 \le x \le 3$

Range: $-3 \le y \le 1$

2.1 Exercise Set

1. Complete the following sentences.

a) For any function, the set of x-values (input) is called the ____________________ .

b) For any function, the set of y-values (output) is called the ____________________ .

c) One value of the domain is paired with exactly one value of the range is a __________________ .

d) Every value of the domain is paired with exactly one value of the range is a __________________ .

e) A set of ordered pairs is called a ____________________ .

f) In a graph, the domain is located on the ________-axis.

g) In a graph, the range is located on the ________-axis.

h) When a relation is graphed, a ______________________ line test is used to determine if the relation is a ______________________ .

i) When a relation is graphed, a ______________________ and ______________________ line test is used to determine if the relation is a______________________ .

2. Determine if the following relations are functions, one-to-one functions or neither.

a)

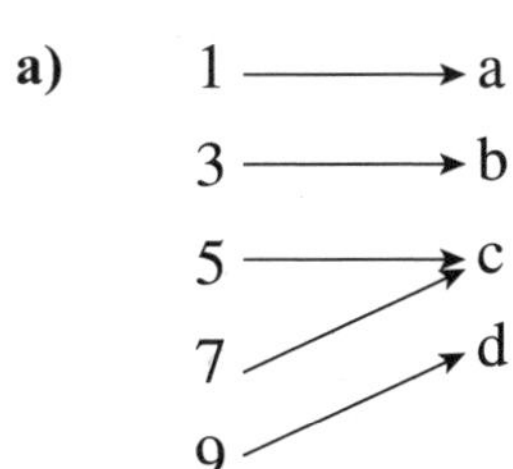

b)

c) **d)**

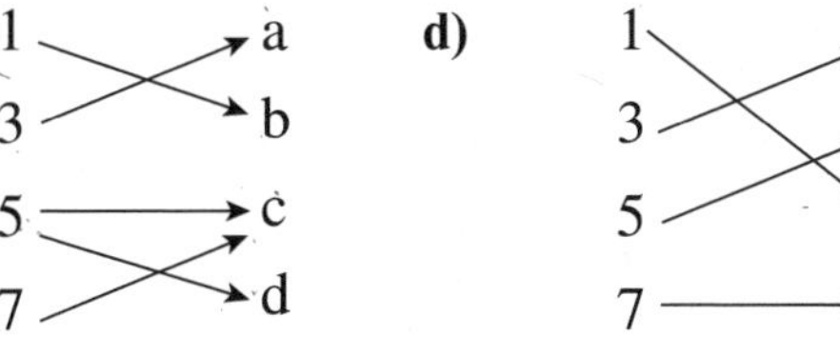

________________ ________________ ________________ ________________

e) **Girls age** (in months) **Weight gain** (grams)

3 → 23.1
7 → 10.3
15 → 7.8
24 → 5.0

f) **Mathematicians** **Birthdays**

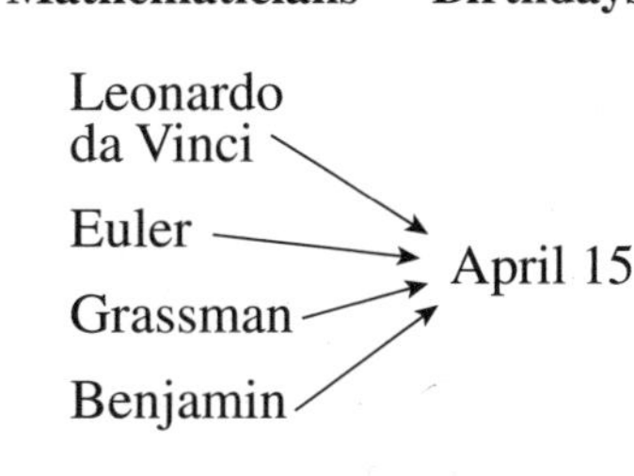

g) **Birthday** **Mathematicians**

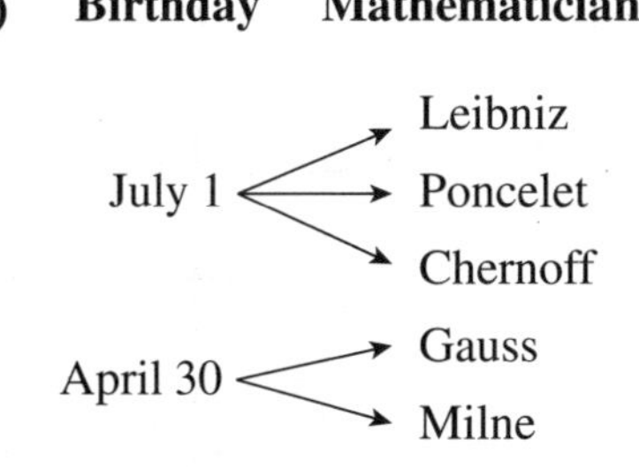

________________ ________________ ________________

h) **Province** **Neighbouring Province**

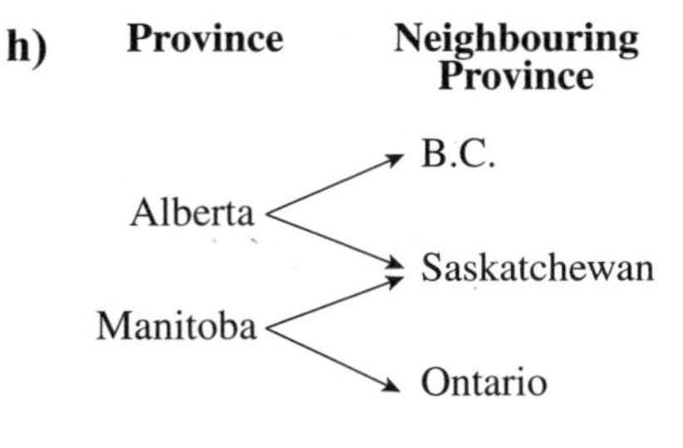

i) **Chase** **Catch**

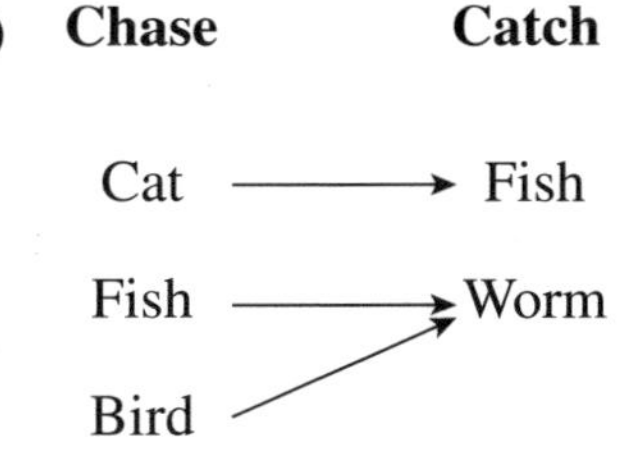

j) **Car** **Cylinder**

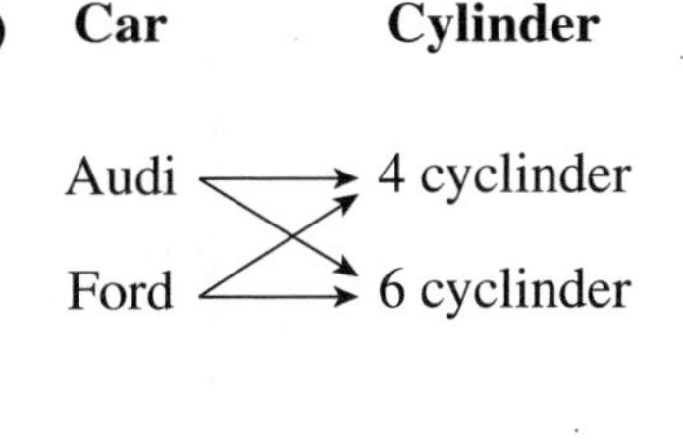

________________ ________________ ________________

3. For each graph, determine the domain, range, and if the graph is a function (yes/no).

a)

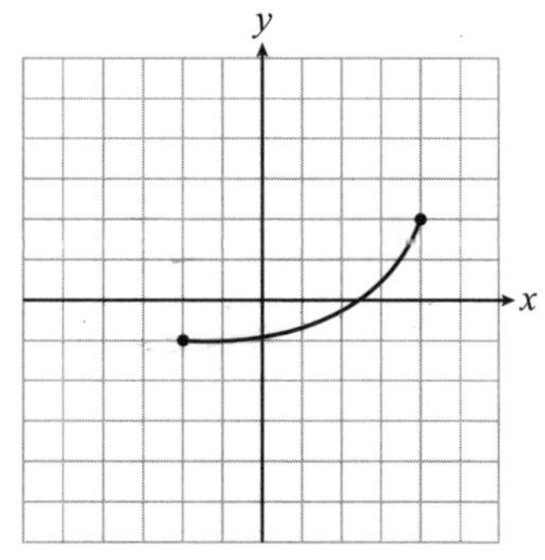

D: ____________

R: ____________

F: ____________

b)

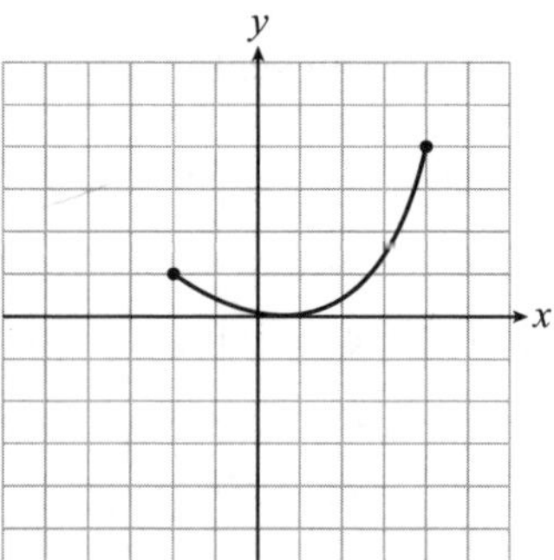

D: ____________

R: ____________

F: ____________

c)

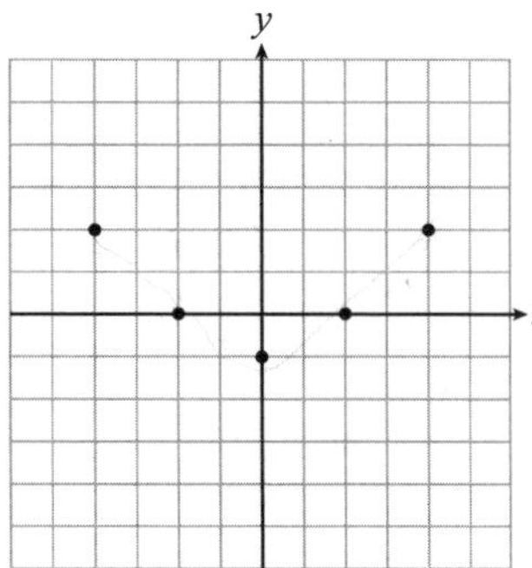

D: ____________

R: ____________

F: ____________

d)

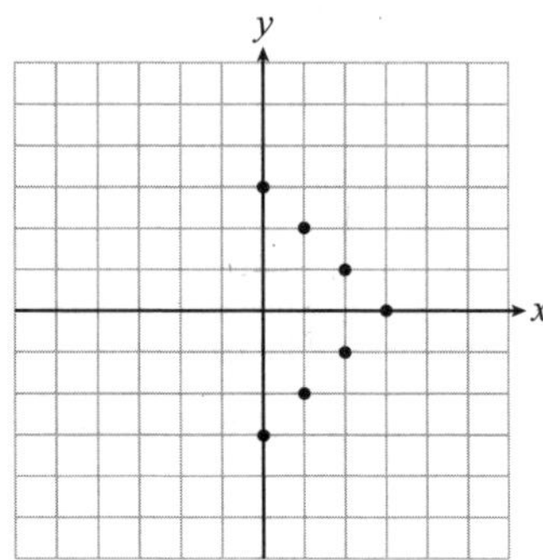

D: ____________

R: ____________

F: ____________

e)

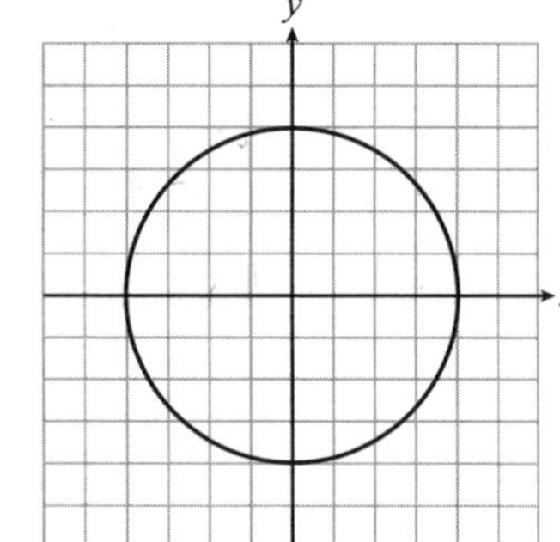

D: ____________

R: ____________

F: ____________

f)

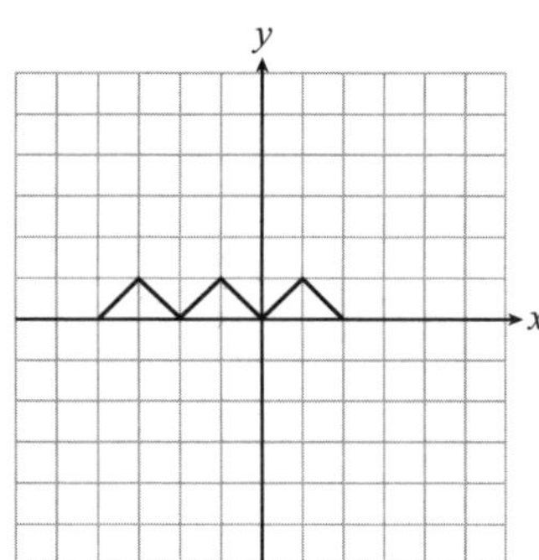

D: ____________

R: ____________

F: ____________

g)

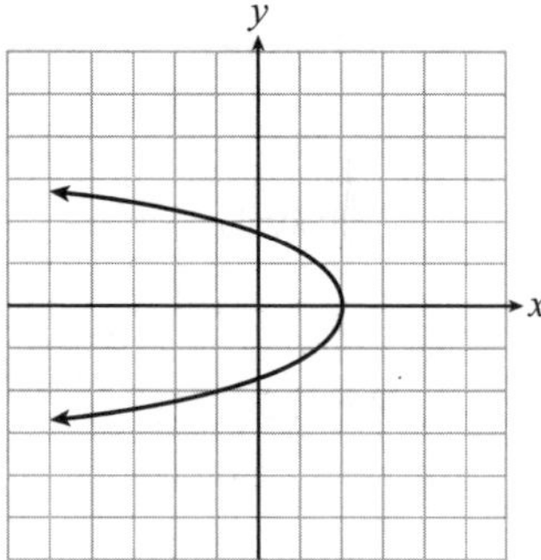

D: ____________

R: ____________

F: ____________

h)

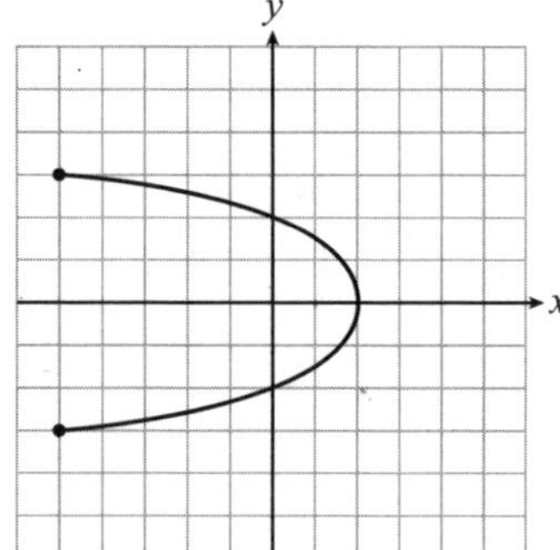

D: ____________

R: ____________

F: ____________

i)

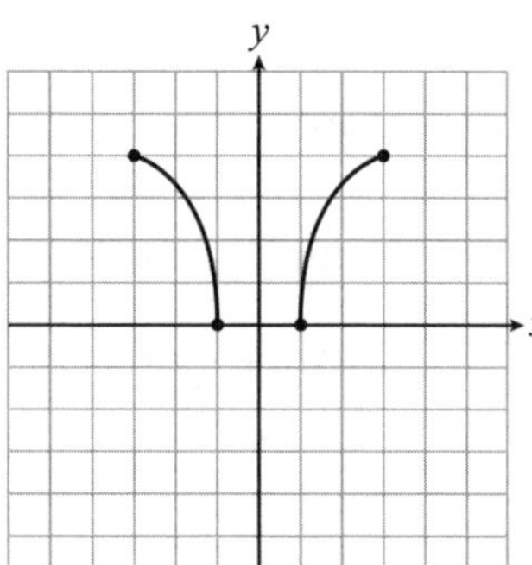

D: ____________

R: ____________

F: ____________

j)

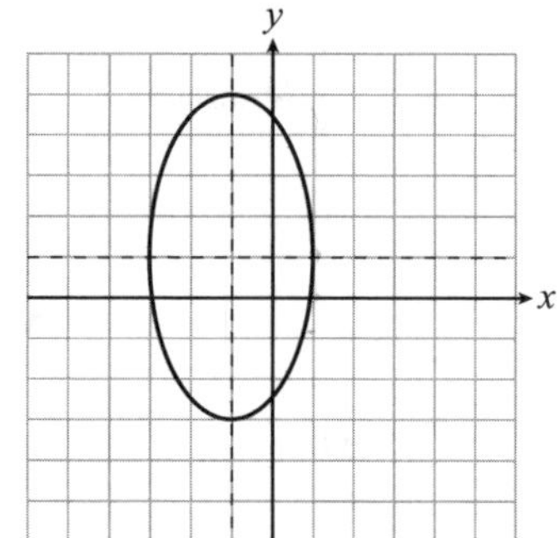

D: ____________

R: ____________

F: ____________

2.2 Arithmetic Combinations of Functions

Any real number can be combined by the operations of addition, subtraction, multiplication, and division to form another real number. This concept can be used with functions in the same way. For example, the functions given by $f(x)=3x+2$ and $g(x)=x^2-4$ can be combined to form the sum, difference, product, and quotient of *f* and *g*.

$$f(x)+g(x)=(3x+2)+(x^2-4) \quad \textit{sum}$$
$$=x^2+3x-2$$
$$f(x)-g(x)=(3x+2)-(x^2-4) \quad \textit{difference}$$
$$=-x^2+3x+6$$
$$f(x)g(x)=(3x+2)(x^2-4) \quad \textit{product}$$
$$=3x^3+2x^2-12x-8$$
$$\frac{f(x)}{g(x)}=\frac{3x+2}{x^2-4},\ x\neq\pm2 \quad \textit{quotient}$$

The domain (*x*-values) of this combination of functions *f* and *g* is the set of real numbers that are common to the domain of *f* and *g*. Therefore, we can state the following:

Sum, Difference, Product, and Quotients of Functions

Let f and g be two functions. Then the **sum** $f+g$, the **difference** $f-g$, the **product** fg, and the **quotient** $\frac{f}{g}$ are functions defined by the following equations:

1. Sum $(f+g)(x)=f(x)+g(x)$
2. Difference $(f-g)(x)=f(x)-g(x)$
3. Product $(fg)(x)=f(x)\cdot g(x)$
4. Quotient $\left(\frac{f}{g}\right)(x)=\frac{f(x)}{g(x)},\ g(x)\neq 0$

Example 1 Compute each expression, given that the functions *f, g, h*, and *k* are defined as follows:

$$f(x)=2x+1,\quad g(x)=x^2-2x+1,\quad h(x)=x^3,\quad k(x)=2$$

a) $(f+g)(x)$

b) $(h-k)(x)$

c) $\left(\frac{kg}{h}\right)(3)$

d) $(fk)(1)-(hg)(2)$

e) $[h\cdot(f+g)](x)$

▶ *Solution:*

a) $(f+g)(x)=f(x)+g(x)=(2x+1)+(x^2-2x+1)=x^2+2$

b) $(h-k)(x)=h(x)-k(x)=x^3-2$

c) $\left(\dfrac{kg}{h}\right)(3)=\dfrac{k(3)\cdot g(3)}{h(3)}=\dfrac{2\cdot 4}{27}=\dfrac{8}{27}$

d) $(fk)(1)-(hg)(2)=f(1)k(1)-h(2)g(2)=3\cdot 2-8\cdot 1=-2$

e) $h(x)\left[f(x)+g(x)\right]=x^3\left[(2x+1)+(x^2-2x+1)\right]=x^3(x^2+2)=x^5+2x^3$

Example 2

Use the graphs of *f*, *g*, and *h* to evaluate the functions.

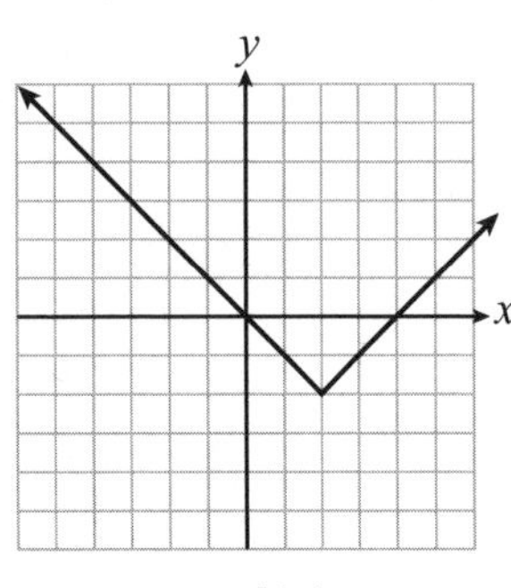

$y=f(x)$

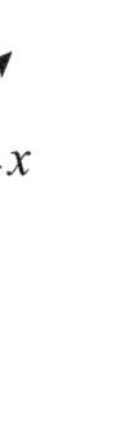

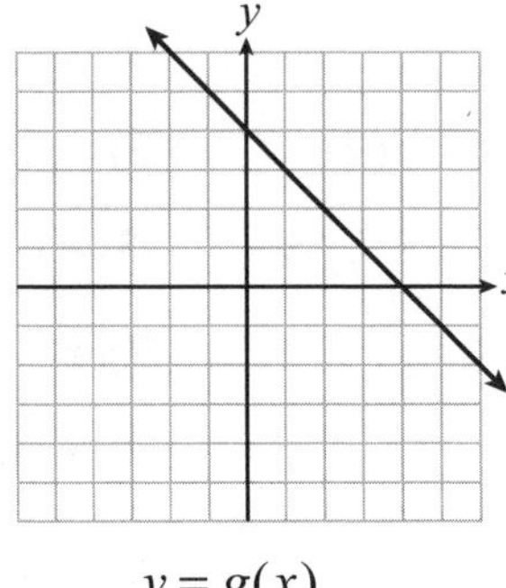

$y=g(x)$

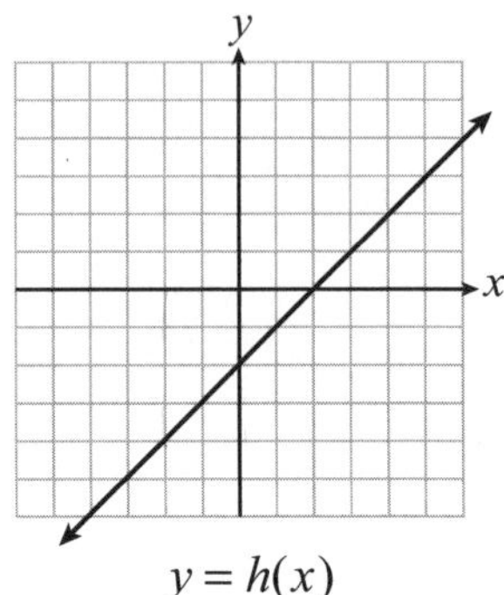

$y=h(x)$

a) $(f+g)(3)$ **b)** $\left(\dfrac{h}{g}\right)(5)$ **c)** $(fgh)(1)$ **d)** graph: $(f-h)(x)$ **e)** graph: $(fg)(x)$

▶ *Solution:*

a) $(f+g)(3)=f(3)+g(3)=-1+1=0$

b) $\left(\dfrac{h}{g}\right)(5)=\dfrac{h(5)}{g(5)}=\dfrac{3}{-1}=-3$

c) $(fgh)(1)=f(1)g(1)h(1)=(-1)(3)(-1)=3$

d) Graph: $(f-h)(x)=f(x)-h(x)$

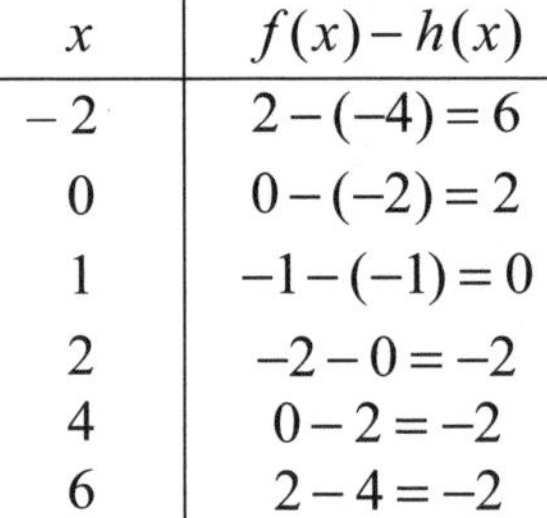

x	$f(x)-h(x)$
-2	$2-(-4)=6$
0	$0-(-2)=2$
1	$-1-(-1)=0$
2	$-2-0=-2$
4	$0-2=-2$
6	$2-4=-2$

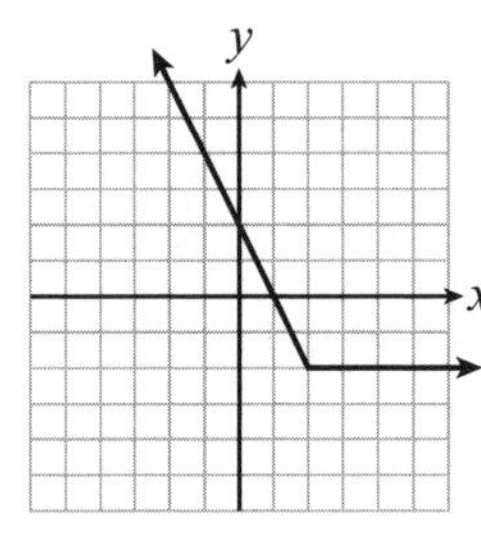

or for $x\le 2$

$$f(x)-h(x)=-x-(x-2)$$
$$=-2x+2$$

for $x\ge 2$

$$f(x)-h(x)=x-4-(x-2)$$
$$=-2$$

e) Graph: $(fg)(x)=f(x)g(x)$

x	$f(x)g(x)$
-1	$1\cdot 5=5$
0	$0\cdot 4=0$
1	$-1\cdot 3=-3$
2	$-2\cdot 2=-4$
3	$-1\cdot 1=-1$
4	$0\cdot 0=0$
5	$1\cdot -1=-1$
6	$2\cdot -2=-4$

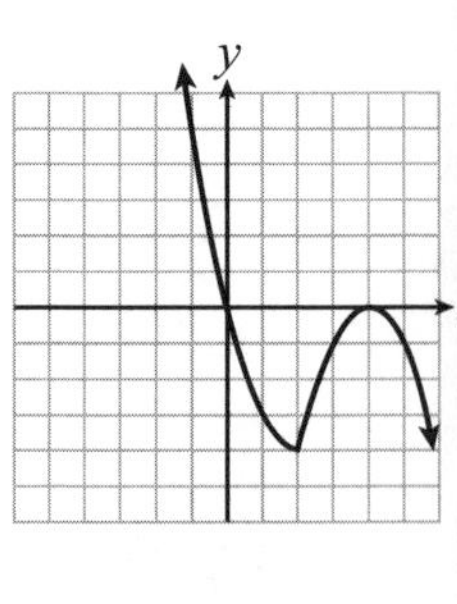

or for $x\le 2$

$$f(x)g(x)=-x(-x+4)=x^2-4x+4-4$$
$$=(x-2)^2-4$$

for $x\ge 2$

$$f(x)g(x)=(x-4)(-x+4)=-x^2+8x-16$$
$$=-(x^2-8x+16)$$
$$=-(x-4)^2$$

2.2 Exercise Set

1. Use the following functions *f, g, h, i, j*, and *k*, to find:

$$f(x)=2x^2+5x+3,\quad g(x)=2x-1,\quad h(x)=3,\quad i(x)=\frac{1}{x},\quad j(x)=x^2-1,\quad k(x)=\frac{2}{x+2}$$

a) $(g+j)(2)$

b) $(f-k)(-2)$

c) $(hi)(3)$

d) $(jk)(-3)$

e) $\left(\frac{g}{f}\right)(4)$

f) $\left(\frac{i}{k}\right)(-4)$

g) $\left(\frac{h}{j}\right)(-2)$

h) $(k-i)(7)$

2. Use the same functions *f, g, h, i, j*, and *k* to find the function and its domain:

$$f(x)=2x^2+5x+3,\quad g(x)=2x-1,\quad h(x)=3,\quad i(x)=\frac{1}{x},\quad j(x)=x^2-1,\quad k(x)=\frac{2}{x+2}$$

a) $(f-g)(x)$

b) $(j+i)(x)$

c) $\left(\frac{i}{h}\right)(x)$

d) $\left(\frac{h}{i}\right)(x)$

e) $(gk)(x)$

f) $\left(\frac{g}{k}\right)(x)$

g) $\left(\frac{f}{j}\right)(x)$

h) $(g\,j)(x)$

3. Find each expression, given that the function of *f, g, h, k* and *l* are defined as follows:

$$f(x)=2x+1, \quad g(x)=2x^2-x-1, \quad h(x)=x^3, \quad k(x)=3, \quad l(x)=x^2-1,$$

a) $\left(\frac{f}{l}\right)(x)-\left(\frac{l}{f}\right)(x)$

b) $\left(\frac{f}{l}\right)(0)-\left(\frac{l}{f}\right)(0)$

c) $[h(f+l)](x)$

d) $(hf)(x)+(hl)(x)$

e) $\left[l(k-h)\right](x)$

f) $(lk)(x)-(lh)(x)$

g) $(g+g)(x)$

h) $(g-g)(x)$

i) $(kg)(x)$

j) $(g+g)(-2)-(kg)(-2)$

4. Find $(f+g)(x)$, $(f-g)(x)$, $(fg)(x)$, $(ff)(x)$, $\left(\frac{f}{g}\right)(x)$, and $\left(\frac{g}{f}\right)(x)$, if:

a) $f(x)=x^2-4,\ g(x)=x+2$

b) $f(x)=2x^2-x-3,\ g(x)=x+1$

c) $f(x)=\sqrt{x},\ g(x)=\frac{1}{x}$

d) $f(x)=\sqrt{x},\ g(x)=x^2$

For questions 5 to 8, use the graph of $y = f(x)$ and $y = g(x)$ to graph:

a) $(f+g)(x)$ b) $(f-g)(x)$ c) $(g-f)(x)$ d) $(-f-g)(x)$ e) $\left(2f+\frac{1}{2}g\right)(x)$

5.

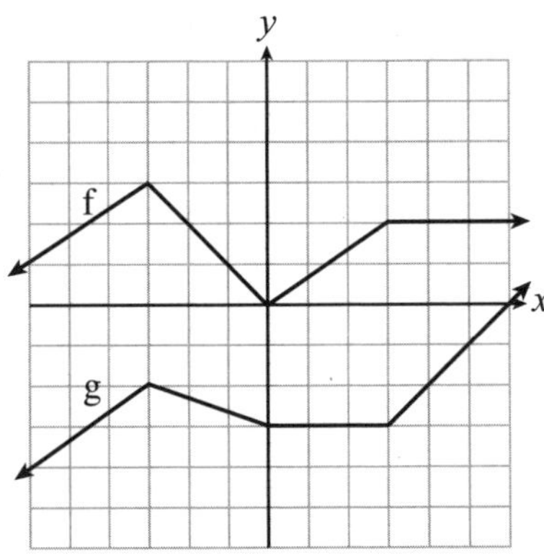

a)

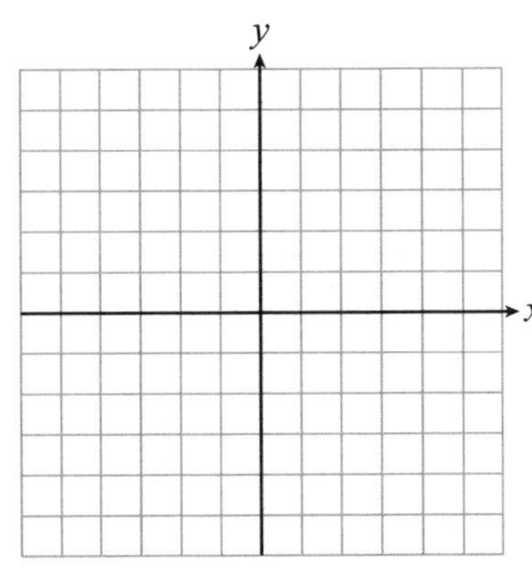

b)

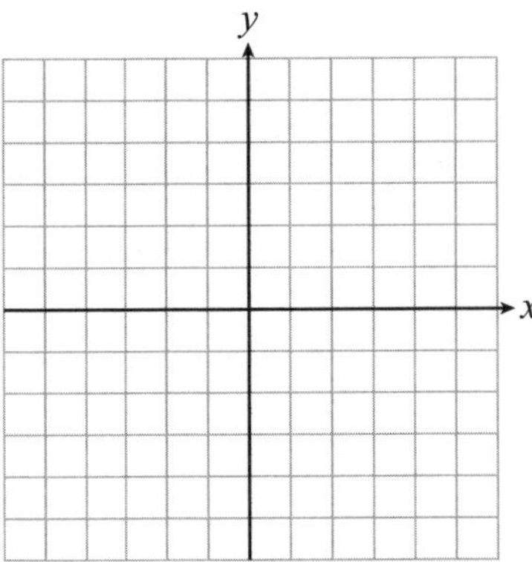

c)

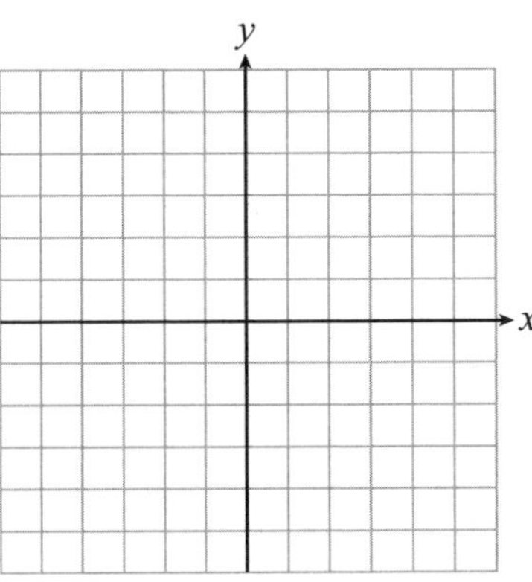

d)

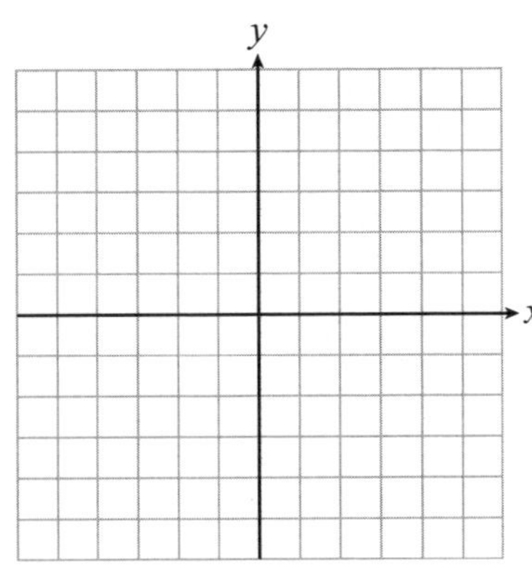

e)

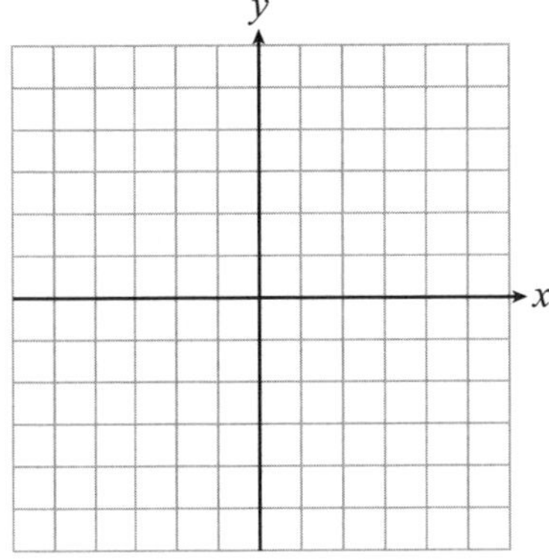

6.

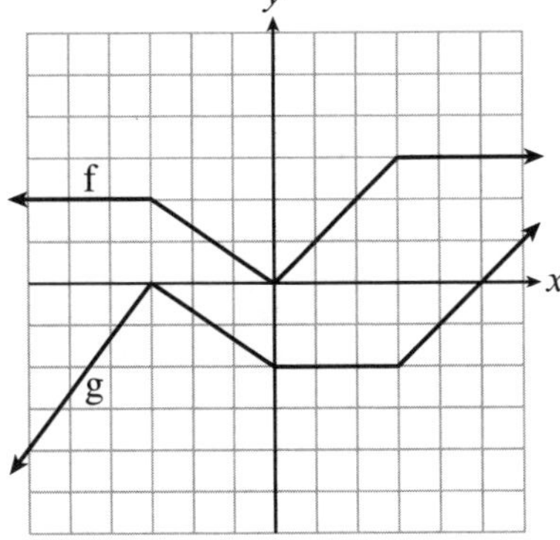

a)

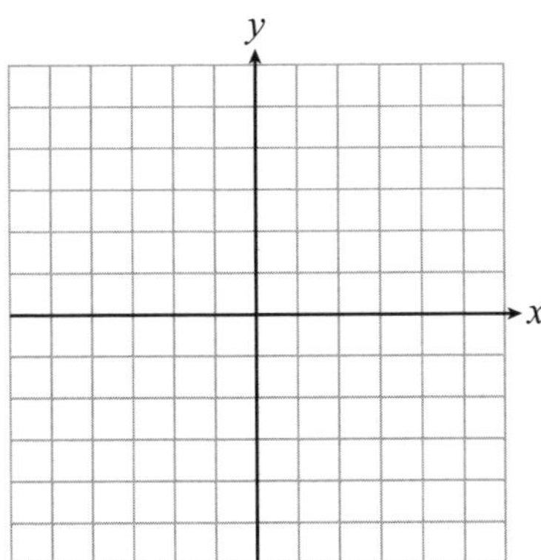

b)

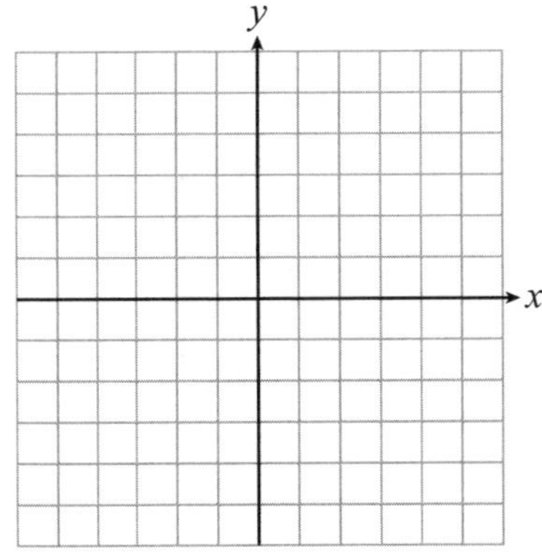

c)

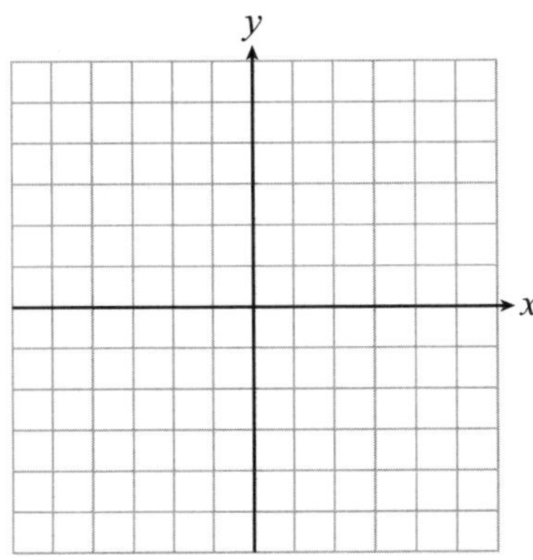

d)

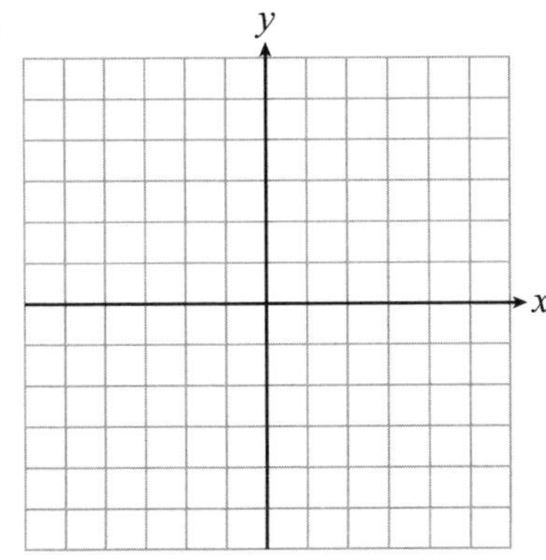

e)

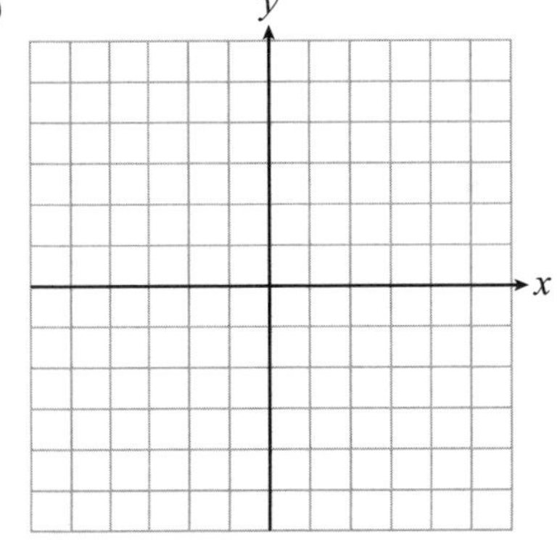

a) $(f+g)(x)$ b) $(f-g)(x)$ c) $(g-f)(x)$ d) $(-f-g)(x)$ e) $\left(2f+\frac{1}{2}g\right)(x)$

7.

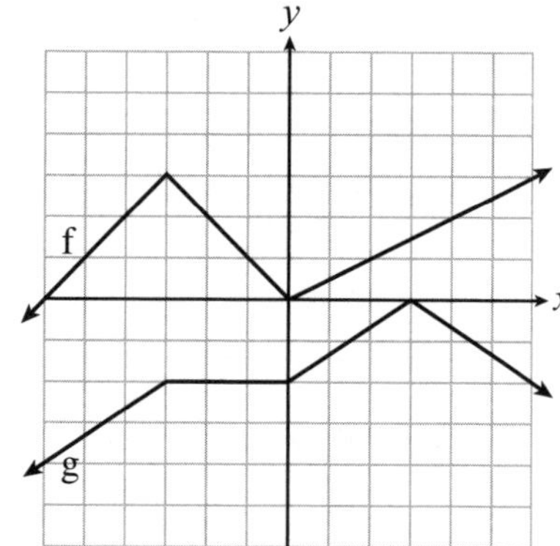

a)

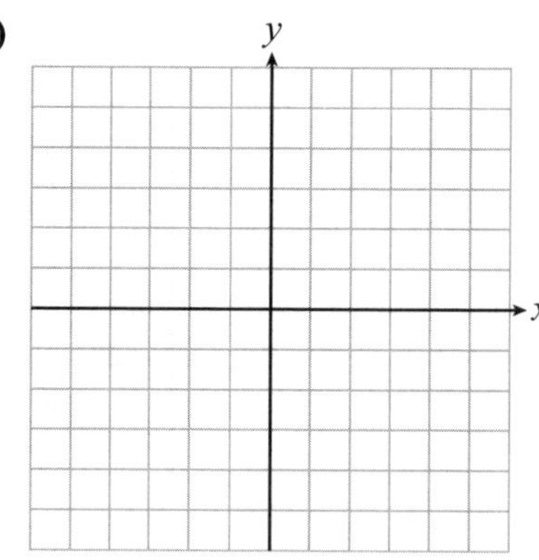

b)

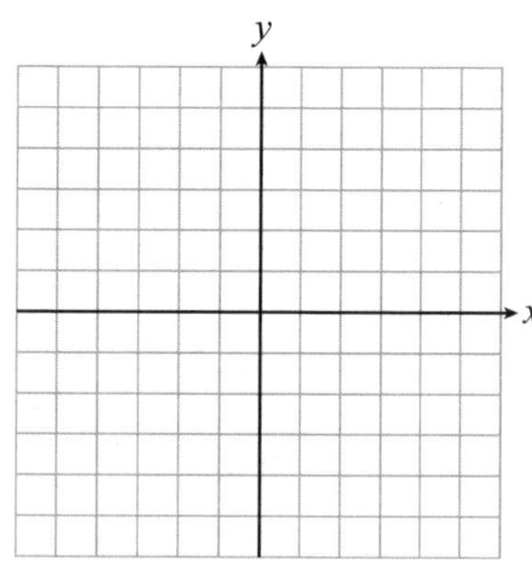

c)

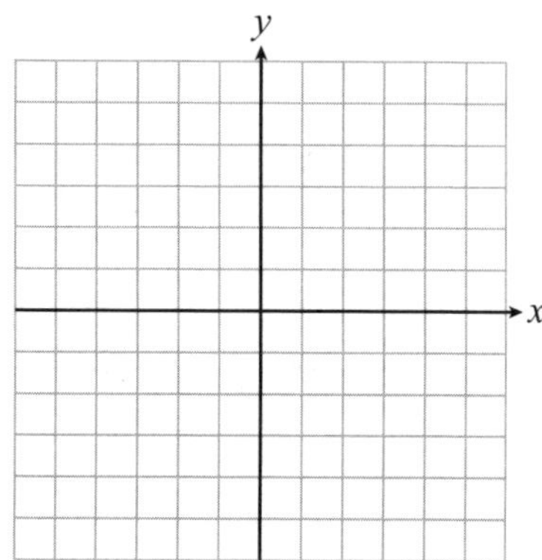

d)

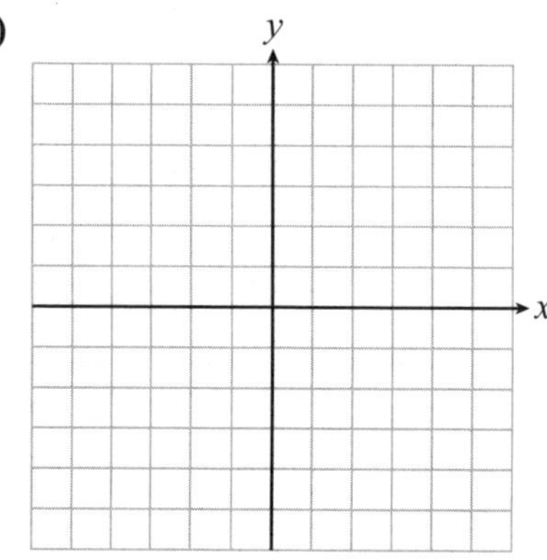

e)

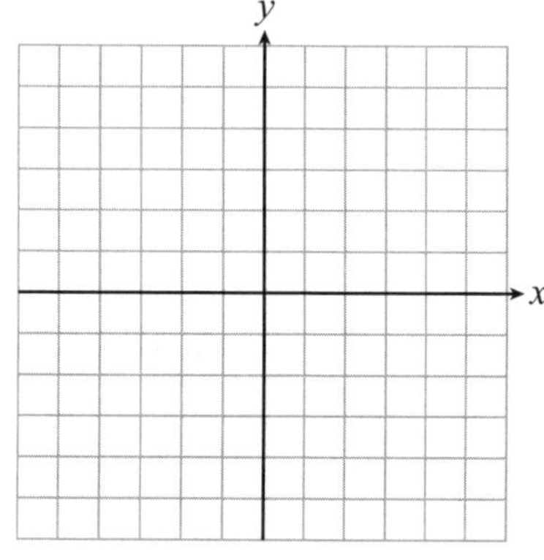

8.

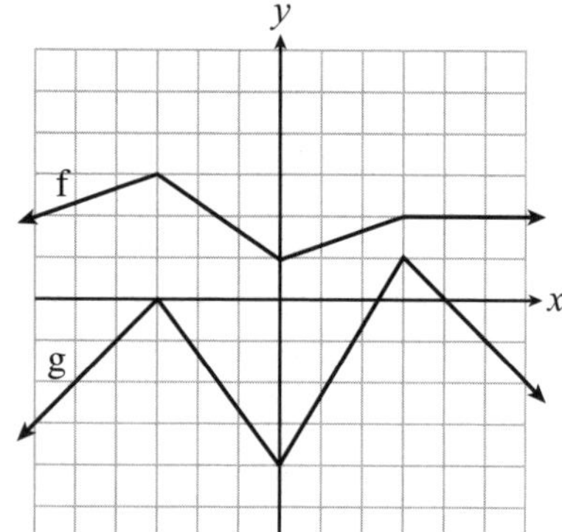

a)

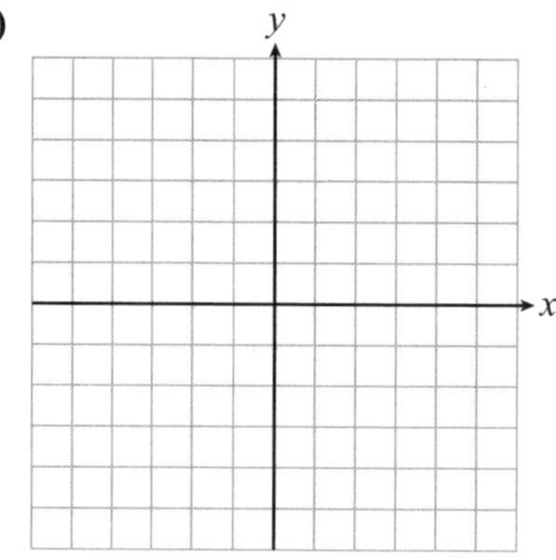

b)

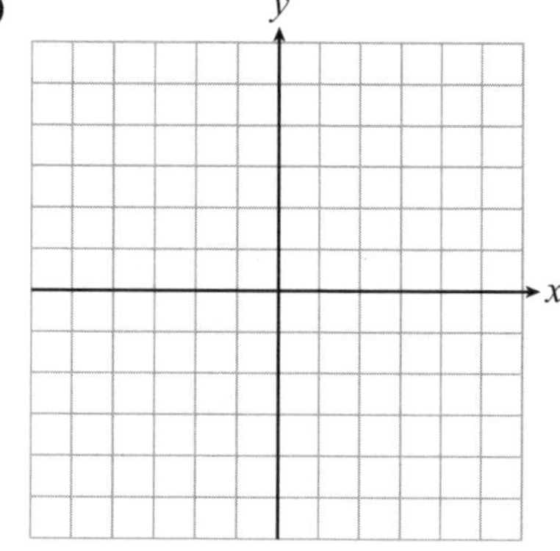

c)

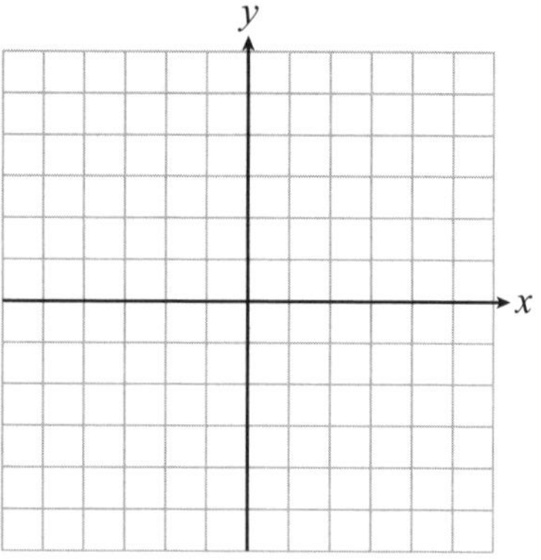

d)

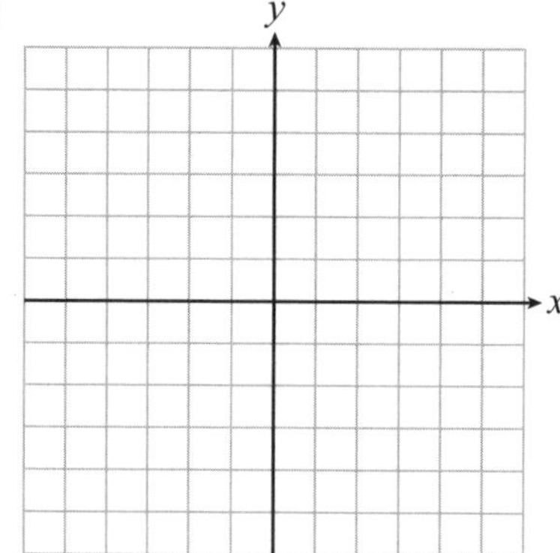

e)

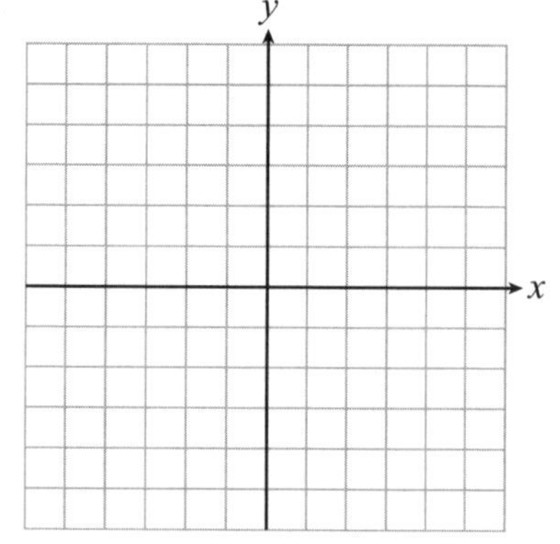

2.3 Composite Functions

We can combine functions by another method, the composition function. This method is based on the algebraic process of substitution. For example, if f and g are two functions defined by:

$$f(x) = x^2 \quad g(x) = 2x - 1$$

Choose any number in the domain of g, say $x = 3$. We can compute $g(3)$:

$$g(3) = 2(3) - 1 = 5$$

Now, let's use the output 5 that g has produced as an input for f. We obtain:

$$f(5) = 5^2 = 25$$

Therefore,

$$f(g(3)) = 25$$

Summarizing,

1. Start with the input value of x and calculate $g(x)$.
2. Use $g(x)$ as an input for f, and calculate $f(x)$, that is, calculate $f(g(x))$.

We use the notation $f \circ g$ to denote the function, read f circle g or f composed with g. The domain of $f \circ g$ consists of those x's in the domain of g whose range values are in the domain of f (i.e., those x's for which $g(x)$ is in the domain of f).

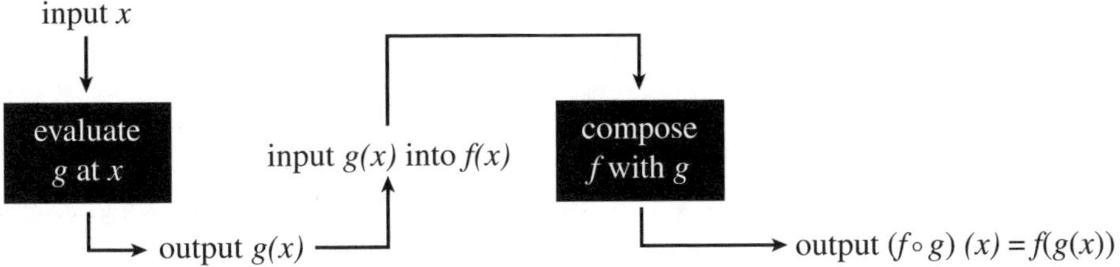

Our formal definition follows:

> **Composite of Functions** $f \circ g$
> The composite function $f \circ g$ of two functions f and g is defined by $(f \circ g)(x) = f(g(x))$.
> For all x in the domain of g such that $g(x)$ is in the domain of f.

i.e., $(f \circ g)(x)$ has the domain restriction of $g(x)$ as well as the domain restriction of the final composite function $(f \circ g)(x)$.

Example 1 If $f(x)=1-x^2$, $g(x)=2x+3$, find

a) $(f\circ g)(x)$ **b)** $(g\circ f)(x)$

▶ *Solution:* **a)** $(f\circ g)(x)=f(g(x))$

$=f(2x+3)$ *substitute* $g(x)$

$=1-(2x+3)^2$ *in* $f(x)$ *change every* x *to* $2x+3$

$=1-(4x^2+12x+9)$ *expand*

$=-4x^2-12x-8$ *simplify*

$g(x)$ and $(f\circ g)(x)$ do not have any domain restriction so the domain is all real numbers.

b) $(g\circ f)(x)=g(f(x))$

$=g(1-x^2)$ *substitute* $f(x)$

$=2(1-x^2)+3$ *in* $g(x)$ *change every* x *to* $1-x^2$

$=2-2x^2+3$ *expand*

$=-2x^2+5$ *simplify*

$f(x)$ and $(g\circ f)(x)$ do not have any domain restrictions so the domain is all real numbers.

Note: $(f\circ g)(x)$ is not the same as $(g\circ f)(x)$.

Example 2 If $f(x)=x^2$ and $g(x)=2x-1$, find $(f\circ g)(-2)$.

▶ *Solution:*

Method 1

$(f\circ g)(x)=f(g(x))$

$=f(2x-1)$

$=(2x-1)^2$

$=4x^2-4x+1$

and therefore

$(f\circ g)(-2)=4(-2)^2-4(-2)+1$

$=25$

Method 2

$(f\circ g)(-2)=f(g(-2))$

$=f(2(-2)-1)$

$=f(-5)$

$=(-5)^2$

$=25$

Example 3 If $f(x)=x^2-1$ and $g(x)=\sqrt{x}$, find $(f\circ g)(x)$, the domain of $f\circ g$ and sketch the graph.

▶ *Solution:* $(f\circ g)(x)=f(g(x))$

$=f(\sqrt{x})$

$=(\sqrt{x})^2-1$

$=x-1$

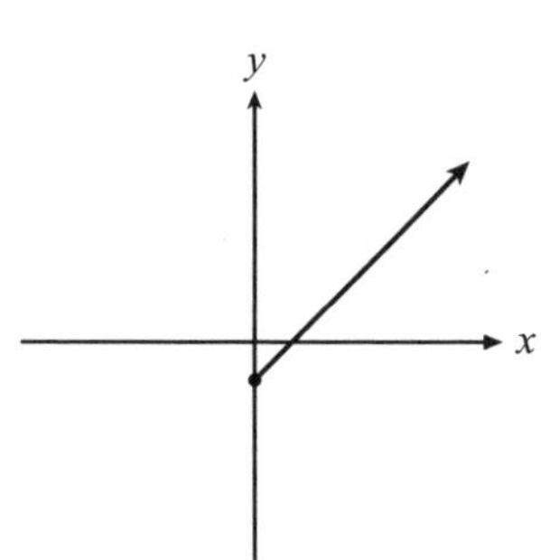

In $g(x)=\sqrt{x}$, there is a domain restriction of $\sqrt{x}\geq 0$.

In $(f\circ g)(x)=x-1$, there appears to be no restriction on x. However, the domain of $(f\circ g)(x)$ is restricted by the domain for $g(x)$ i.e. $x\geq 0$.

Example 4

If $f(x)=\dfrac{x}{x-1}$ and $g(x)=\dfrac{1}{x+1}$, find

a) $(f\circ g)(x)$ and its domain.

b) $(g\circ f)(x)$ and its domain.

▶ *Solution:*

a) $(f\circ g)(x)=f(g(x))=f\left(\dfrac{1}{x+1}\right)$

$$=\frac{\dfrac{1}{x+1}}{\dfrac{1}{x+1}-1}=\frac{\dfrac{1}{x+1}}{\dfrac{1-x-1}{x+1}}=\frac{1}{-x}=-\frac{1}{x}$$

In $g(x)=\dfrac{1}{x+1}$, $x\neq -1$; in $(f\circ g)(x)$, $x\neq 0$

Therefore, the domain of $(f\circ g)(x)$ is $x\neq 0,-1$.

b) $(g\circ f)(x)=g(f(x))=g\left(\dfrac{x}{x-1}\right)$

$$=\frac{1}{\dfrac{x}{x-1}+1}=\frac{1}{\dfrac{x+x-1}{x-1}}=\frac{x-1}{2x-1}$$

In $f(x)=\dfrac{x}{x-1}$, $x\neq 1$; in $(g\circ f)(x)$, $x\neq \dfrac{1}{2}$

Therefore, the domain of $(g\circ f)(x)$ is $x\neq \dfrac{1}{2},1$.

Example 5

If $f=\{(1,d),(3,e)\}$ and $g=\{(a,1),(b,3),(c,5)\}$, find $(f\circ g)(x)$.

▶ *Solution:*

$(f\circ g)(a)=f(g(a))=f(1)=d$

$(f\circ g)(b)=f(g(b))=f(3)=e$

$(f\circ g)(c)=f(g(c))=f(5)$, but 5 is not in the domain $f(x)$

so $(f\circ g)(c)$ cannot be found.

Hence $(f\circ g)(x)=\{(a,d),(b,e)\}$

Example 6 Use the graph of the two functions to find:

a) $(f \circ g)(1)$

b) $(g \circ g)(5)$

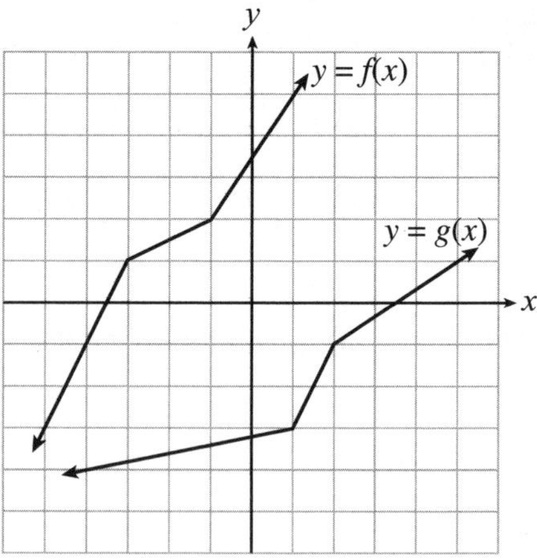

▶ *Solution:*

a) $(f \circ g)(1) = f(g(1))$
$= f(-3)$
$= 1$

b) $(g \circ g)(5) = g(g(5))$
$= g(1)$
$= -3$

Example 7 Compute $\dfrac{f(x+h)-f(x)}{h}$, $h \neq 0$ for $f(x) = 2x^2 + 3$

▶ *Solution:*

$f(x) = 2x^2 + 3$

$f(x+h) = 2(x+h)^2 + 3$ thus

$$\frac{f(x+h)-f(x)}{h} = \frac{\left[2(x+h)^2+3\right]-\left[2x^2+3\right]}{h}$$

$$= \frac{\left[2(x^2+2xh+h^2)+3\right]-\left[2x^2+3\right]}{h}$$

$$= \frac{2x^2+4xh+2h^2+3-2x^2-3}{h}$$

$$= \frac{4xh+2h^2}{h}$$

$$= 4x + 2h$$

Note: *This combining function is a technique that will be extremely useful when studying calculus.*

Decomposing a Composite Function

When decomposing a composite function, we ask ourselves what function (of the composition) is on the inside – the input value – and what function is on the outside – the output value.

Example 8 Given $h(x)=\sqrt{x-2}$, find two functions *f* and *g* so that $(f\circ g)(x)=h(x)$.

▶ *Solution:* We see that $x-2$ is inside the radical, thus $g(x)=x-2$, and the radical is outside, so $f(x)=\sqrt{x}$.

$$\begin{aligned}\text{check } (f\circ g)(x)&=f(g(x))=f(x-2)\\&=\sqrt{x-2}\\&=h(x)\end{aligned}$$

Example 9 Given $h(x)=\sqrt[3]{x+5}$, find functions *f* and *g* so that $h(x)=(f\circ g)(x)$.

▶ *Solution:* Since the formula for $h(x)$ says to first add 5 and then take the cube root, we get

$g(x)=x+5$ and $f(x)=\sqrt[3]{x}$

$$\begin{aligned}\text{Then } (f\circ g)(x)&=f(g(x))\\&=f(x+5)\\&=\sqrt[3]{x+5}\\&=h(x)\end{aligned}$$

Example 10 Given $h(x)=\left(\sqrt{x}+1\right)^3-2$, find two functions *f* and *g* so that $(f\circ g)(x)=h(x)$.

▶ *Solution:* Inside is $\sqrt{x}+1$, thus $g(x)=\sqrt{x}+1$.

Outside is x^3-2, thus $f(x)=x^3-2$.

$$\begin{aligned}\text{check } (f\circ g)(x)&=f(g(x))=f\left(\sqrt{x}+1\right)\\&=\left(\sqrt{x}-1\right)^3-2\\&=h(x)\end{aligned}$$

Note: The solution to decomposing a composite function is ***not*** *unique; other answers are possible, too.*

2.3 Exercise Set

1. What is the domain of the following functions?

a) $f(x)=\dfrac{1}{x-2}$

b) $f(x)=\dfrac{x-3}{x^2-9}$

c) $f(x)=\sqrt{x+2}$

d) $f(x)=\sqrt{3-x}$

e) $f(x)=\dfrac{1}{\sqrt{x}}$

f) $f(x)=\sqrt{x^2-1}$

g) $f(x)=\sqrt{1-x^2}$

h) $f(x)=\sqrt{x(x-2)}$

2. Let $f(x)=2x^2-3x+1,\quad g(x)=x+1,\quad h(x)=5,\quad j(x)=\dfrac{x-1}{x+1}$

Evaluate the following:

a) $(f\circ g)(2)$

b) $(h\circ j)(-3)$

c) $(j\circ h)(2)$

d) $j(g(0))$

e) $h(j(-1))$

f) $f(j(3))$

g) $(h\circ g\circ g)(2)$

h) $(f\circ f\circ f)(-1)$

i) $(j\circ h\circ g)(-3)$

j) $(g\circ j\circ f)(4)$

k) $(f\circ h\circ j)(2)$

l) $j(j(g(f(-2))))$

3. Use f and g by the following table of values to evaluate the following:

x	–2	0	3	7
$f(x)$	0	1	4	6

x	–1	1	4	6
$g(x)$	3	2	–2	–4

a) $f(0)$

b) $g(1)$

c) $(f\circ g)(-1)$

d) $(f\circ g)(4)$

e) $(g\circ f)(0)$

f) $(g\circ f)(7)$

g) $(f\circ g)(1)$

h) $(g\circ f)(-2)$

4. For each pair of functions, find $(f\circ g)(x)$ and $(g\circ f)(x)$. State the domain of each result.

a) $f(x)=\sqrt{x+2}$ and $g(x)=2x-3$

b) $f(x)=\frac{2}{x}$ and $g(x)=\frac{x}{x-1}$

c) $f(x)=x^2-2x$ and $g(x)=x+3$

d) $f(x)=x^2+x-3$ and $g(x)=x+2$

e) $f(x)=\sqrt{x-2}$ and $g(x)=3x+2$

f) $f(x)=|x|-3$ and $g(x)=-2x+3$

g) $f(x)=\frac{3}{x}$ and $g(x)=\frac{1}{x-4}$

h) $f(x)=|x-2|-3$ and $g(x)=\frac{1}{x}$

5. Find two functions $f(x)$ and $g(x)$ such that $h(x)=(f \circ g)(x)$. Answers may vary.

a) $h(x)=(2x-3)^2$

b) $h(x)=\sqrt[3]{3x^2-2}$

c) $h(x)=\dfrac{1}{3x-4}$

d) $h(x)=\dfrac{2}{x^2+4}$

e) $h(x)=\sqrt{x^2+1}+3$

f) $h(x)=\sqrt[3]{3x+4}-1$

g) $h(x)=3(2x-3)^4-(2x-3)^7$

h) $h(x)=3(2x+4)^3+2(2x+4)^6$

6. Sketch the graph of $(f \circ g)(x)$ for the following. State the domain.

a) $f(x)=x^2+1$ and $g(x)=\sqrt{x}$

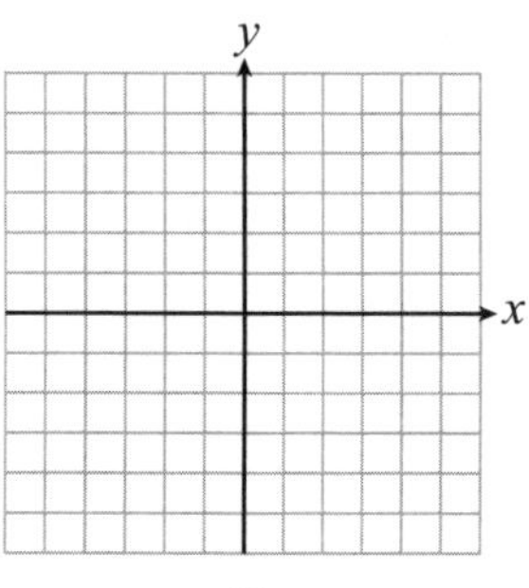

b) $f(x)=x^2+2$ and $g(x)=\sqrt{x-2}$

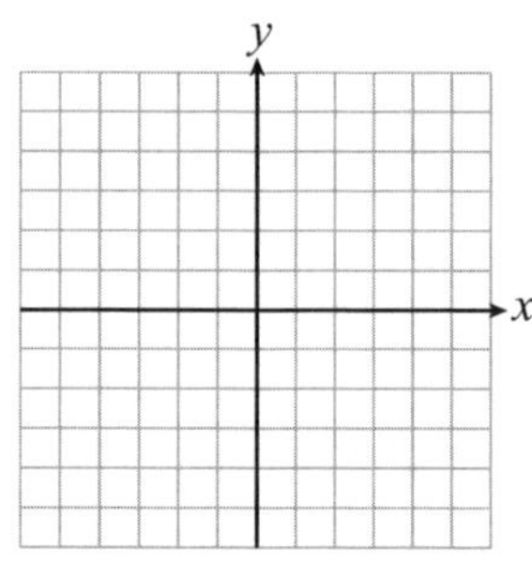

c) $f(x)=1-x^2$ and $g(x)=\sqrt{1-x}$

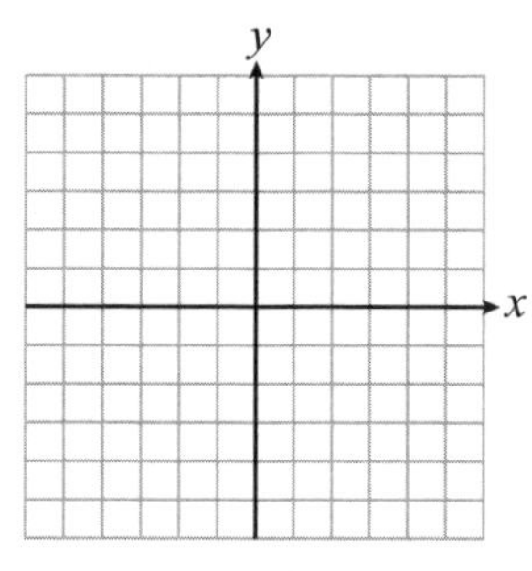

d) $f(x)=x^2+1$ and $g(x)=\sqrt{4-x^2}$

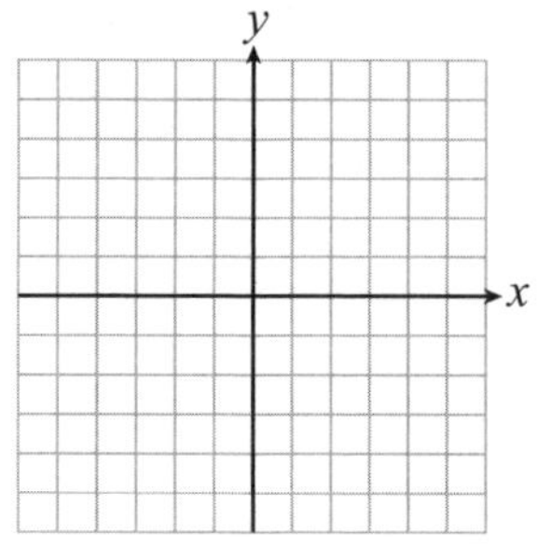

7. The first figure shows the graph of two functions, f and g. The second figure shows the graph of two functions, h and k. Use the graphs to compute the following:

a) $(g \circ f)(-4) =$

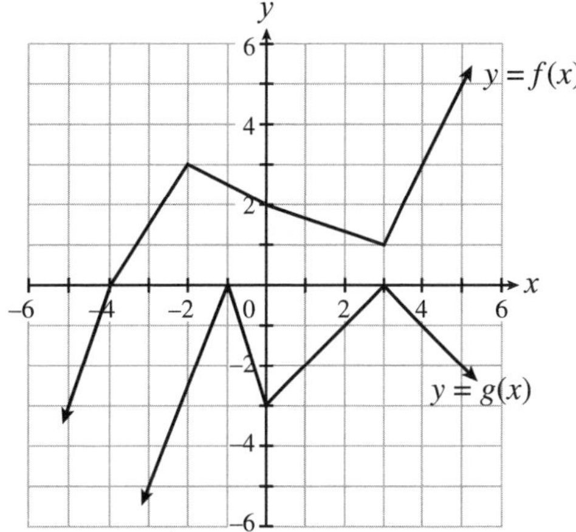

b) $(f \circ g)(3) =$

c) $(f \circ f)(-2) =$

d) $(g \circ g)(3) =$

e) $(g \circ f)(-5) =$

f) $(g \circ f)(-3) =$

g) $h(k(0)) ==$

h) $h(k(-1)) =$

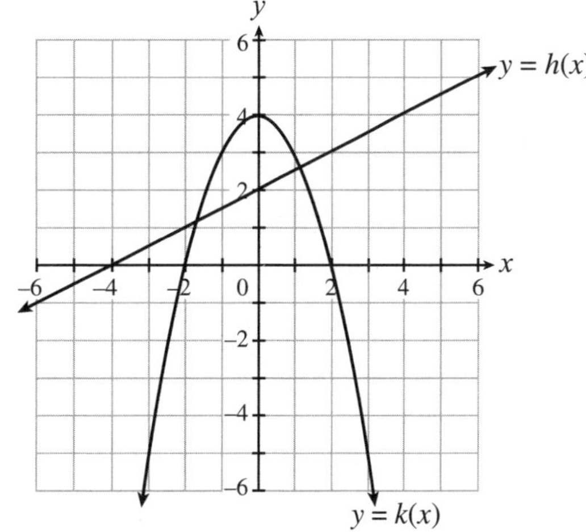

i) $h(k(2)) =$

j) $h(k(-3)) =$

k) $k(h(0)) =$

l) $k(h(2)) =$

m) $k(h(-4)) =$

n) $k(h(-2)) =$

8. If $f = \{ (3, 4), (4, 5), (5, 6), (6, 7) \}$ and $g = \{ (5, 3), (6, 4), (7, -2), (8, 0) \}$, determine:

a) $f \circ g$

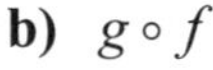

b) $g \circ f$

9. If $f(x) = 3x - 2$ and $g(x) = 3x + b$, find b such $(f \circ g)(x) = (g \circ f)(x)$ for all real numbers x.

10. Find the difference quotient $\frac{f(x+h)-f(x)}{h}, h \neq 0$ for the given function f.

a) $f(x)=2x+3$

b) $f(x)=x^2+x$

c) $f(x)=-3x^2+2x$

d) $f(x)=\frac{1}{x}$

e) $f(x)=\frac{4}{2x-1}$

f) $f(x)=\frac{1}{\sqrt{x}}$

11. A circle is inscribed in a square.

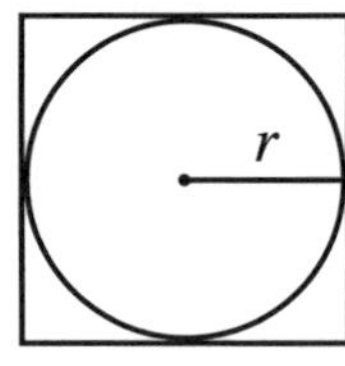

a) Write the radius of the circle as a function of the length x of the sides of the square.

b) Write the area A of the circle as a function of the radius.

c) Find $(A \circ r)(x)$.

12. A baseball diamond is a square 90 ft on each side. A batter is running to first base at a rate of 27 ft/sec.

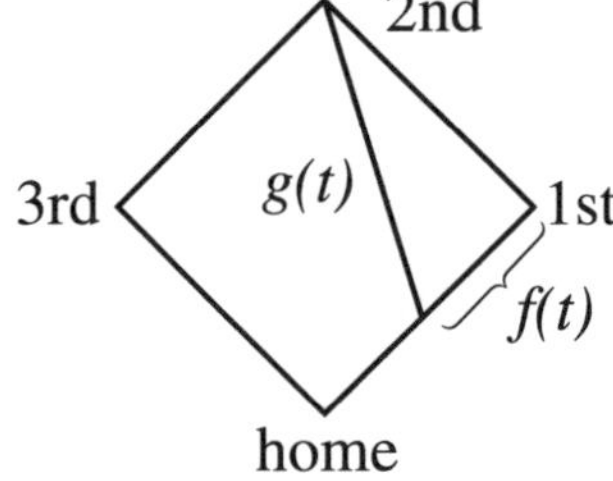

a) Find a function $f(t)$ for the distance x of the batter from first base in terms of time t.

b) Find a function $g(f)$ for the distance the batter is from second base in terms of the distance f.

c) Find $(g \circ f)(t)$ and explain the meaning of the function.

2.4 Transformations of Graphs

Knowing the graph of a basic function, and how to create different functions from these basic functions, is called **transformations**. Types of transformations we will look at are:

- translations – vertical and horizontal shifts of the graph of a function
- compression and expansion of the graph
- reflection of the graph in the x-axis and y-axis

For a function $y = f(x)$, these transformations can result in:

$$y = af[b(x-c)]+d$$

1. Translations, or shifts, are additions or subtractions shown by c or d.
   Expansions, or compressions, are multiplications shown by a or b.
   Reflections occur when the multipliers are negative.

2. Constants a and d, which are "outside" the original function, affect the y-value of the function.
   Constants b and c, which are "inside" the original function, affect the x-value of the function.

The section will introduce each transformation separately. A later section will deal with combining multiple types of transformations.

Translations

A translation is when a graph is shifted in the x or y direction **without** the shape of the graph changing.

a) Vertical translation, $a > 0$

If $a > 0$, for the graph of $y = f(x)$, the graph of:

$y = f(x) + a$ is shifted up "a" units
$y = f(x) - a$ is shifted down "a" units

The following examples show translations for different algebraic functions.

Example 1

Quadratic Graphs

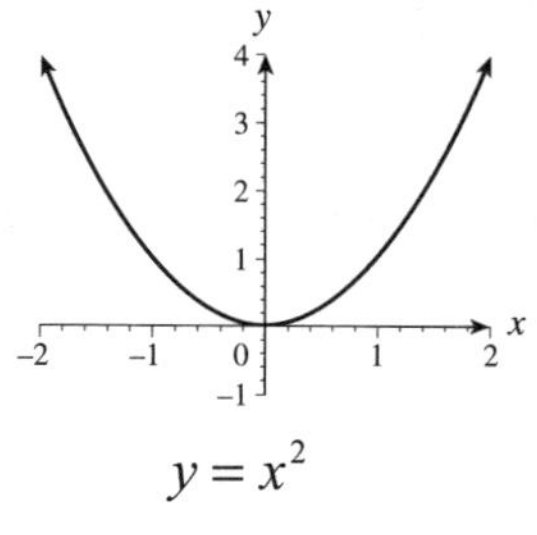

$y = x^2$

$y = f(x)$

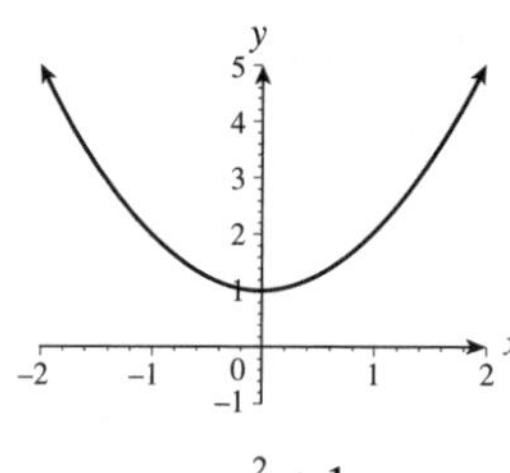

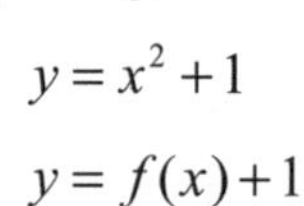

$y = x^2 + 1$

$y = f(x) + 1$

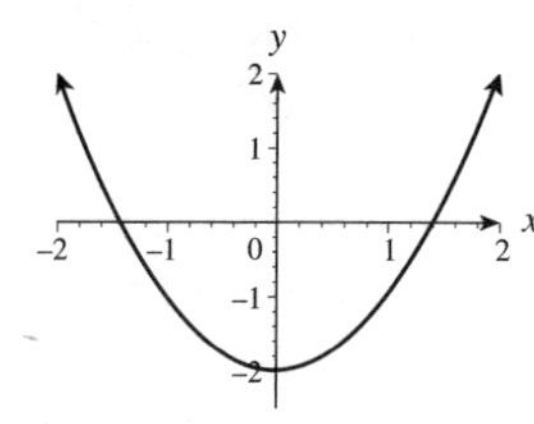

$y = x^2 - 2$

$y = f(x) - 2$

Square Root Graphs

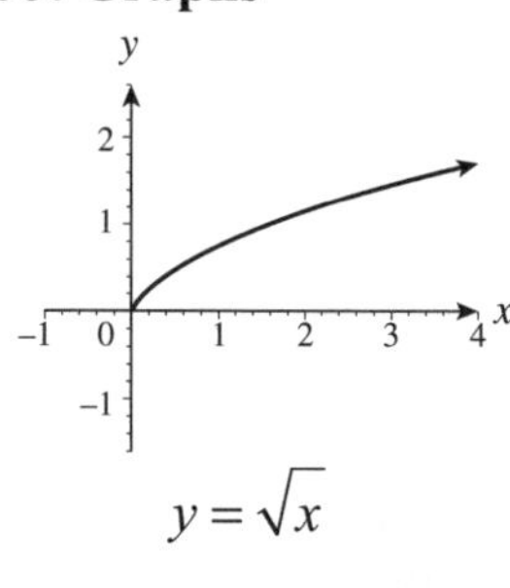

$y = \sqrt{x}$

$y = f(x)$

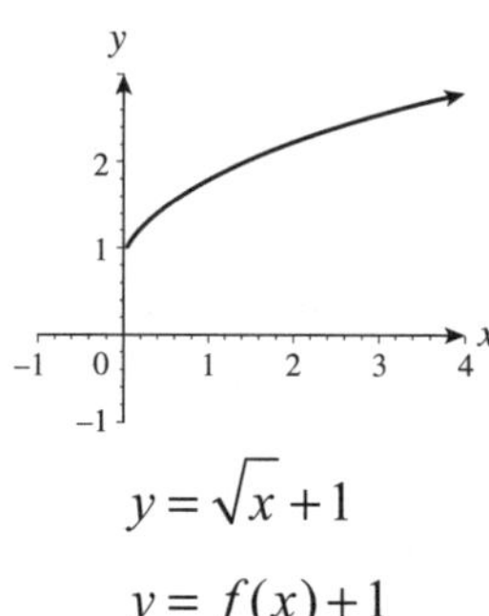

$y = \sqrt{x} + 1$

$y = f(x) + 1$

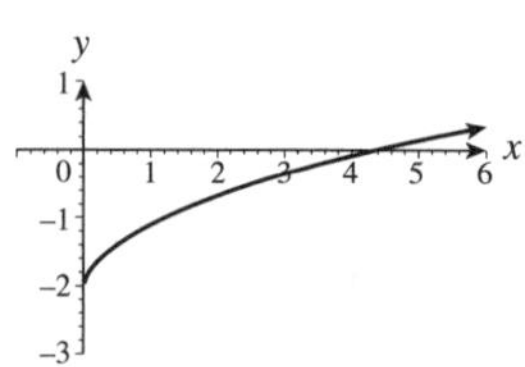

$y = \sqrt{x} - 2$

$y = f(x) - 2$

Absolute Value Graphs

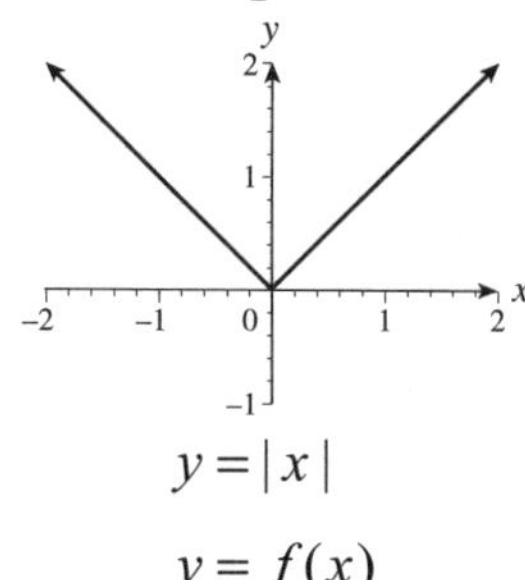

$y = |x|$

$y = f(x)$

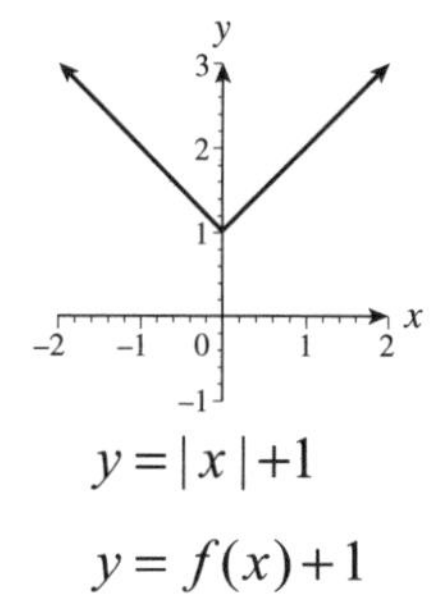

$y = |x| + 1$

$y = f(x) + 1$

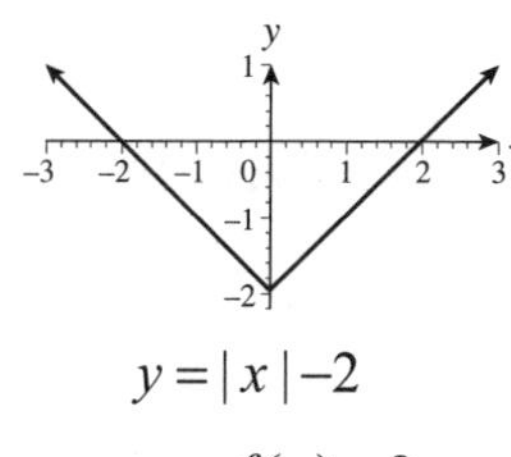

$y = |x| - 2$

$y = f(x) - 2$

Cubic Graphs

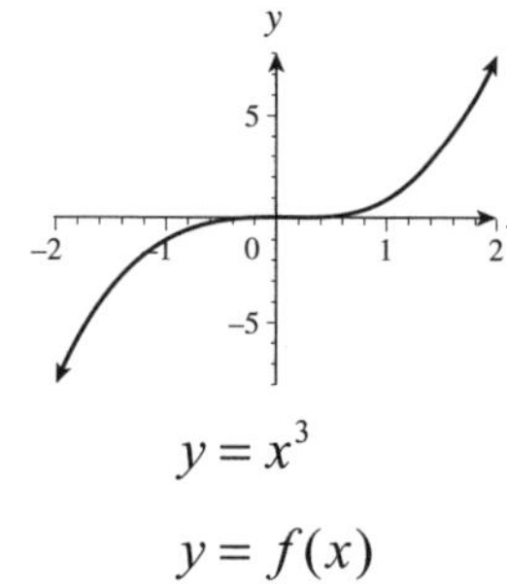

$y = x^3$

$y = f(x)$

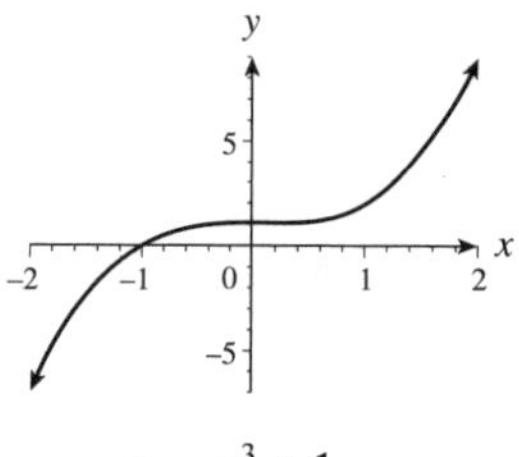

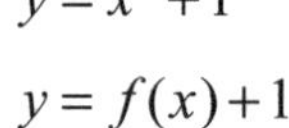

$y = x^3 + 1$

$y = f(x) + 1$

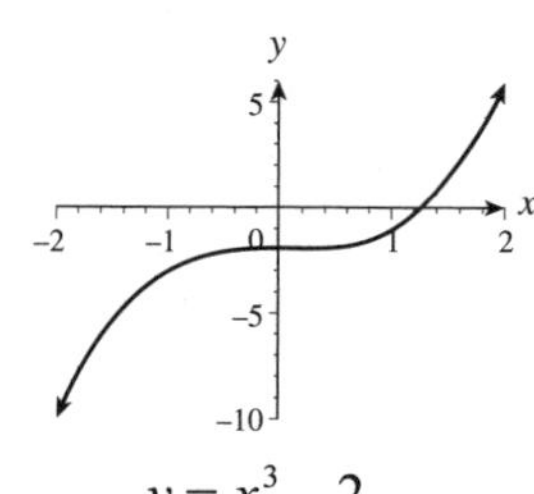

$y = x^3 - 2$

$y = f(x) - 2$

Reciprocal Graphs

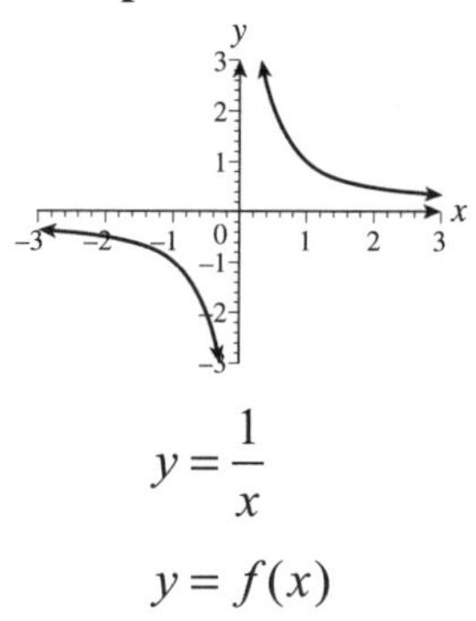

$y = \frac{1}{x}$

$y = f(x)$

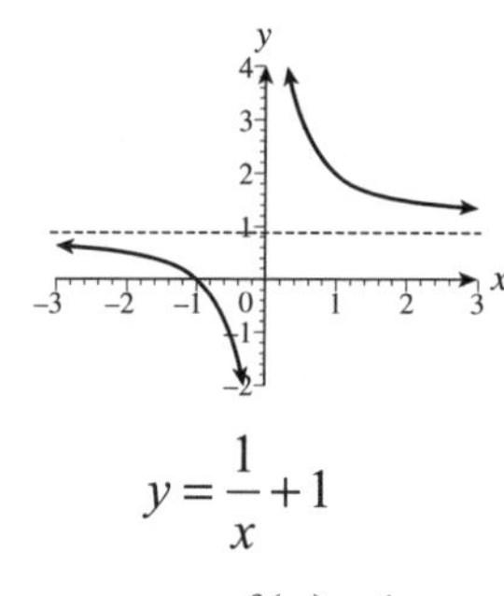

$y = \frac{1}{x} + 1$

$y = f(x) + 1$

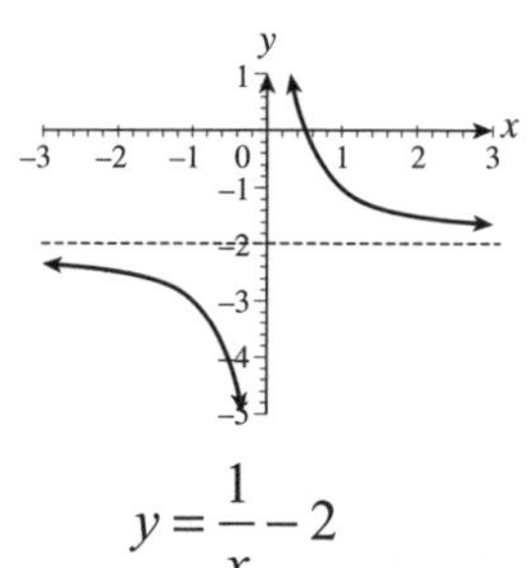

$y = \frac{1}{x} - 2$

$y = f(x) - 2$

b) Horizontal Translations

If $a > 0$, for the graph of $y = f(x)$, the graph of:

$y = f(x+a)$ is shifted left a units
$y = f(x-a)$ is shifted right a units

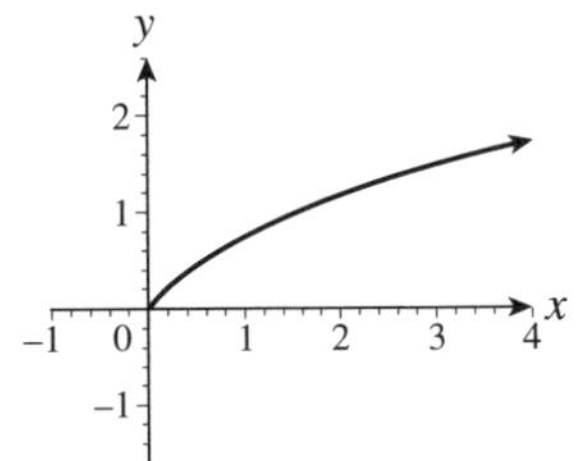

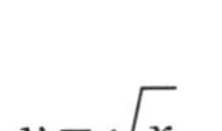

$y = \sqrt{x}$

$y = f(x)$

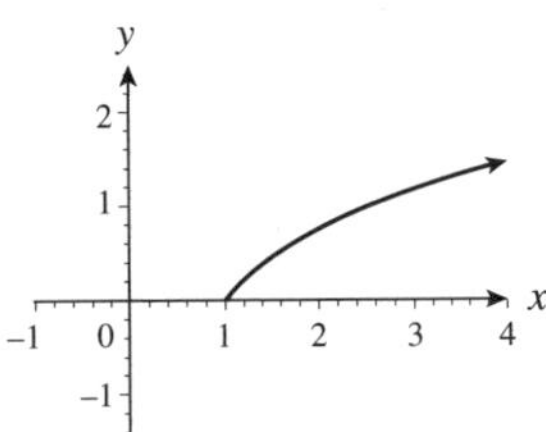

$y = \sqrt{x-1}$

$y = f(x-1)$

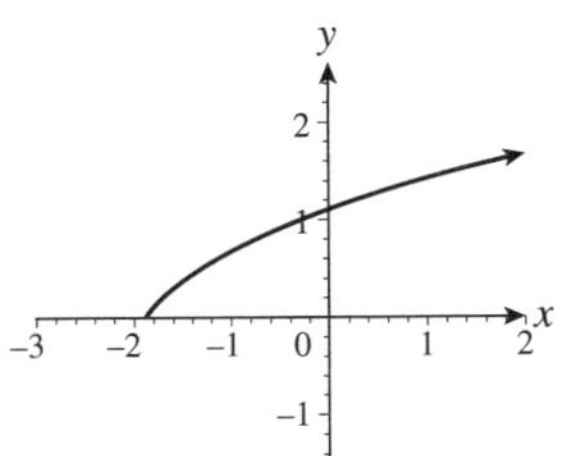

$y = \sqrt{x+2}$

$y = f(x+2)$

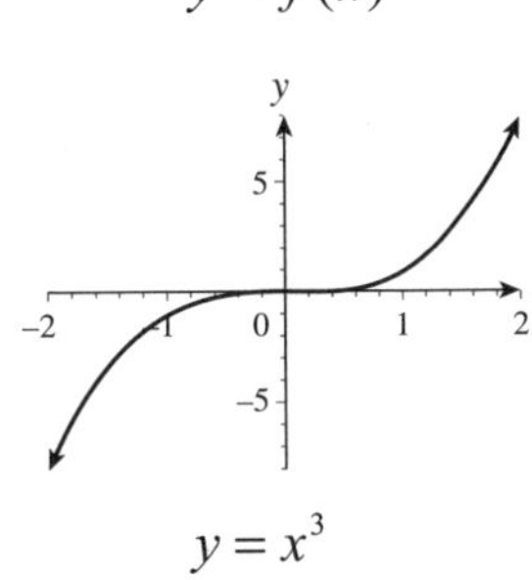

$y = x^3$

$y = f(x)$

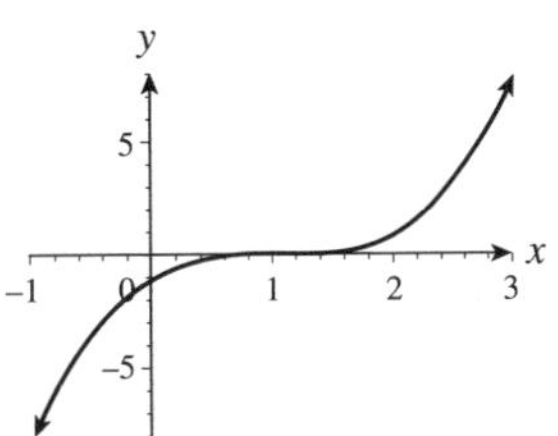

$y = (x-1)^3$

$y = f(x-1)$

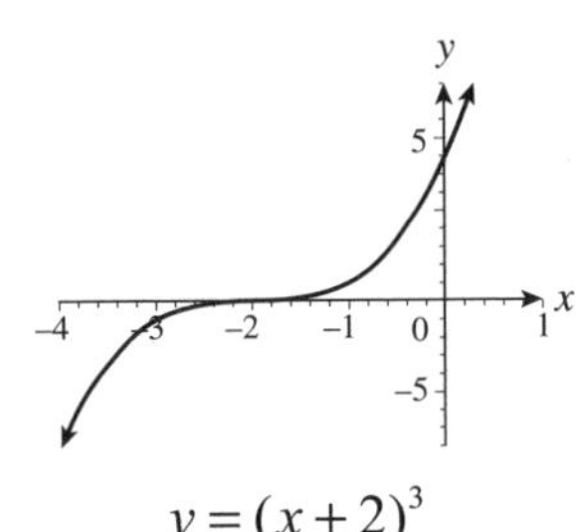

$y = (x+2)^3$

$y = f(x+2)$

The following list summarizes vertical and horizontal translations:

Vertical and Horizontal Translations of $y = f(x)$ with point (m, n)

If $a > 0$:

1.	Vertical translation of a units *upward*	$h(x) = f(x) + a, \ (m, n+a)$
2.	Vertical translation of a units *downward*	$h(x) = f(x) - a, \ (m, n-a)$
3.	Horizontal translation of a units *to the right*	$h(x) = f(x-a), \ (m+a, n)$
4.	Horizontal translation of a units *to the left*	$h(x) = f(x+a), \ (m-a, n)$

Example 2 Write the equation of a function which transforms $f(x) = \sqrt{x}$ by moving 4 units right and 3 units down.

▶ *Solution:* $g(x) = \sqrt{x-4} - 3$

Example 3 What transformations have occurred to change $y = f(x)$ to $y = f(x-2) + 4$?

▶ *Solution:* horizontal translation: 2 units right

vertical translation: 4 units up

Example 4 If (2, 2) is in $y = f(x)$, which point is in $y = f(x+3) - 2$?

▶ *Solution:* 3 units left and 2 units down produces point (–1, 0).

Reflection

The second type of transformation is a **reflection**. The reflections we will discuss are either over the x-axis or over the y-axis.

For the graph of $y = f(x)$, the graph of:
$y = -f(x)$ is a reflection in the x-axis
$y = f(-x)$ is a reflection in the y-axis
$y = -f(-x)$ is a reflection in the x-axis and y-axis

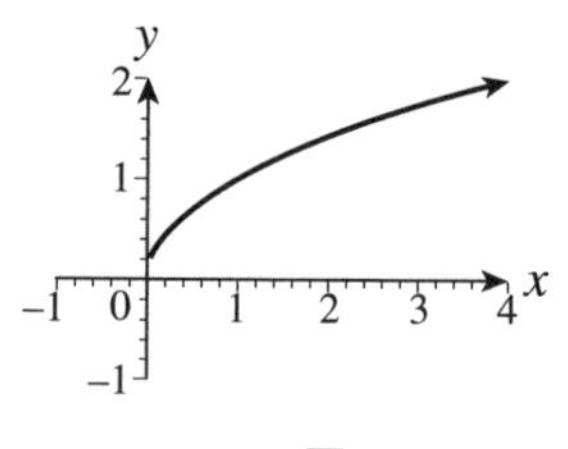

$y = \sqrt{x}$
$y = f(x)$

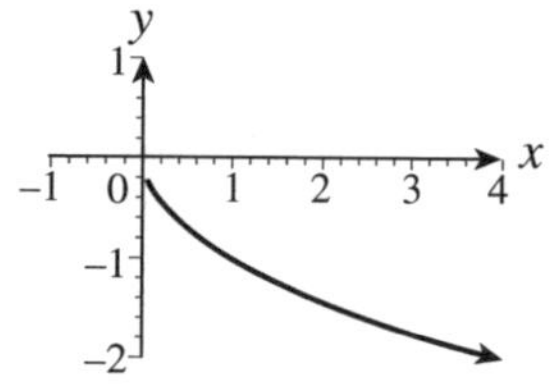

$y = -\sqrt{x}$
$y = -f(x)$

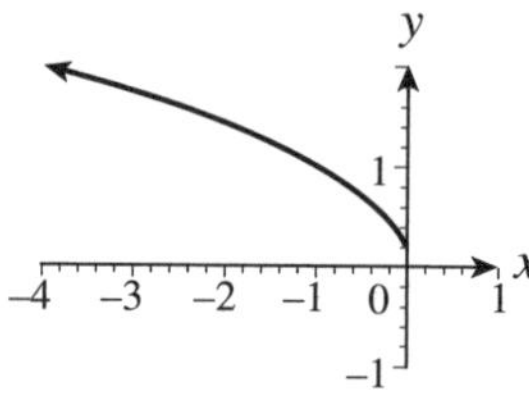

$y = \sqrt{-x}$
$y = f(-x)$

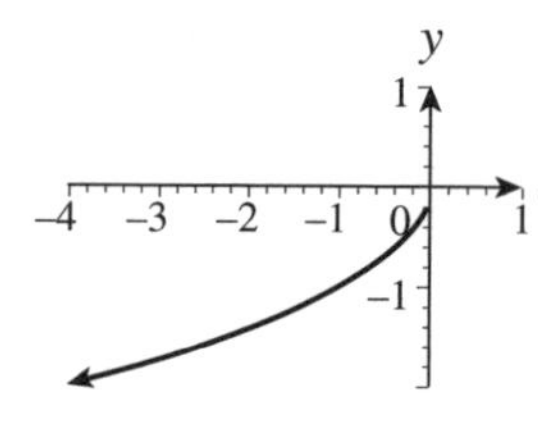

$y = -\sqrt{-x}$
$y = -f(-x)$

Summarizing reflections:

Reflections in the Coordinate Axes

Reflections in the coordinate axes of the graph of $y = f(x)$ with point (m, n) are as follows:

1. Reflection in the x-axis $h(x) = -f(x),\ (m, -n)$
2. Reflection in the y-axis $h(x) = f(-x),\ (-m, n)$

Example 5 Write an equation for the function $y = x^2 + x$ if it is reflected

a) in the x-axis

b) in the y-axis

▶ *Solution:* **a)** $y = -(x^2 + x) = -x^2 - x$

b) $y = (-x)^2 + (-x) = x^2 - x$

Example 6 What transformation has occurred to change $y = x^2 + 2x$ to $y = -(x^2 + 2x)$?

▶ *Solution:* The negative is outside the original function so it affects the y-values which is a reflection on the x-axis.

Example 7 If (3, 2) is on $y = f(x)$, what point is on

a) $y = -f(x)$

b) $y = f(-x)$

c) $y = -f(-x)$

▶ *Solution:* **a)** (3, –2)

b) (–3, 2)

c) (–3, –2)

Absolute Value Function

The domain (x-value) of $y=|f(x)|$ is the same as the domain of $y=f(x)$, but the range (y-value) of $y=|f(x)|$ will be $y=f(x)\geq 0$.

Example

a)

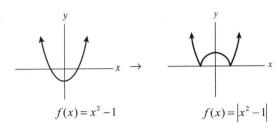

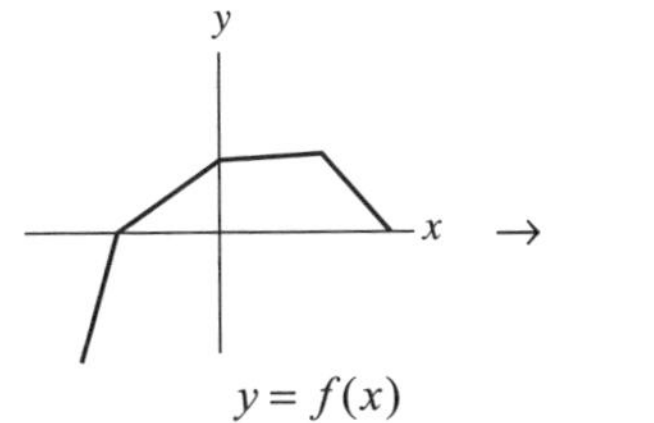

$y=f(x)$

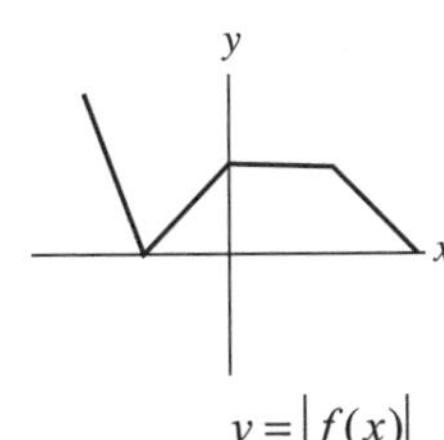

$y=|f(x)|$

b)

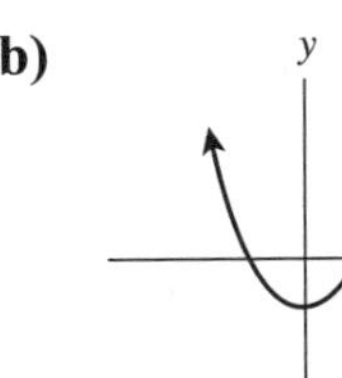

$f(x)=x^2-1$

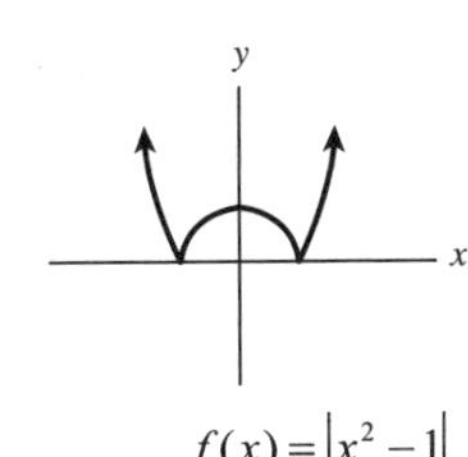

$f(x)=|x^2-1|$

Reciprocal Function

The chart below shows the range relationship between the graph of $y=f(x)$ and the graph of $y=\frac{1}{f(x)}$.

$f(x)$	$\frac{1}{f(x)}$	*Examples*
$f(x)\leq -1$	$-1\leq \frac{1}{f(x)}<0$	$f(x)=-2\rightarrow \frac{1}{f(x)}=-\frac{1}{2}$
$-1\leq f(x)<0$	$\frac{1}{f(x)}\leq -1$	$f(x)=-0.5\rightarrow \frac{1}{f(x)}=\frac{1}{-0.5}=-2$
0	undefined	$f(x)=0\rightarrow \frac{1}{f(x)}=\frac{1}{0}=\infty$
undefined	0	$f(x)=\frac{7}{0}=\infty\rightarrow \frac{1}{f(x)}=\frac{0}{7}=0$
$0<f(x)\leq 1$	$\frac{1}{f(x)}\geq 1$	$f(x)=\frac{3}{4}\rightarrow \frac{1}{f(x)}=\frac{4}{3}$
$f(x)\geq 1$	$0<\frac{1}{f(x)}\leq 1$	$f(x)=\frac{5}{3}\rightarrow \frac{1}{f(x)}=\frac{3}{5}$
$f(x)$ is increasing	$\frac{1}{f(x)}$ is decreasing	$f(x)=1,2,3\rightarrow \frac{1}{f(x)}=1,\frac{1}{2},\frac{1}{3}$
$f(x)$ is decreasing	$\frac{1}{f(x)}$ is increasing	$f(x)=-1,-2,-3\rightarrow \frac{1}{f(x)}=-1,-\frac{1}{2},-\frac{1}{3}$

Example: If $y=f(x)$ has coordinate point (–2, 4), what point is on $y=\frac{1}{f(x)}$?

Solution: The domain (x-value) will not change but the range (y-value) will be a reciprocal value, therefore point is (–2, ¼).

Example: given the graph of $y=f(x)$, graph $y=\frac{1}{f(x)}$.

Function

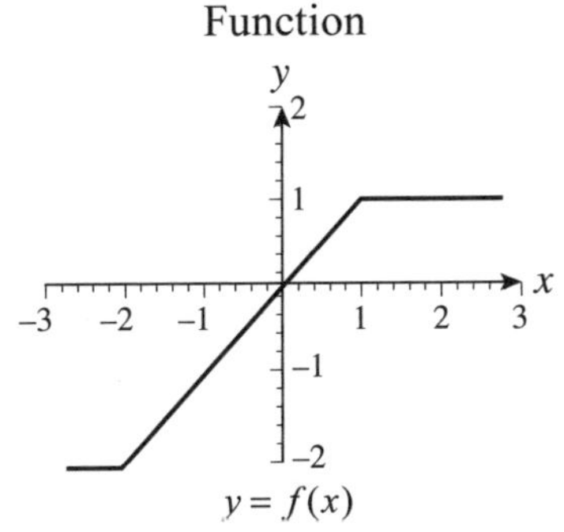

$y=f(x)$

- $f(x)=0\rightarrow \frac{1}{f(x)}=\frac{1}{0}=\infty$, draw asymptote $x=0$
- $f(x)=-2\rightarrow \frac{1}{f(x)}=-\frac{1}{2}$, when $x\leq -2$
- $f(x)=x\rightarrow \frac{1}{f(x)}=\frac{1}{x}$, when $-2<x<0$
- $f(x)=0\rightarrow \frac{1}{f(x)}=\frac{1}{x}$, when $x\geq 1$
- $f(x)=1\rightarrow \frac{1}{f(x)}=1$, when $x\geq 1$
- $f(x)$ is increasing, $\frac{1}{f(x)}$ is decreasing, when $-2<x<1,\quad x\neq 0$

Reciprocal Function

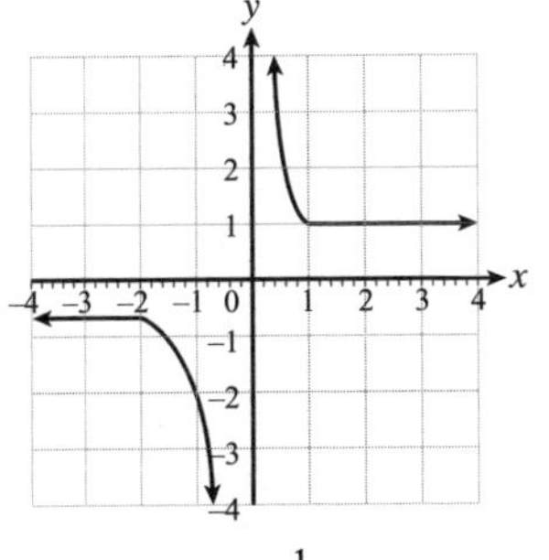

$y=\frac{1}{f(x)}$

Compression and Expansion of Graphs

Horizontal and vertical shifts or reflections leave the shape of the graph unchanged. Compression and expansions of the original graph causes a *distortion* – a change in the shape of the original graph.

a) Vertical compression and expansion

For the graph of $y = f(x)$, the graph of:

$y = a \cdot f(x)$ is a vertical expansion if $a > 1$ (expansion by a factor of a)
$y = a \cdot f(x)$ is a vertical compression if $0 < a < 1$ (compression by a factor of a)

For the graph of $y = f(x)$, the graph of:

$y = 2f(x)$ is a vertical expansion by a factor of 2

$y = \frac{1}{3}f(x)$ is a vertical compression by a factor of $\frac{1}{3}$

Note: In $y = a \cdot f(x)$, you are multiplying the original y-value, $f(x)$, by a, therefore, when $a > 1$, the y-value becomes larger, or expands. When $0 < a < 1$, the y-value gets smaller, or compresses.

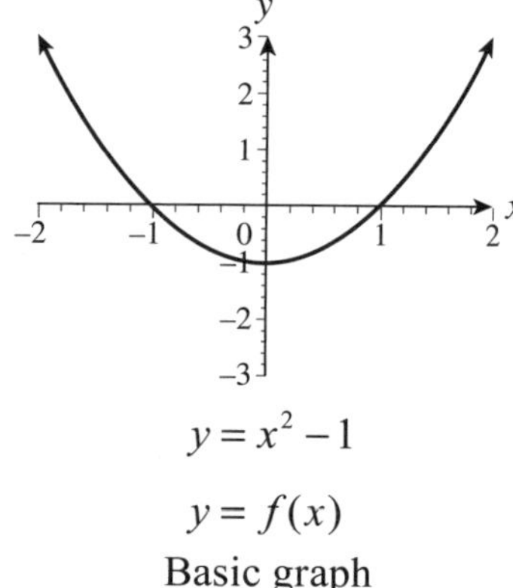

$y = x^2 - 1$

$y = f(x)$

Basic graph

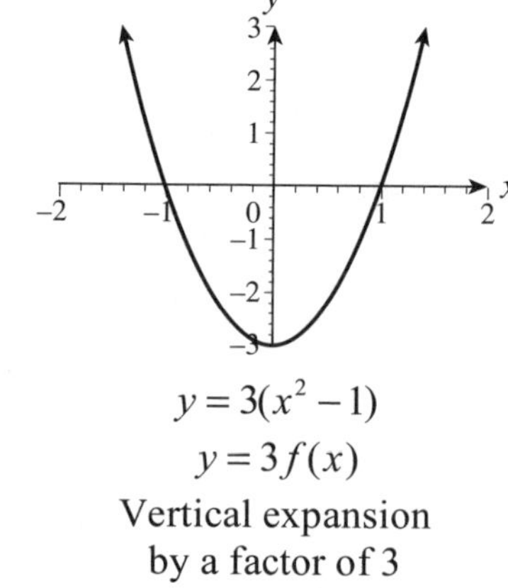

$y = 3(x^2 - 1)$

$y = 3f(x)$

Vertical expansion by a factor of 3

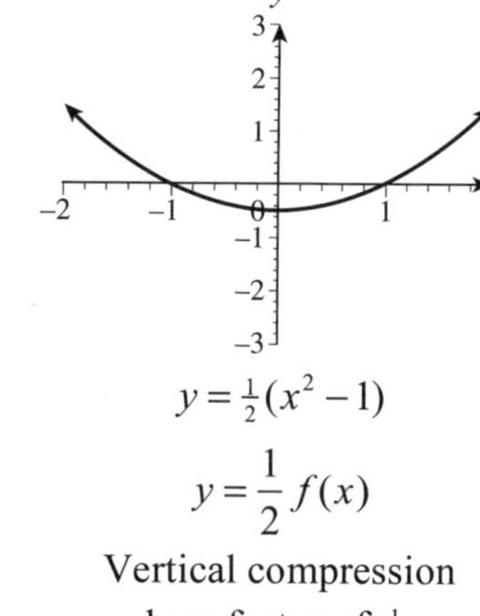

$y = \frac{1}{2}(x^2 - 1)$

$y = \frac{1}{2}f(x)$

Vertical compression by a factor of $\frac{1}{2}$

b) Horizontal compression and expansion

For the graph of $y = f(x)$, the graph of:

$y = f(ax)$ is a horizontal compression if $a > 1$ (by a factor of $\frac{1}{a}$)

$y = f(ax)$ is a horizontal expansion if $0 < a < 1$ (by a factor of $\frac{1}{a}$)

For the graph of $y = f(x)$, the graph of:

$y = f(2x)$ is a horizontal compression by a factor of $\frac{1}{2}$

$y = y = f\left(\frac{1}{3}x\right)$ is a horizontal expansion by a factor of 3

Note: In $y = f(ax)$, you are multiplying the original x-value by a. So when $a > 1$, the x-value becomes smaller, or compresses. When $0 < a < 1$, the x-value get larger, or expands. This note and the one on ***a)*** *above read exactly the same but have opposite outcomes.*

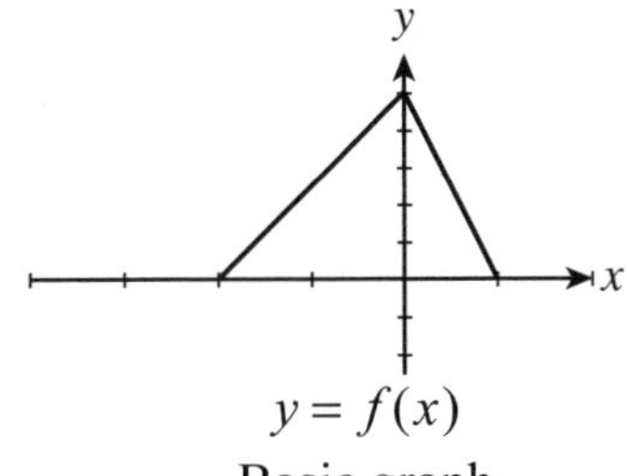

$y = f(x)$
Basic graph

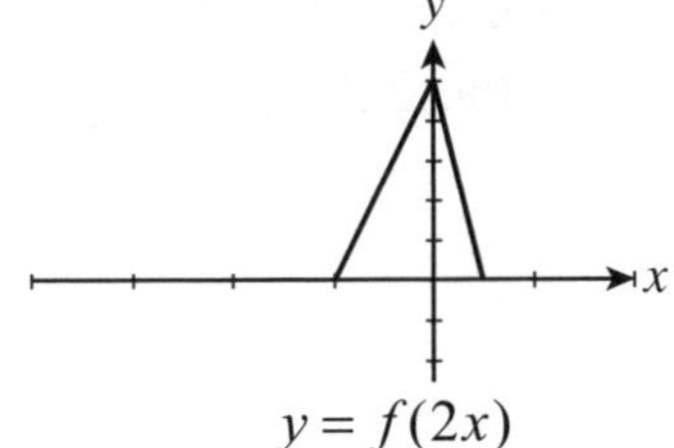

$y = f(2x)$

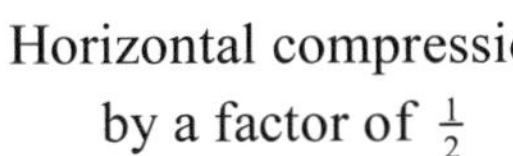

Horizontal compression by a factor of $\frac{1}{2}$

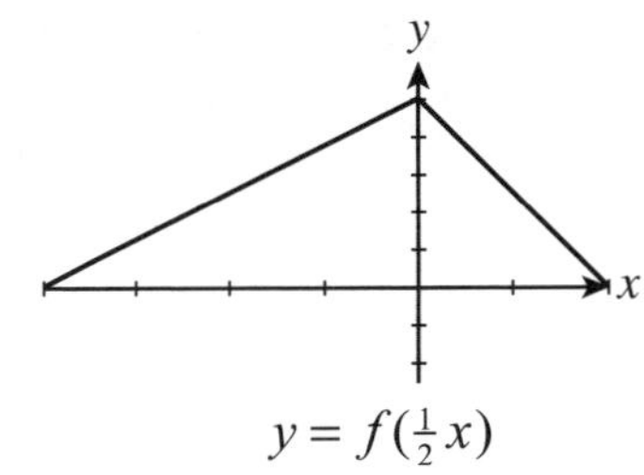

$y = f(\frac{1}{2}x)$
Horizontal expansion by a factor of 2

c) Summary of Vertical and Horizontal Compressions and Expansions of $y = f(x)$

If $a > 1, b > 1$

$y = af(x)$ is a vertical expansion by a factor of a

$y = f(bx)$ is a horizontal compression by a factor of $\frac{1}{b}$

If $0 < a < 1, 0 < b < 1$

$y = af(x)$ is a vertical compression by a factor of a

$y = f(bx)$ is a horizontal expansion by a factor of $\frac{1}{b}$

Example 8 Write an equation for the function $y = \sqrt{x}$, with a

a) vertical expansion by a factor of 2

b) vertical compression by a factor of $\frac{1}{2}$

c) horizontal expansion by a factor of 2

d) horizontal compression by a factor of $\frac{1}{2}$

▶ *Solution:* **a)** $y = 2\sqrt{x}$ **b)** $y = \frac{1}{2}\sqrt{x}$ **c)** $y = \sqrt{\frac{1}{2}x}$ **d)** $y = \sqrt{2x}$

Example 9 What transformation has happened to $y = f(x)$ to produce $y = 3f\left(\frac{1}{4}x\right)$?

▶ *Solution:* Vertical expansion by 3
Horizontal expansion by 4

Example 10 If (3, 1) is on $y = f(x)$, what point is on $y = 2f(4x)$?

▶ *Solution:* This is a horizontal compression by $\frac{1}{4}$ so $3 \to \frac{3}{4}$ and a vertical expansion by 2, so $1 \to 2$.

Point $\left(\frac{3}{4}, 2\right)$

When the shape of the graph changes then we know that an expansion or compression has occurred. Sometimes it is hard to know what transformation has produced the new graph. For instance, graph $y = x^2$ changed to $y = 4x^2$.

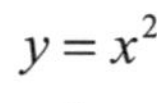

$y = x^2$

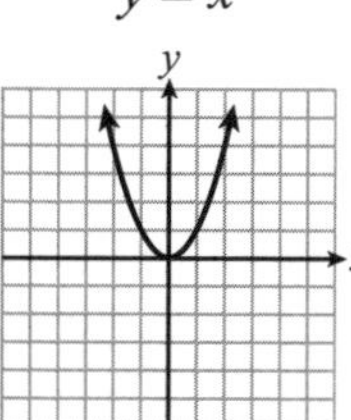

a) $y = 4x^2$

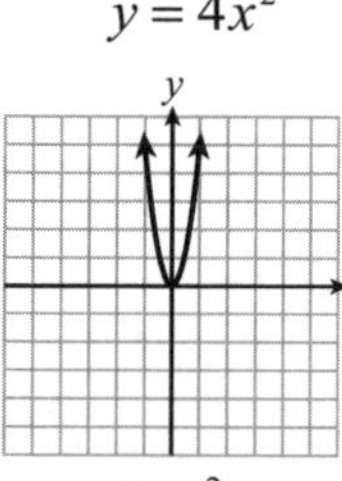

Transforming $y = x^2$ with a vertical expansion by a factor of 4.

b) $y = (2x)^2 = 4x^2$

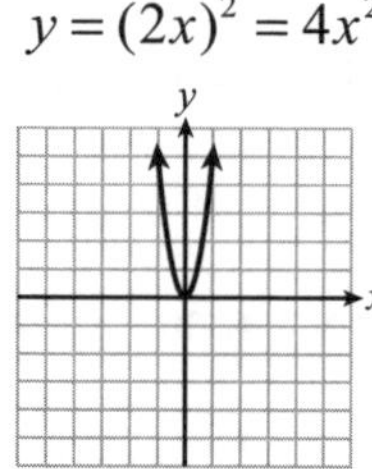

Transforming $y = x^2$ with a horizontal compression by a factor of $\frac{1}{2}$

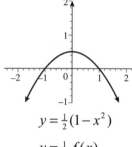

These two transformations were calculated in different ways to reach the final same solution.

Sometimes, however, the graph is such that the transformation is known:

Vertical expansions and compressions leave the x-intercepts the same.
Horizontal expansion and compressions leave the y-intercepts the same.

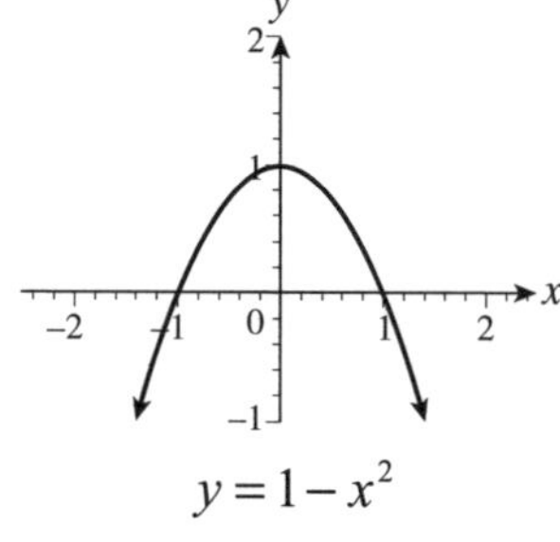

$y = 1 - x^2$

$y = f(x)$

Basic graph

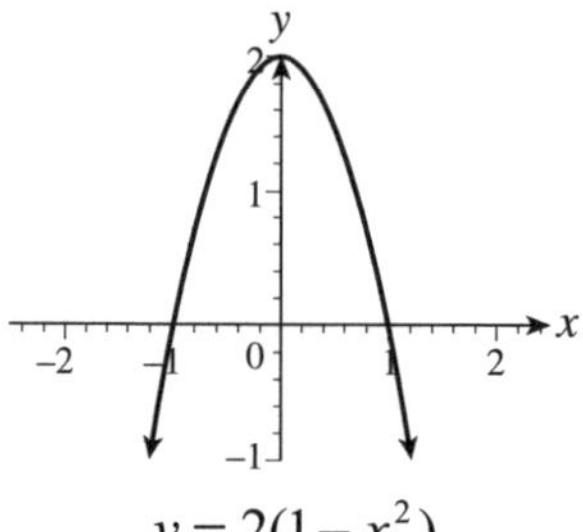

$y = 2(1 - x^2)$

$y = 2f(x)$

Vertical expansion by a factor of 2

Same x-intercept

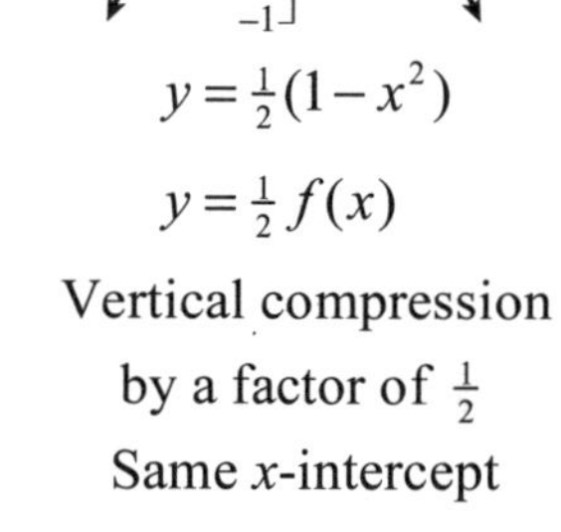

$y = \frac{1}{2}(1 - x^2)$

$y = \frac{1}{2}f(x)$

Vertical compression by a factor of $\frac{1}{2}$

Same x-intercept

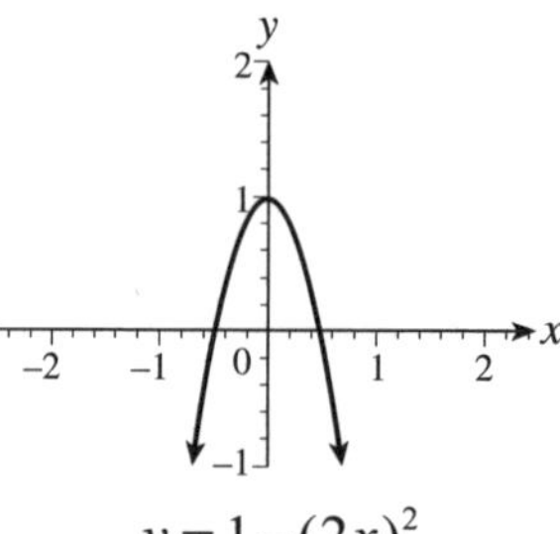

$y = 1 - (2x)^2$

$y = f(2x)$

Horizontal compression by a factor of $\frac{1}{2}$

Same y-intercept

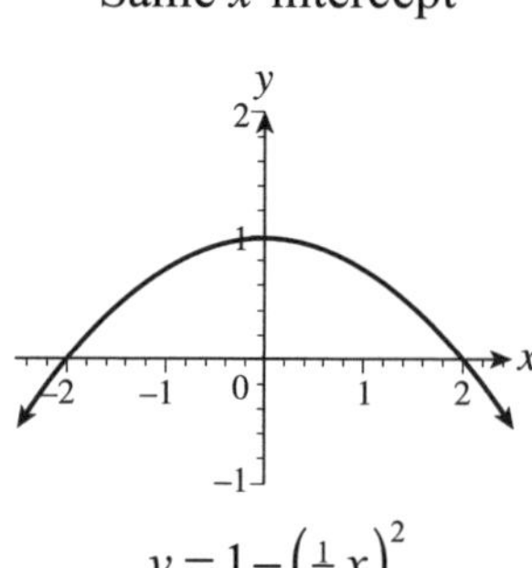

$y = 1 - \left(\frac{1}{2}x\right)^2$

$y = f\left(\frac{1}{2}x\right)$

Horizontal expansion by a factor of 2

Same y-intercept

2.4 Exercise Set

1. Write an equation for the function that is described by the given characteristics.

a) The shape $f(x)=x^2$, moved 4 units to the left and 5 units downward.

b) The shape $f(x)=x^2$, moved 2 units to the right, reflected in the x-axis, and moved 3 units upward.

c) The shape $f(x)=x^3$, moved 2 units to the right and 3 units downward.

d) The shape $f(x)=x^3$, moved 1 unit downward and reflected in the y-axis.

e) The shape of $f(x)=|x|$ moved 6 units upward and 3 units to the left.

f) The shape of $f(x)=|x|$ moved 3 units to the left and reflected in the x-axis.

g) The shape of $f(x)=\sqrt{x}$ moved 7 units to the right and reflected in the x-axis.

h) The shape of $f(x)=\sqrt{x}$ moved 4 units upward and reflected in the y-axis.

2. If $(-3, 1)$ or (a, b) is a point on the graph of $y=f(x)$, what must be a point on the graph of the following?

a) $y=f(x+2)$

b) $y=f(x)+2$

c) $y=f(x-2)-2$

d) $y=-f(x)$

e) $y=f(-x)$

f) $y=-f(-x)$

g) $y=f(-x)-2$

h) $y=-f(x+2)$

3. Use the graph of $f(x)=x$ to write an equation for each function whose graph is shown. Each transformation includes only reflections or expansions/compressions.

a)

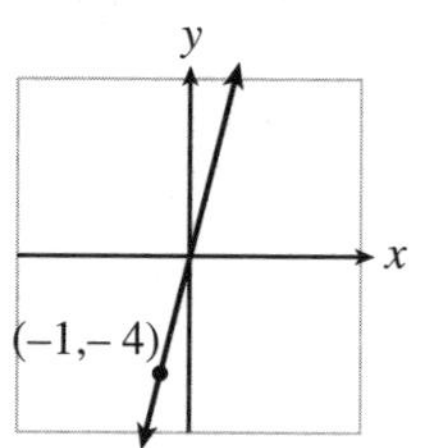

b)

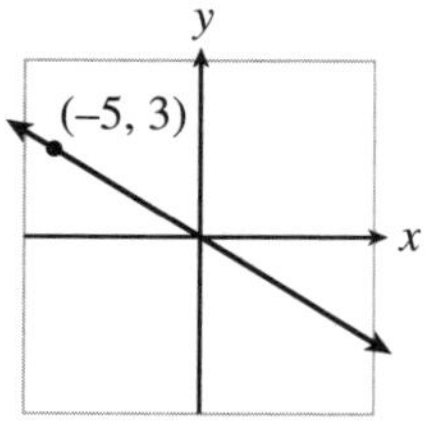

4. Use the graph of $f(x)=x^2$ to write an equation for each function whose graph is shown.

a)

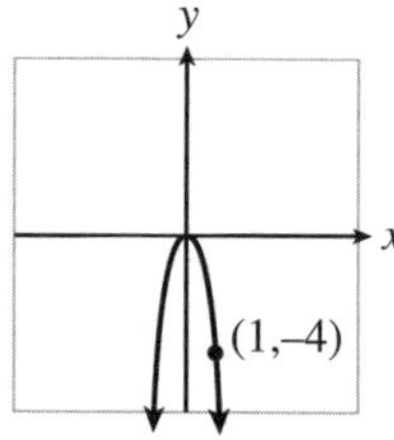

b)

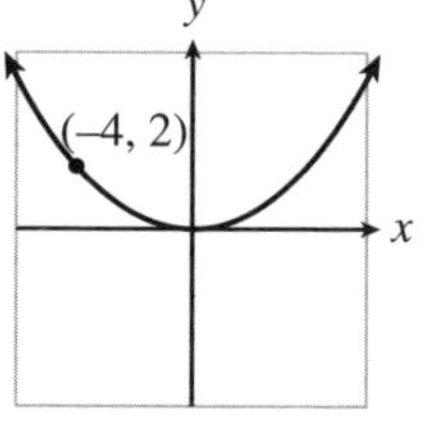

5. Use the graph of $f(x)=x^3$ to write an equation for each function whose graph is shown.

a)

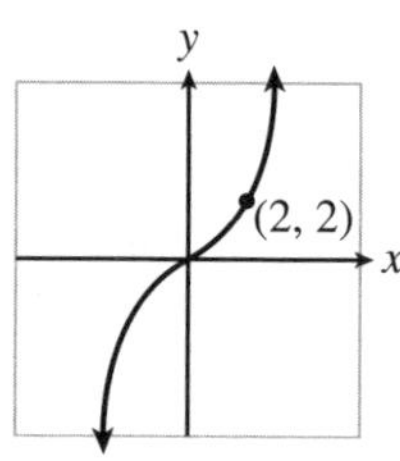

b)

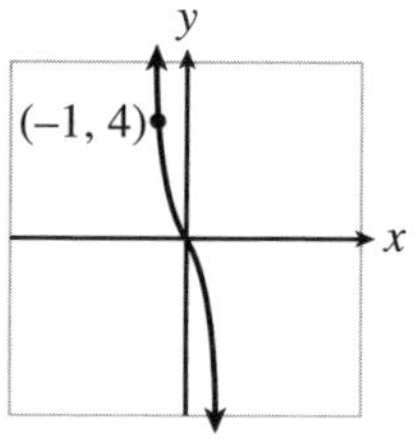

6. Use the graph of $f(x)=|x|$ to write an equation for each function whose graph is shown.

a)

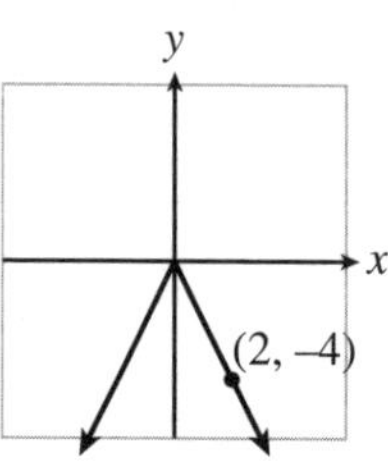

b)

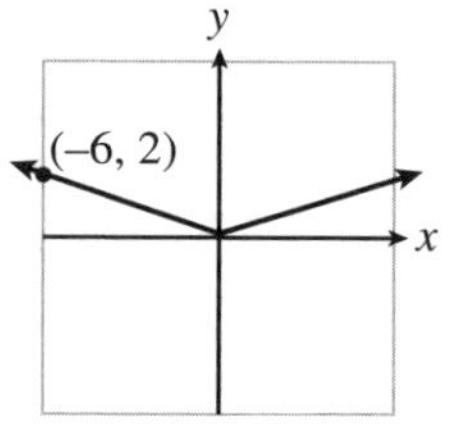

7. Use the graph of $f(x)=\sqrt{x}$ to write an equation for each function whose graph is shown.

a)

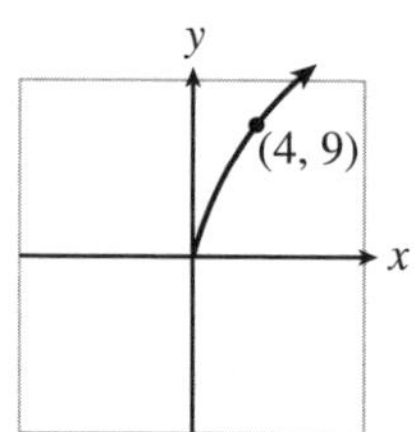

b)

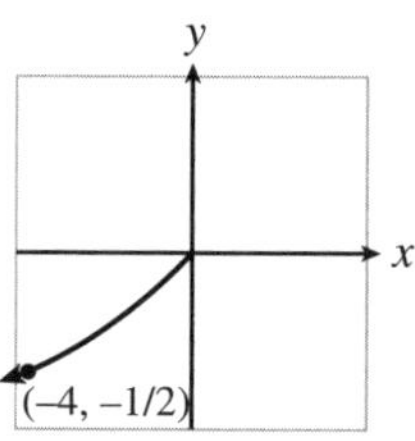

8. Use the graph of $f(x)=x^{\frac{1}{3}}$ to write an equation for each function whose graph is shown.

a)

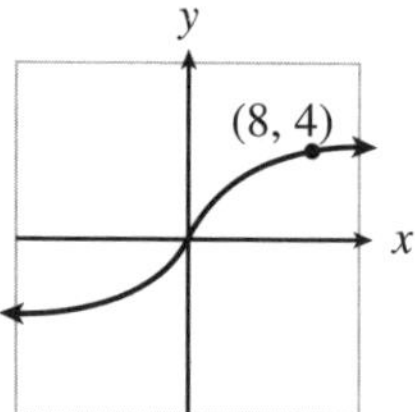

b)

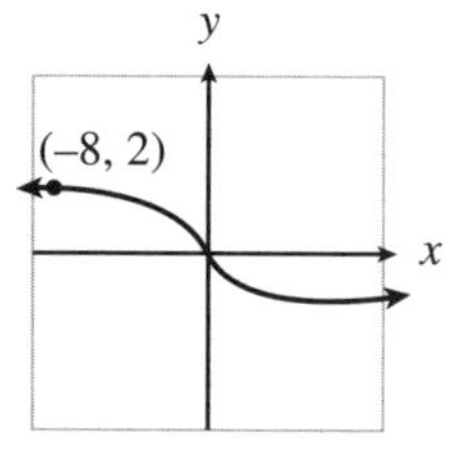

9. Given the graph of $y = f(x)$ below, sketch the graphs of the following:

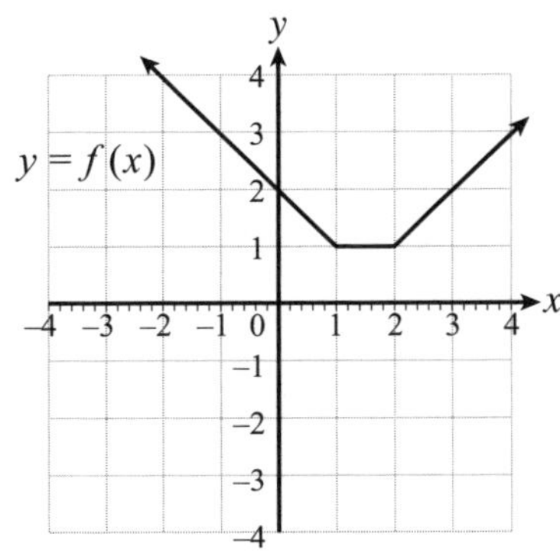

a) $y = -f(x)$

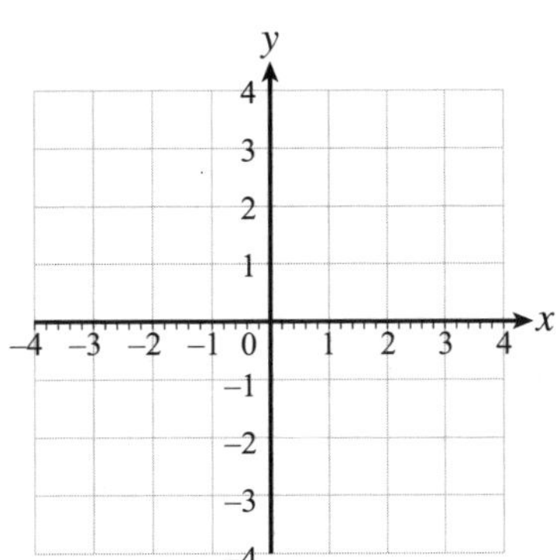

b) $y = f(-x)$

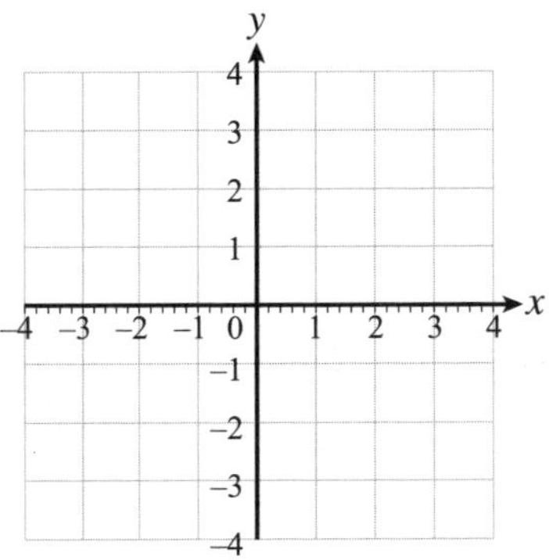

c) $y = -f(-x)$

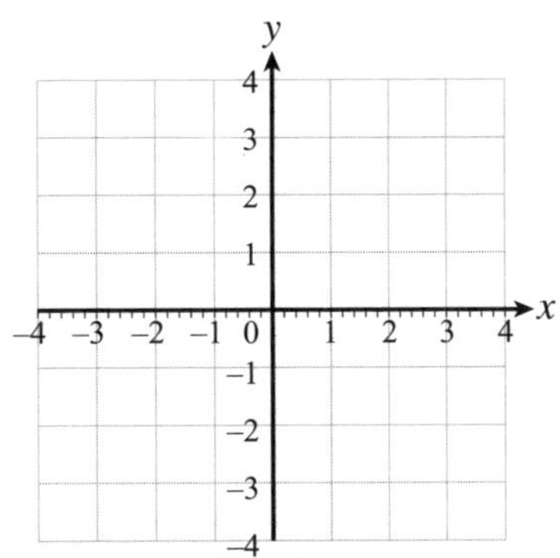

d) $y = f(x+1)$

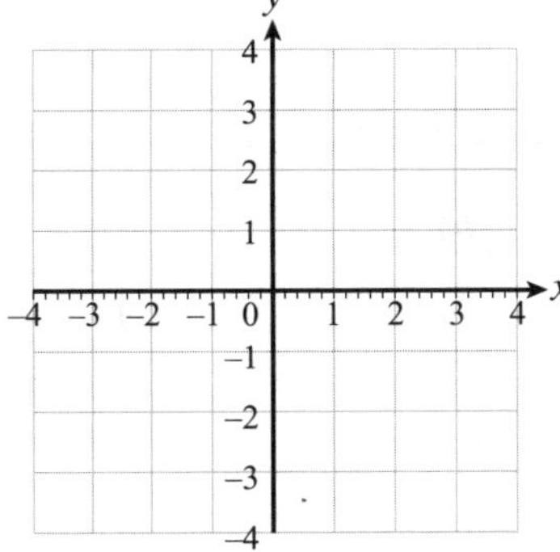

e) $y = f(x) - 2$

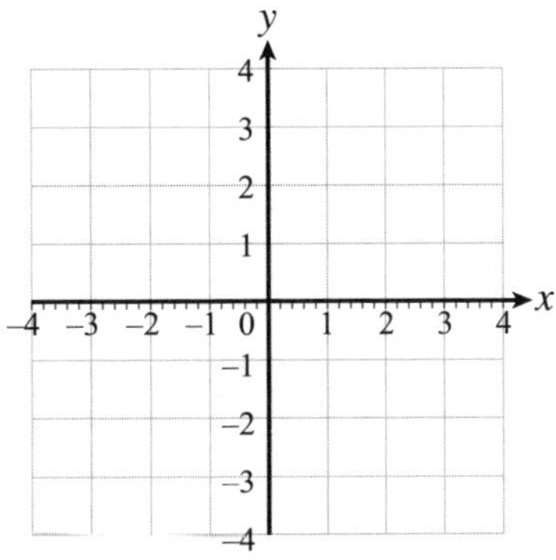

f) $y = f(1-x)$

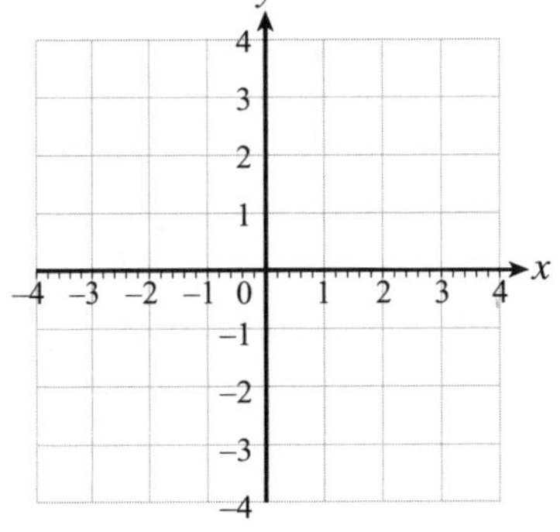

10. If (–2 , 4) is a point on the graph of $y = f(x-1)$, what must be a point on the following graphs?

a) $y = f(x)$

b) $y = -f(x)$

c) $y = f(-x)$

d) $y = f(x)+2$

e) $y = f(x+2)$

f) $y = -f(-x)$

11. What is the range of the Absolute Value Function: $f(x)=\left|4-x^2\right|$?

12. If the point (–1, –2) is on the graph $y = f(x)$, what point is on the graph $y=\left|f(-x)\right|$?

13. If the range of $y = f(x)$ is $-3 \le y \le 1$, what is the range of $y=\left|f(x)\right|$?

14. If the point (–3, –6) is on the graph of $y = f(x)$, determine a point on the graph of $y=3\left|f(x)\right|+1$.

15. Given the graph of $y = f(x)$, graph on the coordinate system $y=\dfrac{1}{f(x)}$.

a)

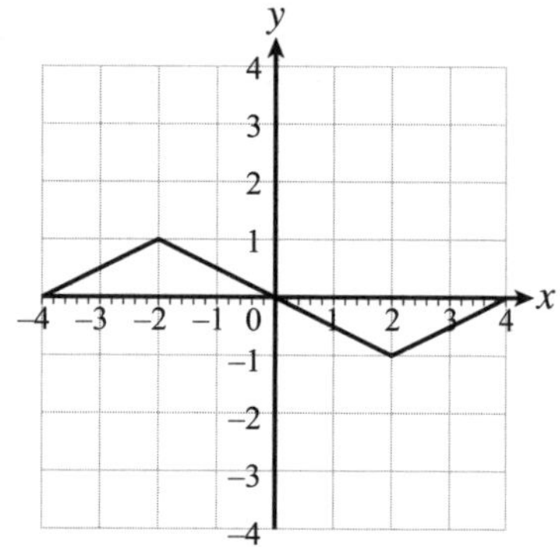

b)

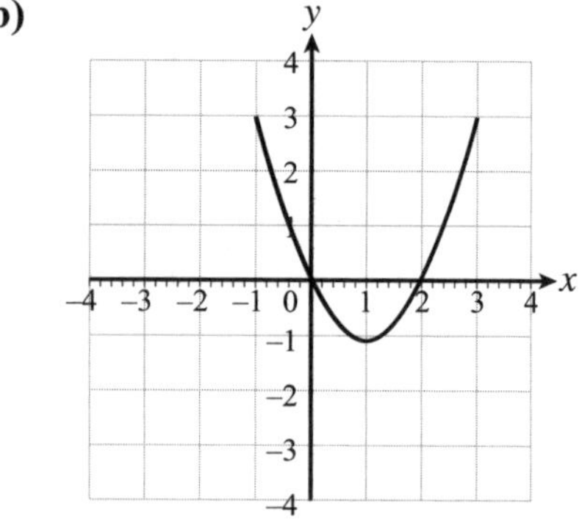

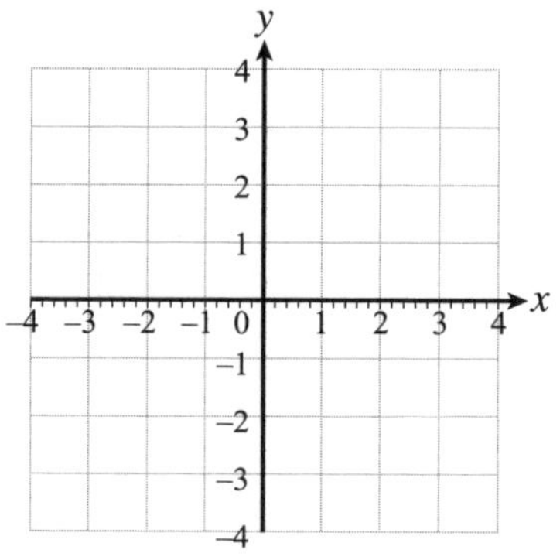

16. If $f(x) \geq 1$, what is the reciprocal function $\dfrac{1}{f(x)}$ value?

17. If the of graph $y = f(x)$ has the restriction of $0 < f(x) \leq 1$, what are the restrictions of $y = \dfrac{1}{f(x)}$?

18. Given the graph of $y = f(x)$ below, sketch the graphs of the following:

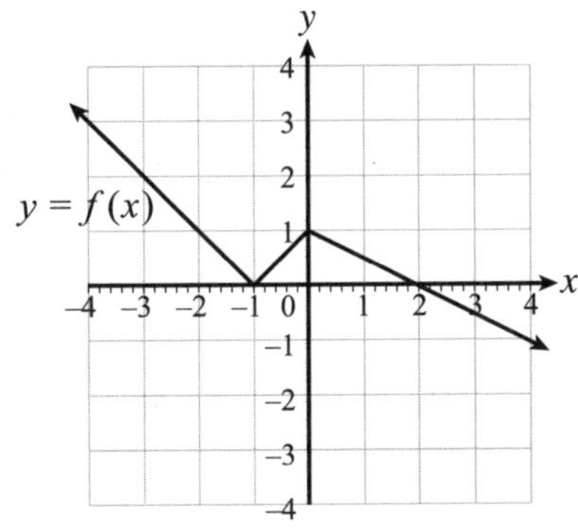

a) $y = 2f(x)$

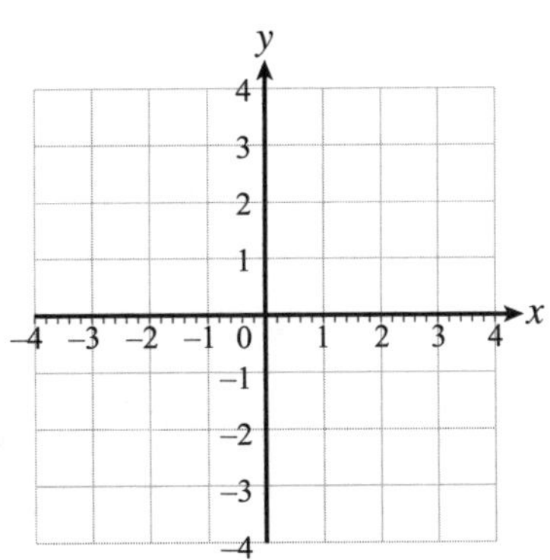

b) $y = f(2x)$

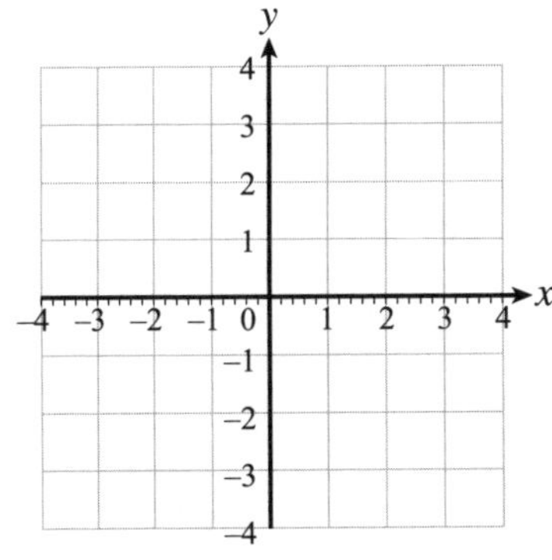

c) $y = -f\left(\dfrac{x}{2}\right)$

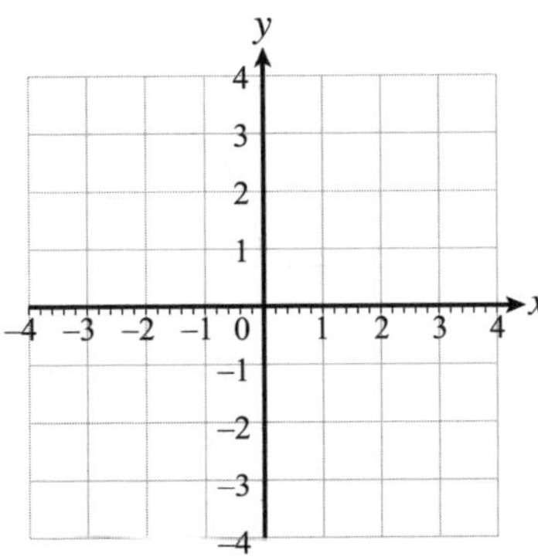

d) $y = -\dfrac{1}{2}f(-x)$

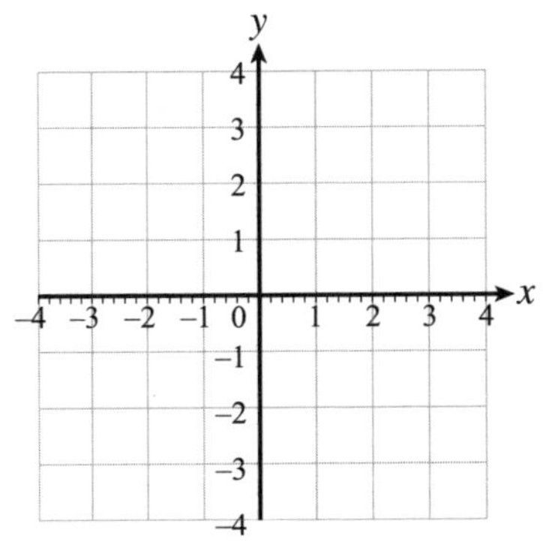

19. Given the graph of $y = f(x)$ below, what equations do the following graphs, *a* to *h*, represent?

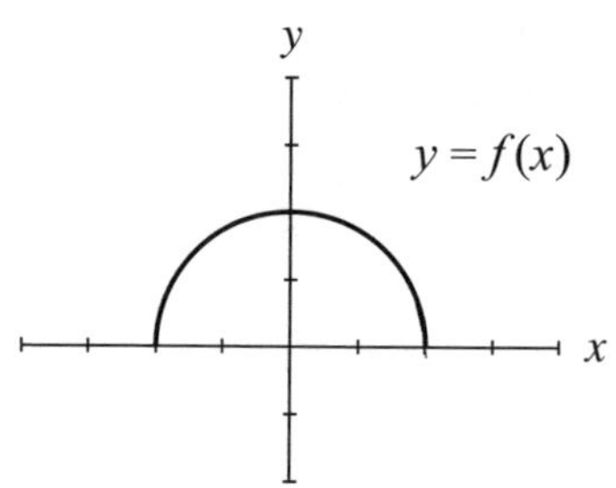

a)

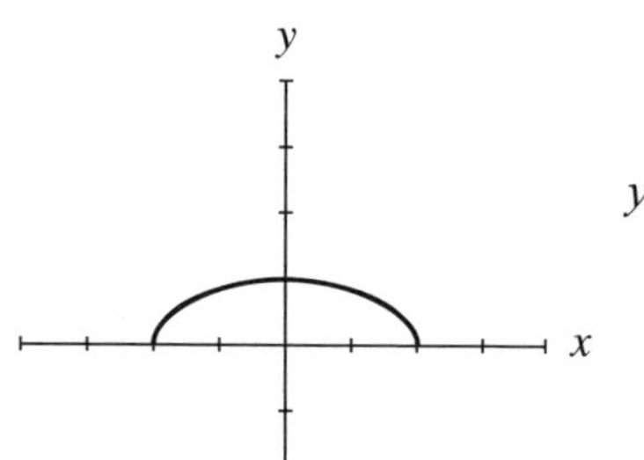

$y =$ ____________

b)

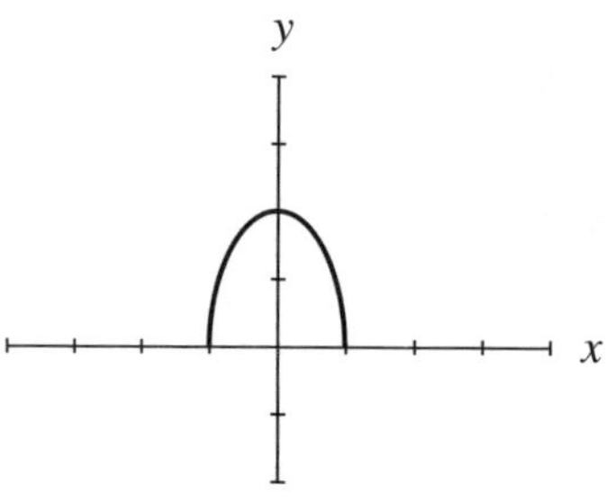

$y =$ ____________

c)

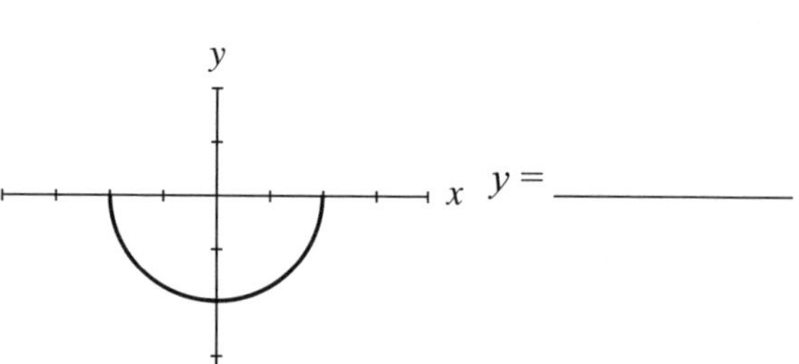

$y =$ ____________

d)

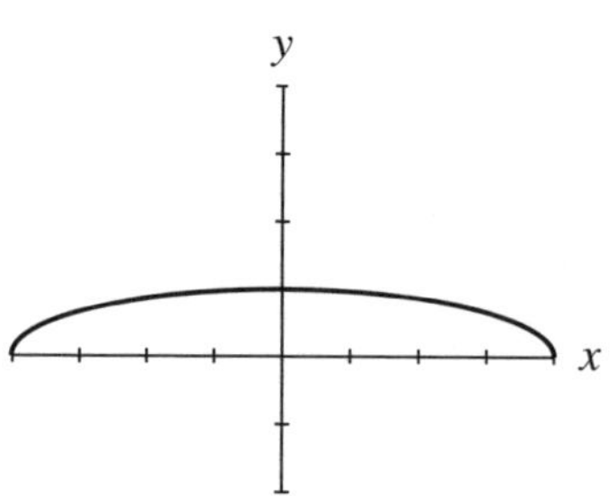

$y =$ ____________

e)

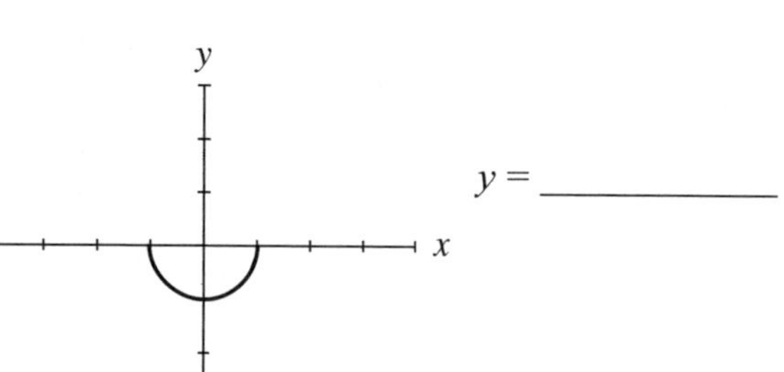

$y =$ ____________

f)

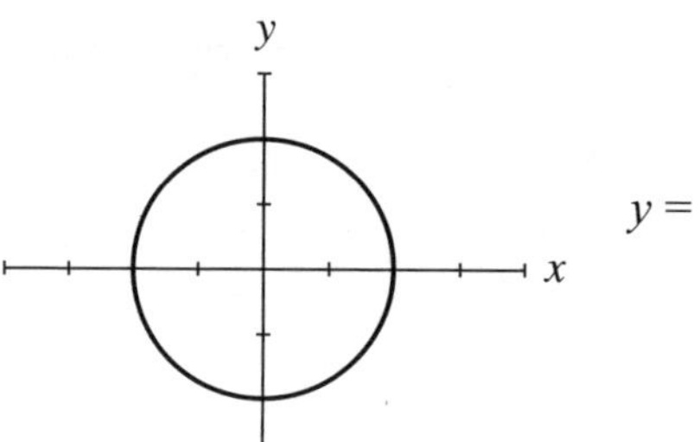

$y =$ ____________

g)

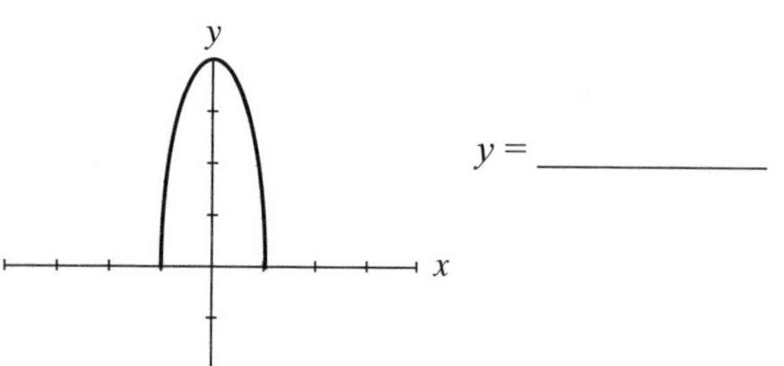

$y =$ ____________

h)

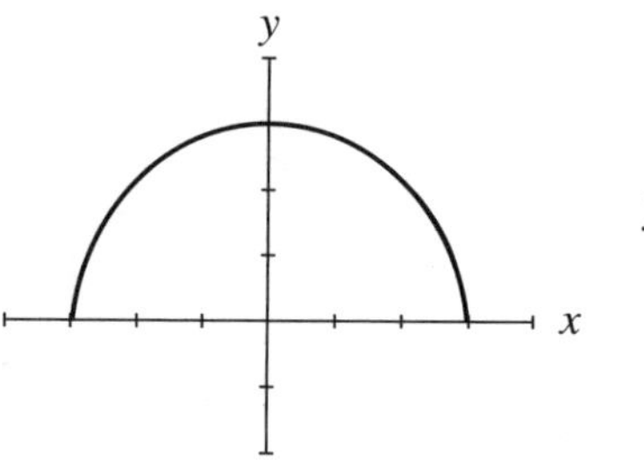

$y =$ ____________

2.5 Inverse Functions

Two functions *f* and *g* that are related such that each "undoes" what the other "does" are said to be inverse functions of one another.

Find Inverse of the Function $y = f(x)$

1. Verify that f is one-to-one (if not, the inverse is not a function).
2. Replace $f(x)$ with y.
3. Interchange x and y. (Change x to y and y to x.)
4. Solve the new equation for y.
5. Replace the new y with $f^{-1}(x)$.

NOTE: The notation f^{-1} is read f-inverse.

*If f is one-to-one, then the inverse f^{-1} is a function, and if f is **not** one-to-one, then the inverse is not a function.*

Example 1 Determine f^{-1} for $f(x) = 2x - 1$

▶ Solution:

$f(x) = 2x - 1$ *function is one-to-one*

$f: y = 2x - 1$ *replace $f(x)$ with y*

$f^{-1}: x = 2y - 1$ *interchange x and y*

$2y = x + 1$ *solve for y*

$y = \frac{x+1}{2}$ *Therefore, $f^{-1}(x) = \frac{x+1}{2}$ replace the new y with $f^{-1}(x)$*

Inverse Function Verification

Two functions *f* and *g* are inverses of each other if and only if

$f\,[g(x)] = x$, for every value of x in the domain of g and

$g\,[f(x)] = x$, for every value of x in the domain of f

Check solution:

$$f(f^{-1}(x)) = f\left(\frac{x+1}{2}\right) = 2\left(\frac{x+1}{2}\right) - 1 = x + 1 - 1 = x$$

$$f^{-1}(f(x)) = f^{-1}(2x-1) = \frac{2x-1+1}{2} = \frac{2x}{2} = x$$

Therefore, $f(x)$ and $f^{-1}(x)$ are inverse functions.

Action of a Function and Its Inverse

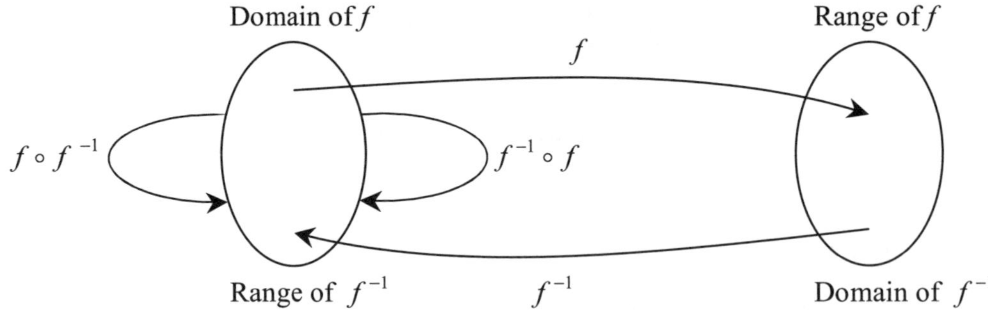

Example 2 Determine g^{-1} for $g(x)=\sqrt{x-1}$

▶ *Solution:*

$g(x)=\sqrt{x-1}$ *function is one-to-one*

$$g: y=\sqrt{x-1}$$

$$g^{-1}: x=\sqrt{y-1}$$

$$: x^2 = y-1$$

$$: y = x^2+1$$

Therefore, $g^{-1}(x)=x^2+1$

The domain and range of $g(x)=\sqrt{x-1}$ has domain : $x \geq 1$, range : $y \geq 0$

The domain and range of $g^{-1}(x)=x^2+1$ must be domain: $x \geq 0$, range : $y \geq 1$

Therefore, $g^{-1}(x)=x^2+1$, $x \geq 0$

Note: $g^{-1}(x)=x^2+1$ *is not a one-to-one function, so cannot have an inverse function. However, with the restriction, $x \geq 0$, it is a one-to-one function, and its inverse is a function* $g(x)=\sqrt{x-1}$.

Check solution:

$$\begin{aligned} g(g^{-1}(x)) &= g(x^2+1) \\ &= \sqrt{x^2+1-1} \\ &= \sqrt{x^2} \\ &= |x| \quad \text{but } x \geq 0 \\ \text{therefore } &= x \end{aligned}$$

$$\begin{aligned} g^{-1}(g(x)) &= g(\sqrt{x-1}) \\ &= (\sqrt{x-1})^2+1 \\ &= x-1+1 \\ &= x \end{aligned}$$

Example 3 Determine h^{-1} of $h(x)=\dfrac{x}{2x-3}$

▶ *Solution:*

$$h(x)=\frac{x}{2x-3}$$
$$h: y=\frac{x}{2x-3}$$
$$h^{-1}: x=\frac{y}{2y-3}$$
$$: x(2y-3)=y$$
$$: 2xy-3x=y$$
$$: 2xy-y=3x$$
$$: y(2x-1)=3x$$
$$: y=\frac{3x}{2x-1}$$

Check solution: $h(h^{-1})=x$ and $h^{-1}(h)=x$

$$h(h^{-1}(x))=h\left(\frac{3x}{2x-1}\right)=\frac{\frac{3x}{2x-1}}{2\left(\frac{3x}{2x-1}\right)-3}=\frac{\frac{3x}{2x-1}}{\frac{6x-6x+3}{2x-1}}=\frac{3x}{3}=x$$

$$h^{-1}(h(x))=h^{-1}\left(\frac{x}{2x-3}\right)=\frac{3\left(\frac{x}{2x-3}\right)}{2\left(\frac{x}{2x-3}\right)-1}=\frac{3x}{2x-2x+3}=\frac{3x}{3}=x$$

Therefore, $h^{-1}(x)=\dfrac{3x}{2x-1}$, $x\neq\dfrac{1}{2}$

Example 4 Determine the inverse of $h(x)=x^2+2$

▶ *Solution:*

$$h(x)=x^2+2$$
$$h: y=x^2+2$$
$$h^{-1}: x=y^2+2$$
$$: y^2=x-2$$
$$: y=\pm\sqrt{x-2}$$

Since $h(x)$ is not a one-to-one function, we expect to get an inverse that is not a function.

$y=\pm\sqrt{x-2}$ is the inverse of $h(x)=x^2+2$ but we cannot write it as $h^{-1}(x)=\pm\sqrt{x-2}$ because $y=\pm\sqrt{x-2}$ is not a function. This happened because $h(x)$ is not a one-to-one function. If $h(x)$ has a domain restriction of $x\geq 0$, then $h(x)$ has an inverse of $h^{-1}(x)=\sqrt{x-2}$. If $h(x)$ has a domain restriction of $x\leq 0$, then $h(x)$ has an inverse of $h^{-1}(x)=-\sqrt{x-2}$.

Check solution:

$$h(h^{-1}(x))=h(\sqrt{x-2})=(\sqrt{x-2})^2+2=x-2+2=x$$

$$h(h^{-1}(x))=h(-\sqrt{x-2})=(-\sqrt{x-2})^2+2=x-2+2=x$$

for $x\geq 0$

$$h^{-1}(h(x))=h^{-1}(x^2+2)=\sqrt{x^2+2-2}=\sqrt{x^2}=|x|=x \text{ since } x\geq 0$$

for $x<0$

$$h^{-1}(h(x))=h^{-1}(x^2+2)=-\sqrt{x^2+2-2}=-\sqrt{x^2}=-|x|=x \text{ since } x<0$$

Conclusion: for $x\geq 0$, $h(x)$ has inverse $\sqrt{x-2}$

for $x<0$, $h(x)$ has inverse $-\sqrt{x-2}$

Graphs of Inverse Functions

Definition: The graphs of f and f^{-1} are symmetric about the line $y = x$.
$f(x)$ is the reflection of $f^{-1}(x)$ on the line $y = x$, and vice versa.

Why are f and f^{-1} mirror images of one another about the line $y = x$? One must remember that the function f^{-1} switches the input and output of f. Thus, a point (a, b) on the graph of f must have the point (b, a) on the graph of f^{-1}. Therefore, the graphs of f and f^{-1} must be reflections of each other about the line $y = x$.

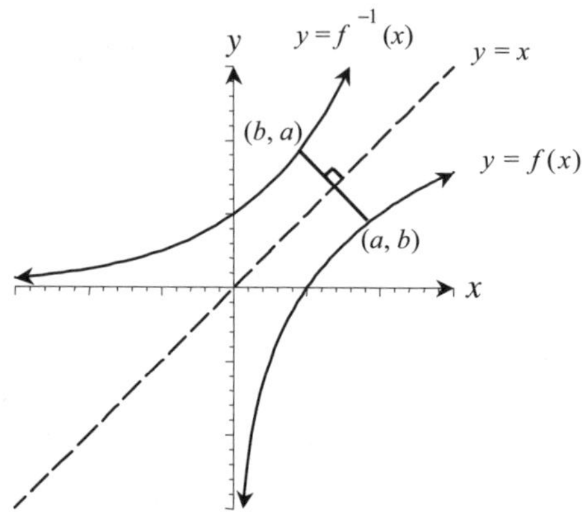

Example 5 Graph the inverse function of $g(x) = x^2,\ x \le 0$.

▶ *Solution:* To find the inverse, we proceed as follow:

$$y = x^2, \quad x \le 0,\ y \ge 0$$
$$x = y^2, \quad x \ge 0,\ y \le 0$$
$$y = \pm\sqrt{x}, \quad x \ge 0,\ y \le 0$$
$$\text{therefore } y = -\sqrt{x}$$

Thus, $g^{-1}(x) = -\sqrt{x},\ x \le 0$

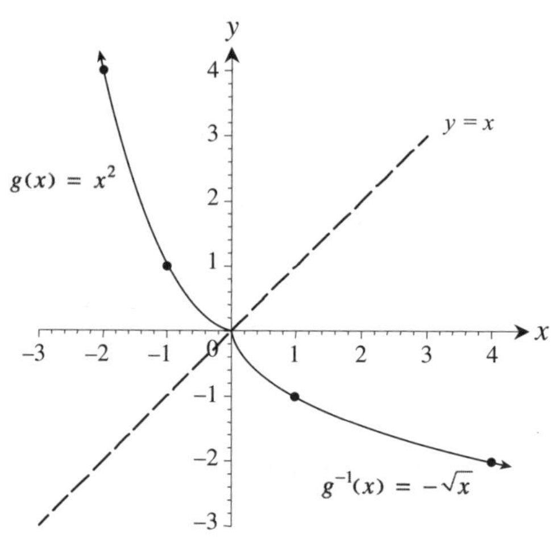

Example 6 $f(x)=2x-3$

a) Determine $f^{-1}(x)$

b) Show $f(f^{-1}(x))=f^{-1}(f(x))=x$

c) Graph f and f^{-1}

▶ *Solution:* **a)**

$$f(x)=2x-3$$
$$f:\ y=2x-3$$
$$f^{-1}:\ x=2y-3$$
$$:2y=x+3$$
$$:\ y=\frac{x+3}{2}$$

Therefore, $f^{-1}(x)=\dfrac{x+3}{2}$

b)

$$f(f^{-1}(x))=f\left(\frac{x+3}{2}\right)=2\left(\frac{x+3}{2}\right)-3=x+3-3=x$$

$$f^{-1}(f(x))=f^{-1}(2x-3)=\frac{(2x-3)+3}{2}=\frac{2x}{2}=x$$

c)

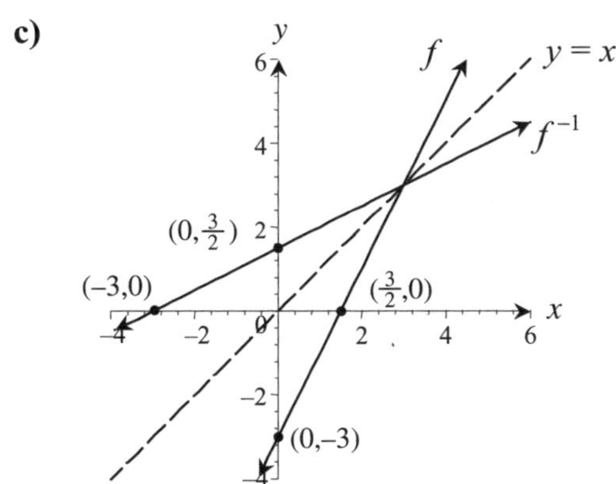

Transformations in Inverse Functions

If $y=f(x)$ has an inverse $y=f^{-1}(x)$, then the following are transformations of the inverse function. When transforming individual points, order is critical: swap the *x*- and *y*-values first and then transform them as normal.

For a point (a, b) in $y=f(x)$

- $y=f^{-1}(x)$ will have a point (b, a)
- $y=f^{-1}(x-1)$ will have a point $(b+1, a)$
- $y=f^{-1}(x)+1$ will have a point $(b, a+1)$
- $y=-2f^{-1}(3x)$ will have a point $\left(\frac{1}{3}b, -2a\right)$

2.5 Exercise Set

1. The following are graphs of functions. Determine which functions have inverse functions. Answer yes or no.

a) 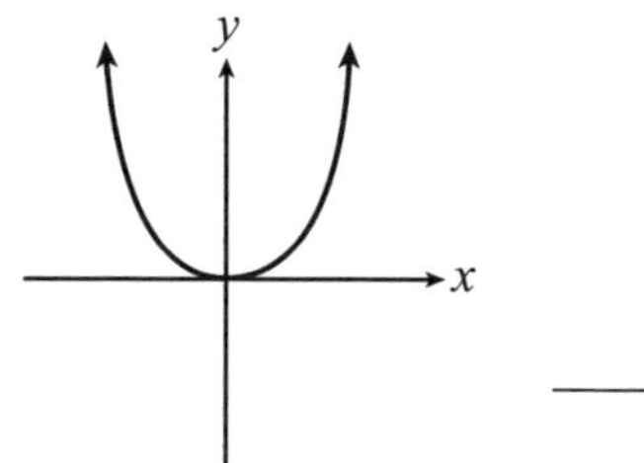

___

b) 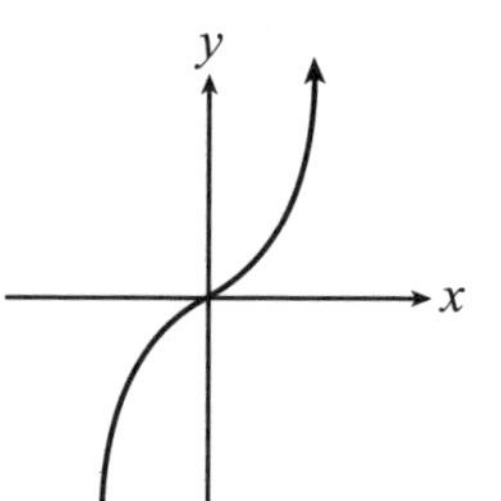

___

c) 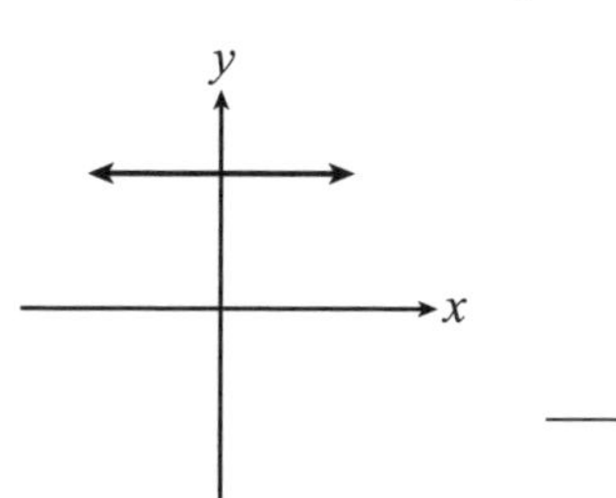

___

d) 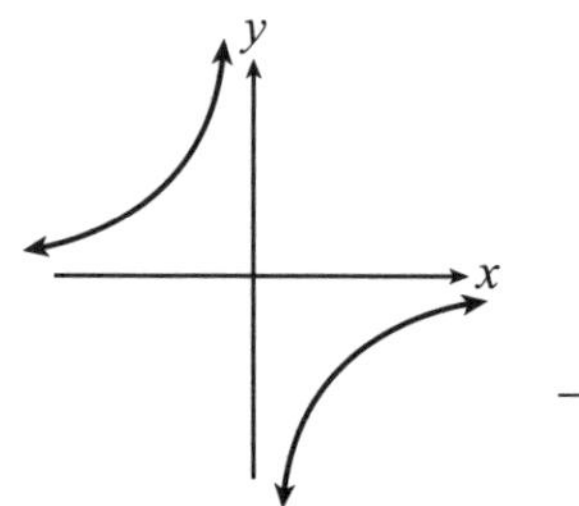

___

e) 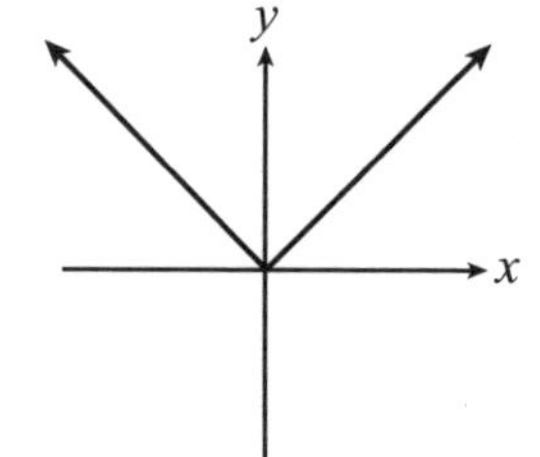

___

f) 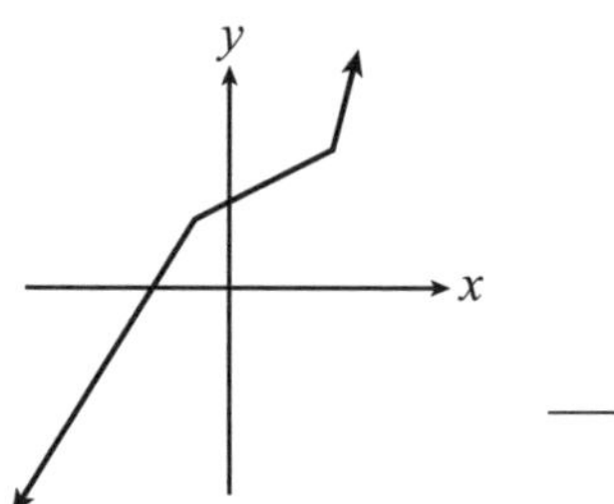

___

2. Determine whether the functions are inverses of each other by calculating $(f \circ g)(x)$ and $(g \circ f)(x)$.

a) $f(x)=\frac{3}{5}x,\ g(x)=\frac{5}{3}x$

b) $f(x)=x-3,\ g(x)=x+3$

c) $f(x)=3-4x,\ g(x)=\frac{3-x}{4}$

d) $f(x)=x^3-2,\ g(x)=\sqrt[3]{x+2}$

e) $f(x)=\sqrt{x-1},\ g(x)=x^2+1$

f) $f(x)=\sqrt[4]{x}, x\geq 0,\ g(x)=x^4$

g) $f(x)=\frac{5x+3}{1-2x},\ g(x)=\frac{x-3}{2x+5}$

h) $f(x)=\sqrt[3]{x+1},\ g(x)=x^3-1$

3. Determine the restrictions on each of the following functions in order for its inverse to be a function.

a) $f(x)=x^2$

b) $f(x)=x^2+2$

c) $f(x)=(x-2)^2$

d) $f(x)=|x+1|-2$

4. Find the inverse of the following functions. State if the inverse is a function, a one-to-one function, or neither.

a) $f(x) = 2x - 3$

b) $f(x) = \sqrt{2x-1}$

c) $f(x) = x^2 + 1$

d) $f(x) = \dfrac{1}{3x-2}$

e) $f(x) = \dfrac{x}{1-x}$

f) $f(x) = \dfrac{2x-1}{3x+2}$

5. Let $f(x) = 2x - 1$, $g(x) = \frac{1}{2}x + 3$, find $f^{-1}(x)$ and $g^{-1}(x)$, then determine:

a) $(f^{-1} \circ g)(x)$

b) $(g^{-1} \circ f^{-1})(x)$

c) $(g \circ f^{-1})(x)$

d) $(f \circ g^{-1})(x)$

e) $(f^{-1} \circ g^{-1})(x)$

f) $(f \circ g)^{-1}(x)$

6. Given the graph of f, on the same grid draw the graph of the inverse of f.

a)

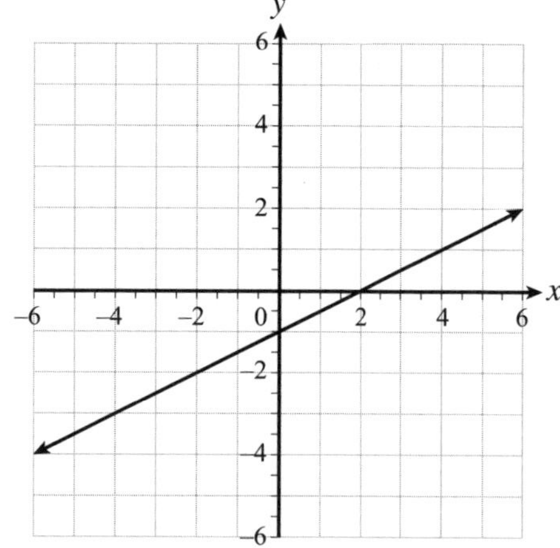

b)

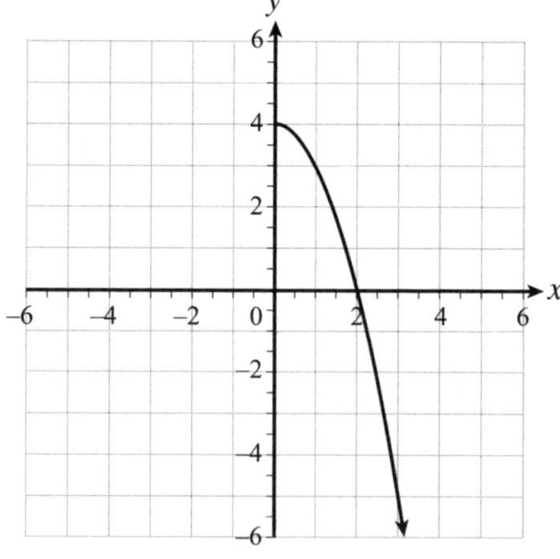

c)

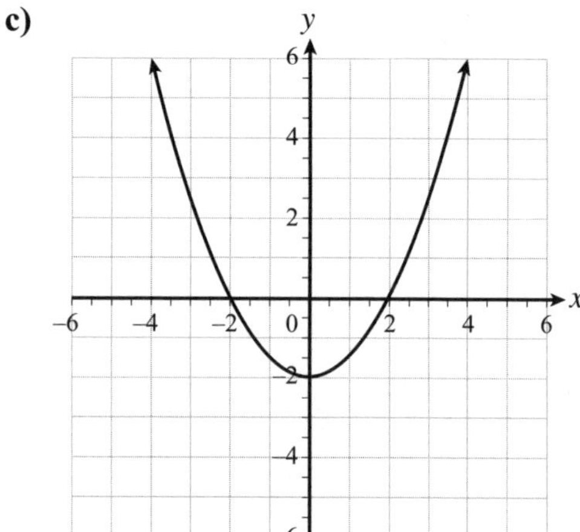

d)

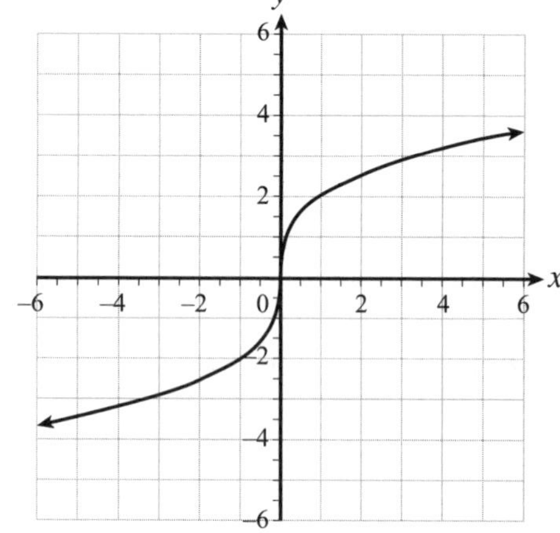

e)

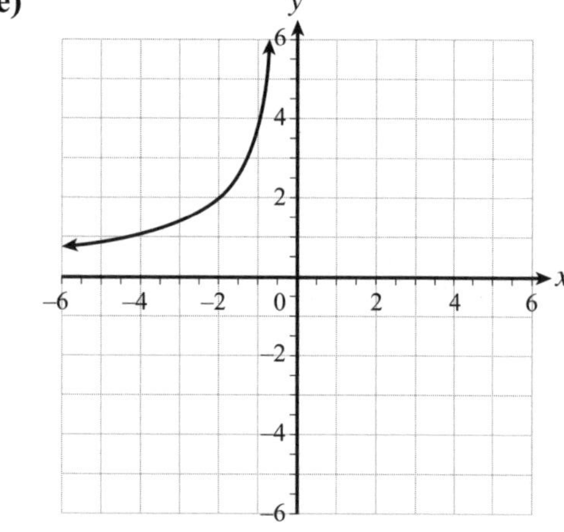

f)

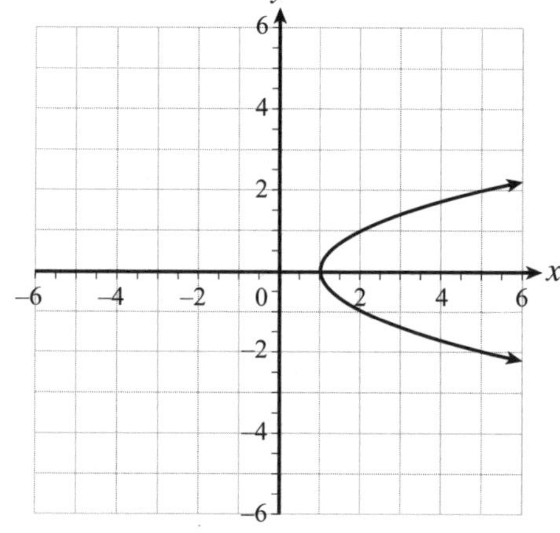

7. If $(-1, 2)$ or (a, b) is a point of the graph of $y = f(x)$, what must be a point on the graph for the following?

a) $y = f^{-1}(x)$

b) $y = f^{-1}(x) - 1$

c) $y = f^{-1}(x+2)$

d) $y = -f^{-1}(-x)$

e) $y = 1 - f^{-1}(-x)$

f) $y = f^{-1}(x+1)$

8. Graph the function and its inverse on a graphic calculator. State if the inverse is a function, a one-to-one function, or neither.

a) $f(x) = 2x - 1$

b) $f(x) = x^2 + 1$

c) $f(x) = x^3 - 1$

d) $f(x) = \sqrt{x^2 - 4}$

9. The function $f(x) = a(-x^3 - x + 2)$ has an inverse function such that $f^{-1}(6) = -2$. Find a.

10. If the graph of f contains points in quadrant I and II, the graph of f^{-1} must contain points in what quadrant?

11. The formulas for Fahrenheit and Celsius temperatures are

$$F = \frac{9}{5}C + 32, \ C = \frac{5}{9}(F - 32)$$

Show that these functions are inverses of each other.

12. Show that for the one-to-one function $f(x) = 2x + 1$ and $g(x) = \frac{1}{4}x - 3$ that $(f \circ g)^{-1}(x) = (g^{-1} \circ f^{-1})(x)$. Does this hold for all one-to-one functions?

2.6 Combined Transformations

We have an understanding of quadratic, square root, absolute value, cubic, reciprocal, general $y = f(x)$ and inverse function graphs plus the transformation of these graphs. We can summarize the transformation steps as follows:

$$y = f(x) \text{ versus } y = a\,f[b(x \pm c)] + d$$

Transforming vertically (affect y-value)

- $a > 1$ is a vertical expansion by a factor of a
- $0 < a < 1$ is a vertical compression by factor of a
- $a < 0$ is a reflection in the x-axis
- $+d$ shift up d units ($d > 0$)
- $-d$ shift down d units ($d > 0$)

Transforming horizontally (affect x-value)

- $b > 1$ is a horizontal compression by a factor of $\frac{1}{b}$
- $0 < b < 1$ is a horizontal expansion by factor of $\frac{1}{b}$
- $b < 0$ is a reflection in the y-axis
- $+c$ shift left c units ($c > 0$)
- $-c$ shift right c units ($c > 0$)

It is important to note that reflections/compressions/expansions always come first in combined functions and relations followed by translations.

Example 1 $y = f(x)$ transformed to $y = -2f(3(x+5)) - 7$

is a vertical – reflection in x-axis (multiply y-value by –1)

– expansion by factor of 2 (multiply y-value by 2)

– translation down 7 (subtract 7 from y-value)

is a horizontal – compression by factor $\frac{1}{3}$ (multiply x-value by $\frac{1}{3}$)

– translation 5 left (subtract 5 from x-value)

Therefore, (6, –3) on $y = f(x)$ is transformed to $\left(6\left(\frac{1}{3}\right) - 5,\ -3(-1)(2) - 7\right) = (-3, -1)$

It is also important to realize that the horizontal expansion/compression factor b must be factored out of the x term.

Example 2 $y = f(2x-6) \rightarrow y = f[2(x-3)]$ is a horizontal compression by factor $\frac{1}{2}$ then 3 to the right.

Solving Combined Equations

There are two methods of solving combined equations:

1. A step-by-step approach using methods learned in sections one to four.
2. Use a method similar to using the quadratic formula for solving a quadratic equation.

If $y = f(x)$ has point (m, n), then $y = af[b(x - c)] + d$ has point $\left(\frac{m}{b} + c, an + d\right)$

Example 3 If the point (3, 2) is on the graph $y = f(x)$, what point is on $y = -4f(6 - 3x) + 1$?

▶ *Solution:* **Method 1**

$y = -4f(6 - 3x) + 1 \rightarrow y = -4f\left[-3(x - 2)\right] + 1$

- – 4 reflects point about the x-axis with vertical expansion by factor of 4, therefore $(3, 2) \rightarrow (3, -8)$
- – 3 reflects point about the y-axis with horizontal compression by factor of $\frac{1}{3}$, therefore, $(3, -8) \rightarrow (-1, -8)$
- $x - 2$ shifts point two units horizontally to the right, therefore $(-1, -8) \rightarrow (1, -8)$
- +1 shifts point one unit vertically up $(1, -8) \rightarrow (1, -7)$. Therefore the point is $(1, -7)$

Method 2

If $y = f(x)$ has point (m, n), then $y = af[b(x - c)] + d$ has point $\left(\frac{m}{b} + c, an + d\right)$

If $y = f(x)$ has point (3, 2), then $y = -4f(6 - 3x) + 1 \rightarrow y = -4f[-3(x - 2)] + 1$

with $a = -4$, $b = -3$, $c = 2$, and $d = 1$, has point $\left(\frac{3}{-3} + 2,\ -4 \cdot 2 + 1\right) = (1, -7)$

Example 4 If the point (–1, 2) is on the graph $y = f^{-1}(x)$, what point is on $y = -3f(8 + 2x) - 1$?

▶ *Solution:* **Method 1**

- If (–1, 2) is on $y = f^{-1}(x)$ then (2, –1) is on $y = f(x)$
- $y = -3f(8 + 2x) - 1 \rightarrow y = -3f(2(x + 4)) - 1$
- –3 reflects point about x-axis with vertical expansion by factor 3, therefore $(2, -1) \rightarrow (2, 3)$
- 2 has horizontal compression by factor of $\frac{1}{2}$ therefore $(2, 3) \rightarrow (1, 3)$
- $x + 4$ shifts point 4 units horizontally to the left therefore $(1, 3) \rightarrow (-3, 3)$
- –1 shifts point 1 unit vertically down therefore $(-3, 3) \rightarrow (-3, 2)$

The point on $y = -3f(8 + 2x) - 1$ is (–3, 2).

Method 2

$y = -3f(2(x + 4) - 1$ with $m = 2$ and $n = -1$ has $a = -3$, $b = 2$, $c = -4$, and $d = -1$

$$\left(\frac{m}{b} + c, an + d\right) = \left(\frac{2}{2} - 4, -3(-1) - 1\right) = (-3, 2)$$

Example 5 Given the graph $y = f(x)$ below, graph $f(x) = -2f[-2(x+1)]+1$

Hint: When doing a problem this difficult, do only ***one*** *or* ***two*** *changes at a time, not all the steps at once or use method 2!*

$y = f(x)$

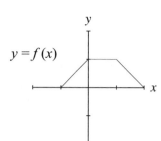

▶ *Solution:* **Method 1** $f(x) = -2\ f[-2\ (x+1)]+1$

Step 1 (-2), Step 2 (-2), Step 3 ($+1$), Step 4 ($+1$)

Step 1

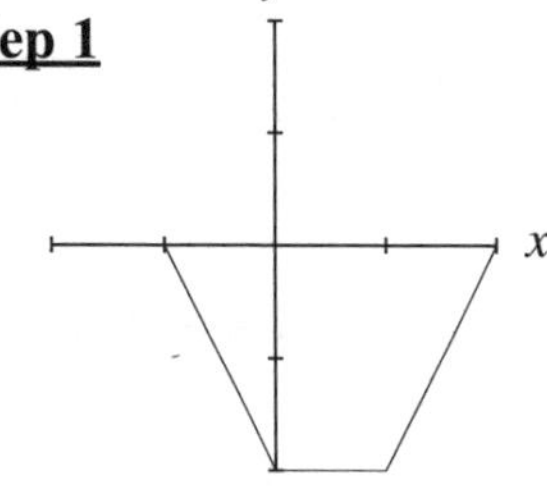

Reflect about x-axis and vertical expansion by a factor of 2

Step 2

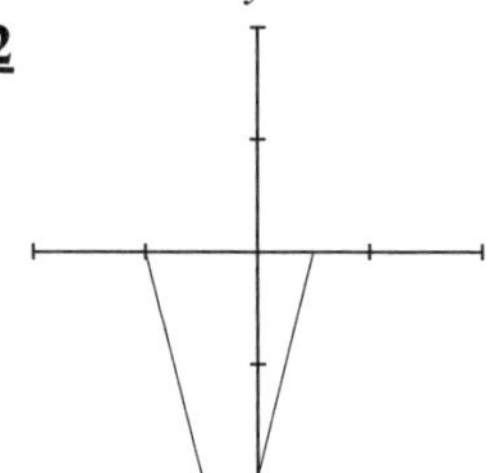

Reflect about y-axis and horizontal compression by a factor of $\frac{1}{2}$

Step 3

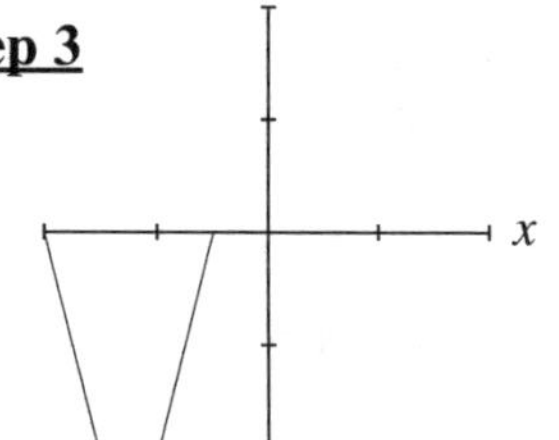

Shift to left 1 unit

Step 4

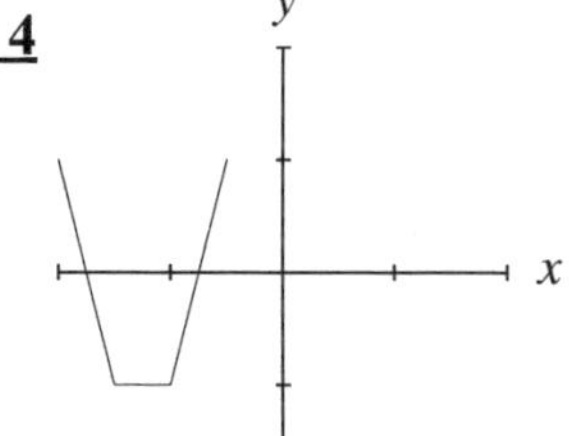

Vertical shift of 1

Method 2

If $y = f(x)$ *has point* (m, n), *then* $y = af[b(x-c)]+d$ *has point* $\left(\frac{m}{b}+c, an+d\right)$

Key reference points of this graph are $(-1, 0)$, $(0, 1)$, $(1, 1)$ and $(2, 0)$

Use these key points to calculate the translated points

(m, n)	$\left(\frac{m}{b}+c,\ an+d\right)$		
$(-1, 0)$	$\left(\frac{-1}{-2}-1, -2\cdot 0+1\right)$	$=$	$\left(-\frac{1}{2}, 1\right)$
$(0, 1)$	$\left(\frac{0}{-2}-1, -2\cdot 1+1\right)$	$=$	$(-1, -1)$
$(1, 1)$	$\left(\frac{1}{-2}-1, -2\cdot 1+1\right)$	$=$	$\left(-\frac{3}{2}, -1\right)$
$(2, 0)$	$\left(\frac{2}{-2}-1, -2\cdot 0+1\right)$	$=$	$(-2, 1)$

Graph of $f(x) = -2\ f[-2\ (x+1)]+1$

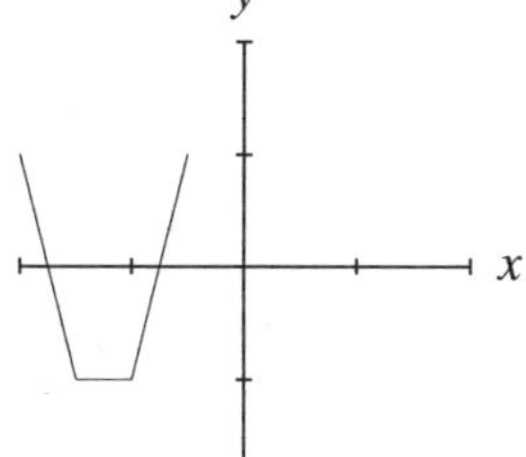

Graph these four points, and join to form the translated graph.

2.6 Exercise Set

1. Suppose $y = f(x)$ has point (a, b). Match the function on the left with the point on the right.

a)	$y = f(x-1)+1$	________	**A**	$(a-1, b)$
b)	$y = f(1-x)$	________	**B**	$(b, 1-a)$
c)	$y = -f(-x)$	________	**C**	$(1-a, b)$
d)	$y = f(x)+1$	________	**D**	$(-a, b)$
e)	$y = f(-x)$	________	**E**	$(-b, a+1)$
f)	$y = -f(x)$	________	**F**	$(a, b+1)$
g)	$y = f(x+1)$	________	**G**	(b, a)
h)	$y = f^{-1}(x)$	________	**H**	$(-a, -b)$
i)	$y = -f^{-1}(x)$	________	**I**	$(b+1, a)$
j)	$y = f^{-1}(x)+1$	________	**J**	$(-b, 1-a)$
k)	$y = f^{-1}(x-1)$	________	**K**	$(b, -a)$
l)	$y = f^{-1}(-x)+1$	________	**L**	$(a, -b)$
m)	$y = -f^{-1}(x)+1$	________	**M**	$(b, a+1)$
n)	$y = -f^{-1}(-x)+1$	________	**N**	$(a+1, b+1)$

2. If points $(4, -2)$ and (a, b) are on the graph of $y = f(x)$, what points must be on the following graphs?

a) $y = f(x-1)-3$

b) $y = -f(-x)+1$

c) $y = -f(x+2)-1$

d) $y = |f(2x)|$

e) $y = \frac{1}{2}f(x-1)+4$

f) $y = -|f(x-2)|$

g) $y = f\left(-\frac{1}{2}x\right)+1$

h) $y = -f(1-x)$

i) $y = f^{-1}(x)+2$

j) $y = f^{-1}(x+1)$

3. If $f(x)=x^2-1$, determine the equation after each of the following transformations:

a) $y=f(x+2)$

b) $y=f(\frac{1}{2}x)+1$

c) $y=-f(x-1)+2$

d) $y=2f(1-x)+3$

e) Expand vertically by a factor of 3

f) Expand horizontally by a factor of 3

4. If $4x^2+y^2=36$, determine the equation after each of the following transformations:

a) Expand horizontally by a factor of 2

b) Compress vertically by a factor of $\frac{1}{3}$

c) Compress horizontally by a factor of $\frac{1}{2}$ and expand vertically by a factor of $\frac{4}{3}$

5. Write an expression for $f(x)$ obtained by reflecting the graph of $g(x)=\frac{1}{2}x-2$ about the:

a) x-axis

b) y-axis

c) line $x=2$

d) line $y=2$

6. Graph the following functions **without** a calculator.

a) $f(x)=-(x-1)^2+3$

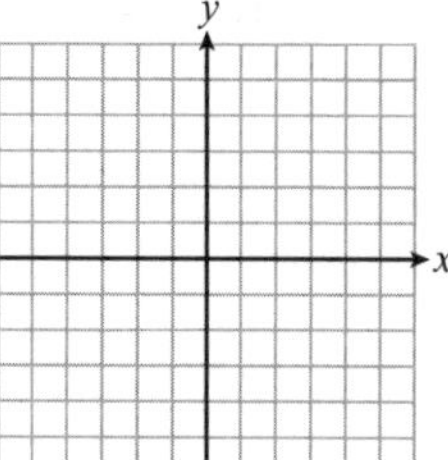

b) $f(x)=3\sqrt{5-x}-5$

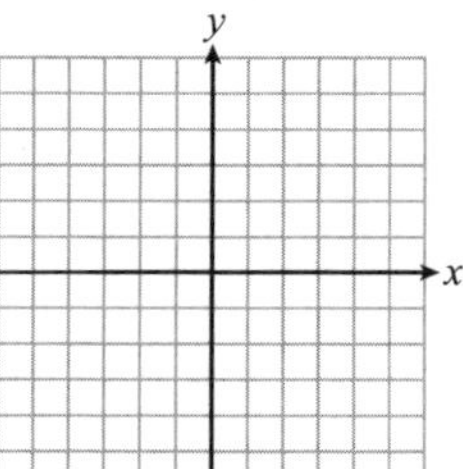

c) $f(x)=-|1-x|+3$

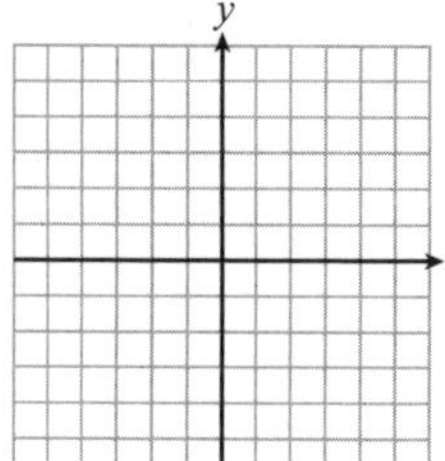

d) $f(x)=-\frac{1}{4}(x+2)^3+1$

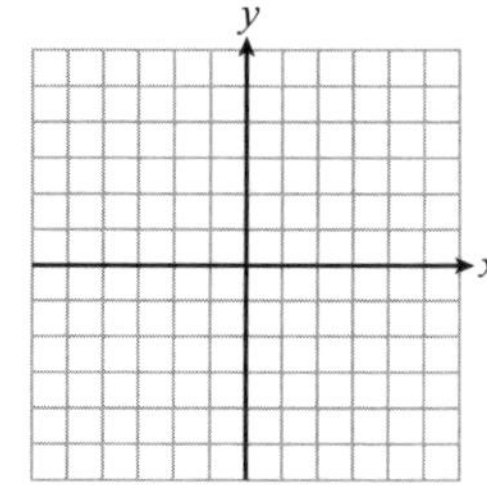

7. Given the graph of $y = f(x)$ below, sketch the graphs of the following:

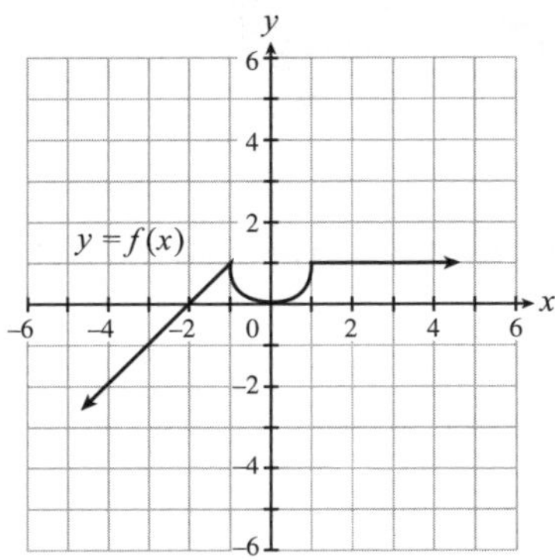

a) $y = f\left(\frac{1}{2}x\right) + 1$

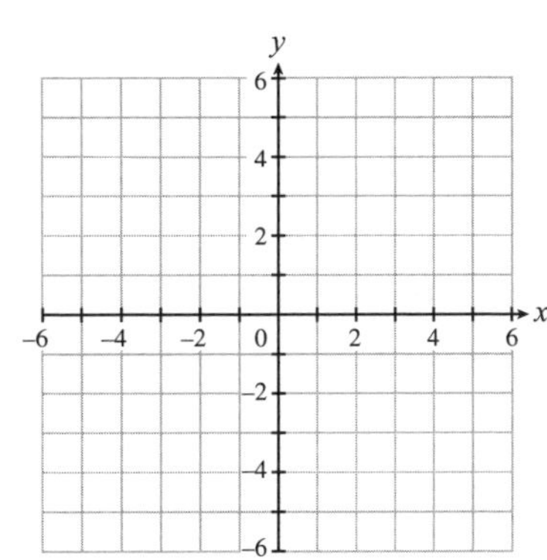

b) $y = -2f(x+2) - 1$

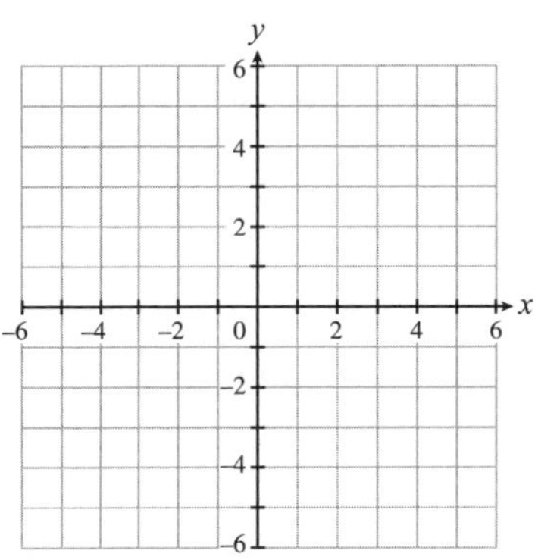

c) $y = 2f\left(\frac{1}{2}x - 1\right) + 1$

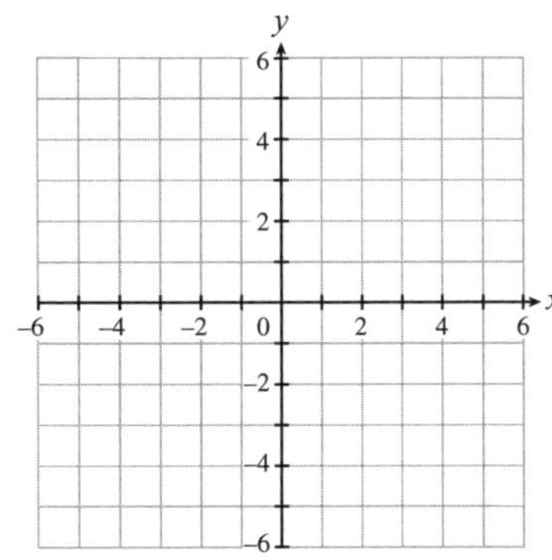

d) $y = 2f(1-x) + 2$

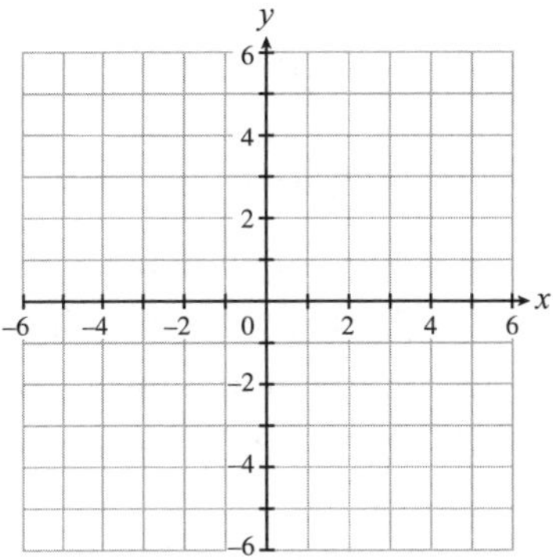

e) $y = -f(2-2x) - 2$

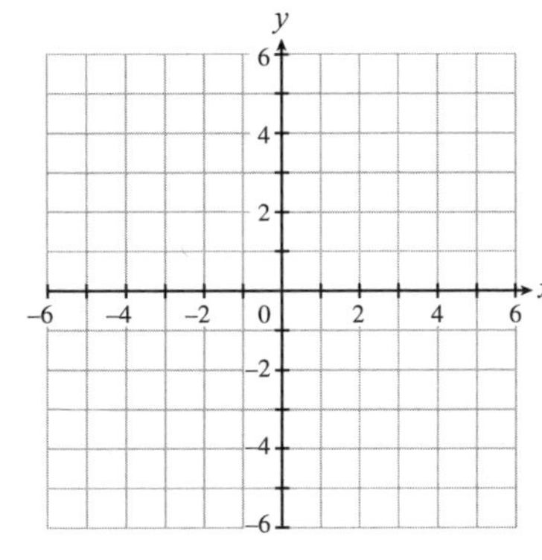

f) $y = -2f(-\frac{1}{2}x - 1) + 1$

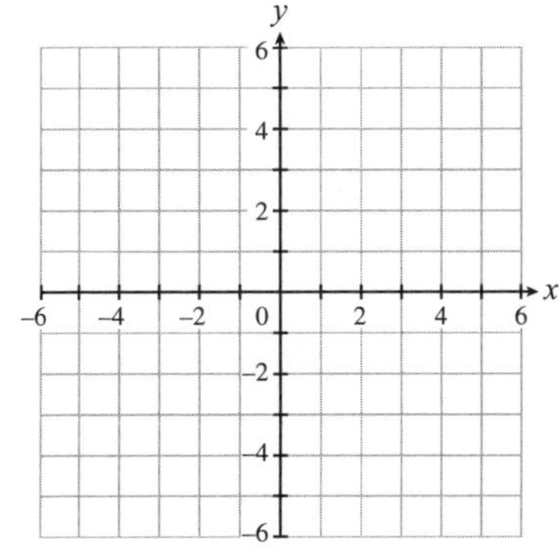

2.7 Chapter Review

Transformations – Multiple-choice Questions

Level A Questions

1. Given $f(x)=x^2+3x-1$ and $g(x)=2x+3$, find $(f-g)(-2)$.

   a) –2
   b) 0
   c) 2
   d) 10

2. The graph of $y=(x+1)^2+2$ compared to the graph of $y=x^2$ has a

   a) vertical downward translation of 2 units and horizontal translation of 1 unit right.
   b) vertical upward translation of 2 units and horizontal translation of 1 unit right.
   c) vertical downward translation of 2 units and horizontal translation of 1 unit left.
   d) vertical upward translation of 2 units and horizontal translation of 1 unit left

3. The graph of $y=-2x^2$ compared to the graph of $y=x^2$ has a

   a) reflection in the x axis and a vertical compression factor of $\frac{1}{2}$ units.
   b) reflection in the y axis and a vertical compression factor of $\frac{1}{2}$ units.
   c) reflection in the x axis and a vertical expansion factor of 2 units.
   d) reflection in the y axis and a vertical expansion factor of 2 units.

4. The graph of $(x-2)^2+(y+3)^2=25$ compared to the graph of $x^2+y^2=25$ has a

   a) horizontal translation of 2 units left and vertical translation of 3 units upward.
   b) horizontal translation of 2 units right and vertical translation of 3 units downward.
   c) horizontal translation of 2 units right and vertical translation of 3 units upward.
   d) horizontal translation of 2 units left and vertical translation of 3 units downward.

5. The graph of $y=-a^x$ compared to the graph of $y=a^x$ has a

   a) reflection in the x-axis.
   b) reflection in the y-axis.
   c) reflection in the line $y=x$.
   d) reflection at the origin.

6. Given the function $y=f(x)$, the graph of $y=f(\frac{1}{2}x)$ will

   a) compress the graph horizontally by a factor of $\frac{1}{2}$ units.
   b) expand the graph horizontally by a factor of 2 units.
   c) compress the graph vertically by a factor of $\frac{1}{2}$ units.
   d) expand the graph vertically by a factor of 2 units.

7. The graph of $y = 2f(3x)$ compared to the graph of $y = f(x)$ has a

a) horizontal compression factor of $\frac{1}{3}$ and a vertical compression factor of $\frac{1}{2}$.

b) horizontal expansion factor of 3 and a vertical compression factor of $\frac{1}{2}$.

c) horizontal compression factor of $\frac{1}{3}$ and a vertical expansion factor of 2.

d) horizontal expansion factor of 3 and a vertical expansion factor of 2.

8. If the graph of $y = f(x)$ has a domain $-3 \le x \le 2$, then the graph of $y = |f(x)|$ has a domain

a) $0 \le x \le 3$
b) $-3 \le x \le 2$
c) $x \ge 0$
d) $x \ge 2$

9. If the graph of $y = f(x)$ has a range $-3 \le f(x) \le 2$, then the graph of $y = |f(x)|$ has a range

a) $0 \le f(x) \le 2$
b) $0 \le f(x) \le 3$
c) $2 \le f(x) \le 3$
d) $f(x) \ge 3$

10. Which equation represents a reflection of the graph $3 - x = 2y^3 + y$ in the line $y = x$?

a) $3 + x = 2y^3 + y$

b) $3 - x = -2y^3 + y$

c) $3 - x = 2y^3 + y$

d) $3 - y = 2x^3 + x$

11. If the point, $(-1,\ 2)$, is on the graph $y = f(x)$, what point is on the graph $x = f(y)$?

a) $(1,\ -2)$
b) $(-2,\ 1)$
c) $(2,\ -1)$
d) $\left(-\frac{1}{2},\ 1\right)$

12. Which equation represents the graph of $y = f(x)$ after it is reflected in the x-axis, then translated vertically 2 units downward?

a) $y = -f(x) + 2$
b) $y = f(-x) + 2$
c) $y = f(-x) - 2$
d) $y = -f(x) - 2$

13. If the graph of $y=f(x)$ has a point on the graph of $(-2, 9)$, then the graph of $x+1=f(y-1)$ must have a point in the graph of

a) $(1, -8)$

b) $(3, -10)$

c) $(8, -1)$

d) $(10, -3)$

14. If $f(x)=x(x-1)$ and $g(x)=x(x^2-1)$, then the restrictions on $\left(\frac{f}{g}\right)(x)$ is:

a) $x \neq 1$

b) $x \neq -1, 1$

c) $x \neq 0, 1$

d) $x \neq -1, 0, 1$

15. Given $f(x)=2x-3$, determine $f^{-1}(x)$, the inverse of $f(x)$

a) $f^{-1}(x)=\frac{1}{2x-3}$

b) $f^{-1}(x)=\frac{x-3}{2x}$

c) $f^{-1}(x)=x+\frac{3}{2}$

d) $f^{-1}(x)=\frac{x+3}{2}$

16. Which equation represents the graph of $y=x^3-x^2-x+1$ after it has been reflected in the x-axis?

a) $y=-x^3-x^2+x+1$

b) $y=-x^3+x^2+x+1$

c) $y=-x^3+x^2+x-1$

d) $y=-x^3+x^2-x+1$

17. Which equation represents the graph of $y=x^3-x^2-x+1$ after it has been reflected in the y-axis?

a) $y=-x^3-x^2+x+1$

b) $y=-x^3+x^2+x+1$

c) $y=-x^3+x^2+x-1$

d) $y=-x^3+x^2-x+1$

18. The point, (a, b), is on the graph of $y=f(x)$, which point must be on the graph $y=\frac{1}{f(x)}$?

a) $\left(\frac{1}{a}, \frac{1}{b}\right)$ **b)** $\left(a, \frac{1}{b}\right)$ **c)** $(-a, -b)$ **d)** (b, a)

19. In which line would the graph of $y = x^3 - 1$ be reflected to obtain the graph of $y = \sqrt[3]{x+1}$?

a) $x = 0$
b) $y = 0$
c) $y = \frac{1}{x}$
d) $y = x$

20. Given $f(x) = x^2 - 4$ determine the *y*-intercept of $y = -2|f(x)|$.

a) –8
b) –6
c) 6
d) 8

21. Which of the following equations does **NOT** have $f(x) = f(-x)$?

a) $y = x^2 + 1$
b) $x^2 + y^2 = 9$
c) $3x^2 - y^2 = 1$
d) $y = (x-1)^2$

Level B Questions

22. The graph of $\left(\frac{x}{2}\right)^2 + (3y)^2 = 9$ compared to the graph of $x^2 + y^2 = 9$ has a

a) horizontal compression factor of $\frac{1}{2}$ and a vertical expansion factor of 3.
b) horizontal compression factor of $\frac{1}{2}$ and a vertical compression factor of $\frac{1}{3}$.
c) horizontal expansion factor of 2 and a vertical compression factor of $\frac{1}{3}$.
d) horizontal expansion factor of 2 and a vertical expansion factor of 3.

23. The graph of $y = \sin\left(\frac{\pi}{2}x + \pi\right)$ compared to the graph of $y = \sin\frac{\pi}{2}x$ has a

a) horizontal translation to the right of π units.
b) horizontal translation to the left of π units.
c) horizontal translation to the right of 2 units.
d) horizontal translation to the left of 2 units

24. The graph of $y = f(x+a) + b$ with $a, b < 0$ compared to the graph of $y = f(x)$ has a

a) horizontal translation to the right of "*a*" units and vertical translation of "*b*" units upward.
b) horizontal translation to the left of "*a*" units and vertical translation of "*b*" units upward.
c) horizontal translation to the right of "*a*" units and vertical translation of "*b*" units downward.
d) horizontal translation to the left of "*a*" units and vertical translation of "*b*" units downward.

25. The graph of $y = -af(x)$, $0 < a < 1$ compared to the graph of $y = f(x)$ has a

a) reflection in the x-axis and a vertical compression of a factor of a.
b) reflection in the x-axis and a vertical expansion of a factor of a.
c) reflection in the y-axis and a vertical compression of a factor of a.
d) reflection in the y-axis and a vertical expansion of a factor of a.

26. Given $f(x) = x^2 - 4$ and $g(x) = \sqrt{4 - x^2}$, then the domain of $(f \circ g)(x)$ is:

a) $x \geq 0$
b) $x \leq -2, x \geq 2$
c) $-2 \leq x \leq 2$
d) all real numbers

27. If $y = f(x)$ has points in quadrant II and III, then the graph of $y = f^{-1}(x)$ must have points in what quadrants?

a) I, IV
b) II, III
c) II, IV
d) III, IV

28. What is the graph $y = \sin(2x + 4)$ translated 2 units to the right?

a) $y = \sin(2x)$
b) $y = \sin(2x + 2)$
c) $y = \sin(2x + 6)$
d) $y = \sin(2x + 8)$

29. Which equation represents the graph of $y = f(-x)$ translated 2 units to the left and down 3 units?

a) $y = f(-x + 2) + 3$
b) $y = f(-x - 2) + 3$
c) $y = f(-x + 2) - 3$
d) $y = f(-x - 2) - 3$

30. If the point, $(-2,\ -6)$, is on the graph of $y = f(x)$, what point is on the graph of $y = -2\,|\,f(x)\,| + 3$?

a) $(-2,\ -9)$
b) $(-2,\ -6)$
c) $(2,\ -9)$
d) $(2,\ -6)$

31. The graph of the function $y = f(x)$ is shown at left, what transformation will produce the graph on the right?

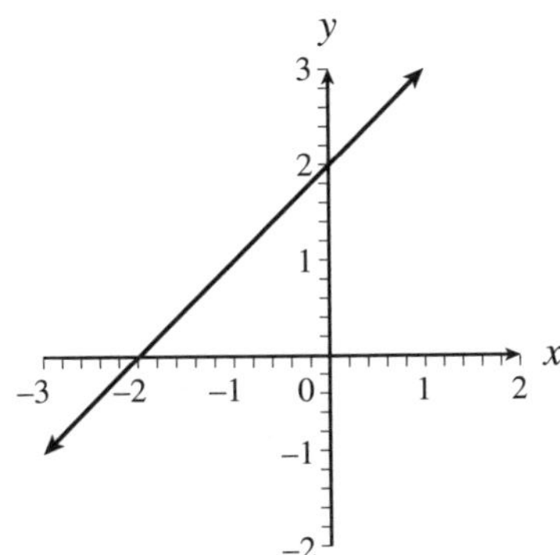
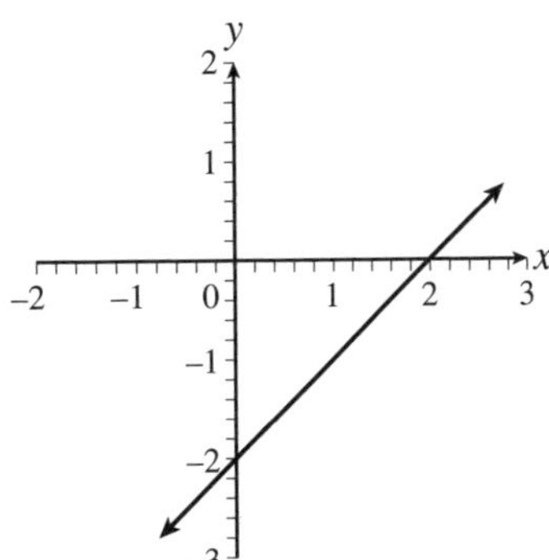

a) $f(-x)$
b) $-f(x)$
c) $f^{-1}(x)$
d) $\dfrac{1}{f(x)}$

32. If $f(x) = 4x^2 + 8$, determine the new equation $g(x)$ after a horizontal expansion by a factor of 2 units.

a) $g(x) = x^2 + 8$
b) $g(x) = 16x^2 + 8$
c) $g(x) = x^2 + 2$
d) $g(x) = 16x^2 + 32$

33. If the point, $(-1,\ -2)$, is on the graph $y = f(x)$, what point is on the graph of $y = |f(-x)|$?

a) $(-1,\ -2)$
b) $(1,\ 2)$
c) $(-1,\ 2)$
d) $(1,\ -2)$

34. If the point, $(-2,\ 4)$, is on the graph of $y = f(x)$, what point is on the graph of $y = f^{-1}(x+1)$?

a) $(3,\ -2)$
b) $(4,\ -3)$
c) $(1,\ -4)$
d) $(5,\ -2)$

35. If the point, $(-2,\ 4)$, is on the graph of $y = f(x)$, what point is on the graph of $y = f^{-1}(-x)$?

a) $(4,\ 2)$
b) $(-4,\ 2)$
c) $(-4,\ -2)$
d) $(4,\ -2)$

36. The function $y=\sqrt{16-x^2}$ is expanded horizontally by a factor of 2, then translated 2 units downward. The transformed function would be

a) $y=\frac{1}{2}\sqrt{4-x^2}-2$

b) $y=\frac{1}{2}\sqrt{64-x^2}-2$

c) $y=2\sqrt{2-x^2}$

d) $y=\frac{1}{2}\sqrt{60-x^2}$

37. If $f(x)=1-\dfrac{1}{x}$, then $f(-n)$ is equal to

a) $f(n)$

b) $\dfrac{1}{f(n)}$

c) $f\left(\dfrac{-1}{n}\right)$

d) $\dfrac{1}{f(n+1)}$

38. If $9x^2+8y^2=36$, determine the equation if its graph has been compressed horizontally by a factor of $\dfrac{1}{3}$ and expanded vertically by a factor of 2.

a) $x^2+2y^2=36$

b) $x^2+32y^2=36$

c) $27x^2+4y^2=36$

d) $81x^2+2y^2=36$

39. The graph, $y=f(x)$, is shown on the left. Determine the equation of the new graph on the right.

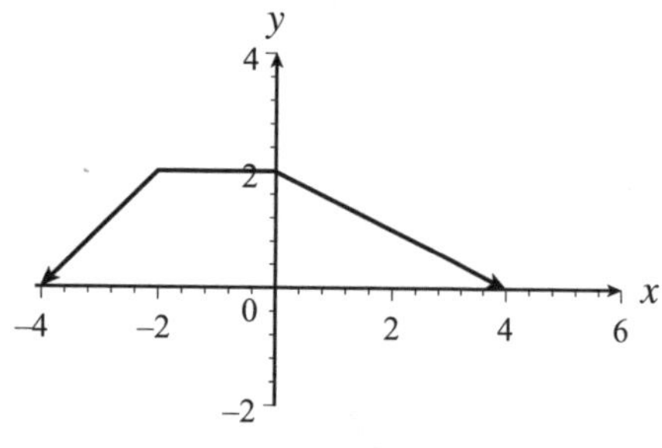

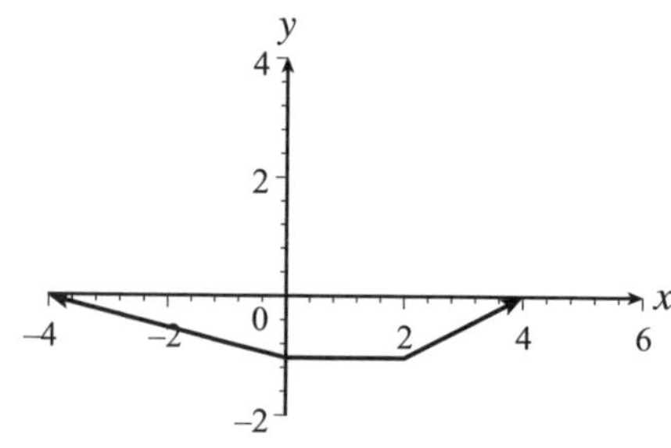

a) $y=-2f(-x)$

b) $y=-\frac{1}{2}f(-x)$

c) $y=-f(-\frac{1}{2}x)$

d) $y=-f(-2x)$

40. The graph, $y=f(x)$, is shown on the left. Determine the equation of the new graph on the right.

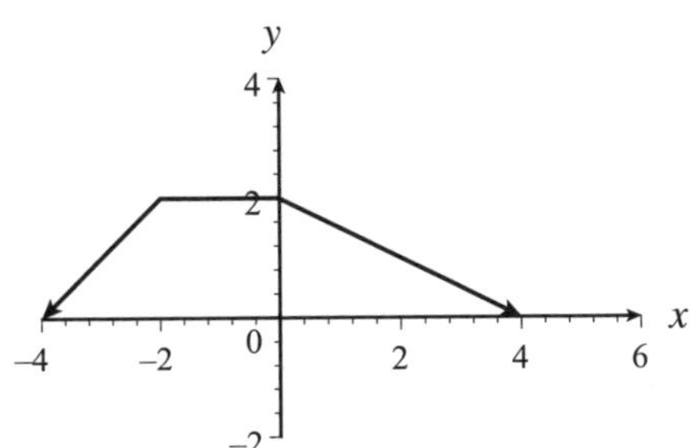

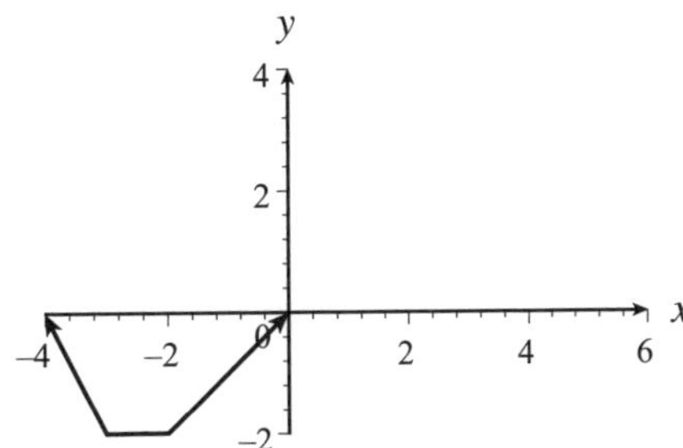

a) $y=-f(2x+4)$
b) $y=f(-2x-4)$
c) $y=-2f(x+2)$
d) $y=-2f(x-2)$

41. The graph, $y=f(x)$, is shown on the left. Determine the equation of the new graph on the right.

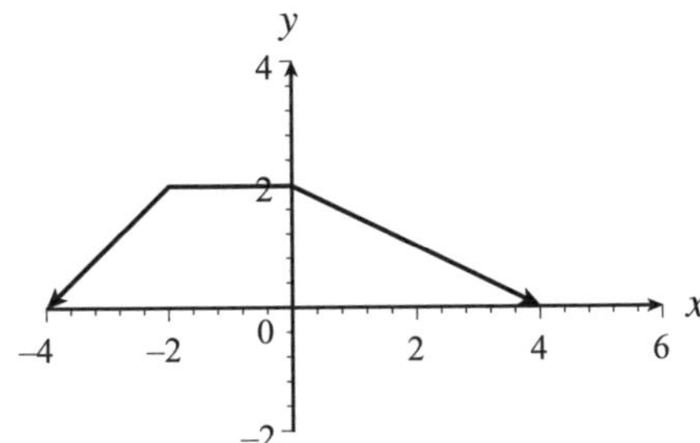

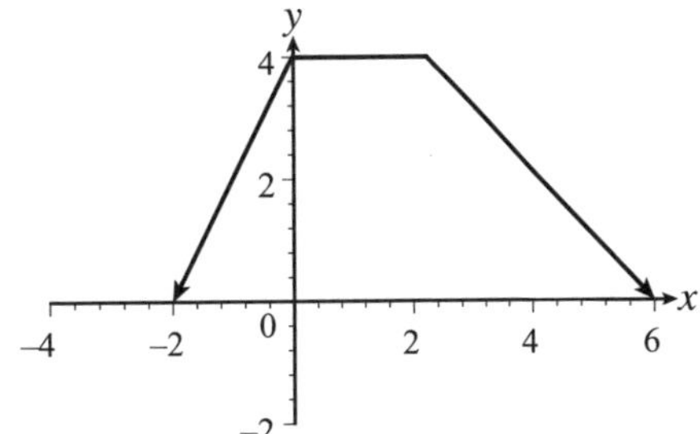

a) $y=f(\frac{1}{2}x+1)$
b) $y=f(\frac{1}{2}x-1)$
c) $y=2f(x+2)$
d) $y=2f(x-2)$

42. Given $f(x)=x^2-9$ determine the y-intercept of $y=|f(x+2)|$.

a) -5
b) -2
c) 2
d) 5

43. If the range of $y=f(x)$ is $-2\le y\le 1$ determine the range of the function $y=-2f(x)-4$.

a) $-8\le y\le 2$
b) $-6\le y\le 0$
c) $-2\le y\le 4$
d) $2\le y\le 8$

44. Given the function $f(x)=(x+1)(x-2)$ which function below will have the same x-intercept as $f(x)$?

a) $y=f(-2x)$
b) $y=-2f(x)$
c) $x=f(y)$
d) $y=\dfrac{1}{f(x)}$

45. In which line would the graph of $f(x)=2x^2-3x$ be reflected to obtain the graph of $g(x)=2x^2+3x$?

a) $x=0$
b) $y=0$
c) $y=x$
d) $y=-x$

46. If the point (8, –6) is on the graph of $y=f(x)$, what point is graphed after the following transformations are performed in the order given?

<u>Step 1</u>: compress horizontally by a factor of $\frac{1}{2}$
<u>Step 2</u>: reflected over the x-axis
<u>Step 3</u>: expanded vertically by a factor of 3
<u>Step 4</u>: reflected in the line $y=x$

a) (2, 16)
b) (9, 12)
c) (18, 4)
d) (18, 16)

Level C Questions

47. Which equation represents the graph of $y=x^3-x^2+x-1$ after it is reflected in both the x-axis and y-axis?

a) $y=x^3-x^2+x-1$
b) $y=x^3+x^2+x-1$
c) $y=-x^3-x^2-x+1$
d) $y=x^3+x^2+x+1$

48. Which equation represents the graph of $y=f(x)$ after it is reflected in the y-axis, then translated horizontally 2 units to the left?

a) $y=-f(x+2)$
b) $y=-f(x-2)$
c) $y=f(-x-2)$
d) $y=f(-x+2)$

49. The graph of $y=\sqrt{a-x}$, $a>0$ compared to the graph of $y=\sqrt{x}$ has a

a) a reflection over the x-axis and a horizontal translation to the right of "a" units.
b) a reflection over the y-axis and a horizontal translation to the right of "a" units.
c) a reflection over the x-axis and a horizontal translation to the left of "a" units.
d) a reflection over the y-axis and a horizontal translation to the left of "a" units.

50. Given $f(x)=\dfrac{x}{3x-1}$, determine $f^{-1}(x)$, the inverse of $f(x)$

a) $f^{-1}(x)=\dfrac{3x-1}{x}$

b) $f^{-1}(x)=\dfrac{x}{3x-1}$

c) $f^{-1}(x)=\dfrac{-x}{3x-1}$

d) $f^{-1}(x)=\dfrac{x}{3x+1}$

51. Given $f(x)=\dfrac{2x}{1-x}$, determine $f^{-1}(x)$, the inverse of $f(x)$.

a) $f^{-1}(x)=\dfrac{x}{x+2}$

b) $f^{-1}(x)=\dfrac{x}{x-2}$

c) $f^{-1}(x)=\dfrac{-x}{x+2}$

d) $f^{-1}(x)=\dfrac{1-x}{2x}$

52. Find two functions f and g such that $(f\circ g)(x)=\dfrac{3}{(5x+2)^2}$

a) $f(x)=\dfrac{3}{x^2}$, $g(x)=5x+2$

b) $g(x)=\dfrac{3}{x^2}$, $f(x)=5x+2$

c) $f(x)=\dfrac{1}{(5x+2)^2}$, $g(x)=3$

d) $g(x)=\dfrac{1}{(5x+2)^2}$, $f(x)=3$

53. The zeroes of a function $y=f(x)$ are $-3,\ 0,\ 2$. Determine the zeroes of the function $y=f(1-x)$.

a) $-4,\ -1,\ 1$

b) $-3,\ -1,\ 2$

c) $-2,\ 1,\ 3$

d) $-1,\ 1,\ 4$

54. Let $f(x)=\dfrac{(2x-1)}{(x-2)}$, then $(f\circ f)(x)$ equals

a) x

b) $-\dfrac{3x+4}{5}$

c) $\dfrac{3x-4}{5}$

d) $x-2$

55. If $(3,\ -4)$ is a point on the graph of $y=f(x)$, what must be a point on the graph of $y=\dfrac{1}{2}f(1-x)-2$?

a) $(-2,\ -4)$

b) $(-2,\ -3)$

c) $(4,\ -4)$

d) $(4,\ 0)$

56. If the point $(-2,\ 4)$ is on the graph of $y=f(x)$, what point is on the graph of $y=-f^{-1}(-x)-2$?

a) $(-6,\ 2)$

b) $(-4,\ 0)$

c) $(-2,\ 6)$

d) $(4,\ -4)$

57. The point (a, b) is on the graph of $y=x^2$, which of the following points in terms of a and b are on the graph $y=-(x-3)^2+1$?

a) $(-a-3,\ b+1)$

b) $(-a+3,\ b+1)$

c) $(a+3,\ -b-1)$

d) $(a+3,\ -b+1)$

58. If $(m,\ n)$ is a point on the graph of $y=f(x)$, determine a point on the graph $y=-f(x-2)+1$

a) $(m-2,\ -n+1)$

b) $(m+2,\ -n+1)$

c) $(-m+2,\ n+1)$

d) $(-m-2,\ n-1)$

59. If the point (a, b) is on the graph of $y = f(x)$, which of the following points is on the graph $y = 2f(4-x)-1$?

a) $(-a+4,\ 2b-1)$
b) $(-a+4,\ 2b+1)$
c) $(a-4,\ 2b-1)$
d) $(a-4,\ 2b+1)$

60. If $f(x) = x^3$, find $(f^{-1} \circ f^{-1})(512)$.

a) –8
b) –2
c) 2
d) 8

61. Given the function $f(x) = 3x+1$, which of the following will have the same *y*-intercept as $f(x)$?

a) $y = -\dfrac{1}{f(x)}$

b) $y = \dfrac{1}{f(x)}$

c) $x = f(y)$

d) $x = \dfrac{1}{f(y)}$

62. If $f(x) = x^2$ and $g(x) = 2x+1$, then $\dfrac{f\left[g(x)\right] - f\left[g(a)\right]}{x-a}$ is

a) $2x+2a+2$
b) $2x-2a+2$
c) $4x-4a+4$
d) $4x+4a+4$

63. Find $(g \circ f)(x)$ if $f(x) = \dfrac{x^2+1}{x^2-1}$ and $g(x) = \dfrac{2x-5}{3x+4}$.

a) $\dfrac{-3x^2+7}{7x^2-1}$

b) $\dfrac{-2x^2+7}{7x^2-1}$

c) $\dfrac{-3x^2+6}{7x^2+1}$

d) $\dfrac{-3x^2+7}{7x^2+1}$

64. If the graph $x^2 + y^2 = 1$ is horizontally expanded by a factor of 3 and vertically compressed by a factor of $\frac{1}{2}$, determine an equation for the new graph.

a) $\frac{x^2}{9} + 4y^2 = 1$

b) $\frac{x^2}{3} + 2y^2 = 1$

c) $3x^2 + \frac{y^2}{2} = 1$

d) $9x^2 + \frac{y^2}{4} = 1$

65. If the point (–4, 8) is on the graph of $y = f(x)$, what point must be on the graph of $y = f(4 - 2x) - 1$?

a) (0, 7)
b) (–4, –3)
c) (4, 7)
d) (6, 7)

66. The function, $y = f(x)$, is shown on the bottom left. The function, $y = af(bx)$, is shown on the bottom right. Determine the values of a and b.

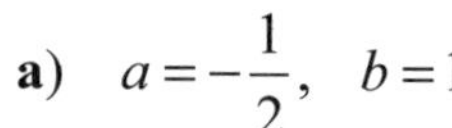

a) $a = -\frac{1}{2}, \quad b = 1$

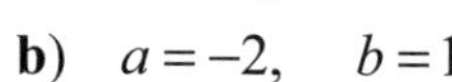

b) $a = -2, \quad b = 1$

c) $a = -1, \quad b = \frac{1}{2}$

d) $a = -1, \quad b = 2$

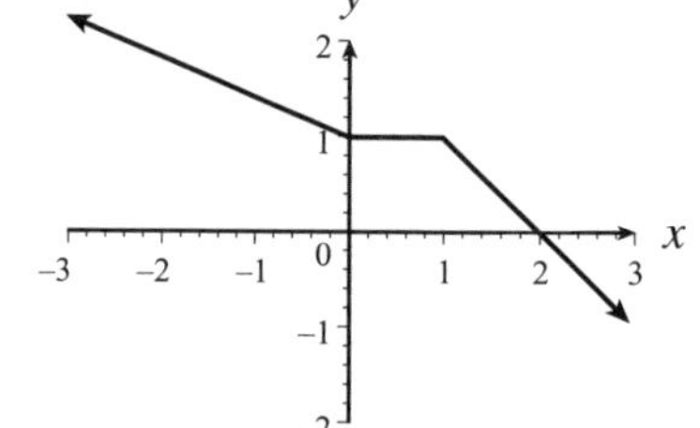

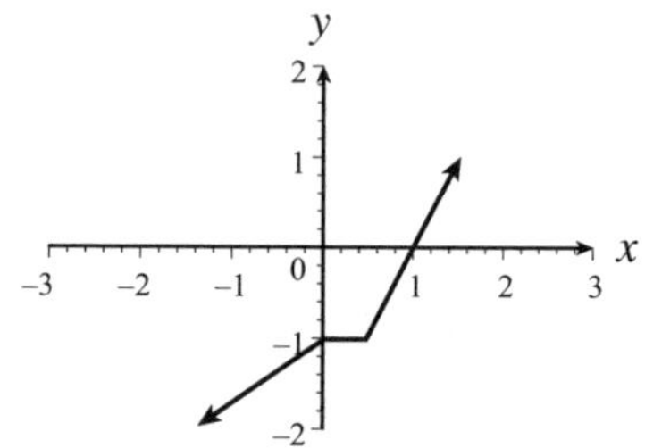

67. The graph of $y = f(x)$ has the restrictions $-2 \le f(x) \le 2$ then the reciprocal graph $y = g(x)$ will have which one of the following restrictions?

a) $g(x) \le -\frac{1}{2}, \quad g(x) \ge \frac{1}{2}$

b) $g(x) \ge -\frac{1}{2}, \quad g(x) \le \frac{1}{2}$

c) $g(x) \le -\frac{1}{2}, \quad g(x) \le \frac{1}{2}$

d) $g(x) \le -2, \quad g(x) \ge 2$

3.1 Polynomials

In this chapter, we will learn to sketch the graphs of polynomial functions and will develop the theory of polynomial equations. But first, we must define a polynomial.

Definition of a Polynomial

Let $a_n, a_{n-1}, a_{n-2,} \cdots, a_2, a_1, a_0$ be real numbers, and *n* a whole number. A polynomial is an expression in the form:

$$a_n x^n + a_{n-1} x^{n-1} + \cdots + a_2 x^2 + a_1 x + a_0 \text{ , with } a_n \neq 0 .$$

The polynomial is of **degree** *n*, with a_n the **leading coefficient**.

A polynomial in standard form is written in descending order of exponents.

The polynomial functions of degrees 0 to 4 have special names.

Example 1

Polynomial in standard form	Degree	Leading Coefficient	Special Name
$f(x) = -5x^4 + 3x^2 + 2x - 7$	4	–5	quartic
$g(x) = 2x^3 - \sqrt{2}x + 4$	3	2	cubic
$h(x) = \sqrt{3}x^2 + 2x - 3$	2	$\sqrt{3}$	quadratic
$j(x) = 2x - 3$	1	2	linear
$k(x) = 5$	0	5	constant

Remember, each exponent of a polynomial must be a whole number defined as $\{0, 1, 2, 3, \ldots\}$, and each coefficient must be a real number.

Example 2

$f(x) = 3x^{-1} + 2x + 5$, not a polynomial, exponent -1 not a whole number.

$g(x) = \sqrt{2}x^3 + \sqrt{-3}x$, not a polynomial, coefficient $\sqrt{-3}$ is not real.

$h(x) = \dfrac{2x-3}{x^2}$, not a polynomial, simplifies to $2x^{-1} - 3x^{-2}$ which gives negative exponents.

$m(n) = 3x - 5x^{\frac{1}{2}}$, not a polynomial, exponent $\dfrac{1}{2}$ not a whole number.

Shape of Polynomial Graphs

The graph of a polynomial function is continuous. A polynomial has no breaks or sharp corners. This means that you can draw the complete graph without lifting your pencil from the paper.

Example 3

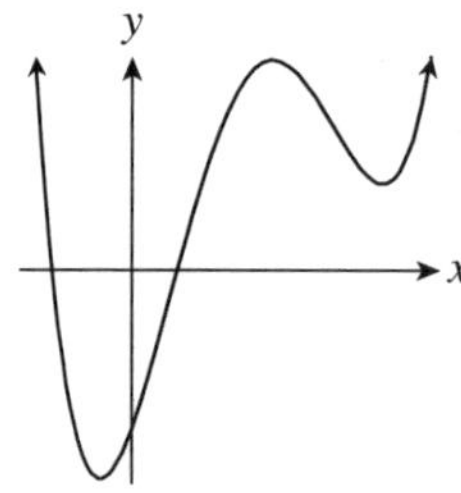

Polynomial function

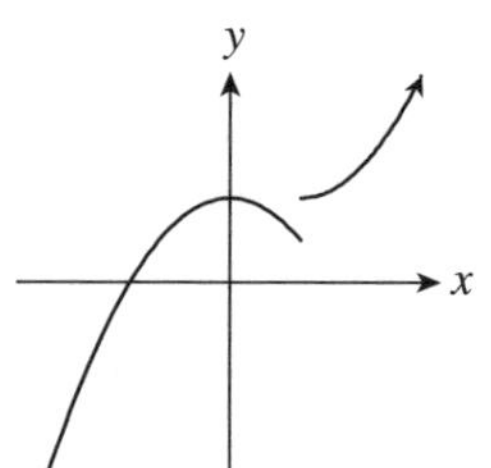

Non-polynomial function – has a break

The graph of a polynomial function has only smooth continuous curves.

Example 4

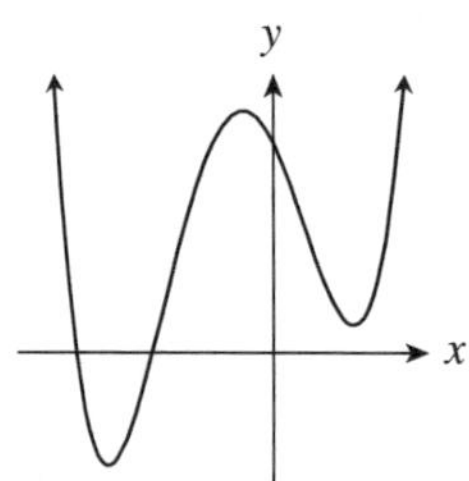

Polynomial function

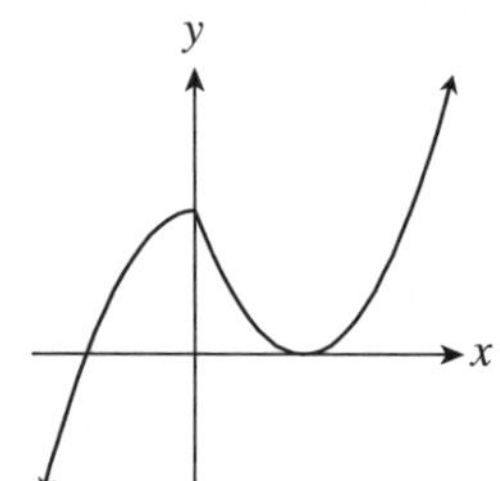

Non-polynomial function – has a corner

Polynomial of the Form $f(x) = x^n$ and $f(x) = -x^n$

Let us look at polynomials of a single term (a monomial) and examine their end behaviour. i.e., whether the graph's y-values are positive or negative for extreme positive and negative x-values.

Example 5

$f(x) = x$

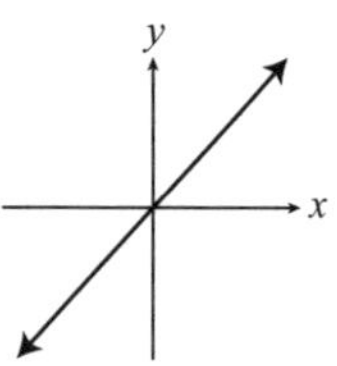

$f(x) = -x$

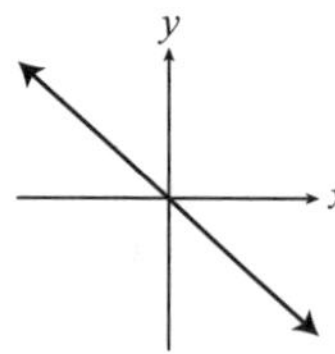

$f(x) = x^2$

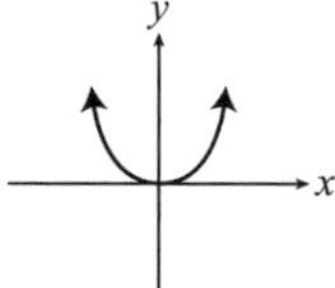

$f(x) = -x^2$

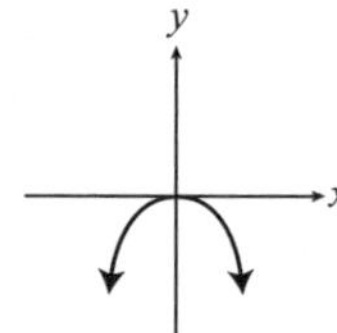

$f(x) = x^3$

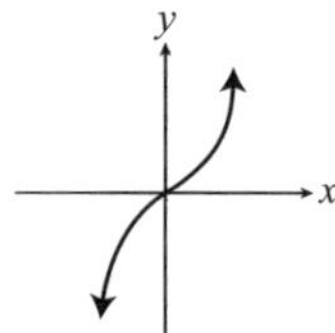

$f(x) = -x^3$

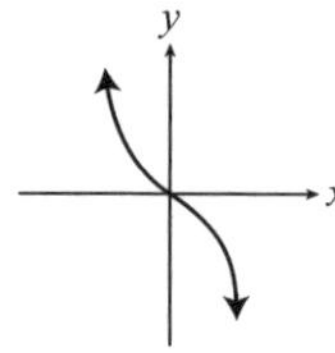

$f(x) = x^4$

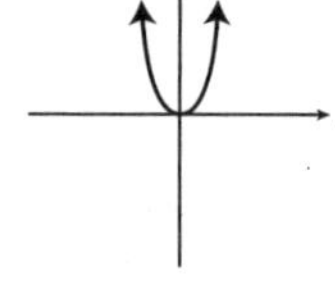

$f(x) = -x^4$

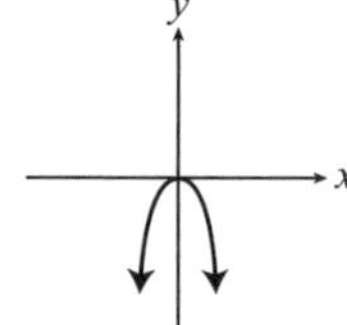

$f(x) = x^5$

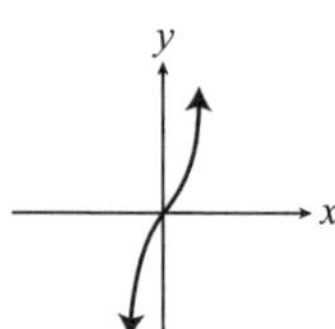

$f(x) = -x^5$

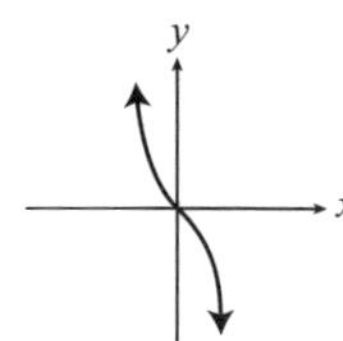

$f(x) = x^6$

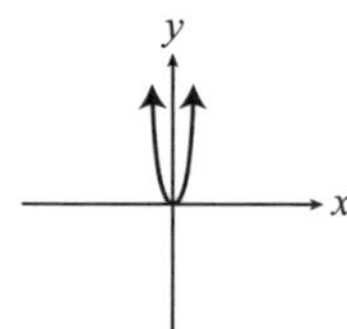

$f(x) = -x^6$

Comparing $f(x) = \pm x^n$ slope of graphs

$f(x) =$	x^n n odd	$-x^n$ n odd	x^n n even	$-x^n$ n even
domain range	all real all real	all real all real	all real $y \geq 0$	all real $y \leq 0$
$x \to \infty$	$f(x)$ increases $f(x) \to \infty$	$f(x)$ decreases $f(x) \to -\infty$	$f(x)$ increases $f(x) \to \infty$	$f(x)$ decreases $f(x) \to -\infty$
$x \to -\infty$	$f(x)$ increases $f(x) \to -\infty$	$f(x)$ decreases $f(x) \to \infty$	$f(x)$ decreases $f(x) \to -\infty$	$f(x)$ increases $f(x) \to \infty$

For $f(x) = x^n$, n an odd integer

Domain – all real numbers

Range – all real numbers

For $f(x) = x^n$, n an even integer

Domain – all real numbers

Range – $y \geq 0$

For $f(x) = -x^n$, n an odd integer

Domain – all real numbers

Range – all real numbers

For $f(x) = -x^n$, n an even integer

Domain – all real numbers

Range – $y \leq 0$

End Behaviour of Polynomials

So far, we have shown the end behaviour of polynomials with one term. What about polynomials with more than one term?

Does the end behaviour of $f(x) = x^4$ and $g(x) = x^4 - 5x^2 + 4$ change?

x	$f(x)$	$g(x)$
0	0	4
2	16	0
–2	16	0
5	625	504
–5	625	504
10	10 000	9 504
–10	10 000	9 504
100	10^8	9.99×10^7
–100	10^8	9.99×10^7

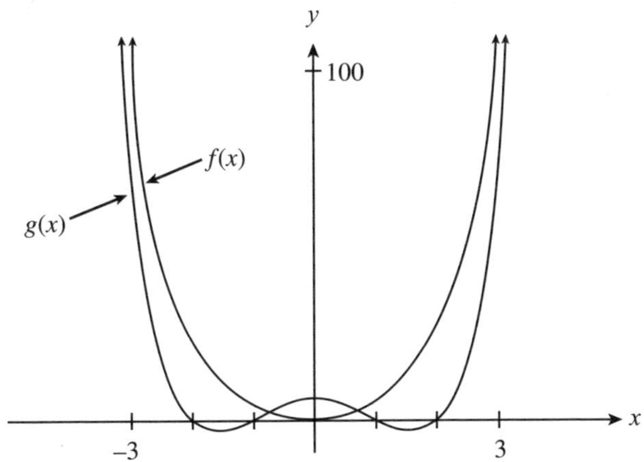

The graphs of the two functions are nearly the same away from the origin. $10^8 \approx 9.99 \times 10^7$. There is only a 0.0000001 difference. We can thus state

End Behaviour of Polynomial Functions

Given a polynomial function

$$f(x) = a_n x^n + a_{n-1} x^{n-1} + \cdots + a_1 x + a_0, \quad a_n \neq 0$$

The end behaviour of $f(x)$ is determined by the leading term of the polynomial, $a_n x^n$.

Degree and Leading Coefficient of Polynomial Functions

When graphing a polynomial function, first examine the leading term $a_n x^n$. The coefficient n will tell you the basic shape of the polynomial. The coefficient a_n will tell you the direction of the polynomial.

a) $y = ax^n + \cdots$, if n is an even whole number and $a > 0$, graph starts up and ends up.

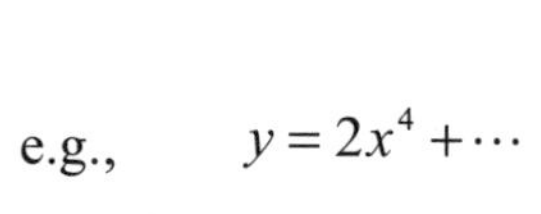

e.g., $y = 2x^4 + \cdots$

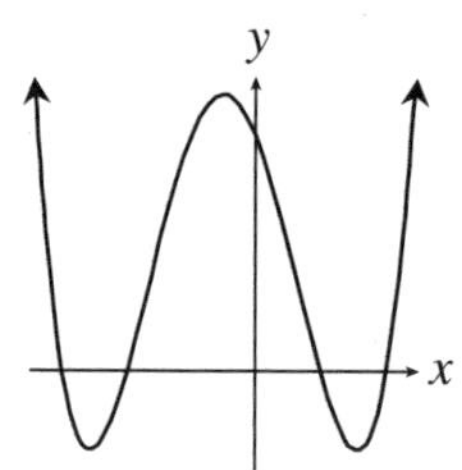

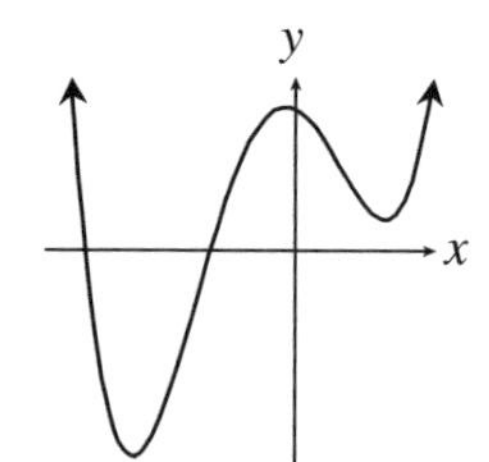

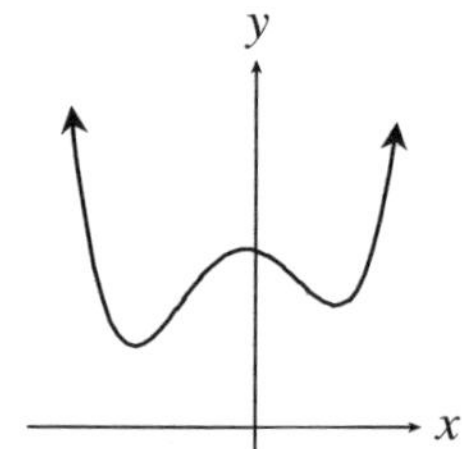

b) $y = ax^n + \cdots$, if n is an even whole number and $a < 0$, graph starts down and ends down.

e.g., $y = -2x^4 + \cdots$

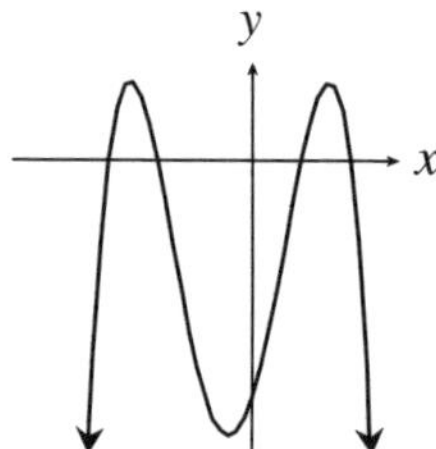

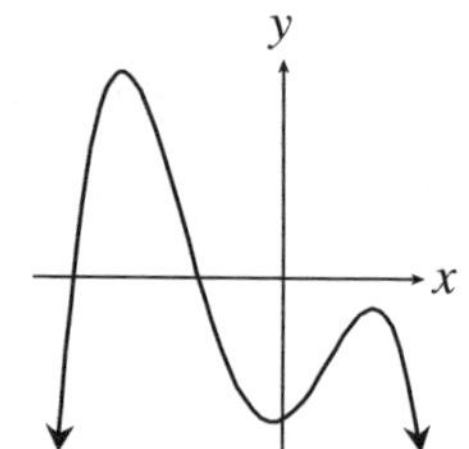

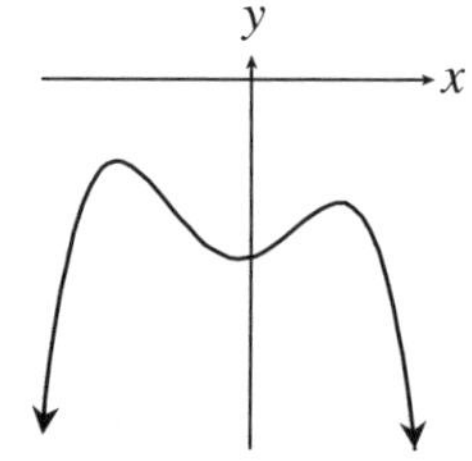

c) $y = ax^n + \cdots$, if n is an odd whole number and $a > 0$, graph starts down and ends up.

e.g., $y = x^3 + \cdots$

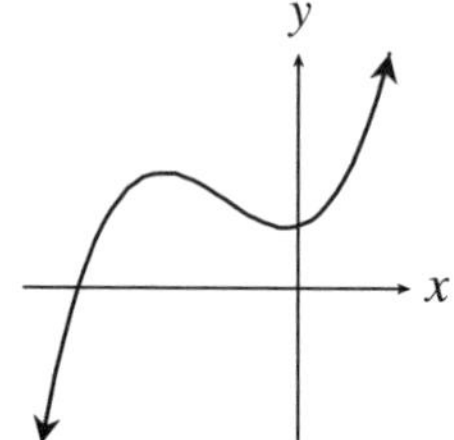

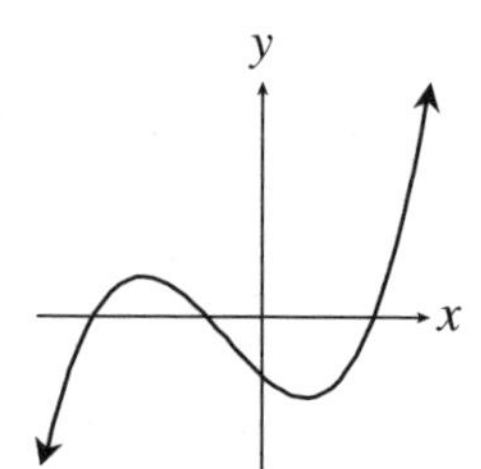

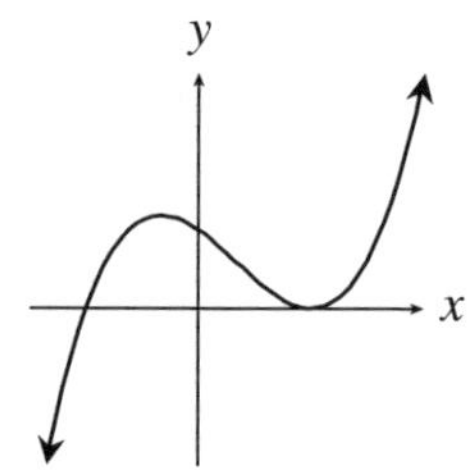

d) $y = ax^n + \cdots$, if n is an odd whole number and $a < 0$, graph starts up and ends down.

e.g., $y = -x^3 + \cdots$

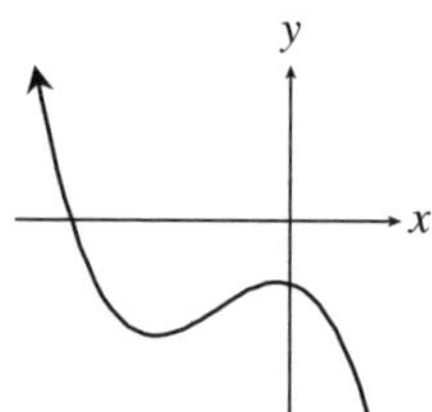

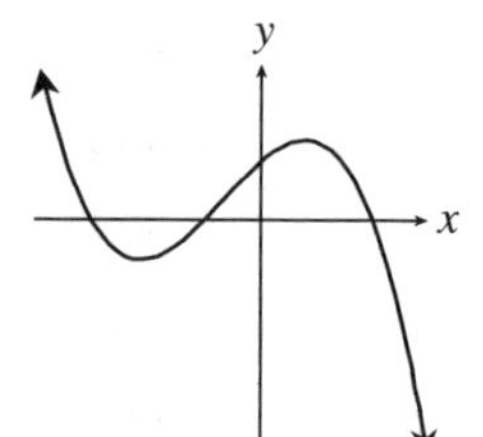

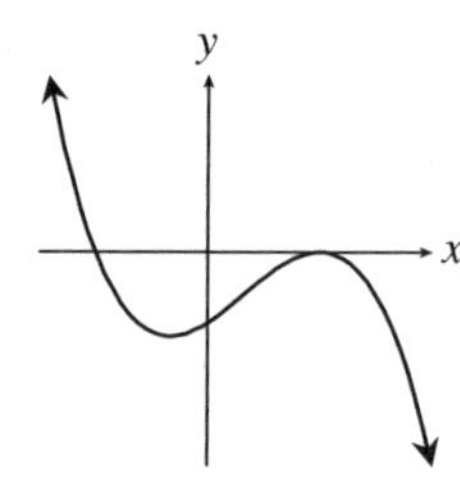

The Degree and Leading Coefficient of Polynomial Functions

If the **degree** of the polynomial is **odd**, the ends will point in **opposite** directions:

a) positive leading coefficient: down on left, up on right

b) negative leading coefficient: up on left, down on right

If the **degree** of the polynomial is **even**, the ends will point in the **same** direction:

a) positive leading coefficient: up on left, up on right

b) negative leading coefficient: down on left, down on right

Constant Value of a Polynomial Function

The next most important item to examine when graphing a polynomial is the constant value, i.e., when $x = 0$. This value tells you where the graph crosses the y-axis.

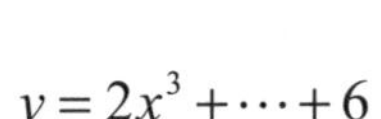

$y = 2x^3 + \cdots + 6$

This graph crosses the y-axis at 6.

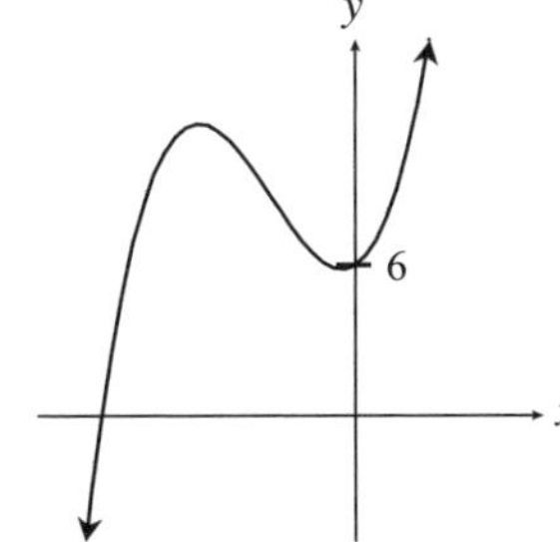

$y = -x^4 + \cdots - 3$

This graph crosses the y-axis at – 3.

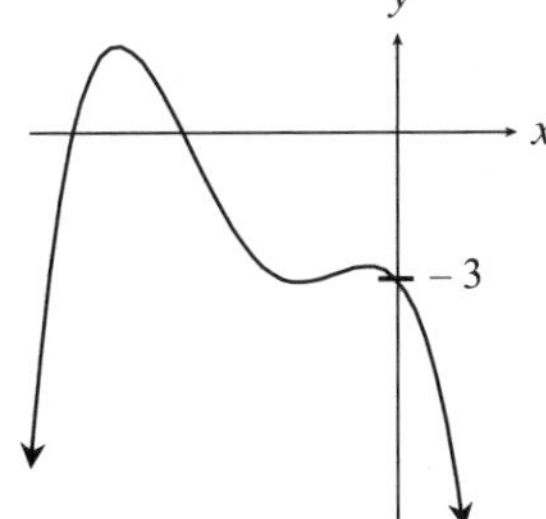

Example 6 Find the y-intercept of the following polynomial functions:

a) $f(x) = -2(x+1)^3$ **b)** $g(x) = (2x-1)(x+4)(x-3)$ **c)** $h(x) = x^4 - 5$

▶ *Solution:* A polynomial will intercept the y-axis by solving $f(0)$.

a) $f(x) = -2(x+1)^3$

$f(0) = -2(0+1)^3$

$f(0) = -2$

y-intercept is (0, –2).

b) $g(x) = (2x-1)(x+4)(x-3)$

$g(0) = (2 \cdot 0 - 1)(0+4)(0-3)$

$g(0) = 12$

y-intercept is (0, 12).

c) $h(x) = x^4 - 5$

$h(0) = 0^4 - 5$

$h(0) = -5$

y-intercept is (0, – 5).

Zeros of a Polynomial Function

The zeros of a polynomial function happen when the graph crosses the x-axis. This statement can be worded in many different ways.

Real Zeros of a Polynomial Function

If $f(x)$ is a polynomial function and a is a real number, the following statements are equivalent:

1. $x = a$ is a zero of the function $f(x)$.
2. $x = a$ is a root of the function $f(x)$.
3. $x = a$ is a solution of the function $f(x) = 0$.
4. $(x - a)$ is a factor of the function $f(x)$.
5. $(a, 0)$ is an x-intercept of the graph $f(x)$.

Example 7 Find the real zeros of

a) $f(x) = -3x^4 + 3x^2$ **b)** $g(x) = x^3 - 2x^2 + x - 2$

▶ *Solution:*

a) $f(x) = -3x^4 + 3x^2$

$= -3x^2(x^2 - 1)$

$= -3x^2(x-1)(x+1) = 0$

$-3x^2 = 0,\ x - 1 = 0,\ x + 1 = 0$

$x = 0, 1, -1$

b) $g(x) = x^3 - 2x^2 + x - 2$

$= x^2(x-2) + (x-2)$

$= (x-2)(x^2+1) = 0$

$x - 2 = 0,\ x^2 + 1 = 0$

$x = 2,\ x^2 + 1$ has no solution

Zeros of a Polynomial Function of Degree *n*

- A polynomial function of degree n has, at most, n real zeros.

An nth degree polynomial, with n an even number, can intersect the x-axis from 0 to n times.

An nth degree polynomial, with n an odd number, can intersect the x-axis from 1 to n times.

Example 8 What is the minimum and maximum number of intersections of the x-axis for the following polynomial function?

a) $y = -2x^5 + \cdots$ **b)** $y = 3x^6 + \cdots$

▶ *Solution:*

a) Minimum intersections 1
Maximum intersections 5

b) Minimum intersections 0
Maximum intersections 6

Turning Points of a Polynomial Function of Degree *n*

- If a polynomial has n turning points, it is of minimum degree $n + 1$.

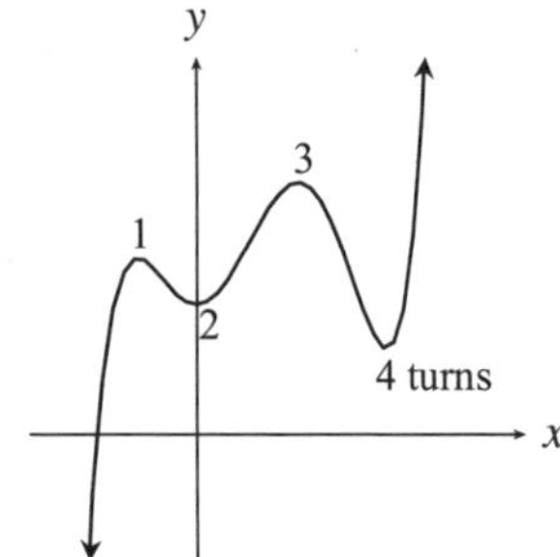

Minimum degree of this polynomial function is 5.

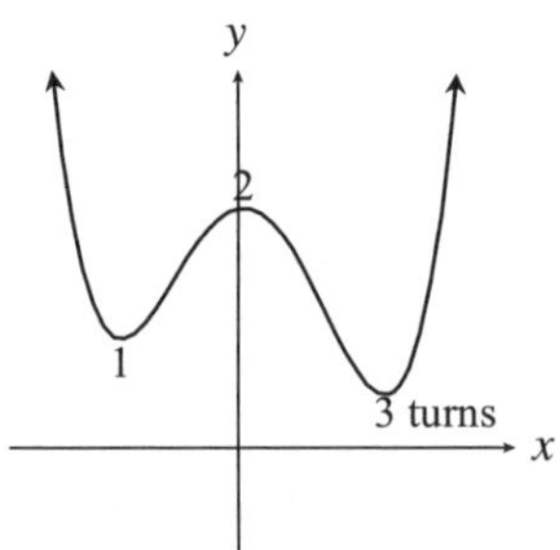

Minimum degree of this polynomial function is 4.

Multiplicity of a Polynomial

If a polynomial is of degree n, it can have at most n distinct solutions. When one solution is repeated r times, the function is said to have a solution of multiplicity r.

Example 9 Find the zeros and multiplicity of the polynomial functions.

a) $f(x) = x^4 + x^3 - 6x^2$ **b)** $g(x) = x^5 + x^4 - 2x^3 - 2x^2 + x + 1$

▶ *Solution:*

a) Has degree 4, thus 0 to 4 zeros

$$\begin{aligned} f(x) &= x^4 + x^3 - 6x^2 \\ &= x^2(x^2 + x - 6) \\ &= x^2(x+3)(x-2) \end{aligned}$$

x^2 has zero at 0, with multiplicity 2
$x+3$ has zero at –3, with multiplicity 1
$x-2$ has zero at 2, with multiplicity 1

b) Has degree 5, thus 1 to 5 zeros

$$\begin{aligned} g(x) &= x^5 + x^4 - 2x^3 - 2x^2 + x + 1 \\ &= x^4(x+1) - 2x^2(x+1) + (x+1) \\ &= (x+1)(x^4 - 2x^2 + 1) \\ &= (x+1)(x^2-1)^2 \\ &= (x+1)(x-1)^2(x+1)^2 \\ &= (x-1)^2(x+1)^3 \end{aligned}$$

$(x-1)^2$ has zero at 1, with multiplicity 2
$(x+1)^3$ has zero at –1, with multiplicity 3

3.1 Exercise Set

1. **a)** The graph of a polynomial function is ______________, which means it has no gaps, breaks, or holes.

   b) For a polynomial of degree "n," if n is an **even** degree it has at most ______________ real zeros and at least ______________ zeros and at most ______________ turning points.

   c) For a polynomial of degree "n," if n is an **odd** degree it has at most ______________ real zeros and at least ______________ zeros and at most ______________ turning points.

   d) If $x = a$ is a zero of a polynomial function then

   - $x = a$ is a __________ of the polynomial equation $f(x) = 0$
   - ____________ is a factor
   - $(a, 0)$ is an __________ of the graph $f(x)$

   e) A polynomial function is written in standard form if its terms are written in ______________ order of exponents from left to right.

2. State whether the following equations are polynomial functions. If yes, state degree, leading coefficient, and special name, if no state reason.

Equation	Polynomial, Yes / No	Degree	Leading Coefficient	Special Name
a) $-2x^3 + x^2 - 5$				
b) $\sqrt{2}x^4 - \sqrt{3x} + 2$				
c) $-\frac{1}{3}x^2 + \sqrt{-2}x + 1$				
d) $3x + 2$				
e) 5				

3. Circle the letter of the following graphs that are polynomials.

a)

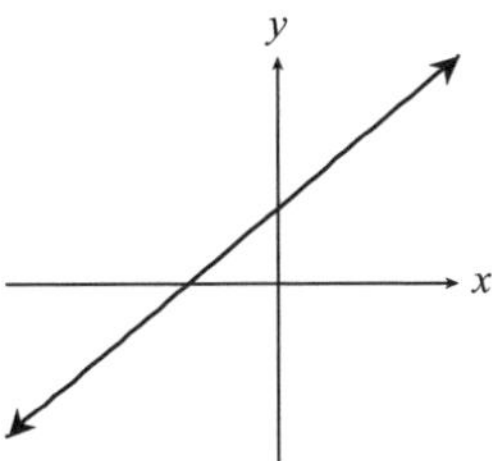

b)

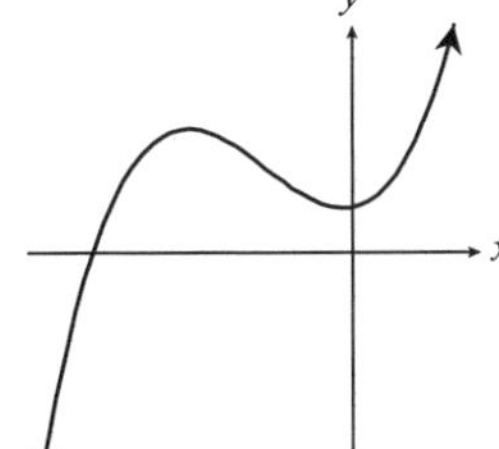

c)

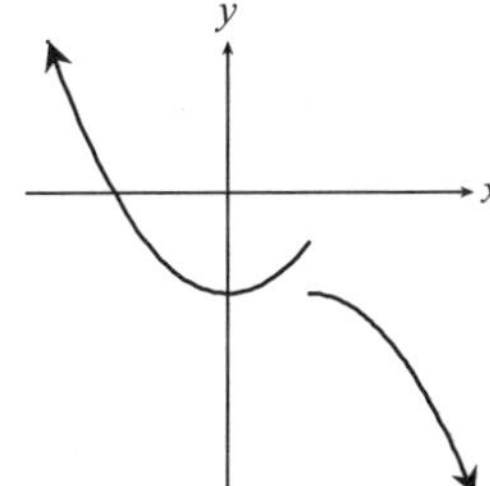

d)

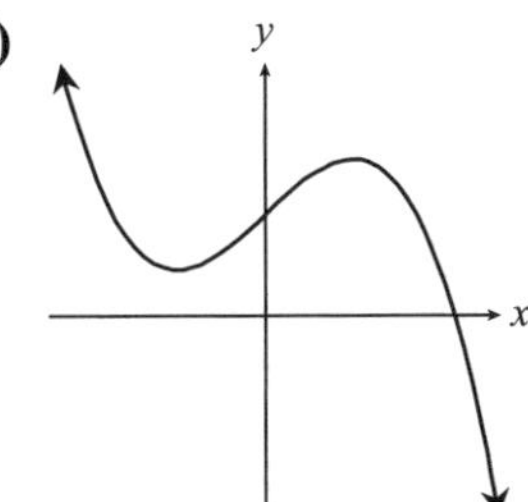

e)

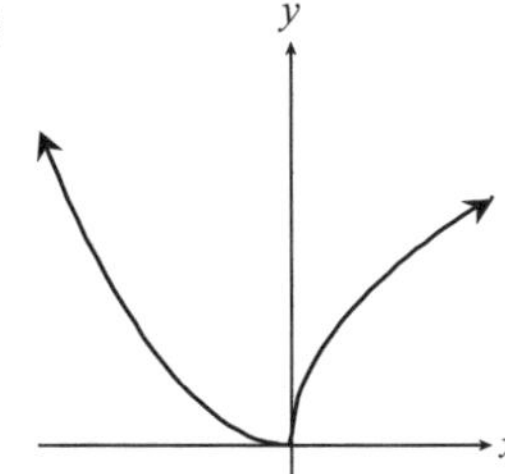

f)

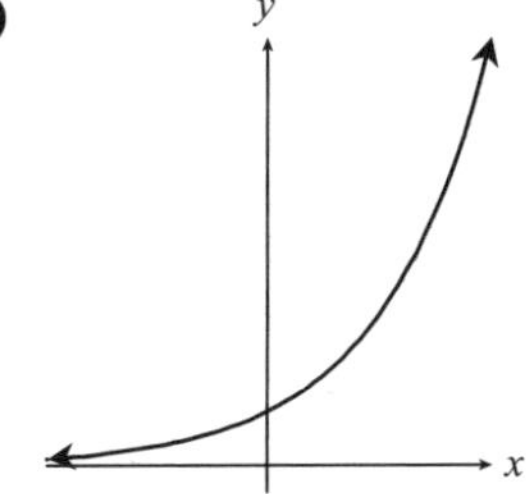

4. What are the real zeros of the following polynomial functions?

a)

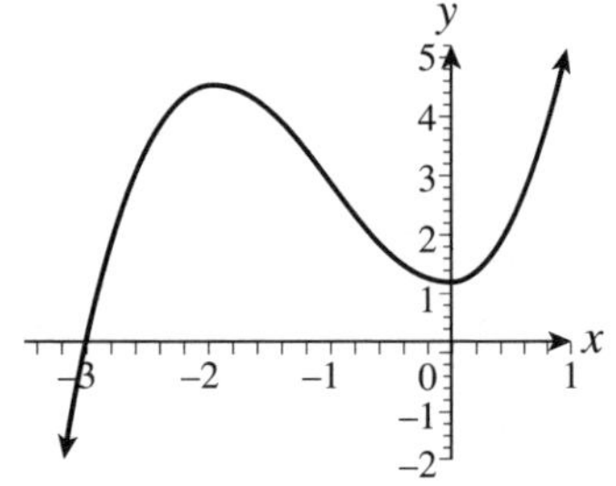

______

b)

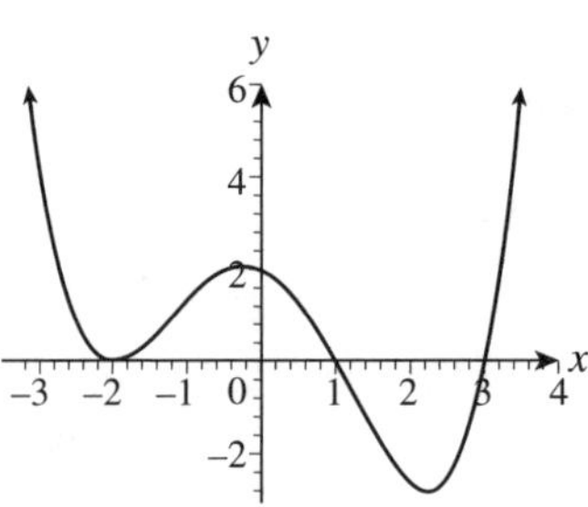

______

5. Determine the max./min. number of zeros for the following polynomials:

a) What is the maximum and minimum number of real roots for:

$3x^5 + ax^4 + bx^2 + 1 = 0$ ______ $3x^6 + ax^4 + bx^2 + 1 = 0$ ______

b) Given a polynomial: $f(x) = a_n x^n + a_{n-1} x^{n-1} + \cdots + a_1 x + a_0$

What is the min. / max. number of zeros if n is an odd number? ______

What is the min. / max. number of zeros if n is an even number? ______

6. Determine whether the following are polynomial functions. If so, state the degree; if not, state the reason.

a) $f(x) = -x^4 + 4x^4 + 2$

b) $f(x) = \sqrt{x}$

c) $f(x) = \dfrac{1}{x}$

d) $f(x) = 0$

e) $f(x) = (x-2)^3$

f) $f(x) = (x+1)^{-2}$

g) $f(x) = x^3 - \sqrt{2}x + \dfrac{1}{3}$

h) $f(x) = 2^{-3}x^2$

i) $f(x) = \sqrt{2}x^2$

j) $f(x) = \dfrac{1}{x+1}$

7. Determine the end behaviour of the polynomial functions.

a) $f(x) = 3x$

b) $f(x) = -3x$

c) $f(x) = 2x + 3x^2$

d) $f(x) = 2x - 3x^2$

e) $f(x) = -2x + x^2 + 3x^3$

f) $f(x) = 2x - x^2 - 3x^3$

g) $f(x) = 3x^4 - x^2 + 1$

h) $f(x) = -3x^4 + x^2 - 1$

i) $f(x) = x^4 + 2x^3 + x^5 - 2$

j) $f(x) = x^4 - 2x^3 - x^5 + 2$

8. Find a function in the form $y = cx^n$ that has the same end behaviour as the given function.

a) $f(x) = -3x^3 - 2x^2 + 1$

b) $g(x) = 2x^3 + x^2 - 1$

c) $h(x) = 2.3x^4 - 4x^2 + 6x$

d) $k(x) = -2.4x^5 + 3x^4 - 2x - 1$

9. Find all the real zeros, and the multiplicity of each zero.

a) $f(x)=x^2-4$

b) $f(x)=(x-4)^2$

c) $g(x)=x^3-4x^2+4x$

d) $g(x)=2x(x^2-2x-1)$

e) $h(x)=x^4-x^3-20x^2$

f) $h(x)=\frac{1}{3}x^4-\frac{1}{3}$

g) $k(x)=x^4+3x^2+2$

h) $k(x)=x^3-4x^2-25x+100$

i) $l(x)=-x^3-3x^2+4x+12$

j) $l(x)=x^3-5x^2-x+5$

k) $m(x)=x^4-2x^2+1$

l) $m(x)=-x^4+3x^2-2$

m) $n(x)=-x^4+4x^3-4x^2$

n) $n(x)=-x^2(x^2-1)+4(x^2-1)$

3.2 Graphing Polynomial Functions

In order to sketch polynomial functions, look at the effect multiplicity of zeros has on the shape of a graph.

a) If $(x-a)$ has multiplicity of 1, the graph of f **crosses** the x-axis directly at x = a.

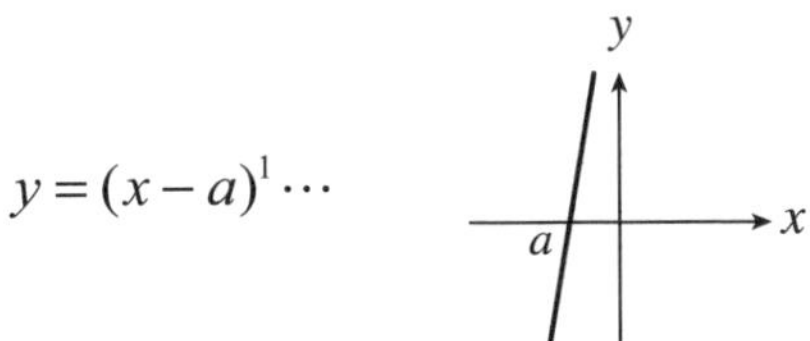

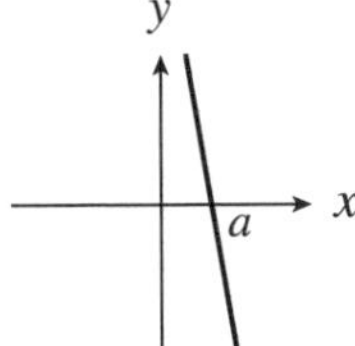

b) If $(x-a)$ has multiplicity of an even number, the graph of f touches the x-axis but does not cross, with this general shape. It bounces at the zero.

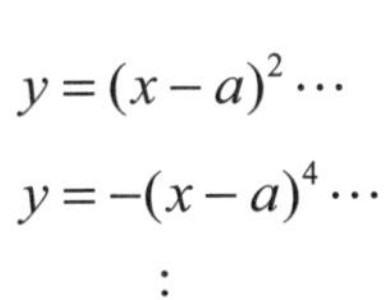

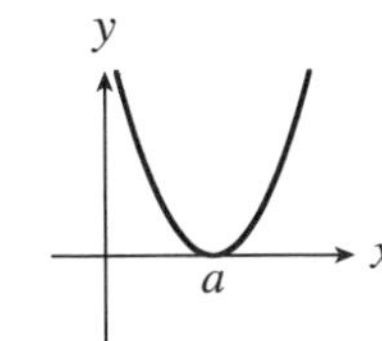

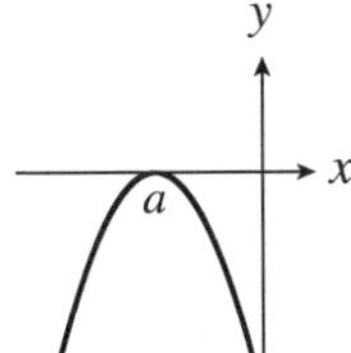

c) If $(x-a)$ has multiplicity of an odd number greater than one, the graph of f crosses the x-axis with this general shape. Looks like it will bounce, but at the zero it changes directions and crosses.

$y=(x-a)^3\cdots$

$y=-(x-a)^5\cdots$

⋮

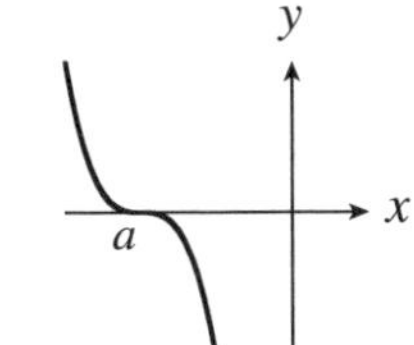

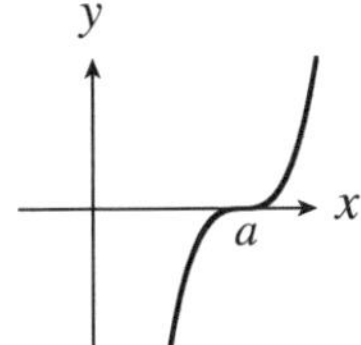

We can now summarize the steps needed to graph a polynomial function:

Summary of Steps in Graphing a Polynomial

Step 1: Find the x-intercept(s) by solving the equation $f(x)=0$, e.g. by factoring.

Step 2: Find the y-intercept by solving $f(0)$.

Step 3: Determine the general shape at each x-intercept.

Step 4: Look at the coefficient and power of the polynomial to determine the end behaviour of the graph of f. (Starts up or down / ends up or down.)

Step 5: Determine the number of turning points.

Step 6: Use the x-value between the x-intercept values to estimate the highs and lows of the graph of $f(x)$.

Step 7: Plot a reasonable number of points and draw a smooth continuous curve.

Example 1 Graph $y = x^2(3-x)(x^2+1)$

▶ Solution:

- Multiply $x^2(3-x)(x^2+1)$ gives $y = -x^5 + \cdots$
- Graph starts up on left and goes down on right.
- Graph has y-intercept of (0, 0).
- Graph has x-intercepts of (0, 0), (3, 0).
- Graph touches but does not go through at $x = 0$ and crosses directly at $x = 3$.
- Plot points.

x	y
–2	100
–1	8
1	4
2	20
2.5	23
4	–272

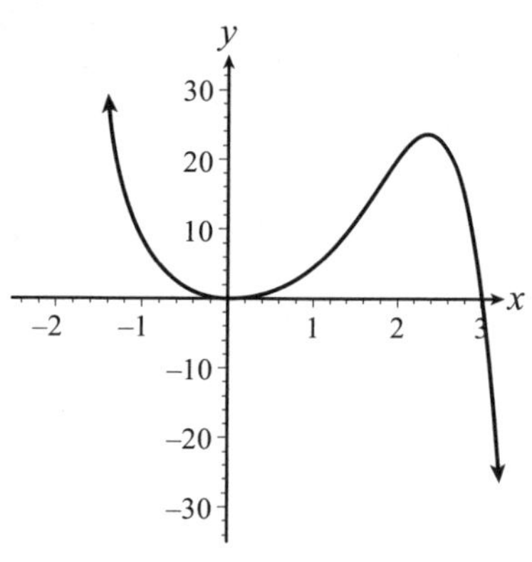

Example 2 Graph $y = (x+1)^2(1-x)(x-2)$

▶ Solution:

- When you multiply the polynomial out, you get $y = -x^4 + \cdots - 2$.
- $-x^4$ therefore the graph starts down and ends down.
- It crosses the y-axis at –2 (when $x = 0$).
- $(x+1)^2$ is an even power; the graph touches but does not cross the x-axis at $x = -1$.
- $(1-x)$ and $(x-2)$ are odd powers; the graph will go through the x-axis at $x = 1$ and $x = 2$.
- Estimate relative maximum at 1.5.
- Draw a smooth unbroken curve.

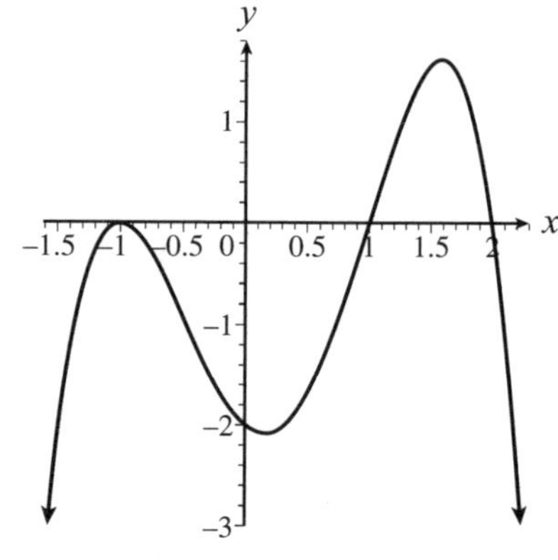

Example 3 Graph $y = (x-3)(x+2)^2(x-1)^3$

▶ Solution:

- Expanding equation gives $y = x^6 + \cdots + 12$.
- $+x^6$ therefore the graph starts up and ends up.
- Crosses y-axis at 12.
- Zeros are at $x = -2, 1, 3$.
- Goes through x-axis at $x = 3$.
- Touches x-axis at $x = -2$ and does not cross because the power of $(x + 2)$ is even.
- Curve shape and goes through at $x = 1$ because the power of $(x - 1)$ is greater than 1 and odd.
- Estimate the highs and lows at $x = -1$ and $2\frac{1}{2}$.
- Draw a smooth unbroken curve.

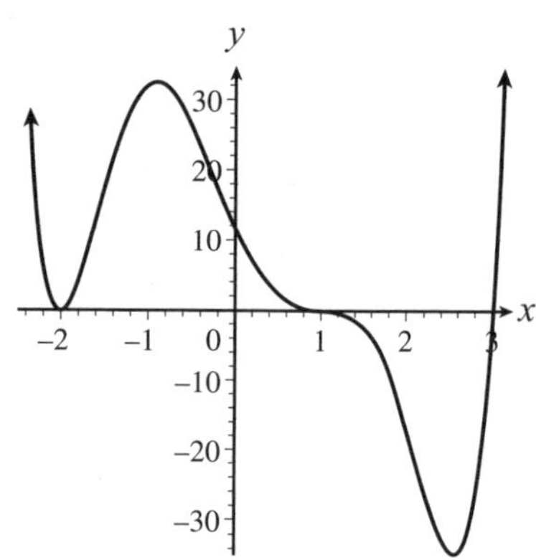

Equation of Polynomial Functions

Our knowledge of multiplicities, x-intercepts, y-intercepts and points of a polynomial function allows us to write the equation of the polynomial function.

Example 4 A polynomial has –1, –1, 0, 2, as its roots, and $p(1) = 5$. What is the equation of the polynomial?

▶ *Solution:* $p(x) = a(x+1)^2 \cdot x \cdot (x-2)$, but $p(1) = 5$

$$p(1) = a(1+1)^2(1)(1-2) = 5$$

$$a(4)(1)(-1) = 5$$

$$a = -\frac{5}{4}, \text{ therefore, } p(x) = -\frac{5}{4}x(x-2)(x+1)^2$$

Example 5 Write an equation of a polynomial in lowest degree that represents the given graph.

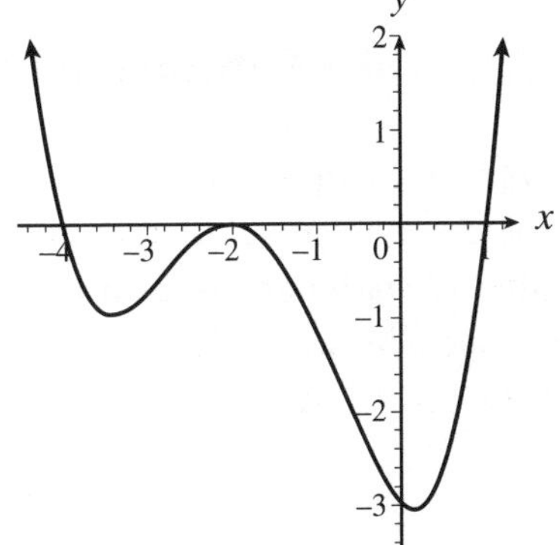

▶ *Solution:*

Zeroes	Multiplicity
–4	1
–2	2
1	1

$p(x) = a(x+4)(x+2)^2(x-1)$

The point (0, –3) is given on the graph.

$p(0) = a(0+4)(0+2)^2(0-1) = -3$ *from graph*

$$-16a = -3$$

$$a = \frac{3}{16}$$

Therefore, $p(x) = \frac{3}{16}(x+4)(x+2)^2(x-1)$

Example 6 Sketch the graph of a polynomial function of lowest degree given the sign diagram.

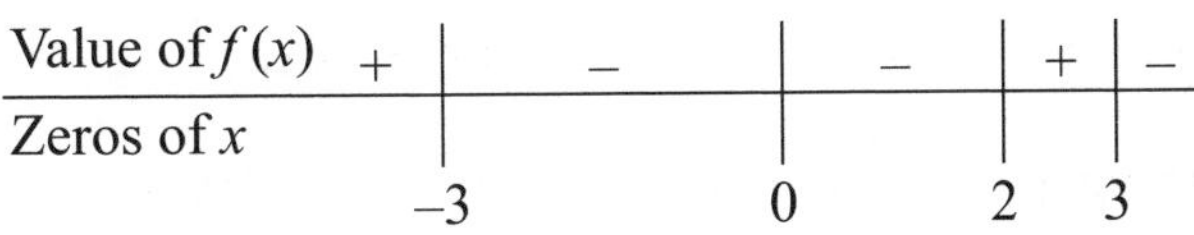

Value of $f(x)$	+	|	–	|	–	|	+	|	–
Zeros of x		–3		0		2		3	

▶ *Solution:* $f(x) = a(x+3)\,x^2(x-2)(x-3)$

$= ax^5 + \cdots$

with $a < 0$

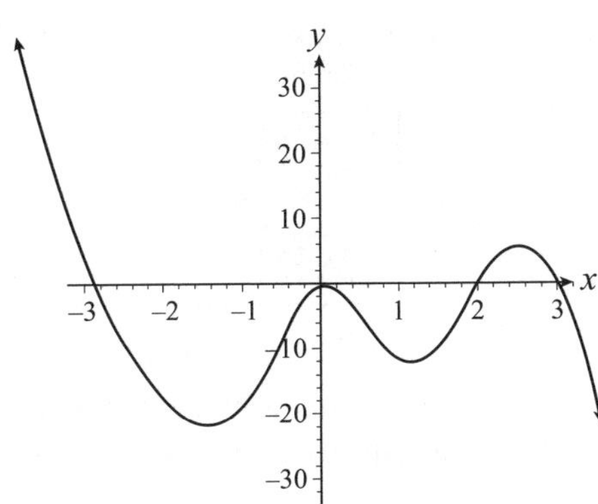

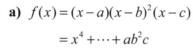

Example 7

a) Sketch the graph of $f(x)=(x-a)(x-b)^2(x-c)$ where $a<b<0<c$.

b) What is the y-intercept?

c) What is the solution of $f(x)>0$?

d) What is the solution of $f(x)\le 0$?

▶ *Solution:*

a) $f(x)=(x-a)(x-b)^2(x-c)$

$=x^4+\cdots+ab^2c$

b) y-intercept $(0, ab^2c)$

c) $f(x)>0$ for $x<a,\ x>c$

d) $f(x)\le 0$ for $a\le x\le c$

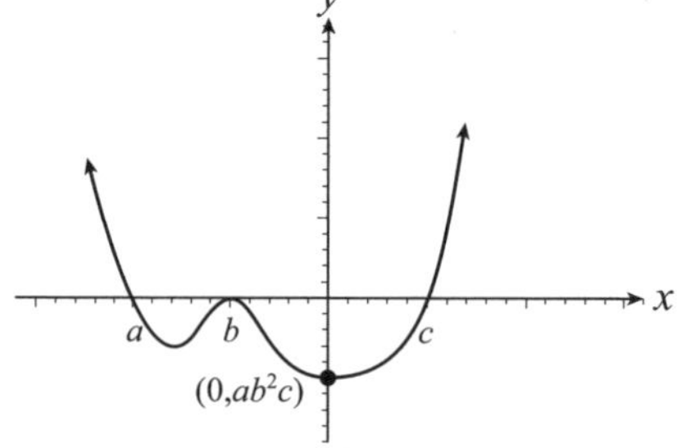

Estimating Zeros of a Polynomial Function without a Graphing Calculator

If $f(a)$ and $f(b)$ have opposite signs (one positive and the other negative) then because of the continuity of a polynomial function there is at least one c between a and b such that $f(c)=0$, that is f has a zero at c.

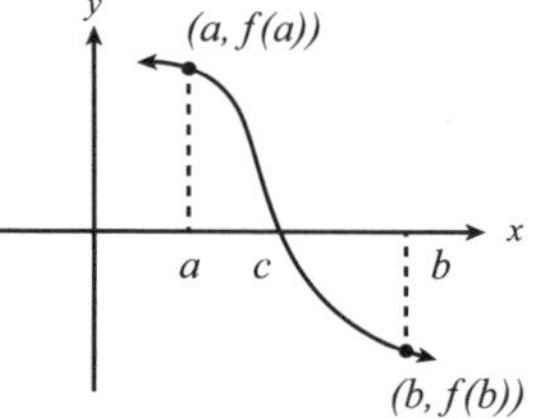

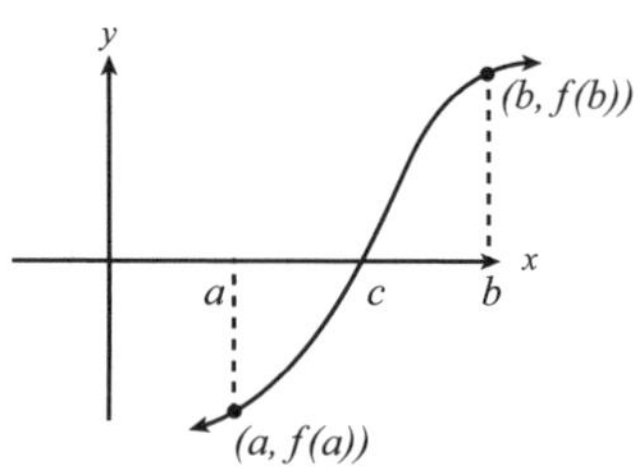

Example 8

Find a positive zero of $f(x)=x^5+2x^4-6x^3+2x-3$ to 1 decimal place.

▶ *Solution:*

$f(x)=x^5+2x^4-6x^3+2x-3$

$f(1)=1^5+2(1)^4-6(1)^3+2(1)-3=-4$

$f(2)=2^5+2\cdot 2^4-6\cdot 2^3+2\cdot 2-3=17$ thus a crossing between $1<x<2$

$f(1.6)=-0.7834$

$f(1.7)=1.8248$ thus a crossing between $1.6<x<1.7$

You can continue this process to get an even more accurate zero.

Graphing Polynomial Functions with a Graphing Calculator

For polynomial functions that are difficult to factor, real zeros can be calculated with a graphing calculator.

Example 9

Determine the real zero of $f(x)=x^5-3x^3+2x+1$.

▶ *Solution:*

Set Window (start with standard window and use Zoom Fit)

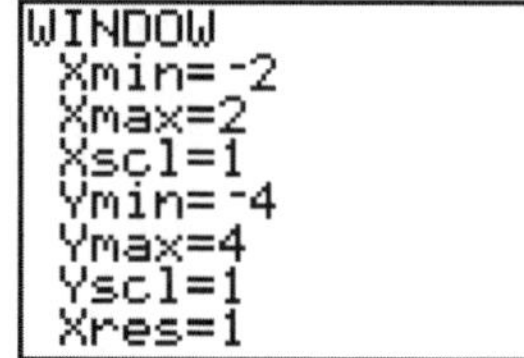

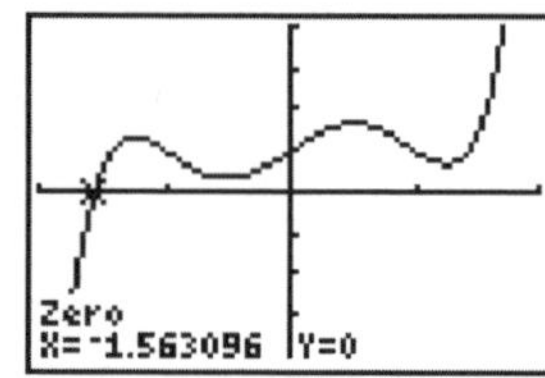

$Y_1=x^5-3x^3+2x+1$

The real zero of $f(x)=x^5-3x^3+2x+1$ is $(-1.563, 0)$ by the calculator's zero function. This is the only one since the graph already has 4 turning points in $-2\le x\le 2$ so there is no possibility of any other crossing.

3.2 Exercise Set

1. What is the minimum degree and number of turning points of the following polynomial graphs?

a)

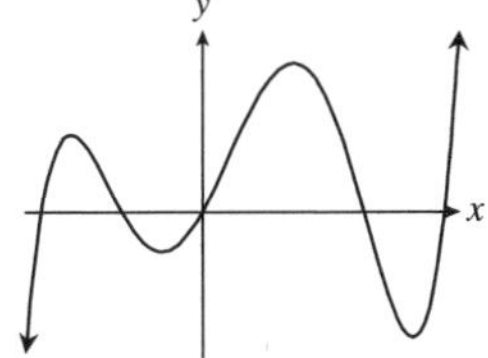

M.D.________

T.P. ________

b)

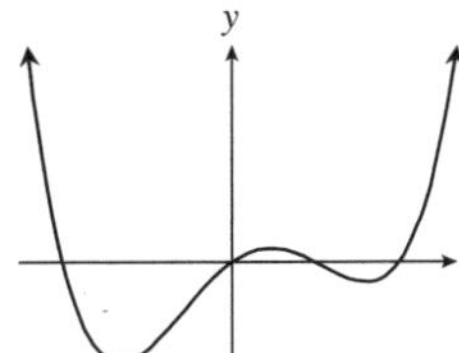

M.D.________

T.P. ________

c)

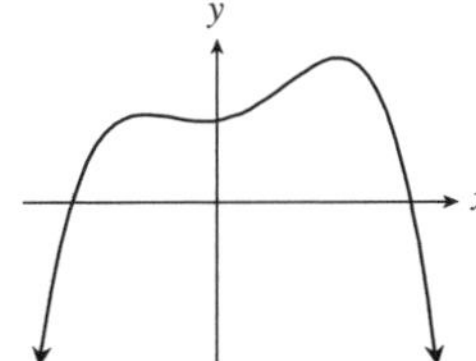

M.D.________

T.P. ________

d)

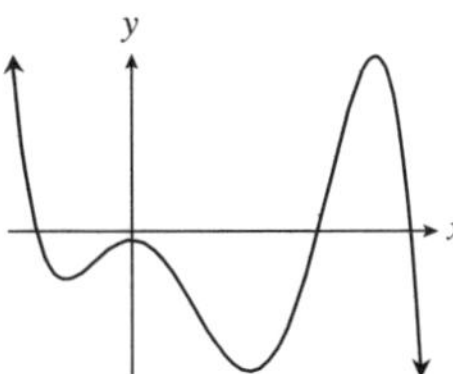

M.D.________

T.P. ________

e)

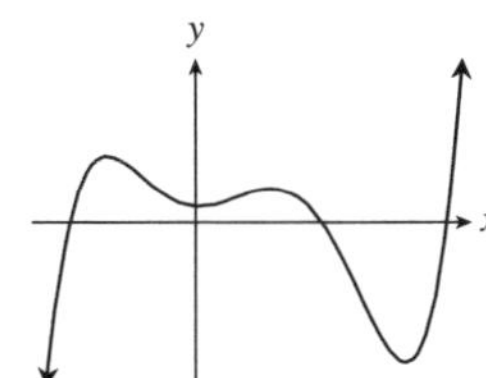

M.D.________

T.P. ________

f)

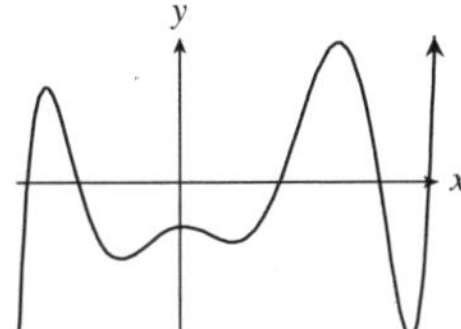

M.D.________

T.P. ________

2. From the table of values below, what is the minimum number of zeros possible for the polynomial function $P(x)$. State at what integer, or between what integers, the zeros occur.

a)

x	–5	–4	–3	–2	–1	0	1	2	3	4
$P(x)$	–25	–8	3	0	–6	–24	–33	–32	–15	5

____

b)

x	–3	–2	–1	0	1	2	3
$P(x)$	–75	–1	3	–6	–15	0	63

____

3. Determine the equation, in factored form, of a polynomial that fits the following graphs.

a)

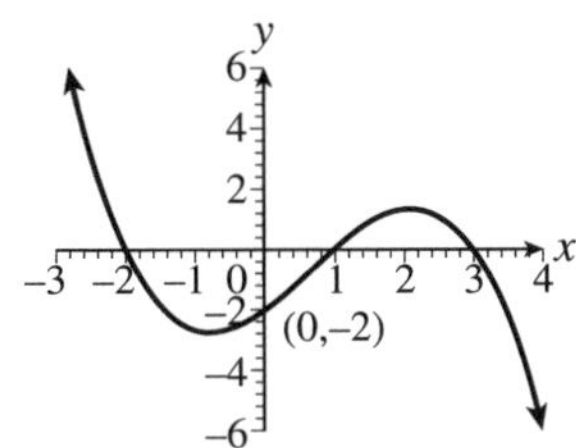

b)

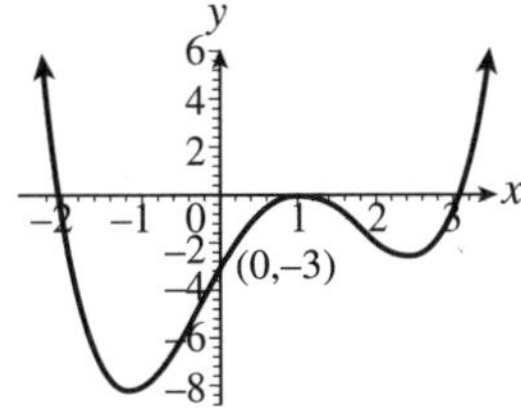

c)

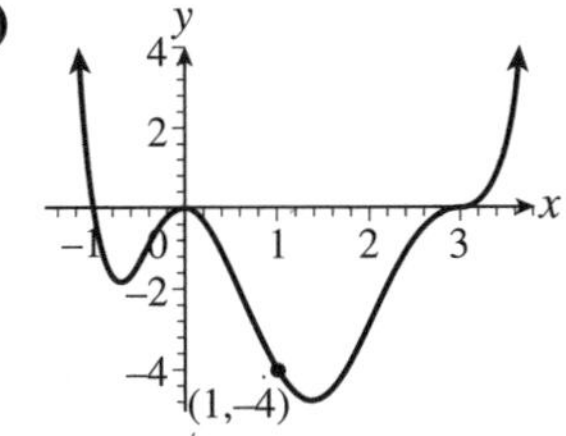

d)

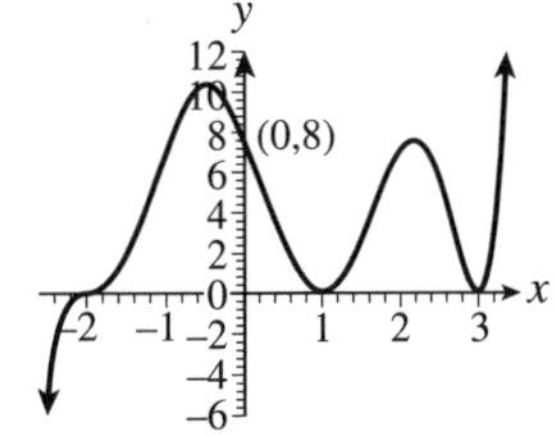

4. Find all values of x such that $f(x) \geq 0$.

a) $f(x) = -\frac{1}{3}x^3$

b) $f(x) = \frac{1}{2}x^3 + 4$

c) $f(x) = -\frac{1}{16}x^4 + 1$

d) $f(x) = x^5 - 1$

e) $f(x) = x^4 - 4x^2$

f) $f(x) = 9x - x^3$

g) $f(x) = -x^3 - 3x^2 + 10x$

h) $f(x) = x^4 - 3x^3 - 4x^2$

i) $f(x) = x(x+1)^2(x-2)(x-4)$

j) $f(x) = x^2(x+1)^2(x-1)$

5. Sketch the graph of a polynomial function of lowest degree.

a)

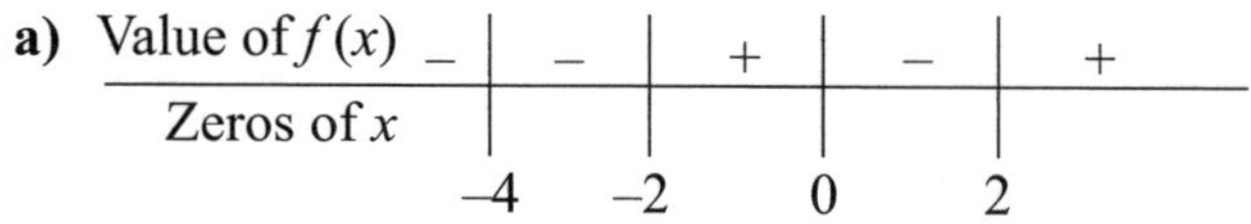

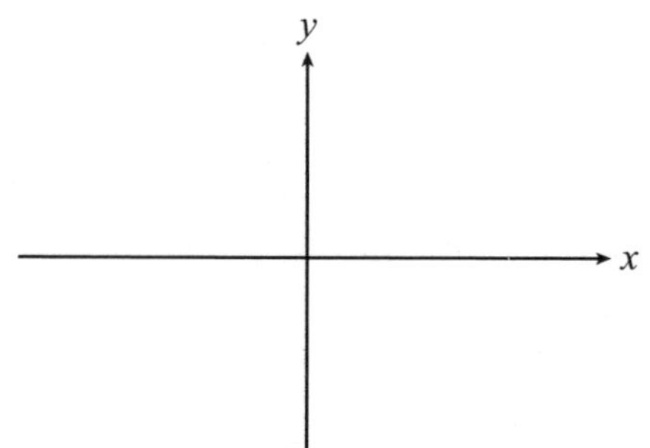

b)

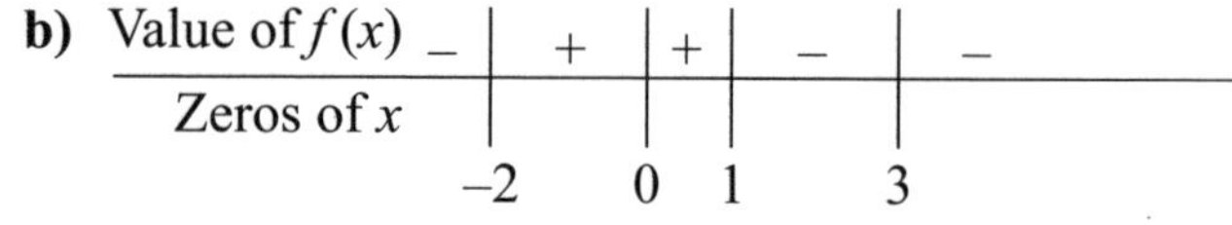

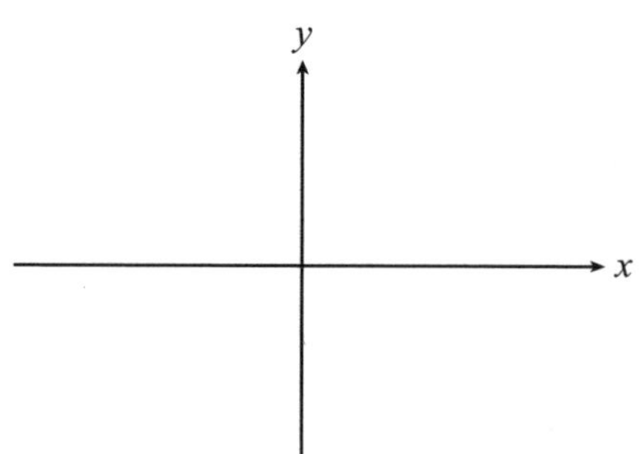

6. Sketch a graph of the following:

a) $f(x) = (x-a)(x-b)^2(x-c)$ where $a < b < 0 < c$

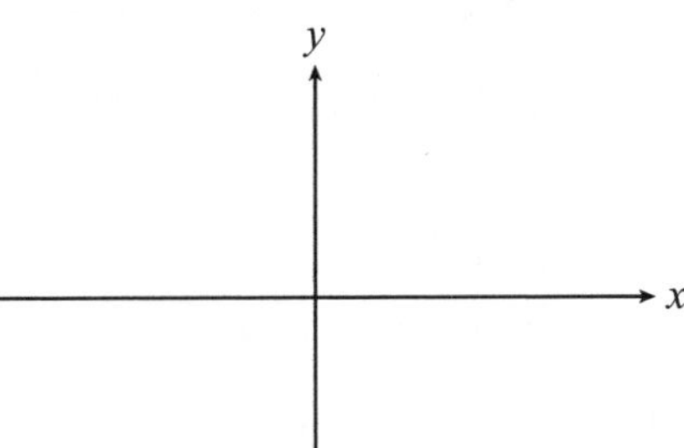

b) $f(x) = (x-a)^3(x-b)(x-c)$ where $a < 0 < b < c$

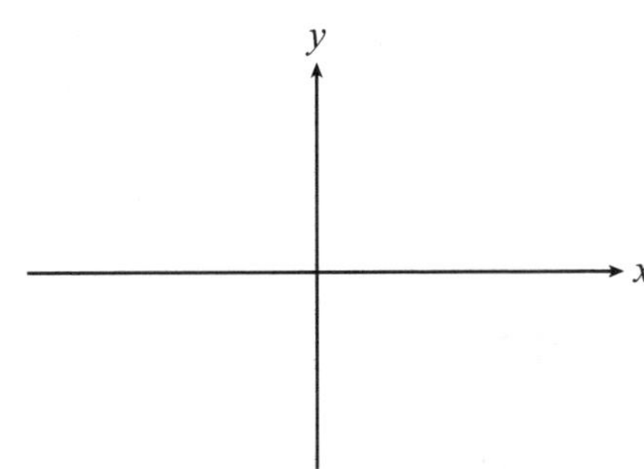

7. Determine the equation of the polynomial in factored form:

a) if the zeros are $-1, -1, 2$ and the y-intercept -4.

b) if the zeros are $0, 0, 1, 1, 1, 2$ and $P(-1) = 12$.

c) if the zeros are $\frac{1}{2}, -\frac{2}{3}, -\frac{2}{3}$ and goes through $(0, -3)$.

d) of degree 4 that has $-\frac{1}{2}$ as a root of multiplicity 3, and $2x^2 - x - 1$ as a factor.

e) of degree 4, whose zeros include 0, 2, which has a factor of $x^2 - 2x - 5$, and whose graph contains the point (3, 12).

f) of the least degree that is symmetric to the y-axis, touches but does not go through the x-axis at (3, 0), and has $P(0) = 27$.

8. If a polynomial function of even degree has a positive leading coefficient and a negative y-intercept, what is the minimum number of real roots it could have?

3.3 Division of Polynomials

This section will look at two methods of dividing polynomials. These division methods will be used to factor and find zeros of polynomial functions. First, we must define the terminology used in division.

Division Terminology

$$\begin{array}{r} 3 \\ 2\overline{)7} \\ \underline{6} \\ 1 \end{array}$$

2 is the divisor
3 is the quotient
7 is the dividend
1 is the remainder

$7 = 2 \cdot 3 + 1$

$$\begin{array}{r} q(x) \\ x-a\overline{)p(x)} \\ \overline{r} \end{array}$$

$x-a$ *is the divisor*
$q(x)$ *is the quotient*
$p(x)$ *is the dividend*
r *is the remainder*

$p(x) = (x-a)q(x) + r$

Long Division

Suppose you are told that the polynomial function $f(x) = 6x^3 - 19x^2 + 11x + 6$ has a zero at $x = 2$. Then $x - 2$ is a factor of $f(x)$. Therefore, $f(x) = (x-2)g(x)$. Let us find $g(x)$ by dividing $f(x)$ by $x - 2$.

$\frac{6x^3}{x}$, $\frac{-7x^2}{x}$, $\frac{-3x}{x}$ — *Divide the highest order term in the dividend by the highest order term in the divisor to get the next term in the quotient.*

$$\begin{array}{rll} & 6x^2 - 7x - 3 & \\ x-2\overline{)} & 6x^3 - 19x^2 + 11x + 6 & \\ & \underline{6x^3 - 12x^2} & \textit{Multiply } 6x^2(x-2) \\ & -7x^2 + 11x & \textit{Subtract; bring down next term } +11x \\ & \underline{-7x^2 + 14x} & \textit{Multiply } -7x(x-2) \\ & -3x + 6 & \textit{Subtract; bring down next term } +6 \\ & \underline{-3x + 6} & \textit{Multiply } -3(x-2) \\ & 0 & \textit{Subtract} \end{array}$$

Then $f(x) = 6x^3 - 19x^2 + 11x + 6$

$= (x-2)(6x^2 - 7x - 3)$

$= (x-2)(2x-3)(3x+1)$ *by factoring the quadratic*

The zeros of $f(x)$ are when $x - 2 = 0$, $2x - 3 = 0$, and $3x + 1 = 0$

$x = 2 \qquad x = \frac{3}{2} \qquad x = -\frac{1}{3}$

*Note: When doing long division, the vast majority of mistakes are **not** made in the division step but in the subtraction step. Please be extra careful in your subtraction steps!*

Example 1 Divide $3x^3 - 2x^2 + 1$ by $x - 2$.

▶ *Solution:* We use zero coefficients for any missing terms so that the subtraction terms line up.

$$
\begin{array}{r l}
\begin{array}{r}
3x^2 + 4x + 8 \\
x-2\,\overline{)\,3x^3 - 2x^2 + 0x + 1} \\
\underline{3x^3 - 6x^2} \qquad\qquad \\
4x^2 + 0x \qquad \\
\underline{4x^2 - 8x} \qquad \\
8x + 1 \\
\underline{8x - 16} \\
17
\end{array}
&
\begin{array}{l}
\\ \\
\textit{Multiply } 3x^2(x-2) \\
\textit{Subtract; bring down next term } +0x \\
\textit{Multiply } 4x(x-2) \\
\textit{Subtract; bring down next term } +1 \\
\textit{Multiply } 8(x-2) \\
\textit{Subtract; this is the remainder}
\end{array}
\end{array}
$$

Thus $3x^3 - 2x^2 + 1 = (x-2)(3x^2 + 4x + 8) + 17$ or $\dfrac{3x^3 - 2x^2 + 1}{x-2} = 3x^2 + 4x + 8 + \dfrac{17}{x-2}$.

Example 2 Divide $3x^4 - 5x^2 + 2x^3 - 1$ by $x^2 - 2x + 3$.

▶ *Solution:* Rewrite the dividend and divisor in descending powers of the variable; use $0x$ as a placeholder.

$$
\begin{array}{r l}
\begin{array}{r}
3x^2 + 8x + 2 \\
x^2 - 2x + 3\,\overline{)\,3x^4 + 2x^3 - 5x^2 + 0x - 1} \\
\underline{3x^4 - 6x^3 + 9x^2} \qquad\qquad\quad \\
8x^3 - 14x^2 + 0x \qquad \\
\underline{8x^3 - 16x^2 + 24x} \qquad \\
2x^2 - 24x - 1 \\
\underline{2x^2 - 4x + 6} \\
-20x - 7
\end{array}
&
\begin{array}{l}
\\ \\
\textit{Multiply } 3x^2(x^2 - 2x + 3) \\
\textit{Subtract; bring down next term } +0x \\
\textit{Multiply } 8x(x^2 - 2x + 3) \\
\textit{Subtract; bring down next term } -1 \\
\textit{Multiply } 2(x^2 - 2x + 3) \\
\textit{Subtract; this is the remainder}
\end{array}
\end{array}
$$

Thus, $\underbrace{3x^4 + 2x^3 - 5x^2 - 1}_{\text{Dividend}} = \underbrace{(x^2 - 2x + 3)}_{\text{Divisor}}\ \underbrace{(3x^2 + 8x + 2)}_{\text{Quotient}} + \underbrace{-20x - 7}_{\text{Remainder}}$

Using the Division Algorithm

$f(x) = d(x) \cdot g(x) + r(x)$ with $f(x)$ – *dividend*

$d(x)$ – *divisor*

$g(x)$ – *quotient*

$r(x)$ – *remainder*

Step 1: Write the dividend and divisor in descending powers of the variable.

Step 2: Insert zero coefficients for missing powers of the variable.

Step 3: Be extremely careful in the subtraction step.

Synthetic Division

There is a shortcut to long division of polynomial functions. It is called **synthetic division**. Synthetic division allows you to carry out calculations in a much simpler and faster manner.

Consider the following problem of dividing:

Divide: $2x^4 - 5x^3 + x - 4$ by $x - 2$

Traditional Long Division Method

Step 1

$$\begin{array}{r} 2x^3 - x^2 - 2x - 3 \\ x-2\overline{)2x^4 - 5x^3 + 0x^2 + x - 4} \\ \underline{2x^4 - 4x^3} \qquad\qquad\qquad \\ -x^3 + 0x^2 \qquad\qquad \\ \underline{-x^3 + 2x^2} \qquad\qquad \\ -2x^2 + x \qquad \\ \underline{-2x^2 + 4x} \qquad \\ -3x - 4 \\ \underline{-3x + 6} \\ -10 \end{array}$$

Simplified without Variables

Step 2

$$\begin{array}{r} 2 \quad -1 \quad -2 \quad -3 \\ -2\overline{)\,2 \quad -5 \quad 0 \quad 1 \quad -4} \\ \underline{2 \quad -4} \qquad\qquad\qquad \\ -1 \quad 0 \qquad\qquad \\ \underline{-1 \quad 2} \qquad\qquad \\ -2 \quad 1 \qquad \\ \underline{-2 \quad 4} \qquad \\ -3 \quad -4 \\ \underline{-3 \quad 6} \\ -10 \end{array}$$

Step 3 Note that the simplified method contains a lot of duplication. Let us eliminate the duplication:

$$\begin{array}{r} 2 \quad -1 \quad -2 \quad -3 \\ -2\overline{)\,2 \quad -5 \quad 0 \quad 1 \quad -4} \\ \underline{-4} \qquad\qquad\qquad \\ 0 \qquad\qquad \\ \underline{2} \qquad\qquad \\ 1 \qquad \\ \underline{4} \qquad \\ -4 \\ \underline{6} \\ -10 \end{array}$$

Step 4 Rather than subtract, let's perform addition by changing the sign of the –2 in the divisor:

$$\begin{array}{r} 2 \quad -1 \quad -2 \quad -3 \\ 2\overline{)\,2 \quad -5 \quad 0 \quad 1 \quad -4} \\ \underline{4} \qquad\qquad\qquad \\ 0 \qquad\qquad \\ \underline{-2} \qquad\qquad \\ 1 \qquad \\ \underline{-4} \qquad \\ -4 \\ \underline{-6} \\ -10 \end{array}$$

Step 5 Compress the entire division into three lines:

$$\begin{array}{r} 2 \quad -1 \quad -2 \quad -3 \\ 2\overline{)\,2 \quad -5 \quad 0 \quad 1 \quad -4} \\ 4 \quad -2 \quad -4 \quad -6 \quad -10 \end{array}$$

Step 6 Combine the quotient row at the top and the remainder at the bottom into a single row and place it at the bottom. Then, turn the division sign inside out:

$$\begin{array}{r|rrrrr} 2 & 2 & -5 & 0 & 1 & -4 \\ & & 4 & -2 & -4 & -6 \\ \hline & 2 & -1 & -2 & -3 & -10 \end{array}$$

Thus, the quotient and remainder is $2x^4 - 5x^3 + x - 4 = (x-2)(2x^3 - x^2 - 2x - 3) - 10$

Example 1 Calculate $3x^3 - 2x^2 + 1 \div (x-2)$ using synthetic division.

▶ *Solution:* Step 1: Write the dividend in descending powers of x. Then copy the coefficients, remembering to insert 0 for any missing power of x.

$$\begin{array}{cccc} 3 & -2 & 0 & 1 \end{array} \quad \text{Row 1}$$

Step 2: Insert the zero of the divisor to the left. Since the divisor is $x-2$, the zero is $x=2$ (which makes $x-2=0$).

$$\begin{array}{c|cccc|l} 2 & 3 & -2 & 0 & 1 & \text{Row 1} \\ & & & & & \text{Row 2} \\ \hline & & & & & \text{Row 3} \end{array}$$

Step 3: Bring the first coefficient 3 down to row 3.

$$\begin{array}{c|cccc|l} 2 & 3 & -2 & 0 & 1 & \text{Row 1} \\ & & & & & \text{Row 2} \\ \hline & 3 & & & & \text{Row 3} \end{array}$$

Step 4: Multiply the first entry in Row 3 by divisor 2, and place the result in Row 2, one column to the right.

$$\begin{array}{c|cccc|l} 2 & 3 & -2 & 0 & 1 & \text{Row 1} \\ & & 6 & & & \text{Row 2} \\ \hline & 3 & & & & \text{Row 3} \end{array}$$

Step 5: Add the entry in Row 2 to the entry above it in Row 1, and enter the sum in Row 3.

$$\begin{array}{c|cccc|l} 2 & 3 & -2 & 0 & 1 & \text{Row 1} \\ & & 6 & & & \text{Row 2} \\ \hline & 3 & 4 & & & \text{Row 3} \end{array}$$

Step 6: Repeat this process of steps 4 and 5 until Row 2 and 3 are filled.

$$\begin{array}{c|cccc|l} 2 & 3 & -2 & 0 & 1 & \text{Row 1} \\ & & 6 & 8 & 16 & \text{Row 2} \\ \hline & 3 & 4 & 8 & 17 & \text{Row 3} \end{array}$$

Quotient: 3 4 8 — Remainder: 17

Quotient $= 3x^2 + 4x + 8$

Remainder $= 17$

Check: $(3x^2 + 4x + 8)(x-2) + 17$

$3x^3 + 4x^2 + 8x - 6x^2 - 8x - 16 + 17$

$3x^3 - 2x^2 + 1$

- $3x^3 - 2x^2 + 1 = (x-2)(3x^2 + 4x + 8) + 17$
- $\dfrac{3x^3 - 2x^2 + 1}{x-2} = 3x^2 + 4x + 8 + \dfrac{17}{x-2}$

Example 2 Divide $P(x)=4x^5-30x^3-50x+2$ by $x+3$.

▶ *Solution:*

$$\begin{array}{r|rrrrrr} -3 & 4 & 0 & -30 & 0 & -50 & 2 \\ & \downarrow & -12 & 36 & -18 & 54 & -12 \\ \hline & 4 & -12 & 6 & -18 & 4 & -10 \end{array}$$

Thus $\dfrac{4x^5-30x^3-50x+2}{x+3}=4x^4-12x^3+6x^2-18x+4+\dfrac{-10}{x+3}$.

Example 3 Find, by synthetic division, k such that $2x^3+x^2-5x+k$ when divided by $x+1$, has a remainder –3.

▶ *Solution:*

$$\begin{array}{r|rrrr} -1 & 2 & 1 & -5 & k \\ & & & & \\ \hline & & & & -3 \end{array} \quad \rightarrow \quad \begin{array}{r|rrrr} -1 & 2 & 1 & -5 & k \\ & & -2 & 1 & 4 \\ \hline & 2 & -1 & -4 & -3 \end{array}$$

$k+4=-3 \rightarrow k=-7$ When $k=-7$, the remainder is –3.

Example 4 Divide $6x^4-7x^3+4x^2-11x+9$ by $2x-1$.

▶ *Solution:* For the synthetic division to work, the coefficent x in the divisor must be 1, so factor the coefficent $2x-1=2(x-\frac{1}{2})$.

So we divide $6x^4-7x^3+4x^2-11x+9$ by $x-\frac{1}{2}$ using synthetic division and then divide that answer by 2.

$$\begin{array}{r|rrrrr} \frac{1}{2} & 6 & -7 & 4 & -11 & 9 \\ & & 3 & -2 & 1 & -5 \\ \hline & 6 & -4 & 2 & -10 & 4 \end{array}$$

thus $\dfrac{6x^4-7x^3+4x^2-11x+9}{x-\frac{1}{2}}=6x^3-4x^2+2x-10+\dfrac{4}{x-\frac{1}{2}}$

But we want to divide by $2(x-\frac{1}{2})$ so need to divide all terms by 2.

$$\frac{6x^4-7x^3+4x^2-11x+9}{2(x-\frac{1}{2})}=\frac{6x^3-4x^2+2x-10}{2}+\frac{4}{2(x-\frac{1}{2})}=3x^3-2x^2+x-5+\frac{4}{2x-1}$$

Notice that the quotient from the synthetic division was divided by 2 but the remainder is unaffected.

Example 5 Divide $x^4+9x^3-5x^2-36x+4$ by x^2-4.

▶ *Solution:* Synthetic division does not work for divisors that are quadratic in form, but x^2-4 factors to $(x-2)(x+2)$.
Therefore, we will divide by these factors.

$$\begin{array}{r|rrrrr} 2 & 1 & 9 & -5 & -36 & 4 \\ & & 2 & 22 & 34 & -4 \\ \hline -2 & 1 & 11 & 17 & -2 & 0 \\ & & -2 & -18 & 2 & \\ \hline & 1 & 9 & -1 & 0 & \end{array}$$

Thus $\dfrac{x^4+9x^3-5x^2-36x+4}{x^2-4}=\dfrac{(x-2)(x+2)(x^2+9x-1)}{x^2-4}=\dfrac{(x-2)(x+2)(x^2+9x-1)}{(x-2)(x+2)}=x^2+9x-1$

3.3 Exercise Set

1. Compute the quotient using long division. Write all answers in two ways:

- dividend = (quotient)(divisor) + remainder
- $\dfrac{\text{dividend}}{\text{divisor}} = (\text{quotient}) + \dfrac{\text{remainder}}{\text{divisor}}$

a) $x-3\overline{\smash{)}x^3-8x^2-3x+2}$

b) $\dfrac{8x^3-1}{2x-1}$

c) $x^2+1\overline{\smash{)}x^5+2x^4-x^3+x^2-3x+4}$

d) $\dfrac{x^4-3x^2+8}{x^2-1}$

e) $x^2-4x-12\overline{\smash{)}x^3+2x^2-13x+10}$

f) $\dfrac{x^3-5x+1}{x^2-2x}$

g) $x^3+3x+2\overline{\smash{)}x^4+6x^3+11x^2+6x}$

h) $\dfrac{x^4+9x^3-5x^2-32x+3}{x^2-3}$

2. Use synthetic division to find the quotient polynomial $Q(x)$ and the remainder R when $P(x)$ is divided by the binomial following it.

a) $P(x)=x^3+2x^2-3x+1$; $x-2$

b) $P(x)=x^3-a^3$; $x-a$

c) $P(x)=4x^3+5x-3$; $x+2$

d) $P(x)=x^5-5x^3+10$; $x-1$

e) $P(x)=0.1x^2+0.2$; $x-2.1$

f) $P(x)=x^5+1$; $x+1$

g) $P(x)=3x^4+x^3-3x+1$; $3x+1$

h) $P(x)=2x^4-x^3+2x-1$; $2x-1$

i) $P(x)=3x^5+2x^4+5x^3-7x-3$; $x+0.8$

j) $P(x)=3x^4-3x^3+2x^2-3x+1$; $x-0.4$

k) $P(x)=x^4-5x^3-4x^2+5x+3$; x^2-1

l) $P(x)=x^5-x^4-8x^3+7x^2+7x-30$; x^2-x-6

3. Divide by synthetic division. Write answer in form $f(x)=c(x)g(x)+r$ where $f(x)$ is the given polynomial and $c(x)$ is the given factor.

a) $4x^3-7x^2-11x+5;\ x+2$

b) $6x^3-16x^2+17x-6;\ 3x-2$

c) $x^3-64;\ x-4$

d) $4x^3+16x^2-23x+15;\ 2x-1$

e) $x^3-4x;\ x-1+\sqrt{3}$

f) $-3x^3+8x^2+10x-8;\ x-2-\sqrt{2}$

g) $x^4-4x^3-15x^2+58x-40;\ x-5$

h) $x^5-2x^4+x^3-5;\ x-2$

i) $x^4+6x^3+11x^2+6x;\ x^2+3x+2$

j) $x^4+9x^3-5x^2-36x+4;\ x^2-4$

k) $x^{3n}+16x^{2n}+64x^n+64;\ x^n+4$
(n is a positive integer)

l) $x^{3n}-9x^{2n}+27x^n-27;\ x^n-3$

4. Use synthetic division to solve for *k* and *m*.

a) When $x^3 + kx + 1$ is divided by $x - 2$, the remainder is –3.

b) When $x^3 - x^2 + kx - 8$ is divided by $x - 4$, the remainder is 0.

c) When $2x^4 + kx^2 - 3x + 5$ is divided by $x - 2$, the remainder is 3.

d) When $x^3 + kx + 6$ is divided by $x + 2$, the remainder is 4.

e) When $x^3 + kx^2 - 2x - 7$ is divided by $x + 1$, the remainder is 5. What is the remainder when it is divided by $x - 1$?

f) When $kx^3 + mx^2 + x - 2$ is divided by $x - 1$, the remainder is 6. When this polynomial is divided by $x + 2$, the remainder is 12.

g) $x^4 + kx^3 - mx + 15$ has no remainder when divided by $x - 1$ and $x + 3$.

h) When $P(x) = 3x^4 + kx^2 + 7$ is divided by $x - 1$, the remainder is the same as when $f(x) = x^4 + kx - 4$ is divided by $x - 2$.

3.4 The Remainder and Factor Theorems

The Remainder Theorem

The remainder obtained in synthetic division has a very important interpretation in evaluating polynomial functions.

By division, we have

$$f(x)=(x-a)q(x)+r \text{ with } r=0 \text{ or a constant value}$$

Evaluate $f(x)$ at $x=a$

$$f(a)=(a-a)q(a)+r$$
$$=r$$

This shows that the value of the polynomial function at $x=a$ is equivalent to the remainder of the polynomial function divided by $(x-a)$.

> **Remainder Theorem**
>
> If the polynomial $P(x)$ is divided by $x-a$, the remainder is $P(a)$.

Example 1 Without dividing, what is the remainder when $P(x)=2x^4-3x^3+2x-3$ is divided by $x-2$?

▶ *Solution:* (by remainder theorem)

$$P(x)=2x^4-3x^3+2x-3$$
$$P(2)=2(2)^4-3(2)^3+2(2)-3$$
$$=9$$

Check by synthetic division:

$$\begin{array}{r|rrrrr} 2 & 2 & -3 & 0 & 2 & -3 \\ & & 4 & 2 & 4 & 12 \\ \hline & 2 & 1 & 2 & 6 & 9 \end{array} \leftarrow \text{remainder}$$

Example 2 For what value of k will the remainder be 5 when $P(x)=x^3-2x^2+x+k$ is divided by $x-2$?

▶ *Solution:*

$$P(2)=(2)^3-2(2)^2+2+k=5$$
$$8-8+2+k=5$$
$$k=3$$

Check by synthetic division:

$$\begin{array}{r|rrrr} 2 & 1 & -2 & 1 & k \\ & & 2 & 0 & 2 \\ \hline & 1 & 0 & 1 & 5 \end{array} \rightarrow k+2=5$$
$$k=3$$

Example 3 Find the remainder when $x^{17}-2x^{12}+7$ is divided by $x+1$.

▶ *Solution:* This problem would be very difficult by division, but using the remainder theorem makes it very easy.

$$x+1=0$$
$$x=-1$$
$$P(x)=x^{17}-2x^{12}+7$$
$$P(-1)=(-1)^{17}-2(-1)^{12}+7$$
$$=-1-2+7$$
$$P(-1)=4$$

Thus, the remainder is 4.

The Factor Theorem

The factor theorem is a direct result of the remainder theorem. If a polynomial $P(x)$ is divided by $(x-a)$ and there is no remainder, that means that $(x-a)$ divides in evenly and is a factor of $P(x)$.

Example 4 $P(x)=3x^4+4x^3-3x^2-3x-10$. Is $(x+2)$ a factor of $P(x)$?

▶ *Solution:* Using the remainder theorem, when $P(x)$ is divided by $(x+2)$ the remainder is $P(-2)$.

$P(-2)=3(-2)^4+4(-2)^3-3(-2)^2-3(-2)-10=48-32-12+6-10=0$

Since $P(-2)=0$ there is no remainder so $(x+2)$ is a factor.

So $3x^4+4x^3-3x^2-3x-10=(x+2)(3x^3-2x^2+x-5)$ and $(x+2)$ is a factor of $P(x)$.

Check by synthetic division:

–2	3	4	–3	–3	–10
		–6	4	–2	10
	3	–2	1	–5	0

So $3x^4+4x^3-3x^2-3x-10=(x+2)(3x^3-2x^2+x-5)$ and $(x+2)$ is a factor of $P(x)$.

Example 5 $P(x)=3x^4+4x^3-3x^2-3x-10$. Is $(x-1)$ a factor of $P(x)$?

▶ *Solution:* Using the remainder theorem, when $P(x)$ is dived by $(x-1)$ the remainder is $P(1)$

$P(1)=3(1)^4+4(1)^3-3(1)^2-3(1)-10=3+4-3-3-10=-9$

Therefore, $(x-1)$ is not a factor of $P(x)$

Check by synthetic division:

1	3	4	–3	–3	–10
		3	7	4	1
	3	7	4	1	–9

So $3x^4+4x^3-3x^2-3x-10=(x-1)(3x^3+7x^2+4x+1)-9$. Since there is a remainder, $(x-1)$ is not a factor of $P(x)$.

We can state:

Factor Theorem

Let *P* be a polynomial function. Then polynomial $P(x)$ has a factor $x-a$ if, and only if, $P(a)=0$.

"If and only if" implies two separate parts to the Factor Theorem:

1. If $P(a)=0$, then $x-a$ is a factor of $P(x)$.
2. If $x-a$ is a factor of $P(x)$, then $P(a)=0$.

Example 6 Does $P(x)=x^3-2x^2+3x-6$ have the factor $x-2$?

▶ *Solution:* Because $x-2$ is of the form $x-a$ with $a=2$, we find the value of $P(2)$

$P(2)=2^3-2(2^2)+3(2)-6=0$, so $(x-2)$ is a factor of $P(x)$

Check by synthetic division:

2	1	–2	3	–6	
		2	0	6	
	1	0	3	0	← remainder is zero

Example 7 Does $P(x) = 2x^4 - 3x^2 + x - 1$ have the factor $x + 1$?

▶ *Solution:*

$$P(-1) = 2(-1)^4 - 3(-1)^2 + (-1) - 1$$
$$= 2 - 3 - 1 - 1$$
$$= -3, \quad P(-1) \neq 0 \text{ so } (x+1) \text{ is not a factor of } P(x)$$

Check by synthetic division:

$\underline{-1}\rvert$	2	0	−3	1	−1
		−2	2	1	−2
	2	−2	−1	2	−3 ← remainder is – 3, not 0

Rational Root Theorem

We will add a third concept of polynomial functions to make finding zeros of a polynomial function easier to find. Recall that rational numbers are your basic fractions , or more formally $\frac{a}{b}$, a, b are integers, $b \neq 0$. We are looking to find divisors that give a remainder of zero.

Consider the factoring of a quadratic equation:

e.g., $3x^2 + 2x - 8 = 0$ The possibilities are

$3x^2 + \cdots - 8$ Possible Factors	Corresponding Zeros
$(3x \pm 1)(x \pm 8)$	$\pm\frac{1}{3}$, ± 8
$(3x \pm 2)(x \pm 4)$	$\pm\frac{2}{3}$, ± 4
$(3x \pm 4)(x \pm 2)$	$\pm\frac{4}{3}$, ± 2
$(3x \pm 8)(x \pm 1)$	$\pm\frac{8}{3}$, ± 1

The possible zeros are $\{\pm 1, \pm 2, \pm 4, \pm 8, \pm\frac{1}{3}, \pm\frac{2}{3}, \pm\frac{4}{3}, \pm\frac{8}{3}\}$

The possible zeros can also be obtained by

$$\frac{\text{possible factors of 8}}{\text{possible factors of 3}} = \frac{\pm 1, \pm 2, \pm 4, \pm 8}{\pm 1, \pm 3} = \{\pm 1, \pm 2, \pm 4, \pm 8, \pm\tfrac{1}{3}, \pm\tfrac{2}{3}, \pm\tfrac{4}{3}, \pm\tfrac{8}{3}\}$$

Test:

$$P(x) = 3x^2 + 2x - 8$$
$$(x+2) \rightarrow P(-2) = 3(-2)^2 + 2(-2) - 8$$
$$= 0$$

or

$\underline{-2}\rvert$	3	2	−8
		−6	8
	3	−4	0

Thus, $(x+2)$ is one factor of

$$3x^2 + 2x - 8 = 0$$
$$(x+2)(3x-4) = 0$$

Therefore, of the 16 possible real roots, the two that worked are $x = -2, \frac{4}{3}$. The Rational Root Theorem works for any polynomial function, not just a quadratic function that was shown in the above example.

Rational Root Theorem

If $f(x)=a_nx^n+a_{n-1}x^{n-1}+\cdots+a_1x+a_0$ is a polynomial function with integer coefficients, every rational zero of $f(x)$ has the form

$$\frac{p}{q},\quad p=\text{factor of constant } a_0$$
$$q=\text{factor of leading coefficient } a_n$$

Thus, possible rational zeros = $\dfrac{\text{factors of constant term}}{\text{factors of leading coefficient}}$

Example 8 Find the zeros of $f(x)=x^3-9x^2+20x-12$.

▶ *Solution:* Possible rational zeros $=\dfrac{\text{factors of }12}{\text{factors of }1}=\dfrac{\pm1,\pm2,\pm3,\pm4,\pm6,\pm12}{\pm1}$

$$=\pm1,\pm2,\pm3,\pm4,\pm6,\pm12$$

Check: $x-1=0\rightarrow x=1$

1⌋	1	−9	20	−12
		1	−8	12
	1	−8	12	0

therefore, $P(x)=x^3-9x^2+20x-12$
$=(x-1)(x^2-8x+12)$
$=(x-1)(x-2)(x-6)$

Remainder zero so $(x-1)$ is one factor of $P(x)$.

Therefore, of the 12 possible roots, the three that worked are $x=1,2,6$.

Example 9 Find the zeros of $f(x)=4x^3+12x^2+5x-6=0$.

▶ *Solution:* Possible rational zeros $=\dfrac{\text{factors of }6}{\text{factors of }4}=\dfrac{\pm1,\pm2,\pm3,\pm6}{\pm1,\pm2,\pm4}$

$$=\pm1,\pm2,\pm3,\pm6,\pm\frac{1}{2},\pm\frac{3}{2},\pm\frac{1}{4},\pm\frac{3}{4}$$

Check $(x+1)$ and $(x-1)$ and show the remainder is not zero.

Check: $x+2=0\rightarrow x=-2$

−2⌋	4	12	5	−6
		−8	−8	6
	4	4	−3	0

therefore, $P(x)=4x^3+12x^2+5x-6=0$
$=(x+2)(4x^2+4x-3)=0$
$=(x+2)(2x-1)(2x+3)=0$

Remainder zero so $(x+2)$ is one factor of $P(x)$.

Therefore, of the 16 possible zeros, the three that worked are $x=-2,\frac{1}{2},-\frac{3}{2}$.

3.4 Exercise Set

1. Find $P(k)$.

a) $P(x)=x^4+3x^3-7x+2$; $k=-2$

b) $P(x)=-2x^4-3x^2-2$; $k=\sqrt{2}$

c) $P(x)=-2x^2+4x+3$; $k=1+\sqrt{2}$

d) $P(x)=x^5-5a^4x+4a^5$; $k=a$

2. Use the remainder theorem to solve for *k* and *m*.

a) When x^3+kx+1 is divided by $x-2$, the remainder is -3.

b) When x^3-x^2+kx-8 is divided by $x-4$, the remainder is 0.

c) When $2x^4+kx^2-3x+5$ is divided by $x-2$, the remainder is 3.

d) When x^3+kx+6 is divided by $x+2$, the remainder is 4.

e) When x^3+kx^2-2x-7 is divided by $x+1$, the remainder is 5. What is the remainder when it is divided by $x-1$?

f) When kx^3+mx^2+x-2 is divided by $x-1$, the remainder is 6. When this polynomial is divided by $x+2$, the remainder is 12.

g) $x^4+kx^3-mx+15$ has no remainder when divided by $x-1$ and $x+3$.

h) When $P(x)=3x^4+kx^2+7$ is divided by $x-1$, the remainder is the same as when $f(x)=x^4+kx-4$ is divided by $x-2$.

3. Use the remainder theorem to solve the following:

a) If a polynomial equation $P(x)$ is divided by $x - a$, what is the value of its remainder?

b) Given $P(x) = x^3 - rx^2 + 3x + r^2$, find all possible values of r so $P(3) = 18$.

c) When the polynomial $x^n + x - 8$ is divided by $x - 2$, there is a remainder of 10. What is the value of n?

d) When $x^2 + 5x - 2$ is divided by $x + a$, the remainder is 8. Find all possible values of "a".

e) When the polynomial $P(x) = kx^{50} + 2x^{30} + 4x + 7$ is divided by $x + 1$, the remainder is 23. Determine the value of the constant, k.

f) Solve for k and m if $P(x) = 2x^3 + 3x^2 + kx + m$ and $P(1) = 8$ and $P(-2) = -13$.

4. Find the missing factors by synthetic division.

a) $2x^3 - 7x^2 + 2x + 3 = (x - 1)(\quad)(\quad)$

b) $x^3 - 3x^2 - 10x + 24 = (x - 2)(\quad)(\quad)$

c) $x^4 + x^3 - 9x^2 - 9x = x(x + 1)(\quad)(\quad)$

d) $2x^4 - 7x^3 + 9x^2 - 5x + 1 = (x - 1)^3(\quad)$

e) $2x^4 + 5x^3 - 11x^2 - 20x + 12 = (x^2 - 4)(\quad)(\quad)$

f) $x^5 - 8x^4 + 25x^3 - 38x^2 + 28x - 8 = (x^2 - 3x + 2)(\quad)(\quad)(\quad)$

5. Solve the following using the factor theorem and rational root theorem as necessary.

a) If 2 is a root of the equation $3x^3 + x^2 - 20x + 12 = 0$, determine the other roots.

b) What are all values of k for which $\frac{1}{2}$ is a zero of $P(x) = -4x^3 + 2x^2 - 2kx + k^3$?

c) If $x = c$ is a root of the polynomial equation $P(x) = 0$, then what must be a factor of $P(x)$?

d) If $x - a$ is a factor of $2x^3 - ax^2 + (1 - a^2)x + 5$, what is a?

e) Determine k so that $x + 1$ is a factor of: $2x^4 + (k+1)x^2 - 6kx + 11$.

f) A polynomial has among its factors, $x^2 - 4$, $x^2 - 2x$, and $x^2 + x - 2$. What is the lowest possible degree of the polynomial?

g) For what number k is k a zero of $f(x) = 2x^3 - kx^2 + (3 - k^2)x - 6$?

h) Find the complete factored form of the following:
$P(x) = x^5 + 3x^4 - 5x^3 - 15x^2 + 4x + 12$
if $P(-2) = P(-1) = P(1) = 0$

i) Factor completely: $x^5 - 3x^4 + 8x^2 - 9x + 3$, if $x - 1$ is a factor.

j) Determine values for a and b such that $x - 1$ is a factor of both $x^3 + x^2 + ax + b$ and $x^3 - x^2 - ax + b$.

3.5 Polynomial Applications

Many real-life situations can be modelled by polynomial functions. The solutions may be rational, and can be solved by methods learned in this chapter. Other solutions are irrational, and can be only solved by a graphing calculator. Here are some examples:

Example 1 A box is constructed such that the length is twice the width and the height is 2 cm longer than the width, with a volume of 350 cm^3. Find the dimensions of the box.

▶ *Solution:*

$V = \text{length} \times \text{width} \times \text{height}$

$= (2x)(x)(x+2) = 350$

$2x^3 + 4x^2 = 350$

$x^3 + 2x^2 - 175 = 0$

Factors of 175 are 1, 5, 7, 25, 35, 175. (Negatives not possible.)

Check: $x = 1$

1⌋	1	2	0	–175
		1	3	3
	1	3	3	–172

Check: $x = 5$

5⌋	1	2	0	–175
		5	35	175
	1	7	35	0

Solve $x^2 + 2x + 35 = 0$ by the quadratic formula

$$x = \frac{-7 \pm \sqrt{7^2 - 4(1)(35)}}{2} = \frac{-7 \pm \sqrt{-91}}{2} \quad \text{no solution}$$

Therefore, $(x-5)(x^2+7x+35) = 0$ so $x = 5$.

Thus, the dimensions are $10\text{ cm} \times 5\text{ cm} \times 7\text{ cm}$.

Example 2 A vitamin capsule has the shape of a right circular cylinder with hemispheres on each end. The total length of the capsule is 14 mm, and its volume is $108\pi\text{ mm}^3$. Find the radius x of the capsule.

▶ *Solution:*

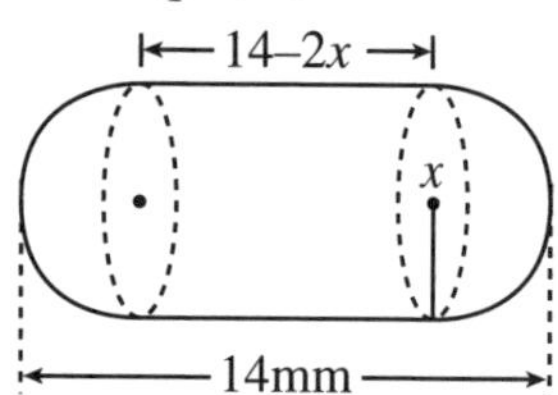

Volume of sphere $= \frac{4}{3}\pi x^3$

Volume of cylinder $= \pi r^2 h = \pi x^2(14 - 2x)$

$$V_{\text{total}} = \frac{4}{3}\pi x^3 + \pi x^2(14-2x) = 108\pi$$

$$\frac{4}{3}x^3 + 14x^2 - 2x^3 = 108$$

$$x^3 - 21x^2 + 162 = 0$$

Possible rational zeros (reject negative zeros) 1, 2, 3, 6, anything after this would make length negative.

Check:

3⌋	1	–21	0	162
		3	–54	–162
	1	–18	–54	0

continue

Solve $x^2 - 18x - 54 = 0$ by the quadratic formula

$$x = \frac{18 \pm \sqrt{18^2 - 4(1)(-54)}}{2} = 9 \pm 3\sqrt{15} = -2.62, 20.62$$

Reject $9 - 3\sqrt{5}$ since a radius cannot be zero.

Reject $9 + 3\sqrt{5}$ since the length of the cylinder cannot be negative.

Thus, the radius of the vitamin capsule is 3 mm.

Example 3 An open rectangular box is constructed by cutting a square of length x from each corner of a 12 cm by 15 cm rectangular piece of cardboard, then folding up the sides. What is the length of the square that must be cut from each corner if the volume is 112 cm^3 (x must be greater than 1)?

▶ *Solution:*

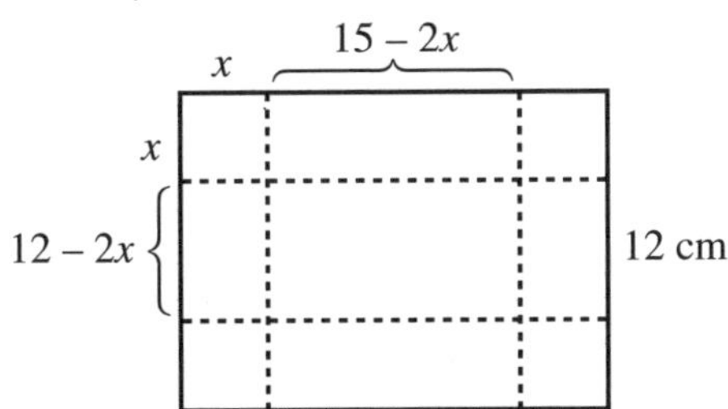

$$V = length \times width \times height$$
$$= (15 - 2x)(12 - 2x)(x) = 112$$
$$4x^3 - 54x^2 + 180x - 112 = 0$$
$$2x^3 - 27x^2 + 90x - 56 = 0$$

Possible rational zeros: 1, 2, 4, 7, 8.
Reject 6 and bigger so width, $12 - 2x$, is positive.

Check: $x = 4$

4	2	–27	90	–56
		8	–76	56
	2	–19	14	0

Solve $2x^2 - 19x + 14 = 0$ by the quadratic formula.

$$x = \frac{19 \pm \sqrt{19^2 - 4(2)(14)}}{4} = \frac{19 \pm \sqrt{249}}{4} = 0.81,\ 8.69$$

Reject 0.81 since it is less than one

Reject 8.69 since it makes length and width negative.

Thus, the volume is $(15 - 2x)(12 - 2x)(x) = 7\text{ cm} \times 4\text{ cm} \times 4\text{ cm} = 112\text{ cm}^3$ and a square of side 4 cm must be cut.

3.5 Exercise Set

1. An open top rectangular box is constructed by cutting a square of length x from each corner of a 12 cm by 15 cm rectangle, and then folding up the sides with $x \geq 2$ cm. What size square must be cut to have a volume of 162 cm^3?

2. What length must be cut if the volume of the box in question 1 is 150 cm^3?

3. A silo is the shape of a cylinder topped by a hemisphere. The overall height of the silo is 12 m. Find the radius if the volume is 360π m^3.

4. A right triangle has the hypotenuse 1 cm longer than one of the sides. Find the length of the sides if the area of the triangle is 6 cm^2.

5. A box is 1 m by 2 m by 3 m. If each side is increased by the same amount, how much must you increase these sides to make the volume 10 times larger?

6. A box measures $(1 \times 1 \times 2)$ m. Each side is increased the same amount. How much is this increase if the volume is increased by six times the original volume?

7. An open top box is made from a piece of cardboard measuring 5 in × 8 in. Cutting out squares from each corner and folding the edges up makes a box with a volume of 14 in^3. How large a square must be cut from each corner?

8. The production of x units produces revenue $R(x)=100x-x^2$ and costs of $C(x)=\frac{1}{3}x^3-6x^2+89x+100$.
At what point does the company make a profit?

9. A shed is constructed in the shape of a cube with a triangular prism forming the roof. The total height of the shed is 6 m, with a volume of 80 m^3. Find the length of the sides of the shed.

10. An open box is made from a piece of cardboard 9 inches by 15 inches, by cutting equal square corners and turning up the sides. Find the maximum volume of the box.

11. A box has a square base; the perimeter of the base plus the height is 120 cm. What length of the base yields a volume of 13 500 cm^3?

12. Calculate the maximum volume of the box in question 11. To achieve this maximum volume, what are the dimensions of the box?

3.6 Chapter Review

Polynomials – Multiple-choice Questions

1. The graph of a cubic polynomial function $y = f(x)$ is shown. Determine the equation of $y = f(x) - 2$.

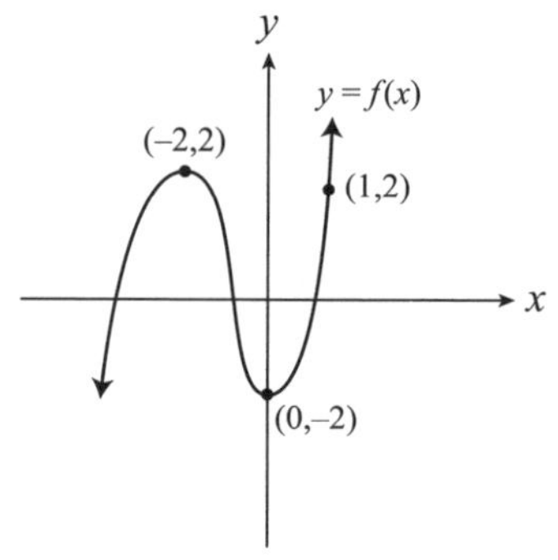

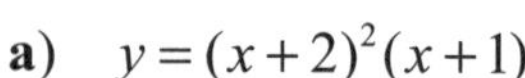

   a) $y = (x+2)^2(x+1)$

   b) $y = (x+2)^2(x-1)$

   c) $y = 2(x+2)^2(x+1)$

   d) $y = 2(x+2)^2(x-1)$

2. Solve $x^3 - 7x - 6 = 0$.

   a) 1, 2, –3
   b) 1, –2, 3
   c) –1, 2, –3
   d) –1, –2, 3

3. If a polynomial $P(x)$ is divided by $x+4$, what is the remainder?

   a) $P(-4)$

   b) $P(4)$

   c) $P(x-4)$

   d) $P(x+4)$

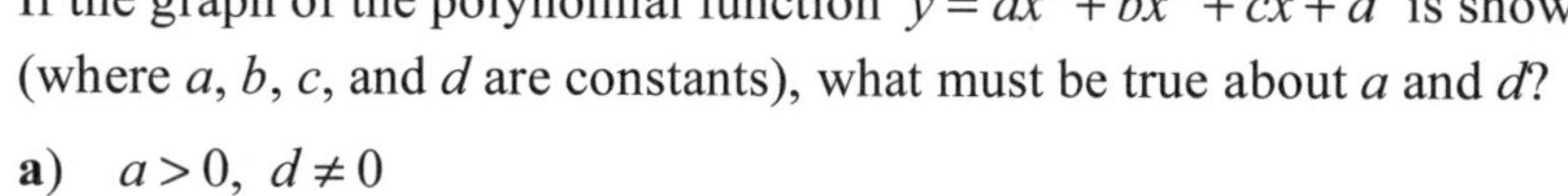

4. If the graph of the polynomial function $y = ax^3 + bx^2 + cx + d$ is shown (where *a*, *b*, *c*, and *d* are constants), what must be true about *a* and *d*?

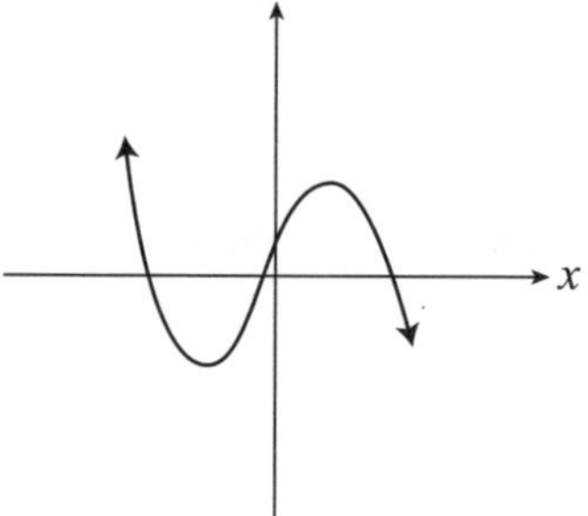

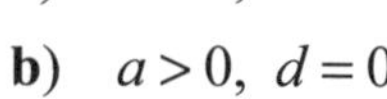

   a) $a > 0,\ d \neq 0$

   b) $a > 0,\ d = 0$

   c) $a < 0,\ d \neq 0$

   d) $a < 0,\ d = 0$

5. From the given graph $f(x)$, determine all values of *x* such that $f(x+2) \geq 0$.

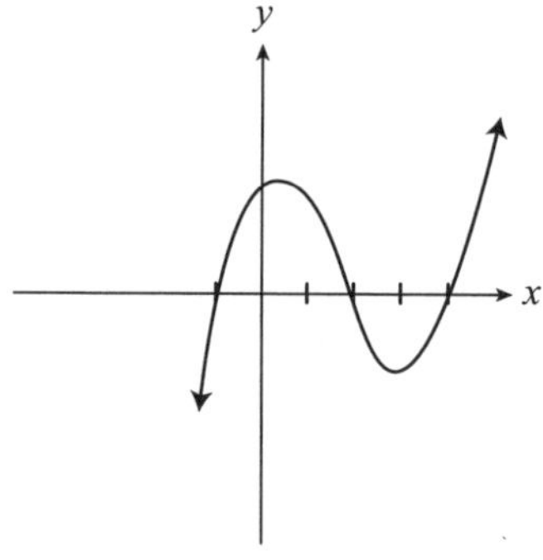

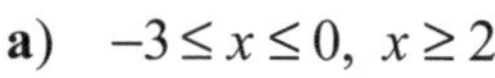

   a) $-3 \leq x \leq 0,\ x \geq 2$

   b) $x \leq -3,\ 0 \leq x \leq 2$

   c) $-1 \leq x \leq 2,\ x \geq 4$

   d) $1 \leq x \leq 3,\ x \geq 6$

6. Determine one factor of the polynomial $x^3 + 2x^2 - 5x - 6$.

a) $x + 2$
b) $x - 3$
c) $x^2 + 4x + 3$
d) $x^2 + 5x + 6$

7. What is the minimum degree of the polynomial graph function?

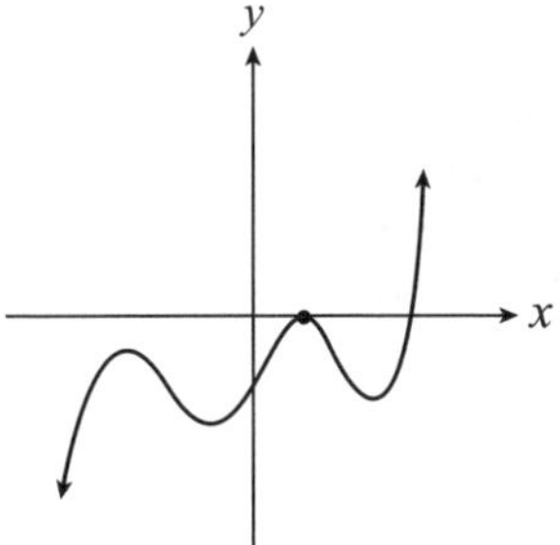

a) 1
b) 2
c) 4
d) 5

8. What is the remainder when $x^{23} - 1$ is divided by $x + 1$?

a) –2
b) –1
c) 0
d) 23

9. Given the graph of $y = f(x)$, which graph best represents $y = x\,f(x)$?

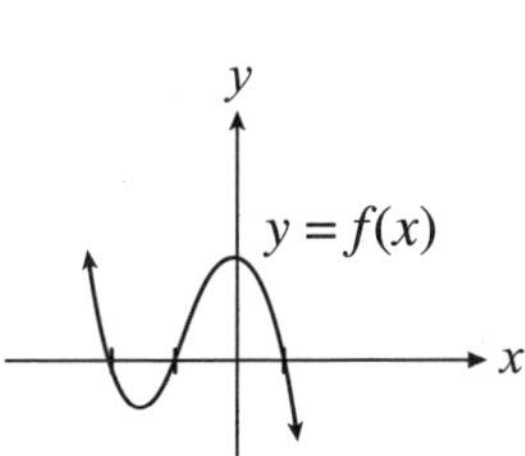

a)

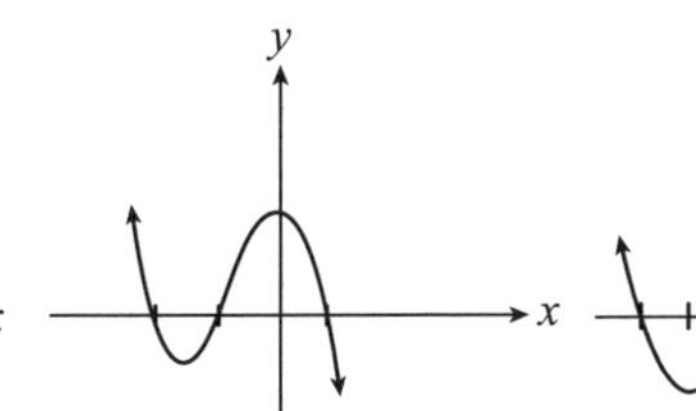

b)

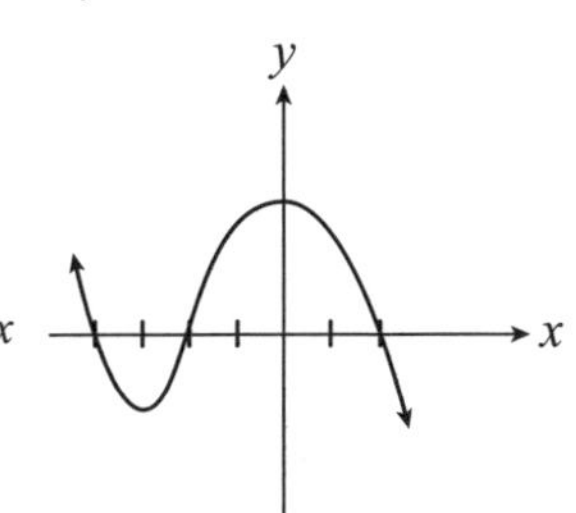

c)

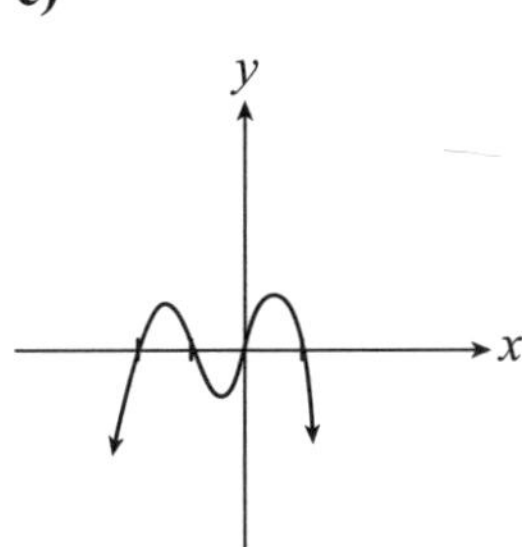

d)

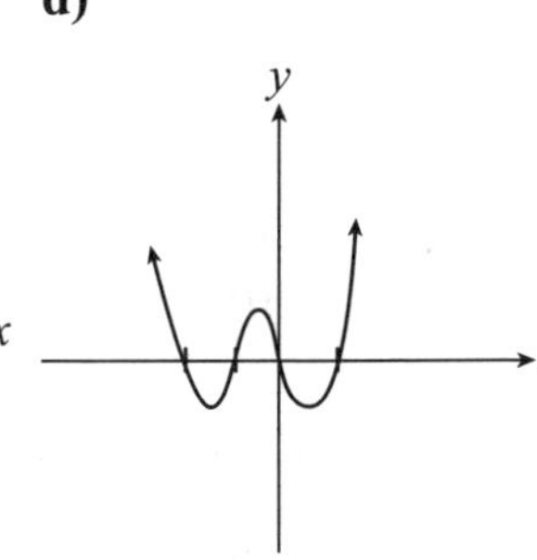

10. Given the graph $y = f(x)$, how many positive zeros has the function $y = f(x + 2) + 1$?

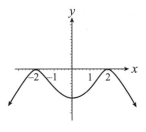

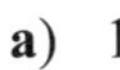

a) 1
b) 2
c) 3
d) 4

11. Which of the following conditions is true for the 3rd degree polynomial function?

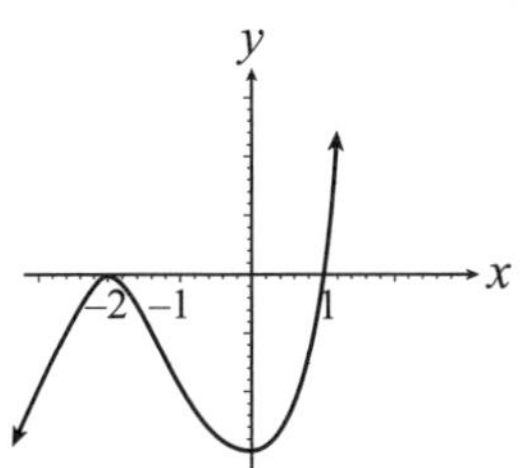

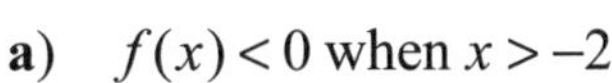

a) $f(x) < 0$ when $x > -2$
b) $f(x) < 0$ when $x > 1$
c) $f(x) > 0$ when $x > -2$
d) $f(x) > 0$ when $x > 1$

12. When $P(x)$ is divided by $x-1$, the remainder is 3. Which of the following must be true?

a) $P(1)=3$
b) $P(3)=1$
c) $P(-1)=3$
d) $P(-3)=1$

13. Determine the largest root of $x^3-30x^2+240x-420=0$.

a) 2.42
b) 9.67
c) 17.91
d) 18.24

14. The graph of $y=P(x)$ is shown. If $R(x)=2P(x-1)$, determine $R(1)$.

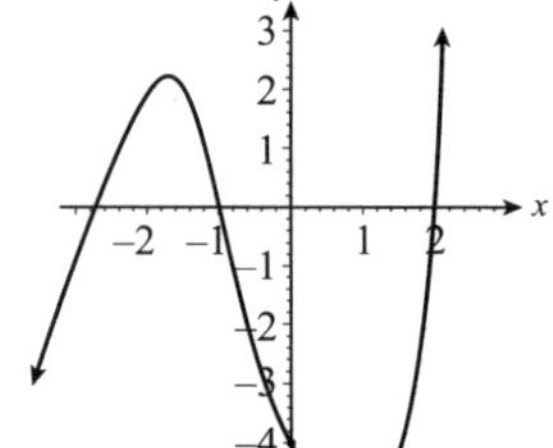

a) –4
b) –5
c) –8
d) –10

15. When a polynomial $P(x)$ is divided by $x+3$, the remainder is 4. Which point must be on the graph?

a) (–3, 4)
b) (4, –3)
c) (–3, –4)
d) (–4, –3)

16. Which of the following is a real zero of the polynomial function $f(x)=x^3-2x+3$?

a) –2.00
b) –1.89
c) 0.82
d) 3.00

17. Determine the number of real roots of the equation $2x(x-3)(x^2+4)=0$.

a) 1
b) 2
c) 3
d) 4

18. If the polynomial function $f(x) = k(x-1)(x+2)^2(x-3)$ passes through the point (2, 5), determine the value of k.

a) $-\frac{16}{5}$

b) $-\frac{5}{4}$

c) $-\frac{4}{5}$

d) $-\frac{5}{16}$

19. Determine an equation of the polynomial function $y = f(x)$ graph.

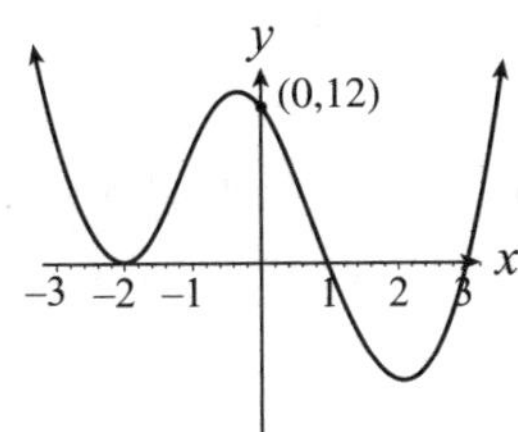

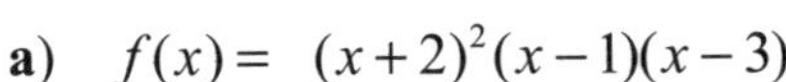

a) $f(x) = (x+2)^2(x-1)(x-3)$

b) $f(x) = (x-2)^2(x+1)(x+3)$

c) $f(x) = -(x+2)^2(x-1)(x-3)$

d) $f(x) = -(x-2)^2(x+1)(x+3)$

20. The following graph represents the polynomial function $y = ax^4 + bx^3 + cx^2 + dx + e$. What conditions must be satisfied by a and e?

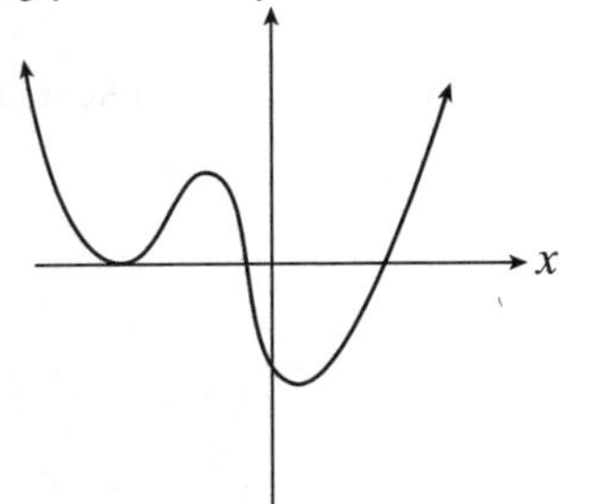

a) $a < 0,\ e < 0$

b) $a < 0,\ e > 0$

c) $a > 0,\ e < 0$

d) $a > 0,\ e > 0$

21. Find the remainder for the following division: $x^2 - 3\overline{)x^4 - 3x^3 + x - 3}$.

a) $-8x - 12$

b) $-8x + 6$

c) $8x - 12$

d) $8x + 6$

22. What is the minimum degree of the polynomial function?

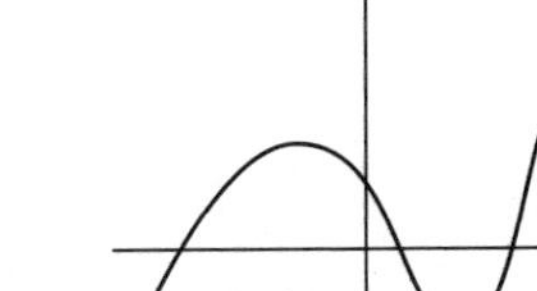

a) 3

b) 4

c) 5

d) 7

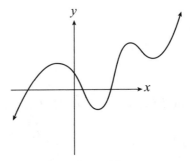

23. When $x^3 - x^2 + kx + 5$ is divided by $x + 2$, the remainder is 1. Find the value of k.

a) –4

b) –1

c) 0

d) 4

24. If $x+3$ is a factor of the polynomial $P(x)$, then which of the following must be true?

a) $P(-3)=0$
b) $P(3)=0$
c) $P(0)=-3$
d) $P(0)=3$

25. If the polynomial $P(x)$, is divided by $x-5$, which of the following represents the remainder?

a) $P(-5)$
b) $P(0)$
c) $P(5)$
d) $P(x)+5$

26. Given that $P(x)$ and $f(x)$ are polynomial functions such that $P(x)=x\,f(x)+k$, determine k if the graph of $P(x)$ is shown.

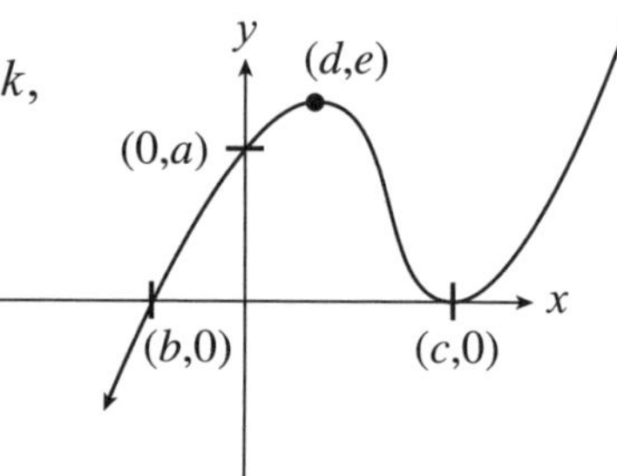

a) a
b) b
c) c
d) e

27. Which graph best represents the function $f(x)=-x(x+4)^2(x-4)^3$?

a)
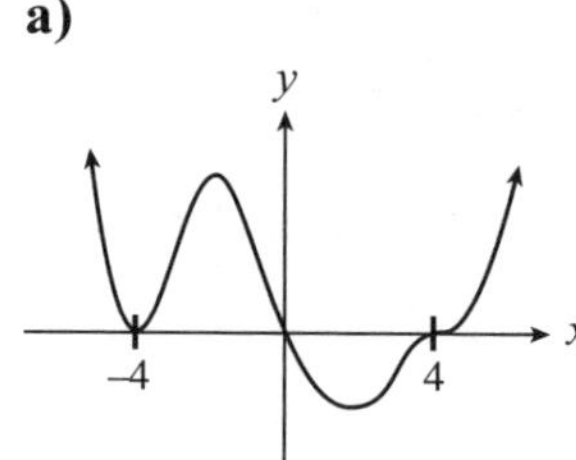

b)
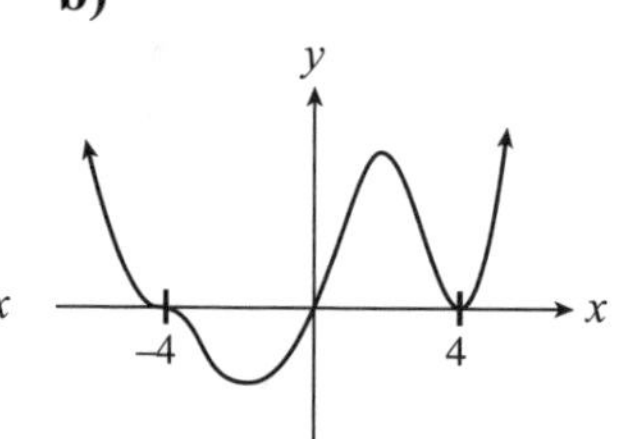

c)
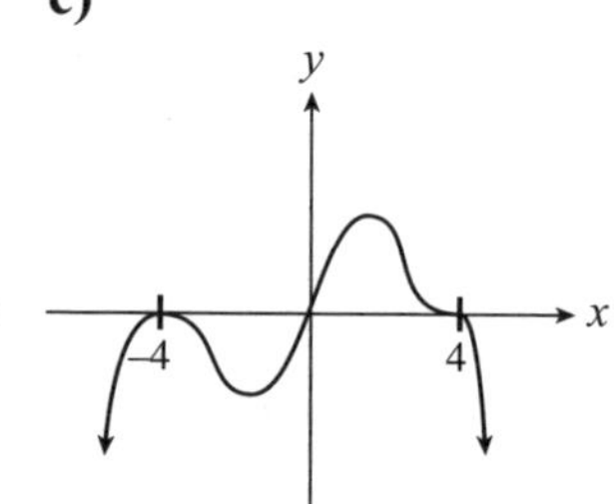

d)
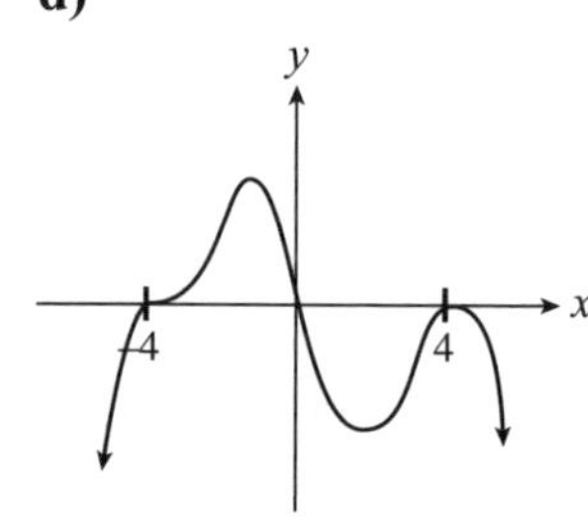

28. If $P(x)$ is a polynomial function where $P(-3)=5$, then which of the following **could not** be a zero of this function?

a) –5
b) –3
c) 3
d) 5

29. The function $P(x)$ is graphed. If $f(x)=2P(x)$, determine the zeros of $f(x)$.

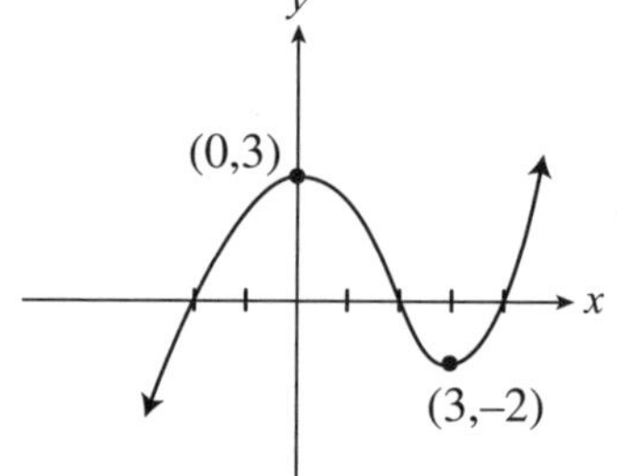

a) –2, 2, 4
b) –4, 4, 8
c) –4, 6
d) –2, 3

30. Determine all the real zeros of the function $P(x)=-2x(x^2+4)(x^2-2)$.

a) $0, \pm\sqrt{2}$
b) $0, \pm 2$
c) $0, \sqrt{2}, 2$
d) $0, \pm\sqrt{2}, \pm 3$

31. What is the minimum number of real roots that a polynomial equation can have if its degree is 5?

a) 0
b) 1
c) 3
d) 5

32. Find the remainder when x^3-2x^2+6 is divided by x^2+x-1.

a) 5
b) $-2x+9$
c) $2x+5$
d) $4x+3$

33. If $P(x)=(x-3)q(x)+r$, determine $P(3)$.

a) $q(3)$
b) $q(-3)$
c) $-r$
d) r

34. Use the graph of the function $y=P(x)$ to solve the equation $P(x-5)+4=0$.

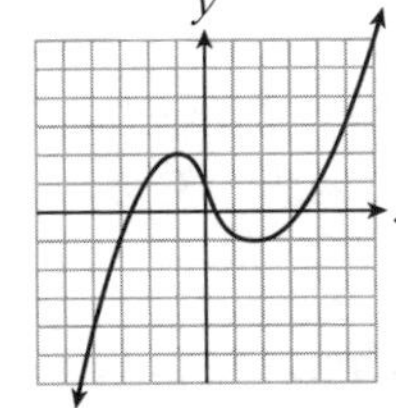

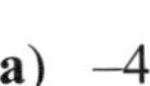
a) -4
b) -1
c) 1
d) 4

35. Given the graph of the cubic polynomial function $y=f(x)$, determine the equation of $y=f(x)-3$.

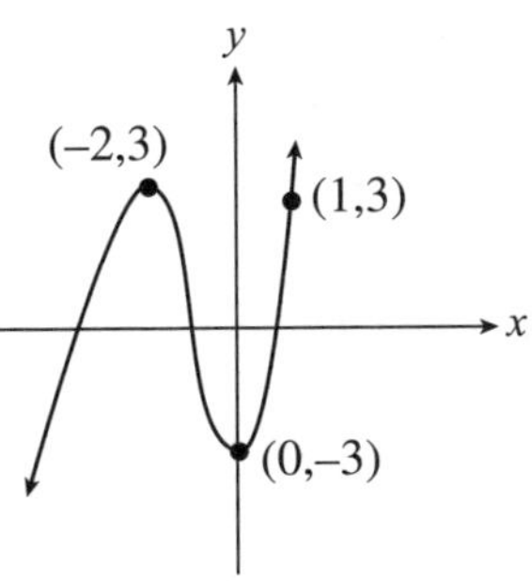

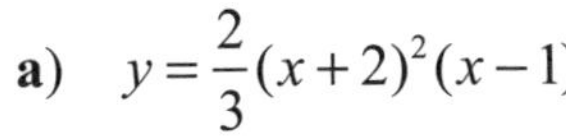
a) $y=\frac{2}{3}(x+2)^2(x-1)$

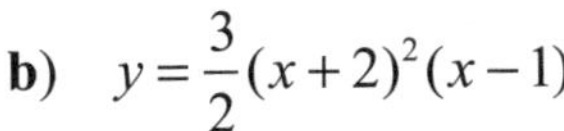
b) $y=\frac{3}{2}(x+2)^2(x-1)$

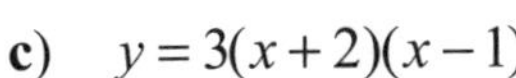
c) $y=3(x+2)(x-1)$

d) $y=3(x+2)(x-1)^2$

36. Determine the remainder: $(x^4 + 3x^3 + 5x^2 + 21x - 13) \div (x^2 + 3x - 2)$.

a) 1
b) –27
c) $12x - 7$
d) $30x - 19$

37. From the graph of $y = f(x)$, find $f(x) = 1$.

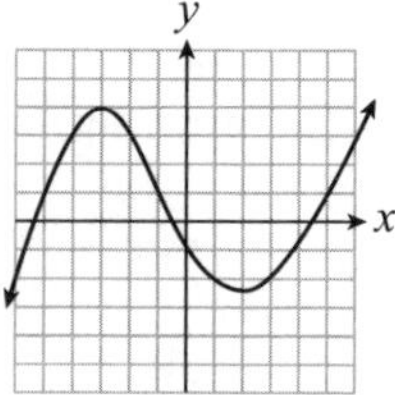

a) –2
b) –1
c) –5, –1, 5
d) –6, 1, 3

38. If $(x+4)$ is a factor of $x^3 + 2x^2 - 11x - 12$, then the remaining two factors are

a) $(x-3)(x-1)$
b) $(x-3)(x+1)$
c) $(x+3)(x-1)$
d) $(x+3)(x+1)$

39. What numbers should replace *a* and *b* in the synthetic division?

$$\begin{array}{r|rrrr} a & 2 & -5 & b & 5 \\ & & 6 & 3 & -3 \\ \hline & 2 & 1 & -1 & 2 \end{array}$$

a) $a = -3,\ b = -4$
b) $a = -3,\ b = 4$
c) $a = 3,\ b = -4$
d) $a = 3,\ b = 4$

40. When the polynomial $P(x) = kx^{40} + 2x^{25} - 4x - 6$ is divided by $x + 1$, the remainder is 23. Determine the value of the constant *k*.

a) 23
b) 27
c) 35
d) 40

41. For what values of *x* does the graph of $y = -(x+1)^2(x-1)(x-3)$ lie above the *x*-axis?

a) $1 < x < 3$
b) $-1 < x < 1,\ x > 3$
c) $x < -1,\ 1 < x < 3$
d) $x < -1,\ -1 < x < 1,\ x > 3$

42. Determine all roots of the equation $x^3+\sqrt{2}x^2-4x-4\sqrt{2}=0$.

a) 2

b) $-\sqrt{2},\ \sqrt{2}$

c) $-\sqrt{2},\ \sqrt{2},\ 2$

d) $-2,\ -\sqrt{2},\ 2$

43. Find a and b if $x+1$ and $x+2$ are both factors of x^3+ax+b.

a) $a=-7,\ b=-6$

b) $a=-7,\ b=6$

c) $a=7,\ b=-6$

d) $a=7,\ b=6$

44. The polynomial $P(x)=ax^3+x^2-13x+k$ has y-intercept 6 and x-intercept 2. Find all other x-intercept(s).

a) $-\frac{1}{2},\ -3$

b) $-\frac{1}{2},\ 3$

c) $\frac{1}{2},\ -3$

d) $\frac{1}{2},\ 3$

45. Determine the values for a and b in the polynomial function $P(x)=x^4+4x^3+ax^2+bx-3$ given that $P(1)=-2.5$ and $P(2)=46$.

a) $a=-5,\ b=-9.5$

b) $a=5,\ b=-9.5$

c) $a=-5,\ b=9.5$

d) $a=5,\ b=9.5$

46. If the polynomial $8x^3+ax^2+16x+3$ is divided by $4x-3$, the quotient is $2x^2+bx+1$ and the remainder is 6. Find the values of a and b.

a) $a=-22,\ b=-4$

b) $a=-22,\ b=4$

c) $a=22,\ b=-4$

d) $a=22,\ b=4$

47. A trinomial function $P(x)$ has three real zeros. Two of the zeros of $P(x)$ are 1 and 2. If $P(5) = 480$ and the y-intercept is 10, find the value of the third zero.

a) $-\frac{7}{5}$

b) $-\frac{5}{7}$

c) $\frac{5}{7}$

d) $\frac{7}{5}$

48. When $x^3 + ax + 3$ is divided by $x + 2$, the remainder is equal to the square of the remainder when the same trinomial is divided by $x - 1$. Determine the value of a.

a) 3, 7
b) 3, –7
c) –3, 7
d) –3, –7

49. When the polynomial function $P(x) = x^4 + ax^2 + bx - 5$ is divided by $x - 2$, the remainder is 12 more than the remainder obtained when $P(x)$ is divided by $x + 1$. If the point (–2, 31) is on the graph of $P(x)$, determine the value of a and b.

a) $a = 4,\ b = -3$

b) $a = -4,\ b = 3$

c) $a = 3,\ b = -4$

d) $a = -3,\ b = 4$

50. A slice 1 cm in width is removed from one side of a cube, then a second slice of the same thickness is removed from a side adjacent to the first slice (not the opposite side). Find the original volume of the cube if the remaining volume is 36 cm^3.

a) 48 cm^3
b) 64 cm^3
c) 80 cm^3
d) 96 cm^3

4.1 Radicals

In our transformation chapter, we observed the variations of the graph $y=\sqrt{x}$. In this chapter, we will investigate radical notation in a more formal way.

If $n \geq 2$ is an integer, and a is a real number, the ***n*^th^ root of *a*** is a number which, when raised to the power of n, equals a.

eg a) the 3rd root of 8 is 2 since $2^3=8$

b) the 3rd root of –8 is –2 since $(-2)^3=-8$

c) the 2nd root of 9 is 3 since $3^2=9$

d) the 2nd root of 9 is –3 since $(-3)^2=9$

e) the 2nd root of –9 does not exist since there is no number x for which $x^2=-9$

eg a) and b) tell us that if n is odd, there is only **one** real number for x for which $x^n=a$. There is always one solution.

eg c) and d) tell us that if n is even and a is positive, there are **two** numbers for which $x^n=a$.

eg e) tells us that if n is even and a is negative, there is **no** real number x for which $x^n=a$.

With this discussion, we can summarize as follows:

Definition of $\sqrt[n]{a}$

Let n be a positive integer greater than 1. Let a be any real number.

1. If $a>0$ and n is even, then $\sqrt[n]{a}$ is the positive n^{th} root of a.
2. If $a<0$ and n is even, then $\sqrt[n]{a}$ does not exist in the real number system.
3. If n is odd, then $\sqrt[n]{a}$ is the nth root of a.
4. $\sqrt[n]{0}=0$

We can formalize the symbol of a radical as follows:

Radical Notation

The number x is the nth root of a if $x^n=a$ and $\sqrt[n]{a}=x$.

$\sqrt[n]{a}$ denotes the principle n^{th} root of a

a is the **radicand**

$\sqrt{}$ is the radical symbol, or the **radical**

the natural number n is the **index**, or the order of the radical

Example 1 Solve the following for x, a real number:

a) $x^2 = 1$, **b)** $x^3 = -27$, **c)** $x^4 = 5$, **d)** $x^4 = -5$, **e)** $x^5 = 5$, and **f)** $x^5 = -5$

▶ *Solution:*

a) $x^2 = 1$
$x = \pm\sqrt{1}$
$= \pm 1$

b) $x^3 = -27$
$x = \sqrt[3]{-27}$
$= -3$

c) $x^4 = 5$
$x = \pm\sqrt[4]{5}$
$\approx \pm 1.5$

d) $x^4 = -5$
$x = \sqrt[4]{-5}$
$= \varnothing$

e) $x^5 = 5$
$x = \sqrt[5]{5}$
≈ 1.38

f) $x^5 = -5$
$x = \sqrt[5]{-5}$
≈ -1.38

Graphing Radicals in the Form $y = a\sqrt{b(x-h)} + k$

Example 2 Graph **a)** $y = \sqrt{x}$, **b)** $y = \sqrt{-x}$, **c)** $y = -\sqrt{x}$, and **d)** $y = -\sqrt{-x}$

▶ *Solution:*

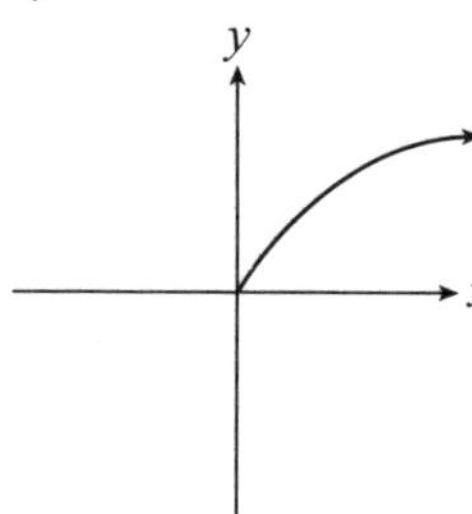

a) Domain: $x \ge 0$ Range: $y \ge 0$

b) Domain: $x \le 0$ Range: $y \ge 0$

c) Domain: $x \ge 0$ Range: $y \le 0$

d) Domain: $x \le 0$ Range: $y \le 0$

Example 3 Graph **a)** $y = \sqrt{x-1}$, **b)** $y = \sqrt{x+1}$, **c)** $y = \sqrt{x} + 1$, and **d)** $y = \sqrt{x} - 1$

▶ *Solution:*

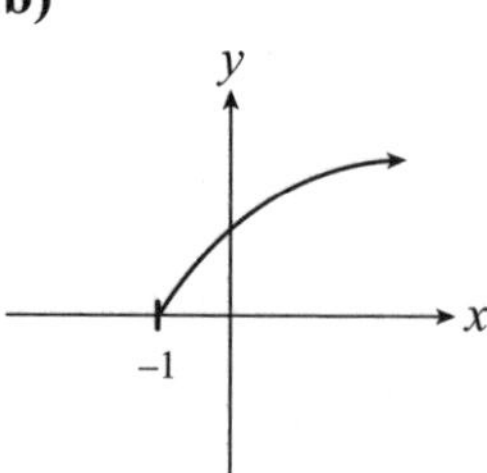

a) Domain: $x \ge 1$ Range: $y \ge 0$

b) Domain: $x \ge -1$ Range: $y \ge 0$

c) Domain: $x \ge 0$ Range: $y \ge 1$

d) Domain: $x \ge 0$ Range: $y \ge -1$

Example 4 Graph $y = \sqrt{x}$, $y = \sqrt{2x}$, $y = \sqrt{\frac{1}{2}x}$

▶ *Solution:*

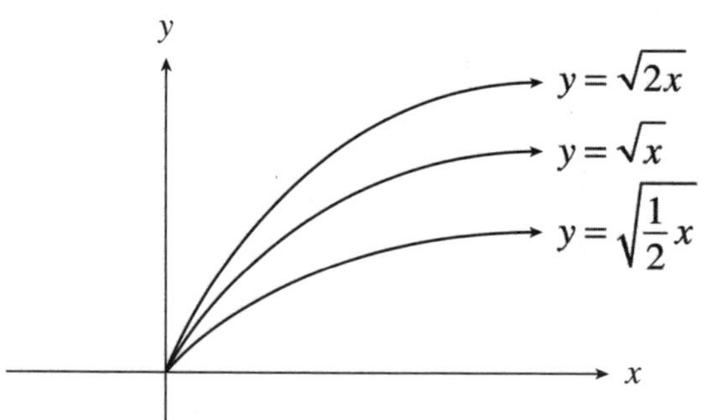

Example 5 Graph **a)** $y = 2\sqrt{4-x} + 1$ and **b)** $y = -\sqrt{2x-4} - 1$

▶ *Solution:*

a) Domain:

$4 - x \geq 0$

$-x \geq -4$

$x \leq 4$

Range:

since $2\sqrt{4-x} \geq 0$ then

$y = 2\sqrt{4-x} + 1$ is

$y \geq 1$

By transformation of

$y = \sqrt{x}$ to $y = 2\sqrt{4-x} + 1 = 2\sqrt{-(x-4)} + 1$

$(a, b) \to (-a+4, 2b+1)$

$(0, 0) \to (4, 1)$

$(1, 1) \to (3, 3)$

$(4, 2) \to (0, 5)$

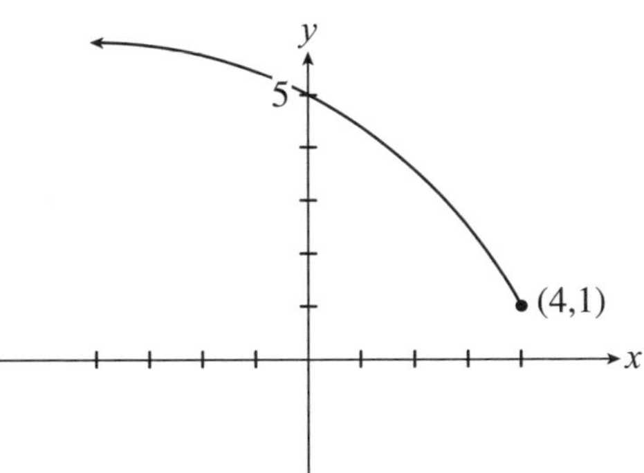

b) Domain:

$2x - 4 \geq 0$

$2x \geq 4$

$x \geq 2$

Range:

since $-\sqrt{2x-4} \leq 0$ then

$y = -\sqrt{2x-4} - 1$ is

$y \leq -1$

By transformation of

$y = \sqrt{x}$ to $y = -\sqrt{2x-4} - 1 = -\sqrt{2(x-2)} - 1$

$(a, b) \to (\frac{1}{2}a + 2, -b-1)$

$(0, 0) \to (2, -1)$

$(1, 1) \to (2.5, -2)$

$(4, 2) \to (4, -3)$

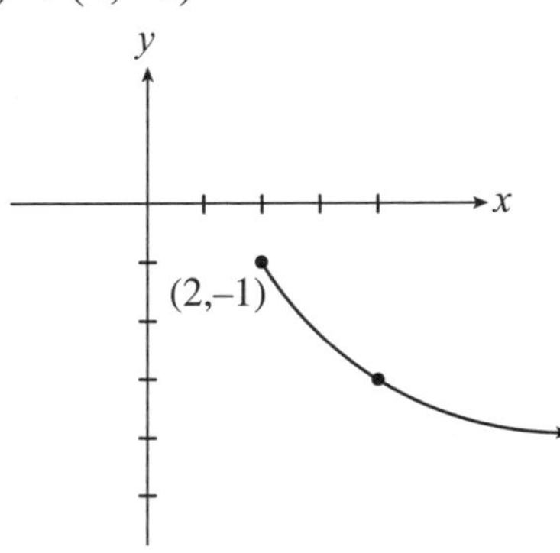

Graphing Radical Functions with Even and Odd Root Indexes

Graphing radical functions with even and odd root indexes will have different domains and ranges. Recall the meaning of the domain and range:

> **Domain and Range**
>
> The **domain** is the set of all real values x, except any value that
>
> 1. causes division by zero
> 2. causes a negative number under a radical symbol with an even index
>
> The **range** is the output value $f(x)$ of the input value x.

Example 6 Find the domain and range of **a)** $y = \sqrt{x}$, **b)** $y = \sqrt[3]{x}$, **c)** $y = \sqrt[4]{x}$, and **d)** $y = \sqrt[5]{x}$.

▶ *Solution:*

a) Domain must have $x \geq 0$; Range is then $y \geq 0$.

b) Domain can be any real number; Range is then any real number.

c) Domain must have $x \geq 0$; Range is then $y \geq 0$.

d) Domain can be any real number; Range is then any real number.

From these examples, we see that negative numbers are excluded from the radicand of any even-order radical, including square roots, fourth roots, etc.

Example 7 Graph **a)** $y=\sqrt{x}$, **b)** $y=\sqrt[3]{x}$, **c)** $y=\sqrt[4]{x}$, and **d)** $y=\sqrt[5]{x}$.

▶ *Solution:*

a) $y=\sqrt{x}$, Domain: $x\geq 0$, Range: $y\geq 0$

x	y
0	0
1	1
2	$\sqrt{2}\approx 1.4$
3	$\sqrt{3}\approx 1.7$
4	2
5	$\sqrt{5}\approx 2.3$
6	$\sqrt{6}\approx 2.4$

b) $y=\sqrt[3]{x}$, Domain and Range: all real numbers

x	y
−8	−2
−4	$\sqrt[3]{-4}\approx -1.6$
−1	−1
0	0
1	1
4	$\sqrt[3]{4}\approx 1.6$
8	2

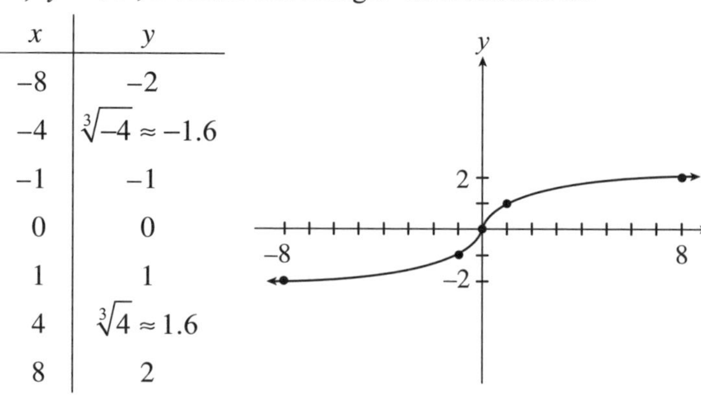

c) $y=\sqrt[4]{x}$, Domain: $x\geq 0$, Range: $y\geq 0$

x	y
0	0
1	1
5	$\sqrt[4]{5}\approx 1.5$
10	$\sqrt[4]{10}\approx 1.8$
16	2

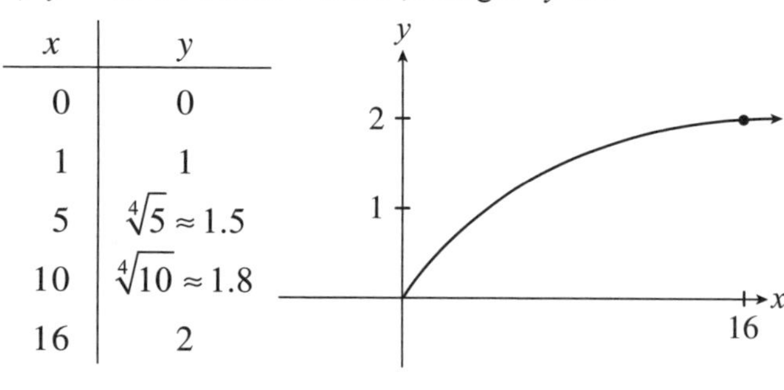

d) $y=\sqrt[5]{x}$, Domain and Range: all real numbers

x	y
−32	−2
−16	$\sqrt[5]{-16}\approx -1.7$
−1	−1
0	0
1	1
16	$\sqrt[5]{16}\approx 1.7$
32	2

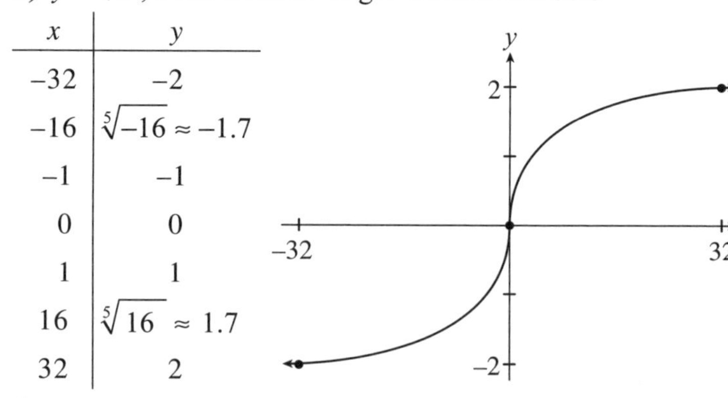

Note: $y=\sqrt{x}=x^{\frac{1}{2}}$, $y=\sqrt[3]{x}=x^{\frac{1}{3}}$, $y=\sqrt[4]{x}=x^{\frac{1}{4}}$, $y=\sqrt[5]{x}=x^{\frac{1}{5}}$ when calculating values with your calculator.

Example 8 Graph **a)** $y=-\sqrt[4]{x-1}-2$ and **b)** $y=-\sqrt[3]{x-1}-2$.

▶ *Solution:*

a) $y=-\sqrt[4]{x-1}-2$, Domain: $x\geq 1$, Range: $y\leq -2$

x	y
1	−2
2	−3
9	$-\sqrt[4]{8}-2\approx -3.7$
17	−4

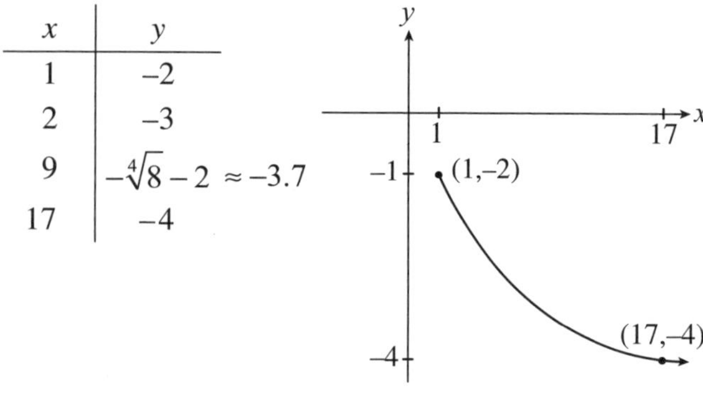

b) $y=-\sqrt[3]{x-1}-2$, Domain and Range: all real numbers

x	y
−7	0
0	−1
1	−2
2	−3
9	−4

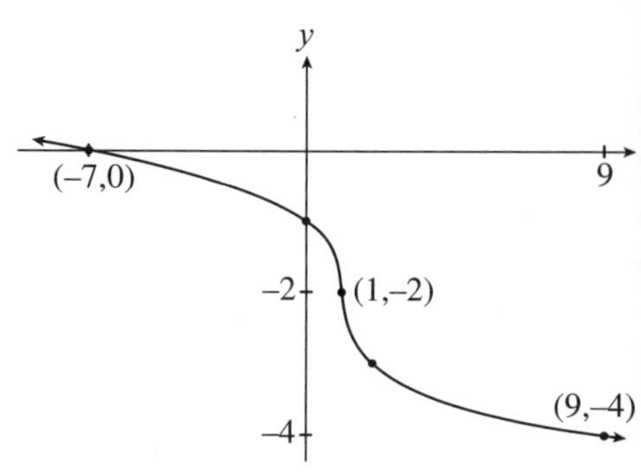

Graphing $y = f(x)$ and $y = \sqrt{f(x)}$

The graphs of $y = f(x)$ and $y = \sqrt{f(x)}$ will have different domains and ranges because of the restriction on an even root function.

Example 9 Graph **a)** $y = x^2$ and $y = \sqrt{x^2}$ and **b)** $y = x^3$ and $y = \sqrt{x^3}$. State the domain and range.

▶ Solution: **a)**

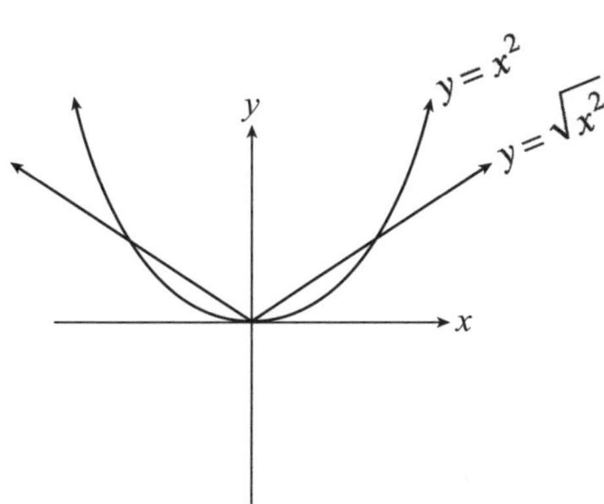

Domain: $y = x^2$; x is all real numbers

Range: $y = x^2$; $y \geq 0$

Domain: $y = \sqrt{x^2}$; x is all real numbers

Range: $y = \sqrt{x^2}$; $y \geq 0$

Note: Graphs of **a)** are equal at (0, 0), (–1, 1), and (1, 1). The domain and range of both graphs are equal because the even root radical has a value in the radical that is always positive.

b)

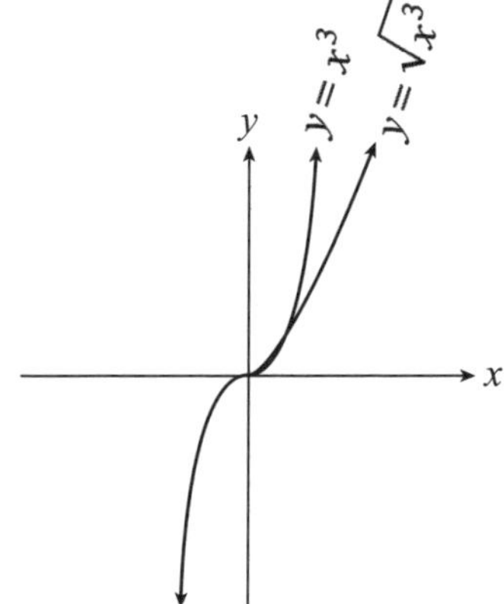

Domain: $y = x^3$; x is all real numbers

Range: $y = x^3$; y is all real numbers

Domain: $y = \sqrt{x^3}$; $x \geq 0$

Range: $y = \sqrt{x^3}$; $y \geq 0$

Note: Graphs of **b)** are equal at (0, 0) and (1, 1). The domain and range of $y = \sqrt{x^3}$ is greater than or equal to zero because the value of an even root radical must be positive, and x^3 is negative for a negative value of x.

Example 10 Graph $f(x)=\frac{1}{2}x^2-2$ and $y=\sqrt{f(x)}$. State the domain and range.

▶ *Solution:*

x	y	$\sqrt{y}$
−4	6	$\sqrt{6}=2.45$
−3	2.5	1.6
−2	0	0
−1	$-\frac{3}{2}$	∅
0	−2	∅
1	$-\frac{3}{2}$	∅
2	0	0
3	2.5	1.6
4	6	$\sqrt{6}=2.45$

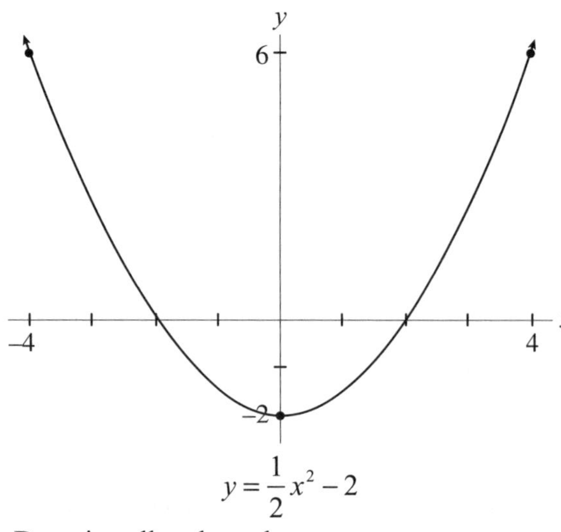

$y=\frac{1}{2}x^2-2$

Domain: all real numbers

Range: $y\geq -2$

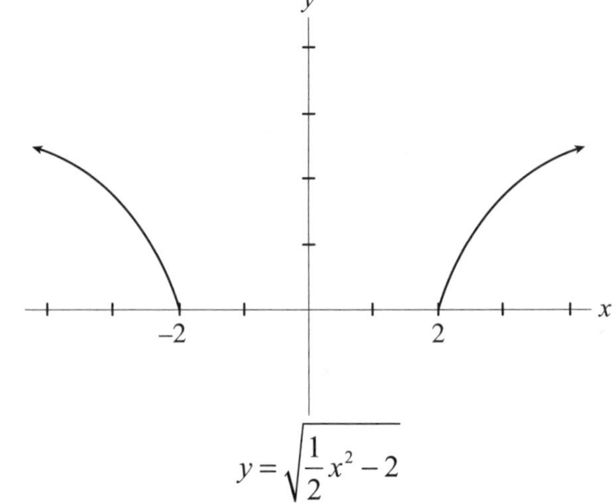

$y=\sqrt{\frac{1}{2}x^2-2}$

Domain: $\frac{1}{2}x^2-2\geq 0$

$$\frac{1}{2}x^2\geq 2$$

$$x^2\geq 4$$

$$x\geq 2,\ x\leq -2$$

Range: $y\geq 0$

Note: The domain and range are quite different. This is because the domain $\frac{1}{2}x^2-2$ has no restriction, but inside an even root radical it must be positive. The range of $y=\frac{1}{2}x^2-2$ depends on the minimum value, but the even root value of a positive radical must be positive or zero.

4.1 Exercise Set

1. Fill in the missing symbols.

a) In the radical notation $\sqrt[n]{x}$, x is called the ____________ .

b) In radical notation, $\sqrt{\quad}$ is called the _______________ .

c) In the radical notation $\sqrt[n]{x}$, n is called the ____________ .

d) The principal n^{th} root of x is written as ______________.

e) $\sqrt{25}=5$ is read the (principal) ______________ root of 25 equals 5.

f) $\sqrt[3]{-27}=-3$ is read the (principal) __________________ root of –27 equals –3.

g) The principal n^{th} root of x is not a real number if n is ________________ and x is ____________.

h) The domain of a real-value function excludes any value of the radicand of an even root to be _______________ .

2. Solve for x.

a) $x^2=9$ ___________ **b)** $x^2=-9$ ___________

c) $x^3=8$ ___________ **d)** $x^3=-8$ ___________

e) $x^4=1$ ___________ **f)** $x^4=-1$ ___________

g) $x^5=32$ ___________ **h)** $x^5=-32$ ___________

3. Simplify each radical.

a) $\sqrt{4x^2},\ x\ge 0$ ___________ **b)** $\sqrt{4x^2},\ x<0$ ___________

c) $\sqrt[3]{27x^3},\ x<0$ ___________ **d)** $\sqrt[3]{-27x^3},\ x\ge 0$ ___________

4. Determine the domain and range of the following functions:

a) $y=x$ **b)** $y=\sqrt{x}$

c) $y=\sqrt{1-x}$ **d)** $y=-\sqrt{x-1}$

e) $y+2=\sqrt{1-x}$ **f)** $y-2=\sqrt{x-1}$

g) $y+3=\sqrt{2x-4}$ **h)** $y-3=-\sqrt{2x+4}$

i) $y=-\sqrt{-2x-4}+3$ **j)** $y=\sqrt{x^2-4}$

k) $y=-\sqrt{4-x^2}$ **l)** $y=-\sqrt{x^3-8}$

5. Match the equation with the graph.

a) $f(x)=\sqrt{-x}$ ______

b) $f(x)=-\sqrt{x}$ ______

c) $f(x)=\sqrt[3]{x}$ ______

d) $f(x)=\sqrt{1-x}$ ______

e) $f(x)=\sqrt{x^2}$ ______

f) $f(x)=-\sqrt{x-1}$ ______

g) $f(x)=-\sqrt{x}-1$ ______

h) $f(x)=1-\sqrt[3]{-x}$ ______

i) $f(x)=1-\sqrt{x-1}$ ______

j) $f(x)=1-\sqrt{1-x}$ ______

k) $f(x)=\sqrt{x^2-1}$ ______

l) $f(x)=1+\sqrt[3]{-x}$ ______

m) $f(x)=-1-\sqrt{1-x}$ ______

n) $f(x)=-1+\sqrt{x+1}$ ______

A

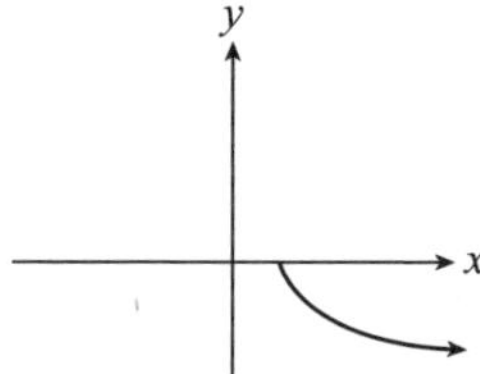

B

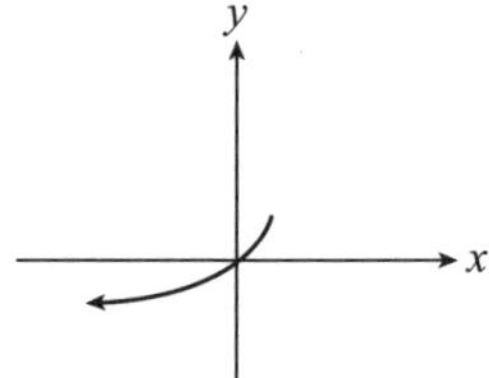

C

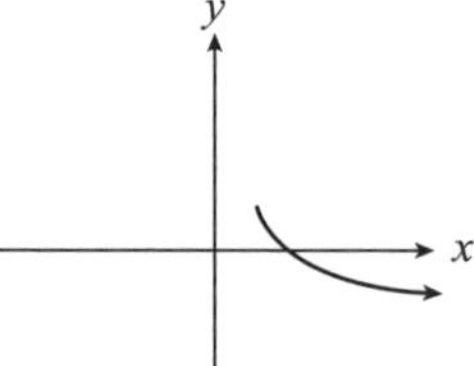

D

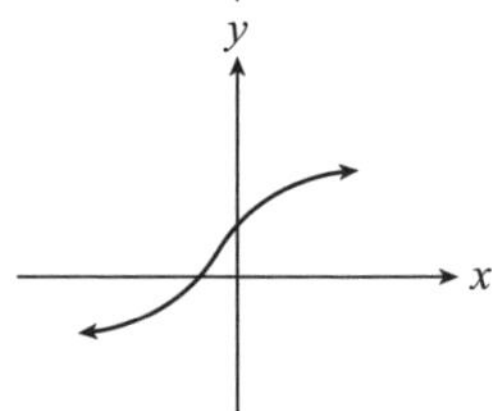

E

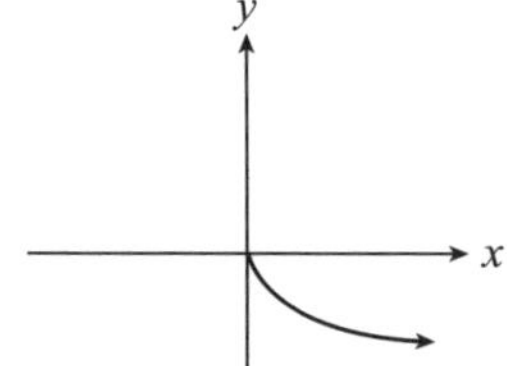

F

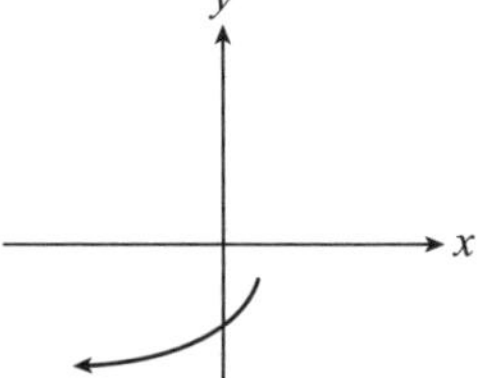

G

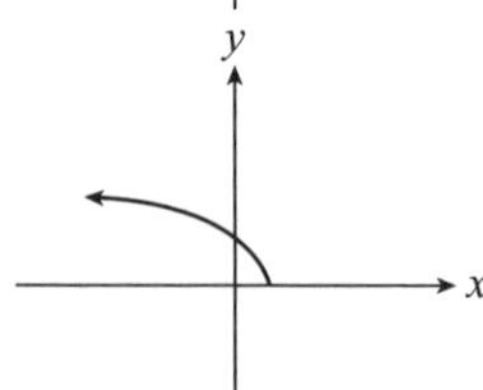

H

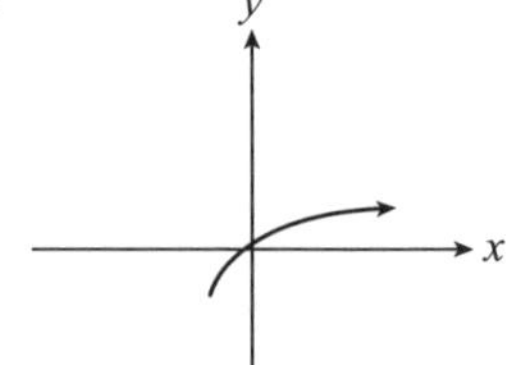

I

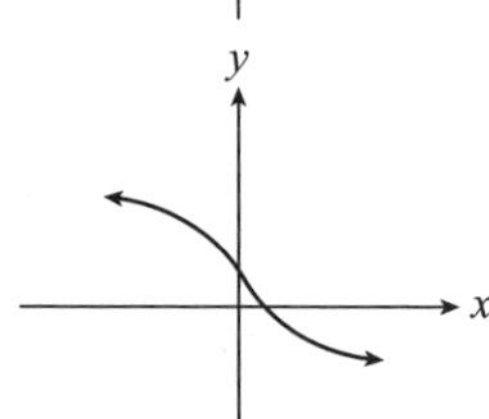

J

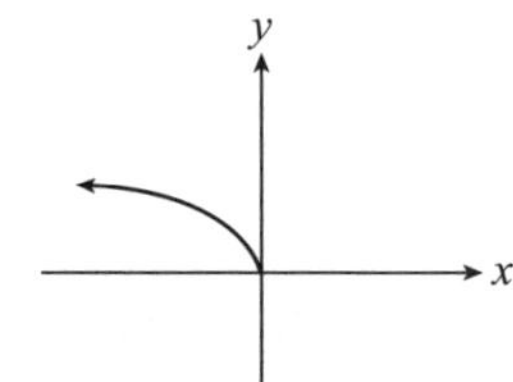

K

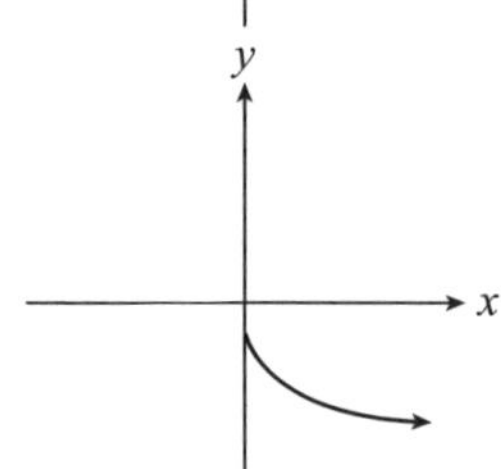

L

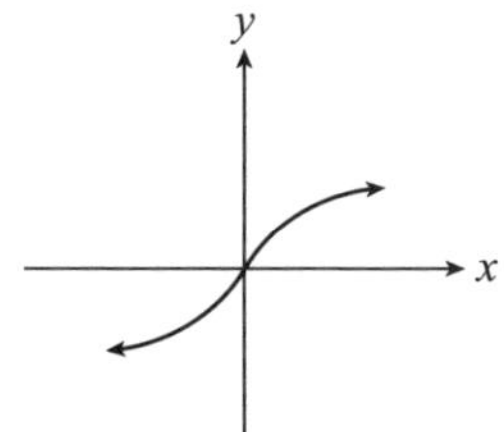

M

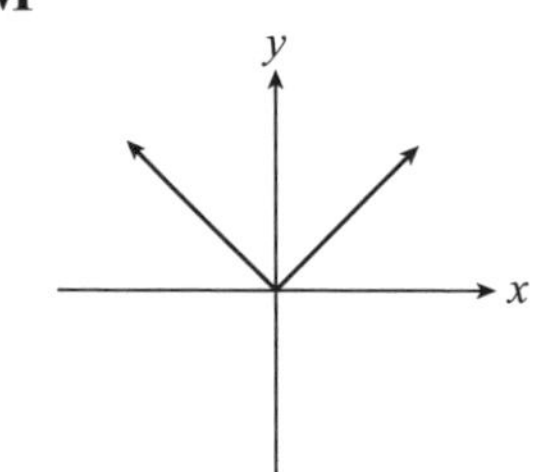

N

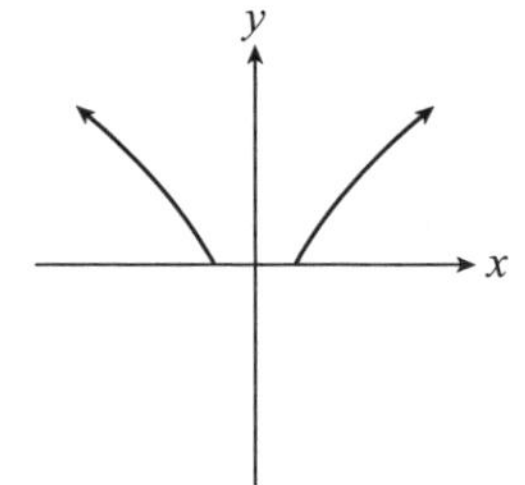

6. Graph the following functions. State the domain and range.

a) $f(x) = 2x$

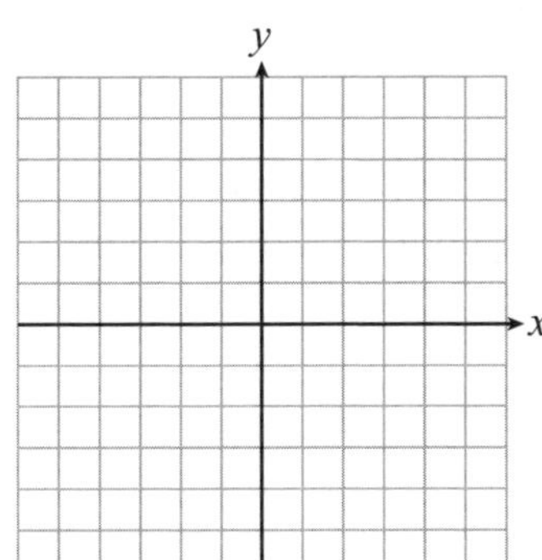

b) $f(x) = \sqrt{2x}$

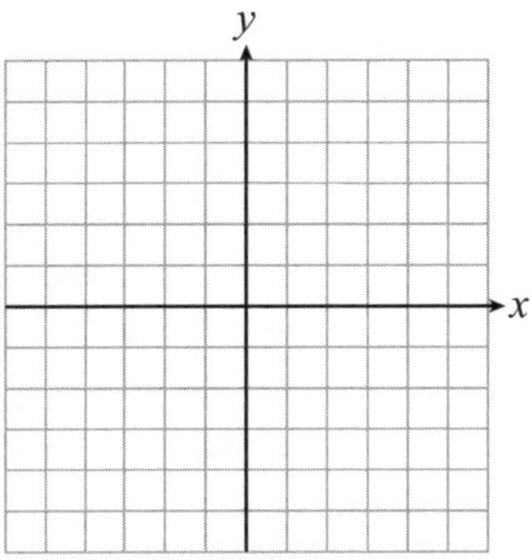

c) $f(x) = 4 - x^2$

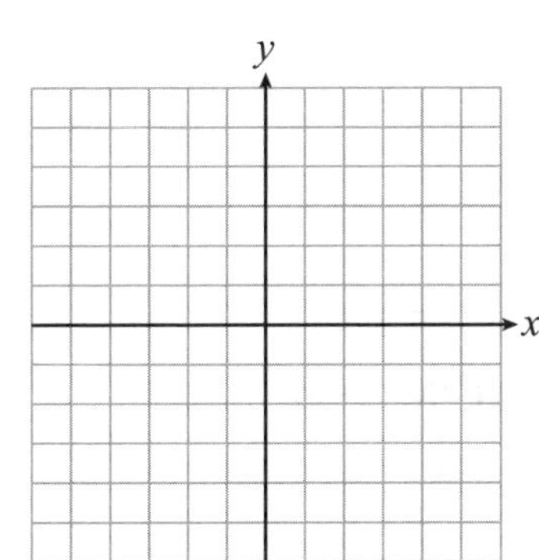

d) $f(x) = \sqrt{4 - x^2}$

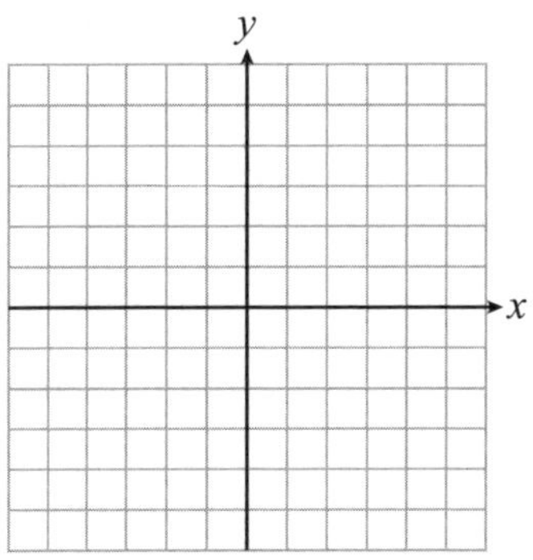

e) $f(x) = \frac{1}{3}x^2 - 3$

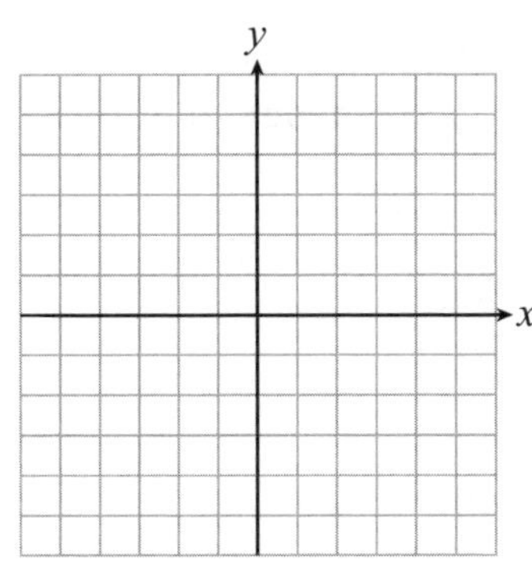

f) $f(x) = \sqrt{\frac{1}{3}x^2 - 3}$

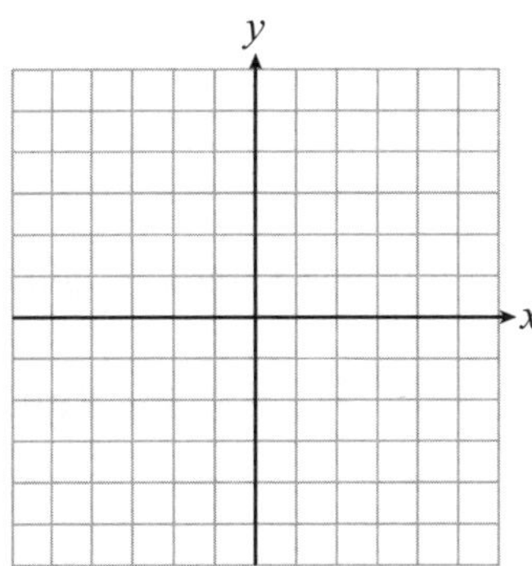

g) $f(x) = -\frac{1}{8}x^3 + 1$

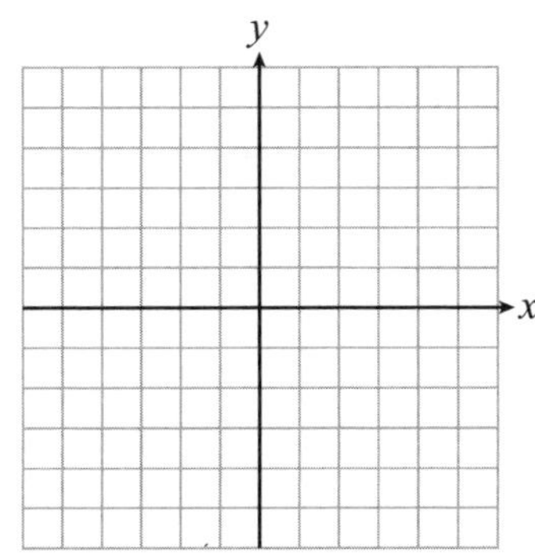

h) $f(x) = \sqrt{-\frac{1}{8}x^3 + 1}$

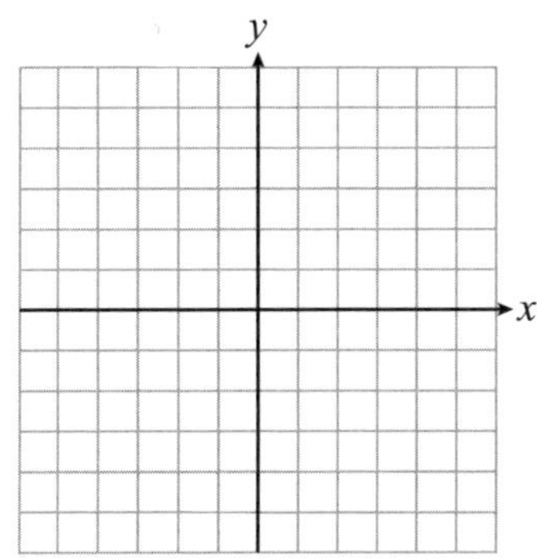

4.2 Graphing and Solving Radical Equations

Equations that contain variables in the radicand are called **radical equations**. Understanding the domain and range restriction allows one to solve radical equations both algebraically and graphically. The key to solving radical equations **graphically** is to make as accurate a graph as possible of where the graph crosses the x-axis with the help of the domain and range.

Solving Radical Equations Graphically

1. Determine domain and range, if possible. (Sometimes range is difficult.)
2. Set radical equation equal to zero.
3. Calculate a set of points $(a, f(a))$ with $f(a) < 0$ and $f(a) > 0$ and when possible $f(a) = 0$.
4. Sketch graph as accurately as possible.
5. Solution(s) is/are zeros(s) of graph.

The key to solving radical equations algebraically is the **power theorem**.

Power Theorem

If $x = y$, then $x^n = y^n$, where n is a positive integer.

Caution: The equation $x = y$ is not always the same as $x^n = y^n$. When using the power theorem, all solutions must be checked. Solutions that do not satisfy the original equation are called **extraneous solutions**; they must be discarded.

The following steps should be used in solving a radical equation:

Solving Equations with Radicals

Step 1. Isolate the radical on one side of the equal sign.

Step 2. Raise both sides of the equation to a power that is equal to the index of the radical.

Step 3. Solve the non-radical equation.

Step 4. Check all possible solutions in the *original equation*, and reject any extraneous solutions.

Consider the following examples:

Example 1 Solve $f(x)=\sqrt{5-x}-2=0$

▶ *Solution:* (Graphically)
Where the function $y=f(x)=0$ is a solution of this equation.

Domain: $5-x\geq 0$

$x\leq 5$

Range: since $5-x\geq 0$

$y\geq -2$

x	y
5	–2
1	0
–4	1

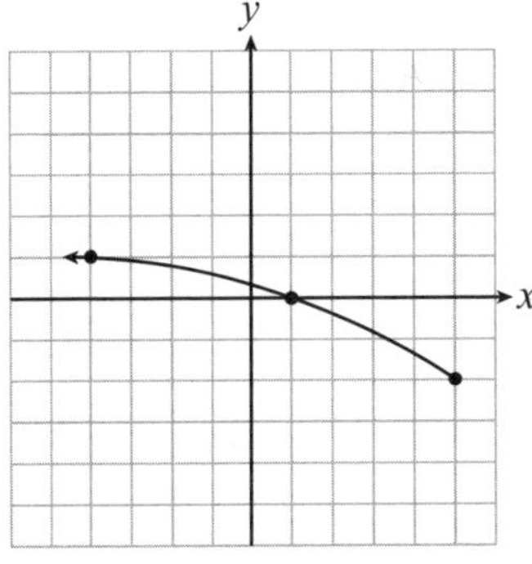

Graph crosses x-axis at 1, solution is $x=1$.

▶ *Solution:* (Algebraically)

$$\sqrt{5-x}-2=0$$
$$\sqrt{5-x}=2$$
$$\left(\sqrt{5-x}\right)^2=(2)^2$$
$$5-x=4$$
$$x=1$$

Check solution:

$$\sqrt{5-x}-2=0$$
$$\sqrt{5-1}-2=0$$
$$2-2=0$$
$$0=0 \quad \textit{accept}$$

Solution is $x=1$.

Example 2 Solve $g(x)=\sqrt{x+6}-x=0$

▶ *Solution:* (Graphically)

Domain: $x+6\geq 0$

$x\geq -6$

x	y
–6	6
–2	4
3	0

Range: difficult to calculate $y\leq 6.25$

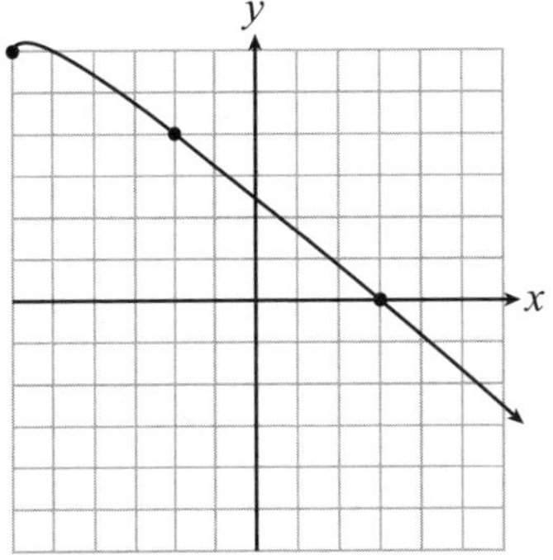

Graph crosses x-axis at 3, solution is $x=3$.

▶ *Solution:* (Algebraically)

$$\sqrt{x+6}-x=0$$
$$\sqrt{x+6}=x$$
$$\left(\sqrt{x+6}\right)^2=x^2$$
$$x+6=x^2$$
$$x^2-x-6=0$$
$$(x-3)(x+2)=0$$
$$x=-2,3$$

Check solution: $x=-2$

$$\sqrt{x+6}-x=0$$
$$\sqrt{-2+6}-(-2)=0$$
$$\sqrt{4}+2=0$$
$$4\neq 0 \quad \textit{reject}$$

Check solution: $x=3$

$$\sqrt{3+6}-3=0$$
$$\sqrt{9}-3=0$$
$$3-3=0$$
$$0=0 \quad \textit{accept}$$

Solution is $x=3$.

Example 3 Solve $f(x)=\sqrt{4x+1}-2=0$

▶ *Solution:* (Graphically)

Domain: $4x+1\geq 0$

$$x\geq -\frac{1}{4}$$

Range: since $\sqrt{4x+1}\geq 0$

$$y\geq -2$$

x	y
$-\frac{1}{4}$	-2
0	-1
1	0.236
2	1
6	3

zero $0<x<1$
Approximate: closer to 1 than 0 since 0.236 is closer to zero than -1.
$x\approx 0.7$

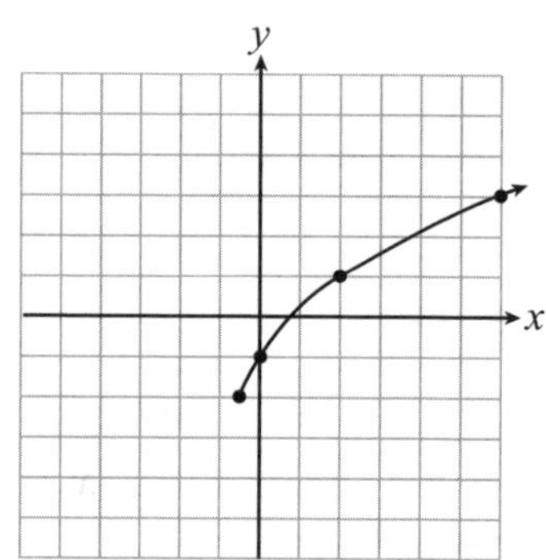

Note: Graphic solution is not as accurate as algebraic when solution is not an integer.

▶ *Solution:* (Algebraically)

$$\sqrt{4x+1}-2=0$$
$$\sqrt{4x+1}=2$$
$$\left(\sqrt{4x+1}\right)^2=2^2$$
$$4x+1=4$$
$$x=\frac{3}{4}$$

Check solution:

$$\sqrt{4x+1}-2=0$$
$$\sqrt{4\left(\frac{3}{4}\right)+1}-2=0$$
$$2-2=0$$
$$0=0 \quad \textit{accept}$$

Solution is $x=\frac{3}{4}$.

Example 4 Solve $f(x)=\sqrt{x+1}-x+2=0$

▶ *Solution:* (Graphically)

Domain: $x+1\geq 0$ Range: difficult to calculate $y\leq 3.25$

$x\geq -1$

x	y
–1	3
0	3
3	1
4	0.236
5	–0.550
8	–3

zero $4<x<5$, closer to 4 than 5 since 0.236 is closer to zero than – 0.550

$x\approx 4.3$

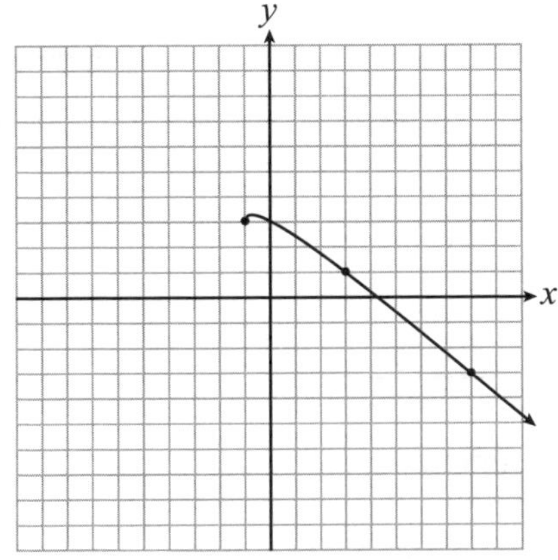

▶ *Solution:* (Algebraically)

$$\sqrt{x+1}-x+2=0$$
$$\sqrt{x+1}=x-2$$
$$\left(\sqrt{x+1}\right)^2=(x-2)^2$$
$$x+1=x^2-4x+4$$
$$x^2-5x+3=0$$
$$x=\frac{5\pm\sqrt{(-5)^2-4(1)(3)}}{2}$$
$$=\frac{5\pm\sqrt{13}}{2}=0.697, 4.303$$

Check solution:

$$\sqrt{x+1}-x+2=0$$
$$\sqrt{0.697+1}-0.697+2=0$$
$$2.606\neq 0 \quad \textit{reject}$$
$$\sqrt{4.303+1}-4.303+2=0$$
$$0=0 \quad \textit{accept}$$

Solution is $x=\frac{5+\sqrt{13}}{2}\approx 4.303$.

4.2 Exercise Set

1. Fill in the missing blanks.

a) A radical equation is an equation that has variables in a ____________ .

b) The Power Theorem states that if $x = y$, then ______________ where n is a positive integer.

c) The reason why we check the solution of radical equations is that when we raise both sides to the nth power it introduces ____________ roots.

2. Use the given graphs to solve each radical equation.

a) $\sqrt{x+6}-2=0$

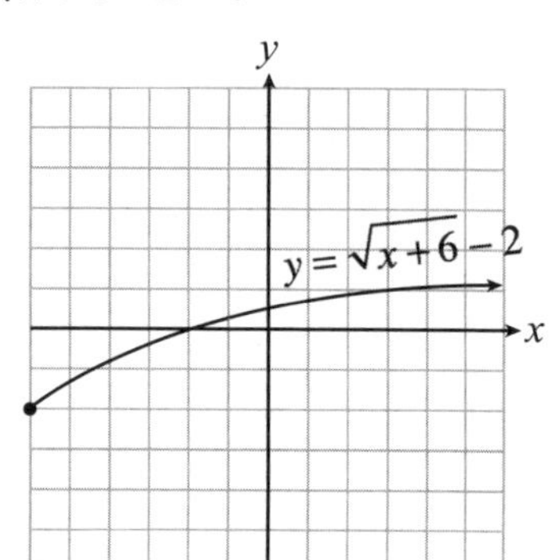

b) $\sqrt{5x-1}=3$

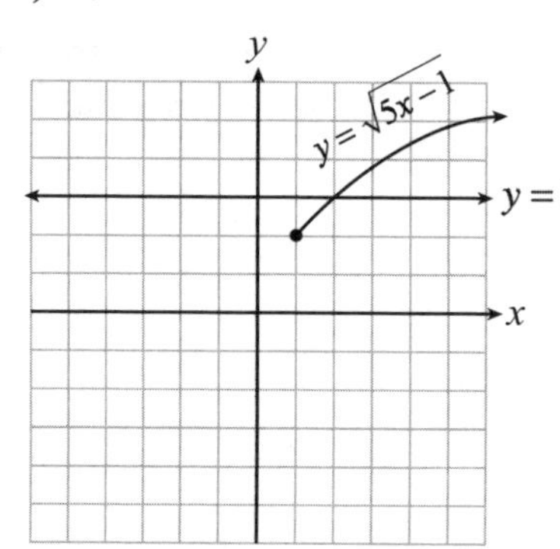

c) $\sqrt[3]{2x+3}+1=0$

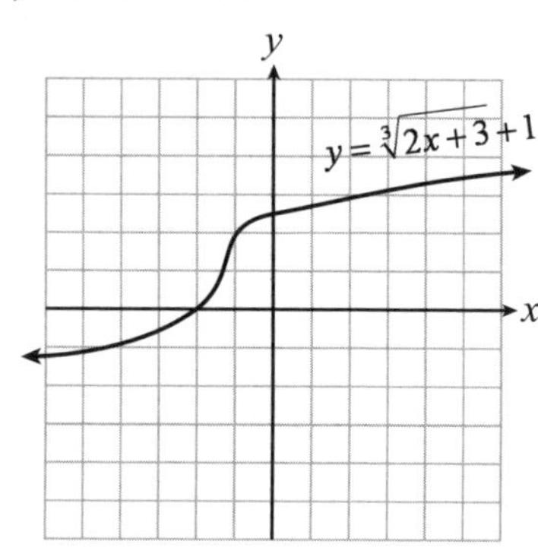

______________ ______________ ______________

3. Determine the x-intercept and y-intercept of the following functions:

a) $f(x)=\sqrt{2x}-4$

b) $f(x)=\sqrt[3]{4x}+2$

c) $f(x)=\sqrt{4x-3}-5$

d) $f(x)=\sqrt[3]{2x-1}-4$

e) $f(x)=\sqrt{2x}+4$

f) $f(x)=\sqrt{4-x}-2$

g) $f(x)=\sqrt{x^2+1}-\sqrt{17}$

h) $f(x)=\sqrt{x^2+6x}-4$

i) $f(x)=\sqrt[4]{x-1}-2$

j) $f(x)=\sqrt{x^2-5x}-6$

4. Determine the x-intercept of the following functions. Check your solutions.

a) $f(x)=\sqrt{13-x}-x+1$

b) $f(x)=\sqrt{2x-3}+x-3$

c) $f(x)=\sqrt{5-5x}+x-1$

d) $f(x)=2x-8+\sqrt{x+1}$

e) $f(x)=\sqrt{x+3}-x-3$

f) $f(x)=\sqrt{x+5}-x+1$

5. Determine between which consecutive integers the zeros of the radical functions occur; answer in form $a<x<b$..

a) $f(x)=\sqrt{x+5}-x$

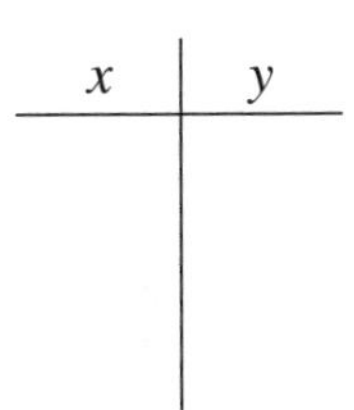

b) $f(x)=\sqrt[3]{2x+1}+2$

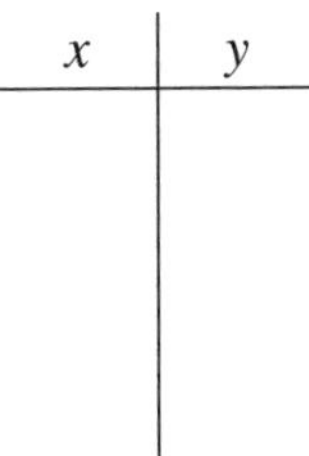

c) $f(x)=\sqrt{2x+6}-x$

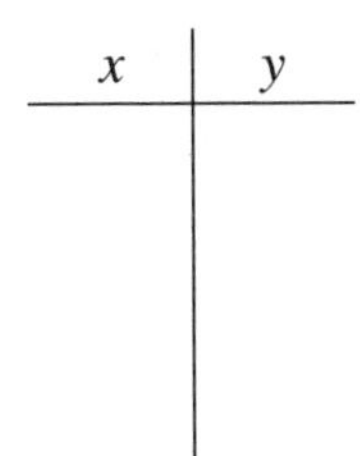

d) $f(x)=\sqrt{x+2}-2x$

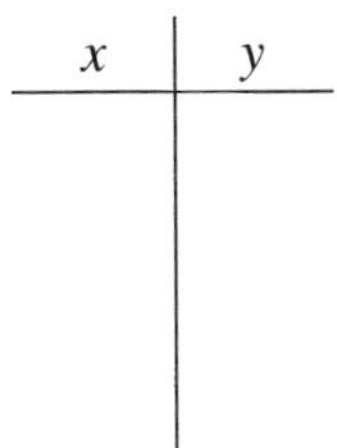

e) $f(x)=\sqrt{4-x}-x$

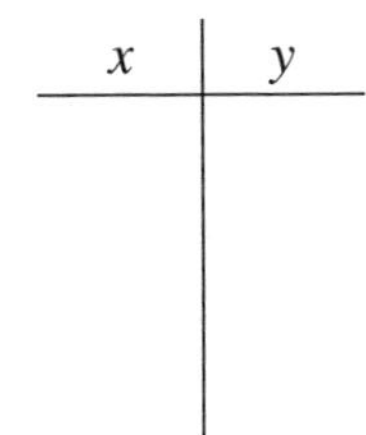

f) $f(x)=\sqrt{10-x}-x-1$

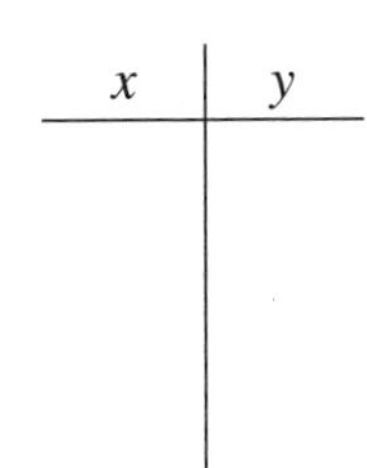

6. Solve the radical equations A) algebraically and B) graphically.

a) $f(x) = \sqrt{2x-3} - 3 = 0$

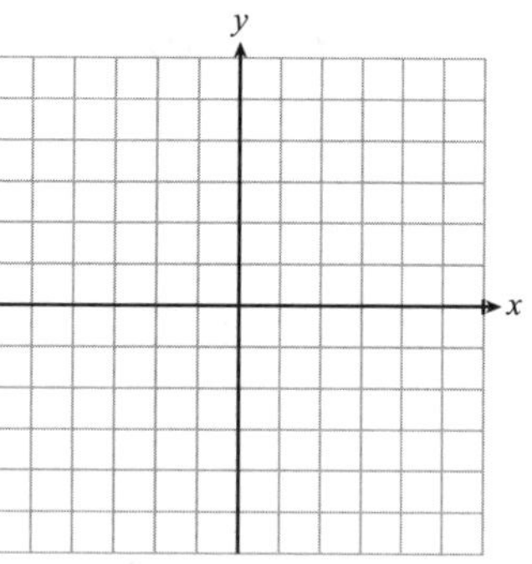

b) $f(x) = \sqrt[3]{x+4} + 1 = 0$

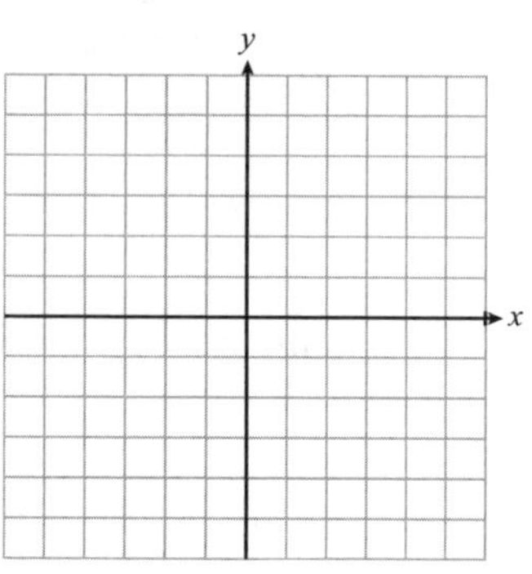

c) $f(x) = \sqrt{1-2x} + 3 = 0$

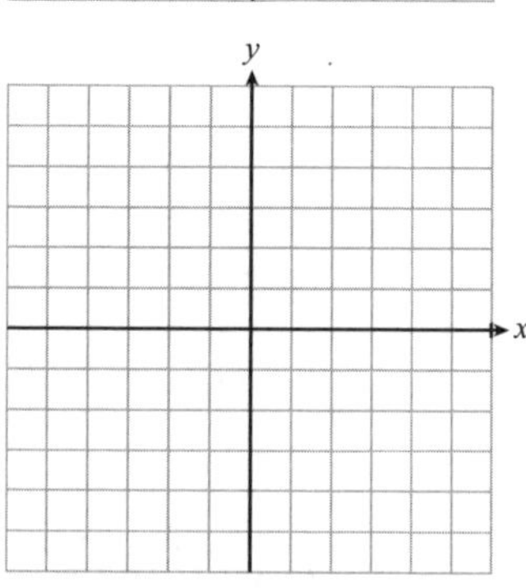

d) $f(x) = x + 8 - \sqrt{4-3x} = 0$

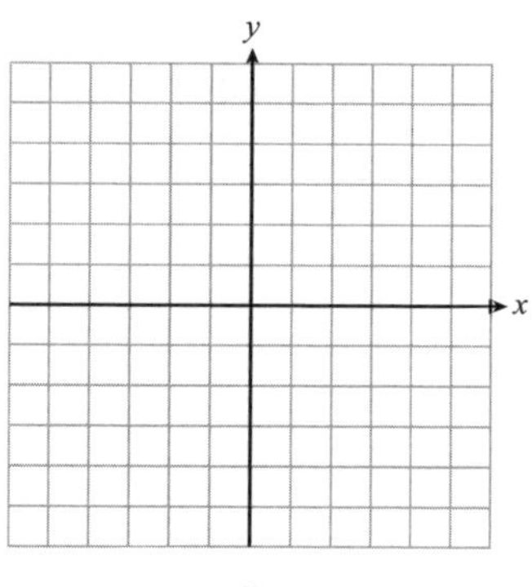

e) $f(x) = \sqrt{x+1} - x - 1 = 0$

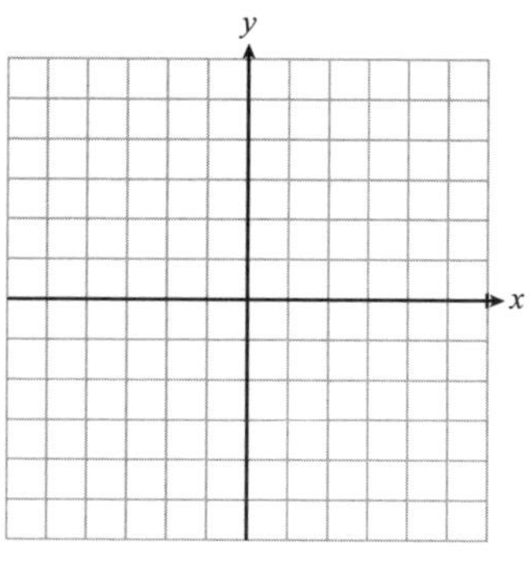

4.3 Rational Functions

A rational **expression** is the ratio of two polynomials. We use rational expressions to define rational functions. A rational function is defined as follows:

> A **Rational Function** is a function of the form:
>
> $f(x)=\dfrac{g(x)}{h(x)}$, where $g(x)$ and $h(x)$ are polynomials, and $h(x)\neq 0$

Example 1

a) $\dfrac{x+2}{x-1}$ This is a rational expression. *Just a ratio of two polynomials.*

b) $y=\dfrac{x+2}{x-1}$ This is a rational function. *Both the numerator and denominator are polynomials.*

c) $y=2x^2-3x+5$ This is a rational function. *This expression can be written* $y=\dfrac{2x^2-3x+5}{1}$. *Both the numerator and denominator are polynomials.*

d) $y=\dfrac{3x-2}{\sqrt{x+3}}$ This is **not** a rational function. *The denominator* $\sqrt{x+3}$ *is not a polynomial.*

Asymptotes

A line is an **asymptote** for a curve if the distance between the line and the curve approaches zero as we move farther and farther along the line.

> **Definition of an Asymptote**
>
> An asymptote of a graph is a vertical or horizontal line that a part of the graph gets very close to (but never reaches).

Example 2 Graph of $f(x)=\dfrac{4}{x}$

- The domain does not include 0.
- The graph is discontinuous; there is a break at $x=0$.
- The graph approaches the vertical line $x=0$ as the graph moves towards the origin.
- The graph approaches the horizontal line $y=0$ as the graph moves away from the origin.

x	$f(x)$
0	undefined
± 4	± 1
± 1	± 4
± 2	± 2
± 6	$\pm \frac{2}{3}$
$\pm \frac{2}{3}$	± 6

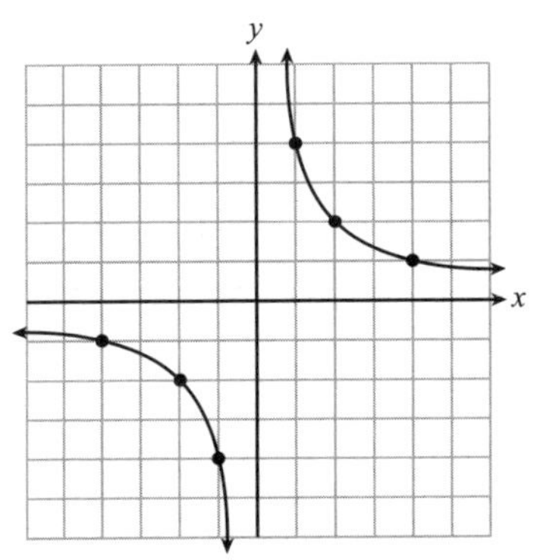

Vertical Asymptotes of Rational Functions

Since the denominator of a rational function cannot be zero, it is the zeros of the denominator which restrict the domain. Vertical asymptotes can be determined by setting the denominator equal to zero and **excluding** those values from the domain of the rational function. We define a vertical asymptote as follows:

> **Vertical Asymptotes of Rational Functions**
>
> Let $f(x)=\dfrac{g(x)}{h(x)}$ be a rational function.
>
> If c is a zero of $h(x)$, then the line $x=c$ is a vertical asymptote of the graph of $f(x)$.

Example 3 Determine the vertical asymptotes of the rational functions.

a) $f(x)=\dfrac{x}{x^2-9}$ **b)** $g(x)=\dfrac{2x+3}{x^3-4x}$

▶ *Solution:*

a) $f(x)=\dfrac{x}{x^2-9}$;

$$x^2-9=0$$
$$(x-3)(x+3)=0$$
$$x=-3,3$$

Vertical asymptotes are $x=-3$ and $x=3$.

b) $g(x)=\dfrac{2x+3}{x^3-4x}$;

$$x^3-4x=0$$
$$x(x-2)(x+2)=0$$
$$x=-2,0,2$$

Vertical asymptotes are $x=-2$, $x=0$, and $x=2$.

Horizontal Asymptotes of Rational Functions

We can examine the end behaviour as $|x|$ becomes very large; as $x\to\infty$ or as $x\to-\infty$. This end behaviour is a **horizontal asymptote**. The following gives the necessary conditions for a rational function to have a horizontal asymptote:

> **Horizontal Asymptote of Rational Functions**
>
> Consider the rational function $f(x)=\dfrac{g(x)}{h(x)}=\dfrac{a_mx^m+\cdots+a_1x+a_0}{b_nx^n+\cdots+b_1x+b_0}$ with $a_m\neq0,\ \ b_n\neq0$
>
> 1. If $m<n$, the line $y=0$ (the x axis) is a horizontal asymptote.
> 2. If $m=n$, the line $y=\dfrac{a_m}{b_n}$ (ratio of leading coefficients) is a horizontal asymptote.
> 3. If $m>n$, there is no horizontal asymptote.

Example 4 Determine, if possible, the horizontal asymptotes of the rational functions:

a) $f(x)=\dfrac{2x}{3x-1}$ **b)** $g(x)=\dfrac{1-2x}{x^2-4x+3}$ **c)** $h(x)=\dfrac{2x^2-3x+1}{x+4}$

▶ *Solution:* **a)** $f(x)=\dfrac{2x}{3x-1}$, divide each term by the highest power of the **denominator**.

$$=\frac{\frac{2x}{x}}{\frac{3x-1}{x}}=\frac{2}{3-\frac{1}{x}}, \text{ as } |x|\to\infty, \frac{2}{3-\frac{1}{\infty}}=\frac{2}{3-0}=\frac{2}{3} \quad \left(\text{Note: } \frac{1}{\infty}=0\right)$$

or leading coefficient of $2x$ is 2, leading coefficient of $3x-1$ is 3, thus horizontal asymptote is $f(x)=\dfrac{2}{3}$.

b) $g(x)=\dfrac{1-2x}{x^2-4x+3}$, divide each term by the highest power of the **denominator**.

$$=\frac{\frac{1}{x^2}-\frac{2x}{x^2}}{\frac{x^2}{x^2}-\frac{4x}{x^2}+\frac{3}{x^2}}=\frac{\frac{1}{x^2}-\frac{2}{x}}{1-\frac{4}{x}+\frac{3}{x^2}}, \text{ as } |x|\to\infty, \frac{\frac{1}{\infty^2}-\frac{2}{\infty}}{1-\frac{4}{\infty}+\frac{3}{\infty^2}}=\frac{0-0}{1-0+0}=\frac{0}{1}=0$$

or if power of numerator < than power of denominator; horizontal asymptote is $f(x)=0$.

c) $h(x)=\dfrac{2x^2-3x+1}{x+4}$, divide each term by the highest power of the **denominator**.

$$=\frac{\frac{2x^2}{x}-\frac{3x}{x}+\frac{1}{x}}{\frac{x}{x}+\frac{4}{x}}=\frac{2x-3+\frac{1}{x}}{1+\frac{4}{x}}, \text{ as } |x|\to\infty, \frac{2(\infty)-3+\frac{1}{\infty}}{1+\frac{4}{\infty}}$$

$$=\frac{\text{infinte number}-3+0}{1+0}=\text{infinite number}$$

or power of numerator > than power of denominator; no horizontal asymptote. Thus, $h(x)$ has no horizontal asymptote.

x-intercept(s) and y-intercept(s) of Rational Functions

To graph a rational function, determining the x- and y-intercepts is very helpful.

Example 5 Determine the x- and y-intercepts of the rational functions:

a) $f(x)=\dfrac{x^2-7x+12}{x^2-4}$ **b)** $g(x)=\dfrac{x^4-1}{x^4+x}$ **c)** $h(x)=\dfrac{x^2-9}{x^2-x-2}$ **d)** $k(x)=\dfrac{1}{x+1}-\dfrac{1}{x-1}+2$

▶ *Solution:*

a) $f(x)=\dfrac{x^2-7x+12}{x^2-4}$;

Let $x=0$, $\dfrac{0^2-7(0)+12}{0^2-4}=-3$, y-intercept is $(0,-3)$

Let $f(x)=0$, $\dfrac{x^2-7x+12}{x^2-4}=0$

$$x^2-7x+12=0$$

$$(x-3)(x-4)=0$$

$x=3, 4$, x-intercepts are $(3,0), (4,0)$

b) $g(x)=\dfrac{x^4-1}{x^4+x}$;

Let $x=0$, $\dfrac{0^4-1}{0^4+0}=$ undefined, no y-intercept

Let $g(x)=0$, $\dfrac{x^4-1}{x^2+x}=0$

$$x^4-1=0$$

$$(x-1)(x+1)(x^2+1)=0$$

$x=1,-1$, x-intercepts are $(-1,0), (1,0)$

c) $h(x)=\dfrac{x^2-9}{x^2-x-2}$;

Let $x=0$, $\dfrac{0^2-9}{0^2-0-2}=\dfrac{9}{2}$, y-intercept is $\left(0,\dfrac{9}{2}\right)$

Let $h(x)=0$, $\dfrac{x^2-9}{x^2-x-2}=0$

$$x^2-9=0$$

$$(x-3)(x+3)=0$$

$x=-3, 3$, x-intercepts are $(-3,0), (3,0)$

d) $k(x)=\dfrac{1}{x+1}-\dfrac{1}{x-1}+2$ LCM: $(x-1)(x+1)$

$$=\frac{(x-1)-(x+1)+2(x+1)(x-1)}{(x+1)(x-1)}=\frac{2x^2-4}{(x-1)(x+1)}$$

Let $x=0$, $\dfrac{2(0^2)-4}{(0-1)(0+1)}=4$, y-intercept is $(0,4)$

Let $k(x)=0$, $\dfrac{2x^2-4}{(x-1)(x+1)}=0$

$$2x^2-4=0$$

$$x^2=2$$

$x=\pm\sqrt{2}$, x-intercepts are $(-\sqrt{2},0), (\sqrt{2},0)$

Holes in Rational Functions

Sometimes a rational function simplifies to a different function and eliminates one or more of the vertical asymptotes.

Example 6

At first glance, $f(x)=\dfrac{x+2}{x^2+x-2}$ appears to have vertical asymptotes at

$$x^2+x-2=0$$
$$(x-1)(x+2)=0$$
$$x=1,-2$$

But when the whole function is considered in the factorization

$$f(x)=\frac{\cancel{x+2}}{\cancel{(x+2)}(x-1)} \text{ reduces to } f(x)=\frac{1}{x-1}$$

There is only one vertical asymptote when $x-1=0$, at $x=1$. However, $x=-2$ is also not allowed in the original function since it makes the denominator 0.

When $x=-2$ in $f(x)=\dfrac{1}{x-1}$, $f(x)=\dfrac{1}{-2-1}=-\dfrac{1}{3}$.

So the point $(-2,-\frac{1}{3})$ is not allowed in the new function. This creates a hole in the graph.

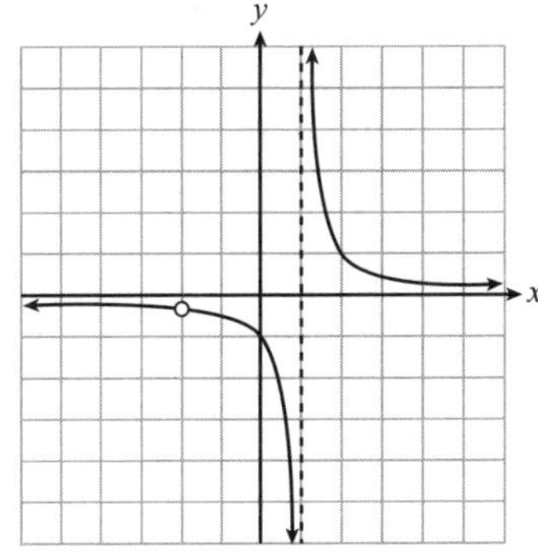

Example 7

Determine the vertical asymptotes and holes of the rational functions:

a) $f(x)=\dfrac{x-3}{x^2-x-6}$ **b)** $g(x)=\dfrac{x^2+2x-8}{x+4}$ **c)** $h(x)=\dfrac{x^2-4}{x^3-4x}$

▶ *Solution:*

a) $f(x)=\dfrac{x-3}{x^2-x-6}$;

$$f(x)=\frac{x-3}{(x-3)(x+2)}=\frac{1}{x+2}$$

Vertical asymptote is $x=-2$. Also, the point $\left(3,\dfrac{1}{5}\right)$ must be excluded since $x=3$ makes the denominator of the original rational function equal to zero.

b) $g(x)=\dfrac{x^2+2x-8}{x+4}$;

$$g(x)=\frac{(x+4)(x-2)}{x+4}=x-2$$

No vertical asymptote. This is a linear equation with the point $(-4,-6)$ omitted.

c) $h(x)=\dfrac{x^2-4}{x^3-4x}$;

$$h(x)=\frac{(x-2)(x+2)}{x(x-2)(x+2)}=\frac{1}{x}$$

Vertical asymptote is $x=0$. Also, the points $\left(-2,-\dfrac{1}{2}\right)$ and $\left(2,\dfrac{1}{2}\right)$ must be excluded.

4.3 Exercise Set

1. Fill in the missing blanks.

a) A rational expression is defined as the ______________________ of two polynomial with the ______________________ not equal to zero.

b) A function defined by $f(x)=\dfrac{g(x)}{h(x)}$, with $g(x)$ and $h(x)$ ______________________ functions and $h(x)\neq 0$, is called a ______________________ function.

c) To determine the excluded values of the domain of a rational function, we find the values for which the ______________________ is equal to __________ .

d) A vertical line that a graph approaches but never touches is called a __________ __________ .

e) A horizontal line that a graph approaches as $|x|\to\infty$ is called a __________ __________ .

f) The graph of a rational function $f(x)=\dfrac{3}{x-2}$ will have a vertical asymptote of ______________ and a horizontal asymptote of ______________ .

2. Find the domain, the x- and y-intercepts, and any holes for each rational function.

a) $y=\dfrac{3x-9}{4x+12}$

b) $y=\dfrac{(x+6)(x+3)}{(x-2)^2}$

c) $y=\dfrac{x^2-8x-9}{x^2-x-6}$

d) $y=\dfrac{(x^2-1)(x+1)}{x^3}$

e) $y=\dfrac{x+2}{x^2+4}$

f) $y=\dfrac{-3x^2+12}{x^2-9}$

g) $y=\dfrac{4}{(x+4)^2}$

h) $y=\dfrac{-x^2+9}{-2x^2+8}$

i) $y=\dfrac{2+x}{x^2+4}$

j) $y=\dfrac{x^2-3x-4}{4+3x-x^2}$

3. The graph of each function is a variation of the graph $f(x)=\frac{1}{x^n}$. In each case, find the horizontal and vertical asymptotes and the x- and y-intercepts.

a) $g(x)=-\frac{4}{x}$

b) $h(x)=-\frac{3}{x^2}$

c) $i(x)=1+\frac{1}{x}$

d) $j(x)=2-\frac{1}{x}$

e) $k(x)=\frac{1}{x^2}-4$

f) $l(x)=-1-\frac{1}{x^2}$

g) $m(x)=-\frac{1}{x+1}$

h) $n(x)=-\frac{2}{(x+1)^2}$

i) $p(x)=\frac{2}{x-1}+3$

j) $q(x)=-\frac{2}{(x+1)^2}+1$

4. What are the vertical and horizontal asymptotes, and any holes in the graph, of the following rational functions?

a) $f(x)=\dfrac{1}{x}$

b) $f(x)=\dfrac{2x}{x+3}$

c) $f(x)=\dfrac{1}{x^2-7x+12}$

d) $g(x)=\dfrac{x^2}{x^2-9}$

e) $h(x)=\dfrac{x}{x^2+1}$

f) $k(x)=\dfrac{x^3}{x^2-x-20}$

g) $p(x)=\dfrac{x^2+3x-1}{4-x^2}$

h) $m(x)=\dfrac{2x^3-18x}{x^3-3x^2-4x}$

i) $n(x)=\dfrac{x^2-4}{2x^3+7x^2-4x}$

j) $t(x)=\dfrac{9-6x}{4x^2-9}$

k) $r(x)=\dfrac{16x-x^3}{2x^3+7x^2-4x}$

l) $s(x)=1-\dfrac{3}{x^2-1}$

4.4 Graphing Rational Functions

The steps in graphing a rational functions are as follows:

Graphing Rational Functions $f(x)=\dfrac{g(x)}{h(x)}, \quad g(x)\neq 0, \quad h(x)\neq 0$

Step 1. Find any vertical asymptote by equating the denominator to 0.

Step 2. Find any horizontal asymptote by dividing all terms by the highest power of x, then assume $\dfrac{1}{\text{infinitely large number}}=0 \quad \left(\dfrac{1}{\infty}=0\right)$.

Step 3. Find x- and y-intercepts, if possible, and holes, if they exist.

Step 4. Make a table of values:

a) Find y-intercept by letting $x = 0$.

b) Choose x values close to vertical asymptotes, and one large positive and negative value of x.

Step 5. Draw a smooth curve through the points.

Example 1 Let $f(x)=\dfrac{2}{x-1}$ **a)** Determine horizontal/vertical asymptotes and **b)** fill in the table.

x	.9	1.1	100	−100	−1	0	2	3
$f(x)$								

c) $f(x)$ $x\to-\infty$ (use large negative numeral); $x\to\infty$ (use large positive numeral)
$x\to1^-$ (left side of 1 but very close); $x\to1^+$ (right side of 1 but very close)

d) Find the x- and y-intercepts, if possible, and **e)** Sketch the graph.

▶ *Solution:* **a)** Horizontal asymptote of $f(x)=\dfrac{2}{x-1}$ is by definition $f(x)=0$

Vertical asymptote of $f(x)=\dfrac{2}{x-1}$ is $x-1=0, x=1$

b)

x	.9	1.1	100	−100	−1	0	2	3
$f(x)$	**−20**	**20**	**.020**	**−.0198**	**−1**	**−2**	**2**	**1**

c) As $x\to-\infty, f(x)\to0^-$ (just less than zero); $x\to\infty, f(x)\to0^+$ (just more than zero)
$x\to1^-, f(x)\to-\infty$ (just less than one); $x\to\infty, f(x)\to1^+$ (just more than one)

d) x-intercept $f(x)=\dfrac{2}{x-1}$, let $f(x)=0$, $\dfrac{2}{x-1}=0$ is undefined; no x-intercept.

y-intercept $f(x)=\dfrac{2}{x-1}$, let $x=0$, $f(0)=\dfrac{2}{0-1}=-2$, $(0,-2)$.

e) Draw asymptotes, plot points and x-intercept. Draw smooth curves.

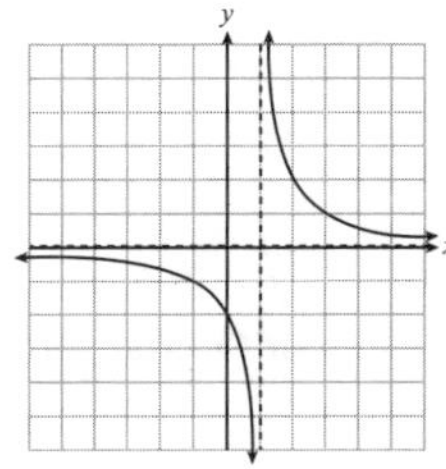

Example 2 Let $f(x)=\dfrac{x^2+x-2}{2+x-x^2}$

a) Determine the vertical and horizontal asymptotes.

b) Fill in the table.

x	−1.01	−.99	1.99	2.01	−1000	1000
$f(x)$						

c) Find the x- and y-intercepts, and holes, if possible.

d) Sketch the graph.

▶ *Solution:*

a) Vertical asymptote: $2+x-x^2=0,\ (2-x)(1+x)=0 \qquad x=-1,2$

Horizontal asymptote:

$$f(x)=\frac{x^2+x-2}{2+x-x^2}=\frac{\frac{x^2}{x^2}+\frac{x}{x^2}-\frac{2}{x^2}}{\frac{2}{x^2}+\frac{x}{x^2}-\frac{x^2}{x^2}}=\frac{1+\frac{1}{x}-\frac{2}{x^2}}{\frac{2}{x^2}+\frac{1}{x}-1}=\frac{1+\frac{1}{\infty}-\frac{2}{\infty^2}}{\frac{2}{\infty^2}+\frac{1}{\infty}-1}=\frac{1+0-0}{0+0-1}=-1$$

thus $f(x)=-1$

or highest power of numerator and denominator are the same.

Coefficients of highest powers are $\dfrac{1}{-1}=-1$, thus $f(x)=-1$.

b)

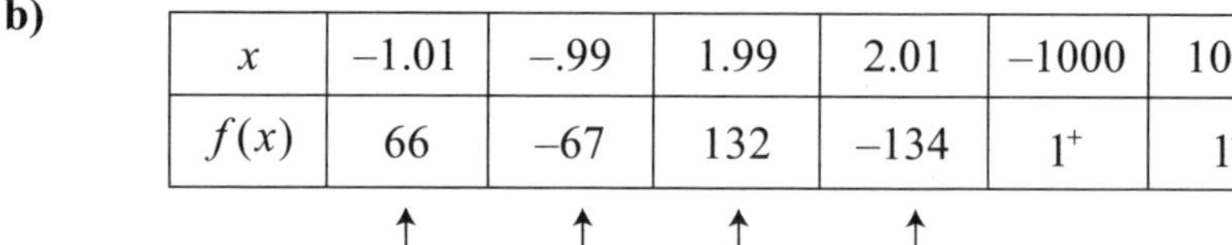

x	−1.01	−.99	1.99	2.01	−1000	1000
$f(x)$	66	−67	132	−134	1^+	1^-

large positive number

large negative number

c) $f(x)=\dfrac{x^2+x-2}{2+x-x^2}$, x-intercept let $f(x)=0$

$$\frac{x^2+x-2}{2+x-x^2}=0,\ x^2+x-2=0$$

$$(x+2)(x-1)=0$$

$$x=-2,1\ \ (-2,0),(1,0)$$

$f(x)=\dfrac{x^2+x-2}{2+x-x^2}$, y-intercept let $x=0$ $\quad f(0)=\dfrac{0^2+0-2}{2+0-0^2}=-1,\ (0,-1)$

d) Draw asymptotes, plot intercepts and points.
Draw smooth curve.

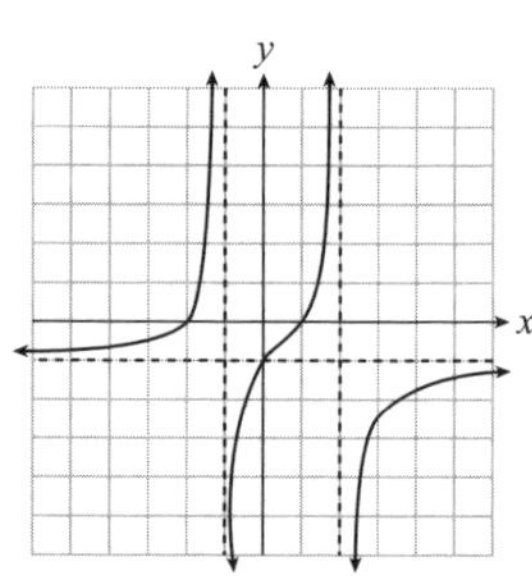

Note: The graph crossed the horizontal asymptote of (0, −1). Horizontal asymptotes are accurate when x is very large, away from the origin, not close to the origin.

Example 3 Find the vertical and horizontal asymptotes of the following, then graph the equation.

a) $f(x)=\dfrac{1}{x-1}$

▶ *Solution:*

Vertical asymptote: $x-1=0,\ x=1$

Horizontal asymptote: $y=0$

(denominator higher power than numerator)

Plot points:

x	0	0.9	1.1	– 10	10
$f(x)$	– 1	– 10	10	– 0.1	0.1

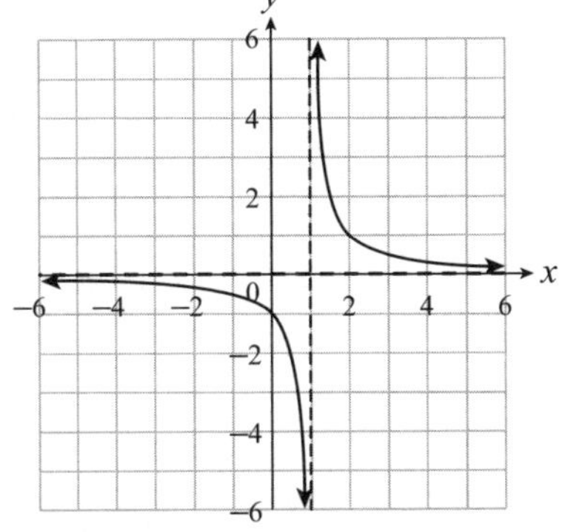

b) $g(x)=\dfrac{2x}{x-1}$

▶ *Solution:*

Vertical asymptote: $x-1=0$, $x=1$

Horizontal asymptote:

$$y=\frac{2x}{x-1}=\frac{\frac{2x}{x}}{\frac{x}{x}-\frac{1}{x}}=\frac{2}{1-\frac{1}{x}}=\frac{2}{1-\frac{1}{\infty}}=\frac{2}{1-0}=2$$

or highest power of numerator and denominator are the same.

Coefficients of highest powers are $\dfrac{2}{1}=2$, thus $f(x)=2$.

Plot points:

x	0	0.9	1.1	– 50	50
$f(x)$	0	– 18	22	1.96	2 .04

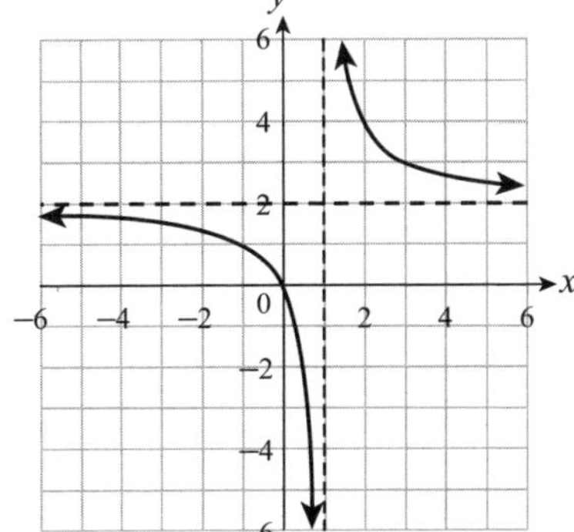

c) $h(x)=\dfrac{2x^2}{x^2+1}$

▶ *Solution:*

Vertical asymptote: $x^2+1=0$, $x^2=-1$, $x=\varnothing$,
no vertical asymptote

Horizontal asymptote:

$$y=\frac{2x^2}{x^2+1}=\frac{\frac{2x^2}{x^2}}{\frac{x^2}{x^2}+\frac{1}{x^2}}=\frac{2}{1+\frac{1}{x^2}}=\frac{2}{1+\frac{1}{\infty^2}}=\frac{2}{1+0}=2$$

or highest power of numerator and denominator are the same.

Coefficients of highest powers are $\dfrac{2}{1}=2$, thus $f(x)=2$.

Plot points:

x	0	– 1	1	5	– 5	– 100	100
$f(x)$	0	1	1	1.9	1.9	2^-	2^-

Note: 2^- means just less than 2.

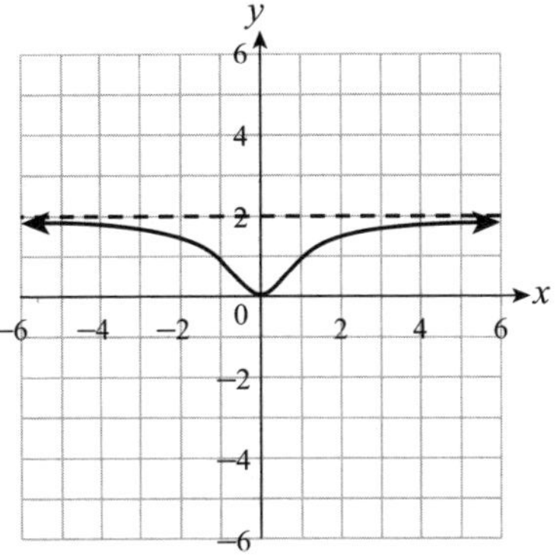

d) $k(x)=\dfrac{2}{x^2-x-2}$

▶ *Solution:* $k(x)=\dfrac{2}{(x-2)(x+1)}$

Vertical asymptotes: $x-2=0$, $x=2$, $x+1=0$, $x=-1$

Horizontal asymptote: $y=0$

Plot points:

x	0	– 0.9	– 1.1	1.9	2.1	– 10	10
$f(x)$	– 1	– 6.9	6.5	– 6.9	6.5	.02	.02

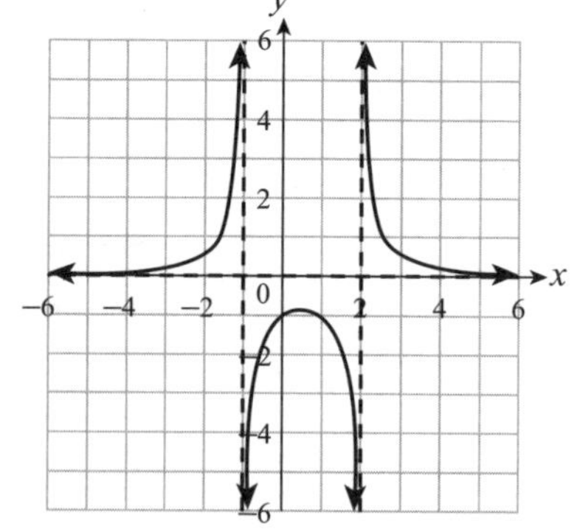

Example 4 Graph the following rational function: $f(x)=\dfrac{x^2-4}{x^2-x-2}$

▶ *Solution:* $f(x)=\dfrac{x^2-4}{x^2-x-2}=\dfrac{(x-2)(x+2)}{(x-2)(x+1)}=\dfrac{x+2}{x+1}$

Vertical asymptotes: $x+1=0$

$x=-1$

Horizontal asymptotes: $f(x)=\dfrac{x+2}{x+1}=\dfrac{\frac{x}{2}+\frac{2}{x}}{\frac{x}{x}+\frac{1}{x}}=\dfrac{1+\frac{2}{x}}{1+\frac{1}{x}}=\dfrac{1+\frac{1}{\infty}}{1+\frac{1}{\infty}}=\dfrac{1+0}{1+0}=1$

or highest power of numerator and denominator are the same coefficients

coefficients of highest powers are $\dfrac{1}{1}=1$, thus $f(x)=1$.

Hole: $f(x)=\dfrac{x+2}{x+1}$, $f(2)=\dfrac{2+2}{2+1}=\dfrac{4}{3}$, $\left(2,\dfrac{4}{3}\right)$

x-intercept: $f(x)=\dfrac{x+2}{x+1}=0$

$x+2=0$

$x=-2$, $(-2,0)$

y-intercept: $f(x)=\dfrac{x+2}{x+1}$

$f(0)=\dfrac{0+2}{0+1}=2$, $(0,2)$

Plot points and Graph:

x	–1.1	–0.9	–100	100
$f(x)$	–9	11	1^-	1^+

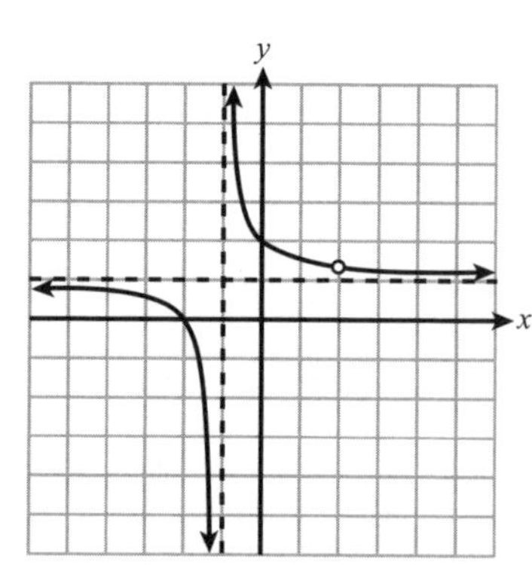

Find Zeros of Rational Functions

Recall a zero, root, and solution of an equation is where the graph crosses the x-axis. In example 1 of this section, we did not have an x-intercept, thus the solution over the real numbers was the empty set. In example 2 of this section, the x-intercept was (1, 0) and (–2 0), thus the solution of this rational equation was $x = 1, -2$. Thus, to find a solution to a rational equation, we set the equation equal to zero, and solve for x.

Example 5 Find the solution to the following rational equations by graphing the function.

a) $f(x) = \dfrac{x^2 - 9}{x^2 - x - 2}$ **b)** $g(x) = \dfrac{1}{x+1} - \dfrac{1}{x-1} + 2$

▶ *Solution:* **a)** Asymptotes are: $x^2 - x - 2 = 0$

$$(x-2)(x+1) = 0$$

$$x = -1, 2, \text{ and } y = 1$$

x-intercepts are: $x^2 - 9 = 0,\ x = \pm 3$

Plot asymptotes and points, then graph.

Therefore, $x = -3,\ 3$ are solutions of the rational function.

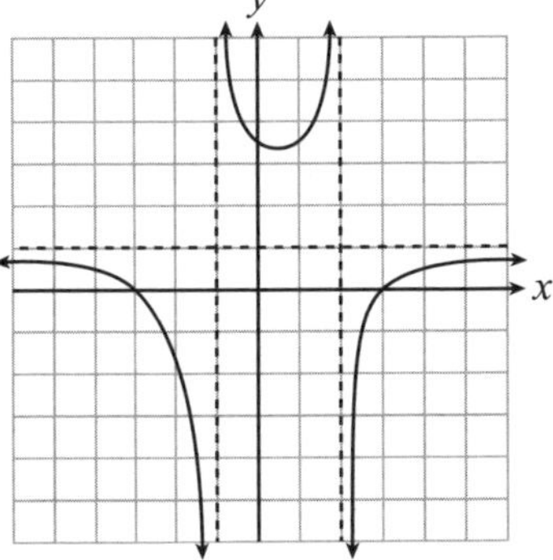

b) $g(x) = \dfrac{1}{x+1} - \dfrac{1}{x-1} + 2$ LCM: $(x-1)(x+1)$

$$= \frac{(x-1) - (x+1) + 2(x+1)(x-1)}{(x+1)(x-1)} = \frac{2x^2 - 4}{(x-1)(x+1)}$$

Asymptotes are: $x = -1, 1,$ and $y = 2$

x-intercepts are: $2x^2 - 4 = 0$

$$x = -\sqrt{2}, \sqrt{2}$$

Plot asymptotes and points, then graph.

Therefore, $x = -1.4$ and 1.4 are solutions of the rational equation.

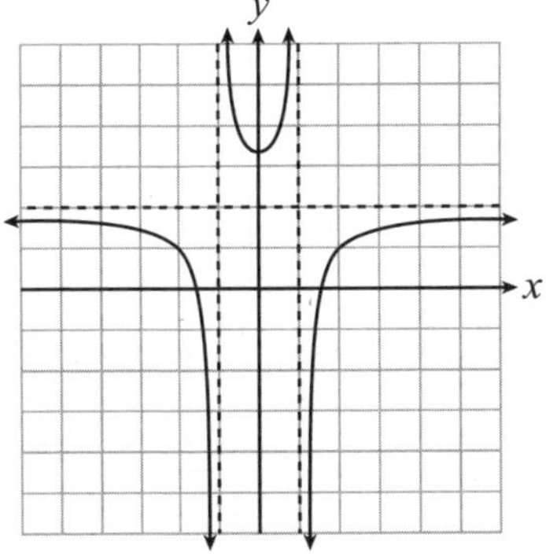

4.4 Exercise Set

1. For the graph of the following functions, find the domain, the vertical and horizontal asymptotes (if any), and approximate the x- and y-intercepts (if any).

a) $y=\dfrac{2x+4}{x-1}$

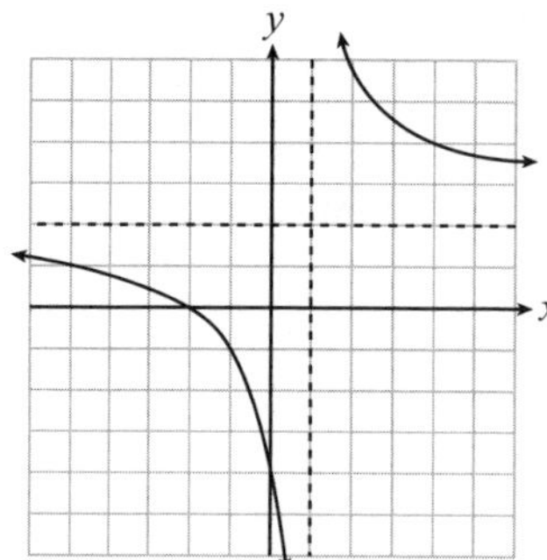

b) $y=\dfrac{4}{x^2-4}$

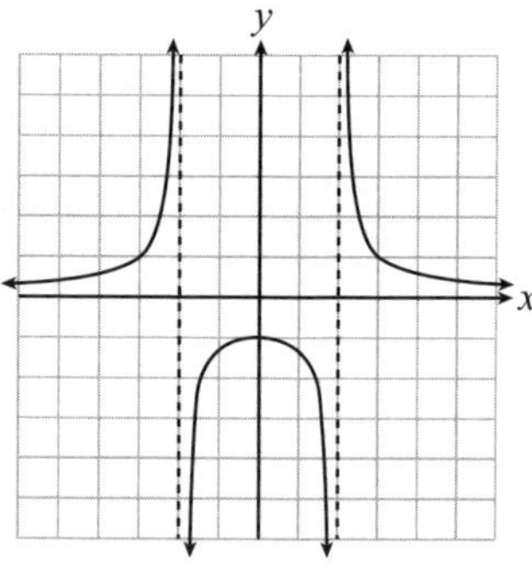

c) $y=\dfrac{x^2-x-2}{x^2+2x-3}$

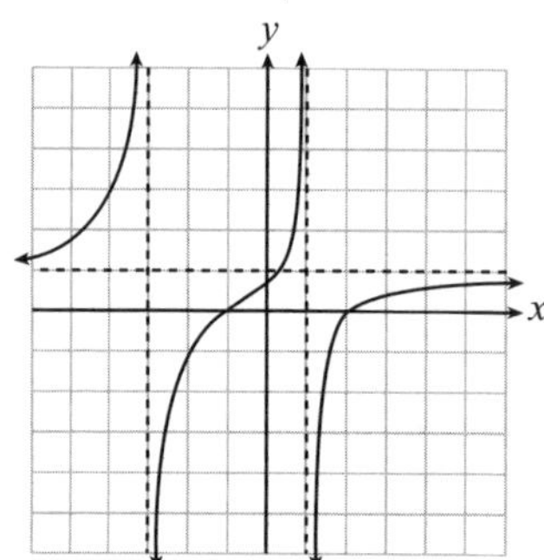

d) $y=\dfrac{3x^2}{x^2+1}$

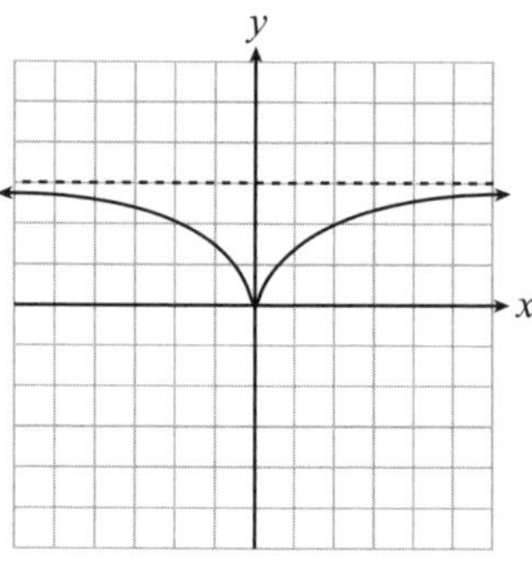

e) $y=\dfrac{1-x}{x^2-x-6}$

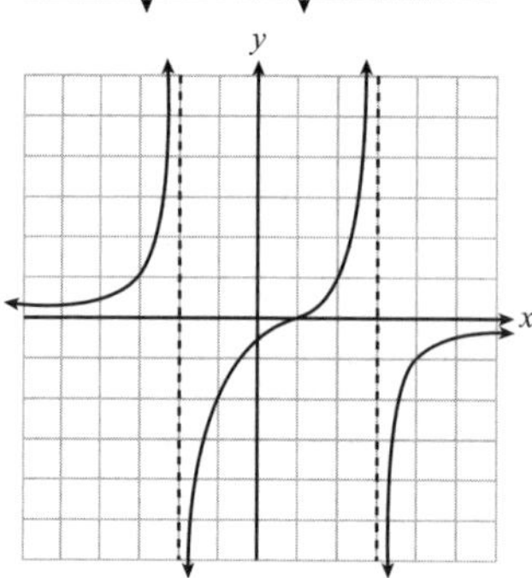

f) $y=\dfrac{x}{x^2-9}+2$

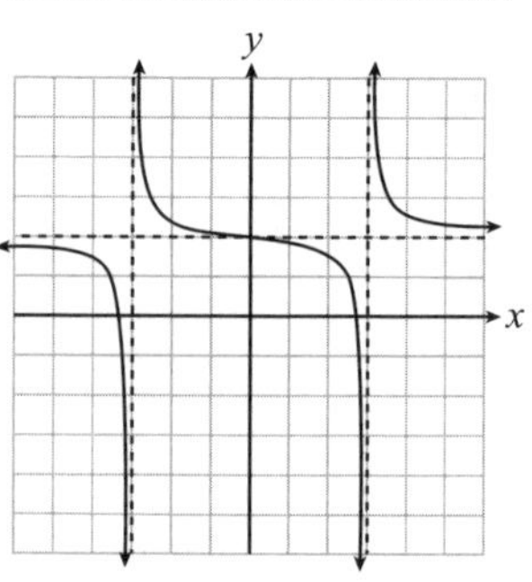

2. Each of the following functions has a "hole" in its graph. Sketch the graph, and show where the hole appears.

a) $f(x)=\dfrac{x^2-4}{x-2}$

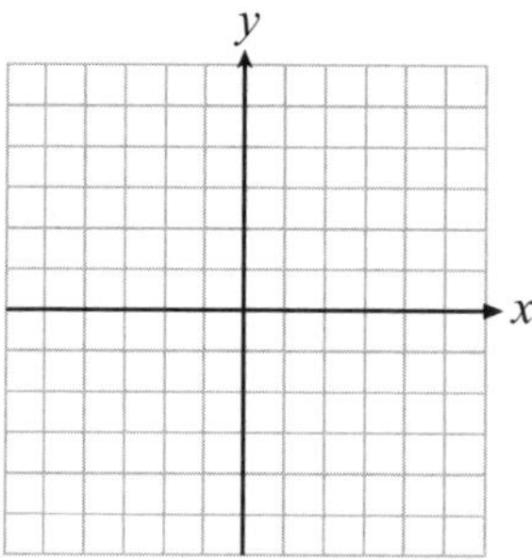

b) $f(x)=\dfrac{x^2-1}{x+1}$

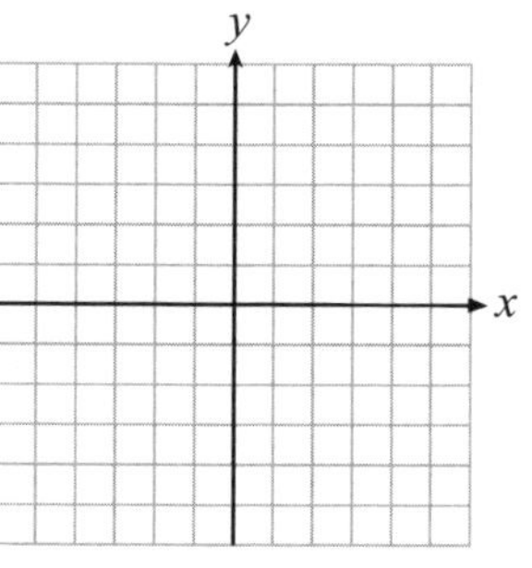

c) $f(x)=\dfrac{x^2-9}{3-x}$

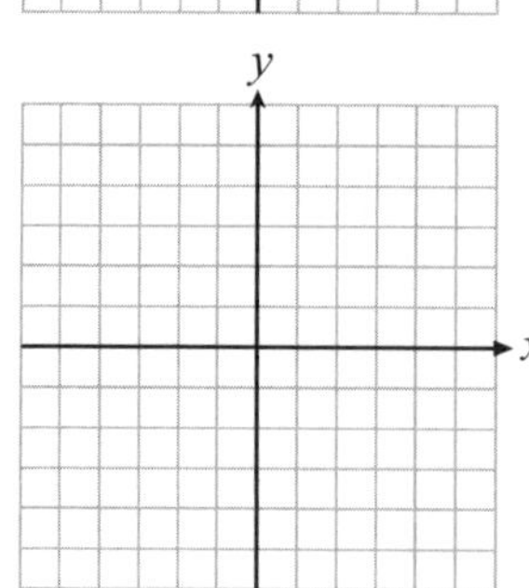

d) $f(x)=\dfrac{4-x^2}{x+2}$

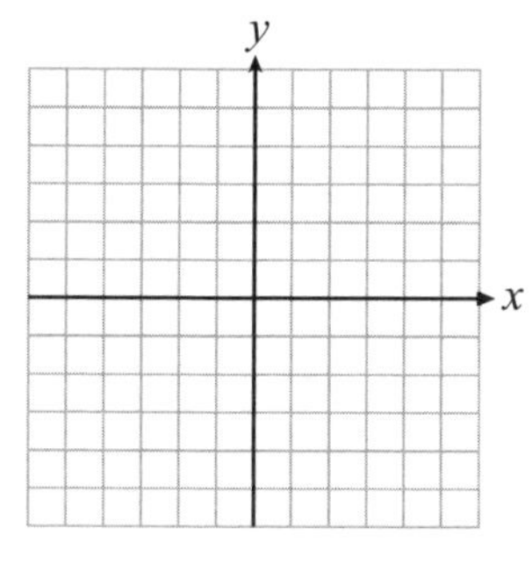

3. For each function, fill in the given table and answer the following:

- What do you observe about the value of $f(x)$ as x approaches the vertical asymptote from the right? From the left?
- What happens to the value of $f(x)$ as x gets very large and positive? Very large and negative?

a) $f(x)=\dfrac{3}{x-1}$

x	0.5	1.5	0.9	1.1	0.99	1.01
$f(x)$						

x	10	100	1000	–10	–100	–1000
$f(x)$						

b) $f(x)=\dfrac{3x^2-1}{x^2}$

x	–0.5	0.5	–0.1	0.1	–0.01	0.01
$f(x)$						

x	10	100	1000	–10	–100	–1000
$f(x)$						

c) $f(x)=\dfrac{x}{x-2}$

x	1.5	2.5	1.9	2.1	1.99	2.01
$f(x)$						

x	10	100	1000	–10	–100	–1000
$f(x)$						

4. Find the zeros (if any) of the rational functions.

a) $f(x)=\dfrac{x^2-4}{x+2}$

b) $g(x)=1-\dfrac{3}{x^2+2}$

c) $h(x)=1-\dfrac{3}{x-3}$

d) $i(x)=-1+\dfrac{4}{x^2+1}$

e) $j(x)=1+\dfrac{4}{x^2+1}$

f) $k(x)=\dfrac{x^3+8}{x^2+4}$

5. Match the rational function with its graph. Do not use a graphing calculator.

a) $f(x)=\dfrac{1}{x-1}$ ______

b) $f(x)=\dfrac{x}{x-1}$ ______

c) $f(x)=\dfrac{-2}{x-1}$ ______

d) $f(x)=\dfrac{1}{x^2}$ ______

e) $f(x)=\dfrac{-x^2}{x^2-1}$ ______

f) $f(x)=\dfrac{x^2}{x^2-1}$ ______

g) $f(x)=\dfrac{x-3}{x-1}$ ______

h) $f(x)=\dfrac{4}{x^2+1}$ ______

i) $f(x)=\dfrac{x}{x^2-4}$ ______

j) $f(x)=\dfrac{x^2-2x}{x^2+2x+1}$ ______

A

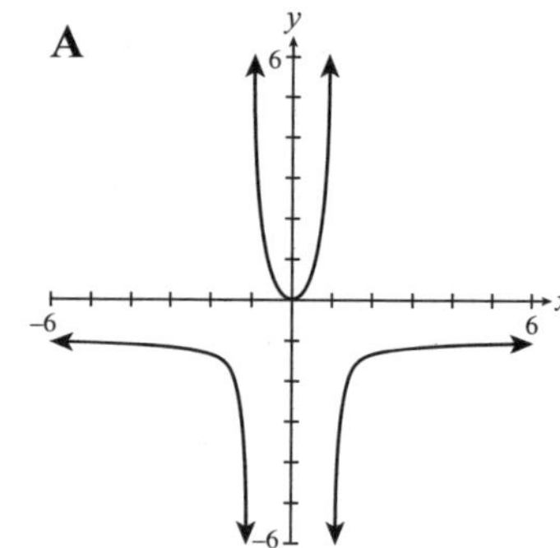

B

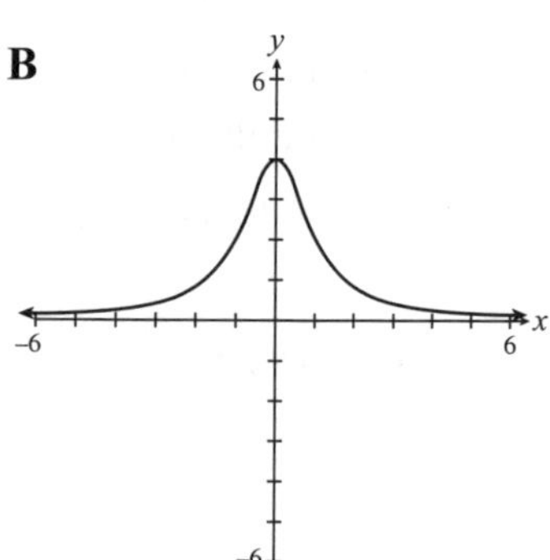

C

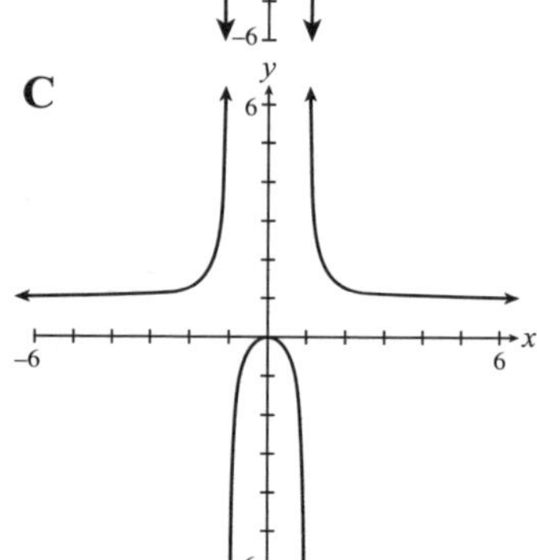

D

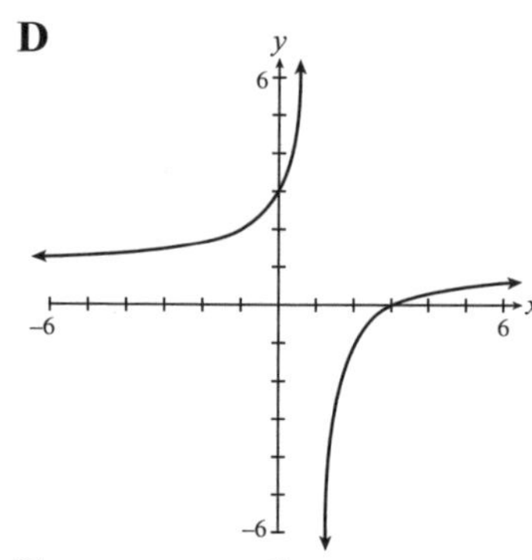

E

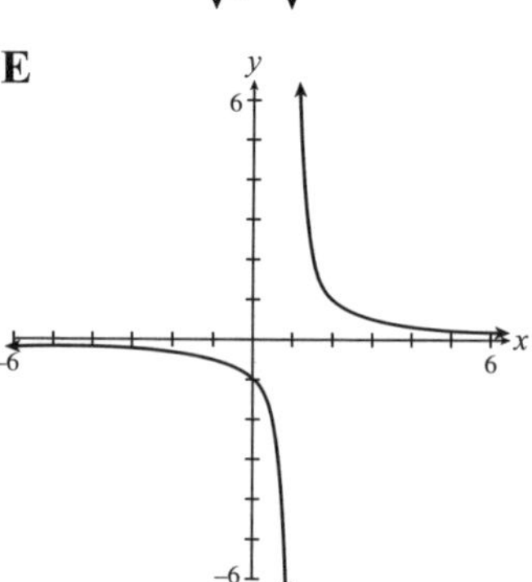

F

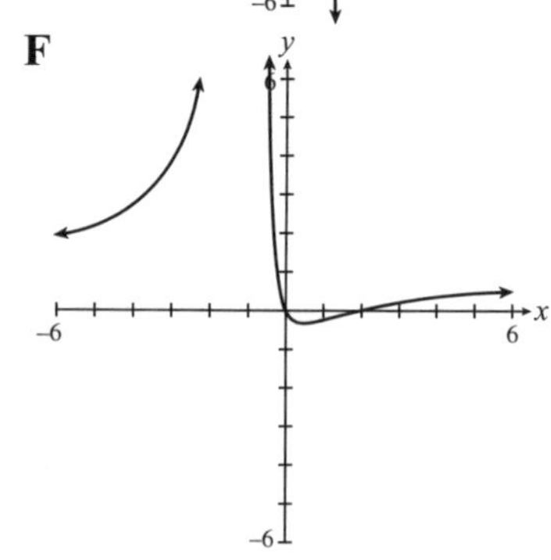

G

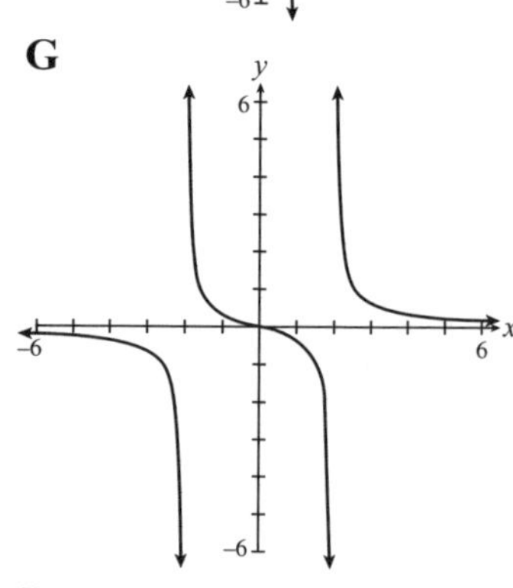

H

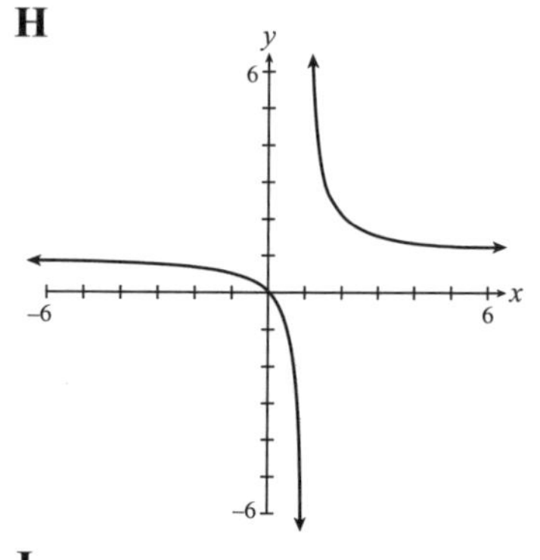

I

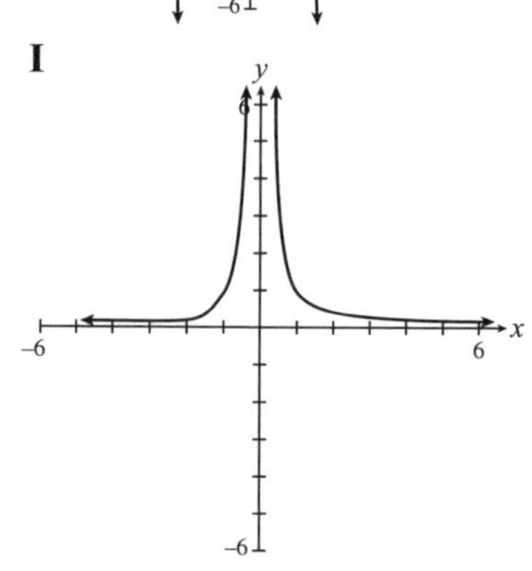

J

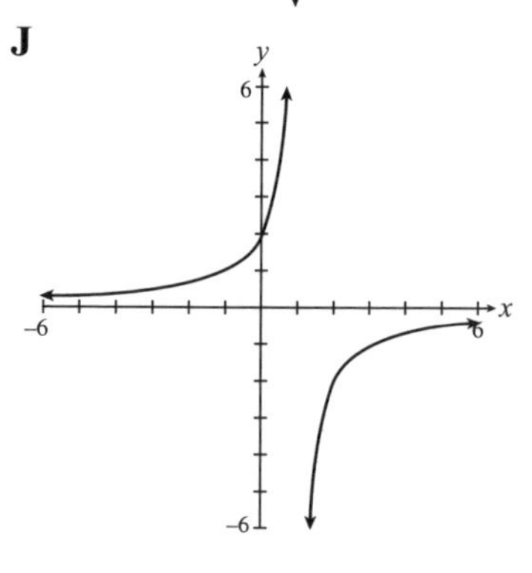

6. Sketch by hand the graph of the rational function. State the domain of the function, identify all intercepts, identify any vertical or horizontal asymptotes and holes. Plot additional solution points as needed.

a) 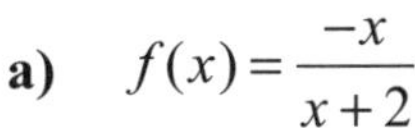 $f(x) = \dfrac{-x}{x+2}$

x						
$f(x)$						

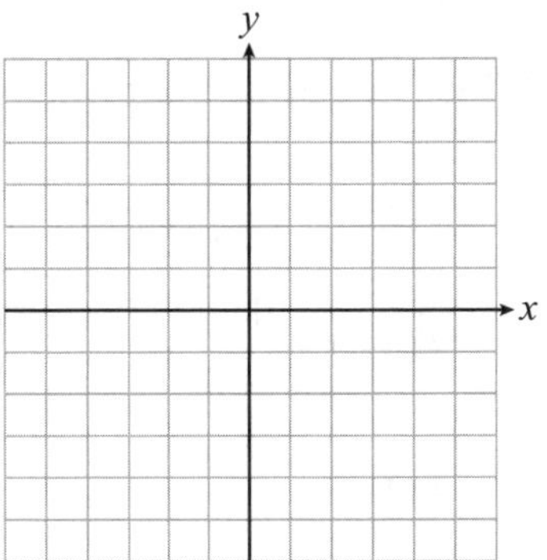

b) $f(x) = \dfrac{x+2}{x-1}$

x						
$f(x)$						

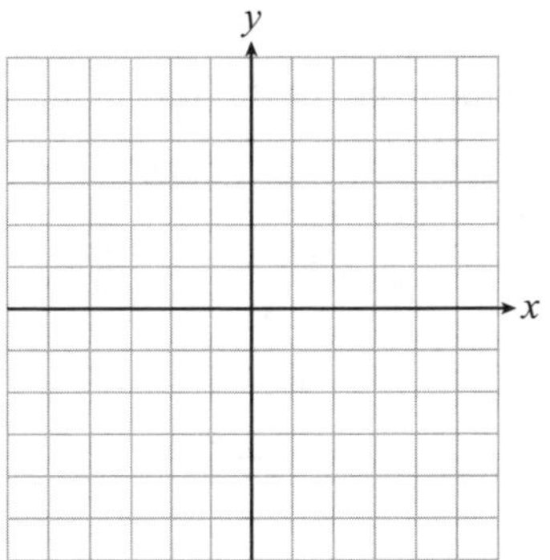

c) $f(x) = \dfrac{x^2+3x+2}{x^2-4}$

x						
$f(x)$						

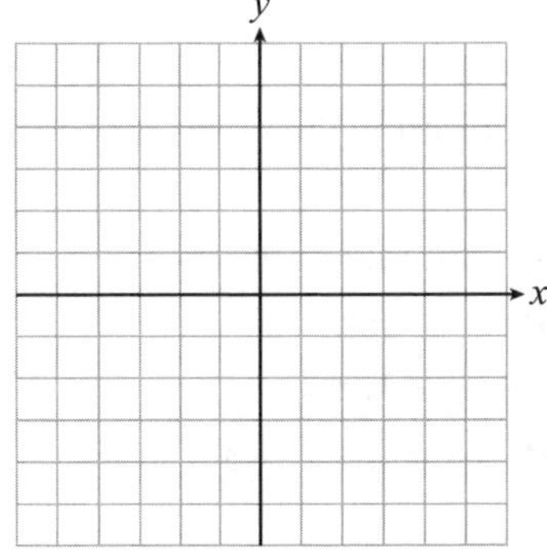

d) $f(x) = \dfrac{x^2}{x^3-9x}$

x						
$f(x)$						

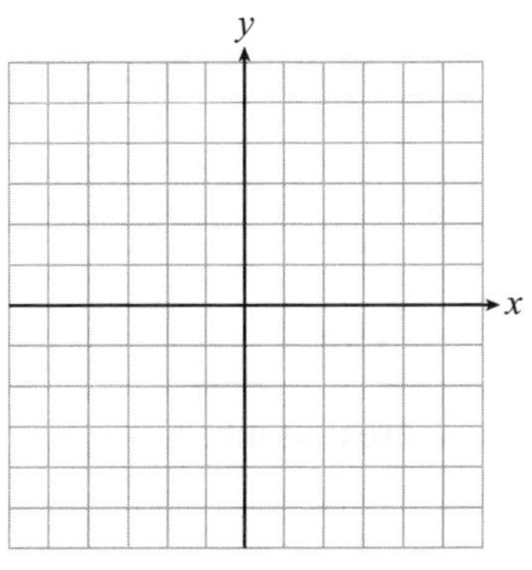

4.5 Chapter Review

1. Which one of the following graphs does not have a vertical asymptote?

   a) $f(x)=\dfrac{1}{x^2+1}$

   b) $f(x)=\dfrac{1}{x^2-3}$

   c) $f(x)=\dfrac{2}{x^2}$

   d) $f(x)=\dfrac{3x+1}{x-5}$

2. Which one of the following graphs does not have a horizontal asymptote?

   a) $f(x)=\dfrac{3x-5}{x+2}$

   b) $f(x)=\dfrac{3x}{x^2-4}$

   c) $f(x)=\dfrac{x^2-4}{x+2}$

   d) $f(x)=\dfrac{x+4}{(x-2)(x+3)}$

3. Determine the domain of the function $f(x)=\dfrac{(x-1)(x+2)(x-3)}{(x-1)(x+2)(x+3)}$.

   a) all real numbers
   b) $x\neq-3$
   c) $x\neq1,-2$
   d) $x\neq1,-2,-3$

4. Determine the domain of $f(x)=\sqrt[n]{ax+b}$, where n is an odd positive integer.

   a) $x\geq-\dfrac{b}{a}$

   b) $x\geq\dfrac{b}{a}$

   c) $-\dfrac{b}{a}\leq x\leq\dfrac{b}{a}$

   d) all real numbers

5. A radical equation $y = \sqrt{ax+b} + cx + d$ can have at most

a) 1 zero
b) 2 zeros
c) 3 zeros
d) 4 zeros

6. Simplify $\sqrt{9x^2}, x \le 0$

a) undefined
b) $-3x$
c) $3x$
d) $\pm 3x$

7. Simplify $\sqrt[3]{-8x^3}$

a) undefined
b) $-2x$
c) $2x$
d) $\pm 2x$

8. Which of the following is not defined over the real number system?

a) $x^5 = 7$
b) $x^5 = -7$
c) $x^6 = 7$
d) $x^6 = -7$

9. Determine the domain of $f(x) = -\sqrt{4 - x^2}$

a) $x \le 0$
b) $x \ge 2$
c) $-2 \le x \le 2$
d) $x \le -2,\ x \ge 2$

10. Determine the range of $f(x) - 3 = -2\sqrt{1 - x}$

a) $y \le -2$
b) $y \le 1$
c) $y \le 2$
d) $y \le 3$

11. Determine the x-intercept of $f(x)=\dfrac{3x^2-3x-6}{x^2+4x+4}$

a) –2
b) –1, 2
c) –3, 6
d) 3, –6

12. Determine the domain of $f(x)=\sqrt{x^2-a^2}$

a) $x \geq a$
b) $x \leq -a,\ x \geq a$
c) $-a \leq x \leq a$
d) all real numbers

13. Which of the following could be the graph below if $a, b > 0$?

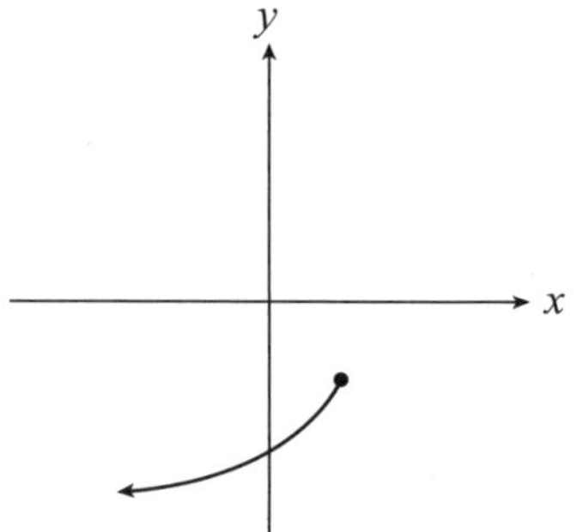

a) $y=-\sqrt{a-x}-b$
b) $y=\sqrt{x-a}-b$
c) $y=\sqrt{a-x}-b$
d) $y=-\sqrt{x-a}-b$

14. The graph $f(x)=\dfrac{x^2-9}{x^2-2x-3}$ has a "hole" at the point

a) (–3, 0)
b) (3, 0)
c) (3, 1)
d) $(3, \frac{3}{2})$

15. Which of the following rational functions has a hole in the graph of the function f?

a) $f(x)=\dfrac{x^2-4}{4-x^2}$

b) $f(x)=\dfrac{x^2-2x-8}{x^2+x-6}$

c) $f(x)=\dfrac{x^2+3x-4}{x^2-2x-3}$

d) $f(x)=\dfrac{x^2-2x-15}{x^2-x-6}$

16. Determine the value of $f(x)$ when $x \to -\infty$ if $f(x)=\dfrac{3x+2}{2x+3}$.

a) $-\dfrac{2}{3}$

b) $\dfrac{2}{3}$

c) 1.5^+
d) 1.5^-

17. Let f be a rational function given by $f(x)=\dfrac{ax^n}{bx^m}$. The graph has a horizontal asymptote of $y=0$ when

a) $n=m$
b) $n<0$
c) $n>m$
d) $n<m$

18. The line $y=b$ is a horizontal asymptote of the graph of $f(x)$ if

a) $x\to b$ as $f(x)\to\infty$ or $f(x)\to-\infty$
b) $x\to b$ as $x\to\infty$ or $x\to-\infty$
c) $f(x)\to b$ as $x\to\infty$ or $x\to-\infty$
d) $f(x)\to b$ as $f(x)\to\infty$ or $f(x)\to-\infty$

19. Which of the following is always true?

a) If $P=Q$ then $P^n=Q^n$, n an integer
b) If $P^n=Q^n$ then $P=Q$, n an integer
c) If $P=Q$ then $P^n=Q^n$, n a positive integer
d) If $P^n=Q^n$ then $P=Q$, n a positive integer

20. Which of the following rational functions describes a graph that is symmetric about the y-axis, has a horizontal asymptote of $y=0$, and a vertical asymptote of $x=0$, with no x- or y-intercepts?

a) $f(x)=\dfrac{-1}{x}$
b) $f(x)=\dfrac{1}{x}$
c) $f(x)=\dfrac{1}{x^2}$
d) $f(x)=\dfrac{1}{x^3}$

21. Which of the following rational functions describes a graph that has a horizontal asymptote $y=-2$ and a vertical asymptote $x=1$ with the y-intercept (0, 0)?

a) $f(x)=\dfrac{-2x}{x-1}$
b) $f(x)=\dfrac{-x}{x-2}$
c) $f(x)=\dfrac{x+2}{x-1}$
d) $f(x)=\dfrac{x-2}{-x}$

Questions 22 to 25

A function is in the form $y = a\sqrt{b(x-h)} + k$ with *a, b, h, k*, constants. What stipulations will produce the following graphs?

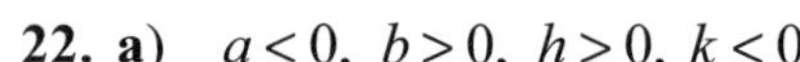

22. **a)** $a<0,\ b>0,\ h>0,\ k<0$
b) $a<0,\ b>0,\ h<0,\ k>0$
c) $a>0,\ b<0,\ h>0,\ k<0$
d) $a>0,\ b<0,\ h<0,\ k>0$

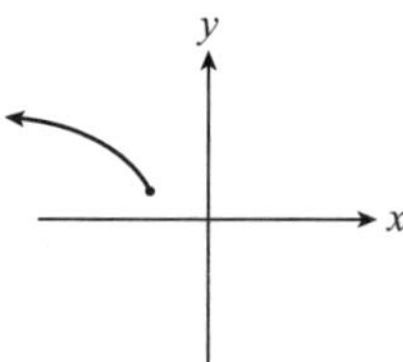

23. **a)** $a<0,\ b>0,\ h>0,\ k>0$
b) $a<0,\ b>0,\ h<0,\ k>0$
c) $a>0,\ b<0,\ h<0,\ k>0$
d) $a<0,\ b<0,\ h>0,\ k<0$

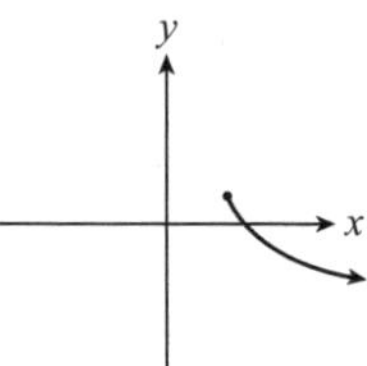

24. **a)** $a<0,\ b<0,\ h<0,\ k<0$
b) $a<0,\ b<0,\ h>0,\ k>0$
c) $a>0,\ b>0,\ h<0,\ k<0$
d) $a>0,\ b>0,\ h>0,\ k>0$

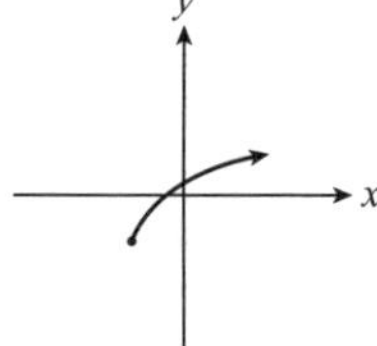

25. **a)** $a<0,\ b<0,\ h>0,\ k<0$
b) $a<0,\ b<0,\ h<0,\ k>0$
c) $a>0,\ b<0,\ h>0,\ k<0$
d) $a<0,\ b>0,\ h>0,\ k<0$

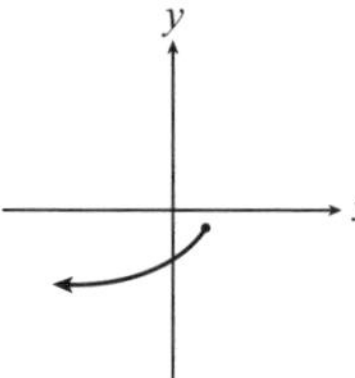

26. Let f be a rational function given by $f(x) = \dfrac{g(x)}{h(x)}$. The graph has a vertical asymptote at the zero of

a) $g(x)$
b) $h(x)$
c) $\dfrac{g(x)}{h(x)}$
d) $\dfrac{h(x)}{g(x)}$

27. An open top box with a square base has a volume of 30 ft^3. The total surface area of the box is

a) $\text{S.A.} = x^2 - \dfrac{60}{x}$

b) $\text{S.A.} = x^2 + \dfrac{60}{x}$

c) $\text{S.A.} = x^2 - \dfrac{120}{x}$

d) $\text{S.A.} = x^2 + \dfrac{120}{x}$

28. Rent-a-Wreck charges $25 per day plus 20 cents per km to rent a car. What is the average cost per x km, $C(x)$?

a) $C(x) = 25 + 0.20x$

b) $C(x) = 25 + \dfrac{0.20}{x}$

c) $C(x) = 25x + 0.20$

d) $C(x) = \dfrac{25}{x} + 0.20$

Questions 29 and 30

A function in the form $f(x) = \dfrac{ax+b}{cx+d}$, with *a, b, c, d* constant and *c* and *d* not zero.

29. What are the x- and y-intercepts of $f(x)$?

a) x-intercept: $\dfrac{-b}{a}$, y-intercept: $\dfrac{a}{c}$

b) x-intercept: $-\dfrac{b}{a}$, y-intercept: $\dfrac{b}{d}$

c) x-intercept: $\dfrac{b}{d}$, y-intercept: $\dfrac{a}{c}$

d) x-intercept: $\dfrac{-b}{a}$, y-intercept: $-\dfrac{d}{c}$

30. What are the horizontal and vertical asymptotes of $f(x)$?

a) horizontal: $y = \dfrac{b}{d}$, vertical: $x = -\dfrac{b}{a}$

b) horizontal: $y = \dfrac{b}{d}$, vertical: $x = -\dfrac{d}{c}$

c) horizontal: $y = \dfrac{a}{c}$, vertical: $x = -\dfrac{b}{a}$

d) horizontal: $y = \dfrac{a}{c}$, vertical: $x = -\dfrac{d}{c}$

LIST OF **WRONGS** AND **RIGHTS**

Probably the main overall rule to keep upper most in your mind when working with logarithms is as follows: **Do not** make up your own rules!

Wrong	**Right**
1. $(\log a)^n = n\log a$	**1.** $(\log a)^n$ cannot be simplified
2. $\log x \cdot \log y = \log xy$	**2.** $\log x \cdot \log y$ cannot be simplified
3. $\log(x+y) = \log x + \log y$	**3.** $\log(x+y)$ cannot be simplified
4. $\log x \cdot \log x = \log x^2$	**4.** $\log x \cdot \log x = (\log x)^2$
5. $\log_y x = \log x - \log y$	**5.** $\log_y x = \dfrac{\log_b x}{\log_b y}$
6. $\dfrac{\log x}{\log y} = \log x - \log y$	**6.** $\dfrac{\log x}{\log y} = \log_y x$
7. $\log\dfrac{x}{2} = \dfrac{\log x}{2}$	**7.** $\log\dfrac{x}{2} = \log x - \log 2$
8. $\dfrac{\log 10}{\log 5} = \dfrac{10}{5} = 2$ or $\dfrac{\log 10}{\log 5} = \log 2$	**8.** $\dfrac{\log 10}{\log 5} = \log_5 10 \approx 1.43$
9. $\dfrac{\log_2 5}{5} = \log_2$	**9.** $\dfrac{\log_2 5}{5}$ cannot be simplified
10. $b^x + b^y = b^{x+y}$	**10.** $b^x + b^y$ cannot be simplified

5.1 Exponents

Logarithms is the study of exponents. Therefore, we must review our exponent properties as our first step in understanding logarithms.

Exponential Function Properties where a and b are positive real numbers and exponents x and y are any real numbers.

1. $b^0 = 1$
2. $b^x \cdot b^y = b^{x+y}$
3. $\dfrac{b^x}{b^y} = b^{x-y}$
4. $\left(b^x\right)^y = b^{xy}$
5. $b^{-x} = \dfrac{1}{b^x}$
6. $\left(\dfrac{a}{b}\right)^{-x} = \left(\dfrac{b}{a}\right)^x = \dfrac{b^x}{a^x}$
7. $\left(ab\right)^x = a^x b^x$
8. $a^x = a^y$ if any only if $x = y$

Example 1 Simplify $\dfrac{4^{6x+1}}{8^{4x+2}}$

▶ *Solution:* $\dfrac{4^{6x+1}}{8^{4x+2}} = \dfrac{2^{2(6x+1)}}{2^{3(4x+2)}} = \dfrac{2^{12x+2}}{2^{12x+6}} = 2^{12x+2-12x-6} = 2^{-4} = \dfrac{1}{2^4} = \dfrac{1}{16}$

Example 2 Solve $9^{2x-3} = 27^{1-x}$

▶ *Solution:* $9^{2x-3} = 27^{1-x} \rightarrow 3^{2(2x-3)} = 3^{3(1-x)} \rightarrow 3^{4x-6} = 3^{3-3x} \rightarrow 4x-6 = 3-3x \rightarrow 7x = 9 \rightarrow x = \dfrac{9}{7}$

Graphing Exponential Functions

To gain a better understanding of exponents, we will look at the graph of $y = b^x$, the exponential function. The base can be any value greater than zero except 1. Therefore, we must look at $0 < b < 1$ and $b > 1$. We define the exponential function and its graph as follows:

Exponential Function

The equation $f(x) = b^x,\ b > 0,\ b \neq 1$ is called an exponential function with base *b*, and *x* any real value.

Exponential Graphs

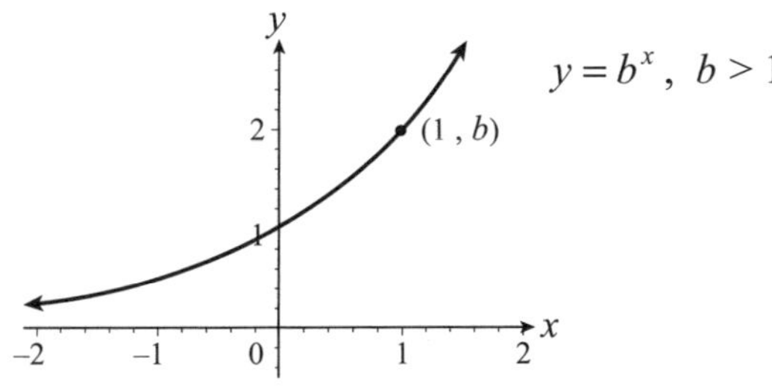

$y = b^x,\ b > 1$

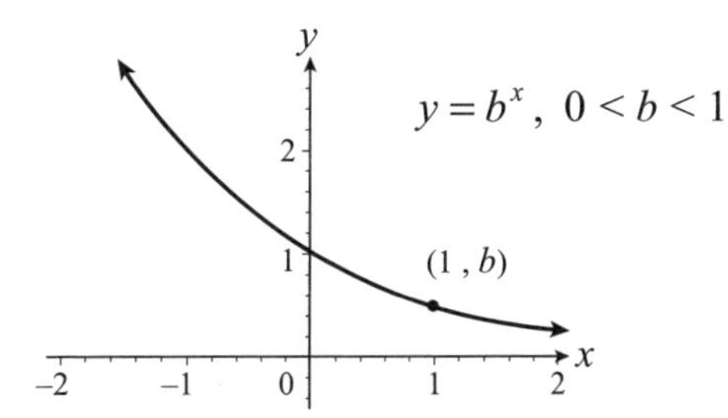

$y = b^x,\ 0 < b < 1$

Basic Properties of Exponential Graphs

Before stating the basic properties of the exponential function graph $y = a^x$, let us define a **horizontal asymptote**:

> **Definition of a Horizontal Asymptote**
>
> The line $y = b$ is a **horizontal asymptote** for the graph $f(x) = a^x$ if $f(x) \to b$ (read $f(x)$ approaches b) as $x \to^+ \infty$ or $x \to^- \infty$. In other words, it is a horizontal line which y approaches as x gets very large or very small.

The basic properties of the graph $f(x) = b^x$ can be stated as follows:

> **Basic Properties of the graph** $f(x) = b^x,\ b > 0,\ b \neq 1$
>
> 1. All graphs go through the point (0, 1), and the graph has no x-intercept.
> 2. The x-axis is a horizontal asymptote with equation $y = 0$
> 3. When $b > 1$, $f(x) = b^x$ is an increasing function
> 4. When $0 < b < 1$, $f(x) = b^x$ is a decreasing function

Example 3 Sketch the graph:

a) $f(x) = \left(\frac{1}{2}\right)^x - 1$ **b)** $g(x) = -3^{x-1} + 1$

► *Solution:* **a)** $f(x) = \left(\frac{1}{2}\right)^x - 1 \to f(x) = 2^{-x} - 1$ This graph is a decreasing function, with the horizontal asymptote shifted down one unit. Asymptote is $f(x) = -1$, with graph going through the origin.

b) $g(x) = -3^{x-1} + 1$ This graph is an decreasing function, with the horizontal asymptote shifted up one unit. Asymptote is $g(x) = 1$. Graph is shifted one unit right from basic graph $y = 3^x$

x	–3	–2	–1	0	1	2	3
$f(x)$	7	3	1	–1	–0.5	–.75	–.875

x	–1	0	1	2	3
$g(x)$	0.89	0.67	0	–2	–8

a)

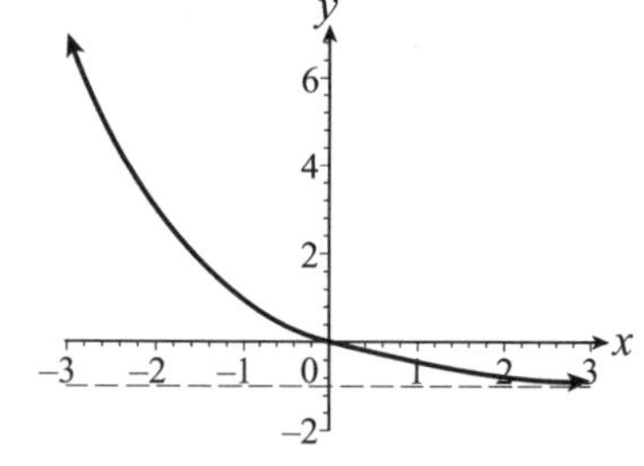

b)

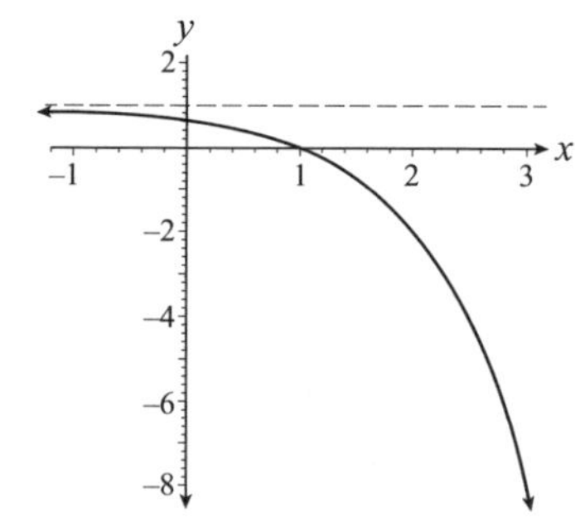

Application of Exponential Functions

Exponential function applications are found in all aspects of life, such as radioactive decay, bacteria growth, spread of epidemics, and compound interest. Such functions are found in variations of the function $f(x)=A(a^x)$ where A is a constant. The compound interest formula shows such a variation.

Compound Interest Formula

Interest calculated on principle plus previously earned interest is called compound interest. If P dollars is deposited at an annually rate r, compounded n times per year, then the compounded amount A is given by the formula:

$$A=P\left(1+\frac{r}{n}\right)^{nt}$$

Where $A=$ final amount

$P=$ principle, or initial amount

$r=$ rate of yearly interest

$n=$ number of times yearly interest is compounded in a year

$t=$ time in years

Example 4 Find the interest earned if \$6500 is deposited in an account paying 6% compounded monthly for five years.

▶ *Solution:* $A=P\left(1+\frac{r}{n}\right)^{nt}$: "compounded monthly" means $n=12$

$=6500\left(1+\frac{0.06}{12}\right)^{12\times5}=8767.53$ Therefore, the interest is $8767.53-6500=\$2267.53$.

Example 5 What initial investment is needed to become a millionaire in 25 years if you receive interest at 12 % compounded quarterly?

▶ *Solution:* $A=P\left(1+\frac{r}{n}\right)^{nt}$: "compounded quarterly" means $n=4$

$1\,000\,000=P\left(1+\frac{0.12}{4}\right)^{4\times25}\rightarrow P=\frac{1\,000\,000}{1.03^{100}}=52\,032.84$

If \$52 032.84 is invested at 12 % for 25 years, the yield is \$1 000 000.

Example 6 What is a better value:

invest \$10 000 at 6% compounded quarterly for 10 years **or**
invest \$10 000 at $6\frac{1}{4}$% compounded annually for 10 years?

▶ *Solution:* $A=10\,000\left(1+\frac{0.06}{4}\right)^{4\times10}=\$18\,140.18$ **or** $A=10\,000\left(1+\frac{0.0625}{1}\right)^{1\times10}=\$18\,335.36$

The investment at $6\frac{1}{4}$% compounded annually is a better investment by \$195.18.

The growth and decay formula is another variation of $f(x) = A(a^x)$.

Growth and Decay Formulas

Growth and decay: $A = A_0(x)^{\frac{t}{T}}$

A – final amount

A_0 – initial amount

x – growth or decay value, e.g., half-life use $\frac{1}{2}$
increase by 10% use 1.1
decrease by 10% use 0.9

t – total time that item is left

T – time of growth or decay, e.g., half-life

Growth and decay: $A = A_0 e^{kt}$

A – final amount

A_0 – initial amount

e – constant ≈ 2.71828

k – proportional constant

t – time

Example 7 The half-life of plutonium-239 is about 25 000 years. How much of a given sample will remain after 2000 years ?

▶ *Solution:* Method 1: $A = A_0(x)^{\frac{t}{T}} \rightarrow A = 1\left(\frac{1}{2}\right)^{\frac{2000}{25000}} \rightarrow A = 0.946$ or 94.6%

Method 2: $A = A_0 e^{kt} \rightarrow \frac{1}{2} = 1 \cdot e^{25000} \rightarrow k = \frac{\ln 0.5}{25000}$

$$A = A_0 e^{\left(\frac{\ln 0.5}{25000}\right)t} \rightarrow A = 1 \cdot e^{\frac{(\ln 0.5)(2000)}{25000}} \rightarrow A = 0.946 \text{ or } 94.6\%$$

Example 8 The number of fruit flies increases by 25% every 3 days. If the population was 2000 fruit flies after 25 days, how many were there initially?

▶ *Solution:* $A = A_0(x)^{\frac{t}{T}} \rightarrow 2000 = A_0(1.25)^{\frac{25}{3}} \rightarrow A_0 = \dfrac{2000}{1.25^{\frac{25}{3}}} = 311$ fruit flies

Summary

- An exponential function is in the form $f(x) = ab^x$, where $b > 1$ or $0 < b < 1, b \neq 1$ and *a, b*, and *x* are real numbers.
- The function is one-to-one; *y*-intercept is (0, 1); domain is all real numbers; range $0 < y < \infty$; asymptote is the *x*-axis: $y = 0$.
- The graph $y = b^{x-h}$, shift graph horizontally right if $h > 0$ and horizontally left if $h < 0$.
- The graph $y = b^x + k$, shift graph vertically upward if $k > 0$ and vertically downward if $k < 0$.

5.1 Exercise Set

1. Simplify

a) $\dfrac{\left(3^{\frac{1}{5}}\right)^{10}\cdot\left(3^{-3}\right)}{9}$

b) $\dfrac{\left(-4x^2y^{-2}\right)^{-3}}{x^{-1}y^2}$

c) $\dfrac{125^{3x-1}\cdot 25^{1-2x}}{\left(\dfrac{1}{5}\right)^{2x-3}}$

d) $\dfrac{2x^4\cdot 3^{5x}-4x^3\cdot 3^{5x}}{x^3-2x^2}$

e) $\left(4^{-x}\cdot 8^x\right)^2$

f) $\dfrac{2^x\left(2^x+2^{-x}\right)-2^x\left(2^x-2^{-x}\right)}{2^{-2}}$

2. Solve for x

a) $4^{x^2-x}=1$

b) $3^{x^2}=9\cdot 3^{-x}$

c) $4^{\sqrt{x+1}}=2^{3x-2}$

d) $4^{-|x+1|}=\dfrac{1}{16}$

e) $4^{-2x+1}=8^{x-4}$

f) $9^{2x-1}=\left(\dfrac{1}{27}\right)^{x+2}$

3. If $y = ab^x$ is defined by the graph below, what is the shape of:

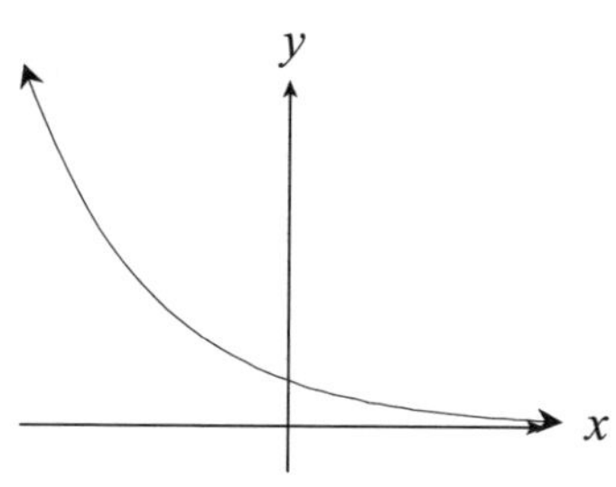

a) $y = -ab^x$

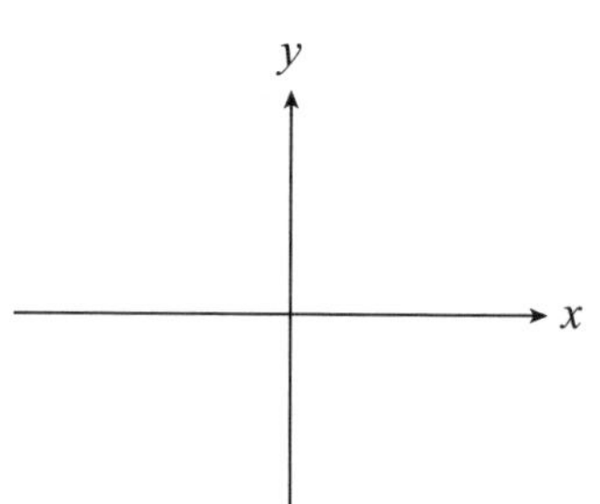

b) $y = ab^{-x}$

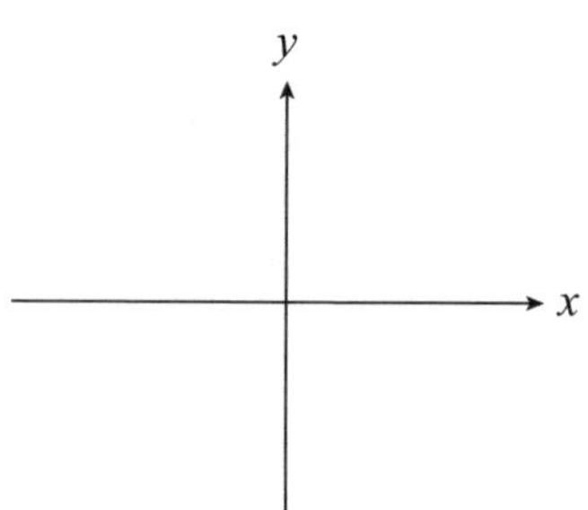

4. Explain how the graphs of the equations below can be obtained from the graph of $y = 3^x$. Then graph the equation, specifying the domain, range, intercept(s), and asymptote.

a) $y = 3^{x+2} - 3$

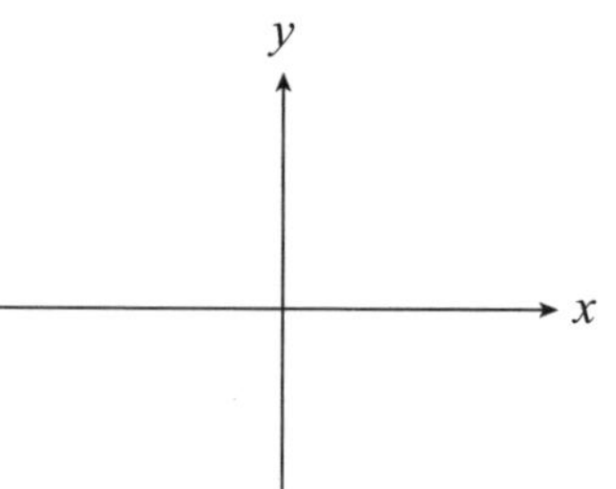

b) $y = \left(\frac{1}{3}\right)^x + 2$

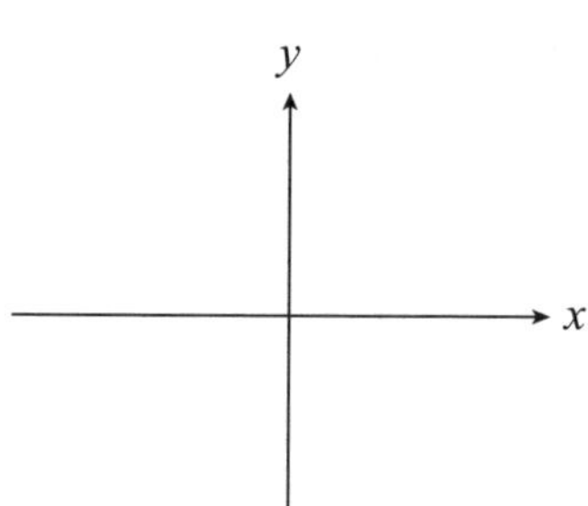

c) $y = -3^{-x}$

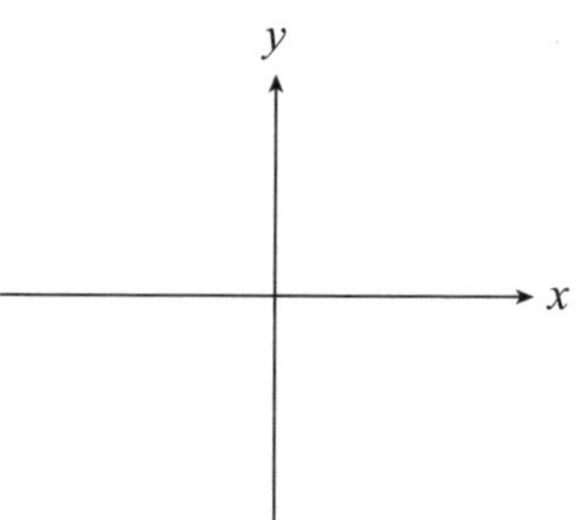

5. Match each exponential equation with the correct graph.

a) $y = 4^{-x}$ ______

b) $y = 3^{-x+1}$ ______

c) $y = 3^{-x} + 1$ ______

d) $y = -4^{-x}$ ______

e) $y = 2^{x+1} - 2$ ______

f) $y = -2^{x+2} + 1$ ______

A

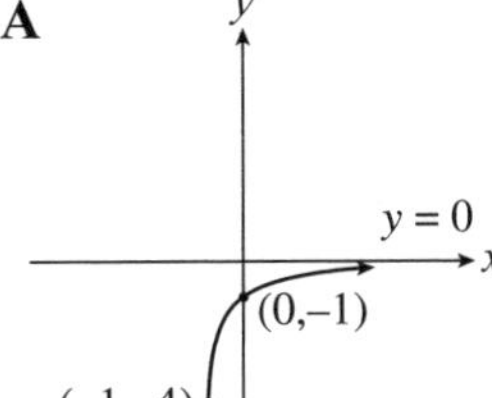

B

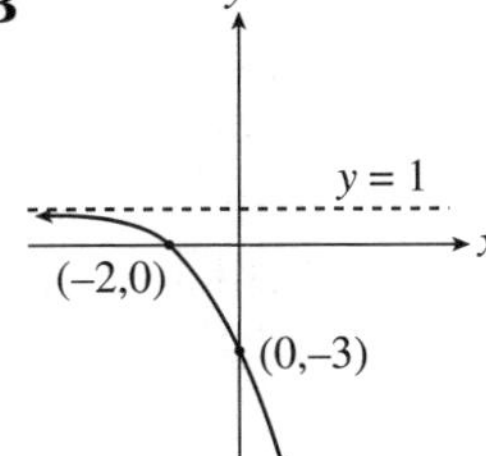

C

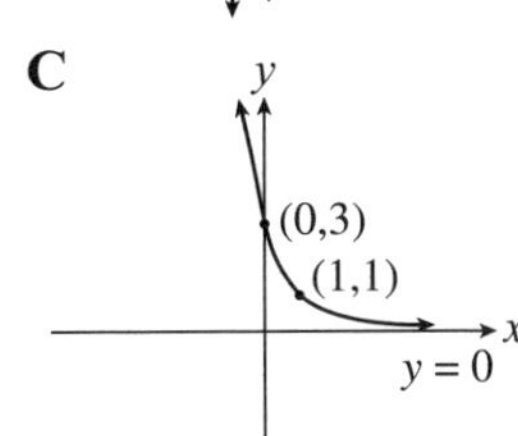

D

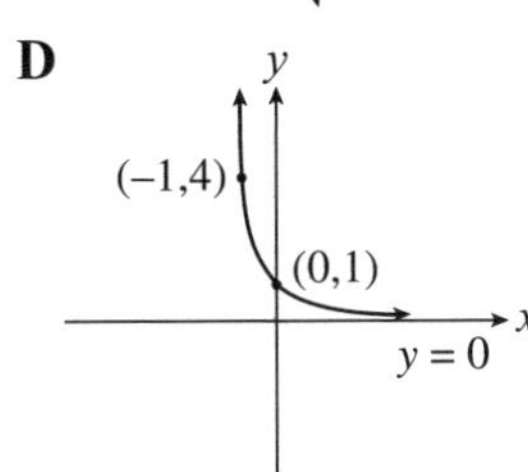

E

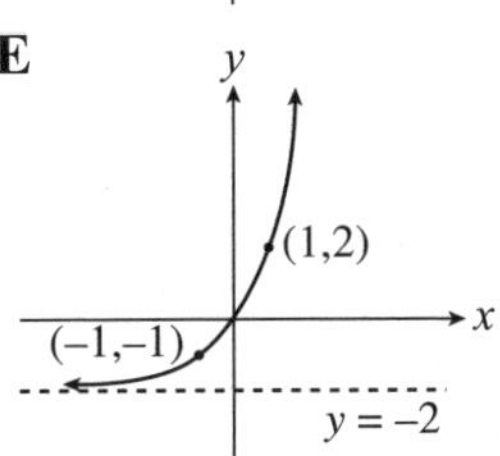

F

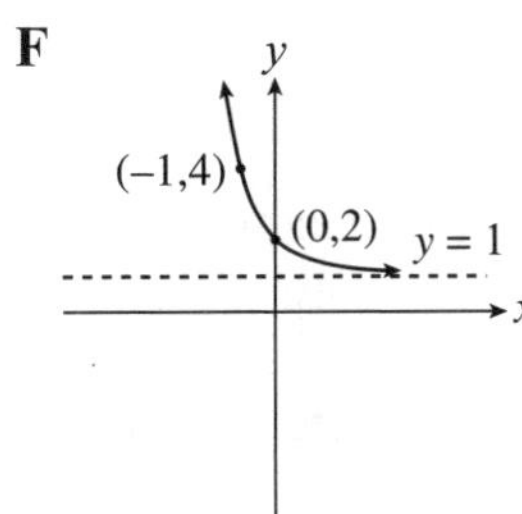

6. Find the base in the exponential function $y = b^x$ that contains the given point.

a) $(-1,\ 3)$ **b)** $\left(\frac{3}{2},\ 27\right)$ **c)** $\left(-\frac{2}{3},\ \frac{1}{9}\right)$

7. Find the exponential function in the form $y = c \cdot 2^{kx}$ that passes through (0 , 4) and (12 , 256).

8. Sketch the graph of $y = 2^x$ and $y = 3^x$ on the same coordinate plane:

x	–3	–2	–1	0	1	2	3
2^x							
3^x							

Comment on $y = 2^x$ and $y = 3^x$ when $x < 0$ and when $x > 0$.

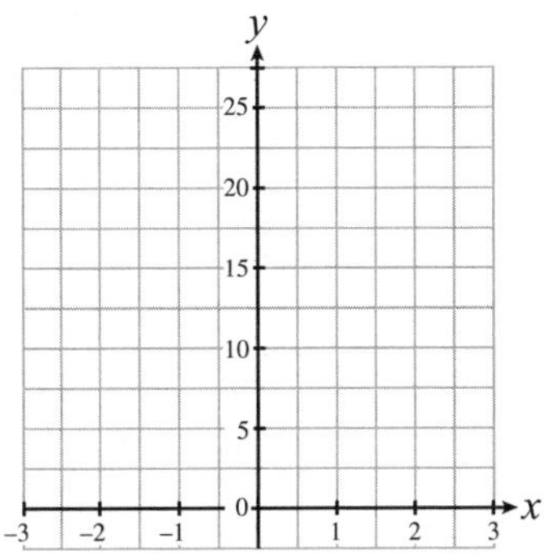

9. Solve:

a) In 1933, an earthquake in Japan measured 8.9 on the Richter scale. How many times more powerful was this earthquake compared to one in the northwest measuring 6.4 on the Richter scale? (The Richter scale is a power of 10 scale.)

b) If an earthquake in San Francisco had an amplitude 1000 times larger than an earthquake that measured 4.9 on the Richter scale, what would the San Francisco earthquake measure?

c) Suppose that \$1000 is invested at an annual rate of 6%, compounded quarterly (4 times per year). Find the total amount in the account after 8 years if no withdrawals are made.

d) Radioactive argon-39 has a half-life of 4 minutes. This means that every 4 minutes one-half of the amount of argon-39 changes into another substance due to radioactive decay. If we initially have 84 grams of argon-39, how much remains after 23 minutes?

e) If \$12 250 is invested in an account paying 9.6% , how much will be in the account at the end of 10 years if the interest is compounded monthly?

f) If the population in Canada is around 30 000 000 people in the year 2000, and if the population continues to grow at 1.9% compounded yearly, what will the population be in the year 2032 to the nearest million?

5.2 Logarithmic Functions and Their Graphs

One of the main concepts learned in the transformation chapter was the inverse function. The following are the major points of an inverse:

1. To have an inverse function, the function must be one-to-one.
2. $f^{-1}(x)$ interchanges the x- and y-coordinates of $f(x)$.
3. The domain of $f(x)$ becomes the range of $f^{-1}(x)$.
4. The range of $f(x)$ becomes the domain of $f^{-1}(x)$.
5. The graphs are a reflection over the line $y = x$.

We will apply this inverse concept to the exponential function $y = b^x$:

1. $y = b^x$ is one-to-one.
2. $x = b^y$ is its inverse.

This inverse function is called the **logarithmic function with base *b***. We thus define a logarithmic function as follows:

Definition of a Logarithmic Function

For $b > 0,\ b \neq 1$ $\qquad y = \log_b x$ is equivalent to $x = b^y, x > 0$

The log to the base b of x is the **exponent** that b must be raised to obtain x. It is the inverse of the exponential function with base b.

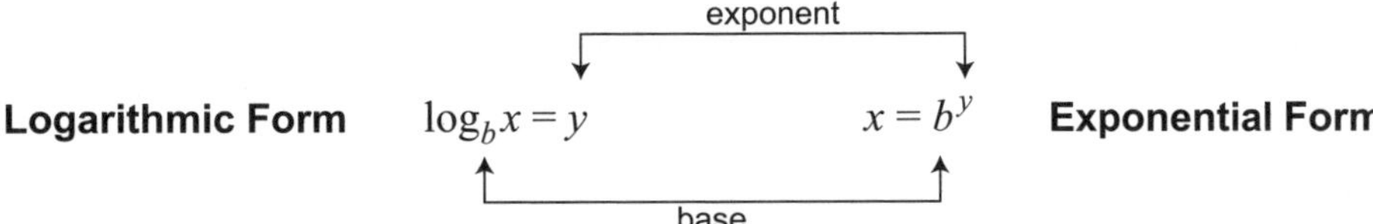

Note: $f(x) = \log_{10} x$ can be written as just $f(x) = \log x$; the 10 is assumed.

Example 1 Change the following from logarithmic form to exponential form:

a) $\log_4 2 = \frac{1}{2}$ **b)** $\log_2 \frac{1}{8} = -3$

▶ *Solution:*

a) $\log_4 2 = \frac{1}{2}$

$2 = 4^{\frac{1}{2}}$

b) $\log_2 \frac{1}{8} = -3$

$\frac{1}{8} = 2^{-3}$

Example 2 Change the following from exponential form to logarithmic form:

a) $3^4 = 81$ **b)** $3^{-2} = \frac{1}{9}$

▶ *Solution:*

a) $3^4 = 81$

$\log_3 81 = 4$

b) $3^{-2} = \frac{1}{9}$

$\log_3 \frac{1}{9} = -2$

Example 3 Determine the numerical value of the following:

a) $\log_4 8$ **b)** $\log_{27} 9$

▶ *Solution:*

a) Let $x = \log_4 8$

$4^x = 8$

$2^{2x} = 2^3$

$2x = 3$

$x = \frac{3}{2}$

b) Let $y = \log_{27} 9$

$27^y = 9$ *change to exponential form*

$3^{3y} = 3^2$ *common base*

$3y = 2$ *exponents equal*

$y = \frac{2}{3}$ *divide*

Example 4 Determine the domain of $y = \log_{x-1}(x+2)$.

▶ *Solution:* Remember, $y = \log_b a$ has $a > 0$ and $b > 0, b \neq 1$.

Thus, $y = \log_{x-1}(x+2)$ has $x + 2 > 0$ and $x - 1 > 0, x - 1 \neq 1$.

$x > -2$ $\quad x > 1$ $\quad x \neq 2$

Take the intersection of these values:

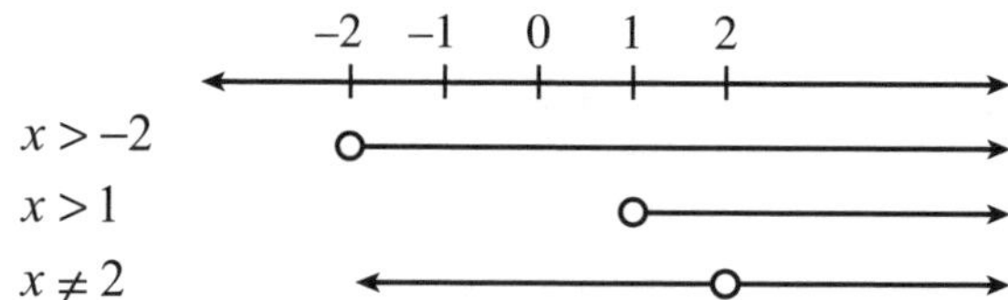

Therefore, $x > 1, x \neq 2$.

The graph would be

Logarithmic Graphs

Basic Properties of the graph $f(x)=\log_b x$, $x>0$, $b>0$, $b\neq 1$

1. All graphs go through the point (1, 0) and the graph has no y-intercept
2. The y-axis is a vertical asymptote with equation $x=0$
3. When $b>1$, $f(x)=\log_b x$ is an increasing function
4. When $0<b<1$, $f(x)=\log_b x$ is a decreasing function

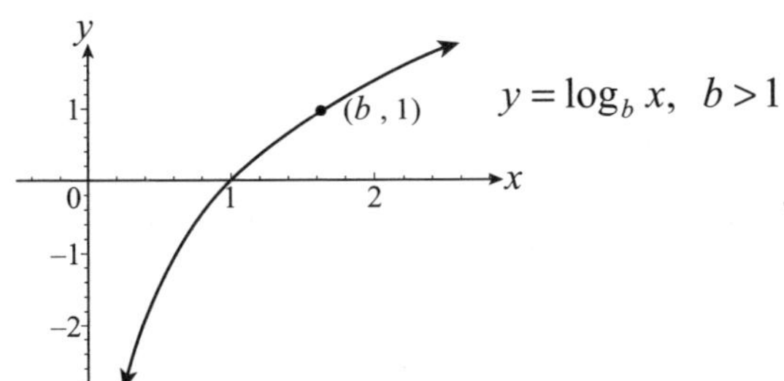

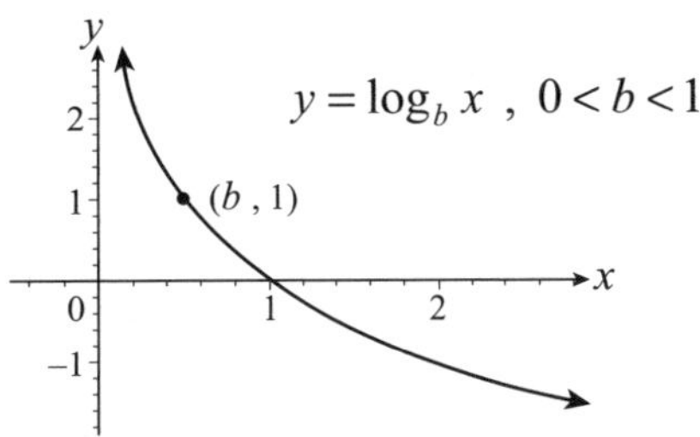

The Function	Proof	
	$y=f(x)=b^x$	*exponential function*
$f(x)=b^x$ and $g(x)=\log_b x$ are inverses	$x=b^y$	*inverse*
	$y=\log_b x$	*logarithmic form*
	$f^{-1}(x)=\log_b x$	$y=f^{-1}(x)$

Graphs of Functions and Their Inverses

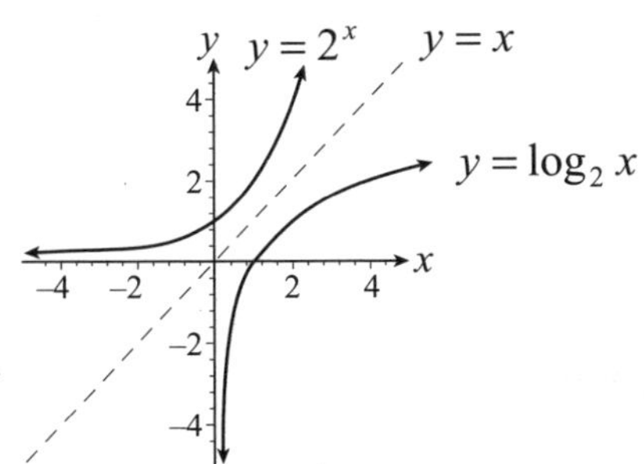

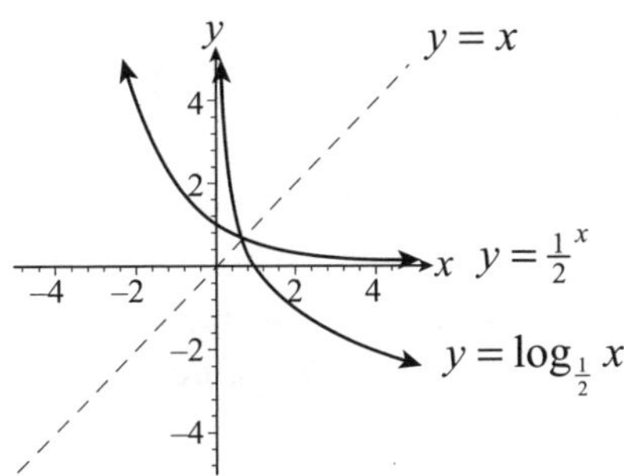

Note: The graphs of $y=b^x$ *and* $y=\log_b x$ *are the inverses of each other. This means that if you draw the line* $y=x$ *and reflect either graph over this line, the graphs will match up.*

Example 4 If the point (2, 5) is on the graph of $y = b^x$, what point is in the graph of $y = \log_b x$?

► *Solution:* Since $y = b^x$ and $y = \log_b x$ are inverses of each other, $y = \log_b x$ must have point (5, 2)

Example 5 Determine the inverse of $f(x) = 2^{x-1} + 3$

► *Solution:*

$f(x) = 2^{x-1} + 3$

Let $y = f(x)$

$y = 2^{x-1} + 3$ *thus the inverse is* $x = 2^{y-1} + 3$

Inverse: $x = 2^{y-1} + 3$

$x - 3 = 2^{y-1}$ *addition*

$\log_2(x-3) = y - 1$ *change from exponential form to logarithmic form*

$y = \log_2(x-3) + 1$ *addition*

$f^{-1}(x) = \log_2(x-3) + 1$

Example 6 Determine the inverse of $f(x) = \log_5(x+1) - 3$

► *Solution:*

$f(x) = \log_5(x+1) - 3$

Let $y = f(x)$

$y = \log_5(x+1) - 3$ *thus the inverse is* $x = \log_5(y+1) - 3$

Inverse: $x = \log_5(y+1) - 3$

$x + 3 = \log_5(y+1)$ *addition*

$y + 1 = 5^{x+3}$ *change from logarithmic form to exponential form*

$y = 5^{x+3} - 1$ *addition*

$f^{-1}(x) = 5^{x+3} - 1$

Note: *The inverse of an exponential equation is a logarithmic equation, and the inverse of a logarithmic equation is an exponential equation.*

5.2 Exercise Set

1. Write the logarithmic equation in exponential form.

a) $\log_4 16 = 2$ __________ **b)** $\log_3 81 = 4$ __________

c) $\log_6 \frac{1}{36} = -2$ __________ **d)** $\log \frac{1}{100} = -2$ __________

e) $\log_{32} 8 = \frac{3}{5}$ __________ **f)** $\log_8 8 = 1$ __________

g) $\log_5 1 = 0$ __________ **h)** $\log 1000 = 3$ __________

i) $\log_8 4 = \frac{2}{3}$ __________ **j)** $\log_4 \frac{1}{8} = -\frac{3}{2}$ __________

2. Write the exponential equation in logarithmic form.

a) $2^4 = 16$ __________ **b)** $8^2 = 64$ __________

c) $16^{\frac{1}{4}} = 2$ __________ **d)** $3^{-2} = \frac{1}{9}$ __________

e) $3^0 = 1$ __________ **f)** $10^{-2} = 0.01$ __________

g) $5^1 = 5$ __________ **h)** $9^{\frac{3}{2}} = 27$ __________

i) $8^{\frac{4}{3}} = 16$ __________ **j)** $\left(\frac{2}{3}\right)^{-4} = \frac{81}{16}$ __________

3. Evaluate the function without using a calculator.

a) $f(x) = \log_2 8$ **b)** $f(x) = \log_4 16$

c) $f(x) = \log_8 2$ **d)** $f(x) = \log_{16} 4$

e) $f(x) = \log_5 1$ **f)** $f(x) = \log_7 7$

g) $f(x) = \log_a a$ **h)** $f(x) = \log_a a^3$

i) $f(x) = \log_b b^{-4}$ **j)** $f(x) = \log_5 0$

4. Find the value of x without using a calculator.

a) $\log_x 27 = 3$

b) $\log_4 x = -3$

c) $\log 1000 = x$

d) $\log_x 8 = 1$

e) $\log_7 x = -2$

f) $\log_9 27 = x$

g) $\log_x 32 = 2$

h) $\log_4 x = 0$

i) $\log_{32} 8 = x$

j) $\log_x 625 = 4$

k) $\log_4 x = \frac{3}{2}$

l) $\log_4 0.25 = x$

m) $\log_{\sqrt{2}} x = 8$

n) $\log_{\sqrt{3}} x = 4$

o) $\log_x \sqrt{3} = \frac{1}{2}$

p) $\log_{3x} 36 = 2$

q) $\log_{\sqrt{2}} 16 = x$

r) $\log_{\sqrt{3}} 9 = x$

s) $\log_7 (x^2 + 24) = 2$

t) $\log(x-2)^2 = -2$

5. Determine the domain of the following logarithmic functions.

a) $f(x) = \log_3 (x-1)$

b) $f(x) = -\log_2 x + 3$

c) $f(x) = \log_{(2-x)} 5$

d) $y = \log_3 (-x)$

e) $y = \log_{x+1} (x-2)$

f) $y = \log_{x-2} (x+1)$

6. Match the logarithmic function on the left with the graph on the right.

a) $f(x) = \log_3(x-1)$ ______

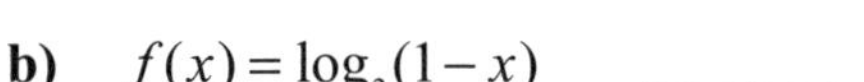

b) $f(x) = \log_3(1-x)$ ______

c) $f(x) = \log_3 x + 2$ ______

d) $f(x) = -\log_3 x$ ______

e) $f(x) = -\log_3(-x)$ ______

f) $f(x) = -\log_3(x+2)$ ______

A

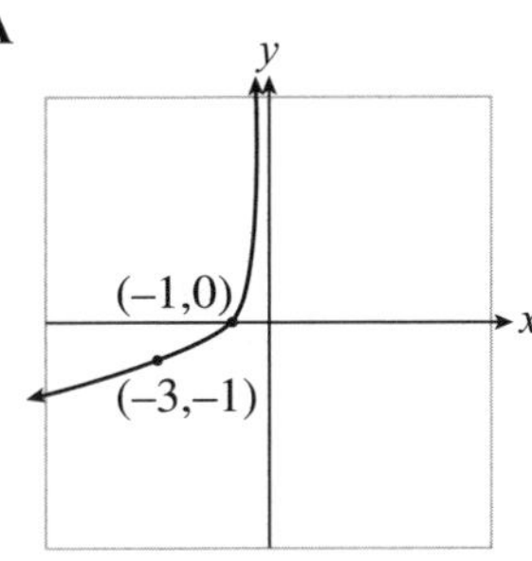

$x = 0$

B

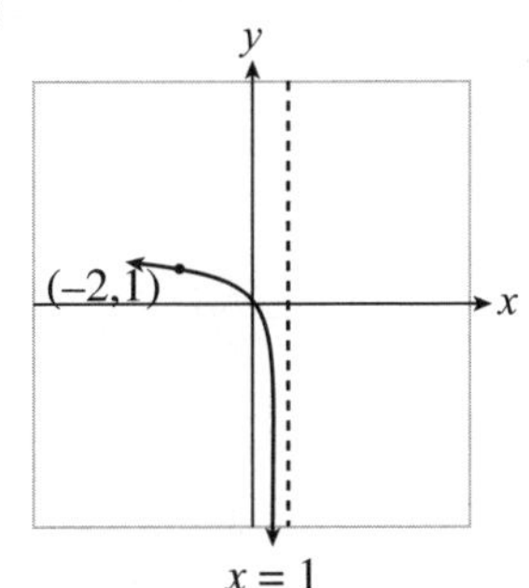

$x = 1$

C

y

(1,2)

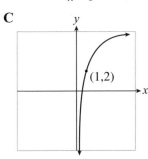

x

$x = 0$

D

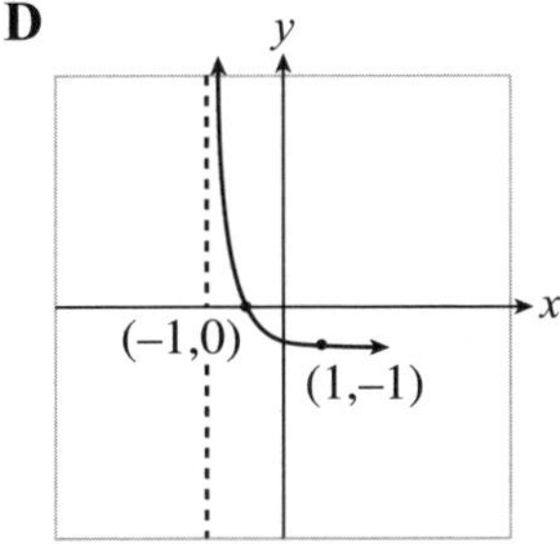

$x = -2$

E

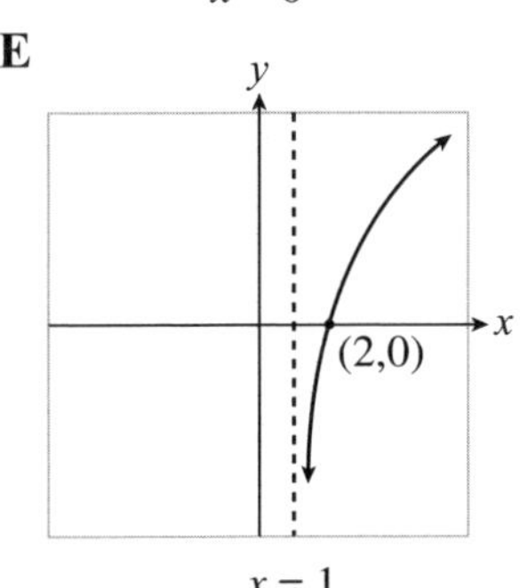

$x = 1$

F

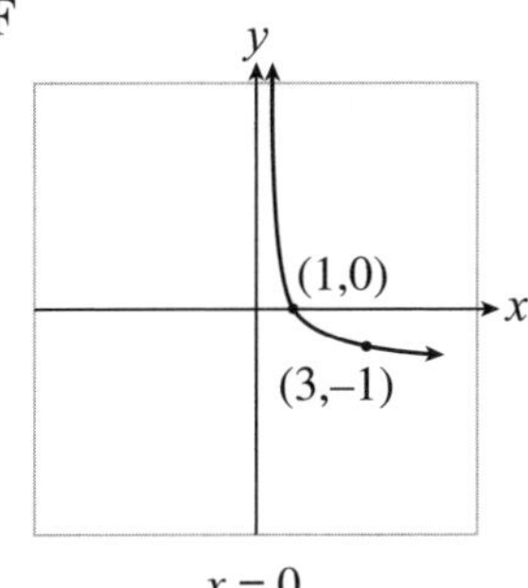

$x = 0$

7. If $y = \log_b a$ is defined by the following graph, what is the shape of:

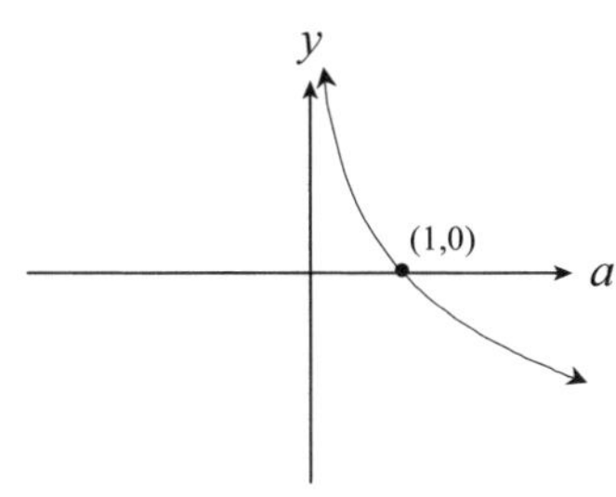

a) $y = -\log_b a$

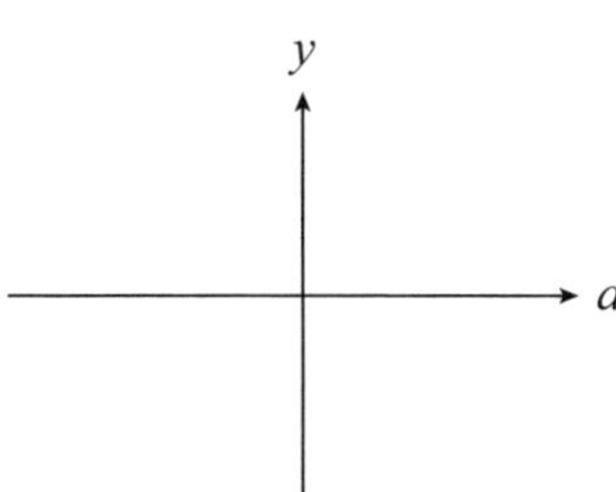

b) $y = \log_b(-a)$

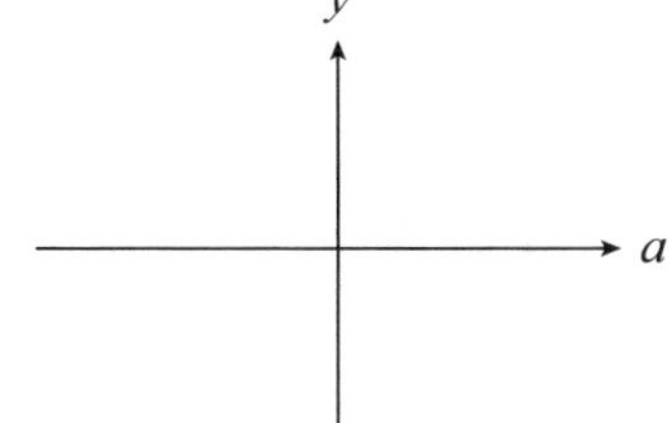

c) $y = \log_{\frac{1}{b}} a$

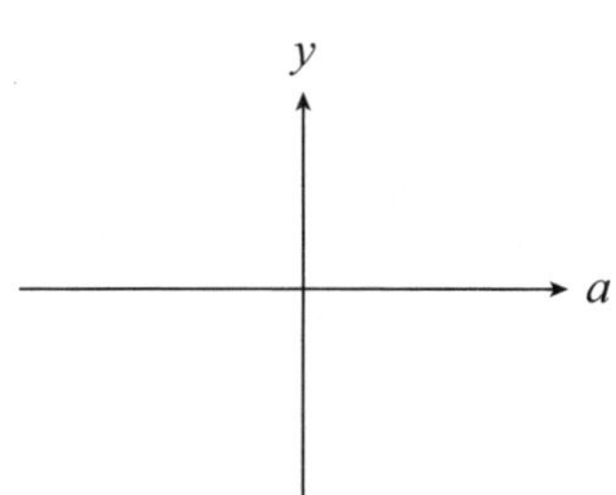

8. If point (a, b) is on the graph of $y = 5^x$, what point satisfies $y = \log_5 x$?

9. If a point on the graph of $y = \log_2 x$ is $(1, 0)$, what point must be on the graph of $y = -\log_2 x$?

10. If (c, d) is a point on the graph of $y = \log_b a$, what point must be on the graph of $y = \log_{\frac{1}{b}} a$?

11. Without using a calculator, between what two integers will we find

a) $\log 1253$

b) $\log 0.025$

12. Graph $y = \log(2 - x)$, labeling any asymptotes and axis crossings.

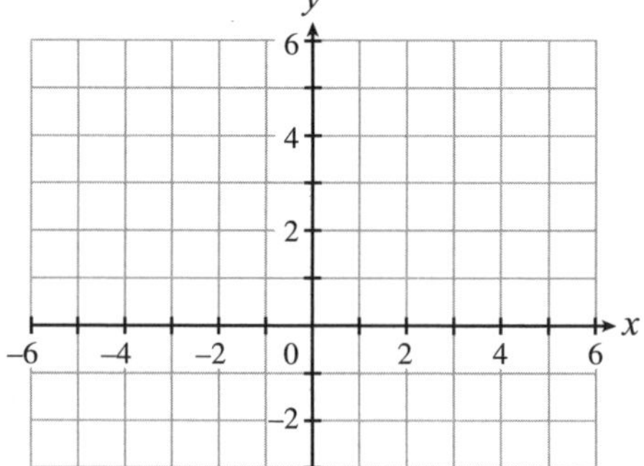

13. Determine the inverse of the following functions:

a) $y = 8^{x-2}$

b) $f(x) = 5^{4x-1} + 6$

c) $y + 1 = \log_3(x - 2)$

d) $f(x) = 2 + \log(5x - 3)$

5.3 Properties of Logarithms

We know that $\log_b 1 = 0$ and $\log_b b = 1$, since the exponential forms of these logarithmic values are $b^0 = 1$ and $b^1 = b$. Let us now derive other important properties.

Try to follow the reasoning in the derivation of these logarithmic rules. They will give you a better understanding of how logarithms work, and the relationship between exponential form and logarithm form.

Product Rule

Let $x = \log_b A$ then $A = b^x$	*logarithmic form to exponential form*
$y = \log_b B$ then $B = b^y$	*logarithmic form to exponential form*
$AB = b^x \cdot b^y = b^{x+y}$	*multiply*
$\log_b AB = x + y$	*exponential form to logarithmic form*
$\log_b AB = \log_b A + \log_b B$	*substitution*

Example 1 Simplify $\log 4 + \log 6$.

▶ *Solution:* $\log 4 + \log 6 = \log(4 \cdot 6) = \log 24$

Quotient Rule

Let $x = \log_b A$ then $A = b^x$	*logarithmic form to exponential form*
$y = \log_b A$ then $B = b^y$	*logarithmic form to exponential form*
$\frac{A}{B} = \frac{b^x}{b^y} = b^{x-y}$	*division*
$\log_b \frac{A}{B} = x - y$	*exponential form to logarithmic form*
$\log_b \frac{A}{B} = \log_b A - \log_b B$	*substitution*

Example 2 Simplify $\log 12 - \log 4$.

▶ *Solution:* $\log 12 - \log 4 = \log\left(\frac{12}{4}\right) = \log 3$

Power Rule

Let $x = \log_b A$ then $A = b^x$	*logarithmic form to exponential form*
$A^n = b^{nx}$	*multiply exponents by n*
$\log_b A^n = nx$	*exponential form to logarithmic form*
$\log_b A^n = n\log_b A$	*substitution*

Example 3 Simplify $\log_2 8$ by power rule.

▶ *Solution:* $\log_2 8 = \log_2 2^3 = 3\log_2 2 = 3$

Change of Base Rule

Let $y = \log_b a$ then $a = b^y$	*logarithmic form to exponential form*
$\log_x a = \log_x b^y$	*take* $\log_x$ *of both sides*
$\log_x a = y\log_x b$	*power rule*
$y = \dfrac{\log_x a}{\log_x b}$	*division*
$\log_b a = \dfrac{\log_x a}{\log_x b}$	*substitution*

Example 4 Find $\log_2 7$ to 3 decimal places

▶ *Solution:* $\log_2 7 = \dfrac{\log_{10} 7}{\log_{10} 2} = \dfrac{\log 7}{\log 2} = \dfrac{0.845}{0.301} = 2.807$

Note: Most calculators have a "log" function, which means $\log_{10}$; they cannot calculate logs of other bases.

We can summarize the basic properties of logarithms as follows:

Properties of Logarithmic Functions (*must-know rules*)

1. $\log_b 1 = 0$
with $b > 0$, $b \neq 1$

2. $\log_b b = 1$

3. $\log_c ab = \log_c a + \log_c b$
with $c > 0$, $c \neq 1$

4. $\log_c \dfrac{a}{b} = \log_c a - \log_c b$

5. $\log_c a^n = n\log_c a$

6. $\log_b a = \dfrac{\log_x a}{\log_x b}$

Using Properties of Logarithms

Example 5 Write each logarithm in terms of $\log 3$ and $\log 5$:

a) $\log 45$ **b)** $\log \frac{25}{3}$

▶ *Solution:*

a)
$$\begin{aligned} \log 45 &= \log(9 \cdot 5) \\ &= \log 9 + \log 5 && \textit{rule 3} \\ &= \log 3^2 + \log 5 && \textit{exponent rule} \\ &= 2\log 3 + \log 5 && \textit{rule 5} \end{aligned}$$

b)
$$\begin{aligned} \log \frac{25}{3} &= \log 25 - \log 3 && \textit{rule 4} \\ &= \log 5^2 - \log 3 && \textit{exponent rule} \\ &= 2\log 5 - \log 3 && \textit{rule 5} \end{aligned}$$

Example 6 Find the exact value of the following:

a) $\log_7 \sqrt[4]{7}$ **b)** $\log_5 5^6 - \log_5 5^2$ **c)** $\log_{\frac{1}{4}} \frac{16^2}{2^{-3}}$

▶ *Solution:*

a)
$$\begin{aligned} \log_7 \sqrt[4]{7} &= \log_7 7^{\frac{1}{4}} \\ &= \frac{1}{4}\log_7 7 && \textit{rule 5} \\ &= \frac{1}{4} && \textit{rule 2} \end{aligned}$$

b)
$$\begin{aligned} \log_5 5^6 - \log_5 5^2 &= 6\log_5 5 - 2\log_5 5 && \textit{rule 4} \\ &= 4\log_5 5 && \textit{subtraction} \\ &= 4 && \textit{rule 2} \end{aligned}$$

c)
$$\begin{aligned} \log_{\frac{1}{4}} \frac{16^2}{2^{-3}} &= \log_{\frac{1}{4}} \frac{(2^4)^2}{2^{-3}} && \textit{exponent rule} \\ &= \log_{\frac{1}{4}} 2^{11} && \textit{exponent rule} \\ &= \frac{\log 2^{11}}{\log \frac{1}{4}} && \textit{rule 6} \\ &= \frac{\log 2^{11}}{\log 2^{-2}} && \textit{exponent rule} \\ &= \frac{11\log 2}{-2\log 2} && \textit{rule 5} \\ &= -\frac{11}{2} && \textit{simplify} \end{aligned}$$

Rewriting Logarithmic Expressions

We can use our knowledge of algebra to expand and condense logarithmic expressions.

Example 7 Expand each logarithmic expression:

a) $\log_5 3x^4y^2$ **b)** $\log\dfrac{\sqrt{2x-5}}{3}$

▶ *Solution:* **a)** $\log_5 \dfrac{3x^4}{y^2} = \log_5 3 + \log_5 x^4 - \log_5 y^2$ *rules 3 and 4*

$= \log_5 3 + 4\log_5 x - 2\log_5 y$ *rule 5*

b) $\log\dfrac{\sqrt{2x-5}}{3} = \log\dfrac{(2x-5)^{\frac{1}{2}}}{3}$

$= \log(2x-5)^{\frac{1}{2}} - \log 3$ *rule 4*

$= \dfrac{1}{2}\log(2x-5) - \log 3$ *rule 5*

Example 8 Condense each logarithmic expression:

a) $\dfrac{1}{3}\log x + 2\log(x-1)$ **b)** $2\log_3(x+4) - \log_3 x$ **c)** $\log 5 + 2\log x - 3\log(x^2+5)$

▶ *Solution:* **a)** $\dfrac{1}{3}\log x + 2\log(x-1) = \log x^{\frac{1}{3}} + \log(x-1)^2$ *rule 5*

$= \log\sqrt[3]{x}(x-1)^2$ *rule 3*

b) $2\log_3(x+4) - \log_3 x = \log_3(x+4)^2 - \log_3 x$ *rule 5*

$= \log_3\dfrac{(x+4)^2}{x}$ *rule 4*

c) $\log 5 + 2\log x - 3\log(x^2+5) = \log 5 + \log x^2 - \log(x^2+5)^3$ *rule 5*

$= \log 5x^2 - \log(x^2+5)^3$ *rule 3*

$= \log\dfrac{5x^2}{(x^2+5)^3}$ *rule 4*

Change of Base

Your calculator has two types of log keys, one for common logarithms with base 10 labelled "LOG" and natural logarithms with base *e* labelled "LN."

Logarithmic Functions	
$y = \log x = \log_{10} x$	Common logarithmic function
$y = \ln x = \log_e x$	Natural logarithmic function

There is no direct way of entering a logarithmic function with a different base, e.g. $\log_2 7$. Therefore, when the base is other than base 10 or base *e*, we use Rule 6 (the change of base property) to evaluate the expression.

Example 9 Evaluate each logarithm to three decimal places:

a) $\log_2 18$ **b)** $\log_{12} 7$ **c)** $\log_6 532$

▶ *Solution:*

a)
$$\log_2 18 = \frac{\log_{10} 18}{\log_{10} 2} = \frac{\log 18}{\log 2}$$ *rule 6*
$$= \frac{1.25527}{0.30103}$$ *use a calculator* *(This step is not necessary when using a calculator.)*
$$= 4.170$$ *simplify*

b)
$$\log_{12} 7 = \frac{\log_{10} 7}{\log_{10} 12} = \frac{\log 7}{\log 12}$$ *rule 6*
$$= \frac{0.84510}{1.07918}$$ *use a calculator*
$$= 0.783$$ *simplify*

c) By common logarithms

$$\log_6 532 = \frac{\log_{10} 532}{\log_{10} 6} = \frac{\log 532}{\log 6}$$
$$= \frac{2.72591}{0.77815}$$
$$= 3.503$$

By natural logarithms

$$\log_6 532 = \frac{\log_e 532}{\log_e 6} = \frac{\ln 532}{\ln 6}$$
$$= \frac{6.27664}{1.79176}$$
$$= 3.503$$

There are other rules of logarithms that can be used. These are quite easy to prove. They are helpful in simple logarithmic expressions but not absolutely needed. All problems with logarithms can be done with just Rules 1 to 6.

Properties of Logarithmic Functions (*helpful rules*)

7. $b^{\log_b a} = a, \quad a > 0$ **8.** $\log_b a = \dfrac{1}{\log_a b}$ **9.** $\log_b a = -\log_{\frac{1}{b}} a$

10. $\log_b \dfrac{1}{x} = -\log_b x$ **11.** $\dfrac{\log_a x}{\log_a y} = \dfrac{\log_b x}{\log_b y}$ **12.** $\log_b x = \log_b y$, if and only if $x = y$

Example 10 Simplify: $\dfrac{1}{\log_2 10} + \dfrac{1}{\log_5 10}$

▶ *Solution:*

$$\begin{aligned} \frac{1}{\log_2 10} + \frac{1}{\log_5 10} &= \log_{10} 2 + \log_{10} 5 && \textit{rule 8} \\ &= \log_{10} 2 \cdot 5 && \textit{rule 3} \\ &= \log_{10} 10 && \textit{multiply} \\ &= 1 && \textit{rule 2} \end{aligned}$$

Example 11 Simplify: $6\log_9 x - 12\log_{27} x$

▶ *Solution:*

$$\begin{aligned} 6\log_9 x - 12\log_{27} x &= \frac{6\log x}{\log 9} - \frac{12\log x}{\log 27} && \textit{rule 6} \\ &= \frac{6\log x}{\log 3^2} - \frac{12\log x}{\log 3^3} && \textit{law of exponents} \\ &= \frac{6\log x}{2\log 3} - \frac{12\log x}{3\log 3} && \textit{rule 5} \\ &= 3\log_3 x - 4\log_3 x && \textit{rule 6} \\ &= -\log_3 x && \textit{subtraction} \end{aligned}$$

Helpful Hints for Simplifying Logarithmic Functions

1. Do not make up your own rules for logarithms. Three of the most common mistakes are as follows:

   $\log(a+b) \neq \log a + \log b$, $(\log a)^2 \neq 2\log a$, $\dfrac{\log a}{\log b} \neq \log a - \log b$

2. Thoroughly understand *must-know rules* rules 1 to 6 of logarithm functions (see p. 216).
3. Apply the properties of logarithms, and write all expressions in logarithmic form.
4. Know how to change from exponential form to logarithmic form, and vice versa.
5. Check the solution for extraneous roots.

5.3 Exercise Set

1. Write the following logarithmic expression in terms of $\log 2$ and $\log 3$:

a) $\log 6$

b) $\log 12$

c) $\log 72$

d) $\log 3200$

e) $\log 0.36$

f) $\log_2 216$

g) $\log 5.4$

h) $\log_6 180$

i) $\log_{18} 2160$

j) $\log_{12} 0.108$

2. Find the exact value of the following logarithmic expressions without the use of a calculator:

a) $\log_3 81$

b) $\log_2 \frac{1}{32}$

c) $\log_2 \sqrt[4]{8}$

d) $\log_5 \sqrt{125}$

e) $\log_9 27^{2.2}$

f) $\log_4 \frac{1}{32}$

g) $(\log_4 8)(\log_{16} 32)$

h) $\dfrac{\log_{27} 81}{\log_{25} 125}$

i) $\log_4 2 + \log_2 32$

j) $\log_9 16 - 2\log_3 2$

3. Use the properties of logarithms to expand the following logarithmic expressions:

a) $\log 100x^2y^3$

b) $\log \dfrac{x^3}{1000y^2}$

c) $\log(x^2+y^3)^4$

d) $\log^4(x^2+y^3)$

e) $\log_5 \dfrac{25x^2y^3}{z}$

f) $\log\sqrt{x^2(x+2)}$

g) $4\log_2(2x)^{12}$

h) $\log_a \sqrt{\dfrac{x^2y+1}{a^3}}$

i) $\log \dfrac{(x^3+y)^3}{x^3}$

j) $\log \sqrt[3]{\dfrac{xy^3}{z^6}}$

4. Condense the expressions to the logarithm of a single quantity:

a) $\log_5 x - \log_5 25$

b) $\log_3 x - 2\log_3 27$

c) $\log\sqrt{x} + \log x^{\frac{3}{2}}$

d) $\log(x^2-1) - \log(x+1) - \log x$

e) $\log(3x^2-5x-2) - \log(x^2-4) - \log(3x+1)$

f) $\log_3(2x-3) - \log_3(2x^2-x-3) + \log_3 3(x+1)$

g) $2\left[\log(x^2-1) - \log(x+1) - \log(x-1)\right]$

h) $\dfrac{3}{2}\log 4x^4 - \dfrac{1}{2}\log y^6$

i) $\dfrac{1}{4}\left[\log(x^2-4) - \log(x-2)\right] - \log x$

j) $\log(x^2-4) - \left[\log(x-2) + \log(x+2)\right]$

5. Simplify:

a) $\log_b x^{\log_x a}$

b) $x^{\log_x 20 - \log_x 4}$

c) $(\log_2 10)(\log 48 - \log 3)$

d) $\dfrac{\log x^3 + \log x^5}{\log x^6 - \log x^3}$

e) $\left(\dfrac{a}{b}\right)^{\log 0.5} \cdot \left(\dfrac{a}{b}\right)^{\log 0.2}$

f) $4^{-2\log_4 3}$

g) $10\log_4 x - 12\log_8 x$

h) $\log \pi + \log \dfrac{\sqrt{2}}{\pi} + \dfrac{1}{2}\log \dfrac{3}{2} - \log \dfrac{\sqrt{3}}{10}$

i) $\log(1-x^3) - \log(1+x+x^2) - \log(1-x)$

j) $\dfrac{\log_a x}{\log_{ab} x} - \dfrac{\log_a x}{\log_b x}$

k) $\dfrac{1}{\log_a x} + \dfrac{1}{\log_b x}$

l) $(\log_5 9)(\log_3 7)(\log_7 5)$

5.4 Exponential and Logarithmic Equations

The two most important rules for solving exponential or logarithmic equations are:

1. $a^x = a^y$ if, and only if, $x = y$.
2. $\log_a x = \log_a y$ if, and only if, $x = y$.

Remember that in $\log_a x, x > 0$ and $a > 0, a \neq 1$. So you must always **check solutions for extraneous roots**. You must also be able to change equations from logarithmic to exponential form, and from exponential form to logarithmic form.

Example 1 Solve by logarithms:

a) $2^x = 8$ **b)** $3^x = 11$

▶ *Solution:*

a)

$$2^x = 8$$
$$\log 2^x = \log 8$$
$$x \log 2 = \log 8$$
$$x = \frac{\log 8}{\log 2}$$
$$x = \frac{0.90309}{0.30103}$$
$$x = 3$$

b)

$3^x = 11$	
$\log 3^x = \log 11$	*if* $a = b$ *then* $\log a = \log b$
$x \log 3 = \log 11$	*power rule*
$x = \dfrac{\log 11}{\log 3}$	*division*
$x = \dfrac{1.04139}{0.47712}$	*calculator*
$x = 2.1827$	*calculator*

Example 2 Solve: $\log(x+3) + \log x = 1$

▶ *Solution:*

$\log(x+3) + \log x = 1$	
$\log x(x+3) = 1$	*product property*
$x(x+3) = 10^1$	*change to exponential form*
$x^2 + 3x - 10 = 0$	*set equal to zero*
$(x+5)(x-2) = 0$	*factor*
$x + 5 = 0$ *or* $x - 2 = 0$	*solve*
$x = -5, 2$	

Check for extraneous roots, $x \neq -5$ since $x > 0$ in $\log x$. Therefore, solution is $x = 2$

Example 3 Solve for x: $\log_3(x+6)-\log_3(x+2)=\log_3 x$

▶ *Solution:*

$$\log_3(x+6)-\log_3(x+2)=\log_3 x$$

$$\log_3(x+6)=\log_3 x+\log_3(x+2) \quad \textit{addition}$$

$$\log_3(x+6)=\log_3 x(x+2) \quad \textit{product property}$$

$$x+6=x(x+2) \quad \log a=\log b \textit{ then } a=b$$

$$x^2+x-6=0 \quad \textit{set equal to zero}$$

$$(x+3)(x-2)=0 \quad \textit{factor}$$

$$x=-3,2 \quad \textit{solve}$$

Check $x\neq -3$ since $\log x>0$. Therefore, solution is $x=2$

Example 4 Solve: $2\log_3 x+\log_3(x-1)=1+\log_3 2x$

▶ *Solution:*

$$2\log_3 x+\log_3(x-1)=1+\log_3 2x$$

$$\log_3 x^2+\log_3(x-1)-\log_3 2x=1 \quad \textit{power property and addition}$$

$$\log_3\frac{x^2(x-1)}{2x}=1 \quad \textit{product and quotient property}$$

$$\log_3\frac{x(x-1)}{2}=1 \quad \textit{simplify}$$

$$\frac{x(x-1)}{2}=3^1 \quad \textit{change from log form to exponential form}$$

$$x^2-x-6=0 \quad \textit{set equal to zero}$$

$$(x-3)(x+2)=0 \quad \textit{factor}$$

$$x=-2,3 \quad \textit{solve}$$

Check $x\neq -2$ since $\log x>0$. Therefore, solution is $x=3$

Example 5 Solve: $x^{\log x}=100x$

▶ *Solution:*

$$x^{\log x}=100x$$

$$\log_x 100x=\log x \quad \textit{change to logarithmic form}$$

$$\frac{\log 100x}{\log x}=\log x \quad \textit{change of base property}$$

$$\log 100x=(\log x)^2 \quad \textit{multiply}$$

$$\log 100+\log x=(\log x)^2 \quad \textit{product rule}$$

$$(\log x)^2-\log x-2=0 \quad \textit{simplify}$$

$$(\log x-2)(\log x+1)=0 \quad \textit{factor}$$

$$\log x=-1,2 \quad \textit{solve}$$

$$x=10^{-1} \text{ or } x=10^2$$

Therefore, $x=\frac{1}{10},100$, check that both solutions work.

Example 6 Solve $3\cdot 2^{x-2}=6^x$ in terms of logarithms.

▶ *Solution:*

$$3\cdot 2^{x-2}=6^x$$

$$\log\left(3\cdot 2^{x-2}\right)=\log 6^x \qquad \textit{if } a=b \textit{ then } \log a=\log b$$

$$\log 3+(x-2)\log 2=x\log 6 \qquad \textit{product and power property}$$

$$\log 3+x\log 2-2\log 2=x\log 6 \qquad \textit{multiply}$$

$$x\log 2-x\log 6=2\log 2-\log 3 \qquad \textit{addition}$$

$$x(\log 2-\log 6)=\log 2^2-\log 3 \qquad \textit{factor and power property}$$

$$x=\frac{\log 4-\log 3}{\log 2-\log 6} \qquad \textit{solve}$$

$$\text{or } x=\frac{\log\frac{4}{3}}{\log\frac{1}{3}}=\frac{\log\frac{4}{3}}{-\log 3} \qquad \textit{simplified solutions}$$

Example 7 Solve for A in terms of B and C: $2\log A-\log B=C$.

▶ *Solution:*

$$2\log A-\log B=C$$

$$\log A^2-\log B=C \qquad \textit{power property}$$

$$\log\frac{A^2}{B}=C \qquad \textit{quotient property}$$

$$\frac{A^2}{B}=10^C \qquad \textit{change to exponential form}$$

$$A^2=B\cdot 10^C \qquad \textit{multiply}$$

$$A=\sqrt{B\cdot 10^C} \qquad \textit{radical}$$

Example 8 If $\log 3=a$ and $\log 8=b$, determine $\log 18$ in terms of a and b.

▶ *Solution:*

$$\log 18=\log 9\cdot 2 \qquad \textit{product property}$$

$$=\log 9+\log 2 \qquad \textit{sum property}$$

$$=\log 3^2+\log 8^{\frac{1}{3}} \qquad \textit{exponent rule}$$

$$=2\log 3+\frac{1}{3}\log 8 \qquad \textit{power property}$$

$$=2a+\frac{1}{3}b \qquad \textit{substitution}$$

5.4 Exercise Set

1. Solve for x. Reject any extraneous roots.

a) $\log_5(2x-1)+\log_5(x-2)=1$

b) $\log_2(2-2x)+\log_2(1-x)=5$

c) $\frac{1}{2}-\log_{16}(x-3)=\log_{16}x$

d) $\log_2(3x+1)+\log_2(x-1)=\log_2(10x+14)$

e) $\log_4(3x^2-5x-2)-\log_4(x-2)=1$

f) $\log x+\log(29-x)=2$

g) $\log_{25}(x-1)+\log_{25}(x+3)=\log_7\sqrt{7}$

h) $2\log(4-x)-\log 3 = \log(10-x)$

i) $2\log_2(x+2)-\log_2(3x-2)=2$

j) $2\log_4 x+\log_4(x-2)-\log_4 2x=1$

2. Express in terms of the stated variable.

a) If $\log x = a$ and $\log y = b$, what is $\log \frac{x^3}{y^2}$ in terms of a and b?

b) If $a = \log_2 3$, find $\log_{16} 81$ in terms of a.

c) If $\log 3 = a$ and $\log 25 = b$, determine an expression for $\log \frac{9}{5}$ in terms of a and b.

d) If $a = \log 2$ and $b = \log 3$, what is $\log \frac{25}{9}$ in terms of a and b?

e) If $\log A = 2$ and $\log B = 3$, what is

(*i*) $\log \frac{A}{B^2}$

(ii) $(\log AB)^2$?

f) If $\log 2 = a$ and $\log 3 = b$, what is $\log_5 12$ in terms of a and b ?

g) If $\log AB = 8$ and $\log B = -4$, then what value does A equal?

h) If $\log 3 = x$, $\log 5 = y$, and $\log 7 = z$, find $\log_2 \sqrt[3]{12.6}$ in terms of x, y, and z.

i) If $\log_8 3 = a$ and $\log_3 5 = b$, find log 5 in terms of a and b.

3. Solve:

a) Solve for B in terms of A and C:
$A = \log 3B - \log C$.

b) Solve for A in terms of B and C:
$1 + \log(AB) = \log C$.

c) Solve for A in terms of B and C:
$3 \log A + \log B = \log C$

d) Solve for x in terms of A, B, and C:
$\log A = \log B - C \log x$.

4. Express the value of x in terms of logs.

a) $2^{3x} = 5^{x-1}$

b) $7^{2x-1} = 17^x$

c) $3^{x-1} = 9 \cdot 10^x$

d) $7^{x-1} = 2 \cdot 5^{1-2x}$

5. Solve for x.

a) $\log_2(\log_8 x) = -1$

b) $\log_2(\log_x(\log_3 27)) = -1$

c) $\log_{\frac{1}{2}}(\log_4(\log_2 x)) = 1$

d) $\log x = \frac{2}{3}\log 27 + 2\log 2 - \log 3$

e) $\log x = \log 2 + 3\log_{\sqrt{10}} y - \log 2z$

f) $2\log x = -\log a + 3\log b + 4\log\frac{1}{c}$

6. Determine an equation for $\log x$ if x equals the following:

a) $x = \frac{a^2}{b^3 \cdot c^{\frac{1}{2}}}$

b) $x = \frac{a^{-2}b^3}{c^{-\frac{1}{2}}}$

c) $x = \frac{\sqrt[3]{a^2} \cdot b^{-\frac{2}{5}}}{c^{\frac{1}{2}}}$

d) $x = \frac{\sqrt{a^5 b}^{-\frac{1}{3}}}{c^3 \cdot d^{-\frac{2}{3}}}$

7. Solve for x.

a) $\log_2 16^{2x+1} = 8$

b) $\log_{16} x + \log_4 x + \log_2 x = 7$

c) $\log_9 x + 3\log_3 x = 7$

d) $2\log_4 x - 3\log_x 4 = 5$

e) $(\log_4 a)(\log_a 2a)(\log_{2a} x) = \log_a a^3$

f) $\sqrt{\log x} = \log\sqrt{x}$

8. Find the fallacy in each of the following "proofs" that $1 > 2$:

a)

$$2 > 1$$
$$\frac{2}{4} > \frac{1}{4}$$
$$\log\frac{1}{2} > \log\frac{1}{4}$$
$$\log\frac{1}{2} > \log\left(\frac{1}{2}\right)^2$$
$$\log\frac{1}{2} > 2\log\frac{1}{2}$$
$$1 > 2$$

b)

$$3 > 2$$
$$3\log\frac{1}{2} > 2\log\frac{1}{2}$$
$$\log\left(\frac{1}{2}\right)^3 > \log\left(\frac{1}{2}\right)^2$$
$$\left(\frac{1}{2}\right)^3 > \left(\frac{1}{2}\right)^2$$
$$\frac{1}{8} > \frac{1}{4}$$
$$1 > 2$$

5.5 Applications of Exponential and Logarithmic Functions

When Albert Einstein was asked what was the most important formula he had encountered, his answer was the **compound interest** formula. Most of our lives revolve around this most important concept.

To derive the formula, suppose P dollars is deposited at rate r for 1 year.

- Then, Interest $I_1 = P \cdot r \cdot 1 = Pr$
- At the end of one year the amount on deposit is $A_1 = P + Pr = P(1+r)$
- If the deposit earns compound interest, then the interest earned the second year is based on the deposit at the end of the first year.

$$I_2 = P(1+r)r \cdot 1 = P(1+r)r$$

- So the total amount on deposit at the end of the second year is

$$\begin{aligned} A_2 &= P(1+r) + P(1+r)r = P(1+r)(1+r) \\ &= P(1+r)^2 \end{aligned}$$

- If we continue this pattern for a third year, then

$$A_3 = P(1+r)^3$$

$$\vdots$$

- If we continue this pattern for t years, then

$$A_t = P(1+r)^t$$

To calculate more frequent (quarterly, monthly, or daily), let n be the number of compounds per year and t the number of years. Then the rate per compound is $\frac{r}{n}$ for t years.

$$A = P\left(1 + \frac{r}{n}\right)^{nt}$$

Let the principle be $P = \$1$ for 1 year at a nominal rate of 100%, to make the algebra simple, then $A = \left(1 + \frac{1}{n}\right)^n$.

As n grows larger and larger, $\left(1 + \frac{1}{n}\right)^n$ approaches e.

Number of Compounds	Amount $\left(1+\frac{1}{n}\right)^n$
$n=1$ (annually)	$\left(1+\frac{1}{n}\right)^1=2$
$n=4$ (quarterly)	$\left(1+\frac{1}{4}\right)^4=2.44$
$n=12$ (monthly)	$\left(1+\frac{1}{12}\right)^{12}=2.61$
$n=365$ (daily)	$\left(1+\frac{1}{365}\right)^{365}=2.7146$
$n=8760$ (hourly)	$\left(1+\frac{1}{8760}\right)^{8760}=2.7181$
$n=31536000$ (each second)	$\left(1+\frac{1}{31536000}\right)^{31536000}=2.71828$
⋮	⋮
$n=$ infinite times	$\left(1+\frac{1}{\infty}\right)^{\infty}=e$

Thus, the formulas for compound interest are

Compound Interest Formulas

(Interest compounded n times per year)	(Interest compounded continuously)
$A=P\left(1+\frac{r}{n}\right)^{nt}$	$A=Pe^{rt}$

Our growth and decay formulas follow the same pattern as compound interest.

Growth and Decay Formulas

Growth and decay: $A = A_0(x)^{\frac{t}{T}}$

A – final amount

A_0 – initial amount

x – growth or decay value, e.g., half-life use $\frac{1}{2}$

increase by 10% use 1.1

decrease by 10% use 0.9

t – total time that item is left

T – time of growth or decay, e.g., half-life

Growth and decay: $A = A_0 e^{kt}$

A – final amount

A_0 – initial amount

e – constant $\approx$ 2.71828...

k – proportional constant

t – time

Example 1

Estimate the time required for \$5000 to grow to \$30 000 if it is invested at 10% compounded **a)** monthly **b)** continuously.

▶ Solution:

a)

$$A = P\left(1+\frac{r}{n}\right)^{nt}$$

$$30\,000 = 5000\left(1+\frac{0.10}{12}\right)^{12t}$$

$$6 = 1\left(1+\frac{0.10}{12}\right)^{12t}$$

$$\log 6 = \log\left(1+\frac{0.10}{12}\right)^{12t}$$

$$\log 6 = 12t\log\left(1+\frac{0.10}{12}\right)$$

$$t = \frac{\log 6}{12\log\left(1+\frac{0.10}{12}\right)}$$

$$= 17.99 \text{ years}$$

b)

$$A = Pe^{rt}$$

$$30\,000 = 5000e^{0.10t}$$

$$6 = e^{0.10t}$$

$$\log_e 6 = 0.10t$$

$$\ln 6 = 0.10t$$

$$t = \frac{\ln 6}{0.10}$$

$$= 17.92 \text{ years}$$

The half-life of plutonium-241 is 13 years. Find the time for 80% of a 5 gram sample to decay.

▶ *Solution:* If 80% decays, then 20% remains. 0.20 of 5 grams = 1 gram.

Method I

$$A = A_0(x)^{\frac{t}{T}}$$

$$1 = 5\left(\frac{1}{2}\right)^{\frac{t}{13}}$$

$$0.2 = \left(\frac{1}{2}\right)^{\frac{t}{13}}$$

$$\log_{\frac{1}{2}} 0.2 = \frac{t}{13}$$

$$t = 13\frac{\log 0.2}{\log\left(\frac{1}{2}\right)}$$

$$= 30.185 \text{ years}$$

Method II

$$A = A_0 e^{kt}$$

$$2.5 = 5e^{k \cdot 13}$$

$$0.5 = e^{13k}$$

$$13k = \ln(0.5)$$

$$k = \frac{\ln(0.5)}{13}$$

$$1 = 5e^{\frac{\ln(0.5)t}{13}}$$

$$0.2 = e^{\frac{\ln(0.5)t}{13}}$$

$$\ln 0.2 = \frac{\ln(0.5)t}{13}$$

$$t = \frac{13\ln(0.2)}{\ln(0.5)}$$

$$= 30.185 \text{ years}$$

Example 3

A hotel is serving roast turkey. At noon, the turkey's temperature was 75°F. At 2:00 p.m. the chef checked the temperature, and it had reached 100°F. If the oven remains constant at 325°F, at what time will the turkey be done if it must reach a temperature of 175°F?

▶ *Solution:*

$$A = A_0(x)^{\frac{t}{T}}$$

$$100 = 75(x)^{\frac{2}{1}}$$ *where x is the rate at which the temperature rises (°F per hr)*

$$x = \sqrt{\frac{100}{75}} = 1.547$$

$$175 = 75(1.1547)^t$$

$$t = \log_{1.1547}\left(\frac{7}{3}\right) = \frac{\log\left(\frac{7}{3}\right)}{\log(1.1547)}$$

$$= 5.89 \text{ hours}$$

The turkey will be ready just before 6:00 p.m., or 5:53 p.m.

5.5 Exercise Set

1. An average new car depreciates 15% in value each year. How long does it take for a new \$40 000 car to depreciate down to \$10 000 in value?

2. If you have \$10 000, how long does it take you to become a millionaire if you invest the full amount at 12% compounded **a)** quarterly **b)** continuously?

3. What interest rate is needed if money is to triple in 15 years if the interest is compounded **a)** semi-annually **b)** continuously?

4. It is estimated that 20% of a certain radioactive substance decays in 30 hours. What is the half-life of this substance?

5. The pH scale measures the acidity (0–7) or alkalinity (7–14) of a solution with 7 being neutral water. It is a logarithm scale in base 10. Thus, a pH of 9 is 10 times more alkaline than a pH of 8, and a pH of 5 is 10 times more acidic than a pH of 6.

   a) If lemon juice has a pH of 2.1, how many times more acidic is it than black coffee which has a pH of 4.8?

   b) If tomato juice, with a pH of 4.2, is 75 times as acidic as milk, what is the pH of milk?

6. If Vancouver has a population of 400 000 and is growing at a rate of 2% annually, and Surrey has a population of 300 000 and is growing at a rate of 3% annually, in how many years will Surrey catch up to Vancouver in population?

7. Find the time needed for money to triple at 8% compounded **a)** daily **b)** continuously.

8. The amount of a chemical in grams that will dissolve in a solution is given by $C = 8e^{0.3t}$ where t is the temperature in Celsius of the solution. Find t when $C = 100$ grams.

9. The population of Toronto is given by $P(t) = 4\ 000\ 000e^{0.012t}$, where $t = 0$ corresponds to year 2000. What year will the population reach 6 400 000?

10. A biologist studying a colony of bacteria determines that a certain culture grows exponentially such that the bacteria doubles every 4 days. If initially the biologist has 1200 bacteria present, how many days does it take before 100 000 bacteria are present?

11. The half-life of radioactive carbon 14 is 5570 years. If 500 milligrams of radioactive carbon 14 are present today, determine the amount present after 2500 years.

12. Prime numbers are integers that are divisible only by one and themselves. The newest largest prime has an added distinction: It is what is known as a Mersenne prime. These rare numbers discovered by Euclid in 350 B.C. can be written using the formula $2^p - 1$, where p is also a prime number. Most prime numbers cannot be written this way. In fact, the newest discovered prime is only the 49th of its kind to be found. This largest prime is $2^{74207281} - 1$. How many digits are in the decimal expansion of this largest prime number?

5.6 Chapter Review

Logarithms – Multiple-choice Questions

Level A Questions

1. Change $\log_a c = b$ to exponential form.

a) $a^b = c$
b) $c^a = b$
c) $b^c = a$
d) $a^c = b$

2. Solve for x: $\log 5 = \log x - \log 2$

a) $\frac{2}{5}$
b) 1
c) $\frac{5}{2}$
d) 10

3. What is the equation of the asymptote of the graph of the function $y = \log_3(x-2)+1$?

a) $x = -2$
b) $x = -1$
c) $x = 2$
d) $x = 3$

4. Simplify: $\dfrac{\log 10^x}{10^{\log x}}$

a) $\frac{1}{10}$
b) 1
c) $\frac{x}{10}$
d) x

5. If $y = \log x$, then $y+2$ equals which of the following?

a) $\log 2x$
b) $\log 100x$
c) $\log(x+2)$
d) $\log(x+100)$

6. Determine an expression for $\log x$ if $x = \dfrac{\sqrt{A}}{3B}$.

a) $\dfrac{\frac{1}{2}\log A}{3\log B}$

b) $\dfrac{\frac{1}{2}\log A}{\log 3 + \log B}$

c) $\frac{1}{2}\log A - \log 3 + \log B$

d) $\frac{1}{2}\log A - \log 3 - \log B$

7. If $\log_a 2 = b$ and $\log_c 5 = d$, then $a^b \cdot c^d$ equals which of the following?

a) $\log_{ac} 7$

b) $\log_{ac} 10$

c) 7

d) 10

8. Write as a simple logarithm: $4\log a^2 - 2\log a$.

a) $\log a^2$

b) $\log a^3$

c) $\log a^4$

d) $\log a^6$

9. Determine an equation of the asymptote of the graph of $y = 2^{x-1} - 4$.

a) $x = -1$

b) $x = 1$

c) $y = -4$

d) $y = 4$

10. Give the domain of the function $y = \log_3(2 - x)$.

a) $x < 0$

b) $x > 0$

c) $x < 2$

d) $x > 2$

11. Solve: $3^{\log x} = \dfrac{1}{27}$

a) $\dfrac{1}{1000}$

b) $\dfrac{1}{9}$

c) 9

d) 1000

12. Solve: $\left(\frac{1}{9}\right)^{2x-1} = 27^{2-x}$

a) -8
b) -4
c) 4
d) 8

13. Solve: $4^{x^2-2x} = 8^{1-x}$

a) $-1, \frac{3}{2}$
b) $-1, \frac{2}{3}$
c) $-\frac{2}{3}, 1$
d) $-\frac{3}{2}, 1$

14. Determine the x- and y-intercepts of $x = \log_3(y+5) - 2$.

a) x-intercept: -0.54, y-intercept: 4.0
b) x-intercept: 0, y-intercept: 4.0
c) x-intercept: 4.0, y-intercept: -0.54
d) x-intercept: 4.0, y-intercept: 0

15. Determine the x-intercept of the function $y = -\log_4(x+8) + \frac{1}{2}$

a) -10
b) -6
c) -1
d) 0

16. Determine the y-intercept of the function $y = \log_2(x+8) - 3$

a) 0
b) 1
c) 2
d) 3

17. Determine the domain of the function $y = -\log(x+2) - 3$

a) $x \geq -2$
b) $x > -2$
c) $x \leq -2$
d) $x < -2$

18. Determine the range of the function $y = -3 \cdot 2^{x-1} + 4$

a) $y < 1$
b) $y > 1$
c) $y < 4$
d) $y > 4$

19. Evaluate: $2\log_x\left(\frac{1}{\sqrt{x}}\right),\quad x>0,\quad x\neq 1$

a) $\sqrt{x}$
b) x
c) -1
d) 1

Level B Questions

20. An earthquake on Haida Gwaii (formerly the Queen Charlotte Islands), B.C. on August 22, 1949 measured 8.1 on thc Richter scale and an earthquake on Baffin Bay in Nunavut (formerly the Northwest Territories) on November 20, 1933 measured 7.4 on the Richter scale. How much more intense was the earthquake on Haida Gwaii compared to the earthquake on Baffin Bay?

a) 0.7
b) 5.0
c) 7.3
d) 50.1

21. Determine an expression for $\log x$ if $x=\frac{\sqrt[3]{a}}{bc^2}$.

a) $\frac{1}{3}\log a-\log b+2\log c$

b) $\frac{1}{3}\log a-2\log b-2\log c$

c) $\frac{1}{3}\log a-\log b-2\log c$

d) $\frac{\frac{1}{3}\log a}{\log b+\log c}$

22. The inverse relation of $y=\log\left(\frac{x}{2}\right)$ is which of the following:

a) $y=20^x$

b) $y=2\cdot 10^x$

c) $y=10^{\frac{2}{x}}$

d) $y=\frac{1}{\log 2-\log x}$

23. Simplify $\log_{\frac{1}{a}}(\sqrt{a})^a$.

a) $-\frac{a}{2}$

b) $\frac{a}{2}$

c) $-\sqrt{a}$

d) $\sqrt{a}$

24. Determine the domain of the function $y = \log_x(x+2)$.

a) $x > -2$
b) $x > 0$
c) $x > 0,\ \ x \neq 1$
d) $x > -2,\ \ x \neq 1$

25. Solve: $\log_3(x+5) - \log_3(x-3) = 2$.

a) -2
b) 2
c) 4
d) $\frac{29}{7}$

26. Express as a single logarithm: $3 - 2\log a + \log b$.

a) $\log\frac{3b}{a^2}$

b) $\log\frac{3}{a^2 b}$

c) $\log\frac{1000b}{a^2}$

d) $\log\frac{1000}{a^2 b}$

27. The point $(m\ ,\ n)$ is on the graph of $f(x) = \log_a x$. What point must be on a variation of the inverse graph $h(x) = a^{-x}$?

a) $(-m,\ -n)$
b) $(-n,\ m)$
c) $(-m,\ n)$
d) $(-n,\ -m)$

28. Solve for x: $(\log_9 x)(\log_5 3) = 1$.

a) $\sqrt{5}$
b) 5
c) 25
d) 81

29. Given $f(x) = 2^{-x}$, determine its inverse $f^{-1}(x)$.

a) $f^{-1}(x) = 2^x$

b) $f^{-1}(x) = -2^x$

c) $f^{-1}(x) = \log_2(-x)$

d) $f^{-1}(x) = \log_2\left(\frac{1}{x}\right)$

30. Solve : $2^{3\log_8 5} = x$

a) 5
b) 25
c) 125
d) $\sqrt[3]{5}$

31. If $f(x) = 6^{x+1} - 2$, find $f^{-1}(x)$, the inverse of $f(x)$.

a) $f^{-1}(x) = \log_6(x+2) - 1$
b) $f^{-1}(x) = \log_6(x+1) - 2$
c) $f^{-1}(x) = \log_6(x-2) + 1$
d) $f^{-1}(x) = \log_6(x-1) + 2$

32. If $f(x) = \log_5(x-1) - 2$, find $f^{-1}(x)$, the inverse of $f(x)$.

a) $f^{-1}(x) = 5^{x-2} - 1$
b) $f^{-1}(x) = 5^{x+2} - 1$
c) $f^{-1}(x) = 5^{x-2} + 1$
d) $f^{-1}(x) = 5^{x+2} + 1$

33. If $\log_{81} x = a$, determine $\log_{27} x$ in terms of a.

a) $\frac{2}{3}a$
b) $\frac{3}{2}a$
c) $\frac{3}{4}a$
d) $\frac{4}{3}a$

34. The half-life of a radioactive substance is 14 years. Determine an expression for the mass of the substance remaining from 50 grams after t years.

a) $0.5(50)^{\frac{14}{t}}$
b) $50\left(\frac{1}{2}\right)^{\frac{14}{t}}$
c) $0.5(50)^{\frac{t}{14}}$
d) $50\left(\frac{1}{2}\right)^{\frac{t}{14}}$

35. Determine the initial investment needed, P, if an interest rate of 12% per annum compounded quarterly yields \$1000 in 5 years.

a) $P = \dfrac{1000}{1.03^5}$

b) $P = \dfrac{1000}{1.04^5}$

c) $P = \dfrac{1000}{1.03^{20}}$

d) $P = \dfrac{1000}{1.04^{20}}$

36. An earthquake in Grand Banks Nova Scotia which measured 7.3 on the Richter scale was 240 times as strong as an earthquake near Vancouver Island. Determine the Richter scale strength of the Vancouver Island earthquake.

a) 2.4
b) 4.9
c) 6.3
d) 9.7

37. The population of Canada is approximately 30 million. Assuming the population is growing continuously, the population P, in millions, t years from now can be determined by the formula $P = 30e^{0.019t}$. What will be the population, in millions, 50 years from now?

a) 75.38
b) 76.83
c) 77.45
d) 77.57

38. A strain of bacteria triples every 5 days. Determine an expression for the initial amount of bacteria if after t days, 200 bacteria are present.

a) $A = \dfrac{200}{3^{\frac{t}{5}}}$

b) $A = \dfrac{200}{3^{\frac{5}{t}}}$

c) $A = 200(3)^{\frac{t}{5}}$

d) $A = 200(3)^{\frac{5}{t}}$

For questions 39 and 40

In chemistry, the pH scale measures the acidity (0–7) or alkalinity (7–14) of a solution. It is a logarithmic scale in base 10. Thus, a pH of 9 is 10 times more alkaline than a pH of 8, and a pH of 5 is 10 times more acidic than a pH of 6.

39. If a solution has a pH of 9.8, how much weaker is a solution with a pH of 8.2?

a) 1.6
b) 4.0
c) 39.8
d) 53.7

40. Determine the pH of a solution that is 160 times more alkaline than a known pH of 8.7.

a) 7.2
b) 10.9
c) 23.5
d) 46.2

41. Determine an equivalent expression for $\log_3\left(\frac{a}{9b^2}\right)$

a) $\log_3 a - 18\log_3 b$

b) $\log_3 a - 9\log_3 b^2$

c) $-2 + \log_3 a - 2\log_3 b$

d) $-2 + \log_3 a + 2\log_3 b$

42. If $\log_2 5 = a$ and $\log_2 3 = b$, determine an expression for $\log_2\left(\frac{25}{72}\right)$ in terms of *a* and *b*

a) $2a - 2b + 3$
b) $2a - 2b - 3$
c) $a^2 - b^2 - 3$
d) $a^2 - b^2 + 3$

43. Express as a single logarithm: $1 - \log\frac{3}{b} - \log c$

a) $\log\frac{10b}{3c}$

b) $\log\frac{30b}{c}$

c) $\log\frac{b}{30c}$

d) $\log\frac{10bc}{3}$

44. Change to logarithmic form: $y = ab^x$

a) $x = \log_b\left(\frac{a}{y}\right)$

b) $x = \log_b\left(\frac{y}{a}\right)$

c) $x = \log_{ab} y$

d) $x = \log_y(ab)$

45. If $\log_2(a-3) = b$, $a > 3$, express a in terms of b.

a) $a = 2^{b-3}$
b) $a = 2^{b+3}$
c) $a = 2^b + 3$
d) $a = 2^b - 3$

Level C Questions

46. If $\log 4 = a$ and $\log 3 = b$, determine an expression for $\log\frac{2}{9}$ in terms of a and b.

a) $\sqrt{a} - 2b$

b) $\frac{a}{2} - 2b$

c) $\frac{a}{4b}$

d) $\frac{\sqrt{a}}{2b}$

47. The graph of the function $y = \log_{x+1}(2-x)$ must observe what restrictions?

a) $x > -1$
b) $x \neq 0$
c) $x > 2,\ x < -1$
d) $-1 < x < 2,\ x \neq 0$

48. When solving algebraically: $2\log(3-x) = \log 2 + \log(22-2x)$, what answer is eliminated by the restriction on logarithms?

a) 5
b) 6
c) 7
d) 8

49. When solving algebraically: $\log_x 12 - \log_x(x-1) = 1$, what answer is eliminated by the restriction on logarithms?

a) -1
b) -2
c) -3
d) -4

50. Solve for x: $\log_5(2x+1)=1-\log_5(x+2)$.

a) -3

b) $\frac{1}{2}$

c) $-\frac{1}{2}$, 3

d) $\frac{1}{2}$, -3

51. If $a=3\log_8 c$ and $b=\log_4 d$, determine an expression for $\frac{c}{d}$ in terms of a and b.

a) 2^{2a-b}

b) 2^{a-2b}

c) $2^{\frac{a}{3}-b}$

d) $2^{\frac{a}{3}-2b}$

52. What equation describes the set of points $(2^a,\ a)$?

a) $x=\log_y 2$

b) $y=\log_x 2$

c) $x=\log_2 y$

d) $y=\log_2 x$

53. Solve for x: $\log_3[\log_x(\log_2 8)]=-1$.

a) 1
b) 3
c) 9
d) 27

54. Given $\log 4=x$ and $\log\frac{1}{3}=y$, determine an expression for $\log 6$ in terms of x and y.

a) $\frac{x}{2}-y$

b) $x-2y$

c) $\frac{-xy}{2}$

d) $\frac{2x}{y}$

55. Solve for x in terms of logarithms: $2^{x-1} = 3^x$.

a) $\dfrac{-\log 2}{\log 2 - \log 3}$

b) $\dfrac{\log 2}{\log 2 - \log 3}$

c) $\dfrac{-\log 3}{\log 2 - \log 3}$

d) $\dfrac{\log 3}{\log 2 - \log 3}$

56. If $\log 2 = a$ and $\log 9 = b$, determine $\log 12$ in terms of a and b.

a) $2a + \dfrac{1}{2}b$

b) $2a - \dfrac{1}{2}b$

c) $\dfrac{1}{2}a + b$

d) $\dfrac{1}{2}a - b$

57. Solve for x: $\dfrac{1}{\log_3 x} - \log_x 27 = 2$.

a) $\dfrac{1}{3}$

b) -3

c) 3

d) 9

58. If $\log_4 3 = x$ and $\log_8 7 = y$, determine $\log_2 21$ in terms of x and y.

a) $x + y$

b) $2x + 3y$

c) $3x + 2y$

d) $6xy$

59. For every 100 metres that a balloon rises, the atmospheric pressure is reduced by 1%. At what balloon height is the atmospheric pressure 15% of the pressure at Earth's surface? (accurate to the nearest 1000 m)

a) 16 000 m

b) 17 000 m

c) 18 000 m

d) 19 000 m

60. If 25% of a radioactive material decays in 40 hours, what is the half-life of the material?

a) 16.60h
b) 20.00h
c) 80.00h
d) 96.38h

61. Solve: $\log_3(2-4x)-\log_3(3-x)=2$

a) -6
b) 5
c) 5.5
d) no solution

62. Solve for x in terms of logarithms: $3a^{x-1}=b^x$

a) $x=\dfrac{\log a-\log 3}{\log a-\log b}$

b) $x=\dfrac{\log a-\log 3}{\log a+\log b}$

c) $x=\dfrac{\log 3a}{\log 3a-\log b}$

d) $x=\dfrac{\log 3a}{\log 3a+\log b}$

63. Solve: $2\log_3(-x)=2-\log_3 4$

a) $-\dfrac{3}{2}$

b) $\dfrac{3}{2}$

c) $\pm\dfrac{3}{2}$

d) no solution

64. What interest rate, compounded monthly, is needed for money to triple in value in 10 years?

a) 9.5%
b) 10.0%
c) 10.5%
d) 11.0%

65. A radioactive substance decays from 600 grams to 200 grams in 10 days. Determine the half-life of the substance.

a) 6.3 d
b) 6.7 d
c) 11.2 d
d) 15.8 d

LIST OF WRONGS AND RIGHTS

On the left are listed some of the mistakes students frequently make in trigonometry calculations.

Wrong	Right
1. $\sin(x+y) = \sin x + \sin y$	1. $\sin(x+y) = \sin x \cos y + \cos x \sin y$
2. $\cos(-x) = -\cos x$	2. $\cos(-x) = \cos x$
3. $\sin(-x) = \sin x$	3. $\sin(-x) = -\sin x$
4. $\sin 2x = 2\sin x$	4. $\sin 2x = 2\sin x \cdot \cos x$
5. $\dfrac{\sin 2x}{2} = \sin x$	5. $\dfrac{\sin 2x}{2} = \dfrac{2\sin x \cos x}{2} = \sin x \cos x$
6. $\sin 2x = 1 \rightarrow \sin x = \frac{1}{2} \rightarrow x = 30°$	6. $\sin 2x = 1 \rightarrow 2x = 90° \rightarrow x = 45°$ etc.
7. $\cos 2x = 1 - 2\sin^2 x \rightarrow$ $\therefore \quad \cos 4x = 2 - 4\sin^2 2x$	7. $\cos 2x = 1 - 2\sin^2 x \rightarrow$ $\therefore \quad \cos 4x = 1 - 2\sin^2 2x$
8. $\sin x + \cos x = 1$	8. $\sin^2 x + \cos^2 x = 1$
9. $\csc x = \dfrac{1}{\cos x}$	9. $\csc x = \dfrac{1}{\sin x}$
10. $\sin^{-1} x = \dfrac{1}{\sin x}$	10. $\sin^{-1} x$ represents the inverse sine function.
11. $\tan kx$ has period of $\dfrac{2\pi}{\lvert k \rvert}$	11. $\sin kx$ and $\cos kx$ have periods of $\dfrac{2\pi}{\lvert k \rvert}$, but $\tan kx$ has period of $\dfrac{\pi}{\lvert k \rvert}$

6.1 Trigonometric Functions

Angles and Their Measures

Angles on a coordinate plane in standard position: Standard position means the initial side is along the positive x-axis with the vertex at the origin. Rotating a ray about the vertex forms an angle θ with an initial side and a terminal side.

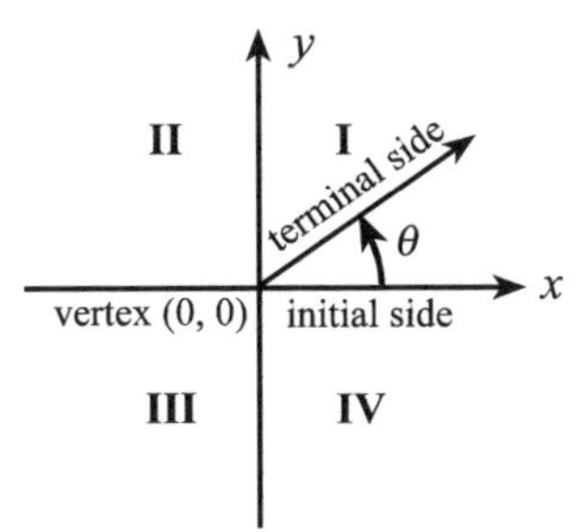

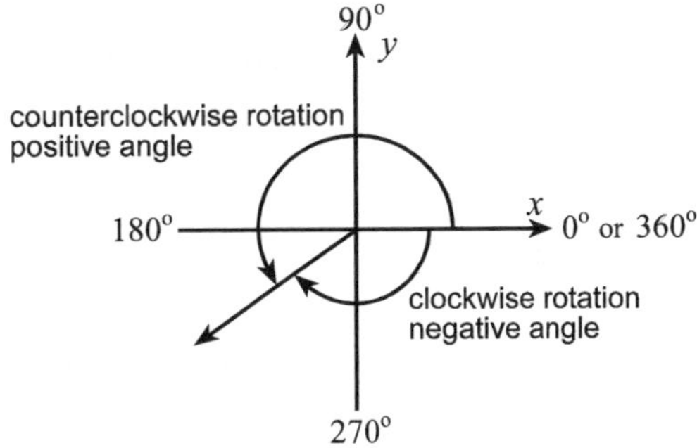

Degree Measures

The measure of an angle is determined by the direction and the amount of rotation from the initial side to the terminal side. The measure you are familiar with is **degrees**. One degree (1°) is formed when a ray is rotated $\frac{1}{360}$ of a revolution in a **counterclock** direction. Thus, one full rotation is 360°.

> **Definition of Degree Measure**
>
> An angle formed by one complete rotation has a measure of 360 degrees (360°).
>
> An angle formed by $\frac{1}{360}$ of a rotation has a measure of **1 degree**. The symbol ° denotes degrees.

Examples of Degree Measures

$\theta = 110°$

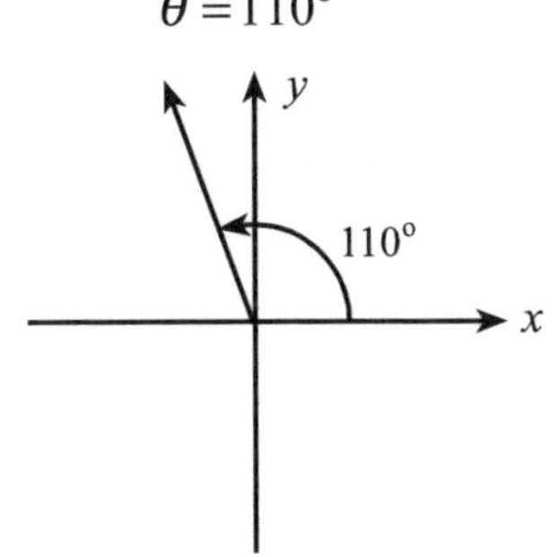

$\theta = -150°$

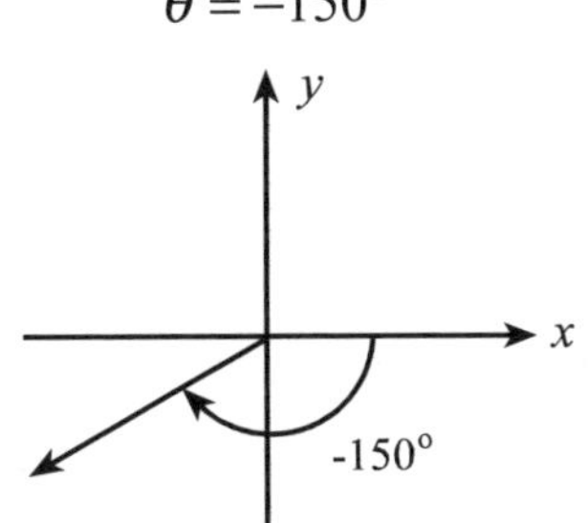

$\theta = 400°$

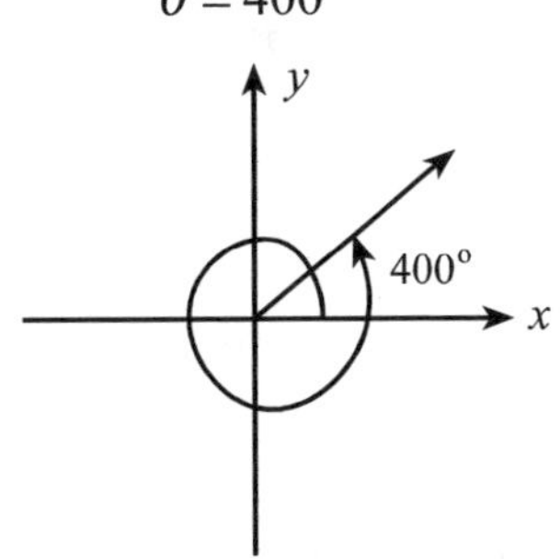

$\theta = -500°$

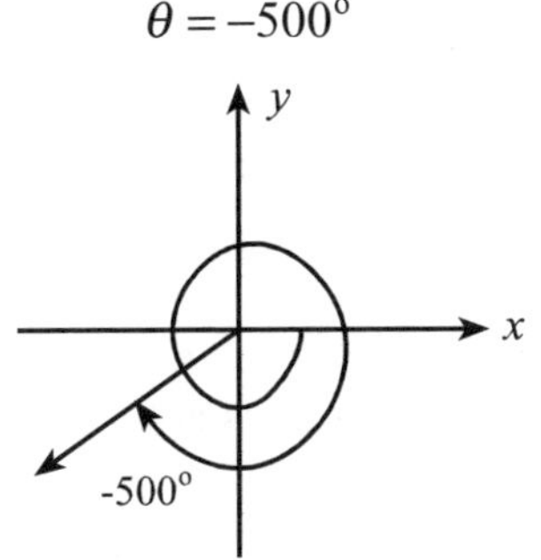

Examples of Special Types of Angles

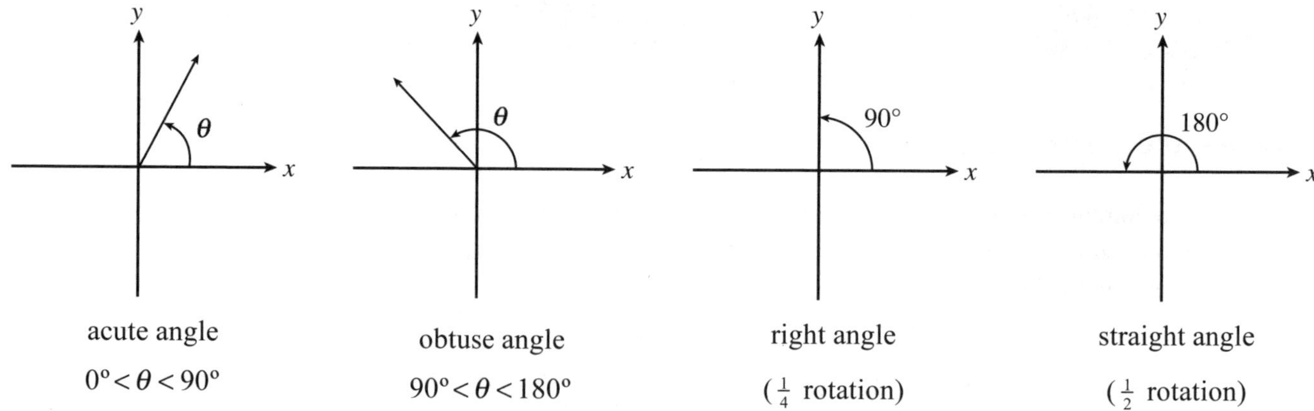

Coterminal Angles

Angles in standard position that have the same initial side and the same terminal side are called **coterminal angles**.

Examples of Coterminal Angles

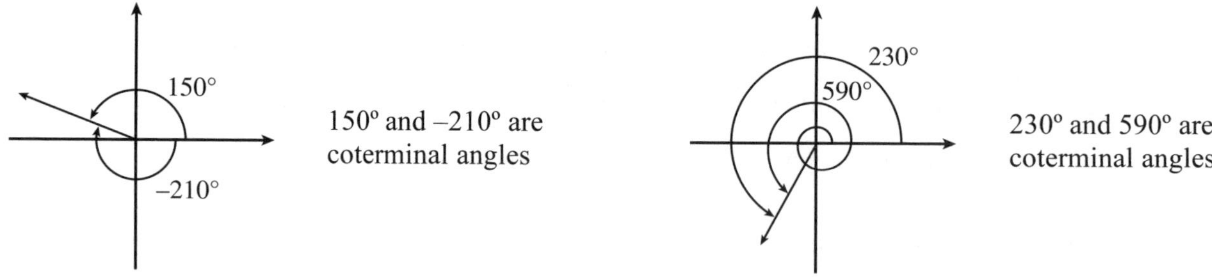

Example 1 Determine two positive and two negative coterminal angles for $465°$.

▶ *Solution:* $465° - 360° = 105°$, $465° + 360° = 825°$, $465° - 2 \times 360° = -255°$, $465° - 3 \times 360° = -615°$

(*infinite number of possible answers*)

Radian Measure and Conversion

Another unit of angle measure is called **radian**. It is more suited to scientific work and engineering applications because a radian is an arc length of a circle.

To define radian measure, we will use a circle with a radius of 1 with centre at the origin.
This circle is called a **unit circle**.

> **Definition of Radian Measure**
>
> An angle of 1 radian is a standard position angle in the counterclockwise direction of arc length 1 on a unit circle.

Example – Unit Circles and Radians

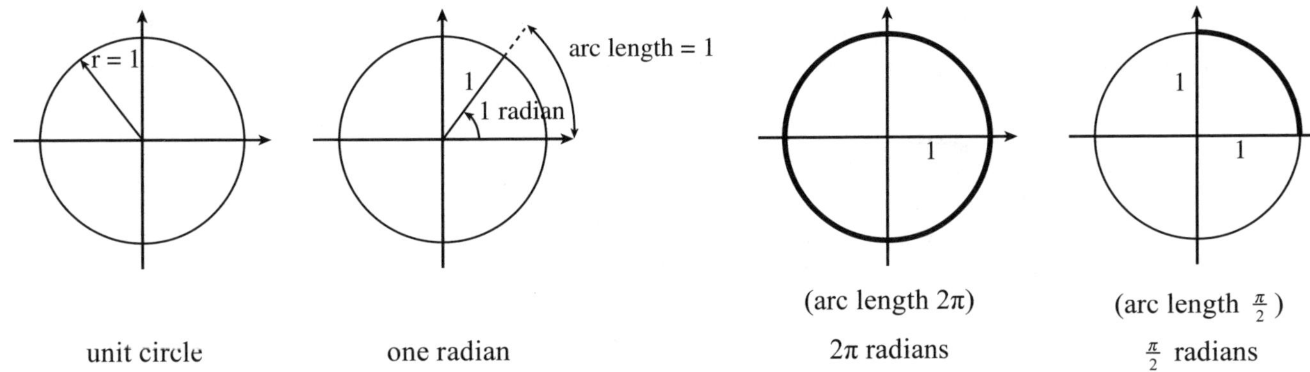

unit circle | one radian | (arc length 2π) 2π radians | (arc length $\frac{\pi}{2}$) $\frac{\pi}{2}$ radians

A circle has $360°$. The circumference of a circle is $C = 2\pi r$. If the radius measure is one, $C = 2\pi$. Then one complete rotation about the unit circle is an arc length of 2π for every $360°$. Therefore, the relationship between degree and radian is $360° = 2\pi$ radians or $180° = \pi$ radians. Thus, we can state:

Conversion Factors: Degrees to Radians and Radians to Degrees

- Conversion factor for degrees to radians: multiply the degree measure by $\dfrac{\pi}{180°}$
- Conversion factor for radians to degrees: multiply the radian measure by $\dfrac{180°}{\pi}$

Example 1 Convert the degree value to radians and radian value to degrees:

a) $240°$ **b)** $72°$ **c)** $\dfrac{3\pi}{4}$ **d)** 2.13

▶ *Solution:*

a) $240° \times \dfrac{\pi}{180°} = \dfrac{4\pi}{3} \approx 4.19$

b) $72° \times \dfrac{\pi}{180°} = \dfrac{2\pi}{5} \approx 1.26$

c) $\dfrac{3\pi}{4} \times \dfrac{180°}{\pi} = 135°$

d) $2.13 \times \dfrac{180°}{\pi} \approx 122°$

Note: In solutions a) and b) the answer is understood to be radians if no symbol is placed after the numerical value.

Arc Length

The length of an arc of a circle is directly proportional to the angle θ and the radius of the circle. If θ is given in radians, then the constant of proportionality is the radius r, thus the arc lengths = $r\theta$.

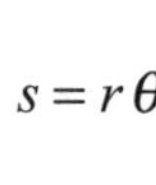

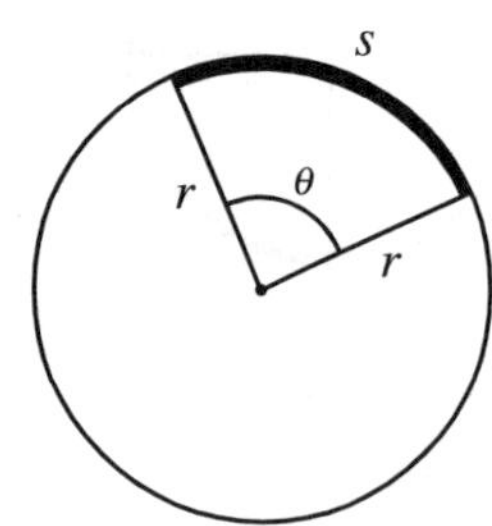

θ = central angle in radians
r = radius
s = arc length

Example 1 Determine the arc length of a circle with radius 5 cm and central angle of 60°.

▶ *Solution:* $60^\circ \times \dfrac{\pi}{180^\circ} = \dfrac{\pi}{3}$ radians, therefore, $\boldsymbol{s = r\theta} = 5 \times \dfrac{\pi}{3} = \dfrac{5\pi}{3} \approx 5.24$ cm.

Example 2 Find the distance travelled by the tip of the second hand on a watch of radius 16 mm as it moves from 0-second mark to the 40-second mark.

▶ *Solution:* From 0 to 40 seconds is $\dfrac{40}{60} = \dfrac{2}{3}$ of a revolution.

Thus, $\theta = \dfrac{2}{3}$ revolution $= \dfrac{2}{3}(2\pi \text{ radians}) = \dfrac{4\pi}{3}$ radians

$$s = r\theta$$

$$= (16 \text{ mm})\left(\frac{4\pi}{3}\right)$$

$$= \frac{64\pi}{3} \text{ mm} \approx 67.0 \text{ mm}$$

Example 3 What is the degree measure of a central angle θ opposite an arc of 18 cm in a circle of radius 6 cm?

▶ *Solution:*

$$s = r\theta$$

$$\theta = \frac{s}{r} = \frac{18 \text{ cm}}{6 \text{ cm}} = 3$$

$$3 \text{ radians} = 3 \times \frac{180^\circ}{\pi}$$

$$= \frac{540^\circ}{\pi} \approx 171.9^\circ$$

6.1 Exercise Set

1. Determine if the angle is in quadrant I, II, III, IV or not in a quadrant for the following standard position angles.

a) 150° __________ **b)** –150° __________

c) 314° __________ **d)** –314° __________

e) 612° __________ **f)** –537° __________

g) 1100° __________ **h)** 6325° __________

i) 810° __________ **j)** –900° __________

2. Find the degree measure of each angle.

a) $\frac{1}{8}$ rotation __________ **b)** $\frac{1}{5}$ rotation __________

c) $\frac{5}{6}$ rotation __________ **d)** $\frac{9}{8}$ rotations __________

e) $\frac{7}{5}$ rotations __________ **f)** $\frac{7}{6}$ rotations __________

3. Find the radian measure of each angle.

a) $\frac{1}{6}$ rotation __________ **b)** $\frac{3}{4}$ rotation __________

c) $\frac{2}{3}$ rotation __________ **d)** $2\frac{1}{4}$ rotations __________

e) $\frac{13}{12}$ rotations __________ **f)** $\frac{11}{8}$ rotations __________

4. Determine a positive and a negative coterminal angle.

a) 150° __________ **b)** –150° __________

c) 314° __________ **d)** –314° __________

e) 612° __________ **f)** –537° __________

g) 1100° __________ **h)** 6325° __________

i) 810° __________ **j)** –900° __________

5. Convert from degrees to radians. Express answer in terms of π.

a) 45° ______ **b)** 90° ______

c) 150° ______ **d)** 240° ______

e) 300° ______ **f)** 360° ______

g) 405° ______ **h)** 420° ______

i) 450° ______ **j)** 630° ______

6. Convert from degrees to radians. Express answer to 3 decimal places.

a) 70° ______ **b)** 37.5° ______

c) 130° ______ **d)** $\frac{90^\circ}{\pi}$ ______

e) 400° ______ **f)** 527° ______

g) -248° ______ **h)** 718° ______

i) 1025° ______ **j)** -1349° ______

7. Convert from radians to degrees.

a) $\frac{\pi}{3}$ ______ **b)** $\frac{5\pi}{6}$ ______

c) $\frac{3\pi}{4}$ ______ **d)** $\frac{11\pi}{6}$ ______

e) $\frac{17\pi}{6}$ ______ **f)** $\frac{21\pi}{4}$ ______

g) $\frac{11\pi}{3}$ ______ **h)** $\frac{20\pi}{3}$ ______

i) $\frac{31\pi}{6}$ ______ **j)** $\frac{23\pi}{4}$ ______

8. Convert from radians to degrees. Give answers to 1 decimal place.

a) 3 ______________ **b)** – 4 ______________

c) 2.7 ______________ **d)** – 1.2 ______________

e) 8.2 ______________ **f)** – 12.8 ______________

9. Find the radius of a circle if an arc of 3 subtends an angle of 30° on the circle.

10. Find the arc length of a sector of a circle with radius 15 cm if the sector angle is 130°.

11. Find the angle in degrees if an arc length of 5 cm has a radius of 6 cm

12. As the time changes from 2:00 to 2:30 on a dial-face clock,

a) determine the change in radian measure of the minute hand.

b) determine the change in radian measure of the hour hand.

13. A horse on a merry-go-round is 4 m from the centre. How many metres does Kate travel on the horse if the merry-go-round makes 15 revolutions before stopping?

14. A flywheel makes 12 revolutions per minute (rpm). How many seconds does it take for the flywheel to turn through 216°?

15. The Earth rotates about an axis through its poles, making one revolution per day. The radius of Earth is approximately 6400 kilometres. What distance is traversed by a point on Earth's surface at the equator during any 8-hour interval as a result of Earth's rotation about its axis?

16. What distance does a bird travel when flying due south from 40° north latitude to 20° north latitude?

6.2 Trigonometric Function of Acute Angles

We have learned from studying trigonometry in grades 10 and 11 that for a fixed acute angle θ in a right triangle, the ratio of the length of the sides does not depend on the size of the triangle. The ratios depend on the measure of θ, therefore we can define trigonometric functions in terms of θ. Each ratio of a pair of lengths of sides of a right triangle is given a special name.

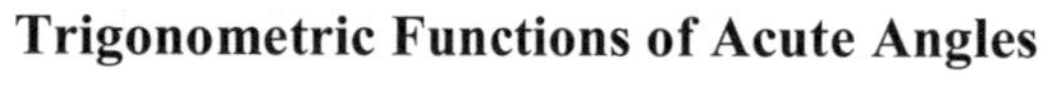

Trigonometric Functions of Acute Angles

For a given acute angle θ

Sine: $\sin\theta = \dfrac{\text{opposite}}{\text{hypotenuse}}$ Cosecant: $\csc\theta = \dfrac{\text{hypotenuse}}{\text{opposite}}$

Cosine: $\cos\theta = \dfrac{\text{adjacent}}{\text{hypotenuse}}$ Secant: $\sec\theta = \dfrac{\text{hypotenuse}}{\text{adjacent}}$

Tangent: $\tan\theta = \dfrac{\text{opposite}}{\text{adjacent}}$ Cotangent: $\csc\theta = \dfrac{\text{adjacent}}{\text{opposite}}$

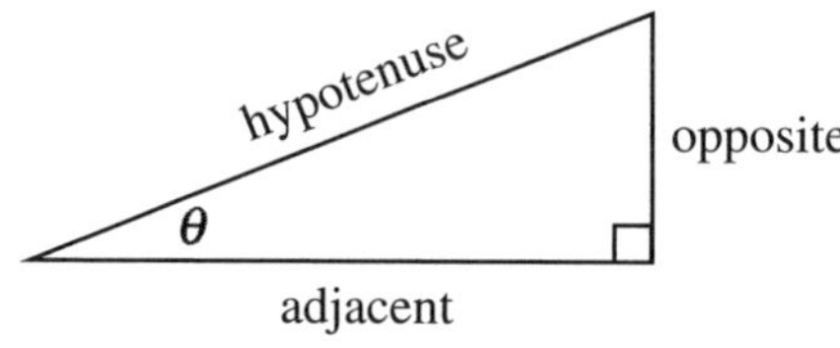

Consider an angle θ in standard positon with $P(x, y)$ a point on the terminal side of θ. Then, by Pythagorean theorem, $x^2 + y^2 = r^2$ or $r = \sqrt{x^2 + y^2}$. The values of x, y and r determine the six trigonometric ratios for angle θ.

Trigonometry Ratios

If θ is an angle in standard position with $P(x, y)$ a point on the terminal side of θ, then the six trigonometric ratios of angles θ are defined as follows:

$\sin\theta = \dfrac{y}{r}$ $\csc\theta = \dfrac{r}{y}$

$\cos\theta = \dfrac{x}{r}$ $\sec\theta = \dfrac{r}{x}$

$\tan\theta = \dfrac{y}{x}$ $\csc\theta = \dfrac{x}{y}$

where $r = \sqrt{x^2 + y^2}$

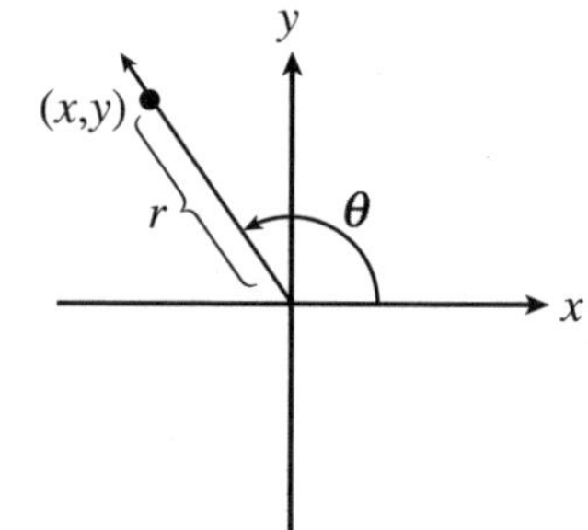

Algebraic Signs of the Trigonometric Functions

When selecting a point $P(x, y)$ on the terminal side of angle θ, the quadrant in which θ is found will determine the algebraic sign of the trigonometric function. It will be either positive or negative.

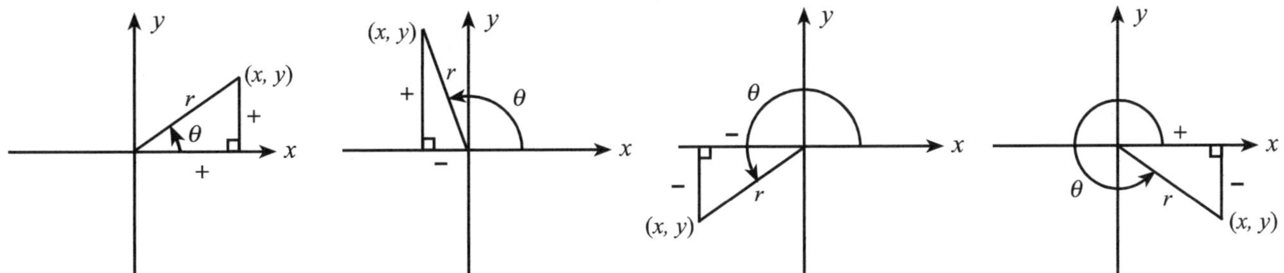

Remember, $r=\sqrt{x^2+y^2}$ is always positive. Since $\sin\theta$ and $\csc\theta$ are always ratios of y and r, then $\sin\theta$ and $\csc\theta$ are positive where y is positive. Similarly, $\cos\theta$ and $\sec\theta$ are positive where x is positive. Also, since tan and cot are ratios of x and y, $\tan\theta$ and $\cot\theta$ are positive when x and y are both positive, or x and y are both negative, because a negative divided by a negative is positive.

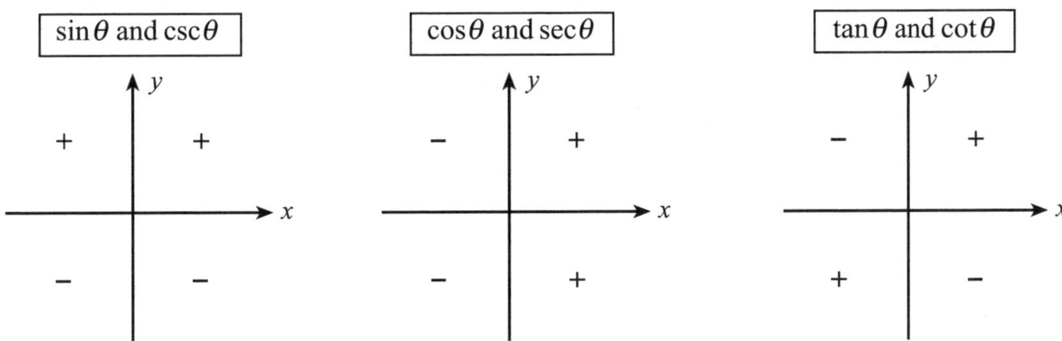

Example 1 What quadrant has $\sin\theta<0$, $\tan\theta>0$?

▶ *Solution:* $\sin\theta<0$ in quadrant III and IV, $\tan\theta>0$ in quadrant I and III, therefore, answer found in quadrant III.

Example 2 Determine $\cos\theta$ if $\csc\theta=-\frac{3}{2}$ and $\tan\theta<0$.

▶ *Solution:* $\csc\theta<0$ in quadrant III and IV, $\tan\theta<0$ in quadrant II and IV, therefore answer is found in quadrant IV. $\cos\theta$ is positive in quadrant IV.

$x^2+(-2)^2=3^2 \rightarrow x=\sqrt{5}$,

therefore $\cos\theta=\frac{\sqrt{5}}{3}$

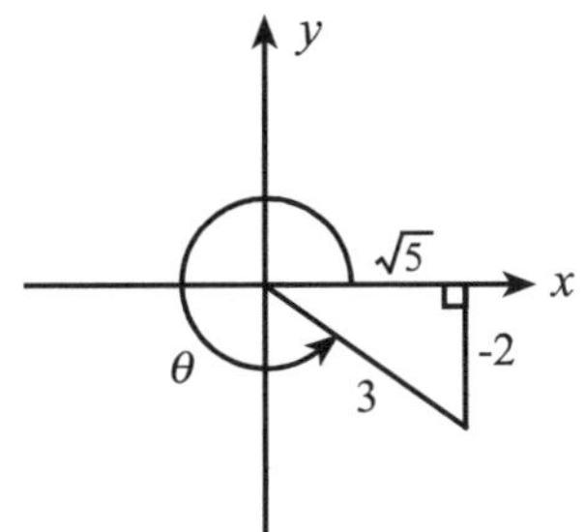

Example 3 Determine $\cot\theta$ if $\sin\theta = \frac{2}{5}$ and $\cos\theta < 0$.

▶ *Solution:* $\cos\theta < 0$ in quadrant II and III, $\sin\theta > 0$ in quadrant I and II, therefore answer found in quadrant II.

$x^2 + 2^2 = 5^2 \rightarrow x = -\sqrt{21}$ (x is negative in quadrant II)

therefore $\cot\theta = \frac{-\sqrt{21}}{2}$

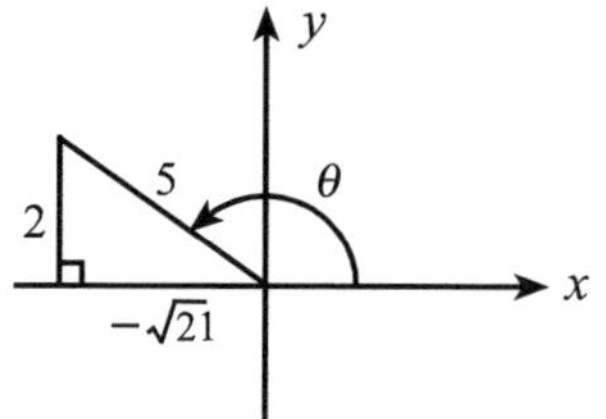

Example 4 Determine $\sec\theta$ if $\cot\theta = -\frac{2}{3}$.

▶ *Solution:* $\cot\theta < 0$ in quadrant II and IV

$r^2 = (-2)^2 + 3^2$

$r = \sqrt{13}$

therefore, $\sec\theta = -\frac{\sqrt{13}}{2}$ or $\sec\theta = \frac{\sqrt{13}}{2}$

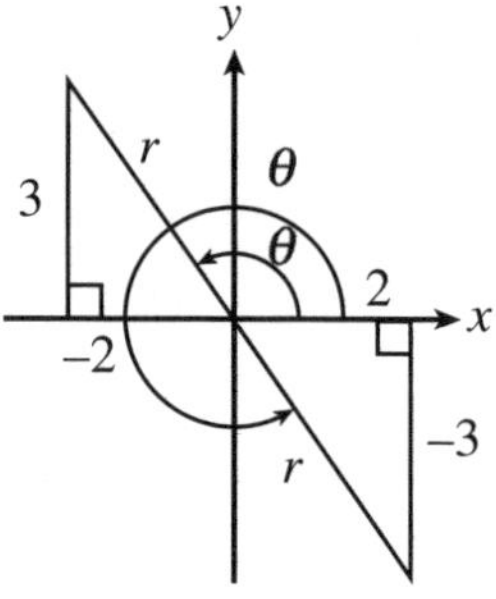

Example 5 Given the point (2, – 1) on the terminal side of angle θ, determine the value of all 6 trigonometric functions.

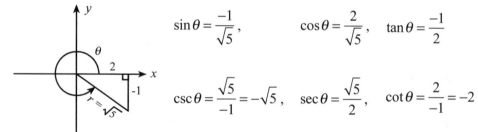

▶ *Solution:* $r^2 = (-1)^2 + 2^2$,

$r = \sqrt{5}$,

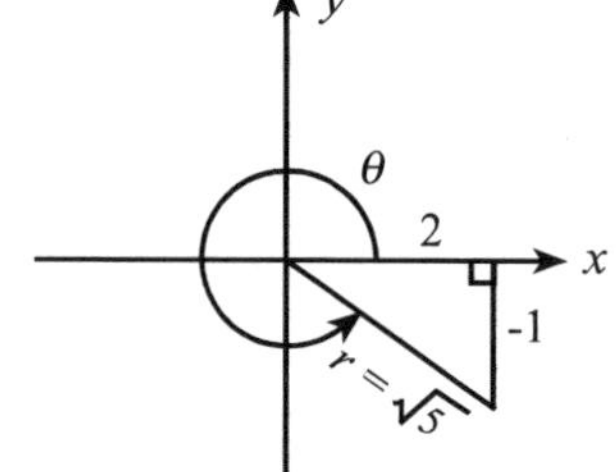

$\sin\theta = \frac{-1}{\sqrt{5}}$, $\cos\theta = \frac{2}{\sqrt{5}}$, $\tan\theta = \frac{-1}{2}$

$\csc\theta = \frac{\sqrt{5}}{-1} = -\sqrt{5}$, $\sec\theta = \frac{\sqrt{5}}{2}$, $\cot\theta = \frac{2}{-1} = -2$

Example 6 Determine $\sin\theta$ and $\cos\theta$ if θ is an angle in standard position whose terminal side is the graph $2x + 5y = 0,\ x \le 0$.

▶ *Solution:* Graph $2x + 5y = 0,\ x \le 0$

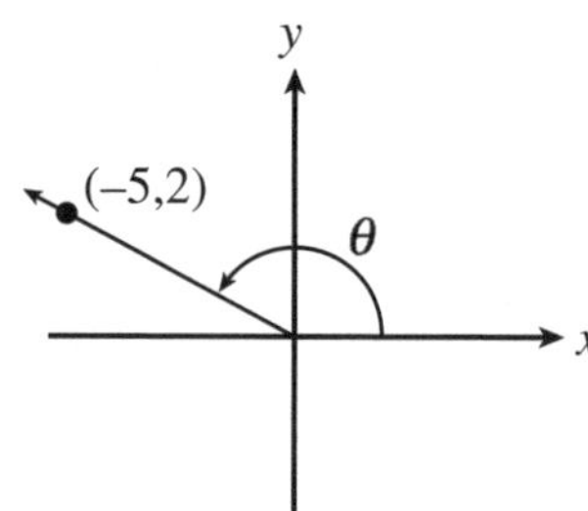

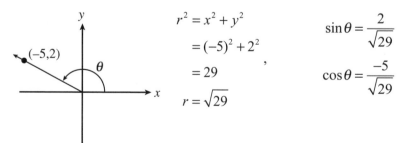

$$\begin{aligned} r^2 &= x^2 + y^2 \\ &= (-5)^2 + 2^2 \\ &= 29 \\ r &= \sqrt{29} \end{aligned},$$

$\sin\theta = \frac{2}{\sqrt{29}}$

$\cos\theta = \frac{-5}{\sqrt{29}}$

Example 7 Determine the coordinate of the point 8 units from the origin in quadrant III and $\tan\theta = \frac{3}{4}$.

▶ *Solution:* Graph $\tan\theta = \frac{3}{4}$ in quadrant III. (Note: $x = -4, y = -3$)

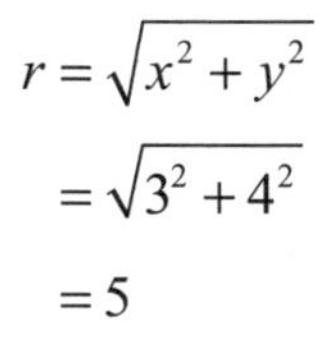

$$r = \sqrt{x^2 + y^2} = \sqrt{3^2 + 4^2} = 5$$

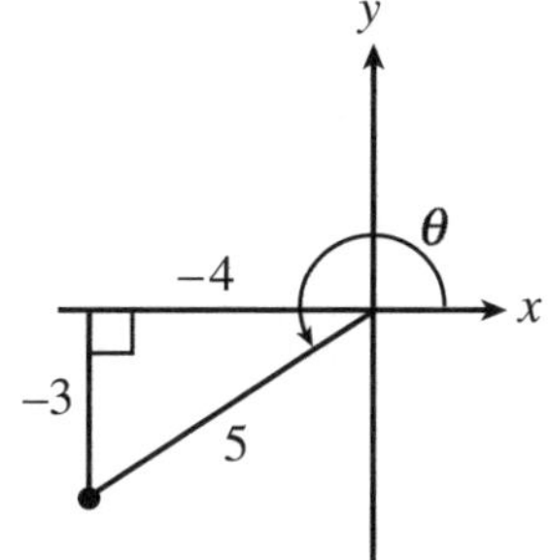

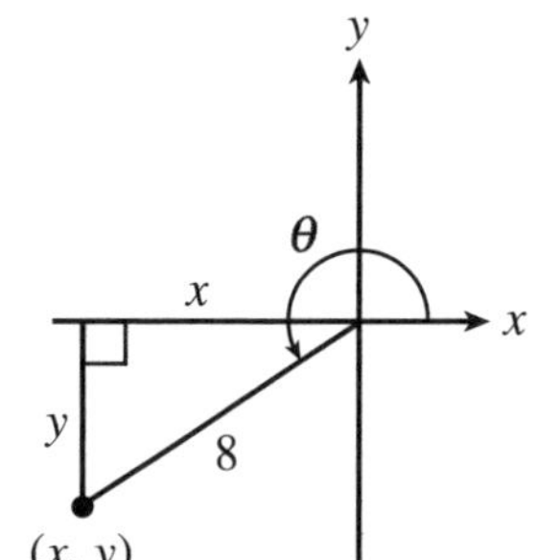

by proportion

$$\frac{-4}{5} = \frac{x}{8};\ x = \frac{-32}{5}$$

$$\frac{-3}{5} = \frac{y}{8};\ y = \frac{-24}{5}$$

Thus, coordinates $(x, y) = \left(-\frac{32}{5}, -\frac{24}{5}\right)$.

Example 8 If $\sin\theta = \frac{2}{3}$, find **a)** $\csc\theta$ and **b)** $\cos(90° - \theta)$.

▶ *Solution:* **a)** $\sin\theta$ and $\csc\theta$ are reciprocals of each other, therefore if $\sin\theta = \frac{2}{3}$, $\csc\theta = \frac{3}{2}$.

b)

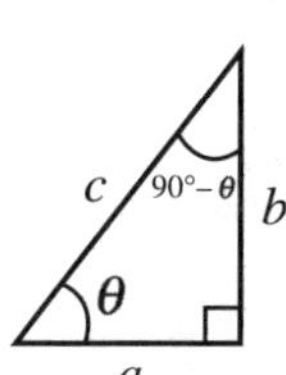

$\sin\theta = \frac{b}{c}$, $\cos(90° - \theta) = \frac{b}{c}$

Thus $\sin\theta = \cos(90° - \theta)$,

So $\cos(90° - \theta) = \frac{2}{3}$

Note: $\sin\theta = \cos(90° - \theta)$, $\cos\theta = \sin(90° - \theta)$, $\tan\theta = \cot(90° - \theta)$
$\cot\theta = \tan(90° - \theta)$, $\sec\theta = \csc(90° - \theta)$, $\csc\theta = \sec(90° - \theta)$
using the same reasoning as example 8b) above.

Example 9 Find all angles θ, $0° \le \theta < 360°$ such that $\sin\theta = -\cos\theta$.

▶ *Solution:* $\sin\theta > 0$ and $\cos\theta < 0$ in quadrant II with opposite = – adjacent

$\sin\theta < 0$ and $\cos\theta > 0$ in quadrant IV with adjacent = – opposite

The opposite and adjacent leg of the triangle must be the same length.

This must be a 45° reference angle in quadrants II and IV.

Thus, $\theta = 135°$ and $315°$.

6.2 Exercise Set

1. Find the missing dimensions of a right triangle with sides a and b and hypotenuse c.

a) $a = 5, b = 12, c =$ ______ **b)** $a = 2, b = 3, c =$ ______

c) $a = 15, c = 17, b =$ ______ **d)** $b = 2\sqrt{2}, c = 3, a =$ ______

e) $c = 3\sqrt{5}, b = 6, a =$ ______ **f)** $c = \sqrt{17}, a = 2\sqrt{2}, b =$ ______

2. Determine the quadrant in which θ lies for the following.

a) $\sin\theta > 0, \quad \sec\theta > 0$ _____ **b)** $\tan\theta < 0, \quad \cos\theta > 0$ _____

c) $\csc\theta > 0, \quad \cot\theta < 0$ _____ **d)** $\cos\theta < 0, \quad \csc\theta < 0$ _____

e) $\sin\theta < 0, \quad \tan\theta < 0$ _____ **f)** $\cot\theta > 0, \quad \sec\theta < 0$ _____

g) $\tan\theta < 0, \quad \csc\theta > 0$ _____ **h)** $\cos\theta > 0, \quad \sec\theta < 0$ _____

i) $\sin\theta < 0, \quad \cot\theta < 0$ _____ **j)** $\tan\theta < 0, \quad \sec\theta > 0$ _____

3. Find the value of the indicated functions.

a) $\csc\theta = 2, \ \sin\theta =$ ______ **b)** $\cos\theta = -\frac{2}{3}, \ \sec\theta =$ ______

c) $\tan\theta = -5, \ \cot\theta =$ ______ **d)** $\sin\theta = -0.23, \ \csc\theta =$ ______

e) $\sec\theta = 2.35, \ \cos\theta =$ ______ **f)** $\cot\theta = -2.4, \ \tan\theta =$ ______

4. Find the acute angle θ, for the trigonometric function.

a) $\sin 30° = \cos\theta, \ \theta =$ ______ **b)** $\tan 65° = \cot\theta, \ \theta =$ ______

c) $\sec 25° = \csc\theta, \ \theta =$ ______ **d)** $\cos\frac{\pi}{4} = \sin\theta, \ \theta =$ ______

e) $\cot\frac{\pi}{6} = \tan\theta, \ \theta =$ ______ **f)** $\csc\frac{\pi}{3} = \sec\theta, \ \theta =$ ______

5. A point P on the terminal side of θ is shown in the figures below. Evaluate the six trigonometric functions of θ.

a)

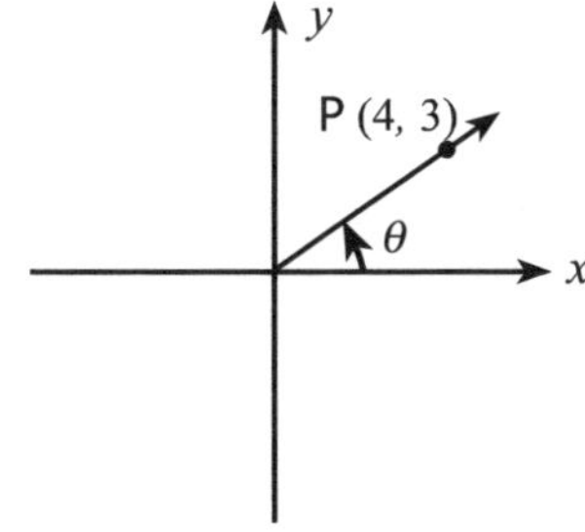

$\sin\theta =$ ______, $\cos\theta =$ ______

$\tan\theta =$ ______, $\cot\theta =$ ______

$\sec\theta =$ ______, $\csc\theta =$ ______

b)

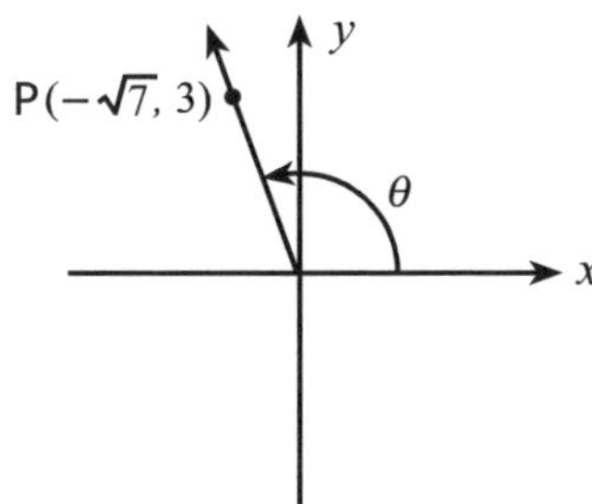

$\sin\theta =$ ______, $\cos\theta =$ ______

$\tan\theta =$ ______, $\cot\theta =$ ______

$\sec\theta =$ ______, $\csc\theta =$ ______

c)

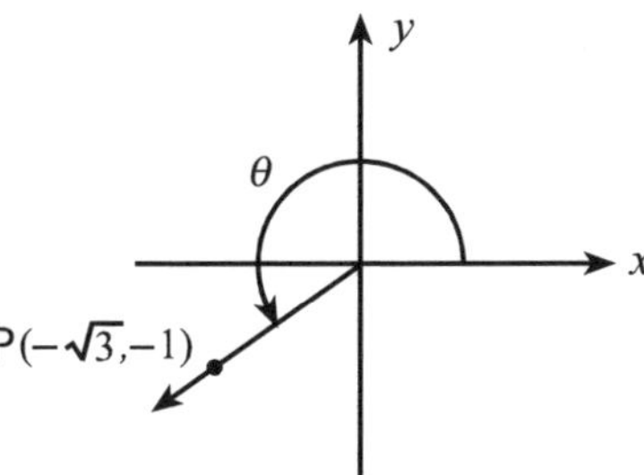

$\sin\theta =$ ______, $\cos\theta =$ ______

$\tan\theta =$ ______, $\cot\theta =$ ______

$\sec\theta =$ ______, $\csc\theta =$ ______

d)

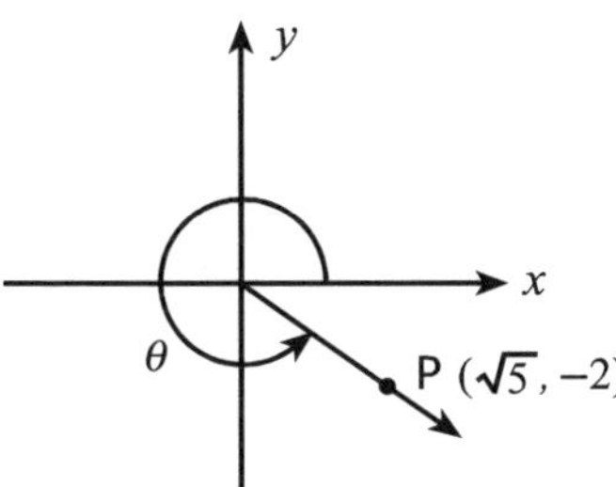

$\sin\theta =$ ______, $\cos\theta =$ ______

$\tan\theta =$ ______, $\cot\theta =$ ______

$\sec\theta =$ ______, $\csc\theta =$ ______

e)

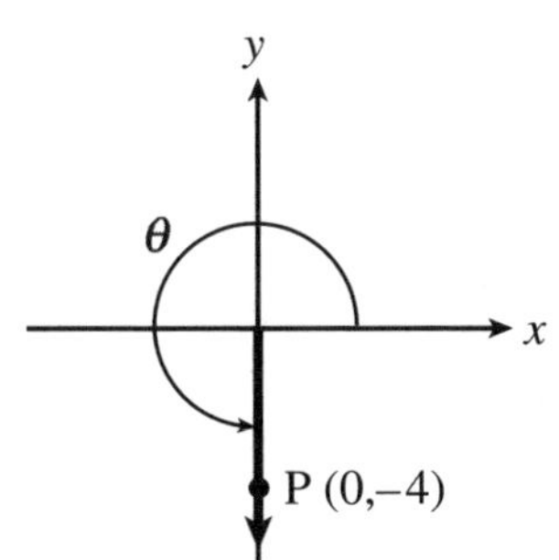

$\sin\theta =$ ______, $\cos\theta =$ ______

$\tan\theta =$ ______, $\cot\theta =$ ______

$\sec\theta =$ ______, $\csc\theta =$ ______

6. The value of one trigonometric function is given. Determine the other 5 trigonometric functions.

a) $\sin\theta = \frac{5}{13}$, θ is in quadrant I

$\sin\theta = \frac{5}{13}$, $\cos\theta =$ ______

$\tan\theta =$ ______, $\cot\theta =$ ______

$\sec\theta =$ ______, $\csc\theta =$ ______

b) $\tan\theta = \frac{8}{15}$, θ is in quadrant III

$\sin\theta =$ ______, $\cos\theta =$ ______

$\tan\theta = \frac{8}{15}$, $\cot\theta =$ ______

$\sec\theta =$ ______, $\csc\theta =$ ______

c) $\sec\theta = \frac{3}{2}$, θ is in quadrant IV

$\sin\theta =$ ______, $\cos\theta =$ ______

$\tan\theta =$ ______, $\cot\theta =$ ______

$\sec\theta = \frac{3}{2}$, $\csc\theta =$ ______

d) $\csc\theta = 3$, $\tan\theta < 0$

$\sin\theta =$ ______, $\cos\theta =$ ______

$\tan\theta =$ ______, $\cot\theta =$ ______

$\sec\theta =$ ______, $\csc\theta = 3$

e) $\cot\theta = -2.4$, $\sin\theta > 0$

$\sin\theta =$ ______, $\cos\theta =$ ______

$\tan\theta =$ ______, $\cot\theta = -2.4$

$\sec\theta =$ ______, $\csc\theta =$ ______

f) $\cos\theta = -0.238$, $\tan\theta > 0$

$\sin\theta =$ ______, $\cos\theta = -0.238$

$\tan\theta =$ ______, $\cot\theta =$ ______

$\sec\theta =$ ______, $\csc\theta =$ ______

7. Find the six trigonometric functions of θ if θ is an angle in standard position whose terminal side is the graph of the given relation.

a) $3x+5y=0,\ x\geq 0$

$\sin\theta=$ ______, $\cos\theta=$ ______

$\tan\theta=$ ______, $\cot\theta=$ ______

$\sec\theta=$ ______, $\csc\theta=$ ______

b) $2x-3y=0,\ y\leq 0$

$\sin\theta=$ ______, $\cos\theta=$ ______

$\tan\theta=$ ______, $\cot\theta=$ ______

$\sec\theta=$ ______, $\csc\theta=$ ______

c) $\sqrt{5}x+2y=0,\ y\leq 0$

$\sin\theta=$ ______, $\cos\theta=$ ______

$\tan\theta=$ ______, $\cot\theta=$ ______

$\sec\theta=$ ______, $\csc\theta=$ ______

d) $x=0,\ y\leq 0$

$\sin\theta=$ ______, $\cos\theta=$ ______

$\tan\theta=$ ______, $\cot\theta=$ ______

$\sec\theta=$ ______, $\csc\theta=$ ______

8. Determine the coordinates of the point at the given distance from the origin in the stated quadrant, if θ is its position angle.

a) 10; II; $\sin\theta=\frac{3}{5}$

b) 3; III; $\tan\theta=1$

c) 8; I; $\sec\theta=2$

d) 8; II; $\csc\theta=\frac{13}{5}$

9. Let B be an acute angle with $\sin B = a$.
Find $\csc B$ and $\cos(90° - B)$ in terms of a.

10. Let P be an acute angle with $\cos P = b$.
Find $\sec P$ and $\sin\left(\frac{\pi}{2} - P\right)$ in terms of b.

11. The terminal side of angle θ in standard position goes through the intersection point of the given curves. Find $\sin\theta$ and $\cos\theta$.

a) $2x - y = 10$ $\sin\theta =$ ______
$3x + y = 5$ $\cos\theta =$ ______

b) $y = x^2 + 4x$ $\sin\theta =$ ______
$y = -4x - 16$ $\cos\theta =$ ______

12. Find all angles θ, $0° \le \theta \le 360°$ for which $\sin\theta = \cos\theta$.

13. If $1 + \sin\theta = 3\sin\theta$, $\tan\theta < 0$. Find $\cos\theta$.

14. Show that: $h = \dfrac{d}{\cot\alpha - \cot\beta}$

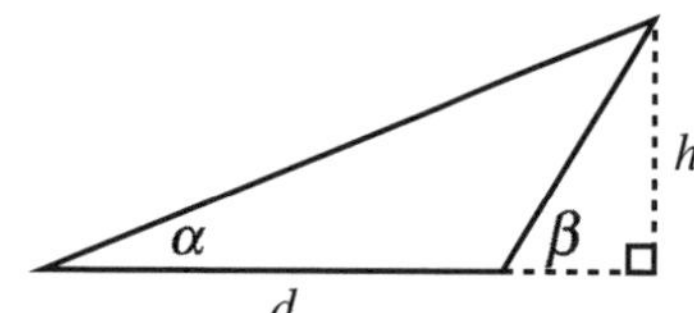

15. Show that: $h = \dfrac{d}{\cot\alpha + \cot\beta}$

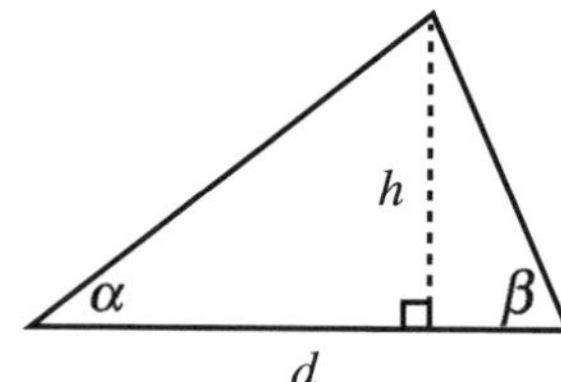

6.3 Trigonometric Function – General & Special Angles

Quadrantal Angles

Quadrantal angles are angles with their terminal side lying along a coordinate axis, either the x-axis or the y-axis. To evaluate the trigonometric functions of a quadrantal angle, we select any arbitrary point other than the origin. The easiest point to pick is a point 1 unit from the origin. Then apply the definitions of the six trigonometric ratios.

Angles of $0°, 90°, 180°, 270°$ or $0, \frac{\pi}{2}, \pi, \frac{3\pi}{2}$

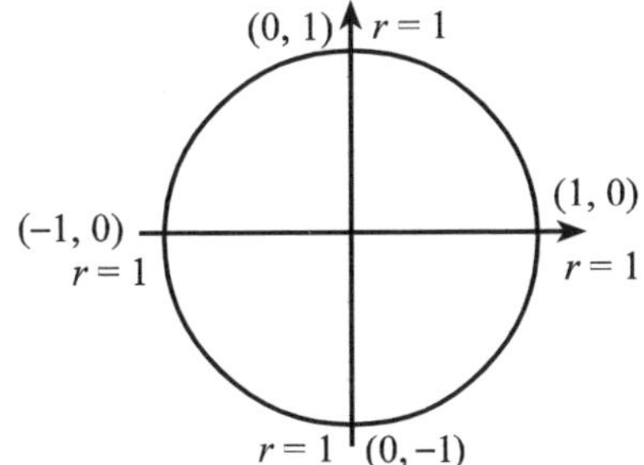

The x-value is the adjacent value in the ordered pair.
The y-value is the opposite value in the ordered pair.
The r-value will be 1 all around the circle.

Example 1 Find **a)** $\cos 0°$ **b)** $\tan 90°$ **c)** $\sin \pi$ **d)** $\csc \frac{3\pi}{2}$

▶ *Solution:*

a) $\cos 0° = \frac{\text{adjacent}}{\text{radius}} = \frac{x}{r} = \frac{1}{1} = 1$

b) $\tan 90° = \frac{\text{opposite}}{\text{adjacent}} = \frac{y}{x} = \frac{1}{0} = \text{undefined}$

c) $\sin \pi = \frac{\text{opposite}}{\text{radius}} = \frac{y}{r} = \frac{0}{1} = 0$

d) $\csc \frac{3\pi}{2} = \frac{\text{radius}}{\text{opposite}} = \frac{r}{y} = \frac{1}{-1} = -1$

Using the procedure of the above examples, we can verify the following entries:

θ	$\sin\theta$	$\cos\theta$	$\tan\theta$	$\cot\theta$	$\sec\theta$	$\csc\theta$
$0°$ or 0	0	1	0	undefined	1	undefined
$90°$ or $\frac{\pi}{2}$	1	0	undefined	0	undefined	1
$180°$ or π	0	−1	0	undefined	−1	undefined
$270°$ or $\frac{3\pi}{2}$	−1	0	undefined	0	undefined	−1

We may obtain the values of other trigonometric functions for other quadrantal angles using the idea of coterminal angles.

Example 2 Evaluate **a)** $\cos 540^\circ$ **b)** $\tan 6\pi$ **c)** $\csc\frac{9\pi}{2}$

▶ *Solution:* **a)** Find a coterminal angle θ, $0^\circ \le \theta^\circ < 360^\circ$

$$540^\circ - 360^\circ = 180^\circ$$

$$\text{Thus, } \cos 540^\circ = \cos 180^\circ = \frac{\text{adjacent}}{\text{hypotenuse}} = \frac{-1}{1} = -1$$

b) Find a coterminal angle θ, $0 \le \theta < 2\pi$

$$6\pi - 3(2\pi) = 0$$

$$\text{Thus, } \tan 6\pi = \tan 0 = \frac{\text{opposite}}{\text{adjacent}} = \frac{0}{1} = 0$$

c) Find a coterminal angle θ, $0 \le \theta < 2\pi$

$$\frac{9\pi}{2} - 2(2\pi) = \frac{\pi}{2}$$

$$\text{Thus, } \csc\frac{9\pi}{2} = \csc\frac{\pi}{2} = \frac{\text{hypotenuse}}{\text{opposite}} = \frac{1}{1} = 1$$

Special Angles: 30°, 45°, and 60°

By using the relationship between an isosceles right triangle and an equilateral triangle, we can find exact values of 30°, 45° and 60° angles by applying Pythagoras' theorem.

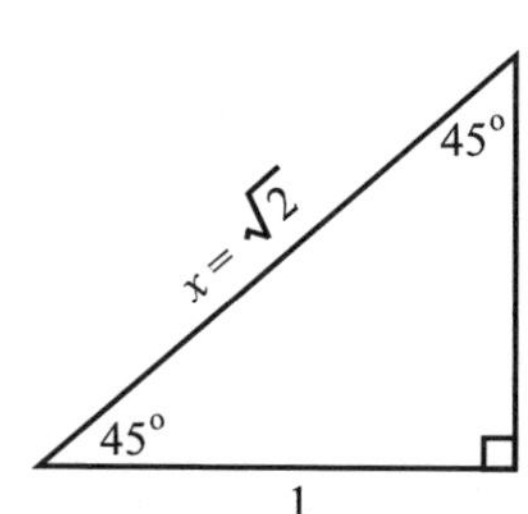

$$x^2 = 1^2 + 1^2$$
$$x = \sqrt{2}$$

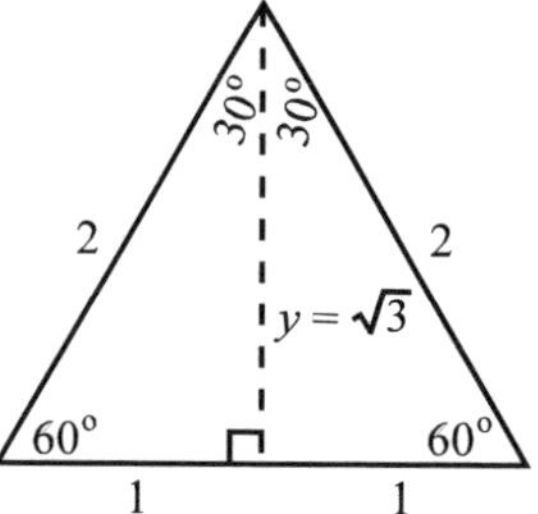

→

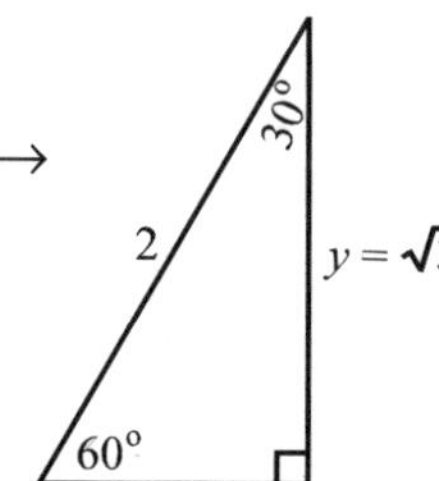

$$y^2 + 1^2 = 2^2$$
$$y = \sqrt{3}$$

Example 3 Evaluate **a)** $\sin 60^\circ$ **b)** $\sec\frac{\pi}{4}$ **c)** $\tan\frac{\pi}{6}$

▶ *Solution:* **a)** $\sin 60^\circ = \frac{\text{opposite}}{\text{hypotenuse}} = \frac{\sqrt{3}}{2}$

b) $\sec\frac{\pi}{4} = \frac{\text{hypotenuse}}{\text{adjacent}} = \frac{\sqrt{2}}{1} = \sqrt{2}$

c) $\tan\frac{\pi}{6} = \frac{\text{opposite}}{\text{adjacent}} = \frac{1}{\sqrt{3}} = \frac{1}{\sqrt{3}} \cdot \frac{\sqrt{3}}{\sqrt{3}} = \frac{\sqrt{3}}{3}$ (both answers are acceptable)

Using the procedure of the previous example, we can verify the following entries:

θ	$\sin\theta$	$\cos\theta$	$\tan\theta$	$\cot\theta$	$\sec\theta$	$\csc\theta$
30° or $\frac{\pi}{6}$	$\frac{1}{2}$	$\frac{\sqrt{3}}{2}$	$\frac{1}{\sqrt{3}}$	$\sqrt{3}$	$\frac{2}{\sqrt{3}}$	2
45° or $\frac{\pi}{4}$	$\frac{1}{\sqrt{2}}$	$\frac{1}{\sqrt{2}}$	1	1	$\sqrt{2}$	$\sqrt{2}$
60° or $\frac{\pi}{3}$	$\frac{\sqrt{3}}{2}$	$\frac{1}{2}$	$\sqrt{3}$	$\frac{1}{\sqrt{3}}$	2	$\frac{2}{\sqrt{3}}$

Reference Angles

The concept of reference angles was introduced in grade 11. We shall formally state its definition:

> **Definition of a Reference Angle**
>
> For angle θ in standard position, the **reference angle** is the positive acute angle θ' that is formed with the terminal side of θ and the x-axis.
>
> *A reference angle is* $0^\circ \le \theta' \le 90^\circ$ *or* $0 \le \theta' \le \frac{\pi}{2}$

Diagram of Reference Angles in Quadrants I, II, III, and IV

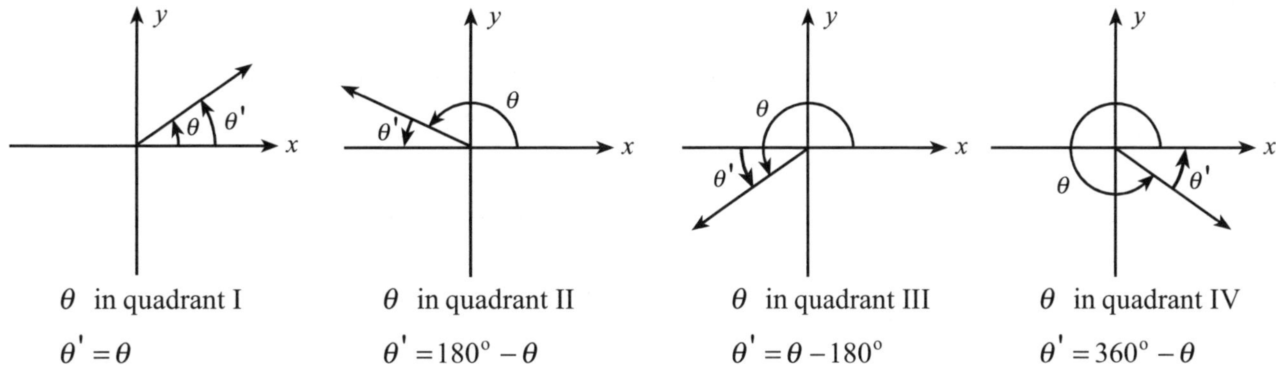

Remember the quadrants where the trigonometric functions are positive and negative, from the previous section:

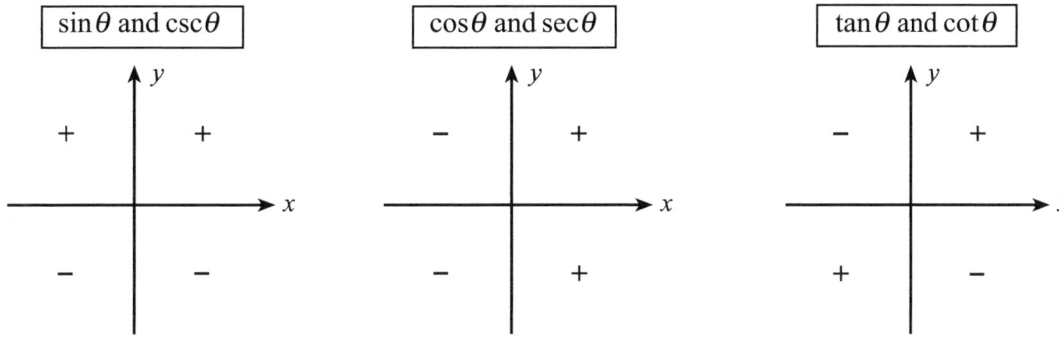

Example 4 Determine the exact value of **a)** $\sin 240^\circ$ **b)** $\sec\frac{5\pi}{3}$ **c)** $\tan\left(-\frac{19\pi}{6}\right)$

▶ *Solution:* **a)** $\sin 240^\circ$ is in quadrant III in which $\sin\theta < 0$.

The reference angle for 240° is $240^\circ - 180^\circ = 60^\circ$, therefore, $\sin 240^\circ = -\sin 60^\circ = \frac{-\sqrt{3}}{2}$.

b) $\sec\frac{5\pi}{3}$ is in quadrant IV in which $\sec\theta > 0$.

The reference angle for $\frac{5\pi}{3}$ is $2\pi - \frac{5\pi}{3} = \frac{\pi}{3}$, therefore, $\sec\frac{5\pi}{3} = \sec\frac{\pi}{3} = \frac{2}{1} = 2$.

c) $\tan\left(-\frac{19\pi}{6}\right) = \tan\left(-\frac{19\pi}{6} + 4\pi\right) = \tan\left(-\frac{19\pi}{6} + \frac{24\pi}{6}\right) = \tan\frac{5\pi}{6}$ is in quadrant II in which $\tan\theta < 0$

The reference angle for $\frac{5\pi}{6}$ is $\pi - \frac{5\pi}{6} = \frac{\pi}{6}$, therefore, $\tan\left(\frac{-19\pi}{6}\right) = -\tan\frac{\pi}{6} = -\frac{1}{\sqrt{3}}$

Finding θ

To find θ for special angles is the reverse process of reference angles.

Example 5 Find the smallest positive θ in degree and radian measures **a)** $\sin\theta = -\frac{\sqrt{3}}{2}$ **b)** $\sec\theta = -\sqrt{2}$.

▶ *Solution:* **a)** $\sin\theta < 0$ in quadrants III and IV. The smallest angle is quadrant III.

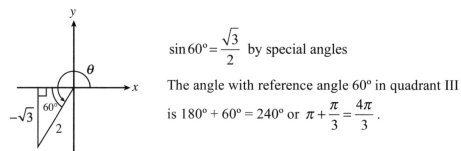

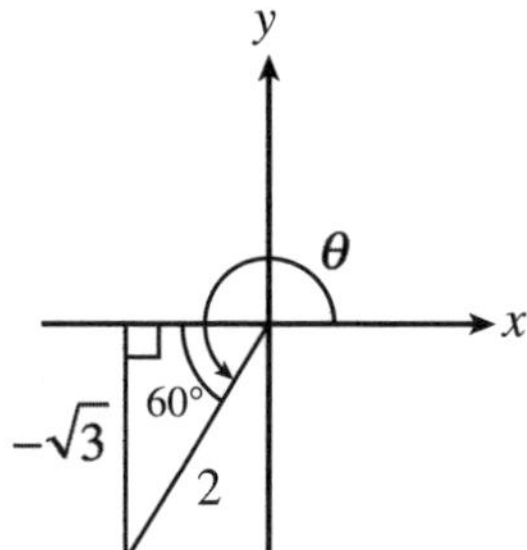

$\sin 60^\circ = \frac{\sqrt{3}}{2}$ by special angles

The angle with reference angle 60° in quadrant III is $180^\circ + 60^\circ = 240^\circ$ or $\pi + \frac{\pi}{3} = \frac{4\pi}{3}$.

b) $\sec\theta < 0$ in quadrants II and III. The smallest angle is quadrant II.

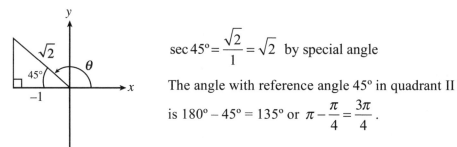

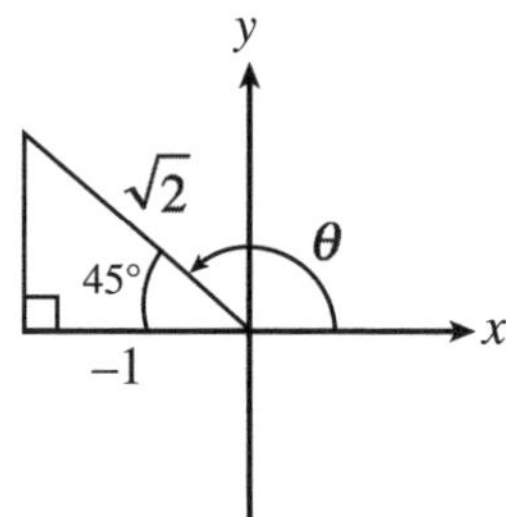

$\sec 45^\circ = \frac{\sqrt{2}}{1} = \sqrt{2}$ by special angle

The angle with reference angle 45° in quadrant II is $180^\circ - 45^\circ = 135^\circ$ or $\pi - \frac{\pi}{4} = \frac{3\pi}{4}$.

Example 6 Find exactly all θ, $0° \le \theta < 360$ for which $\tan\theta = \frac{1}{\sqrt{3}}$.

▶ *Solution:* $\tan\theta > 0$ in quadrants I and III.

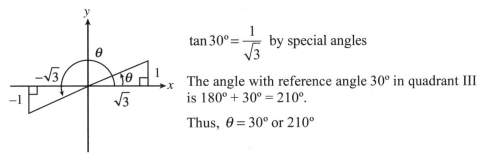

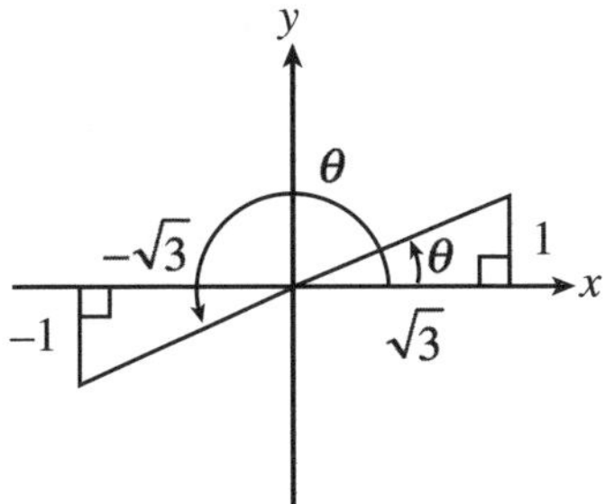

$\tan 30° = \frac{1}{\sqrt{3}}$ by special angles

The angle with reference angle 30° in quadrant III is $180° + 30° = 210°$.

Thus, $\theta = 30°$ or $210°$

Example 7 Find exactly all x, $0 \le x < 2\pi$ for which $\csc x = \frac{-2}{\sqrt{3}}$.

▶ *Solution:* $\csc x < 0$ in quadrants III and IV.

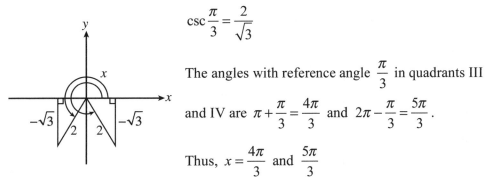

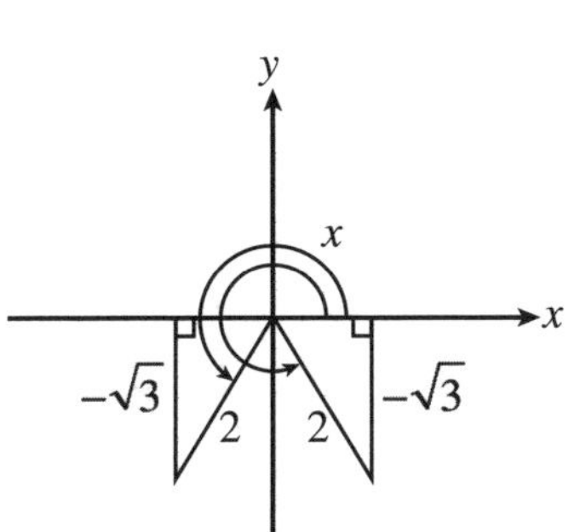

$\csc\frac{\pi}{3} = \frac{2}{\sqrt{3}}$

The angles with reference angle $\frac{\pi}{3}$ in quadrants III and IV are $\pi + \frac{\pi}{3} = \frac{4\pi}{3}$ and $2\pi - \frac{\pi}{3} = \frac{5\pi}{3}$.

Thus, $x = \frac{4\pi}{3}$ and $\frac{5\pi}{3}$

Example 8 Find exactly all x, $0 \le x < 2\pi$ for which $\sec x = -2$.

▶ *Solution:* $\sec x < 0$ in quadrants II and III.

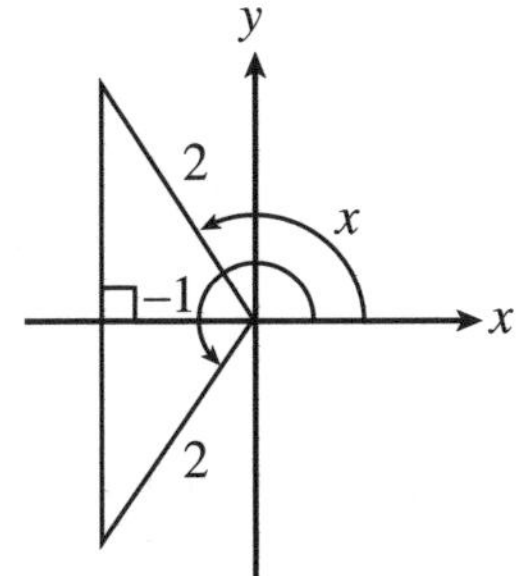

$\sec\frac{\pi}{3} = 2$ by special angles

The angles with reference angle $\frac{\pi}{3}$ in quadrants II and III are $\pi - \frac{\pi}{3} = \frac{2\pi}{3}$ and $\pi + \frac{\pi}{3} = \frac{4\pi}{3}$.

Thus, $x = \frac{2\pi}{3}$ and $\frac{4\pi}{3}$

All Special Angles

Degrees	Radians	$\sin\theta$	$\cos\theta$	$\tan\theta$	$\cot\theta$	$\sec\theta$	$\csc\theta$
0°	0	0	1	0	∞	1	∞
30°	$\frac{\pi}{6}$	$\frac{1}{2}$	$\frac{\sqrt{3}}{2}$	$\frac{\sqrt{3}}{3}$	$\sqrt{3}$	$\frac{2\sqrt{3}}{3}$	2
45°	$\frac{\pi}{4}$	$\frac{\sqrt{2}}{2}$	$\frac{\sqrt{2}}{2}$	1	1	$\sqrt{2}$	$\sqrt{2}$
60°	$\frac{\pi}{3}$	$\frac{\sqrt{3}}{2}$	$\frac{1}{2}$	$\sqrt{3}$	$\frac{\sqrt{3}}{3}$	2	$\frac{2\sqrt{3}}{3}$
90°	$\frac{\pi}{2}$	1	0	∞	0	∞	1
120°	$\frac{2\pi}{3}$	$\frac{\sqrt{3}}{2}$	$-\frac{1}{2}$	$-\sqrt{3}$	$-\frac{\sqrt{3}}{3}$	-2	$\frac{2\sqrt{3}}{3}$
135°	$\frac{3\pi}{4}$	$\frac{\sqrt{2}}{2}$	$-\frac{\sqrt{2}}{2}$	-1	-1	$-\sqrt{2}$	$\sqrt{2}$
150°	$\frac{5\pi}{6}$	$\frac{1}{2}$	$-\frac{\sqrt{3}}{2}$	$-\frac{\sqrt{3}}{3}$	$-\sqrt{3}$	$-\frac{2\sqrt{3}}{3}$	2
180°	π	0	-1	0	∞	-1	∞
210°	$\frac{7\pi}{6}$	$-\frac{1}{2}$	$-\frac{\sqrt{3}}{2}$	$\frac{\sqrt{3}}{3}$	$\sqrt{3}$	$-\frac{2\sqrt{3}}{3}$	-2
225°	$\frac{5\pi}{4}$	$-\frac{\sqrt{2}}{2}$	$-\frac{\sqrt{2}}{2}$	1	1	-2	$-\sqrt{2}$
240°	$\frac{4\pi}{3}$	$-\frac{\sqrt{3}}{2}$	$-\frac{1}{2}$	$\sqrt{3}$	$\frac{\sqrt{3}}{3}$	-2	$-\frac{2\sqrt{3}}{3}$
270°	$\frac{3\pi}{2}$	-1	0	∞	0	∞	-1
300°	$\frac{5\pi}{3}$	$-\frac{\sqrt{3}}{2}$	$\frac{1}{2}$	$-\sqrt{3}$	$-\frac{\sqrt{3}}{3}$	2	$-\frac{2\sqrt{3}}{3}$
315°	$\frac{7\pi}{4}$	$-\frac{\sqrt{2}}{2}$	$\frac{\sqrt{2}}{2}$	-1	-1	$\sqrt{2}$	$-\sqrt{2}$
330°	$\frac{11\pi}{6}$	$-\frac{1}{2}$	$\frac{\sqrt{3}}{2}$	$-\frac{\sqrt{3}}{3}$	$-\sqrt{3}$	$\frac{2\sqrt{3}}{3}$	-2

Being able to calculate all values of this chart quickly allows for more success in the trigonometry unit. There are only two triangles plus x-axis and y-axis values which give the 96 special angles listed above.

The 45° - 45° - 90° triangle

The 30° - 60° - 90° triangle

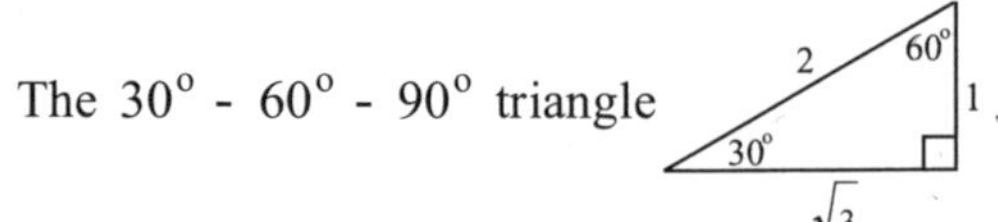

6.3 Exercise Set

1. Find the reference angle θ' for each angle θ.

a) $150°$ __________ **b)** $-150°$ __________

c) $314°$ __________ **d)** $-314°$ __________

e) $612°$ __________ **f)** $-537°$ __________

g) $1100°$ __________ **h)** $6325°$ __________

i) $810°$ __________ **j)** $-900°$ __________

k) $\frac{7\pi}{6}$ __________ **l)** $-\frac{21\pi}{4}$ __________

m) $-\frac{19\pi}{5}$ __________ **n)** $\frac{24\pi}{7}$ __________

o) $\frac{17\pi}{3}$ __________ **p)** $\frac{16\pi}{5}$ __________

2. Determine the exact value of each trigonometric function. Do not use a calculator.

a) $\sin 120°$ __________ **b)** $\cot 135°$ __________

c) $\cos 330°$ __________ **d)** $\tan 660°$ __________

e) $\csc 1125°$ __________ **f)** $\sec\frac{\pi}{6}$ __________

g) $\sin\frac{5\pi}{4}$ __________ **h)** $\tan\frac{11\pi}{6}$ __________

i) $\csc\frac{19\pi}{6}$ __________ **j)** $\cot\frac{13\pi}{3}$ __________

k) $\cot(-240°)$ __________ **l)** $\sec(-945°)$ __________

m) $\cos\left(\frac{-5\pi}{3}\right)$ __________ **n)** $\tan\left(\frac{-29\pi}{6}\right)$ __________

o) $\sin\left(\frac{-20\pi}{3}\right)$ __________ **p)** $\csc\left(\frac{-27\pi}{4}\right)$ __________

3. For which values of θ, $0° \le \theta < 360$, is each of the following undefined?

a) $\sin\theta$ ____________ b) $\cos\theta$ ____________

c) $\tan\theta$ ____________ d) $\cot\theta$ ____________

e) $\sec\theta$ ____________ f) $\csc\theta$ ____________

4. For which values of θ, $0° \le \theta < 2\pi$, is each of the following undefined?

a) $\sin\theta$ ____________ b) $\cos\theta$ ____________

c) $\tan\theta$ ____________ d) $\cot\theta$ ____________

e) $\sec\theta$ ____________ f) $\csc\theta$ ____________

5. Find the smallest positive θ in degree measure for which

a) $\sin\theta = -\frac{1}{2}$ ____________ b) $\tan\theta = -\sqrt{3}$ ____________

c) $\csc\theta = -\frac{2}{\sqrt{3}}$ ____________ d) $\sec\theta = -\sqrt{2}$ ____________

e) $\cot\theta = -\frac{1}{\sqrt{3}}$ ____________ f) $\cos\theta = \frac{-\sqrt{3}}{2}$ ____________

6. Find the smallest positive x in radian measure for which

a) $\sin x = \frac{-\sqrt{3}}{2}$ ____________ b) $\cot x = -\sqrt{3}$ ____________

c) $\csc x = -\sqrt{2}$ ____________ d) $\sec x = -\frac{2}{\sqrt{3}}$ ____________

e) $\tan x = -1$ ____________ f) $\cos x = -\frac{1}{2}$ ____________

7. Find the exact value of each expression without using a calculator. Note: $(\sin\theta)^2 = \sin^2\theta$.

a) $\sin 60^\circ$ ____________ **b)** $2\sin 30^\circ \cos 30^\circ$ ____________

c) $\sin^2\frac{\pi}{6}+\cos^2\frac{\pi}{6}$ ____________ **d)** $\sin^2\frac{\pi}{4}+\cos^2\frac{\pi}{4}$ ____________

e) $\sec^2 60^\circ - \tan^2 60^\circ$ ____________ **f)** $\csc^2\frac{\pi}{6}-\cot^2\frac{\pi}{6}$ ____________

g) $2\sin^2\frac{\pi}{6}$ ____________ **h)** $1-\cos\frac{\pi}{3}$ ____________

i) $\tan\frac{\pi}{3}$ ____________ **j)** $\dfrac{2\tan\frac{\pi}{6}}{1-\tan^2\frac{\pi}{6}}$ ____________

8. Find an angle x such that $x \neq y, 0 \leq x < 2\pi$ and $\sin x = \sin y$.

a) $y=\frac{\pi}{6}$ ____________ **b)** $y=\frac{7\pi}{4}$ ____________

c) $y=\frac{11\pi}{6}$ ____________ **d)** $y=\frac{4\pi}{3}$ ____________

9. Find an angle x such that $x \neq y, 0 \leq x < 2\pi$ and $\cos x = \cos y$.

a) $y=\frac{\pi}{6}$ ____________ **b)** $y=\frac{7\pi}{4}$ ____________

c) $y=\frac{7\pi}{6}$ ____________ **d)** $y=\frac{4\pi}{3}$ ____________

10. Find an angle x such that $x \neq y, 0 \leq x < 2\pi$ and $\tan x = \tan y$.

a) $y=\frac{\pi}{6}$ ____________ **b)** $y=\frac{7\pi}{4}$ ____________

c) $y=\frac{11\pi}{6}$ ____________ **d)** $y=\frac{4\pi}{3}$ ____________

11. Determine all possible values of x by special angles, $0 \le x < 2\pi$.

a) $\cos x = \frac{\sqrt{3}}{2}$ __________

b) $\sin x = -\frac{1}{2}$ __________

c) $\tan x = -1$ __________

d) $\csc x = 2$ __________

e) $\sec x = -\sqrt{2}$ __________

f) $\sin x = -1$ __________

g) $\cot x = \text{undefined}$ __________

h) $\cos x = 0$ __________

i) $\csc x = \text{undefined}$ __________

j) $\sec x = -1$ __________

k) $\cot x = -\frac{1}{\sqrt{3}}$ __________

l) $\csc x = -\sqrt{2}$ __________

12. Find exact values of $\sin 3x$ and $\sin\left(\frac{x}{3}\right)$ for the given values of x.

a) $x = 0$

b) $x = \frac{\pi}{2}$

c) $x = -\frac{\pi}{2}$

d) $x = -\pi$

13. Find exact values of $\cos 3x$ and $\cos\left(\frac{x}{3}\right)$ for the given values of x.

a) $x = 0$

b) $x = \frac{\pi}{2}$

c) $x = -\frac{\pi}{2}$

d) $x = -\pi$

14. Choose various special angle values of $\sin\theta$ and $\sin(-\theta)$. How does the value of $\sin(-\theta)$ compare to the value of $\sin\theta$?

15. Choose various special angle values of $\cos\theta$ and $\cos(-\theta)$. How does the value of $\cos(-\theta)$ compare to the value of $\cos\theta$?

6.4 Graphing Basic Trigonometric Functions

The Unit Circle

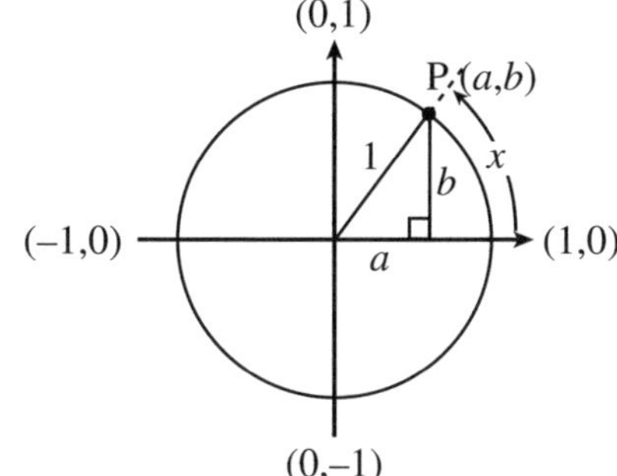

The equation of the unit circle by Pythagoras' theorem is $a^2 + b^2 = 1$.

Thus, $\sin x = \dfrac{\text{opposite}}{\text{hypotenuse}} = \dfrac{b}{1} = b$; $\cos x = \dfrac{\text{adjacent}}{\text{hypotenuse}} = \dfrac{a}{1} = a$

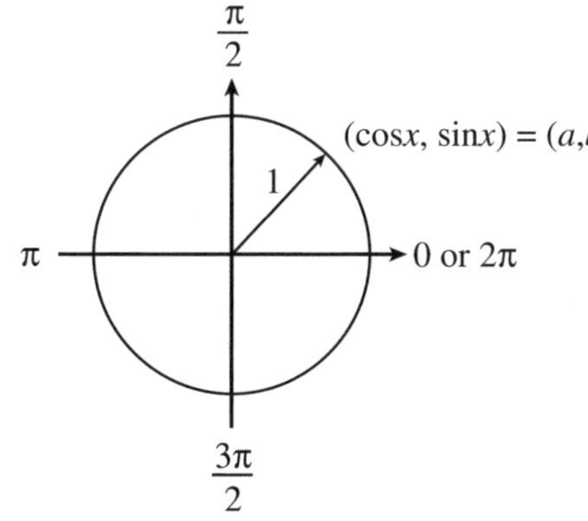

As x varies from:	$y = \sin x = b$ varies from:	$y = \cos x = a$ varies from
0 to $\frac{\pi}{2}$	0 to 1	1 to 0
$\frac{\pi}{2}$ to π	1 to 0	0 to –1
π to $\frac{3\pi}{2}$	0 to –1	–1 to 0
$\frac{3\pi}{2}$ to 2π	–1 to 0	0 to 1

To graph $y = \sin x$ and $y = \cos x$ from 0 to 2π, we will look at its values on the x- and y-axis, plus the special angle values in the 4 quadrants.

Graphing $y = \sin x$ for $0 \le x \le 2\pi$

x'	0	$\frac{\pi}{6}$	$\frac{\pi}{4}$	$\frac{\pi}{3}$	$\frac{\pi}{2}$
$\sin x$	0	$\frac{1}{2}$	$\frac{1}{\sqrt{2}} = 0.71$	$\frac{\sqrt{3}}{2} = 0.87$	1

Quadrant I

Values in quadrants II, III, and IV can be calculated by reference angles.

Sine is positive in quadrants I and II.
Sine is negative in quadrant III and IV.

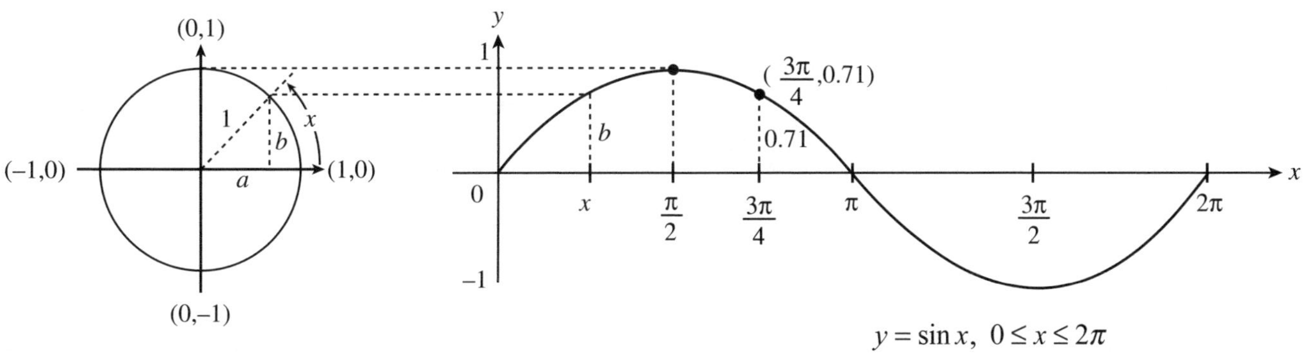

$y = \sin x,\ 0 \le x \le 2\pi$

Graphing $y = \cos x$ for $0 \le x \le 2\pi$

x	0	$\frac{\pi}{6}$	$\frac{\pi}{4}$	$\frac{\pi}{3}$	$\frac{\pi}{2}$
$\cos x$	1	$\frac{\sqrt{3}}{2}=0.87$	$\frac{1}{\sqrt{2}}=0.71$	$\frac{1}{2}$	0

Quadrant I

Values in quadrants II, III, and IV can be calculated by reference angles.

Cosine is positive in quadrants I and IV.
cosine is negative in quadrant II and III.

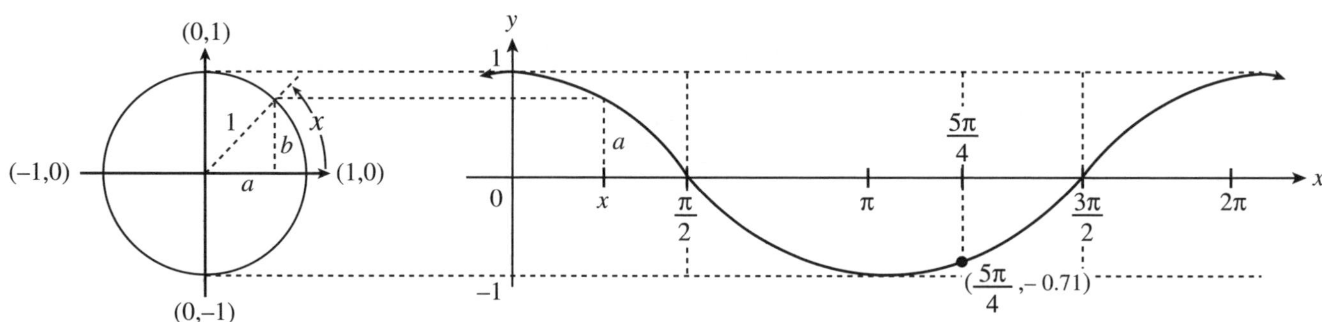

The graphs of $y = \sin x$ and $y = \cos x$ extend horizontally to infinity in both directions, repeating at successive intervals. Each repeated interval is called a **period**.

Definition of a Period

A function f is periodic if there is a positive number P such that $f(x+P) = f(x)$ for all x in the domain. The length of the shortest interval over which the function repeats itself is known as the **period**.

We can summarize as follows:

Graph of $\boldsymbol{y = \sin x}$

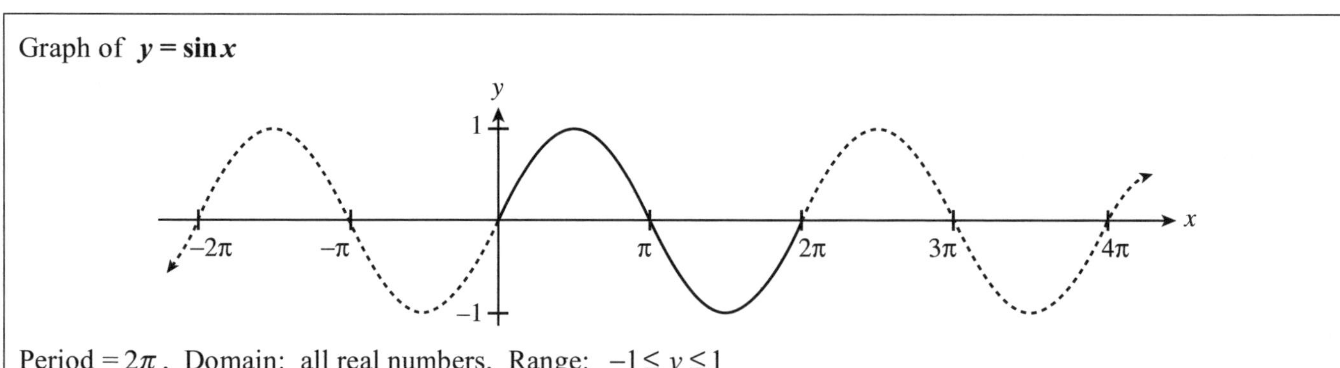

Period $= 2\pi$, Domain: all real numbers, Range: $-1 \le y \le 1$

Graph of $\boldsymbol{y = \cos x}$

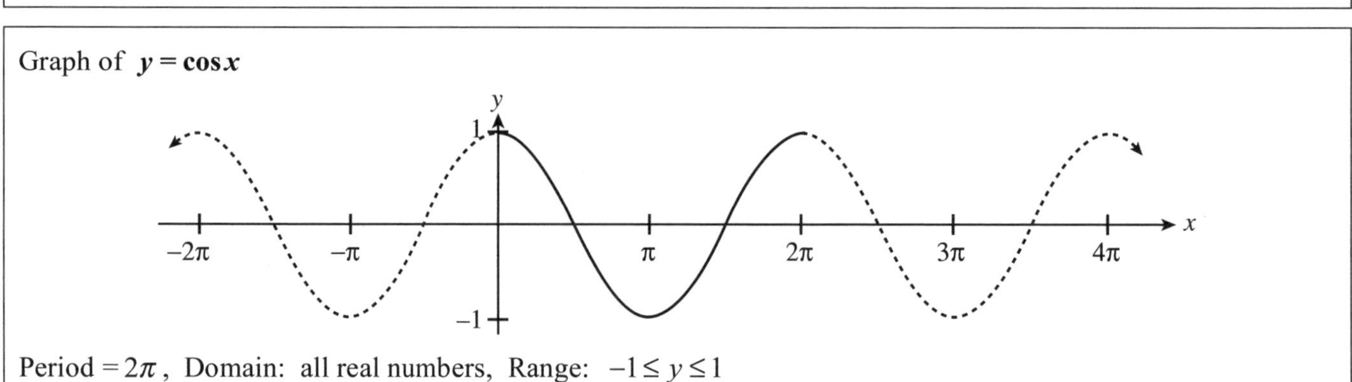

Period $= 2\pi$, Domain: all real numbers, Range: $-1 \le y \le 1$

Amplitude

Let us compare the graphs of $y = \sin x$ and $y = a\sin x$. The graph of $y = a\sin x$ can be obtained by multiplying $y = \sin x$ by a. The absolute value of a, written $|a|$, is the amplitude of the function.

Compare amplitudes of $y = \sin x$, $y = -2\sin x$, and $y = \frac{1}{2}\sin x$, $0 \le x \le 2\pi$.

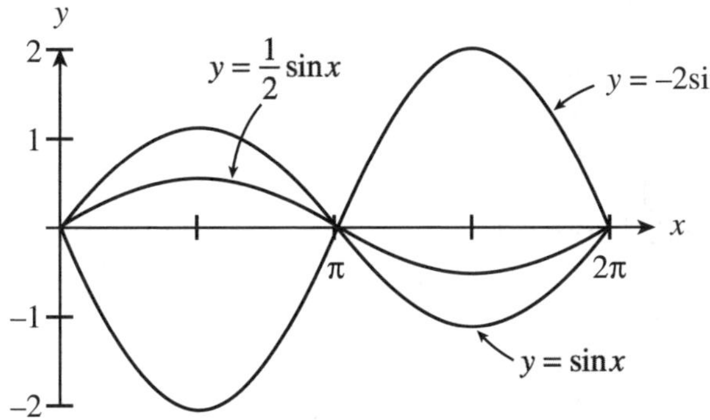

$y = \sin x$; amplitude $|a| = |1| = 1$

$y = -2\sin x$; amplitude $|a| = |-2| = 2$

$y = \frac{1}{2}\sin x$; amplitude $|a| = |\frac{1}{2}| = \frac{1}{2}$

In general, we can define amplitude as follows:

> **Definition of Amplitude**
>
> Let f be a periodic trigonometric function, and let m and M denote the minimum and maximum values of the function. Then, the amplitude of f is
>
> $$\frac{M-m}{2}$$

Periods

Let us compare the graphs of $y = \sin x$ and $y = \sin bx$.

For $y = \sin x$, $0 \le x < 2\pi$ before the graph repeats
period is 2π

For $y = \sin bx$, $0 \le bx < 2\pi$ before the graph repeats
$0 \le x < \frac{2\pi}{|b|}$ (divide by b)
period is $\frac{2\pi}{|b|}$ (period is always positive)

> Period for $y = \sin bx$ or $y = \cos bx$ is
>
> $$\text{Period} = \frac{2\pi}{|b|}$$

Compare the period of $y = \sin x$, $y = \sin 2x$, and $y = \sin\frac{x}{2}$, $0 \le x \le 2\pi$

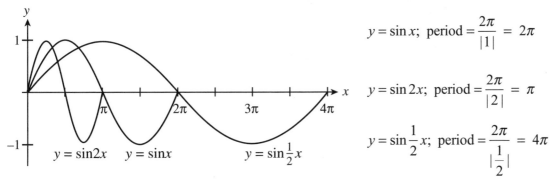

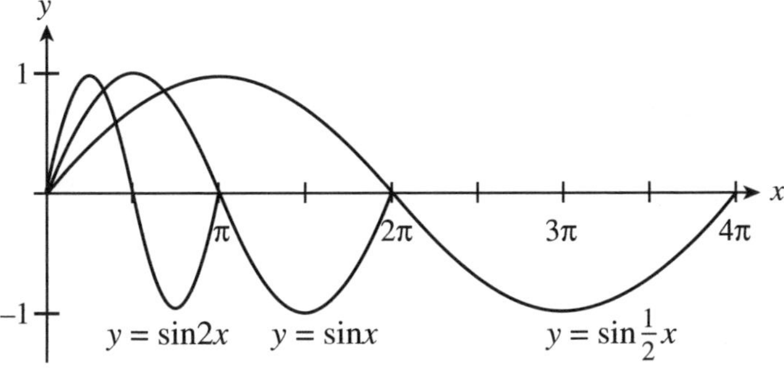

$y = \sin x$; period $= \frac{2\pi}{|1|} = 2\pi$

$y = \sin 2x$; period $= \frac{2\pi}{|2|} = \pi$

$y = \sin\frac{1}{2}x$; period $= \frac{2\pi}{|\frac{1}{2}|} = 4\pi$

Phase Shift

Let us compare the graphs of $\mathbf{y=\sin x}$, $\mathbf{y=\sin(bx-c)}$ and $\mathbf{y=\sin b(x-c)}$.

$\mathbf{y=\sin x}$ has a period of 2π going from 0 to 2π.

$\mathbf{y=\sin(bx-c)}$ has a period of 2π going from $bx-c=0$ to $bx-c=2\pi$

$$bx=c \qquad bx=c+2\pi$$

$$x=\frac{c}{b} \qquad x=\frac{c}{b}+\frac{2\pi}{b}$$

phase shift period

Therefore, $y=\sin(bx-c)$ has a phase shift of $\frac{c}{b}$.

If $\frac{c}{b}>0$, shift to right, if $\frac{c}{b}<0$, shift to left

$\mathbf{y=\sin b(x-c)}$ has a period of 2π going from $b(x-c)=0$ to $b(x-c)=2\pi$

$$x-c=0 \qquad x-c=\frac{2\pi}{b}$$

$$x=c \qquad x=c+\frac{2\pi}{b}$$

phase shift period

Therefore, $y=\sin b(x-c)$ has a phase shift of c.
If $c>0$, shift to right, if $c<0$, shift to left

Compare the phase shift of $y=\sin x$, $y=\sin\left(2x-\frac{\pi}{2}\right)=\sin 2\left(x-\frac{\pi}{4}\right)$, $0\le x\le\frac{9\pi}{4}$.

$y=\sin x$ has no phase shift

$y=\sin\left(2x-\frac{\pi}{2}\right)$ has a phase shift of $2x-\frac{\pi}{2}=0\rightarrow 2x=\frac{\pi}{2}\rightarrow x=\frac{\pi}{4}$

$y=\sin 2\left(x-\frac{\pi}{4}\right)$ also has a phase shift of $2\left(x-\frac{\pi}{4}\right)=0\rightarrow x-\frac{\pi}{4}=0\rightarrow x=\frac{\pi}{4}$

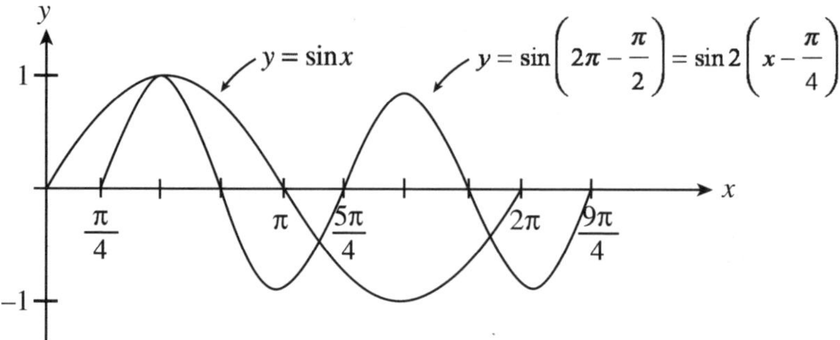

Thus $y=\sin\left(2x-\frac{\pi}{2}\right)$ and $y=\sin 2\left(x-\frac{\pi}{2}\right)$ have a period of π and a phase shift of $\frac{\pi}{4}$ to the right.

Vertical Displacement

Let us compare the graphs of $y = \sin x$ and $y = \sin x + d$.

If $d > 0$, shift vertically upward d units

If $d < 0$, shift vertically downward d units

Compare $y = \sin x$ and $y = \sin x - 2, 0 \le x \le 2\pi$

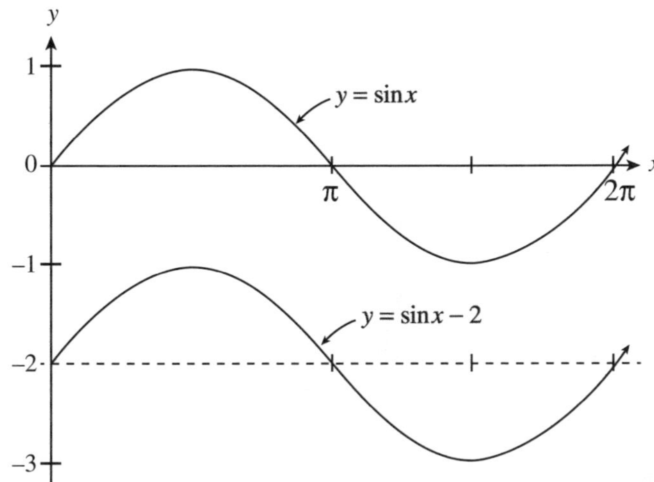

$y = \sin x$; no vertical shift

$y = \sin x - 2$; shift vertically down 2 units

Summary of the Forms $f(x) = a\sin(bx - c) + d$ **and** $f(x) = a\cos(bx - c) + d$
or $f(x) = a\sin b(x - c) + d$ **and** $f(x) = a\cos b(x - c) + d$

Assume $a \ne 0$ and $b > 0$

Amplitude: $|a|$,

Period: $\frac{2\pi}{b}$,

Phase Shift: $bx - c = 0$

$x = \frac{c}{b}$, $\frac{c}{b} > 0$ shift right

$\frac{c}{b} < 0$ shift left

or $b(x - c) = 0$

$x = c, c > 0$ shift right

$c < 0$ shift left

Vertical Displacement: d, $d > 0$ shift upward

$d < 0$ shift downward

Example 1 Find the amplitude, period, phase shift and vertical displacement of

a) $y = -3\cos\left(\frac{3}{2}x + \frac{\pi}{2}\right) + 1$ **b)** $y = 2\sin\frac{\pi}{6}(x - 2) - 3$

▶ *Solution:*

a) amplitude: $|a| = |-3| = 3$

period: $\frac{2\pi}{|b|} = \frac{2\pi}{\left|\frac{3}{2}\right|} = \frac{4\pi}{3}$

phase shift: $\frac{3}{2}x + \frac{\pi}{2} = 0, x = -\frac{\pi}{3}$

shift left $\frac{\pi}{3}$

v.d.: $d = 1$, upward

b) amplitude: $|a| = |2| = 2$

period: $\frac{2\pi}{|b|} = \frac{2\pi}{\left|\frac{\pi}{6}\right|} = 12$

phase shift: $\frac{\pi}{6}(x - 2) = 0, x = 2$

shift right 2

v.d.: $d = -3$, downward

Example 2 Graph $y = -2\cos\frac{\pi}{4}(x+3) + 1$ for one period.

Step 1: What is the amplitude, period, phase shift and vertical displacement?

$$a = |-2| = 2\,,\quad p = \frac{2\pi}{\frac{\pi}{4}} = 8\,,\quad \text{p.s: } \tfrac{\pi}{4}(x+3) = 0 \rightarrow x = -3\,,\quad \text{v.d.} = 1$$

Step 2: Recognize this is a reflection of a cosine graph in the x-axis.

Step 3: Draw coordinate system and label:

p.s. = 3: One full period will start at x = – 3,
and end at x = –3 + 8 = 5.

p = 8: Divide period into 4 equal parts.

v.d. = 1: Midline y = 1.

a = 2: The curve will oscillate between:
maximum y = 1 + 2 = 3
minimum y = 1 – 2 = – 1

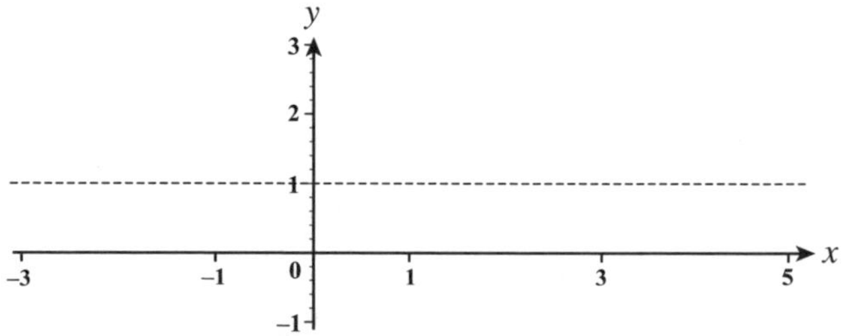

Step 4: If step 3 is done correctly, the graph is virtually done. The basic graph of cosine is known, so just fill in the 5 points and draw the curve.

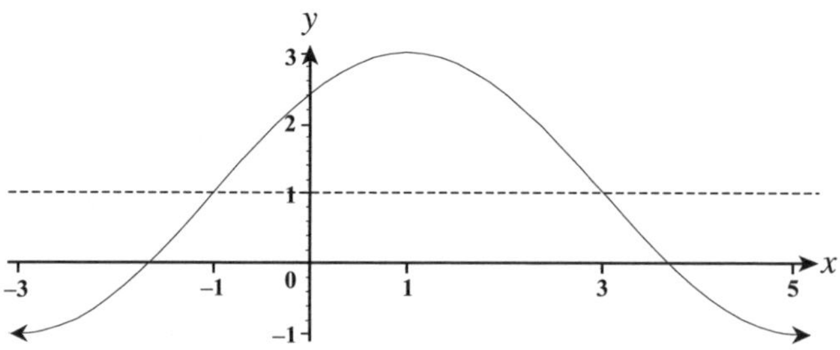

Step 5: Check your graph; if you put $x = -3\,,\ -1\,,\ 1,\ 3\,,\ 5$ into $\frac{\pi}{4}(x+3)$ you have to get $0,\ \frac{\pi}{2},\ \pi,\ \frac{3\pi}{2}$ and 2π or there is something wrong with your graph.

Example 3 Write an equation for the following graph in terms of both sine and cosine.

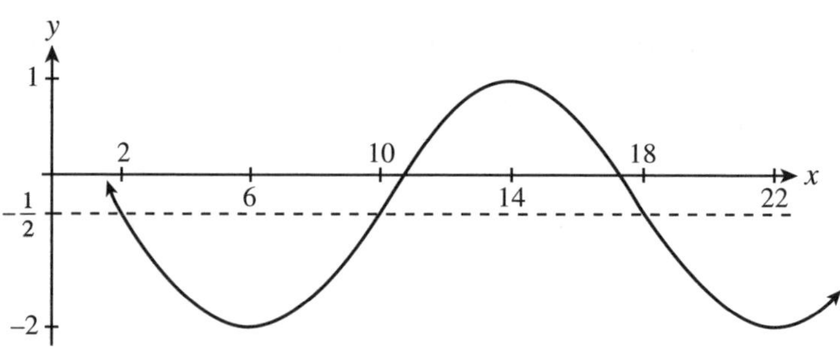

From graph: amplitude: $\frac{3}{2}$, period: 16, vertical displacement: $-\frac{1}{2}$

start at $x = 2$: $y = -\frac{3}{2}\sin\frac{\pi}{8}(x-2) - \frac{1}{2}$

start at $x = 10$: $y = \frac{3}{2}\sin\frac{\pi}{8}(x-10) - \frac{1}{2}$

(many answers)

start at $x = 6$: $y = -\frac{3}{2}\cos\frac{\pi}{8}(x-6) - \frac{1}{2}$

start at $x = 14$: $y = \frac{3}{2}\cos\frac{\pi}{8}(x-14) - \frac{1}{2}$

(many answers)

Graphing $y = \tan x$

By definition, $\tan x = \dfrac{\text{opposite}}{\text{adjacent}}$. Thus, the graph of $y = \tan x$ is undefined where the adjacent side is zero since a number divided by zero is undefined. Two such values are $x = \dfrac{\pm\pi}{2} \approx \pm 1.5708$. We can examine this more closely with the following table:

x	$-\dfrac{\pi}{2}$	-1.57	-1.5	-1	0	1	1.5	1.57	$\dfrac{\pi}{2}$
$\tan x$	undefined	-1256	-14.1	-1.56	0	1.56	14.1	1256	undefined

Graph of $y = \tan x$

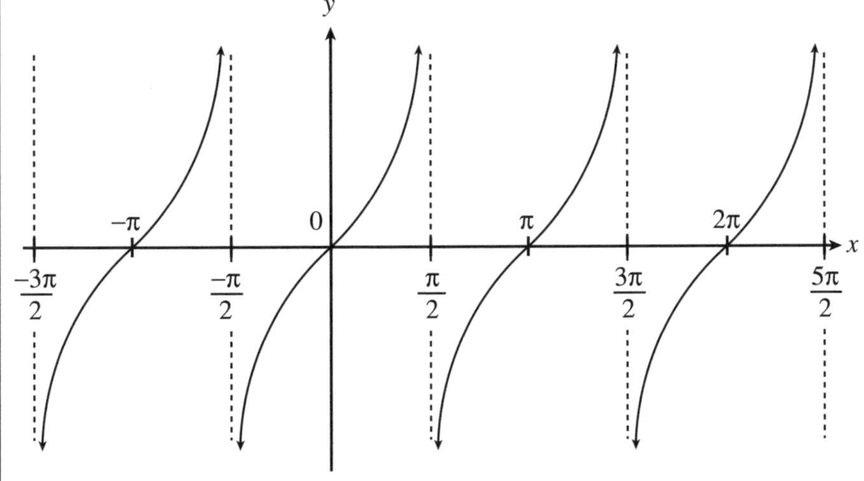

Period: π

Domain: all real numbers except $\dfrac{\pi}{2} \pm n\pi$, n an integer

Range: all real numbers

Note: no amplitude

Period

Let us compare the graph of $y = \tan x$ and $y = \tan bx$.
$y = \tan x$ has a period of π.
Thus, $y = \tan bx$ has a period of $bx = 0$ to $bx = \pi$

$$x = 0 \qquad x = \frac{\pi}{b}$$

> Period for $y = \tan bx$ is
>
> Period $= \dfrac{\pi}{|b|}$

Therefore the period of $y = \tan bx$ is $\dfrac{\pi}{|b|}$, period is always positive.

Example 4 Find the period of **a)** $y = \tan 2x$ and **b)** $y = \tan \frac{1}{2}x$.

▶ *Solution:*

a) $P = \dfrac{\pi}{|b|} = \dfrac{\pi}{|2|} = \dfrac{\pi}{2}$

b) $P = \dfrac{\pi}{|b|} = \dfrac{\pi}{\left|\frac{1}{2}\right|} = 2\pi$

6.4 Exercise Set

1. Which function below matches the description given?

amplitude	**A)** 2	**B)** 3	**C)** 2	**D)** 3	**E)** 3	**F)** 2
period	π	π	3π	3π	$\frac{4\pi}{3}$	$\frac{2\pi}{3}$
phase shift	$\frac{\pi}{3}$	$-\frac{\pi}{6}$	$-\frac{2\pi}{3}$	$-\frac{3\pi}{4}$	$\frac{\pi}{3}$	$\frac{\pi}{6}$
vertical displacement	–2	2	–2	3	3	–3

$f(x) = 2\cos\frac{2}{3}\left(x + \frac{2\pi}{3}\right) - 2$ __________ $g(x) = 3\cos\left(\frac{2}{3}x + \frac{\pi}{2}\right) + 3$ __________

$h(x) = -2\sin 2\left(x - \frac{\pi}{3}\right) - 2$ __________ $i(x) = -2\cos\left(3x - \frac{\pi}{2}\right) - 3$ __________

$j(x) = -3\sin 2\left(x + \frac{\pi}{6}\right) + 2$ __________ $k(x) = 3\sin\left(\frac{3}{2}x - \frac{\pi}{2}\right) + 3$ __________

2. Which functions have $f(x) = g(x)$ for all x?

a) $f(x) = \sin x$ __________ **A** $g(x) = \cos(-x + \pi)$

b) $f(x) = -\sin x$ __________ **B** $g(x) = -\sin\left(x - \frac{\pi}{2}\right)$

c) $f(x) = \cos x$ __________ **C** $g(x) = \cos\left(x - \frac{\pi}{2}\right)$

d) $f(x) = -\cos x$ __________ **D** $g(x) = \cos\left(x + \frac{\pi}{2}\right)$

3. State the amplitude, period, phase shift and vertical displacement for the graph of each function

a) $y = \frac{1}{3}\sin\left(2x + \frac{\pi}{3}\right) - 1$ **b)** $y = -\frac{1}{2}\sin\pi\left(x + \frac{3}{4}\right) + 1$

c) $y = -4\cos\frac{\pi}{3}(x - 1) + 2$ **d)** $y = -\cos 2\left(\frac{\pi}{6} - x\right)$

e) $y = 3\sin\left(\frac{2\pi}{3} - \pi x\right) - 2$ **f)** $y = \frac{3}{2}\cos 2\left(x + \frac{\pi}{4}\right)$

4. What is the period of

a) $y = 2\tan\frac{1}{3}x$ __________ **b)** $y = -2\tan\frac{\pi}{2}x$ __________

5. Write an equation in the form $y = a\sin b(x-c)$ and $y = a\cos b(x-c)$ for the least non-negative real number c, with $a > 0$ and $b > 0$ for the following graphs.

a)

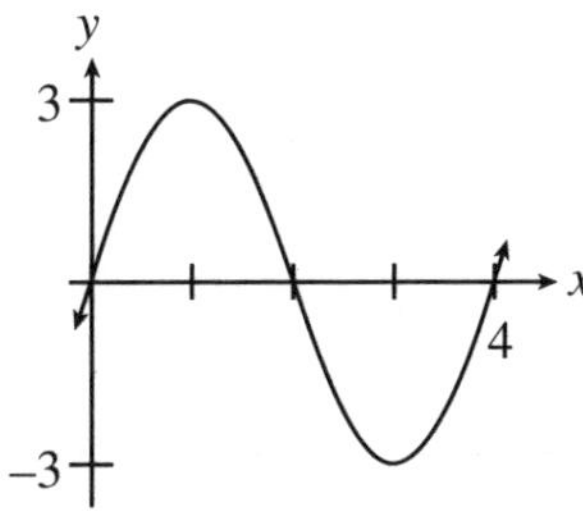

b)

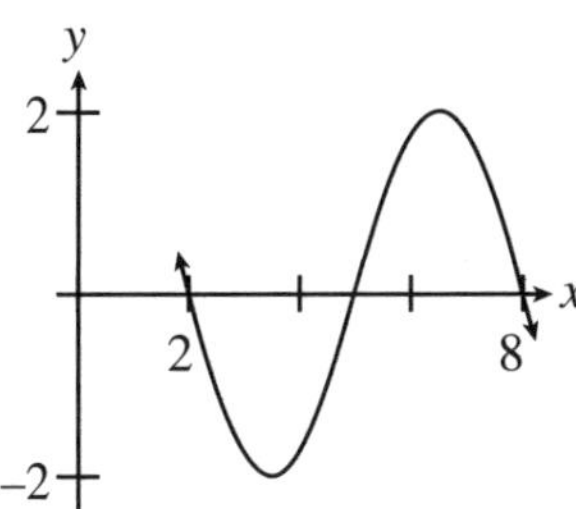

c)

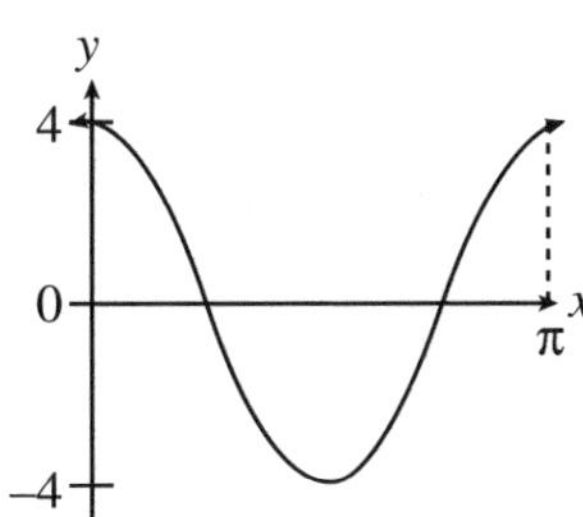

d)

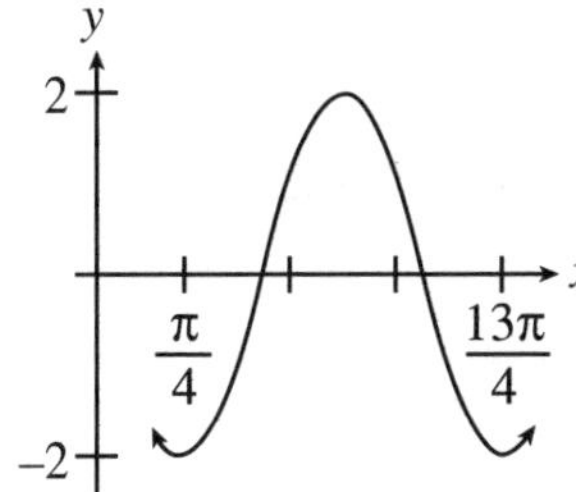

e)

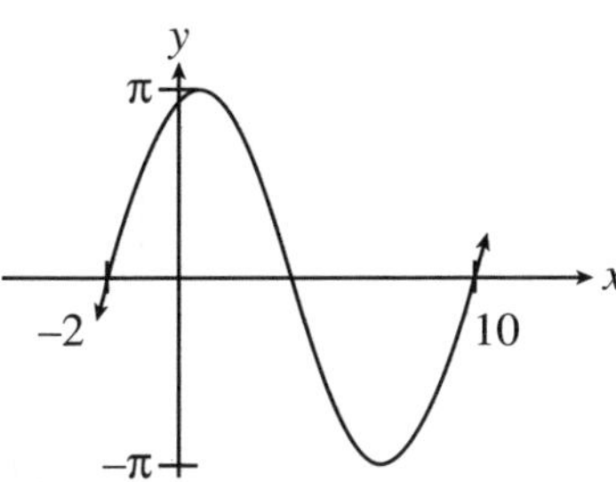

f)

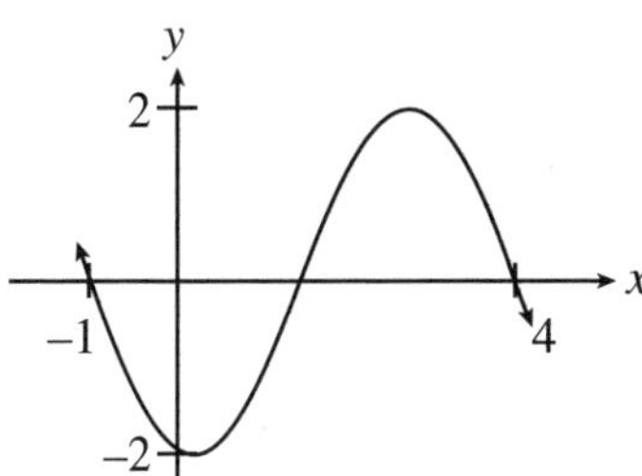

g)

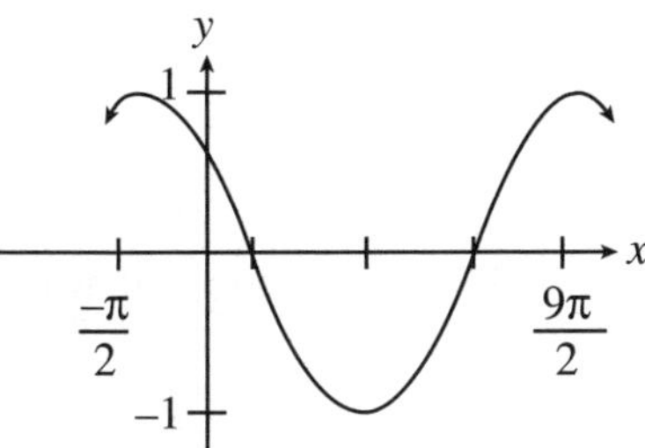

h)

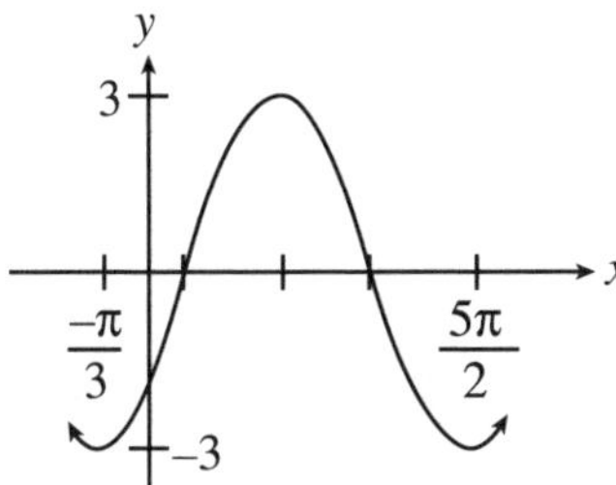

i)

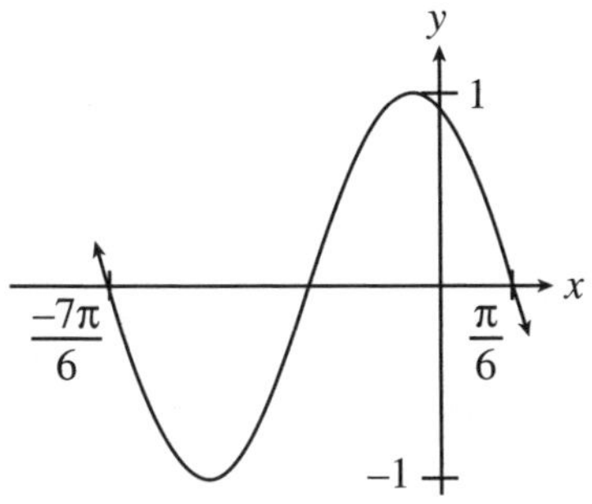

j)

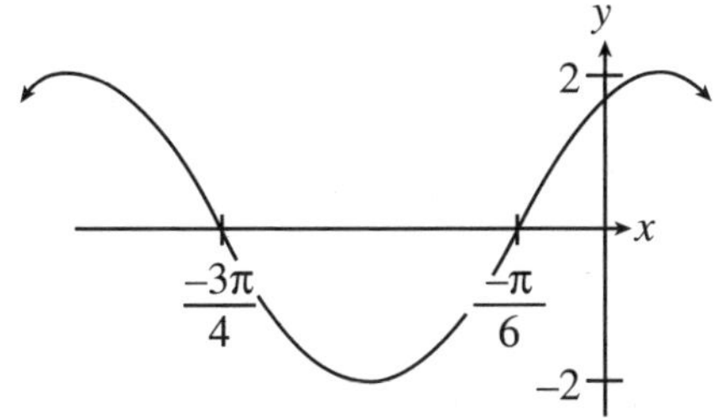

6. Accurately sketch at least one complete period of the curve $y = -3\sin\frac{\pi}{3}(x+2)+1$

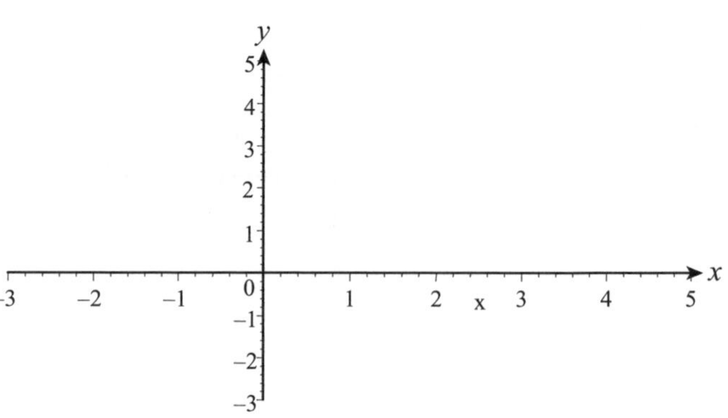

7. Accurately sketch at least one complete period of the curve $y = 2\cos\left(\frac{\pi}{2}x+\pi\right)-1$.

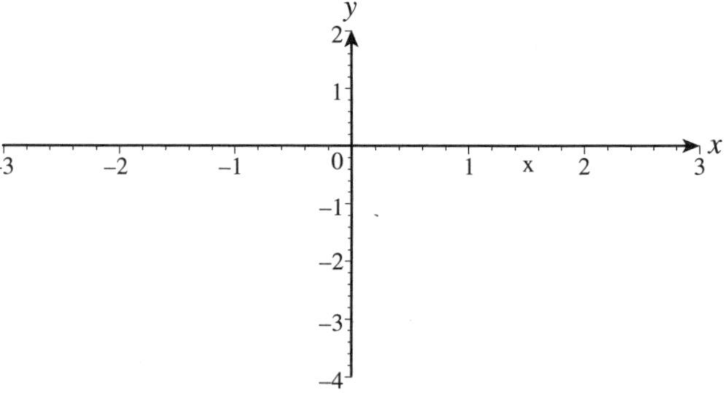

8. Find a function in the form $y = a\sin bx + c$ if it has a maximum point of (2 , 3) and the closest minimum point of $(6, -7)$.

9. Find a function in the form $y = a\cos b(x-c)+d$ if it has a maximum point of (2 , 3) and the closest minimum point of $(6, -7)$.

10. a) The graph below describes the function $y = a\sin b(x+c)+d$. Write a sine equation which describes the graph if ***(i)*** $a > 0$ ***(ii)*** $a < 0$

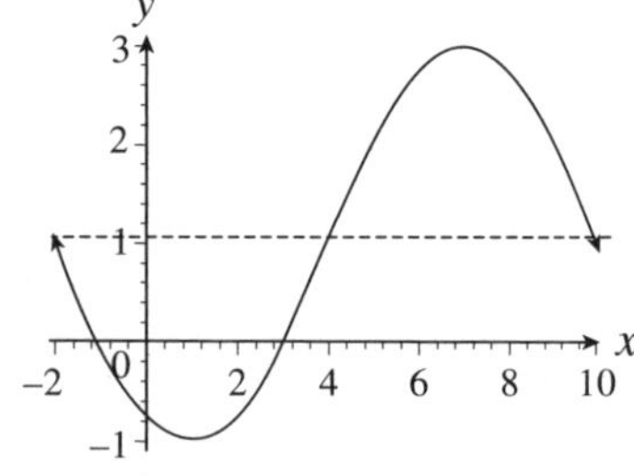

(i) ______________________________

(ii) ______________________________

b) The graph can also describe the function $y = a\cos b(x+c)+d$. Write a cosine equation which describes the graph if ***(i)*** $a > 0$ ***(ii)*** $a < 0$.

(i) ______________________________ **(ii)** ______________________________

6.5 Application of Periodic Functions

The periodic values of the sine and cosine functions are found in nature. A motion involving a pattern that is repeated at fixed time intervals is called **harmonic motion**. Examples of harmonic motion are pendulums, objects suspended from a spring, a Ferris wheel, the amount of daylight during a year, tides, heart beat, radio waves, etc.

Example 1 A weight is attached to a spring and set in motion by stretching the spring and releasing it. The distance (cm) the spring is from its rest position at time t (sec) is given by the equation $d = 5\sin(4\pi t)$

a) How many cycles per second does the spring make?

b) Graph the spring for one period.

c) At what time will the first maximum and minimum extremes of the cycles occur?

▶ *Solution:* **a)** $P = \frac{2\pi}{b} = \frac{2\pi}{4\pi} = \frac{1}{2}$ second. Thus, the spring makes 2 cycles per second.

b)

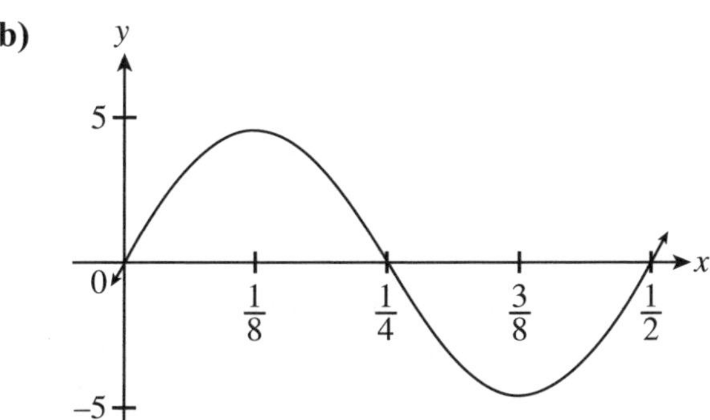

c) If the period is $\frac{1}{2}$ the maximum of 5 cm will occur at $\frac{1}{4}$ of the period: $\frac{1}{4} \times \frac{1}{2} = \frac{1}{8}$ seconds and the minimum will occur at $\frac{3}{4}$ of the period: $\frac{3}{4} \times \frac{1}{2} = \frac{3}{8}$ seconds.

Example 2 The voltage E of an electrical circuit has an amplitude of 220 volts and a frequency of 60 cycles per second. If $E = 220$ when $t = 0$, find a periodic equation in terms of cosine that describes this voltage.

▶ *Solution:* If the frequency is 60 cycles per second, then the period is $\frac{1}{60}$ seconds.

$$P = \frac{2\pi}{b} = \frac{1}{60}$$

$$b = 120\pi$$

Thus, the equation is $E = 220\cos(120\pi t)$.

Example 3 The monthly sales of a seasonal product are approximated by

$$S = 760 + 480\cos\frac{\pi t}{6}$$

where t is the time in months, with $t = 1$ corresponding to January. Graph the function and state what months exceed 1000 units of sales.

▶ *Solution:* $P = \dfrac{2\pi}{b} = \dfrac{2\pi}{\frac{\pi}{6}} = 12$, vertical displacement = 760, amplitude = 480

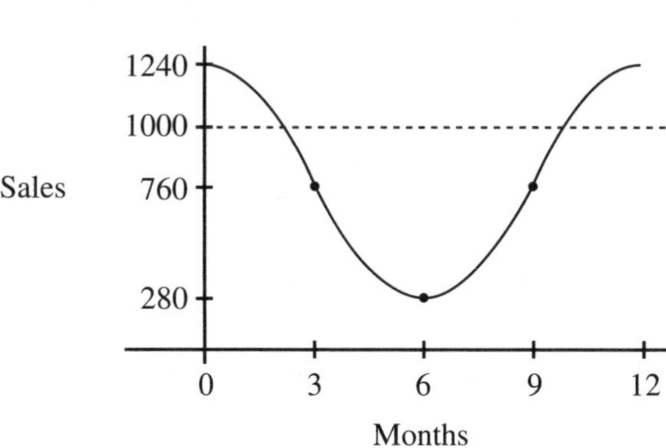

$$760 + 480\cos\frac{\pi t}{6} > 1000$$

$$480\cos\frac{\pi}{6}t > 240$$

$$\cos\frac{\pi}{6}t > \frac{1}{2}$$

cosine equal $\frac{1}{2}$ at $\frac{\pi}{3}$ and $\frac{5\pi}{3}$

$$\frac{\pi}{6}t = \frac{\pi}{3} \quad \text{and} \quad \frac{\pi}{6}t = \frac{5\pi}{3}$$

$$t = 2 \qquad\qquad t = 10$$

Thus, January, November, and December exceed 1000 unit of sales.
In February and October there are exactly 1000 units of sales.

Example 4 A Ferris wheel has a radius of 20 m and rotates every 60 seconds. A rider enters the seat at the lowest point of the Ferris wheel, 3 m above the ground. Find a cosine function that gives the height h, after t seconds of motion for the rider and find at what time the rider first reaches a height of 30 m.

▶ *Solution:* amplitude = 20, period = $\dfrac{2\pi}{b} = 60$, $b = \dfrac{\pi}{30}$, vertical displacement is 20 + 3 = 23; upside-down standard cosine function, no phase shift.

Therefore, $h = -20\cos\left(\dfrac{\pi}{30}t\right) + 23$

By graphing calculator set in radian mode

Set Window

```
WINDOW
 Xmin=0
 Xmax=60
 Xscl=5
 Ymin=-10
 Ymax=50
 Yscl=5
 Xres=5
```

Graph $Y_1 = -20\cos\left(\dfrac{\pi x}{30}\right) + 23$

$Y_2 = 30$

Intersection
X=18.414553 Y=30

It takes 18.4 seconds for the rider to be above 30 m.

6.5 Exercise Set

1. Assume that the simple harmonic motion of a spring is described by the equation

$$S = 4\cos\left(\frac{\pi t}{2}\right)$$

where S is in cm and t is in seconds. When during the time $0 \le t \le 8$ is the spring passing through the origin?

2. The voltage E in an electrical circuit is given by $E = 4\cos 60\pi t$, where t is time measured in seconds.

a) Find the amplitude and period.

b) The reciprocal of the period, called the frequency, is the number of periods completed in one second. Find the frequency.

3. The temperature in Whitehorse, Yukon is given by

$$T = 35\sin\left[\left(\frac{2\pi}{365}\right)(x-100)\right] + 27$$

where $x = 1$ is January 1st and $x = 365$ is December 31st. Use your graphing calculator to find what days of the year the temperature was below 0°.

4. Sales of snowmobiles are seasonal. Suppose sales in Camrose, Alberta are approximated by

$$S = 200 + 200\cos\left[\frac{\pi}{6}(t+2)\right]$$

where t is time in months with $t = 0$ corresponding to January. For what month are sales equal to 0?

5. The longest day of the year in Victoria, BC is 15 hours on June 21; the shortest day of 9 hours is on December 21; with 12 hours on March 21 and Sept 21. Write a sine equation for the number of daylight hours as a function of the day of the year.

6. A normal adult breathes in and exhales about 0.84 litres of air every 4 seconds with the minimal amount in the lungs of 0.08 litres at $t = 0$. Write a cosine equation with $0 \le t \le 8$ and find the time of maximum air capacity in this interval.

7. If the voltage E in an electrical circuit has an amplitude of 110 volts and a period of $\frac{1}{60}$ seconds, and $E = 110$ when $t = 0$, find a periodic equation in terms of cosine that describes this voltage.

8. The pedals on a bicycle have a maximum height of 30 cm above the ground and a minimum distance of 8 cm above the ground. A person pedals at a constant rate of 20 cycles per minute.

a) What is the period in seconds for this periodic function?

b) Determine an equation for this periodic function.

9. A Ferris wheel of radius 25 metres, placed one metre above the ground, varies sinusoidally with time. The Ferris wheel makes one rotation every 24 seconds, with a person sitting 26 metres from the ground and rising when it starts to rotate.

a) Write a sinusoidal function that describes the function from a person's starting position.

b) How high above the ground would a person be 16 seconds after the Ferris wheel starts moving?

c) How many seconds on each rotation is a person more than 35 metres in the air?

10. Tides are a periodic rise and fall of water in the ocean. A low tide of 4.2 metres in White Rock, B.C. occurs at 4:30 a.m., and the next high tide of 11.8 metres occurs at 11:30 a.m. the same day.

a) Write a sinusoidal function that describes the tide flow.

b) What is the tide height at 1:15 p.m. that same day?

11. A spring modelling a sinusoidal function rests 1.6 metres above the ground. If the mass on the spring is pulled 1.1 metres below its resting position and then released, it requires 0.5 seconds to move from the maximum position to its minimum position. Assuming friction and air resistance are neglected,

a) write an equation in terms of cosine that describes this periodic function.

b) what height is the spring 2.3 seconds after being released?

12. A tsunami, usually called a tidal wave, is a very fast moving ocean wave caused by earthquakes that occur underwater. The water will first move down from its normal level, then move an equal distance above the normal level, then finally back to normal. The period of this tsunami is 16 minutes with an amplitude of 8 metres. The normal depth of water at Crescent Beach, B.C. is 6 metres.

a) What is the maximum and minimum height of water caused by the tsunami at Crescent Beach?

b) Write a periodic model of the tsunami when it first reaches Crescent Beach.

c) If you were in a boat out in the ocean, how would the tsunami affect you?

6.6 Chapter Review

Trigonometry (Part I) – Multiple-choice Review Questions

1. Determine the amplitude and period of $y = -2\cos\left(\frac{\pi}{2}x - \pi\right) + 3$.

   a) -2 ; 1
   b) 2 ; 1
   c) -2 ; 4
   d) 2 ; 4

2. Determine the phase shift and vertical displacement of $y = -2\cos\left(\frac{\pi}{2}x - \pi\right) + 3$.

   a) $-\pi$; 3
   b) π ; -3
   c) -2 ; 3
   d) 2 ; 3

3. Determine the period of $y = \tan\frac{\pi}{3}x$.

   a) $\frac{1}{3}$
   b) $\frac{2}{3}$
   c) 3
   d) 6

4. Given a circle with radius 6 cm and length of arc 12 cm, determine the sector angle to the nearest degree.
   a) 2°
   b) 29°
   c) 108°
   d) 115°

5. If $\csc x = -\frac{2}{\sqrt{3}}$ and $\tan x < 0$, determine $\cos x$.

   a) $-\frac{\sqrt{3}}{2}$
   b) $-\frac{1}{2}$
   c) $\frac{1}{2}$
   d) $\frac{\sqrt{3}}{2}$

6. If $(2,-3)$ is on the terminal side of standard position angle θ, what is the value of $\sec\theta$?

a) $-\frac{\sqrt{13}}{2}$

b) $-\frac{\sqrt{13}}{3}$

c) $\frac{\sqrt{13}}{3}$

d) $\frac{\sqrt{13}}{2}$

7. Determine the smallest positive angle θ, in radians, such that $\csc\theta=-\sqrt{2}$

a) $\frac{\pi}{4}$

b) $\frac{3\pi}{4}$

c) $\frac{5\pi}{4}$

d) $\frac{7\pi}{4}$

8. Convert 10 radians to a degree value between $0°$ and $360°$.

a) 33°

b) 148°

c) 213°

d) 303°

9. Determine the exact value of $\csc\frac{5\pi}{3}$.

a) $-\frac{2\sqrt{3}}{3}$

b) $-\frac{\sqrt{3}}{3}$

c) $\frac{\sqrt{3}}{3}$

d) $\frac{2\sqrt{3}}{3}$

10. Determine the value of $\cot\frac{17\pi}{6}$

a) $-\sqrt{3}$

b) $-\frac{1}{\sqrt{3}}$

c) $\frac{1}{\sqrt{3}}$

d) $\sqrt{3}$

11. Determine the quadrant in which the terminal arm of θ lies for $\sec\theta<0$, $\tan\theta>0$

a) quadrant I

b) quadrant II

c) quadrant III

d) quadrant IV

12. Determine the reference angle for $-\dfrac{7\pi}{6}$

a) $-\frac{\pi}{6}$

b) $\frac{\pi}{6}$

c) $\frac{5\pi}{6}$

d) $\frac{7\pi}{6}$

13. Determine $\sec\theta$ if the terminal arm of angle θ in standard position intersects the unit circle at point (a, b).

a) a

b) b

c) $\frac{1}{a}$

d) $\frac{1}{b}$

14. Determine the maximum value of $y = -a\sin x - b, \quad a,\ b > 0$

a) $-a - b$

b) $-a + b$

c) $a - b$

d) $a + b$

15. Determine the minimum value of the function $y = a\sin x - b, \quad a, b > 0.$

a) $-a - b$

b) $-a + b$

c) $a - b$

d) $a + b$

16. What is the value of $\tan B$ if $\cos B = -\dfrac{3}{5}$ and $\pi \le B < \dfrac{3\pi}{2}$?

a) $-\frac{4}{3}$

b) $-\frac{3}{4}$

c) $\frac{3}{4}$

d) $\frac{4}{3}$

17. Solve: $\sec x = \dfrac{-2\sqrt{3}}{3}, \qquad 0 \le x < 2\pi$

a) $\frac{2\pi}{3}, \frac{4\pi}{3}$

b) $\frac{2\pi}{3}, \frac{5\pi}{3}$

c) $\frac{5\pi}{6}, \frac{7\pi}{6}$

d) $\frac{5\pi}{6}, \frac{11\pi}{6}$

18. The height, h, in metres, of a certain Ferris wheel seat above the ground at time, t, in seconds, after the ride is started is given by the formula $h(t) = 25\sin\frac{\pi}{30}(t-10)+26$. Use the graph of the function to determine the number of seconds in the first minutes the rider is above 40 m.

a) 15.7 sec.
b) 18.6 sec.
c) 26.3 sec.
d) 34.3 sec.

19. For $f(x) = \cos bx,\ b>0,$ find the smallest positive value of x that produces a minimum value for $f(x)$.

a) 0
b) $\frac{\pi}{2b}$
c) $\frac{\pi}{b}$
d) $\frac{3\pi}{2b}$

20. Determine the values of x if $\csc x = -1.325$, $0 \le x < 2\pi$

a) 2.42, 4.00
b) 2.64, 3.88
c) 3.86, 5.55
d) 4.00, 5.43

21. Determine the value of $\csc x$ if $\tan x = -a$, where $a > 0$, $\cos x < 0$

a) $\frac{-\sqrt{a^2+1}}{a}$
b) $\frac{\sqrt{a^2+1}}{a}$
c) $\frac{-\sqrt{a^2-1}}{a}$
d) $\frac{\sqrt{a^2-1}}{a}$

22. Determine the value of $\cos\theta$ if $\csc\theta = \frac{a}{b}$, where $\tan\theta < 0$ and $\sec\theta > 0$.

a) $\frac{\sqrt{a^2-b^2}}{a}$
b) $\frac{-\sqrt{a^2-b^2}}{a}$
c) $\frac{\sqrt{b^2-a^2}}{b}$
d) $\frac{-\sqrt{b^2-a^2}}{b}$

23. Determine the value of $\sec\theta$ if $\cot\theta = -a$, where $a > 0$ and $\sin\theta < 0$.

a) $\frac{\sqrt{a^2+1}}{a}$
b) $-\frac{\sqrt{a^2+1}}{a}$
c) $\frac{a+1}{a}$
d) $-\frac{a+1}{a}$

24. A cosine curve has a maximum point at $(2,\ 16)$ and the nearest minimum point to the right of this point is at $(7,\ 4)$. Which of the following is an equation for this curve?

a) $y = 6\cos\frac{\pi}{5}(x-2)+10$

b) $y = 6\cos\frac{\pi}{5}(x+2)+10$

c) $y = 6\cos\frac{2\pi}{5}(x-2)+10$

d) $y = 6\cos\frac{2\pi}{5}(x+2)+10$

25. Determine an equation for the function below

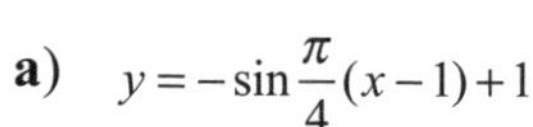

a) $y = -\sin\frac{\pi}{4}(x-1)+1$

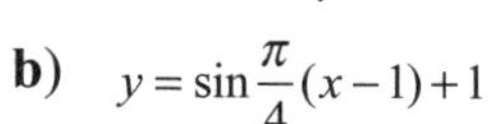

b) $y = \sin\frac{\pi}{4}(x-1)+1$

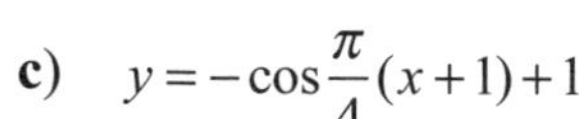

c) $y = -\cos\frac{\pi}{4}(x+1)+1$

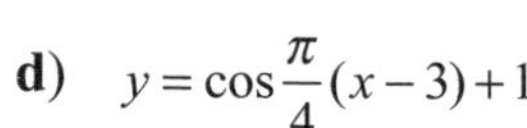

d) $y = \cos\frac{\pi}{4}(x-3)+1$

26. Evaluate $\cot\frac{2\pi}{5}$

a) 0.203
b) 0.325
c) 1.021
d) 3.078

27. Find θ, to the nearest degree, if θ terminates in quadrant II and $\sec\theta = -2.202$.

a) 117°
b) 142°
c) 153°
d) no value satisfies the equation

28. The graph of the function $f(x) = \cos x$ is translated 3 units left. What is the equation of the shifted function?

a) $f(x) = \cos(x+3)$
b) $f(x) = \cos(x-3)$
c) $f(x) = \cos x + 3$
d) $f(x) = \cos x - 3$

29. A circle has a radius 10 cm. Determine the **area** of a sector (pre-shaded region) of the circle that has a central angle of 2.1 radians.

a) 21
b) 105
c) 150
d) 210

30. Solve $\sec x = 3.45,\ 0 \le x < 2\pi$.

a) 0.29, 2.85
b) 0.29, 5.99
c) 1.28, 1.86
d) 1.28, 5.01

31. The point (a, b) is the point of intersection of the terminal arm of angle θ in standard position and the unit circle centred at (0, 0). Which expression represents $\csc\theta$?

a) $\frac{1}{a}$

b) a

c) $\frac{1}{b}$

d) b

32. Determine the minimum value of the function $f(x) = a\cos x + d$, where $a > 0$ and $d > 0$.

a) $a - d$
b) $d - a$
c) $2a - d$
d) $d - 2a$

33. Determine the equations of the asymptotes of the function $y = \tan bx,\ b > 0$.

a) $x = \frac{n\pi}{b}$; n an integer

b) $x = \frac{n\pi}{2b}$; n an integer

c) $x = \frac{\pi}{b} + \frac{n\pi}{b}$; n an integer

d) $x = \frac{\pi}{2b} + \frac{n\pi}{b}$; n an integer

34. A wheel of radius 20 cm has its centre 25 cm above the ground. It rotates once every 10 seconds. Determine an equation for the height, h, above the ground of a point on the wheel at time t seconds if this point has a minimum height at $t = 0$ seconds.

a) $h = -20\cos\frac{\pi}{10}t + 5$

b) $h = -20\cos\frac{\pi}{5}t + 5$

c) $h = -20\cos\frac{\pi}{10}t + 25$

d) $h = -20\cos\frac{\pi}{5}t + 25$

35. The function $h(t) = 3.9\sin 0.16\pi(t - 3) + 6.5$ gives the depth of water h metres, at any time, t hours, during a certain day. A freighter needs at least 8 metres of water to dock safely. How many hours in the 24-hour interval starting at $t = 0$ during which the freighter can dock safely?

a) 3.79
b) 4.68
c) 7.57
d) 9.36

For questions 36 and 37

A Ferris wheel has a radius of 25 m and rotates every 80 seconds. A rider enters the seat at the lowest point of the Ferris wheel 2 metres above the ground.

36. Determine a sinusoidal function that gives the height h, after t seconds of motion for the rider

a) $h = -25\sin\left(\frac{\pi}{40}t\right) + 27$

b) $h = 25\sin\left(\frac{\pi}{40}t\right) + 27$

c) $h = -25\cos\left(\frac{\pi}{40}t\right) + 27$

d) $h = 25\cos\left(\frac{\pi}{40}t\right) + 27$

37. At what time does the rider first reach a height of 35 m?

a) 4.1 sec.
b) 14.5 sec.
c) 24.1 sec.
d) 54.5 sec.

For questions 38, 39 and 40

38. At White Rock pier, the maximum depth of 8 meters occurred at 4:00 a.m. on July 1, with the minimum depth of 2 meters occurring 6 hours later. Determine a sinusoidal curve in terms of sine for this function.

a) $d(t) = -5\sin\frac{\pi}{6}(t-1) + 3$

b) $d(t) = -3\sin\frac{\pi}{6}(t-1) + 5$

c) $d(t) = 3\sin\frac{\pi}{6}(t-1) + 5$

d) $d(t) = 5\sin\frac{\pi}{6}(t-1) + 3$

39. What was the depth of water at White Rock pier at 12 noon on July 1?

a) 2.5 meters
b) 3 meters
c) 3.5 meters
d) 4 meters

40. Determine the first time on July 1 that the water reached a depth of 7 meters.

a) 2:24 a.m.
b) 2:39 a.m.
c) 5:22 a.m.
d) 5:36 a.m.

7.1 Trigonometric Identities and Equations

In this chapter, we will mainly work with equations and identities. An equation is true for **some** values of the variable (e.g., $\sin x - 1 = 0$). An identity is true for **all** values of the variable. Although there are infinitely many trigonometric identities, there are a number of **basic** identities that will serve as our focus of attention.

Verifying Identities

The six trigonometric ratios that we have established from the last chapter are:

Trigonometric Ratios

If θ is an angle in standard position with $P(x, y)$ on the terminal side of θ, then the six trigonometric ratios are

1. $\sin\theta = \frac{y}{r}$
2. $\cos\theta = \frac{x}{r}$
3. $\tan\theta = \frac{y}{x}$
4. $\csc\theta = \frac{r}{y}$
5. $\sec\theta = \frac{r}{x}$
6. $\cot\theta = \frac{x}{y}$

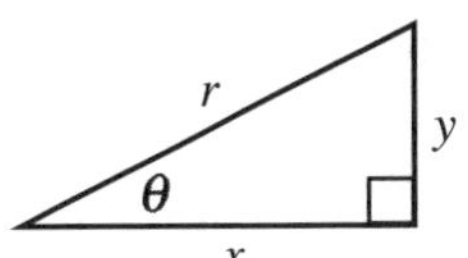

Where $r = \sqrt{x^2 + y^2}$

Our definition of the six trigonometric ratios allows us to find the following products:

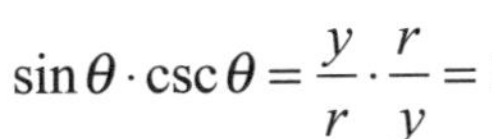

$$\sin\theta \cdot \csc\theta = \frac{y}{r} \cdot \frac{r}{y} = 1$$

$$\cos\theta \cdot \sec\theta = \frac{x}{r} \cdot \frac{r}{x} = 1$$

$$\tan\theta \cdot \cot\theta = \frac{y}{x} \cdot \frac{x}{y} = 1$$

When the product of two numbers of the same values equal one, they are said to be reciprocals of each other. Thus, we can state:

The Reciprocal Identities

1. $\csc\theta = \frac{1}{\sin\theta}$
2. $\sec\theta = \frac{1}{\cos\theta}$
3. $\cot\theta = \frac{1}{\tan\theta}$

These three relationships are examples of **trigonometric identities**. An identity is an equation that is true for **all** allowable replacement values of the variable.

Using the basic definition of the sine and cosine functions:

$$\frac{\sin\theta}{\cos\theta}=\frac{\frac{y}{r}}{\frac{x}{r}}=\frac{y}{r}\cdot\frac{r}{x}=\frac{y}{x}=\tan\theta$$

$$\frac{\cos\theta}{\sin\theta}=\frac{\frac{x}{r}}{\frac{y}{r}}=\frac{x}{r}\cdot\frac{r}{y}=\frac{x}{y}=\cot\theta$$

The Quotient Identities

$$\tan\theta=\frac{\sin\theta}{\cos\theta} \qquad \cot\theta=\frac{\cos\theta}{\sin\theta}$$

Next, we examine $\sin^2\theta+\cos^2\theta$. Remember $\sin^2\theta$ means $(\sin\theta)^2$.

$\sin^2\theta+\cos^2\theta=\left(\frac{y}{r}\right)^2+\left(\frac{x}{r}\right)^2=\frac{y^2+x^2}{r^2}$, but $x^2+y^2=r^2$ from our definition of trigonometric ratios.

Thus, $\sin^2\theta+\cos^2\theta=\frac{y^2+x^2}{r^2}=\frac{y^2+x^2}{x^2+y^2}=1$

If we start with the identity $\sin^2\theta+\cos^2\theta=1$ and divide each term by $\cos^2\theta$, we obtain the following:

$$\sin^2\theta+\cos^2\theta=1$$

$$\frac{\sin^2\theta}{\cos^2\theta}+\frac{\cos^2\theta}{\cos^2\theta}=\frac{1}{\cos^2\theta}$$

$$\left(\frac{\sin\theta}{\cos\theta}\right)^2+\left(\frac{\cos\theta}{\cos\theta}\right)^2=\frac{1}{\cos^2\theta}$$

$$\tan^2\theta+1=\sec^2\theta$$

If we start with $\sin^2\theta+\cos^2\theta=1$ and divide each term by $\sin^2\theta$, we obtain the following:

$$\sin^2\theta+\cos^2\theta=1$$

$$\frac{\sin^2\theta}{\sin^2\theta}+\frac{\cos^2\theta}{\sin^2\theta}=\frac{1}{\sin^2\theta}$$

$$\left(\frac{\sin\theta}{\sin\theta}\right)^2+\left(\frac{\cos\theta}{\sin\theta}\right)^2=\frac{1}{\sin^2\theta}$$

$$1+\cot^2\theta=\csc^2\theta$$

These three identities are called the **Pythagorean Identities**.

The Pythagorean Identities

$\sin^2\theta+\cos^2\theta=1$ $\quad 1+\tan^2\theta=\sec^2\theta$ $\quad 1+\cot^2\theta=\csc^2\theta$

Summarizing these eight identities:

Fundamental Trigonometric Identities

1. $\csc\theta=\dfrac{1}{\sin\theta}$ **2.** $\sec\theta=\dfrac{1}{\cos\theta}$

3. $\cot\theta=\dfrac{1}{\tan\theta}$ **4.** $\tan\theta=\dfrac{\sin\theta}{\cos\theta}$

5. $\cot\theta=\dfrac{\cos\theta}{\sin\theta}$ **6.** $\sin^2\theta+\cos^2\theta=1$

7. $1+\tan^2\theta=\sec^2\theta$ **8.** $1+\cot^2\theta=\csc^2\theta$

We can now use these eight identities to simplify trigonometric expressions.

Strategies for Simplifying a Trigonometric Expression

1. Get a common denominator.

Algebra	Trigonometry
$a+\dfrac{b}{c}$	$\sin x+\dfrac{\sin x}{\cos x}$
$\dfrac{a\cdot c}{c}+\dfrac{b}{c}$	$\dfrac{\sin x\cdot\cos x}{\cos x}+\dfrac{\sin x}{\cos x}$
$\dfrac{ac+b}{c}$	$\dfrac{\sin x\cos x+\sin x}{\cos x}$

2. Factor.

	Algebra		Trigonometry
a)	$1-x^2$	**a)**	$1-\sin^2 x$
	$(1-x)(1+x)$		$(1-\sin x)(1+\sin x)$
b)	x^2-y^2	**b)**	$\sec^2 x-\tan^2 x$
	$(x-y)(x+y)$		$(\sec x-\tan x)(\sec x+\tan x)$

3. Change all terms to sine and cosine.

a) $\dfrac{\sin x}{\csc x}+\dfrac{\cos x}{\sec x}$

$\sin x\cdot\sin x+\cos x\cdot\cos x$ — $\dfrac{1}{\csc x}=\sin x$ *and* $\dfrac{1}{\sec x}=\cos x$

$\sin^2 x+\cos^2 x$ — *multiply*

1 — *Pythagorean identity*

b) $\dfrac{\tan x}{\sec x}$

$\tan x\cdot\cos x$ — $\dfrac{1}{\sec x}=\cos x$

$\dfrac{\sin x}{\cos x}\cdot\cos x$ — $\tan x=\dfrac{\sin x}{\cos x}$

$\sin x$ — *cancel*

4. Conjugate (multiply by the complement)

Algebra

$$\frac{\sqrt{2}}{\sqrt{5}+\sqrt{2}}$$

$$\frac{\sqrt{2}}{\left(\sqrt{5}+\sqrt{2}\right)}\cdot\frac{\left(\sqrt{5}-\sqrt{2}\right)}{\left(\sqrt{5}-\sqrt{2}\right)}$$

$$\frac{\sqrt{2}\left(\sqrt{5}-\sqrt{2}\right)}{5-2}$$

$$\frac{\sqrt{10}-2}{3}$$

Trigonometry

$$\frac{1}{1-\cos x}$$

$$\frac{1}{(1-\cos x)}\cdot\frac{(1+\cos x)}{(1+\cos x)}$$

$$\frac{1+\cos x}{1-\cos^2 x}$$

$$\frac{1+\cos x}{\sin^2 x}$$

(If $\sin^2 x+\cos^2 x=1$ then $\sin^2 x=1-\cos^2 x$.)

Example 1 Simplify **a)** $(\sec^2 x-1)\cot^2 x$ **b)** $\dfrac{2\cos x}{1-\sin^2 x}$

▶ *Solution:*

a) $(\sec^2 x-1)\cot^2 x$

$\tan^2 x\cdot\cot^2 x$

$\tan^2 x\cdot\dfrac{1}{\tan^2 x}$

1

b) $\dfrac{2\cos x}{1-\sin^2 x}$

$\dfrac{2\cos x}{\cos^2 x}$

$\dfrac{2}{\cos x}$

$2\sec x$

Example 2 Simplify **a)** $\frac{\sin x}{1+\cos x}+\frac{\sin x}{1-\cos x}$ **b)** $\frac{1+\sin x}{\cos x}-\frac{\cos x}{1-\sin x}$

▶ *Solution:*

a)

$$\frac{\sin x}{1+\cos x}+\frac{\sin x}{1-\cos x}$$

$$\frac{\sin x}{1+\cos x}\cdot\frac{(1-\cos x)}{(1-\cos x)}+\frac{\sin x}{1-\cos x}\cdot\frac{(1+\cos x)}{(1+\cos x)}$$

$$\frac{\sin x(1-\cos x)}{1-\cos^2 x}+\frac{\sin x(1+\cos x)}{1-\cos^2 x}$$

$$\frac{\sin x(1-\cos x)}{\sin^2 x}+\frac{\sin x(1+\cos x)}{\sin^2 x}$$

$$\frac{1-\cos x}{\sin x}+\frac{1+\cos x}{\sin x}$$

$$\frac{1-\cos x+1+\cos x}{\sin x}$$

$$\frac{2}{\sin x}$$

$$2\csc x$$

b)

$$\frac{1+\sin x}{\cos x}-\frac{\cos x}{1-\sin x}$$

$$\frac{1+\sin x}{\cos x}\cdot\frac{(1-\sin x)}{(1-\sin x)}-\frac{\cos x}{(1-\sin x)}\cdot\frac{\cos x}{\cos x}$$

$$\frac{1-\sin^2 x}{\cos x(1-\sin x)}-\frac{\cos^2 x}{\cos x(1-\sin x)}$$

$$\frac{1-\sin^2 x-\cos^2 x}{\cos x(1-\sin x)}$$

$$\frac{1-(\sin^2 x+\cos^2 x)}{\cos x(1-\sin x)}$$

$$\frac{1-1}{\cos x(1-\sin x)}$$

$$0$$

Example 3 Simplify **a)** $\frac{\sin x\cos x+\sin x}{\cos x+\cos^2 x}$ **b)** $\frac{\cos x\cot x+\cos x}{\cot x+\cot^2 x}$

▶ *Solution:*

a)

$$\frac{\sin x\cos x+\sin x}{\cos x+\cos^2 x}$$

$$\frac{\sin x(\cos x+1)}{\cos x(1+\cos x)}$$

$$\frac{\sin x}{\cos x}$$

$$\tan x$$

b)

$$\frac{\cos x\cot x+\cos x}{\cot x+\cot^2 x}$$

$$\frac{\cos x(\cot x+1)}{\cot x(1+\cot x)}$$

$$\frac{\cos x}{\cot x}$$

$$\cos x\cdot\tan x$$

$$\cos x\cdot\frac{\sin x}{\cos x}$$

$$\sin x$$

Example 4 Determine the restriction on $\tan x+\csc x$, for $0\le x<2\pi$.

▶ *Solution:* A trigonometric expression, like an algebraic expresssion, cannot have zero in the denominator.

$$\tan x+\csc x=\frac{\sin x}{\cos x}+\frac{1}{\sin x}$$

$\cos x=0$ at $\frac{\pi}{2}$ and $\frac{3\pi}{2}$, $\sin x=0$ at 0 and π

Thus $\tan x+\csc x$ cannot have values of 0, $\frac{\pi}{2}$, π, and $\frac{3\pi}{2}$, $0\le x<2\pi$.

7.1 Exercise Set

1. Match the identities.

a) $\cot x$ _____

b) $\tan x$ _____

c) $\sec x$ _____

d) $\csc x$ _____

e) $\tan^2 x$ _____

f) $1+\tan^2 x$ _____

g) $\sin^2 x$ _____

A $\dfrac{1}{\sin x}$

B $\dfrac{1}{\cos x}$

C $\dfrac{\sin x}{\cos x}$

D $\dfrac{1}{\cos^2 x}$

E $\dfrac{1}{\cot^2 x}$

F $\dfrac{\cos x}{\sin x}$

G $\dfrac{1}{\sin^2 x}$

H $1-\cos^2 x$

2. Write with a common denominator, and simplify if possible.

a) $\dfrac{3}{2\sin x}-\dfrac{4}{\sin^2 x}$

b) $\dfrac{1}{1-\sin x}+\dfrac{1}{\sin x}$

c) $\dfrac{1+\dfrac{1}{\tan x}}{\dfrac{1}{\tan^2 x}}$

d) $\dfrac{1}{\sin^2 x}-1$

e) $\sin x+\dfrac{\cos^2 x}{\sin x}$

f) $\dfrac{1}{1+\cos x}+\dfrac{1}{1-\cos x}$

g) $\dfrac{\cos x}{1+\sin x}+\dfrac{1+\sin x}{\cos x}$

h) $\tan x-\dfrac{\sec^2 x}{\tan x}$

3. Factor then simplify if possible.

a) $1-\sin^2 x$

b) $\sec^2 x-\tan^2 x$

c) $\tan^2 x-\tan^2 x\sin^2 x$

d) $\sec^2 x+\sec^2 x\tan^2 x$

e) $\sin^2 x\sec^2 x-\sin^2 x$

f) $\dfrac{\csc^2 x-1}{\csc x-1}$

g) $\cot^4 x+2\cot^2 x+1$

h) $1-2\sin^2 x+\sin^4 x$

i) $\sin^4 x-\cos^4 x$

j) $\sec^3 x-\sec^2 x-\sec x+1$

4. Multiply and simplify.

a) $(\sin x+\cos x)^2$

b) $\sin x(\csc x-\sin x)$

c) $(\csc x-1)(\csc x+1)$

d) $(2-2\cos x)(2+2\cos x)$

e) $(\csc x-\cot x)(\csc x+\cot x)$

f) $(\tan x+\sec x)(\tan x-\sec x)$

5. Rewrite the given expression in terms of $\sin x$ only.

a) $\sin^2 x - \cos^2 x$

b) $\sec^2 x$

c) $\dfrac{\tan x + \sec x}{\cos x}$

d) $\dfrac{\sin x + \tan x}{1 + \sec x}$

6. Rewrite the given expression in terms of cosine only.

a) $\sin^2 x - \cos^2 x$

b) $(\sec x + 1)(\sec x - 1)$

c) $\sin x(\csc x - \sin x)$

d) $\dfrac{\cot x + \csc x}{\sin x}$

7. Rewrite in terms of sine and cosine only.

a) $\csc x + \cot x$

b) $\sec x + \tan x$

c) $\dfrac{1}{\tan x + \cot x}$

d) $\sec x - \dfrac{\cos x}{1 + \sin x}$

8. Determine all restrictions for $0 \le x < 2\pi$.

a) $\dfrac{\cot x}{1 + \sin x}$

b) $\dfrac{\sec x}{1 - \cos x}$

c) $\dfrac{1}{2\cos^2 x + \cos x - 1}$

d) $\cot x + \tan x$

9. Simplify the following trigonometric expressions.

a) $(\sec x \cdot \csc x - \cot x)(\sin x - \csc x)$

b) $\dfrac{\dfrac{\cot x + 1}{\cot x} - 1}{\dfrac{\cot x - 1}{\cot x} - 1}$

c) $\dfrac{\tan^2 x}{\cos^2 x + \sin^2 x + \tan^2 x}$

d) $\dfrac{\cos x \cdot \tan x + \sin x}{2 \tan x}$

e) $\dfrac{1 - \sec^2 x}{\sec^2 x} - \cos^2 x$

f) $\dfrac{\sec x - \cos x}{\csc x - \sin x}$

g) $\dfrac{\cot x (\sin x + \tan x)}{\csc x + \cot x}$

h) $\dfrac{\sec x - \cos x}{\tan x}$

i) $\dfrac{\sec^2 x (1 + \csc x) - \tan x (\sec x + \tan x)}{\csc x (1 + \sin x)}$

j) $\dfrac{\csc^2 x + \sec^2 x}{\csc x \ \sec x}$

k) $\dfrac{\cos x + \cot x}{1 + \csc x}$

l) $\dfrac{\sec x}{\tan x + \cot x}$

7.2 Verifying Trigonometric Identities

In this section, we will show methods for proving (or verifying) trigonometric identities. The key to proving identities is to use the eight fundamental identities with our algebra rules to rewrite trigonometric expressions.

Before going on, let us distinguish between an **expression**, an **equation** and an **identity**.

Expression: An expression has no equal signs. It is merely the sum and product of functions.

Equation: An equation is a statement that is true for a set of specific values.

Example: $\sin x = 1$ only at $x = \frac{\pi}{2}, \frac{5\pi}{2}, \ldots$ etc. is a conditional statement.

Identity: An identity is an equation that is true for all real values.

Example:
$$2x+1 = 2x+1$$
$$2(x-3) = 2x-6$$
$$\tan x = \frac{\sin x}{\cos x}$$

Verifying an identity is quite different from solving an equation. The following rules are very helpful:

Helpful Rules for Proving (Verifying) Identities

1. Change all trigonometric values to sine and cosine.
2. Write an expression with a common denominator.
3. Remember the conjugate step and how to factor.
4. Work with one side of an equation at a time, but work from the more complicated side first.

Note: There is no one way to prove an identity. The more complicated the identity, the more variation in methods can be found.

An identity has been proved when the bottom statement on the left side of the identity is the same as the bottom statement on the right side of the identity.

Example 1 Prove the identity: $\dfrac{\csc^2\theta - 1}{\csc^2\theta} = \cos^2\theta$

▶ *Solution:*

$$\frac{\csc^2\theta - 1}{\csc^2\theta} = \cos^2\theta$$

$$\frac{\cot^2\theta}{\csc^2\theta} = \qquad 1+\cot^2\theta = \csc^2\theta \textit{ thus } \csc^2\theta - 1 = \cot^2\theta$$

$$\frac{\cos^2\theta}{\sin^2\theta}\cdot\sin^2\theta = \qquad \cot\theta = \frac{\cos\theta}{\sin\theta} \textit{ and } \frac{1}{\csc\theta} = \sin\theta$$

$$\cos^2\theta =$$

Note: The bottom statement on the left side = the bottom statement on the right side thus the identity has been proved.

Alternate Solution:

$$\frac{\csc^2\theta - 1}{\csc^2\theta} = \cos^2\theta$$

$$\frac{\csc^2\theta}{\csc^2\theta} - \frac{1}{\csc^2\theta} = \qquad \textit{separate denominator}$$

$$1 - \sin^2\theta = \qquad \textit{divide and } \frac{1}{\csc\theta} = \sin\theta$$

$$\cos^2\theta = \qquad \sin^2\theta + \cos^2\theta = 1 \textit{ thus } 1 - \sin^2\theta = \cos^2\theta$$

same — identity proved

Example 2 Prove the identity: $\dfrac{1}{1-\cos\alpha} + \dfrac{1}{1+\cos\alpha} = 2\csc^2\alpha$

▶ *Solution:*

$$\frac{1}{1-\cos\alpha} + \frac{1}{1+\cos\alpha} = 2\csc^2\alpha$$

$$\frac{1\cdot(1+\cos\alpha)}{(1-\cos\alpha)(1+\cos\alpha)} + \frac{1\cdot(1-\cos\alpha)}{(1+\cos\alpha)(1-\cos\alpha)} = \frac{2}{\sin^2\alpha} \qquad \textit{common denominator is } (1-\cos\alpha)(1+\cos\alpha) \textit{ and } \csc\alpha = \frac{1}{\sin\alpha}$$

$$\frac{1+\cos\alpha+1-\cos\alpha}{(1-\cos\alpha)(1+\cos\alpha)} = \qquad \textit{common denominator}$$

$$\frac{2}{1-\cos^2\alpha} = \qquad \textit{add and multiply}$$

$$\frac{2}{\sin^2\alpha} = \qquad \sin^2\alpha + \cos^2\alpha = 1 \textit{ thus } 1-\cos^2\alpha = \sin^2\alpha$$

same — identity proved

Example 3 Prove the identity: $\tan x + \cot x = \sec x \csc x$

▶ *Solution:*

$$\tan x + \cot x = \sec x \csc x$$

$$\frac{\sin x}{\cos x} + \frac{\cos x}{\sin x} = \frac{1}{\cos x} \cdot \frac{1}{\sin x}$$ *change to sine and cosine*

$$\frac{\sin x}{\cos x} \cdot \frac{\sin x}{\sin x} + \frac{\cos x}{\sin x} \cdot \frac{\cos x}{\cos x} = \frac{1}{\sin x \cos x}$$ *common denominator is* $\sin x \cos x$

$$\frac{\sin^2 x + \cos^2 x}{\sin x \cos x} =$$ *write with common denominator*

$$\frac{1}{\sin x \cdot \cos x} =$$ $\sin^2 x + \cos^2 x = 1$

same

Example 4 Prove the identity: $\csc x + \cot x = \dfrac{\sin x}{1 - \cos x}$

▶ *Solution:*

$$\csc x + \cot x = \frac{\sin x}{1 - \cos x}$$

$$\frac{1}{\sin x} + \frac{\cos x}{\sin x} = \frac{\sin x(1 + \cos x)}{(1 - \cos x)(1 + \cos x)}$$ *left side change to sine and cosine*
right side use conjugate step

$$\frac{1 + \cos x}{\sin x} = \frac{\sin x(1 + \cos x)}{1 - \cos^2 x}$$ *left side common denominator*
right side multiply

$$= \frac{\sin x(1 + \cos x)}{\sin^2 x}$$ $\sin^2 x + \cos^2 x = 1$ *thus* $1 - \cos^2 x = \sin^2 x$

$$= \frac{1 + \cos x}{\sin x}$$ *cancel*

same

Example 5 Prove the identity: $\dfrac{\tan^2 x}{1 + \sec x} = \dfrac{1 - \cos x}{\cos x}$

▶ *Solution:*

$$\frac{\tan^2 x}{1 + \sec x} = \frac{1 - \cos x}{\cos x}$$

$$\frac{\sec^2 x - 1}{1 + \sec x} =$$ $1 + \tan^2 x = \sec^2 x$ *thus* $\tan^2 x = \sec^2 x - 1$

$$\frac{(\sec x - 1)(\sec x + 1)}{1 + \sec x} =$$ *factor*

$$\sec x - 1 =$$ *cancel*

$$\frac{1}{\cos x} - 1 =$$ $\sec x = \dfrac{1}{\cos x}$

$$\frac{1 - \cos x}{\cos x} =$$ *write with common denominator*

same

7.2 Exercise Set

Prove the following identities.

1. $\sin^2 x - \cos^2 x = 2\sin^2 x - 1$

2. $\sin x + \cos x \cot x = \csc x$

3. $\dfrac{1}{\cos x} - \cos x = \dfrac{\sin^2 x}{\cos x}$

4. $\dfrac{1}{\sec x \tan x} = \csc x - \sin x$

5. $\dfrac{\cos^4 x - \sin^4 x}{1 - \tan^4 x} = \cos^4 x$

6. $\dfrac{\sec^4 x - 1}{\tan^2 x} = 2 + \tan^2 x$

7. $\dfrac{\sin x + \cos x}{\csc x + \sec x} = \sin x \cos x$

8. $\dfrac{\cos x + \sin x}{\cos x - \sin x} = \dfrac{1 + \tan x}{1 - \tan x}$

9. $\dfrac{\sec x}{1-\cos x} = \dfrac{\sec x + 1}{\sin^2 x}$

10. $\dfrac{\sin\theta + \cos\theta\cot\theta}{\cos\theta\csc\theta} = \sec\theta$

11. $\dfrac{1+\sec\theta}{\sin\theta + \tan\theta} = \csc\theta$

12. $\dfrac{\sec x}{1-\sin x} = \dfrac{1+\sin x}{\cos^3 x}$

13. $\cos^2 x = \dfrac{1-2\sin^2 x}{1-\tan^2 x}$

14. $\dfrac{\tan x}{\tan x + \sin x} = \dfrac{1-\cos x}{\sin^2 x}$

15. $\dfrac{1-\cos\theta}{\sin\theta} = \dfrac{1}{\csc\theta+\cot\theta}$

16. $\dfrac{\sec x}{1-\cos x} = \dfrac{\sec x+1}{\sin^2 x}$

17. $\dfrac{\sin^2 x-\tan x}{\cos^2 x-\cot x} = \tan^2 x$

18. $\cos^2 x-\sin^2 x = \dfrac{\cot x-\tan x}{\cot x+\tan x}$

19. $\csc x-\dfrac{\sin x}{1+\cos x} = \cot x$

20. $\cot x-\tan x = \dfrac{2\cos^2 x-1}{\sin x\cos x}$

21. $\dfrac{1-\sin x}{1+\sin x}=(\sec x-\tan x)^2$

22. $\dfrac{\cos x}{\csc x+1}+\dfrac{\cos x}{\csc x-1}=2\tan x$

23. $\tan x(\csc+1)=\dfrac{\cot x}{\csc x-1}$

24. $\dfrac{\csc x+\cot x}{\tan x+\sin x}=\cot x\csc x$

25. $\dfrac{\cos x-\cos y}{\sin x+\sin y}+\dfrac{\sin x-\sin y}{\cos x+\cos y}=0$

26. $\csc^2\left(\dfrac{\pi}{2}-x\right)-1=\tan^2 x$

7.3 Trigonometric Equations

A trigonometric equation differs from a trigonometric identity in that it is true only for **some** values of the variable, not for all values of the variable. In this section, we will develop methods for solving trigonometric equations from simple types of equations to types that must be factored or solved by quadratic equation.

There are two types of solutions:

1. Conditional solutions — usually $0 \le x < 2\pi$
2. General form solutions

Example 1 Solve: $2\sin x - 1 = 0$, **a)** $0 \le x < 2\pi$ **b)** general form

$\sin x > 0$ in quadrants I and II.

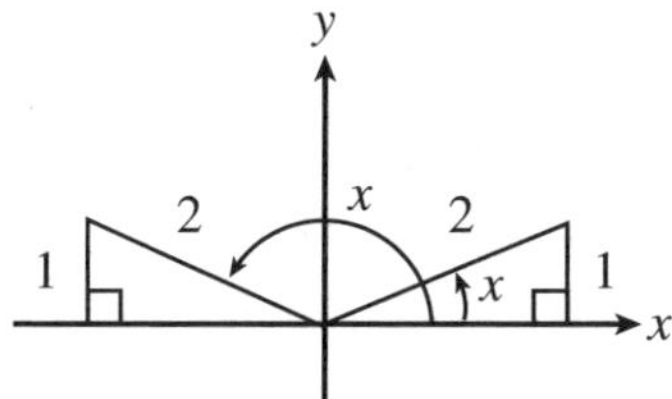

▶ Solution:

a) $2\sin x - 1 = 0$

$$\sin x = \frac{1}{2}$$

by special angles $x = \sin^{-1}\left(\frac{1}{2}\right)$

$$= \frac{\pi}{6}, \frac{5\pi}{6}$$

a) solutions are : $\frac{\pi}{6}, \frac{5\pi}{6}$

b) $2\sin x - 1 = 0$

$$\sin x = \frac{1}{2}$$

Since $\sin x$ has a period of 2π, there are infinitely many other solutions which can be written as $2n\pi$. Thus, the general form

b) solutions are: $\frac{\pi}{6} + 2n\pi$, $\frac{5\pi}{6} + 2n\pi$, n is an integer.

Example 2 Solve: $\cos x + \sqrt{2} = -\cos x$, **a)** $0 \le x < 2\pi$ **b)** general form

▶ Solution:

$$\cos x + \sqrt{2} = -\cos x$$

$$2\cos x = -\sqrt{2}$$

$$\cos x = -\frac{\sqrt{2}}{2}$$

by special angles $x = \cos^{-1}\left(-\frac{\sqrt{2}}{2}\right)$

$$= \frac{3\pi}{4}, \frac{5\pi}{4}$$

$\cos x < 0$ in quadrants II and III.

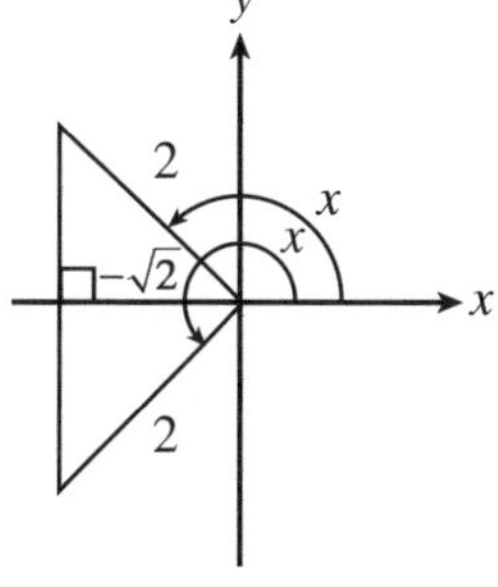

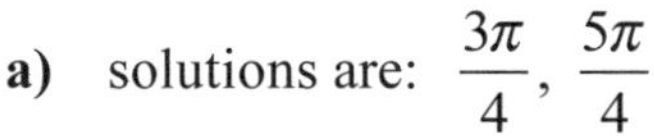
a) solutions are: $\frac{3\pi}{4}, \frac{5\pi}{4}$

b) solutions are: $\frac{3\pi}{4} + 2n\pi$, $\frac{5\pi}{4} + 2n\pi$; n an integer

Example 3 Solve: $\sqrt{3}\tan x + 1 = 0$, **a)** $0 \le x < 2\pi$ **b)** general form

▶ *Solution:*

$$\sqrt{3}\tan x + 1 = 0$$
$$\sqrt{3}\tan x = -1$$
$$\tan x = -\frac{1}{\sqrt{3}}$$

by special angles $x = \tan^{-1}\left(-\frac{1}{\sqrt{3}}\right)$

$$= \frac{5\pi}{6}, \frac{11\pi}{6}$$

a) solutions are: $\frac{5\pi}{6}, \frac{11\pi}{6}$

b) Since $\tan x$ has a period of π, $\frac{5\pi}{6}$ and $\frac{11\pi}{6}$ are symmetric and are π units apart.
The general solution is $\frac{5\pi}{6} + n\pi$; n an integer.

Example 4 Solve: $\sin x \tan x = 2\tan x$, **a)** $0 \le x < 2\pi$ **b)** general form

▶ *Solution:*

$$\sin x \tan x = 2\tan x$$
$$\sin x \tan x - 2\tan x = 0$$
$$\tan x(\sin x - 2) = 0$$
$$\tan x = 0, \sin x = 2$$

$\sin x = 2$ has no solution since $-1 \le \sin x \le 1$
so $\tan x = 0$
by special angles $x = \tan^{-1} 0$
$= 0, \pi$

a) solutions are: $0, \pi$

b) solution is: $n\pi$; n an integer.

Example 5 Solve: $\sec^2 x - \sec x - 2 = 0$, **a)** $0 \le x < 2\pi$ **b)** general form

▶ *Solution:*

$$\sec^2 x - \sec x - 2 = 0$$
$$(\sec x - 2)(\sec x + 1) = 0$$

$\sec x - 2 = 0$ or $\sec x + 1 = 0$

$\sec x = 2$ | $\sec x = -1$

$x = \sec^{-1}(2)$ | $x = \sec^{-1}(-1)$

$= \frac{\pi}{3}, \frac{5\pi}{3}$ | $= \pi$

a) solutions are: $\frac{\pi}{3}, \pi, \frac{5\pi}{3}$

b) $\frac{\pi}{3} + 2n\pi, \pi + 2n\pi, \frac{5\pi}{3} + 2n\pi$; n an integer (acceptable answer). If you look carefully, $\frac{\pi}{3}$, π, and $\frac{5\pi}{3}$ are $\frac{2\pi}{3}$ units apart.

Therefore, a better solution is $\frac{\pi}{3} + \frac{2n\pi}{3}$; n an integer.

Example 6 Solve: $2\cos^2 x + 3\sin x - 3 = 0$, **a)** $0 \le x < 2\pi$ **b)** general form

▶ *Solution:*

$$2\cos^2 x + 3\sin x - 3 = 0$$
$$2(1-\sin^2 x) + 3\sin x - 3 = 0$$
$$2\sin^2 x - 3\sin x + 1 = 0$$
$$(2\sin x - 1)(\sin x - 1) = 0$$

Change all terms to the same trig function using an identity.

$$2\sin x - 1 = 0 \quad \text{or} \quad \sin x - 1 = 0$$

$$\sin x = \frac{1}{2} \qquad x = \sin^{-1}\left(\frac{1}{2}\right) = \frac{\pi}{6}, \frac{5\pi}{6}$$

$$\sin x = -1 \qquad x = \sin^{-1}(-1) = \frac{3\pi}{2}$$

a) solutions are: $\frac{\pi}{6}, \frac{5\pi}{6}, \frac{3\pi}{2}$

b) Using the same reasoning as Example 5, solution is: $\frac{\pi}{6} + \frac{2n\pi}{3}$; n an integer.

Example 7 Solve: $\cos x + 1 = \sin x$; **a)** $0 \le x < 2\pi$ **b)** general form

▶ *Solution:*

$$\cos x + 1 = \sin x$$
$$(\cos x + 1)^2 = \sin^2 x$$
$$\cos^2 x + 2\cos x + 1 = 1 - \cos^2 x$$
$$2\cos^2 x + 2\cos x = 0$$
$$2\cos x(\cos x + 1) = 0$$
$$\cos x = 0, \ \cos x = -1$$

$$x = \cos^{-1}(0) = \frac{\pi}{2}, \frac{3\pi}{2} \qquad x = \cos^{-1}(-1) = \pi$$

Since we had to square each side to solve the equation, we must check solutions.

check

$$\cos x + 1 = \sin x \qquad \cos\frac{\pi}{2} + 1 = \sin\frac{\pi}{2} \qquad 0 + 1 = 1 \qquad 1 = 1 \ \textit{accept}$$

$$\cos x + 1 = \sin x \qquad \cos\frac{3\pi}{2} + 1 = \sin\frac{3\pi}{2} \qquad 0 + 1 = -1 \qquad 1 \ne -1 \ \textit{reject}$$

$$\cos x + 1 = \sin x \qquad \cos\pi + 1 = \sin\pi \qquad -1 + 1 = 0 \qquad 0 = 0 \ \textit{accept}$$

a) solutions are: $\frac{\pi}{2}, \pi$

b) solutions are: $\frac{\pi}{2} + 2n\pi, \pi + 2n\pi$; n an integer.

Example 8 Solve: $2\sin 3\theta + 1 = 0$, **a)** $0° \le x < 360°$ **b)** general form

▶ *Solution:* **a)** $2\sin 3\theta + 1 = 0$

$$2\sin 3\theta = -1$$

$$\sin 3\theta = -\frac{1}{2}$$

$$3\theta = \sin^{-1}\left(-\frac{1}{2}\right)$$

$3\theta = 210°$, $3\theta = 330°$, $3\theta = 210° + 360°$, $3\theta = 330° + 360°$, $3\theta = 210° + 2(360°)$, $3\theta = 330° + 2(360°)$

$\theta = 70°$ $\theta = 110°$ $\theta = 190°$ $\theta = 230°$ $\theta = 310°$ $\theta = 350°$

Solutions are: 70°, 110°, 190°, 230°, 310°, and 350°

b) $3\theta = 210° + 360° n$ $3\theta = 330° + 360° n$

$\theta = 70° + 120° n$ $\theta = 110° + 120° n$; n an integer

Example 9 Solve: $4\tan\frac{x}{2} + 4 = 0$, **a)** $0 \le x < 2\pi$ **b)** general form

▶ *Solution:* **a)** $4\tan\frac{x}{2} + 4 = 0$

$$4\tan\frac{x}{2} = -4$$

$$\tan\frac{x}{2} = -1$$

$$\frac{x}{2} = \tan^{-1}(-1)$$

$\frac{x}{2} = \frac{3\pi}{4}$, $\frac{x}{2} = \frac{7\pi}{4}$

$x = \frac{3\pi}{2}$, $x = \frac{7\pi}{2}$, but $\frac{7\pi}{2}$ is not $0 \le x < 2\pi$

Therefore, solution is only $\frac{3\pi}{2}$.

b) $\frac{x}{2} = \frac{3\pi}{4} + n\pi$ (tangent has a period of π)

$$x = \frac{3\pi}{2} + 2n\pi$$

solution is: $\frac{3\pi}{2} + 2n\pi$; n an integer

Example 10 Solve: $\csc^2 x - 2\cot x - 4 = 0$, **a)** $0 \le x < 2\pi$ **b)** general form

▶ *Solution:* **a)**

$$\csc^2 x - 2\cot x - 4 = 0$$
$$1 + \cot^2 x - 2\cot x - 4 = 0$$
$$\cot^2 x - 2\cot x - 3 = 0$$
$$(\cot x - 3)(\cot x + 1) = 0$$
$$\cot x = 3,\ \cot x = -1$$

$\cot x = 3$

$\tan x = \dfrac{1}{3}$

$x = \tan^{-1}\left(\dfrac{1}{3}\right)$

$= 0.3218, 0.3218 + \pi = 3.4633$

$\cot x = -1$

$\tan x = -1$

$x = \tan^{-1}(-1)$

$= \dfrac{3\pi}{4}, \dfrac{7\pi}{4}$

Therefore, solutions are 0.3218, 3.4633, $\dfrac{3\pi}{4}, \dfrac{7\pi}{4}$.

b) Solutions are $x = 0.3218 + n\pi$ and $x = \dfrac{3\pi}{4} + n\pi$; n an integer

Example 11 Solve: $\cos^2 x - 3\cos x - 2 = 0$, **a)** $0 \le x < 2\pi$ **b)** general form

▶ *Solution:* **a)** By quadratic formula

$$\cos x = \frac{-(-3) \pm \sqrt{(-3)^2 - 4(1)(-2)}}{2}$$
$$= 3.5616 \text{ or } -0.5616$$

Reject 3.5616 as $-1 \le \cos x \le 1$

To obtain reference angle $\cos x = 0.5616$

$$x = \cos^{-1}(0.5616)$$
$$= 0.9745$$

cosine is negative in quadrants II and III
quadrant II, $x = \pi - 0.9745 = 2.1671$
quadrant III, $x = \pi + 0.9745 = 4.1161$
Therefore, solutions are 2.1671, 4.1161

b) Solutions are $2.167 + 2n\pi$, and $4.116 + 2n\pi$; n an integer

Example 12 Solve: $6\sin^2 2x - \sin 2x - 1 = 0$, **a)** $0 \le x < 2\pi$ **b)** general form

▶ *Solution:* **a)**

$$6\sin^2 2x - \sin 2x - 1 = 0$$
$$(2\sin 2x - 1)(3\sin 2x + 1) = 0$$
$$\sin 2x = \frac{1}{2}, \ \sin 2x = -\frac{1}{3}$$

$$2x = \sin^{-1}\left(\frac{1}{2}\right)$$
$$2x = \frac{\pi}{6}, \ \frac{5\pi}{6}, \ \frac{\pi}{6} + 2\pi, \ \frac{5\pi}{6} + 2\pi$$
$$x = \frac{\pi}{12}, \ \frac{5\pi}{12}, \ \frac{13\pi}{12}, \ \frac{17\pi}{12}$$

$$2x = \sin^{-1}\left(\frac{1}{3}\right); \text{ ref. angle } 0.3398$$
$$2x = \pi + 0.3398, \ 3\pi + 0.3398, \ 2\pi - 0.3398, \text{ and } 4\pi - 0.3398$$
$$2x = 3.481, \ 5.943, \ 9.765, \ 12.227$$
$$x = 1.741, \ 2.972, \ 4.883, \ 6.113$$

Therefore, solutions are $\frac{\pi}{12}, \ \frac{5\pi}{12}, \ \frac{13\pi}{12}, \ \frac{17\pi}{12}$, 1.741, 2.972, 4.883, 6.113

b) $2x = \frac{\pi}{6} + 2n\pi$ $\quad 2x = \frac{5\pi}{6} + 2n\pi$ $\quad 2x = 3.481 + 2n\pi$ $\quad 2x = 5.943 + 2n\pi$

$x = \frac{\pi}{12} + n\pi$ $\quad x = \frac{5\pi}{12} + n\pi$ $\quad x = 1.741 + n\pi$ $\quad x = 2.972 + n\pi$

Therfore, solutions are $\frac{\pi}{12} + n\pi, \ \frac{5\pi}{12} + n\pi, \ 1.741 + n\pi, \ 2.972 + n\pi$; n an integer.

Example 13 Solve: $\sin^2 2x - \sin 2x - 2 = 0$, **a)** $0 \le x < 2\pi$ **b)** general form

▶ *Solution:* **a)**

$$\sin^2 2x - \sin 2x - 2 = 0$$
$$(\sin 2x + 1)(\sin 2x - 2) = 0$$

$\sin 2x = -1, \ \sin 2x = 2,$ *reject* $\sin 2x = 2$ *since* $-1 \le \sin 2x \le 1$

$$\sin 2x = -1$$
$$2x = \sin^{-1}(-1)$$
$$2x = \frac{3\pi}{2}, \qquad 2x = \frac{3\pi}{2} + 2\pi = \frac{7\pi}{2}$$
$$x = \frac{3\pi}{4} \qquad x = \frac{7\pi}{4}$$

Therefore, solutions are $\frac{3\pi}{4}, \ \frac{7\pi}{4}$.

b) $2x = \frac{3\pi}{2} + 2n\pi, \quad 2x = \frac{7\pi}{2} + 2n\pi$

$x = \frac{3\pi}{4} + n\pi, \quad x = \frac{7\pi}{4} + n\pi$

Therefore, solutions are $\frac{3\pi}{4} + n\pi$ and $\frac{7\pi}{4} + n\pi$; n an integer.

7.3 Exercise Set

1. Solve **i)** $0 \le x < 2\pi$ **ii)** general form.

a) $\sin x = \frac{\sqrt{3}}{2}$

b) $\cos x = \frac{\sqrt{2}}{2}$

c) $\tan x = \frac{1}{\sqrt{3}}$

d) $\cot x = \frac{1}{\sqrt{3}}$

e) $\sec x = \frac{2}{\sqrt{3}}$

f) $\csc x = 2$

g) $\sin x = -\frac{1}{2}$

h) $\cos x = -1$

i) $\tan x = -\sqrt{3}$

j) $\cot x = 0$

k) $\sec x = -\sqrt{2}$

l) $\csc x = -\frac{2}{\sqrt{3}}$

2. Solve **i)** $0 \le x < 2\pi$ **ii)** general form.

a) $\sin x = 0.6234$

b) $\cos x = 0.4821$

c) $\tan x = 1.7258$

d) $\cot x = 0.7238$

e) $\sec x = 3.1743$

f) $\csc x = 1.5243$

g) $\sin x = -0.4173$

h) $\cos x = -0.4821$

i) $\tan x = -0.3124$

j) $\cot x = -1.1482$

k) $\sec x = -1.9105$

l) $\csc x = -2.3124$

3. How many solutions do the following equations have for $0 \le x < 2\pi$?

a) $\sin 3x = -\dfrac{1}{4}$ ____________ **b)** $\sin 3x = -1$ ____________

c) $\sin \dfrac{1}{2}x = \dfrac{1}{3}$ ____________ **d)** $\cos \dfrac{1}{2}x = \dfrac{1}{3}$ ____________

e) $\tan^2 2x = 1$ ____________ **f)** $\sin bx = \dfrac{1}{2}$ ____________

4. Solve **i)** $0 \le x < 2\pi$ **ii)** general form.

a) $\sin 2x = \dfrac{\sqrt{3}}{2}$

b) $\tan 3x = -1$

c) $\sec \dfrac{x}{2} = -\dfrac{2}{\sqrt{3}}$

d) $\sin 2x = -0.4173$

e) $\tan 2x = 1.7258$

f) $\tan bx = 1.7258$, b an integer

5. Solve the equations algebraically; give exact values for x when possible.

i) $0 \le x < 2\pi$

ii) The general solutions over the set of real numbers.

a) $2\cos x + 1 = 0$

b) $(2\sin x - 1)(\cos x + 1) = 0$

c) $\sqrt{2}\cos^2 x - \cos x = 0$

d) $4\sin^2 x = 3$

e) $\sin^2 x = \sin x$

f) $6\sin^2 x + 11\sin x - 10 = 0$

g) $5\cos^2 x + 6\cos x - 8 = 0$

h) $2\cos^2 x - \cos x = 1$

5. i) $2\cos^2 x - 3\cos x - 2 = 0$

j) $2\tan^2 x + 5\tan x + 2 = 0$

k) $\tan^2 x - 2\tan x - 3 = 0$

l) $\cot^2 x - \cot x - 6 = 0$

m) $\tan x - 2\tan x \cdot \sin x = 0$

n) $3\sin^2 x + 4\sin x - 4 = 0$

o) $\sec^2 x - 3\sec x + 2 = 0$

p) $2\cos^2 x - 3\sin x - 3 = 0$

5. q) $3\csc x - \sin x - 2 = 0$

r) $3\sin x = \sqrt{3}\cos x$

s) $\sin x \tan 2x = \sin\ x$

t) $3\sin^2 2x - 2\sin 2x - 1 = 0$

6. Solve by the graphic calculator:

a) $\tan x - \sin 3x = 1\,, \qquad 0 \le x < 2\pi$

b) $\sin 3x - \cos 2x = -1\,, \qquad 0 \le x < 2\pi$

c) $\cot 2x + \tan \frac{1}{2}x = 0\,, \qquad 0 \le x < 2\pi$

7.4 Sum and Difference Identities

Proof of the Sum and Difference Identities for Sine, Cosine and Tangent

We begin by deriving a formula for $\cos(A-B)$.

Draw a unit circle

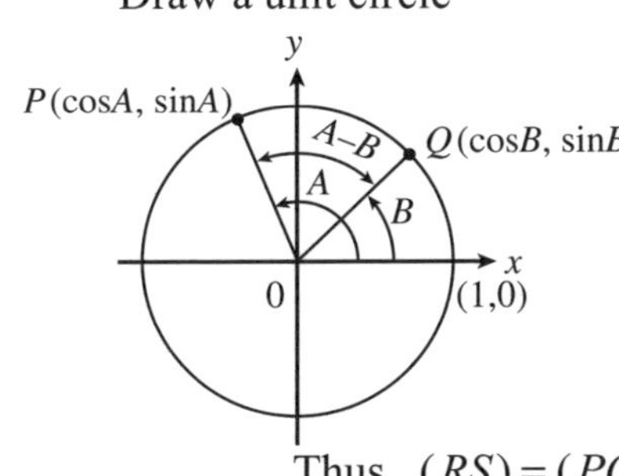

Rotate angle $(A-B)$ to start on x-axis

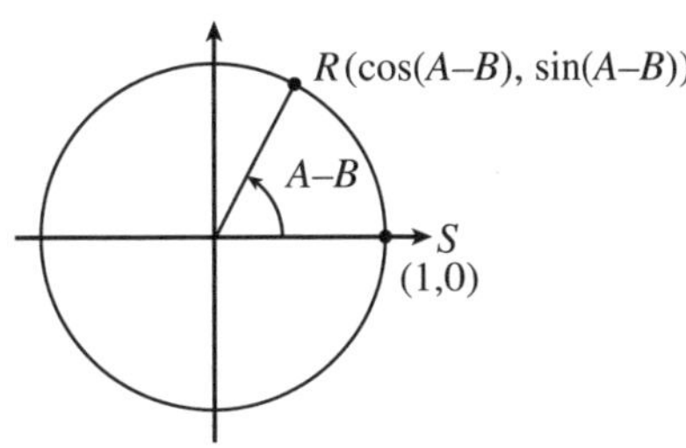

$$\text{Thus } (RS)=(PQ)$$

$$(RS)^2=(PQ)^2$$

$$\left[\cos(A-B)-1\right]^2+\left[\sin(A-B)-0\right]^2=(\cos A-\cos B)^2+(\sin A-\sin B)^2$$

$$\cos^2(A-B)-2\cos(A-B)+1+\sin^2(A-B)=\cos^2 A-2\cos A\cos B+\cos^2 B+\sin^2 A-2\sin A\sin B+\sin^2 B$$

$$(\sin^2(A-B)+\cos^2(A-B))+1-2\cos(A-B)=(\sin^2 A+\cos^2 A)+(\sin^2 B+\cos^2 B)-2\cos A\cos B-2\sin A\sin B$$

$$1+1-2\cos(A-B)=1+1-2\cos A\cos B-2\sin A\sin B$$

$$-2\cos(A-B)=-2\left[\cos A\cos B+\sin A\sin B\right]$$

$$\boxed{\cos(A-B)=\cos A\cos B+\sin A\sin B}$$

Recall that $\cos(-x)=\cos x$ and $\sin(-x)=-\sin x$

$$\cos(A-B)=\cos A\cos B+\sin A\sin B$$

$$\text{then } \cos(A-(-B))=\cos A\cos(-B)+\sin A\sin(-B)$$

$$\boxed{\cos(A+B)=\cos A\cos B-\sin A\sin B}$$

Recall that $\sin x=\cos\left(\dfrac{\pi}{2}-x\right)$ and $\cos x=\sin\left(\dfrac{\pi}{2}-x\right)$

$$\sin(A+B)=\cos\left(\frac{\pi}{2}-(A+B)\right)$$

$$=\cos\left(\left(\frac{\pi}{2}-A\right)-B\right)$$

$$=\cos\left(\frac{\pi}{2}-A\right)\cos B+\sin\left(\frac{\pi}{2}-A\right)\sin B$$

$$\boxed{\sin(A+B)=\sin A\cos B+\cos A\sin B}$$

and $\sin(A+(-B)) = \sin A\cos(-B) + \cos A\sin(-B)$

$$\boxed{\sin(A-B) = \sin A\cos B - \cos A\sin B}$$

$$\tan(A+B) = \frac{\sin(A+B)}{\cos(A+B)} = \frac{\sin A\cos B + \cos A\sin B}{\cos A\cos B - \sin A\sin B}$$

$$= \frac{\dfrac{\sin A\cos B}{\cos A\cos B} + \dfrac{\cos A\sin B}{\cos A\cos B}}{\dfrac{\cos A\cos B}{\cos A\cos B} - \dfrac{\sin A\sin b}{\cos A\cos B}} \quad \textit{divide each term by} \cos A\cos B$$

$$\boxed{\tan(A+B) = \frac{\tan A + \tan B}{1 - \tan A\tan B}}$$

If $\sin(-x) = -\sin x$ and $\cos(-x) = \cos x$ then $\tan(-x) = \dfrac{\sin(-x)}{\cos(-x)} = \dfrac{-\sin x}{\cos x} = -\tan x$

$$\text{thus } \tan(A+(-B)) = \frac{\tan A + \tan(-B)}{1 - \tan A\tan(-B)}$$

$$\boxed{\tan(A-B) = \frac{\tan A - \tan B}{1 + \tan A\tan B}}$$

We summarize the formulas, each of which is an identity, as follows:

Sum and Difference Identities

$$\sin(A+B) = \sin A\cos B + \cos A\sin B$$

$$\sin(A-B) = \sin A\cos B - \cos A\sin B$$

$$\cos(A+B) = \cos A\cos B - \sin A\sin B$$

$$\cos(A-B) = \cos A\cos B + \sin A\sin B$$

$$\tan(A+B) = \frac{\tan A + \tan B}{1 - \tan A\tan B}$$

$$\tan(A-B) = \frac{\tan A - \tan B}{1 + \tan A\tan B}$$

Even–Odd and Cofunction Identities

with $\sin(-A) = -\sin A$, $\cos(-A) = \cos A$, $\tan(-A) = -\tan A$

$\sin\left(\dfrac{\pi}{2} - A\right) = \cos A$, $\cos\left(\dfrac{\pi}{2} - A\right) = \sin A$, $\tan\left(\dfrac{\pi}{2} - A\right) = \cot A$

$\csc\left(\dfrac{\pi}{2} - A\right) = \sec A$, $\sec\left(\dfrac{\pi}{2} - A\right) = \csc A$, $\cot\left(\dfrac{\pi}{2} - A\right) = \tan A$

The sum and difference identities, with the even-odd and cofunction identities, can be used to solve a wide variety of problems in trigonometry. The following examples show some of the ways they can be used.

Example 1 Find the exact value of $\cos 105°$.

▶ *Solution:*

$$\cos 105° = \cos(60° + 45°) = \cos 60° \cos 45 - \sin 60° \sin 45°$$
$$= \frac{1}{2} \cdot \frac{\sqrt{2}}{2} - \frac{\sqrt{3}}{2} \cdot \frac{\sqrt{2}}{2}$$
$$= \frac{\sqrt{2}}{4} - \frac{\sqrt{6}}{4}$$
$$= \frac{\sqrt{2} - \sqrt{6}}{4}$$

Example 2 Simplify $\dfrac{\tan\frac{2\pi}{5} - \tan\frac{3\pi}{20}}{1 + \tan\frac{2\pi}{5}\tan\frac{3\pi}{20}}$.

▶ *Solution:*

$$\frac{\tan\frac{2\pi}{5} - \tan\frac{3\pi}{20}}{1 + \tan\frac{2\pi}{5}\tan\frac{3\pi}{20}} = \tan\left(\frac{2\pi}{5} - \frac{3\pi}{20}\right) = \tan\left(\frac{\pi}{4}\right) = 1$$

Example 3 Given $\sin A = -\frac{3}{5}$, A in quadrant III and $\cos B = \frac{5}{13}$, B in quadrant IV, find $\sin(A + B)$.

▶ *Solution:*

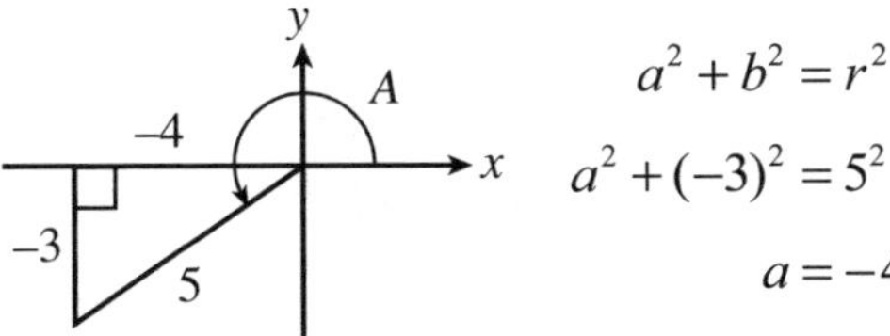

$$a^2 + b^2 = r^2$$
$$a^2 + (-3)^2 = 5^2$$
$$a = -4$$

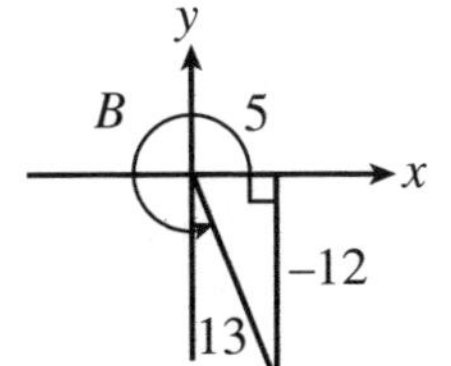

$$a^2 + b^2 = r^2$$
$$5^2 + b^2 = 13^2$$
$$b = -12$$

$$\sin(A + B) = \sin A \cos B + \cos A \sin B$$
$$= \left(-\frac{3}{5}\right)\left(\frac{5}{13}\right) + \left(-\frac{4}{5}\right)\left(-\frac{12}{13}\right)$$
$$= -\frac{15}{65} + \frac{48}{65}$$
$$= \frac{33}{65}$$

Example 4 Solve: $\sin\left(x+\frac{\pi}{4}\right)+\sin\left(x-\frac{\pi}{4}\right)=-1,\ 0\le x<2\pi$.

▶ *Solution:*

$$\sin\left(x+\frac{\pi}{4}\right)+\sin\left(x-\frac{\pi}{4}\right)=-1$$

$$\left(\sin x\cos\frac{\pi}{4}+\cos x\sin\frac{\pi}{4}\right)+\left(\sin x\cos\frac{\pi}{4}-\cos x\sin\frac{\pi}{4}\right)=-1$$

$$2\sin x\cos\frac{\pi}{4}=-1$$

$$2\sin x\left(\frac{\sqrt{2}}{2}\right)=-1$$

$$\sin x=-\frac{1}{\sqrt{2}}$$

$$x=\frac{5\pi}{4},\ \frac{7\pi}{4}$$

Example 5 Prove the identity: $\sin(A+B)+\sin(A-B)=2\sin A\sin B$.

▶ *Solution:*

$$\sin(A+B)+\sin(A-B)=2\sin A\cos B$$

$$(\sin A\cos B+\cos A\sin B)+(\sin A\cos B-\cos A\sin B)=$$

$$\sin A\cos B \quad + \quad \sin A\cos B \quad =$$

$$2\sin A\cos B=$$

same

Example 6 Find the general form of the solution of $2\tan x+\tan(\pi-x)=\sqrt{3}$.

▶ *Solution:*

$$2\tan x+\tan(\pi-x)=\sqrt{3}$$

$$2\tan x+\frac{\tan\pi-\tan x}{1+\tan\pi\tan x}=\sqrt{3}$$

$$2\tan x+\frac{0-\tan x}{1+0}=\sqrt{3}$$

$$\tan x=\sqrt{3}$$

$$x=\tan^{-1}(\sqrt{3})=\frac{\pi}{3},\ \frac{4\pi}{3}$$

$$x=\frac{\pi}{3}+n\pi;\ n\text{ is an integer}$$

Example 7 Determine the amplitude, period, and phase shift of $f(x)=3\sqrt{2}\sin 2x\cos\frac{\pi}{4}+3\sqrt{2}\cos 2x\sin\frac{\pi}{4}$.

▶ *Solution:* To find the amplitude, period, and phase shift, the function needs to be rewritten as a single trigonometric function.

$$\begin{aligned} f(x)&=3\sqrt{2}\sin 2x\cos\frac{\pi}{4}+3\sqrt{2}\cos 2x\sin\frac{\pi}{4}\\ &=3\sqrt{2}\left(\sin 2x\cos\frac{\pi}{4}+\cos 2x\sin\frac{\pi}{4}\right)\\ &=3\sqrt{2}\sin\left(2x+\frac{\pi}{4}\right)\\ &=3\sqrt{2}\sin 2\left(x+\frac{\pi}{8}\right)\end{aligned}$$

Amplitude: $3\sqrt{2}$

Period: $\frac{2\pi}{2}=\pi$

Phase Shift: $2\left(x+\frac{\pi}{8}\right)=0$, $x+\frac{\pi}{8}=0$, $x=-\frac{\pi}{8}$

or $2x+\frac{\pi}{4}=0$, $2x=-\frac{\pi}{4}$, $x=-\frac{\pi}{8}$

Example 8 Simplify: $\csc(90°-\theta)\sec(360°-\theta)-\tan(720°+\theta)\cot(450°-\theta)$.

▶ *Solution:*

$$\csc(90°-\theta)\sec(360°-\theta)-\tan(720°+\theta)\cot(450°-\theta)$$

$$\frac{1}{\sin(90°-\theta)}\cdot\frac{1}{\cos(360°-\theta)}-\tan(720°+\theta)\cdot\frac{\cos(450°-\theta)}{\sin(450°-\theta)}$$

$$\frac{1}{\cos\theta}\cdot\frac{1}{\underbrace{\cancel{\cos 360°}}_{1}\cos\theta+\underbrace{\cancel{\sin 360°}}_{0}\sin\theta}-\frac{\overbrace{\cancel{\tan 720°}}^{0}+\tan\theta}{1-\underbrace{\cancel{\tan 720°}}_{0}\tan\theta}\cdot\frac{\overbrace{\cancel{\cos 450°}}^{0}\cos\theta+\overbrace{\cancel{\sin 450°}}^{1}\sin\theta}{\underbrace{\cancel{\sin 450°}}_{1}\cos\theta-\underbrace{\cancel{\cos 450°}}_{0}\sin\theta}$$

$$\frac{1}{\cos\theta}\cdot\frac{1}{1\cdot\cos\theta+0\cdot\sin\theta}-\frac{0+\tan\theta}{1-0\cdot\tan\theta}\cdot\frac{0\cdot\cos\theta+1\cdot\sin\theta}{1\cdot\cos\theta-0\cdot\sin\theta}$$

$$\frac{1}{\cos\theta}\cdot\frac{1}{\cos\theta}-\tan\theta\cdot\frac{\sin\theta}{\cos\theta}$$

$$\frac{1}{\cos^2\theta}-\frac{\sin^2\theta}{\cos^2\theta}$$

$$\frac{1-\sin^2\theta}{\cos^2\theta}$$

$$\frac{\cos^2\theta}{\cos^2\theta}$$

$$1$$

7.4 Exercise Set

1. Find the exact value of each expression.

a) $\sin 15^\circ$

b) $\cos(-75^\circ)$

c) $\tan\frac{5\pi}{12}$

d) $\cot\frac{11\pi}{12}$

e) $\sec\frac{19\pi}{12}$

f) $\csc(-105^\circ)$

2. Simplify each expression.

a) $\sin 24^\circ \cos 36^\circ + \cos 24^\circ \sin 36^\circ$

b) $\cos 55^\circ \cos 10^\circ + \sin 55^\circ \sin 10^\circ$

c) $\dfrac{\tan\frac{\pi}{5} - \tan\frac{\pi}{30}}{1 + \tan\frac{\pi}{5}\tan\frac{\pi}{30}}$

d) $\sin\frac{23\pi}{18}\cos\frac{\pi}{9} - \cos\frac{23\pi}{18}\sin\frac{\pi}{9}$

e) $\cos\frac{\pi}{8}\cos\frac{7\pi}{8} + \sin\frac{\pi}{8}\sin\frac{7\pi}{8}$

f) $\dfrac{\tan\frac{2\pi}{9} + \tan\frac{\pi}{9}}{1 - \tan\frac{2\pi}{9}\tan\frac{\pi}{9}}$

g) $\dfrac{\sin 3x}{\csc x} - \dfrac{\cos 3x}{\sec x}$

h) $\cos(A+B)\cdot\cos B + \sin(A+B)\cdot\sin B$

i) $\tan^2(\frac{\pi}{2} - x)\cdot\sec^2 x - \sin^2(\frac{\pi}{2} - x)\cdot\csc^2 x$

j) $\sin\left(\frac{\pi}{3} - x\right)\cdot\cos\left(\frac{\pi}{3} + x\right) + \cos\left(\frac{\pi}{3} - x\right)\cdot\sin\left(\frac{\pi}{3} + x\right)$

3. Find the exact value of each expression.

a) $\tan x = 3$, find $\tan\left(x+\frac{\pi}{4}\right)$

b) $\sin x = \frac{4}{5}$, x in quadrant I, find $\sin\left(x+\frac{\pi}{6}\right)$

c) $\cos x = \frac{12}{13}$, x in quadrant I, find $\cos\left(x+\frac{2\pi}{3}\right)$

d) If both A and B are third quadrant angles, and $\cos B = -\frac{12}{13}$, what is the value of $\sin(A-B)$ if $\sin A = -\frac{3}{5}$?

e) Given that $\sin A = \frac{12}{13}$ is in quadrant II, and $\sec B = \frac{5}{4}$ is in quadrant IV, what is the value of $\cos(A+B)$?

f) Given that $\tan A = \frac{5}{12}$ is in quadrant III, and $\cos B = -\frac{3}{5}$ is in quadrant II, what is the value of $\sin(A-B)$?

4. Find the solution, $0° \le \theta < 360°$, or $0 \le x < 2\pi$, for each equation.

a) $\cos\theta\cos 10° - \sin\theta\sin 10° = \frac{1}{2}$

b) $\sin\theta\cos 12° + \cos\theta\cos 78° = \frac{\sqrt{3}}{2}$

c) $\cos 3x\cos x + \sin 3x\sin x = 0$

d) $2\tan x + \tan(\pi - x) = \sqrt{3}$

e) $\sqrt{2}\sin 3x\cos 2x = 1 + \sqrt{2}\cos 3x\sin 2x$

f) $\cos\left(x+\frac{\pi}{4}\right) + \cos\left(x-\frac{\pi}{4}\right) = 1$

5. Prove the identities.

a) $\sin(A+B)-\sin(A-B)=2\sin B\cos A$

b) $\dfrac{\sin(A+B)}{\cos(A-B)}=\dfrac{\cot A+\cot B}{1+\cot A\cot B}$

c) $\dfrac{\sin(A-B)}{\sin B}+\dfrac{\cos(A-B)}{\cos B}=\dfrac{\sin A}{\sin B\cos B}$

d) $\dfrac{1+\tan A}{\tan\left(A+\dfrac{\pi}{4}\right)}=1-\tan A$

e) $\sin(A+B)\sin(A-B)=\sin^2 A-\sin^2 B$

f) $\cos(A+B)\cos(A-B)=\cos^2 A-\sin^2 B$

g) $\sec(A+B)=\dfrac{\sec A\sec B}{1-\tan A\tan B}$

h) $\csc(A-B)=\dfrac{\csc A\csc B}{\cot B-\cot A}$

6. Simplify

a) $\cos(90° - A)\sin(180° - B) + \cos(360° - A)\sin(90° - B)$

b) $\cos(A - 90°)\sin(90° - B) - \sin(B - 270°)\cos(90° - A)$

c) $\tan(90° - A)\tan(180° - A)\sec A + \csc B\sin(90° - B)\csc(90° - B)$

d) $\sec(180° - A)\csc(270° - A) - \cot(630° + A)\tan(540° - A)$

7. Find the amplitude, period, and phase shift of the following trigonometric functions.

a) $y = \cos 3x\cos x - \sin 3x\sin x$

b) $y = -2\sin 2x\cos\frac{\pi}{3} + 2\cos 2x\sin\frac{\pi}{3}$

c) $y = 3\sin\frac{\pi}{6}x\cos\frac{\pi}{3} + 3\cos\frac{\pi}{6}x\sin\frac{\pi}{3}$

d) $y = -\sin\frac{\pi}{4}x\sin\frac{\pi}{2} - \cos\frac{\pi}{4}x\cos\frac{\pi}{2}$

8. Consider the expression $\tan(\frac{\pi}{2} + x)$. Why can't we use the identity for $\tan(A + B)$ to express it as a function of x alone?

9. Show $\tan\left(\frac{\pi}{2} + x\right) = -\cot x$

7.5 Double-Angle Identities

The sum and difference identities may be used to develop several other trigonometric identities.

The sum formula for sine states that

$$\sin(A+B) = \sin A\cos B + \cos A\sin B$$

If we replace B with A in this formula, then we obtain

$$\sin(A+A) = \sin A\cos A + \cos A\sin A$$

$$\boxed{\sin 2A = 2\sin A\cos A}$$

This is called the double-angle formula for sine. We can use this same process to develop double-angle formulas for cosine and tangent.

$$\cos(A+B) = \cos A\cos B - \sin A\sin B$$

Again, replace B with A in this formula, then we obtain

$$\cos(A+A) = \cos A\cos A - \sin A\sin A$$

$$\boxed{\cos 2A = \cos^2 A - \sin^2 A}$$

Starting with the double-angle formula for cosine, and replacing $\sin^2 A$ with $1-\cos^2 A$, since $\sin^2 A + \cos^2 A = 1$, we obtain

$$\begin{aligned}\cos 2A &= \cos^2 A - \sin^2 A \\ &= \cos^2 A - (1-\cos^2 A)\end{aligned}$$

$$\boxed{\cos 2A = 2\cos^2 A - 1}$$

Again, starting with the double-angle formula for cosine, and replacing $\cos^2 A$ with $1-\sin^2 A$, we obtain

$$\begin{aligned}\cos 2A &= \cos^2 A - \sin^2 A \\ &= 1-\sin^2 A - \sin^2 A\end{aligned}$$

$$\boxed{\cos 2A = 1-2\sin^2 A}$$

For tangent, we obtained the following:

$$\tan(A+B)=\frac{\tan A+\tan B}{1-\tan A\tan B}$$

Again, we replace B with A in the formula:

$$\tan(A+A)=\frac{\tan A+\tan A}{1-\tan A\tan A}$$

$$\boxed{\tan 2A=\frac{2\tan A}{1-\tan^2 A}}$$

Summarizing the double-angle formulas:

Double-Angle Formulas

$$\sin 2A=2\sin A\cos A$$

$$\begin{aligned}\cos 2A&=\cos^2 A-\sin^2 A\\&=2\cos^2 A-1\\&=1-2\sin^2 A\end{aligned}$$

$$\tan 2A=\frac{2\tan A}{1-\tan^2 A}$$

The double-angle formulas have a variety of uses. The following examples show some of the ways double-angle formulas can be used.

Example 1 Solve: $\cos 2x=2\sin^2 x,\ 0\le x<2\pi$.

▶ *Solution:*

$$\cos 2x=2\sin^2 x$$

$$1-2\sin^2 x=2\sin^2 x$$ *pick the best one of the three double-angle identities for cosine*

$$4\sin^2 x=1$$

$$\sin^2 x=\frac{1}{4}$$

$$\sin x=\pm\frac{1}{2}$$

Thus $x=\sin^{-1}\left(\frac{1}{2}\right)$, $x=\sin^{-1}\left(-\frac{1}{2}\right)$

$=\frac{\pi}{6},\frac{5\pi}{6}$ $\quad=\frac{7\pi}{6},\frac{11\pi}{6}$ *by special angles*

Therefore, solutions are $\frac{\pi}{6}$, $\frac{5\pi}{6}$, $\frac{7\pi}{6}$, and $\frac{11\pi}{6}$.

Example 2 Use the double-angle formula to simplify **a)** $12\sin 4x\cos 4x$ **b)** $4-8\cos^2 6x$ **c)** $\dfrac{4\tan 3x}{1-\tan^2 3x}$.

▶ *Solution:*

a)
$$\begin{aligned}12\sin 4x\cos 4x &= 6(2\sin 4x\cos 4x)\\ &= 6\sin 2(4x)\\ &= 6\sin 8x\end{aligned}$$

b)
$$\begin{aligned}4-8\cos^2 6x &= -4(2\cos^2 6x-1)\\ &= -4\cos 2(6x)\\ &= -4\cos 12x\end{aligned}$$

c)
$$\begin{aligned}\frac{4\tan 3x}{1-\tan^2 3x} &= 2\left(\frac{2\tan 3x}{1-\tan^2 3x}\right)\\ &= 2\tan 2(3x)\\ &= 2\tan 6x\end{aligned}$$

Example 3 Prove the identity: $\dfrac{\sin 6x}{1+\cos 6x}=\tan 3x$.

▶ *Solution:* Proof

$$\frac{\sin 6x}{1+\cos 6x} = \tan 3x$$

$$\frac{2\sin 3x\cos 3x}{1+(2\cos^2 3x-1)} = \frac{\sin 3x}{\cos 3x}$$

$$\frac{2\sin 3x\cos 3x}{2\cos^2 3x} =$$

$$\frac{\sin 3x}{\cos 3x} =$$

same

Example 4 Given $\sin x=-\dfrac{12}{13}$ in quadrant III, find $\tan 2x$.

▶ *Solution:*

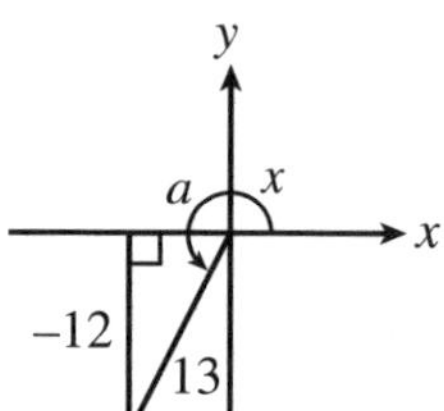

$$a^2+(-12)^2=13^2$$
$$a=-5$$

$$\begin{aligned}\tan 2x &= \frac{2\tan x}{1-\tan^2 x}\\ &= \frac{2\left(\frac{-12}{-5}\right)}{1-\left(\frac{-12}{-5}\right)^2}\\ &= -\frac{120}{119}\end{aligned}$$

Power-Reducing Identities

The power-reducing identities are just the double angle identities written in a different way.
If we take the double-angle identity $\cos 2x = 1 - 2\sin^2 x$ and solve for $\sin^2 x$:

$$\cos 2x = 1 - 2\sin^2 x$$

$$2\sin^2 x = 1 - \cos 2x$$

$$\boxed{\sin^2 x = \frac{1-\cos 2x}{2}}$$

Because the identity expresses a sine function of the second power in terms of a cosine function of the first power, it is called a **power-reducing identity**.

Repeat the double-angle identity with $\cos 2x = 2\cos^2 x - 1$ and solve for $\cos^2 x$:

$$\cos 2x = 2\cos^2 x - 1$$

$$2\cos^2 x = 1 + \cos 2x$$

$$\boxed{\cos^2 x = \frac{1+\cos 2x}{2}}$$

To write tangent we use the identity $\tan\theta = \dfrac{\sin\theta}{\cos\theta}$, thus

$$\tan^2 x = \frac{\sin^2 x}{\cos^2 x} = \frac{\frac{1-\cos 2x}{2}}{\frac{1+\cos 2x}{2}} = \frac{1-\cos 2x}{1+\cos 2x}$$

$$\boxed{\tan^2 x = \frac{1-\cos 2x}{1+\cos 2x}}$$

Power-Reducing Formulas

$$\sin^2 A = \frac{1-\cos 2A}{2} \quad \text{or} \quad \frac{1}{2}(1-\cos 2A)$$

$$\cos^2 A = \frac{1+\cos 2A}{2} \quad \text{or} \quad \frac{1}{2}(1+\cos 2A)$$

$$\tan^2 A = \frac{1-\cos 2A}{1+\cos 2A}$$

7.5 Exercise Set

1. Simplify each expression.

a) $8\sin 5x\cos 5x$

b) $4\sin\frac{x}{2}\cos\frac{x}{2}$

c) $2\sin^2 2x-2\cos^2 2x$

d) $\frac{8\tan 4x}{1-\tan^2 4x}$

e) $\sec 8x(\sin^2 4x-\cos^2 4x)$

f) $2\sin 6x(\cos^2 3x-\sin^2 3x)$

g) $\frac{1}{2}\cot 4x(1-\tan^2 4x)$

h) $\frac{1}{4}\sec 6x\csc 6x$

i) $4\sin^2\frac{x}{2}-2$

j) $2\cos^2 8x-1$

k) $\frac{\sin 6x}{2\sin 3x}$

l) $\sin 4x\csc 2x-2\cos 2x$

m) $\sin 4x-(\sin 2x+\cos 2x)^2$

n) $\sin^4 3x-\cos^4 3x$

o) $\frac{2}{1-\cos 8x}$

p) $\frac{4}{\tan 3x-\cot 3x}$

2. Solve, $0 \le x < 2\pi$

a) $\sin 2x + \cos x = 0$

b) $\sin x + \cos 2x = 1$

c) $3\cos 2x + 2\sin^2 x = 2$

d) $\sin 2x = \cot x$

e) $\csc^2 x = 2\sec 2x$

f) $\tan x - \cot x = 2$

g) $\tan 2x + \tan x = 0$

h) $4\sin^2 x = 2 - \cos^2 2x$

i) $\cos 4x + 2\cos^2 2x = 2$

j) $\csc^2 x = 2\sec 2x$

3. Prove the identities.

a) $\cot x - \tan x = \dfrac{4\cos^2 x - 2}{\sin 2x}$

b) $\dfrac{\sin 4x - \sin 2x}{\cos 4x + \cos 2x} = \tan x$

c) $\tan 2x = \dfrac{2}{\cot x - \tan x}$

d) $\dfrac{\cot x - \cos x}{1 - \sin x} = \dfrac{\sin 2x}{1 - \cos 2x}$

e) $\cot 2x = \dfrac{\cot^2 x - 1}{2\cot x}$

f) $\dfrac{\cos 2x}{1 - \sin 2x} = \dfrac{1 + \tan x}{1 - \tan x}$

4. If $\sin x = -\frac{3}{5}$ in quadrant III, find

a) $\sin 2x$ **b)** $\cos 2x$ **c)** $\tan 2x$

5. If $\tan x = -3$ in quadrant II, find

a) $\sin 2x$ **b)** $\cos 2x$ **c)** $\sec 2x$

6. Write $\cos 3x$ in terms of $\cos x$.

7. Write $\cos 4x$ in terms of $\cos x$.

8. Write $\sin 5x$ in terms of $\sin x$.

9. Write $\tan^4 x$ in terms of a first power.

10. Write $\sin^2 x \cos^4 x$ in terms of the first power of cosine.

11. Write $\sin^4 x + \cos^4 x$ in terms of the first power of cosine.

12. Find y.

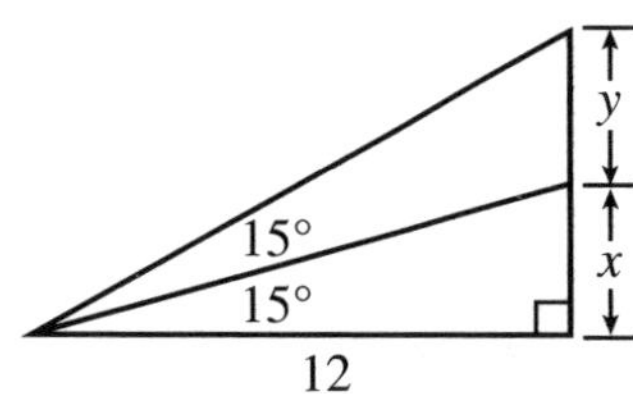

13. Find x.

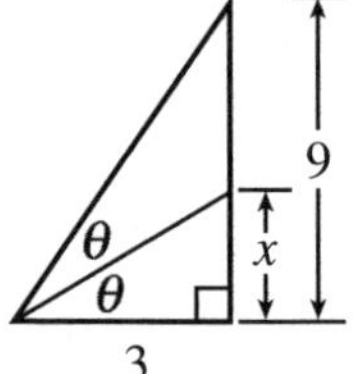

14. Find h.

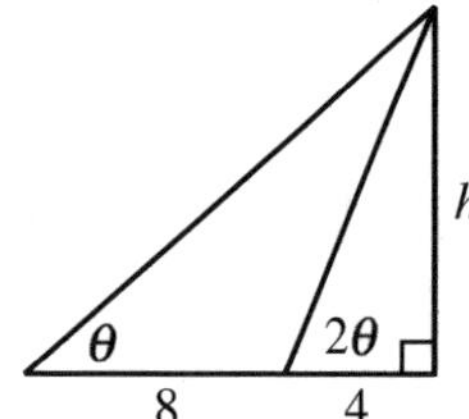

15. Find x.

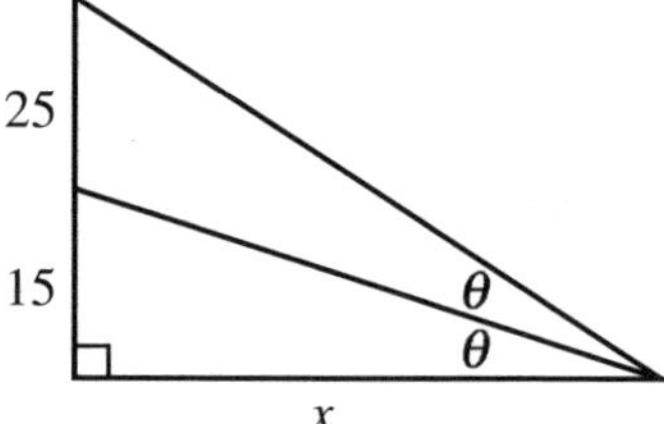

7.6 Chapter Review

Trigonometry (Part II) – Multiple-choice Review Questions

1. Which of the following is equivalent to: $1-\cos 2x$?

a) $\sin 2x$

b) $\cos^2 x$

c) $-2\cos^2 x$

d) $2\sin^2 x$

2. Simplify: $\sin^4\theta-\cos^4\theta$

a) -1
b) $-\cos 2\theta$
c) $\cos 2\theta$
d) $-\cos 4\theta$

3. Simplify: $\cos(90°+\alpha)$

a) $-\sin\alpha$
b) $-\cos\alpha$
c) $\sin\alpha$
d) $\cos\alpha$

4. How many solutions are there for the equation $4\cos\frac{1}{2}x=1,\ 0\le x<2\pi$?

a) 0
b) 1
c) 2
d) 4

5. An equivalent expression for $\tan(x+y)-\tan x\tan y\tan(x+y)$ is

a) $\tan x-\tan y$

b) $\tan y-\tan x$

c) $\tan x+\tan y$

d) $\tan x\tan y-\tan y\tan x$

6. Simplify: $\dfrac{\sin 2x}{1+\cos 2x}$

a) $\tan x$
b) $\csc x$
c) $\sec x$
d) $\cot x$

7. Which expression is equivalent to: $\dfrac{\sin 6x}{\sin 3x}$?

a) $\sin 2x$
b) $2\cos 3x$
c) $2\sin 3x$
d) $3\cos 3x$

8. Simplify: $\cos\frac{x}{3}\sin\frac{x}{3}$

a) $\frac{1}{2}\sin\frac{2}{3}x$

b) $2\sin\frac{x}{3}$

c) $2\sin\frac{2}{3}x$

d) $\tan\frac{x}{3}$

9. Simplify: $\sin^2 x+\cos^2 x+\cot^2 x$

a) $\csc^2 x$
b) $\sec^2 x$
c) $\tan^2 x$
d) $2\sin^2 x$

10. Simplify: $-1-\cos^2 x+\sin^2 x$

a) -2
b) 0
c) 2
d) $-2\cos^2 x$

11. Which expression is **NOT** an equivalent expression for $\cos(2x+\pi)$?

a) $2\sin^2 x-1$
b) $\cos^2 x-\sin^2 x$
c) $1-2\cos^2 x$
d) $\sin^2 x-\cos^2 x$

12. If $\tan x$ is undefined, then which of the following is correct?

a) $\sin x\neq 0$, $\cos x\neq 0$
b) $\sin x=0$, $\cos x\neq 0$
c) $\sin x\neq 0$, $\cos x=0$
d) $\sin x=0$, $\cos x=0$

13. Simplify: $\cos 5x \sin 3x + \sin 5x \cos 3x$

a) $\cos 2x$
b) $\cos 8x$
c) $\sin 2x$
d) $\sin 8x$

14. Determine the *y*-intercept of $f(x) = -3\sin(\pi + x)$

a) -3
b) 0
c) 3
d) π

15. Solve: $2^x = \cot x$, $0 \le x < 2\pi$

a) 0.59, 3.25
b) 0.59, 3.14, 3.25
c) 0.61, 3.27
d) 3.02

16. Solve: $\cot x - \sin 3x = 0$, $0 \le x < 2\pi$

a) 3.14
b) 1.96 , 4.33
c) 2.01 , 4.38
d) 1.96 , 3.14, 4.33

17. Determine the maximum value of $y = -a\sin x - b$, $a,\ b > 0$

a) $-a - b$
b) $-a + b$
c) $a - b$
d) $a + b$

18. Determine the minimum value of the function $y = a\sin x - b$, $a, b > 0$.

a) $-a - b$
b) $-a + b$
c) $a - b$
d) $a + b$

19. Simplify: $\dfrac{\cos^3 A - \cos A}{\sin^3 A}$

a) $\cot A$
b) $-\cot A$
c) $\tan A$
d) $-\tan A$

20. Simplify: $\dfrac{\sin(x-\frac{\pi}{2})+\sin(\frac{\pi}{2}-x)}{\tan^2 x-\cot^2 x}$.

a) -2
b) 0
c) $-2\cos x$
d) $2\cos x$

21. What is/are the restriction(s) for the expression: $\dfrac{\csc x}{\cos x}$?

a) $\csc x \neq 0$
b) $\cos x \neq 0$
c) $\sin x \neq 0$
d) $\sin x \neq 0, \quad \cos x \neq 0$

22. Simplify: $\cos\dfrac{x}{4}\cos\dfrac{x}{3}-\sin\dfrac{x}{4}\sin\dfrac{x}{3}$

a) $\sin\dfrac{x}{12}$
b) $\sin\dfrac{7x}{12}$
c) $\cos\dfrac{x}{12}$
d) $\cos\dfrac{7x}{12}$

23. How many solutions does $\cos^2 x=\dfrac{1}{a}$ have, $a>1, \quad 0\leq x<2\pi$?

a) 1
b) 2
c) 3
d) 4

24. How many solutions does the following equation have over the interval, $0°\leq\theta<360°$.

$$(a\sin\theta-a)(\tan^3\theta-b)=0 \text{ with } b>0$$

a) 2
b) 3
c) 4
d) 5

25. How many solutions does the equation $(2\sin 3x-1)(\cos 2x+1)=0$ have over the interval, $0\leq x<2\pi$?

a) 3
b) 6
c) 8
d) 10

26. Simplify: $\dfrac{1+\sec x}{\tan x+\sin x}$

a) $\csc x$
b) $\sec x$
c) $\tan x$
d) $\cot x$

27. Simplify: $\dfrac{\cos x}{1-\sin x}-\dfrac{1}{\cos x}$

a) $\tan x$
b) $\cot x$
c) $\sec x$
d) $\csc x$

28. Determine the range of $y=-2\csc\frac{\pi}{4}x+1$, $\quad 4\le x<6$

a) $y<-1$
b) $y\le -1$
c) $y>3$
d) $y\ge 3$

29. Determine the general solution for $\sin 2x=1$.

a) $\frac{\pi}{4}+n\pi$, n an integer

b) $\frac{\pi}{4}+2n\pi$, n an integer

c) $\frac{\pi}{2}+n\pi$, n an integer

d) $\frac{\pi}{2}+2n\pi$, n an integer

30. Determine the period of the graph of $y=1-2\sin^2 6x$?

a) $\dfrac{\pi}{6}$

b) $\dfrac{\pi}{3}$

c) π
d) 2π

31. Simplify: $\dfrac{\csc^2 x-1}{\sec^2 x-1}$

a) $2\tan^2 x$
b) $2\cot^2 x$
c) $\tan^4 x$
d) $\cot^4 x$

32. Determine the restrictions for $\dfrac{\cot x}{2+3\cos x}$

a) $\cos x \neq \frac{2}{3}, \quad \cos x \neq 0$

b) $\cos x \neq -\frac{2}{3}, \quad \cos x \neq 0$

c) $\cos x \neq \frac{2}{3}, \quad \sin x \neq 0$

d) $\cos x \neq -\frac{2}{3}, \quad \sin x \neq 0$

33. Determine the number of solutions for $(a\sin x + b)(a\tan x + a)(a\sec x - b) = 0$ where $0 \le x < 2\pi$ if $0 < a < b$

a) 3
b) 4
c) 5
d) 6

34. Simplify: $8\sin^2 6x - 4$

a) $-4\cos 3x$
b) $4\cos 3x$
c) $-4\cos 12x$
d) $4\cos 12x$

35. For $f(x) = \cos bx$, $b > 0$, find the smallest positive value of x that produces a minimum value for $f(x)$.

a) 0

b) $\frac{\pi}{2b}$

c) $\frac{\pi}{b}$

d) $\frac{3\pi}{2b}$

36. If $A = 90° - B$ simplify $\sin A\cos B + \cos A\sin B$

a) 0
b) 1
c) $\cos 2B$
d) $\sin 2B$

37. Simplify $\sec(\pi - x)$

a) $-\sec x$
b) $-\csc x$
c) $\csc x$
d) $\sec x$

38. Determine the range of the function $y = -4\sin 6x\cos 6x$

a) $-2 \le y \le 2$
b) $0 \le y \le 2$
c) $0 \le y \le 4$
d) $-4 \le y \le 4$

39. Simplify: $\dfrac{\csc^2 x+\sec^2 x}{\csc^2 x-\sec^2 x}$

a) $\cos 2x$
b) $\sin 2x$
c) $\csc 2x$
d) $\sec 2x$

40. Simplify: $\cos\left(\dfrac{\pi}{6}+x\right)\cdot\cos\left(\dfrac{\pi}{6}-x\right)-\sin\left(\dfrac{\pi}{6}+x\right)\cdot\sin\left(\dfrac{\pi}{6}-x\right)$

a) 0
b) $\dfrac{1}{2}$
c) $\dfrac{\sqrt{3}}{2}$
d) $\dfrac{2\pi}{3}$

41. When $y=6\sin x\cos^3 x+6\sin^3 x\cos x$ is changed to the form $y=A\sin Bx$ then the values of A and B are:

a) $A=2,\quad B=2$
b) $A=2,\quad B=3$
c) $A=3,\quad B=2$
d) $A=3,\quad B=3$

42. Simplify: $\dfrac{\sin A}{1+\cos A}-\dfrac{1-\cos A}{\sin A}$

a) 0
b) $2\csc A$
c) $2\csc A$
d) $\dfrac{2\sin A}{1+\cos A}$

43. If $\sin A=\dfrac{1}{3}$ and A is in quadrant II, then $\sin 2A$ has what value?

a) $-\dfrac{2}{3}$
b) $\dfrac{2}{3}$
c) $-\dfrac{4\sqrt{2}}{9}$
d) $\dfrac{4\sqrt{2}}{9}$

44. What is the value of $\sin(A+B)$ if $\sin A=-\dfrac{3}{5}$ and $\cos B=\dfrac{3}{5}$, with both A and B fourth quadrant angles?

a) -1
b) $-\dfrac{7}{25}$
c) $-\dfrac{24}{25}$
d) $\dfrac{7}{25}$

45. Determine the general solution for $\tan bx = -\sqrt{3}$.

a) $\frac{2\pi}{3}+\frac{n\pi}{b}$, n an integer

b) $\frac{2\pi}{3b}+\frac{n\pi}{b}$, n an integer

c) $\frac{2\pi}{3}+\frac{2n\pi}{b}$, n an integer

d) $\frac{2b\pi}{3}+bn\pi$, n an integer

46. Simplify: $\cos\left(x+\frac{\pi}{2}\right)-\cos\left(x-\frac{\pi}{2}\right)$

a) 0
b) $-2\sin x$
c) $2\sin x$
d) $2\cos x$

47. Solve: $8\sin^4 x+2\sin^2 x-1=0$, $0°\le x<360°$
a) 30°, 150°
b) 60°, 120°
c) 30°, 150°, 210°, 330°
d) 60°, 120°, 240°, 300°

48. Simplify: $(\sin x-\cos x)^2-(\sin x+\cos x)^2$
a) 0
b) $-\sin 2x$
c) $\sin 2x$
d) $-2\sin 2x$

49. Determine the general solution for $\cos 2x = -\frac{1}{2}$.

a) $\frac{\pi}{3}+\frac{\pi}{2}n$, $\frac{2\pi}{3}+\frac{\pi}{2}n$, n an integer

b) $\frac{\pi}{3}+\pi n$, $\frac{2\pi}{3}+\pi n$, n an integer

c) $\frac{5\pi}{12}+\frac{\pi}{2}n$, $\frac{7\pi}{12}+\frac{\pi}{2}n$, n an integer

d) $\frac{5\pi}{12}+\pi n$, $\frac{7\pi}{12}+\pi n$, n an integer

50. Determine the general solution of $\cos x+2\cos^2 x=0$

a) $x=n\pi$, $x=\frac{2\pi}{3}+2n\pi$, $x=\frac{4\pi}{3}+2n\pi$, n an integer

b) $x=\frac{\pi}{2}+n\pi$, $x=\frac{2\pi}{3}+2n\pi$, $x=\frac{4\pi}{3}+2n\pi$, n an integer

c) $x=n\pi$, $x=\frac{5\pi}{6}+2n\pi$, $x=\frac{7\pi}{6}+2n\pi$, n an integer

d) $x=\frac{\pi}{2}+n\pi$, $x=\frac{5\pi}{6}+2n\pi$, $x=\frac{7\pi}{6}+2n\pi$, n an integer

8.1 Linear Equations Review

A curve developed from the intersection of a plane with a double right circular cone is referred to as a **conic**. The specific types of conic curves are: circles, parabolas, ellipses, and hyperbolas. The **double right circular cone** will be used to generate the four conics.

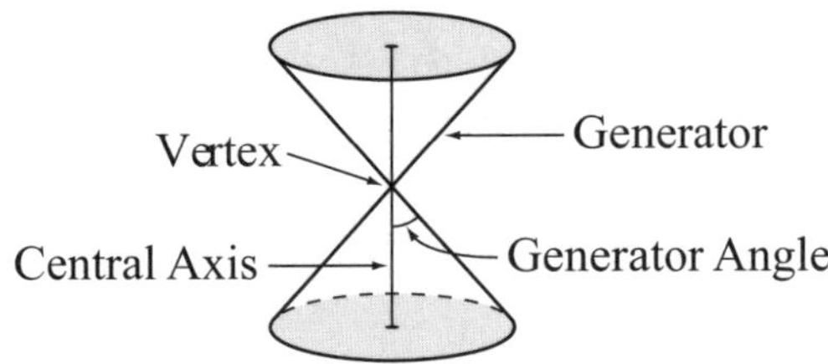

The equation of all conic sections have the general form $Ax^2 + Cy^2 + Dx + Ey + F = 0$, where at least one of the coefficients of A and C is not zero. The graph of these equations fall into four main categories: a circle, a parabola, an ellipse, and a hyperbola. They can also produce a point, a pair of lines, or no graph at all. These graphs are called **conic sections**, because each one is the intersection of a plane and a right-circular cone.

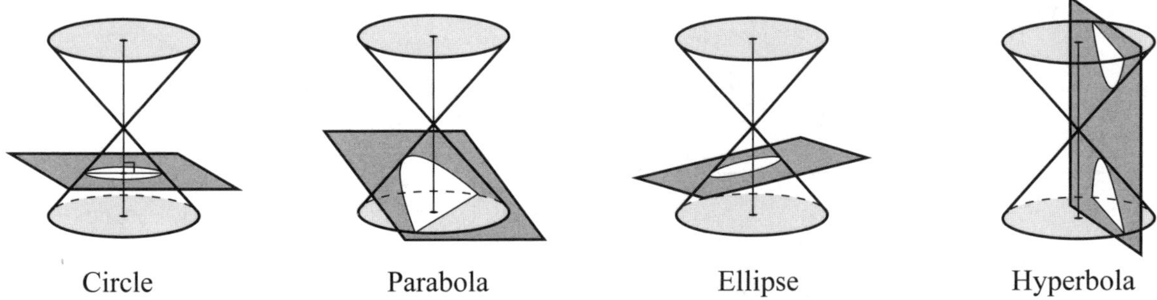

Before studying the four conics, the formulas that connect two points must be reviewed.

Distance Formula

The distance formula is used to find the distance between two points on a rectangular coordinate system. Points are labeled as ordered pairs $P(x_1, y_1)$ and $Q(x_1, y_1)$, then the Pythagorean theorem is used to develop the formula.

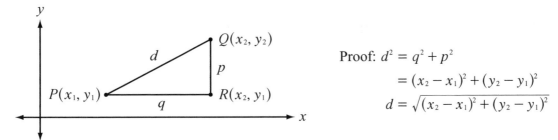

y, $Q(x_2, y_2)$, d, p, $P(x_1, y_1)$, $R(x_2, y_1)$, q, x

Proof: $d^2 = q^2 + p^2$

$$= (x_2 - x_1)^2 + (y_2 - y_1)^2$$

$$d = \sqrt{(x_2 - x_1)^2 + (y_2 - y_1)^2}$$

The Distance Formula

The distance d between two points (x_1, y_1) and (x_2, y_2) is:

$$d = \sqrt{(x_2 - x_1)^2 + (y_2 - y_1)^2}$$

Example 1 Find the distance between $A(-2,6)$ and $B(5,3)$

► *Solution*:

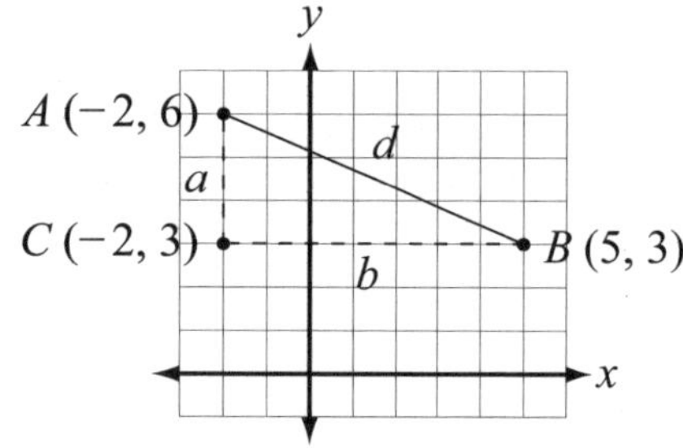

Method 1: By reasoning

$d^2 = a^2 + b^2$

$d = \sqrt{a^2 + b^2}$

$d(AC) = 3,\ d(BC) = 7$

$d = \sqrt{3^2 + 7^2}$

$= \sqrt{58}$

Method 2: By distance formula

$d = \sqrt{(x_2 - x_1)^2 + (y_2 - y_1)^2}$

$= \sqrt{(5-(-2))^2 + (3-6)^2}$

$= \sqrt{49+9}$

$= \sqrt{58}$

Midpoint of a Line Segment

A point M lies midway between the ordered pairs $P(x_1, y_1)$ and $Q(x_2, y_2)$. Point M is called the midpoint of segment PQ.

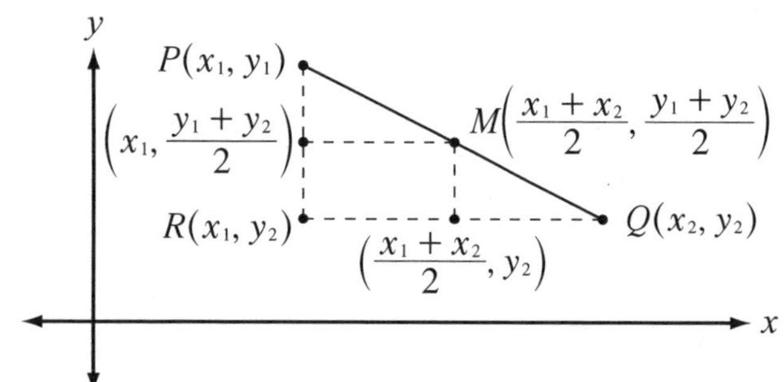

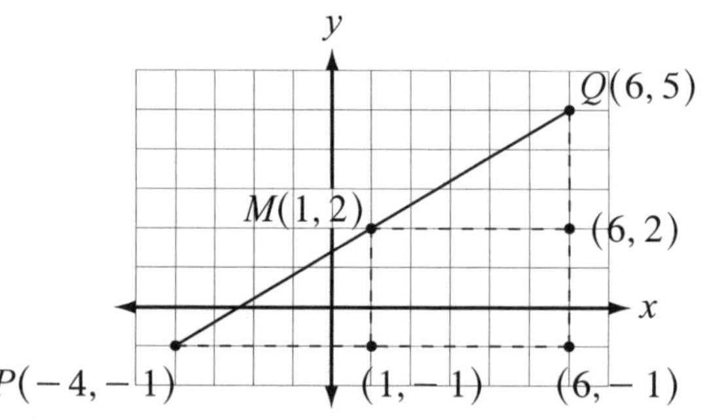

> **Midpoint Formula**
>
> The midpoint of a line segment with endpoints at $P(x_1, y_1)$ and $Q(x_2, y_2)$ is the point M with coordinates:
>
> $$M = \left(\frac{x_1 + x_2}{2}, \frac{y_1 + y_2}{2}\right)$$

Example 2 Find the midpoint of the segment joining $(7, -2)$ and $(-1, 4)$.

► *Solution*: $M_x = \frac{x_1 + x_2}{2} = \frac{7 + (-1)}{2} = 3,\ M_y = \frac{y_1 + y_2}{2} = \frac{-2 + 4}{2} = 1$. The midpoint is $(3, 1)$.

Example 3 One endpoint of a line segment AB is $A(3,4)$. If the midpoint is $M(-2,3)$, what are the coordinates of B?

► *Solution*: $M_x = \frac{x_1 + x_2}{2} \rightarrow -2 = \frac{x_1 + 3}{2} \rightarrow x_1 + 3 = -2 \cdot 2 \rightarrow x_1 = -7$

$M_y = \frac{y_1 + y_2}{2} \rightarrow 3 = \frac{y_1 + 4}{2} \rightarrow y_1 + 4 = 3 \cdot 2 \rightarrow y_1 = 2$

The coordinate of B is $(-7, 2)$.

Equation of a Line

Recall from Math 10 that writing the equation of a line requires the slope and a point on the line, or two points on the line.

The slope formula is $m = \dfrac{\text{rise}}{\text{run}} = \dfrac{\text{vertical change}}{\text{horizontal change}} = \dfrac{y_2 - y_1}{x_2 - x_1}$

Example 4 Find the equation of a line with point $(2, -4)$ and slope, $m = -\dfrac{2}{3}$

► *Solution*: The equation $y - y_1 = m(x - x_1)$ is the point slope equation of a line.

	or	
$y - y_1 = m(x - x_1)$		$y = mx + b$
$y - (-4) = -\frac{2}{3}(x - 2)$		$-4 = -\frac{2}{3}(2) + b$
$3(y + 4) = -2(x - 2)$		$b = -4 + \frac{4}{3}$
$3y + 12 = -2x + 4$		$= -\frac{8}{3}$
$2x + 3y = -8$		$y = -\frac{2}{3}x - \frac{8}{3}$
(Standard Form)		(Slope Intercept Form)

Example 5 Find the equation of the line going through $(-2, 5)$ and $(4, 3)$.

► *Solution*: $m = \dfrac{y_2 - y_1}{x_2 - x_1} = \dfrac{5 - 3}{-2 - 4} = \dfrac{2}{-6} = -\dfrac{1}{3}$

Using $(4, 3)$:

	or	
$y_2 - y_1 = m(x_2 - x_1)$		$y = mx + b$
$y - 3 = -\frac{1}{3}(x - 4)$		$3 = -\frac{1}{3}(4) + b$
$3(y - 3) = -1(x - 4)$		$b = 3 + \frac{4}{3}$
$3y - 9 = -x + 4$		$= \frac{13}{3}$
$x + 3y = 13$		$y = -\frac{1}{3}x + \frac{13}{3}$
(Standard Form)		(Slope Intercept Form)

Example 6 A line passes through the point $(-3, 2)$.

a) Write the equation of the line if it is parallel to the x-axis.

b) Write the equation of the line if it is parallel to the y-axis.

► *Solution*: **a)** The line parallel to the x-axis must be $y = 2$, with $m = 0$.

$y - 2 = 0(x + 3) \rightarrow y = 2$

b) The line parallel to the y-axis must be $x = -3$, with $m = \varnothing$

The equation of the line cannot be written because of the undefined slope.

8.1 Exercise Set

1. Find the distance between the two given points A and B to two decimal places.

a) $A(-3, 5)$ and $B(6, -2)$

b) $A(1.3, 4.7)$ and $B(-4.5, -2.8)$

c) $A\left(\frac{1}{4}, -2\right)$ and $B\left(-3, -\frac{1}{3}\right)$

d) $A(\sqrt{2}, -\sqrt{3})$ and $B(4\sqrt{2}, -3\sqrt{3})$

2. Find the midpoint between the two given points A and B.

a) $A(5, -2)$ and $B(-5, -2)$

b) $A\left(\frac{3}{5}, \frac{2}{3}\right)$ and $B\left(\frac{1}{2}, -3\right)$

c) $A(-7, 4)$ and $B(7, -4)$

d) $A(a, -b)$ and $B(c, d)$

3. The endpoint A and the midpoint M of a line segment AB are given. Find the coordinates of the other endpoint B.

a) $A(2, 5)$ and $M(4, 6)$

b) $A(1, -6)$ and $M(-4, 5)$

c) $A(4, -4)$ and $M(4, 4)$

d) $A(-6, 3)$ and $M(0, 0)$

4. Determine the equation of the line with goes through the given points.

a) $(-3, 5)$ and $(1, -5)$ **b)** $(\sqrt{2}, -\sqrt{2})$ and $(-3\sqrt{2}, -5\sqrt{2})$

5. Determine the equation of the line with every point equal distance from the given points.

a) $(-5, 3)$ and $(7, 2)$ **b)** $(2, -6)$ and $(-8, -2)$

6. Determine the type of triangle with the given vertices.

a) $A(14, -1)$, $B(10, -7)$, and $C(6, -1)$ **b)** $D(-3, 2)$, $E(-1, 5)$, and $F(-6, 4)$

7. Find the area of the shaded rectangle.

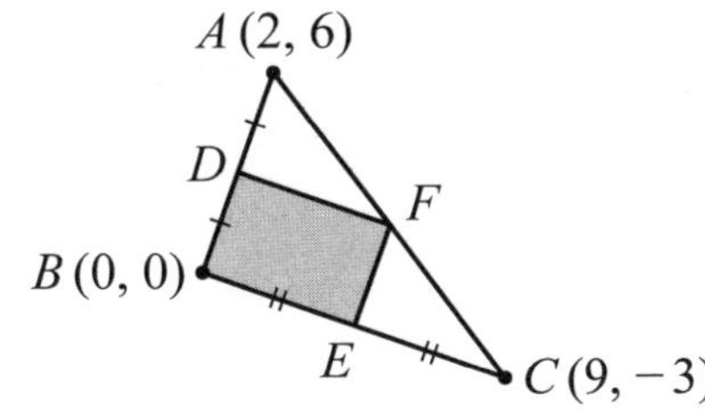

8. Point M and N are midpoints of AC and BC. Find the length of MN.

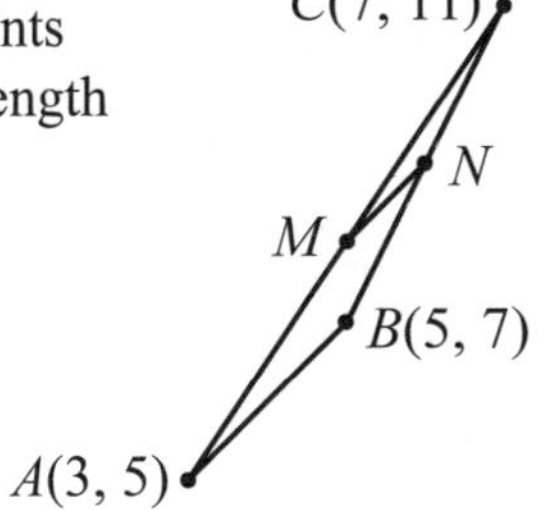

8.2 Circles

Where a plane cuts a circular cone perpendicular to the axis, a circle is formed.

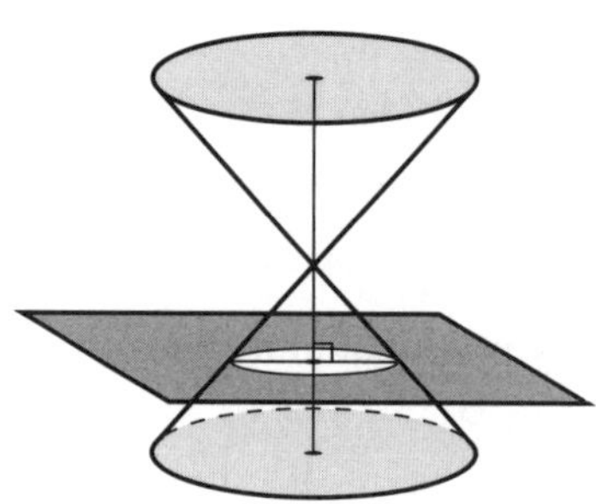

Circle with Centre at the Origin

The locus definition of a circle is the set of points at an equal distance from a given point (the centre).

The Standard Equation of a Circle with Centre at (0, 0)

The graph of any equation that can be written in the form

$$x^2 + y^2 = r^2$$

is a circle with radius r, and centre at (0, 0).

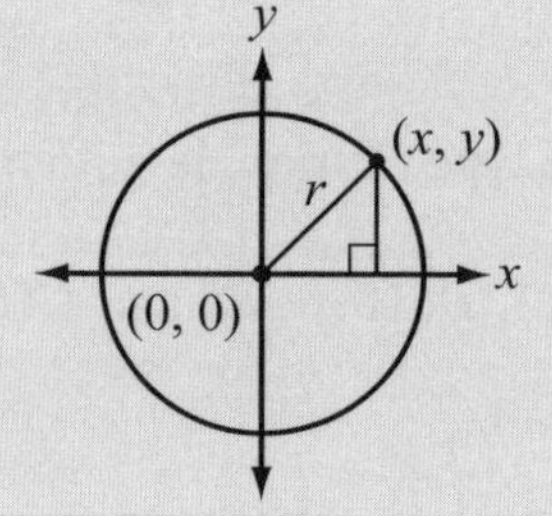

Example 1 Write the equation for the circle.

a)

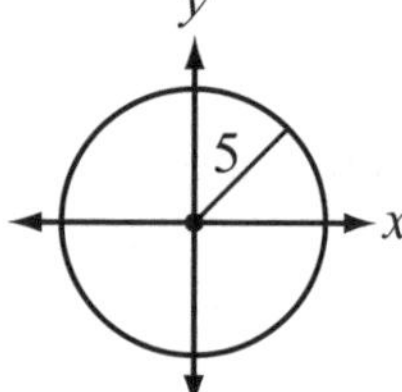

b)

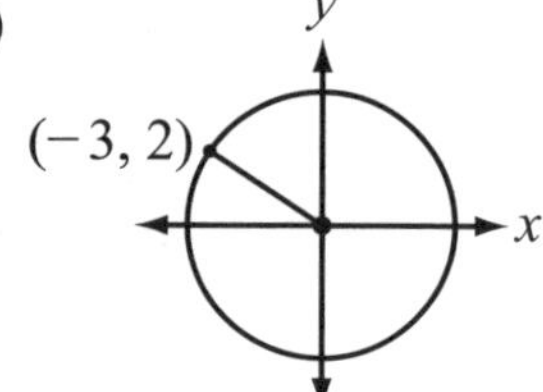

► *Solution*:

a) $x^2 + y^2 = 5^2$

$x^2 + y^2 = 25$

b) $r = \sqrt{(-3-0)^2 + (2-0)^2}$

$= \sqrt{9+4}$

$= \sqrt{13}$

$x^2 + y^2 = (\sqrt{13})^2$

$x^2 + y^2 = 13$

Circle with Centre at (*h*, *k*)

By distance formula: $r = \sqrt{(x-h)^2 + (y-k)^2} \rightarrow r^2 = (x-h)^2 + (y-k)^2$

The Standard Equation of a Circle with Centre at (h, k)

The graph of any equation that can be written in the form

$$(x-h)^2 + (y-k)^2 = r^2$$

This is a circle with radius r, and centre at (h, k).

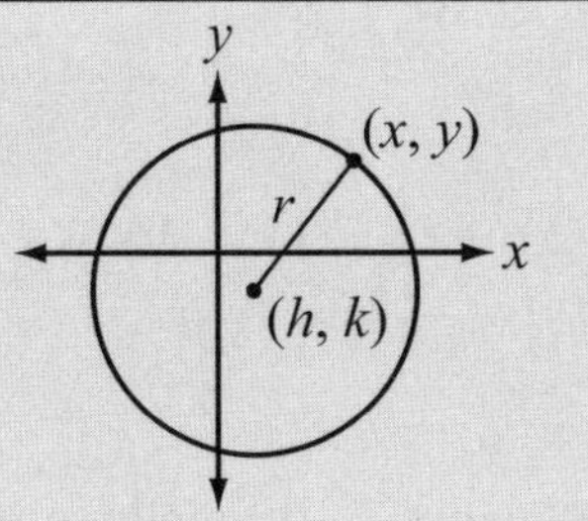

General Form of a Circle

The general form of all conics is $Ax^2 + Cy^2 + Dx + Ey + F = 0$. To be a circle, $A \cdot C > 0$ and $A = C$.
For example: $4x^2 + 4y^2 + 2x - 3y + 1 = 0$ is a circle.

Example 2 Determine the equation of a circle with centre $(3, -1)$ that passes through $(7, 4)$.

► *Solution*: By the distance formula, $r = \sqrt{(7-3)^2 + (4+1)^2} = \sqrt{41}$

Therefore the equation is $(x-3)^2 + (y+1)^2 = 41$

Example 3 Sketch the part of the circle given by each equation.

a) $y + 1 = \sqrt{9 - (x-2)^2}$ **b)** $x - 2 = -\sqrt{9 - (y+1)^2}$

► *Solution*: **a)**

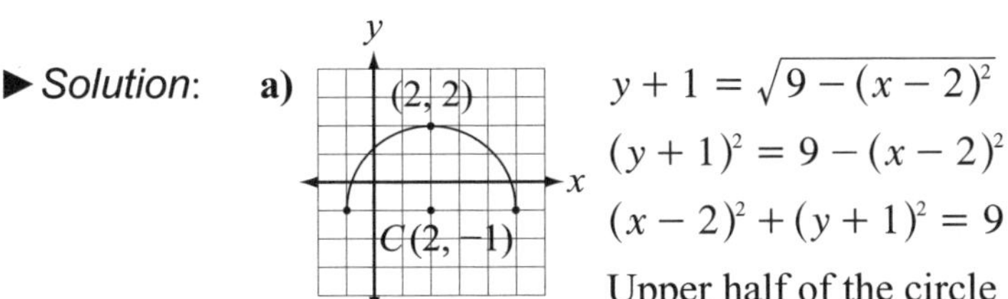

$y + 1 = \sqrt{9 - (x-2)^2}$

$(y+1)^2 = 9 - (x-2)^2$

$(x-2)^2 + (y+1)^2 = 9$

Upper half of the circle

b)

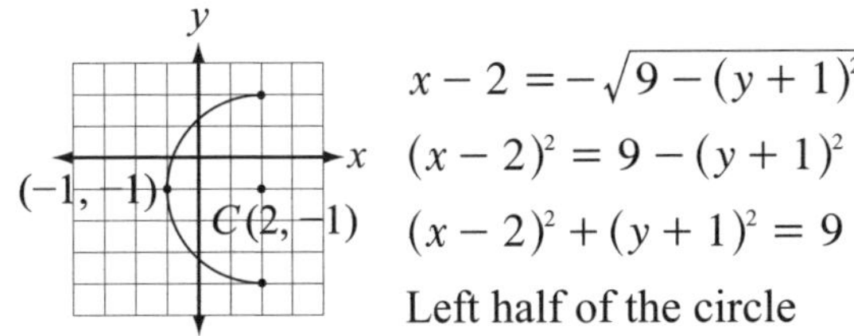

$x - 2 = -\sqrt{9 - (y+1)^2}$

$(x-2)^2 = 9 - (y+1)^2$

$(x-2)^2 + (y+1)^2 = 9$

Left half of the circle

Example 4 Find the centre and radius of the circle $x^2 + y^2 - 14x + 6y - 6 = 0$.

► *Solution*: First, change the equation from general form to standard form. Since standard form consists of perfect squares, complete the square for each variable.

$x^2 + y^2 - 14x + 6y - 6 = 0$	
$x^2 + y^2 - 14x + 6y = 6$	*Add 6 to both sides of the equation*
$(x^2 - 14x + \_\_) + (y^2 + 6y + \_\_) = 6$	*Separate the terms containing x and y*
$(x^2 - 14x + 49) + (y^2 + 6y + 9) = 6 + 49 + 9$	*divide the middle term by 2 and square it*
$(x-7)^2 + (y+3)^2 = 64$	*Rewrite quadratic expression in factored form*

Therefore, the centre of the circle is $(7, -3)$, and the radius is $r = 8$.

8.2 Exercise Set

1. Find the coordinates of the centre of the circle and it's radius.

a) $x^2 + y^2 - 25 = 0$

b) $x^2 + y^2 = 7$

c) $(x+2)^2 + (y-3)^2 = 16$

d) $2(x+3)^2 + 2y^2 = 18$

2. Find the equation of the circle, given the centre C and radius r.

a) $C(0,0),\ r = 3$

b) $C(-3,4),\ r = 5$

c) $C(-4,-2),\ r = \sqrt{7}$

d) $C(0,-3),\ r = \sqrt{5}$

3. Graph the circle.

a) $(x-3)^2 + (y+2)^2 = 4$

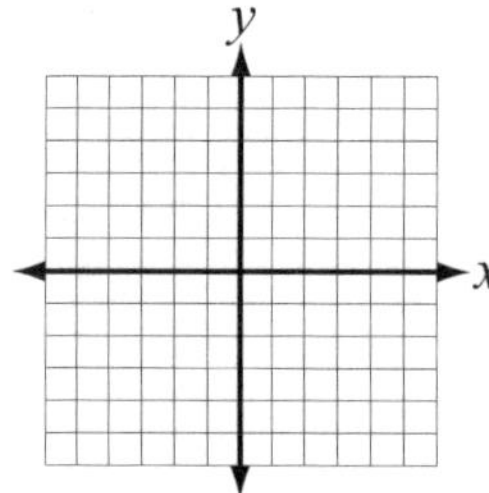

b) $(x+1)^2 + (y-2)^2 = 10$

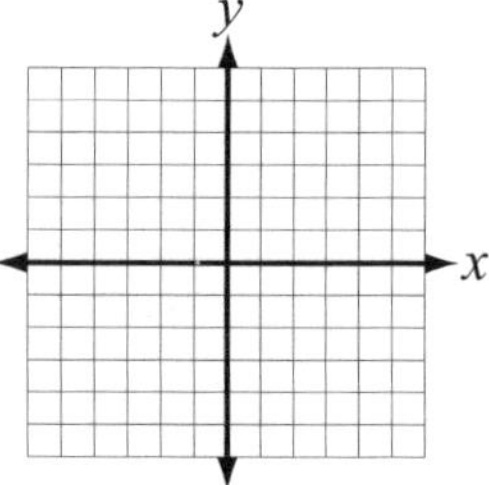

4. Find the centre and radius of the circle.

a) $x^2 + y^2 + 6x - 2y + 1 = 0$

b) $2x^2 + 2y^2 + 4x - 8y + 2 = 0$

c) $9x^2 + 9y^2 + 6x - 6y - 142 = 0$

d) $4x^2 - 12x + 4y^2 - 30 = 0$

5. Find the general form of the standard form equation of a circle.

a) $(x-1)^2+(y+3)^2=9$

b) $(x+2)^2+(y-4)^2=7$

6. The circle $x^2+y^2=9$ is shifted 4 units to the left and 1 unit up, plus the radius is increased by 2 units. What is the equation of the new circle?

7. The diameter of a circle has endpoints $(2,-7)$ and $(-4,1)$. What is the equation of the circle?

8. For what real value, k, will the equation $x^2+y^2-2x+4y+k=0$ describe a circle with radius 4?

9. For what value(s) of the constant, m, would the conic $x^2/(m+4)^2+y^2/9^2=1$ be a circle?

10. Write the equation of a circle with radius 5, and centre at the intersection of $3x+y=1$ and $2x+3y=-4$.

11. A circle has its centre on the y-axis and contains the points $(1,5)$ and $(7,4)$. Find the coordinates of the centre of the circle.

12. Determine the equation of the circle with centre $(2,6)$, that is tangent to the line $y=x+2$.

13. A circle intersects the x-axis at -12 and 2; it intersects the y-axis at -2 and 12. What is the equation of the circle?

8.3 Parabolas

The graph of a quadratic function $y = Ax^2 + Bx + C,\ A \neq 0$, is called a parabola. The path of a ball tossed in the air makes a parabolic shape, as do the support cables of a suspension bridge and the lens of a telescope.

Definition of a Parabola

A parabola is the set of all points in a plane equidistant from a line (called the **directrix**) and a fixed point F (called the **focus**) that is not on the line.

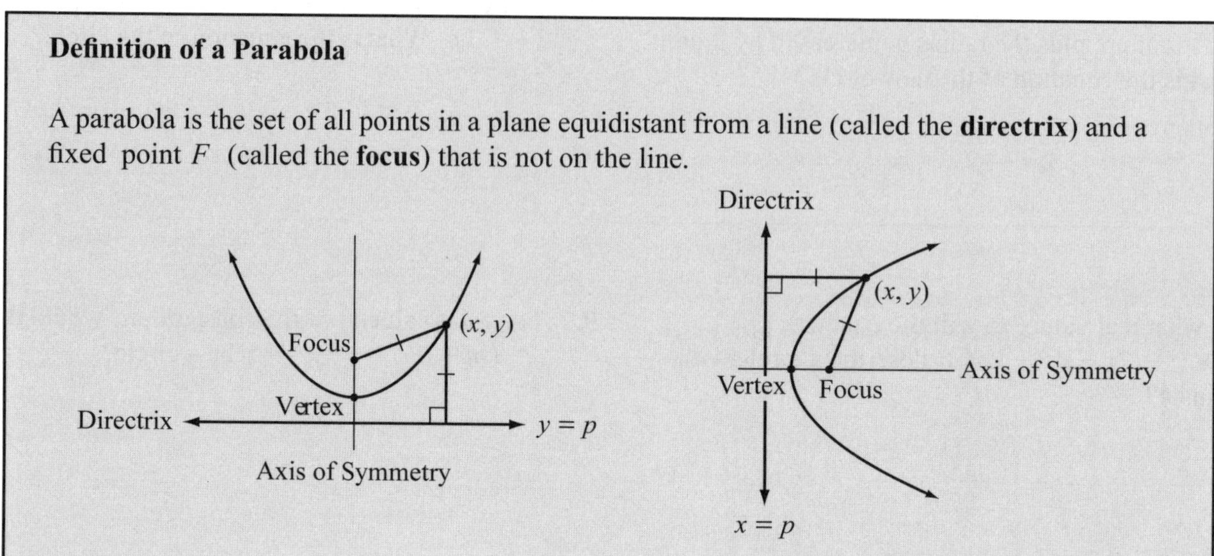

The equation of a parabola can be obtained by combining the definition above with the distance formula. The easiest way to obtain the equation is with the vertex at $(0, 0)$, and the focus at $(0, p)$, with directrix $y = -p$ or with the focus at $(p, 0)$ and directrix $x = -p$.

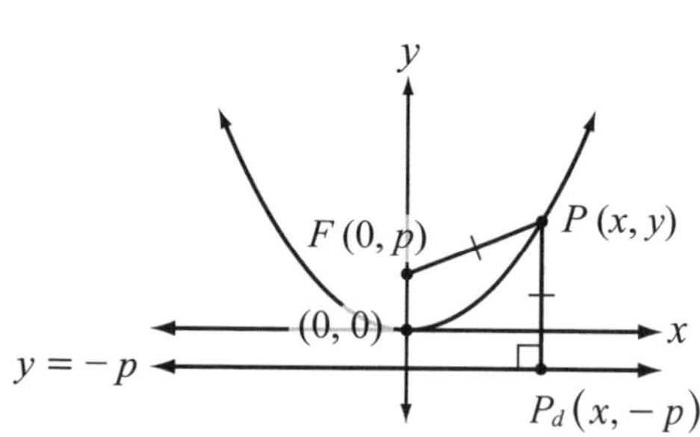

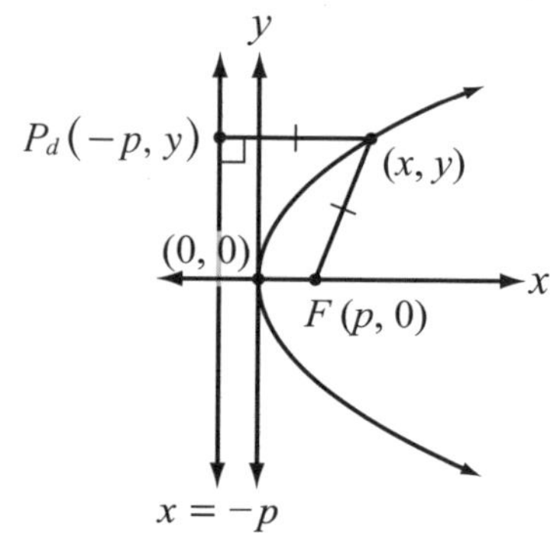

$$FP = PP_d$$
$$\sqrt{(x-0)^2 + (y-p)^2} = \sqrt{(x-x)^2 + (y+p)^2}$$
$$(x-0)^2 + (y-p)^2 = (x-x)^2 + (y+p)^2$$
$$x^2 + y^2 - 2py + p^2 = y^2 + 2py + p^2$$
$$x^2 - 2py = 2py$$
$$x^2 = 4py$$

$$FP = PP_d$$
$$\sqrt{(x-p)^2 + (y-0)^2} = \sqrt{(x+p)^2 + (y-y)^2}$$
$$(x-p)^2 + (y-0)^2 = (x+p)^2 + (y-y)^2$$
$$x^2 - 2px + p^2 + y^2 = x^2 + 2px + p^2$$
$$-2px + y^2 = 2px$$
$$y^2 = 4px$$

The **focus-directrix** forms of a vertical and horizontal parabola with centre at $(0, 0)$ are $4py = x^2$, and $4px = y^2$.

Focus-Directrix Form of the Equation of a Parabola with Vertex $(0, 0)$

	Vertical Parabola	Horizontal Parabola
Equation:	$4py = x^2$	$4px = y^2$
Focus:	$(0, p)$	$(p, 0)$
Directrix:	$y = -p$	$x = -p$
$p > 0$:	parabola opens up	parabola opens to the right
$p < 0$:	parabola opens down	parabola opens to the left

Example 1 A parabola has vertex $(0, 0)$, and passes through $(-4, 2)$.

a) Find the equation so that it opens up. **b)** Find the equation so that it opens to the left.

▶ *Solution*: **a)**

$$\begin{aligned} 4py &= x^2 \\ 4p(2) &= (-4)^2 \\ 8p &= 16 \\ p &= 2 \\ 4(2)y &= x^2 \\ 8y &= x^2 \end{aligned}$$

b)

$$\begin{aligned} 4px &= y^2 \\ 4p(-4) &= 2^2 \\ -16p &= 4 \\ p &= -\tfrac{1}{4} \\ 4(-\tfrac{1}{4})x &= y^2 \\ -x &= y^2 \end{aligned}$$

Focus-Directrix Form of the Equation of a Parabola with Vertex (h, k)

	Vertical Parabola	Horizontal Parabola
Equation:	$4p(y-k) = (x-h)^2$	$4p(x-h) = (y-k)^2$
Focus:	$(h, k+p)$	$(h+p, k)$
Directrix:	$y = k - p$	$x = h - p$
Axis of Symmetry:	$x = h$	$y = k$
$p > 0$:	parabola opens up	opens to the right
$p < 0$:	parabola opens down	opens to the left

Example 2 Find the equation of a parabola that opens up, has a vertex at $(4, 5)$, and passes through $(0, 7)$.

▶ *Solution*:

$$\begin{aligned} 4p(y-k) &= (x-h)^2 \\ 4p(y-5) &= (x-4)^2 \\ 4p(7-5) &= (0-4)^2 \\ 8p &= 16 \\ p &= 2 \end{aligned}$$

The equation of the parabola is $8(y-5) = (x-4)^2$

Example 3 Find the vertex, focus, directrix, and axis of symmetry of $x^2 - 6x + 12y - 15 = 0$. Sketch the graph of the parabola.

► *Solution*: Change the equation from general form to focus-directrix form.

$$x^2 - 6x + 12y - 15 = 0$$
$$x^2 - 6x + \_\_\_ = -12y + 15$$
$$x^2 - 6x + 9 = -12y + 15 + 9$$
$$(x-3)^2 = -12y + 24$$
$$(x-3)^2 = -12(y-2)$$

Therefore $4p = -12 \rightarrow p = -3$

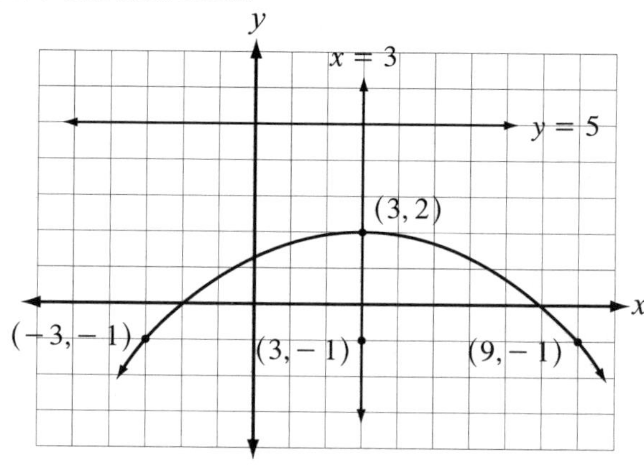

Vertex: $(3, 2)$ Focus: $(h, k+p) = (3, -1)$

Directrix: $y = k - p = 5$ Axis of Symmetry: $x = h = 3$

Example 4 Find the equation of two parabolas that both have a vertex at $(2, 4)$ and pass through $(0, 0)$. Sketch the graphs labelling the vertex, focus, directrix, and axis of symmetry.

► *Solution*: Opens down:

$$4p(y-k) = (x-h)^2, \; p < 0$$
$$4p(y-4) = (x-2)^2$$
$$4p(0-4) = (0-2)^2$$
$$-16p = 4$$
$$p = -\frac{1}{4}$$

Equation: $-(y-4) = (x-2)^2$

or $y - 4 = -(x-2)^2$

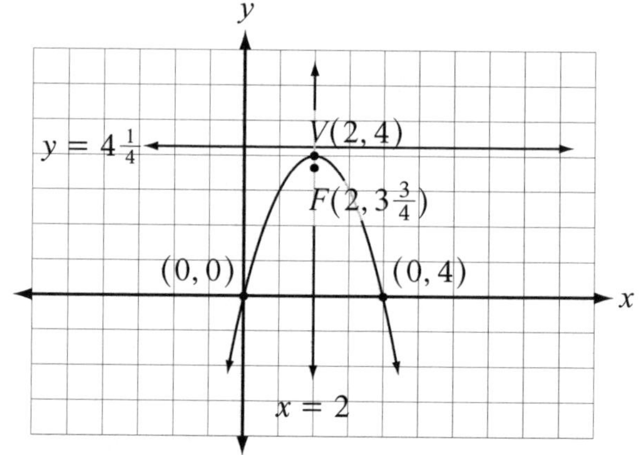

Opens left:

$$4p(x-h) = (y-k)^2, \; p < 0$$
$$4p(x-2) = (y-4)^2$$
$$4p(0-2) = (0-4)^2$$
$$-8p = 16$$
$$p = -2$$

Equation: $-8(x-2) = (y-4)^2$

or $x - 2 = -\frac{1}{8}(y-4)^2$

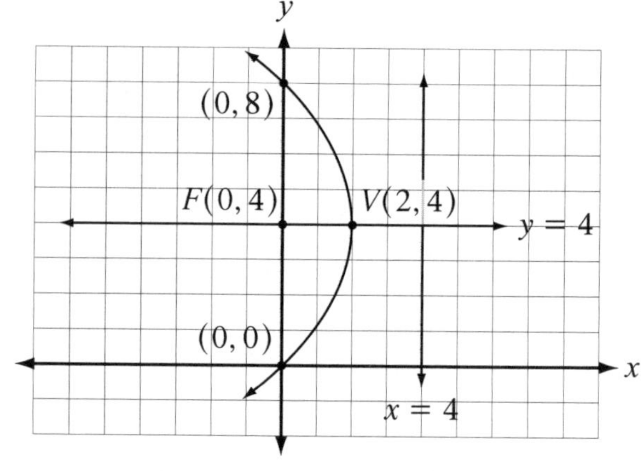

8.3 Exercise Set

1. Find the vertex, focus, directrix, and axis of symmetry of each parabola. A rough sketch may be helpful.

a) $16y = x^2$

b) $-16x = y^2$

c) $16x = (y+2)^2$

d) $-8(y+3) = x^2$

e) $-12(y+1) = (x-2)^2$

f) $-12(x+2) = (y-1)^2$

2. Find the equation of each parabola.

a) Vertex $(0, 0)$, Focus $(0, -4)$

b) Vertex $(3, -5)$, Directrix $y = -1$

c) Focus $(5, 3)$, Directrix $x = -1$

d) Focus $(-2, 1)$, Directrix $y = -3$

e) Vertex $(3, 1)$, Passes through $(4, 3)$ and $(2, 3)$

f) Vertex $(3, -2)$, Passes through $(5, 2)$ and $(5, -6)$

3. Determine the vertex, focus, directrix, and axis of symmetry of each general form parabola.

a) $f(x) = x^2 + 4x + 9$

b) $f(x) = -\frac{1}{8}x^2 - x - 3$

c) $4y = x^2 + 6x + 5$

d) $y^2 + 16x - 6y = 7$

e) $x^2 + 2x + 8y - 15 = 0$

f) $y^2 - 4y = 12x + 8$

4. Determine the equation of $-(y-4)=(x-3)^2$ flipped over the line $y=4$ and moved down two units.

5. If the graph of $y=(x+4c)^2+1$ lies three units horizontally left of the graph $y-1=x^2$, determine the numerical value of c.

6. Find the equation of the parabola passing through $(1,1)$ with vertex $(-2,-3)$ and with a vertical axis of symmetry.

7. The cross section of a TV satellite is shown. Find the focal point of the parabolic dish.

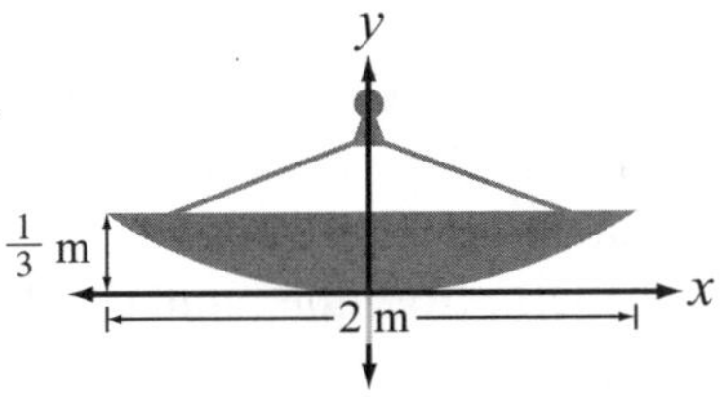

y
$\frac{1}{3}$ m
2 m
x

8. The cable between the towers of a suspension bridge have the shape of a parabola with a vertex 15 feet above the roadway. Find the equation of the parabola.

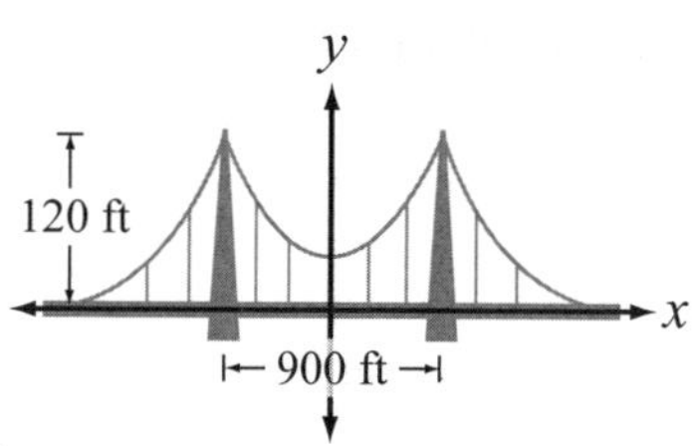

9. The Gateway Arch in St. Louis has a shape that approximates a parabola. Find the width of the arch 60 metres above the ground.

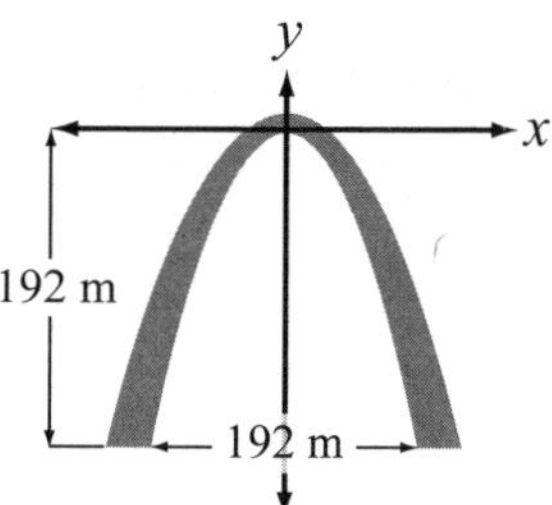

10. The cross-section of a tunnel for a two lane highway that is 10 metres wide has an arch the shape of a parabola. The tunnel is 5 metres high at a distance 1 metre from the tunnel's edge. Find the height of the tunnel.

11. The central cable of a suspension bridge forms a parabolic arch. The cable is suspended from the top of two supporting towers 250 metres apart. The top of the towers are 50 metres above the road and the lowest point on the cable is midway from towers and 3 metres above the road. Find the height of the cable above the road 30 metres from a tower.

8.4 Ellipses

Over 300 years ago the astronomer, Johannes Kepler discovered that the Earth, and other planets, do not revolve around the Sun in a circular motion, but in an elliptical motion.

If you stand at a certain spot in a room that has an oval ceiling, you can hear someone whispering metres away because of the reflective properties of an ellipse. The point at which the two people stand is called the focus of the ellipse (together they are called the foci). This reflective property also applies to light and radiation, giving the ellipse powerful applications in science, medicine, acoustics, and other areas.

Definition of an Ellipse

An ellipse is the set of all points P in a plane such that the sum of the distances from P to the fixed points F_1 and F_2 is a positive constant.

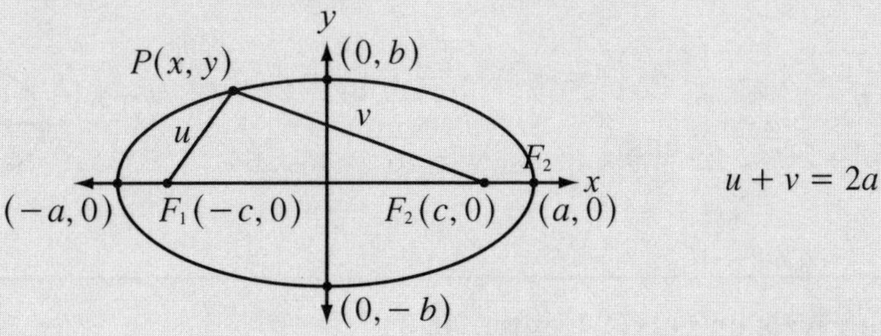

$u + v = 2a$

Proof:

$u + v = 2a$	*Definition of an ellipse*
$\sqrt{(x+c)^2 + (y-0)^2} + \sqrt{(x-c)^2 + (y-0)^2} = 2a$	*Substituting the distance formula*
$(\sqrt{(x+c)^2 + y^2})^2 = (2a - \sqrt{(x-c)^2 + y^2})^2$	*Regrouping and squaring*
$(x+c)^2 + y^2 = 4a^2 - 4a\sqrt{(x-c)^2 + y^2} + (x-c)^2 + y^2$	*Simplifying*
$\cancel{x^2} + 2cx + \cancel{c^2} + \cancel{y^2} = 4a^2 - 4a\sqrt{(x-c)^2 + y^2} + \cancel{x^2} - 2cx + \cancel{c^2} + \cancel{y^2}$	*Multiplying*
$4cx - 4a^2 = -4a\sqrt{(x-c)^2 + y^2}$	*Simplifying and regrouping*
$(a^2 - cx)^2 = (a\sqrt{(x-c)^2 + y^2})^2$	*Dividing by -4*
$a^4 - 2a^2cx + a^2x^2 = a^2(x^2 - 2cx + c^2 + y^2)$	
$a^4 - \cancel{2a^2cx} + c^2x^2 = a^2x^2 - \cancel{2a^2cx} + a^2c^2 + a^2y^2$	
If $P(x, y)$ is moved to point $(0, b)$ it is easily seen that $a^2 = b^2 + c^2$	*By Pythagorean theorem*
$a^4 + (a^2 - b^2)x^2 = a^2x^2 + a^2(a^2 - b^2) + a^2y^2$	*Substituting*
$\cancel{a^4} + \cancel{a^2x^2} - b^2x^2 = \cancel{a^2x^2} + \cancel{a^4} - a^2b^2 + a^2y^2$	*Canceling*
$-b^2x^2 = -a^2b^2 + a^2y^2$	*Simplifying*
$\frac{a^2y^2}{a^2b^2} + \frac{b^2x^2}{a^2b^2} = \frac{a^2b^2}{a^2b^2}$	*Dividing*
$\frac{x^2}{a^2} + \frac{y^2}{b^2} = 1$ with $a^2 = b^2 + c^2$, and $a > b > 0$	

The Ellipse: Major Axis on x-axis, Centre $(0, 0)$

The standard equation of an ellipse with its centre at the origin and major axis (horizontal) on the x-axis is:

$$\frac{x^2}{a^2} + \frac{y^2}{b^2} = 1 \text{ with } a > b > 0$$

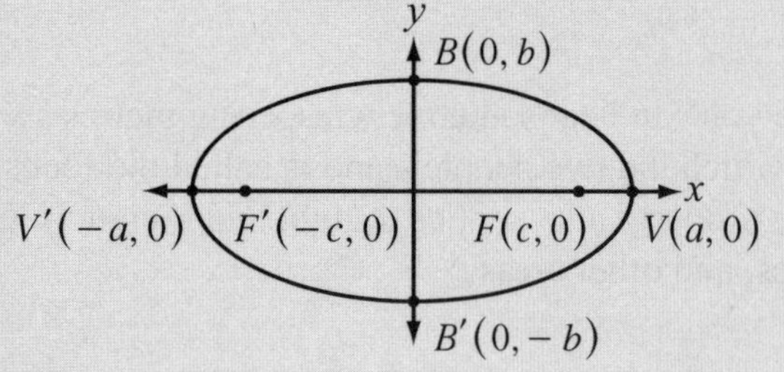

Vertices (ends of the major axis): $V(a, 0)$ and $V'(-a, 0)$
Length of major axis: $2a$
Ends of the minor axis: $B(0, b)$ and $B'(0, -b)$
Length of minor axis: $2b$
Foci: $F(c, 0)$ and $F'(-c, 0)$ with $a^2 = b^2 + c^2$

Example 1 Find the equation of an ellipse with its centre at the origin, major axis length of 10 units on the x-axis, and minor axis length of 6 units. Graph the ellipse, including the two foci.

► *Solution*: $\frac{x^2}{a^2} + \frac{y^2}{b^2} = 1 \rightarrow \frac{x^2}{5^2} + \frac{y^2}{3^2} = 1 \rightarrow \frac{x^2}{25^2} + \frac{y^2}{9^2} = 1$

$a^2 = b^2 + c^2 \rightarrow 25 = 9 + c^2 \rightarrow c^2 = 16 \rightarrow c = \pm 4$

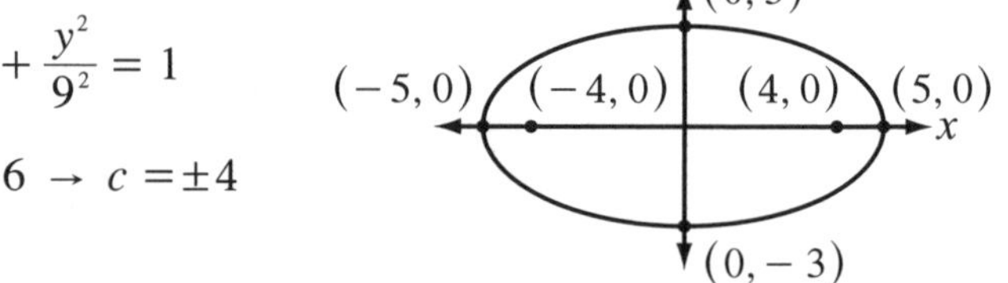

The Ellipse: Major Axis on y-axis, Centre $(0, 0)$

The standard equation of an ellipse with its centre at the origin and major axis (vertical) on the y-axis is:

$$\frac{x^2}{b^2} + \frac{y^2}{a^2} = 1 \text{ with } a > b > 0$$

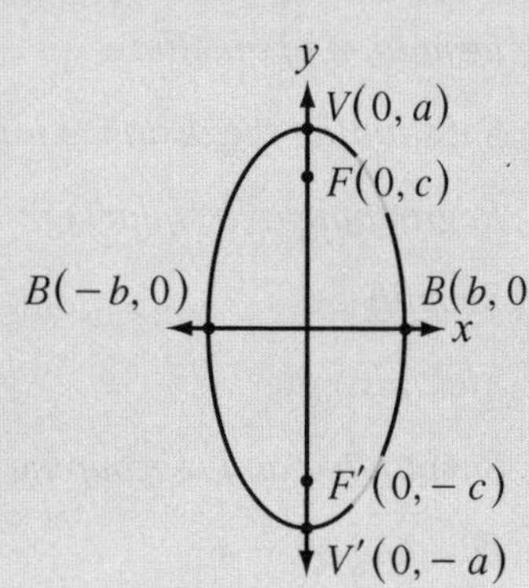

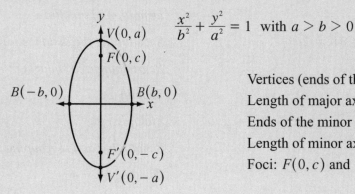

Vertices (ends of the major axis): $V(0, a)$ and $V'(0, -a)$
Length of major axis: $2a$
Ends of the minor axis: $B(b, 0)$ and $B'(-b, 0)$
Length of minor axis: $2b$
Foci: $F(0, c)$ and $F'(0, -c)$ with $a^2 = b^2 + c^2$

Example 2 Find the equation of the ellipse with its centre at the origin, focus $(0, 3\sqrt{2})$, and minor axis of length 6 units. Graph the equation including the focal points.

► *Solution*: Focus $(0, 3\sqrt{2})$ is on the y-axis, so the major axis is vertical.
Minor axis is 6 units: $B(3, 0)$ and $B'(-3, 0)$
$a^2 = b^2 + c^2$
$a^2 = 3^2 + (3\sqrt{2})^2 = 9 + 18 = 27$
$a = \pm\sqrt{27} = \pm 3\sqrt{3}$
The equation is: $\frac{x^2}{3^2} + \frac{y^2}{(3\sqrt{3})^2} = 1 \rightarrow \frac{x^2}{9} + \frac{y^2}{27} = 1$

y
$(0, 3\sqrt{3})$
$(0, 3\sqrt{2})$
$(-3, 0)$
$(3, 0)$
x
$(0, -3\sqrt{2})$
$(0, -3\sqrt{3})$

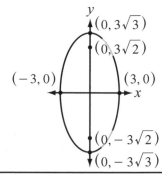

The Ellipse: Major Axis Horizontal, Centre (h, k)

The standard equation of an ellipse with centre (h, k) and major axis horizontal is:

$$\frac{(x-h)^2}{a^2} + \frac{(y-k)^2}{b^2} = 1 \text{ with } a > b > 0$$

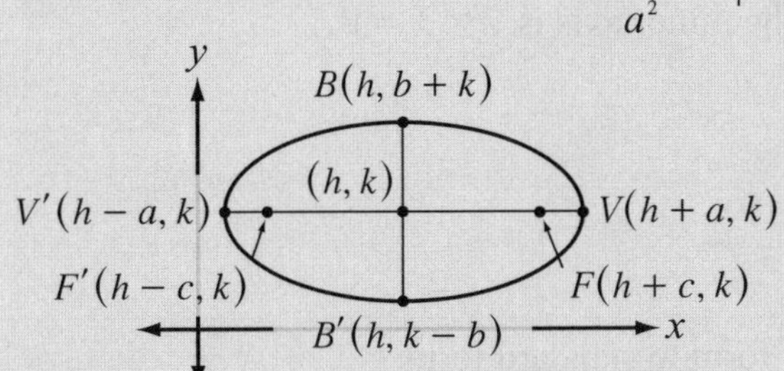

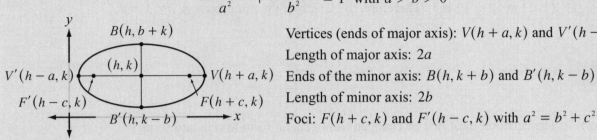

Vertices (ends of major axis): $V(h+a, k)$ and $V'(h-a, k)$
Length of major axis: $2a$
Ends of the minor axis: $B(h, k+b)$ and $B'(h, k-b)$
Length of minor axis: $2b$
Foci: $F(h+c, k)$ and $F'(h-c, k)$ with $a^2 = b^2 + c^2$

Example 3 Find the equation of the ellipse with foci $(10, -2)$ and $(4, -2)$, and an endpoint on the minor axis at $(7, 0)$.

► *Solution*: If the foci are $(10, -2)$ and $(4, -2)$, then the centre is $(7, -2)$ with $c = 3$.

If $(7, 0)$ is a minor endpoint, then $b = 2$.

$a^2 = b^2 + c^2 \rightarrow a^2 = 2^2 + 3^2 = 13$

$$\frac{(x-7)^2}{13} + \frac{(y+2)^2}{4} = 1$$

The Ellipse: Major Axis Vertical, Centre (h, k)

The standard equation of an ellipse with centre (h, k) and major axis vertical is:

$$\frac{(x-h)^2}{b^2} + \frac{(y-k)^2}{a^2} = 1 \text{ with } a > b > 0$$

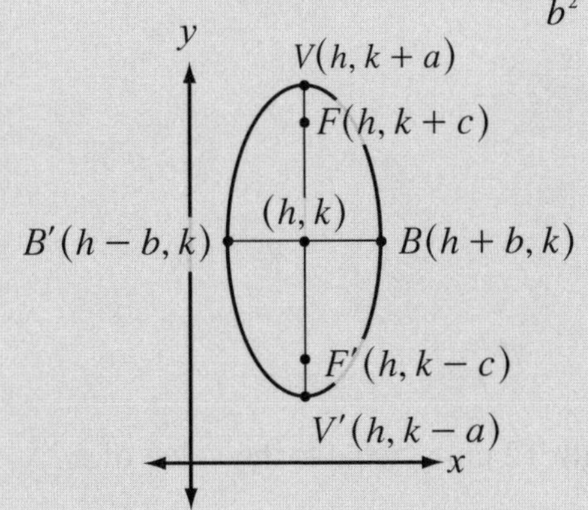

Vertices (ends of major axis): $V(h, k+a)$ and $V'(h, k-a)$
Length of major axis: $2a$
Ends of the minor axis: $B(h+b, k)$ and $B'(h-b, k)$
Length of minor axis: $2b$
Foci: $F(h, k+c)$ and $F'(h, k-c)$ with $a^2 = b^2 + c^2$

Example 4 Find the equation of the ellipse with focus $(-3, 8)$ and vertices $(-3, 10)$ and $(-3, 2)$.

► *Solution*: If the vertices are $(-3, 10)$ and $(-3, 2)$, then the centre is $(-3, 6)$ with $a = 4$

The focus is $(-3, 8)$ with $c = 2$

$a^2 = b^2 + c^2 \rightarrow 4^2 = b^2 + 2^2 \rightarrow b^2 = 12$

$$\frac{(x+3)^2}{12} + \frac{(y-6)^2}{16} = 1$$

Example 5 An ellipse with vertices $(5,2)$ and $(-3,2)$ passes through the point $(1,-1)$. Determine the length of the minor axis.

► *Solution*: If $(5,2)$ and $(-3,2)$ are vertices, then the centre of the ellipse is $(1,2)$. The distance from $(1,2)$ to $(1,-1)$ is 3. Therefore, the length of the minor axis is $2\times3=6$.

Example 6 Graph the ellipse $16x^2+4y^2+96x-8y+84=0$.

► *Solution*: The equation must first be changed from general form to standard form.

$$16x^2+4y^2+96x-8y+84=0$$
$$16(x^2+6x+\_\_\_)+4(y^2-2y+\_\_\_)=-84$$
$$16(x^2+6x+9)+4(y^2-2y+1)=-84+144+4$$
$$16(x+3)^2+4(y-1)^2=64$$
$$\frac{(x+3)^2}{4}+\frac{(y-1)^2}{16}=1$$

Centre $(-3,1)$ Vertex $(-3,5)$ and $(-3,-3)$

Minor axis points $(-5,1)$ and $(-1,1)$

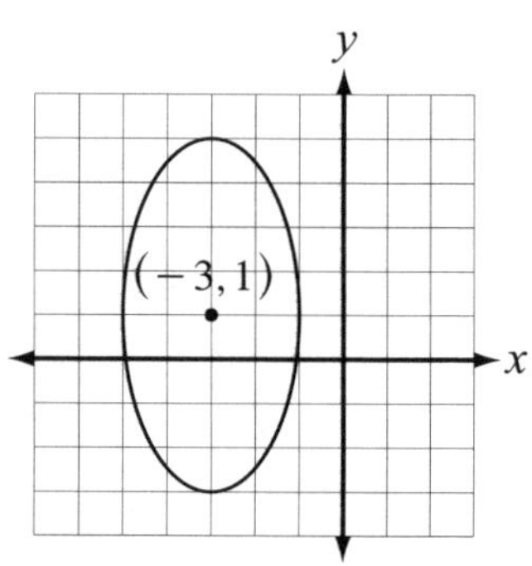

Example 7 Write $\frac{(x-1)^2}{16}+\frac{y^2}{25}=1$ in general form $Ax^2+By^2+Cx+Dy+E=0$.

► *Solution*:

$$\frac{(x-1)^2}{16}+\frac{y^2}{25}=1$$
$$400\left(\frac{(x-1)^2}{16}+\frac{y^2}{25}=1\right)$$
$$25(x-1)^2+16y^2=400$$
$$25(x^2-2x+1)+16y^2=400$$
$$25x^2-50x+25+16y^2=400$$
$$25x^2+16y^2-50x-375=0$$

Example 8 If $2kx^2+ky^2=1$ is an ellipse with a major axis of length 12 units, what is the value of k?

► *Solution*: $2kx^2+ky^2=1 \rightarrow \frac{x^2}{\frac{1}{2k}}+\frac{y^2}{\frac{1}{k}}=1$. Since $\frac{1}{k}>\frac{1}{2k}$, the major axis is the y-axis.

The general formula for an ellipse is $\frac{x^2}{b^2}+\frac{y^2}{a^2}=1$, with the length of the major axis $2a$.

Therefore, $a^2=\frac{1}{k}$, but $2a=12 \rightarrow a=6$, so $\frac{1}{k}=36 \rightarrow k=\frac{1}{36}$

Check: $2kx^2+ky^2=1 \rightarrow 2\left(\frac{1}{36}\right)x^2+\frac{1}{36}y^2=1 \rightarrow \frac{x^2}{18}+\frac{y^2}{36}=1$

8.4 Exercise Set

1. Write the equation of the ellipse that has its centre at the origin.

a) Focus: $(0, -4)$, Vertex: $(0, -6)$

b) Major axis: 10 units, on x-axis, Minor axis: 8 units

c) Focus: $(4, 0)$, Major axis: 10 units

d) Focus: $(2, 0)$, 4 is half the length of minor axis

e) Foci: $(4, 0)$ and $(-4, 0)$, $\frac{c}{a} = \frac{2}{5}$

f) Vertices: $(0, 6)$ and $(0, -6)$, $\frac{2b^2}{a} = 4$

2. Determine the centre, vertices, minor axis points, and foci of the ellipse.

a) $4x^2 + 9y^2 - 16x + 18y - 11 = 0$

b) $x^2 + 2y^2 - 10x + 8y + 29 = 0$

c) $9x^2 + 4y^2 + 54x - 8y + 49 = 0$

d) $36x^2 + 64y^2 + 108x - 128y - 431 = 0$

3. Write the standard form equation in general form.

a) $\dfrac{(x+2)^2}{4}+\dfrac{(y-1)^2}{16}=1$

b) $\dfrac{(x-3)^2}{64}+\dfrac{(y+1)^2}{32}=1$

4. The area of an ellipse $x^2/a^2 + y^2/b^2 = 1$ is given by $A = \pi ab$. Find the area of the ellipse $4x^2 + 9y^2 = 36$.

5. The Earth moves in an elliptical orbit, with the Sun at one focal point of an ellipse with the perihelion (closest distance) is 146 million km away, and the aphelion (farthest distance) is 152 million km away. Write an equation for the orbit of the Earth around the Sun.

6. The eccentricity of a conic section is a measure of its roundness. A circle has an eccentricity of $e = 0$. Ellipses have an eccentricity of $0 < e < 1$. The eccentricity of a conic section is defined as $e = c/a$. Determine which ellipse is closest to being circular: $x^2/25 + y^2/9 = 1$ or $x^2/36 + y^2/16 = 1$.

7. The Moon has an orbit that is an ellipse with the Earth at one focus. If the major axis of the orbit is 608 000 km and the eccentricity is $e = 11/200$, what is the greater distance the Moon can be from Earth?

8. Any sound from one focus of an ellipse reflects off the ellipse directly back to the other focus. Find the distance sound travels from F_1 to F_2 in the diagram.

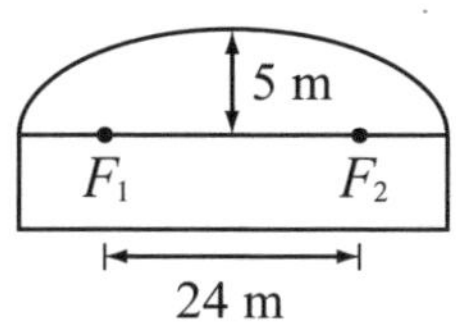

9. A hall 50 metres in length is to be designed as a elliptical whispering gallery. If the foci are located 20 metres from the centre, how high will the ceiling be at the centre?

10. A canal with a cross-section of a semi-ellipse, has a width of 20 metres and is 5 metres deep at the centre. Find the equation for the ellipse, and use it to find the depth 2 metres from the edge.

11. An arch in the form of half an ellipse is 60 feet wide and 20 feet high at the centre. Find the height of the arch at intervals of 10 feet along its width.

12. The major axis of an ellipse has endpoints $(8, 4)$ and $(-4, 4)$. If the ellipse passes through the origin, what must be the equation of the ellipse?

13. The definition of a focal width AA' is the width of a chord passing through a focus and is perpendicular to the major axis. What is the focal width of $x^2/a^2 + y^2/b^2 = 1$ in terms of a and b?

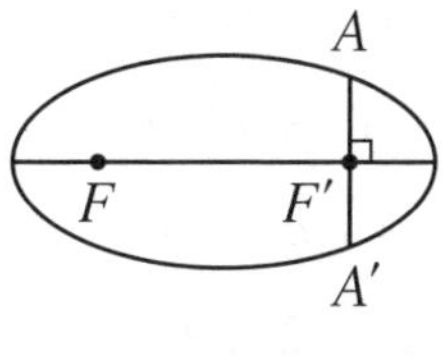

8.5 Hyperbolas

When a jet plane breaks the sound barrier, it sends out a visible vapour cloud and an explosion, called a sonic boom. This shock wave forms one branch of a curve called a hyperbola.

Hyperbolas have many practical applications. The LORAN (Long Range Navigation) is a radio navigation system based on a hyperbola used to determine the location of ships and planes. Hyperbolic mirrors are used in some telescopes, and have the property that a beam of light directed at one focus will be reflected to the second focus. To understand the applications of hyperbolas, the analytic definition must be defined.

Definition of a Hyperbola

A hyperbola is the set of all points in a plane such that the difference of the distance from two fixed points F_1 and F_2 is a constant.

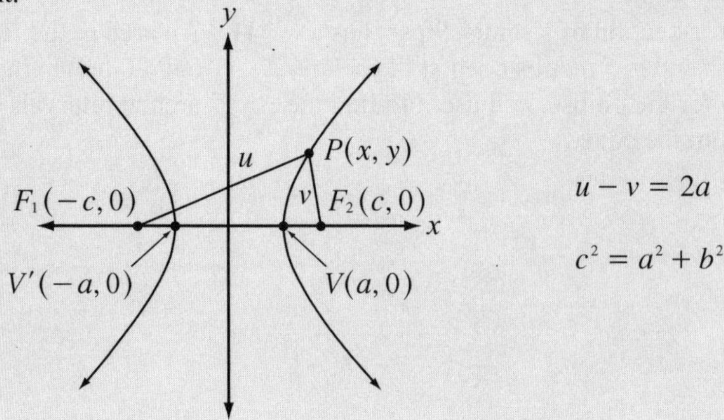

$u - v = 2a$

$c^2 = a^2 + b^2$

Proof:

$u - v = 2a$

$\sqrt{(x+c)^2 + (y-0)^2} - \sqrt{(x-c)^2 + (y-0)^2} = 2a$

$\left(\sqrt{(x+c)^2 + y^2}\right)^2 = \left(2a + \sqrt{(x-c)^2 + y^2}\right)^2$

$(x+c)^2 + y^2 = 4a^2 + 4a\sqrt{(x-c)^2 + y^2} + (x-c)^2 + y^2$

$\cancel{x^2} + 2cx + \cancel{c^2} + \cancel{y^2} = 4a^2 + 4a\sqrt{(x-c)^2 + y^2} + \cancel{x^2} - 2cx + \cancel{c^2} + \cancel{y^2}$

$\cancel{4}cx - \cancel{4}a^2 = \cancel{4}a\sqrt{(x-c)^2 + y^2}$

$(cx - a^2)^2 = \left(a\sqrt{(x-c)^2 + y^2}\right)^2$

$c^2x^2 - 2a^2cx + a^4 = a^2(x^2 - 2cx + c^2 + y^2)$

$c^2x^2 - \cancel{2a^2cx} + a^4 = a^2x^2 - \cancel{2a^2cx} + a^2c^2 + a^2y^2$

$(a^2 + b^2)x^2 + a^4 = a^2x^2 + a^2(a^2 + b^2) + a^2y^2$

$\cancel{a^2x^2} + b^2x^2 + \cancel{a^4} = \cancel{a^2x^2} + \cancel{a^4} + a^2b^2 + a^2y^2$

$\frac{b^2x^2}{a^2b^2} - \frac{a^2y^2}{a^2b^2} = \frac{a^2b^2}{a^2b^2}$

$\frac{x^2}{a^2} - \frac{y^2}{b^2} = 1$ with $c^2 = a^2 + b^2$

The Hyperbola: Foci on x-axis, Centre at $(0, 0)$

The standard equation of a hyperbola with centre at the origin and foci on the x-axis is:

$$\frac{x^2}{a^2} - \frac{y^2}{b^2} = 1 \text{ with } c^2 = a^2 + b^2$$

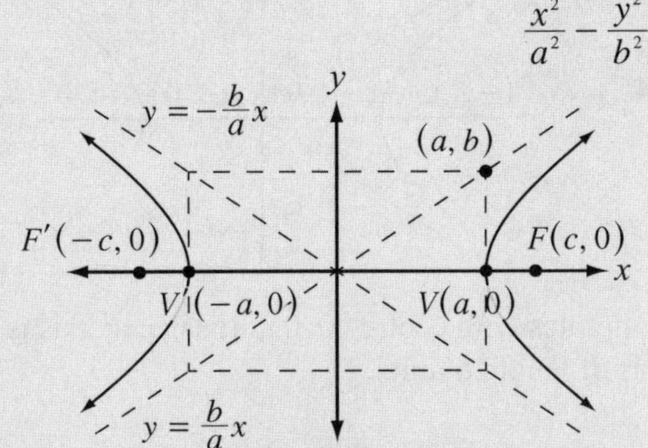

Vertices: $V(a, 0)$ and $V'(-a, 0)$
Foci: $F(c, 0)$ and $F'(-c, 0)$

The Hyperbola: Foci on y-axis, Centre at $(0, 0)$

The standard equation of a hyperbola with centre at the origin and foci on the y-axis is:

$$\frac{y^2}{a^2} - \frac{x^2}{b^2} = 1 \text{ with } c^2 = a^2 + b^2$$

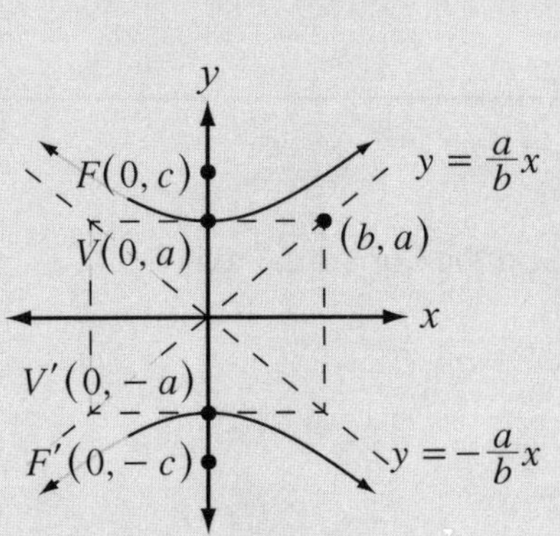

Vertices: $V(0, a)$ and $V'(0, -a)$
Foci: $F(0, c)$ and $F'(0, -c)$

Asymptotes of a Hyperbola

The graph of the hyperbola with equation $\frac{x^2}{9} - \frac{y^2}{4} = 1$ is shown.

From the equation, it is seen that $a^2 = 9 \rightarrow a = 3$ and $b^2 = 4 \rightarrow b = 2$

The dashed lines are asymptotes of the graph.

The values of a and b are used to find the equations of the asymptote lines: $y = \pm\frac{b}{a}x \rightarrow y = \frac{2}{3}x$ and $y = -\frac{2}{3}x$.

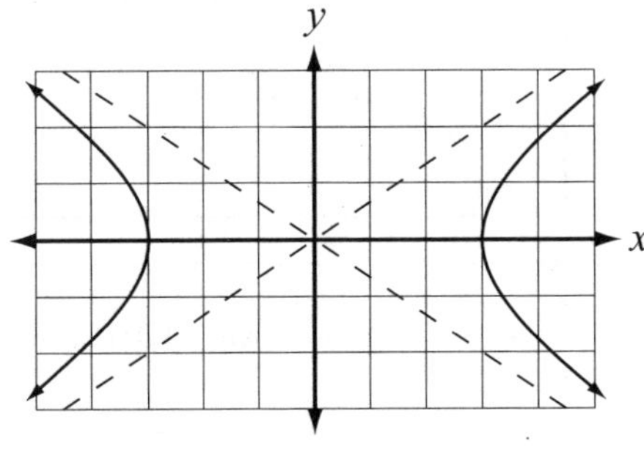

The asymptotes provide information about the end behavior of the graph. The hyperbola gets closer and closer to the asymptotes the further from the centre. If the asymptotes meet at right angles, the hyperbola is called a **rectangular hyperbola**. The equation of the asymptotes with centre at the origin would be $y = \pm x$, since $a = b$.

Transverse and Conjugate Axis of a Hyperbola

The hyperbola is drawn using the equations of the asymptotes as guides.

The segment VV' is called the **transverse axis**. $VV' = 2a$

The segment BB' is called the **conjugate axis**. $BB' = 2b$

The rectangle is called the **fundamental rectangle**.

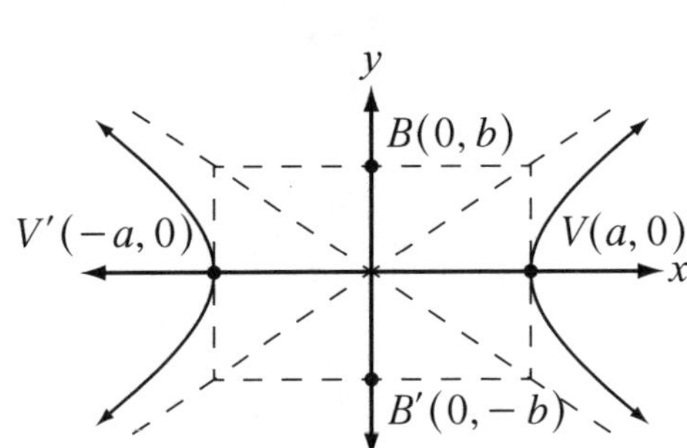

Example 1 Graph the equation $\frac{x^2}{16} - \frac{y^2}{9} = 1$. Label the vertices, foci, and asymptote lines.

► *Solution*: $a^2 = 16 \rightarrow a = \pm 4,\ b^2 = 9 \rightarrow b = \pm 3$

Asymptotes: $y = \pm\frac{b}{a} \rightarrow y = \frac{3}{4}x$ and $y = -\frac{3}{4}x$

$c^2 = a^2 + b^2 = 16 + 9 = 25 \rightarrow c = \pm 5$

Foci: $(5, 0)$ and $(-5, 0)$

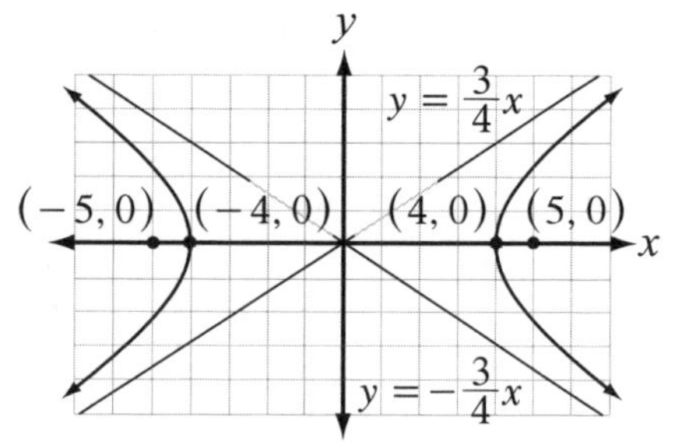

Example 2 Write the equation of the hyperbola and its asymptotes with centre $(0, 0)$, transverse axis is vertical with length 6 units and conjugate axis is of length 8 units.

► *Solution*: Vertices: $V(0, 3)$ and $V'(0, -3)$ Conjugate: $B(4, 0)$ and $B'(-4, 0)$

$\frac{y^2}{a^2} - \frac{x^2}{b^2} = 1 \rightarrow \frac{y^2}{3^2} - \frac{x^2}{4^2} = 1 \rightarrow \frac{y^2}{9} - \frac{x^2}{16} = 1$

Asymptotes: $y = \pm\frac{a}{b} \rightarrow y = \frac{3}{4}x$ and $y = -\frac{3}{4}x$

The Hyperbola: Transverse Axis Horizontal, Centre at (*h, k*)

The standard equation of a hyperbola with centre at (h, k) and foci on the horizontal axis is:

$$\frac{(x-h)^2}{a^2} - \frac{(y-k)^2}{b^2} = 1 \text{ with } c^2 = a^2 + b^2$$

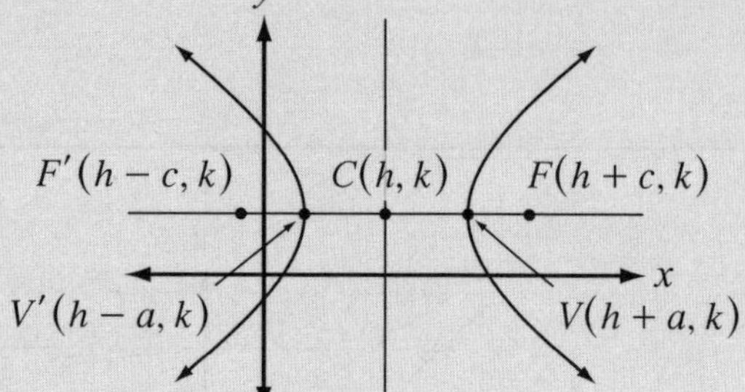

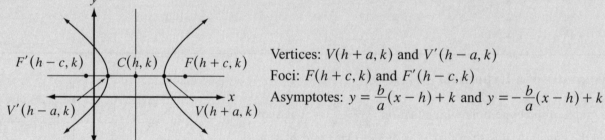

Vertices: $V(h + a, k)$ and $V'(h - a, k)$

Foci: $F(h + c, k)$ and $F'(h - c, k)$

Asymptotes: $y = \frac{b}{a}(x - h) + k$ and $y = -\frac{b}{a}(x - h) + k$

The Hyperbola: Transverse Axis Vertical, Centre at (*h, k*)

The standard equation of a hyperbola with centre at (h, k) and foci on the vertical axis is:

$$\frac{(y-k)^2}{a^2} - \frac{(x-h)^2}{b^2} = 1 \text{ with } c^2 = a^2 + b^2$$

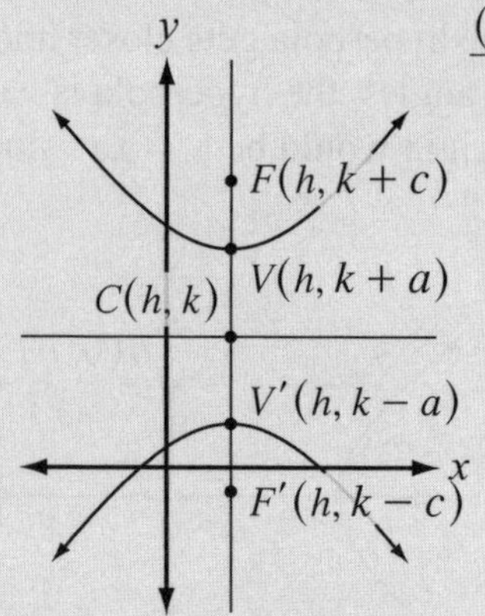

Vertices: $V(h, k + a)$ and $V'(h, k - a)$

Foci: $F(h, k + c)$ and $F'(h, k - c)$

Asymptotes: $y = \frac{a}{b}(x - h) + k$ and $y = -\frac{a}{b}(x - h) + k$

Example 3 Find the equation of the hyperbola with centre $(-3, 4)$, vertex $(-1, 4)$, and focus $(3, 4)$.

► *Solution*: The transverse axis is horizontal.

$$\frac{(x+3)^2}{a^2} - \frac{(y-4)^2}{b^2} = 1 \qquad a = -1-(-3) = 2,\ c = 3-(-3) = 6$$

$$\frac{(x+3)^2}{2^2} - \frac{(y-4)^2}{b^2} = 1 \qquad b^2 = c^2 - a^2 = 6^2 - 2^2 = 32$$

The equation of the hyperbola is $\frac{(x+3)^2}{4} - \frac{(y-4)^2}{32} = 1$

Example 4 Find the equation of the asymptotes for $y^2 - 4x^2 + 6y + 32x = 59$.

► *Solution*: Change the equation from general form to standard form.

$$y^2 - 4x^2 + 6y + 32x = 59$$

$$y^2 + 6y + \_\_\_ - 4(x^2 - 8x + \_\_\_) = 59$$

$$y^2 + 6y + 9 - 4(x^2 - 8x + 16) = 59 + 9 - 64$$

$$(y+3)^2 - 4(x-4)^2 = 4$$

$$\frac{(y+3)^2}{4} - \frac{(x-4)^2}{1} = 1 \text{ with } a = 2,\ b = 1$$

Asymptotes: $y = \pm\frac{a}{b}x + c \rightarrow y = \pm\frac{2}{1}x + c$, with centre $(4, -3)$.

$$y = 2x + c \qquad y = -2x + c$$

$$-3 = 2(4) + c \qquad -3 = -2(4) + c$$

$$c = -11 \qquad c = 5$$

The asymptotes are $y = 2x - 11$ and $y = -2x + 5$

Example 5 Find the equation of the hyperbola if the difference between $P(x, y)$ and the points $(1, -3)$ and $(1, 7)$ is always 6 for every point $P(x, y)$.

► *Solution*: $(1, -3)$ and $(1, 7)$ are foci of a hyperbola with a vertical transverse axis.

The centre is $\left(1, \frac{-3+7}{2}\right) = (1, 2)$

$$\frac{(y-2)^2}{a^2} - \frac{(x-1)^2}{b^2} = 1, \text{ with } 2a = 6 \rightarrow a = 3$$

$$\frac{(y-2)^2}{9} - \frac{(x-1)^2}{b^2} = 1$$

Foci at $(1, -3)$ and $(1, 7)$, so $2c = 7 - (-3) = 10 \rightarrow c = 5,\ b^2 = c^2 - a^2 = 25 - 9 = 16$

The equation is $\frac{(y-2)^2}{9} - \frac{(x-1)^2}{16} = 1$

8.5 Exercise Set

1. Find an equation of a hyperbola in the form $\frac{x^2}{m} - \frac{y^2}{n} = 1$ or $\frac{y^2}{n} - \frac{x^2}{m} = 1$, $m, n > 0$, with centre at the origin, and the given conditions.

a) The transverse axis is on the x-axis
The length of the transverse axis is 12 units
The length of the conjugate axis is 20 units

b) The transverse axis is on the y-axis
The length of the transverse axis is 6 units
The distance of the foci from the centre is 5 units

c) The conjugate axis is on the x-axis
The length of the conjugate axis is 10 units
The distance of the foci from centre is $\sqrt{70}$ units

d) The conjugate axis is on the y-axis
The length of the conjugate axis is 14 units
The distance of the foci from the centre is $\sqrt{200}$ units

2. Find the equation of the asymptotes of each hyperbola.

a) $\frac{x^2}{25} - \frac{y^2}{9} = 1$

b) $\frac{y^2}{25} - \frac{x^2}{9} = 1$

c) $\frac{(x-5)^2}{25} - \frac{(y+1)^2}{9} = 1$

d) $\frac{(y+1)^2}{25} - \frac{(x-3)^2}{9} = 1$

3. Write the equation of each hyperbola.

a) Vertices $(4, 0)$ and $(-4, 0)$; Focus $(6, 0)$

b) Centre $(-2, 4)$; Vertex $(-2, 2)$; Focus $(-2, 8)$

c) Vertices $(0, 4)$ and $(0, 0)$
Passes through point $(\sqrt{5}, -1)$

d) Foci $(-2, 12)$ and $(-2, -4)$; $\frac{c}{a} = \frac{4}{3}$

e) Centre $(-1, 3)$; $a^2 = 4$; $b^2 = 16$

f) Centre $(3, -1)$; y-intercept is -1
x-intercept is $(3 + (3\sqrt{5})/2)$

4. Determine the centre, vertices, and asymptotes of the hyperbola. Sketch the graph.

a) $4x^2 - y^2 + 8x - 4y - 4 = 0$

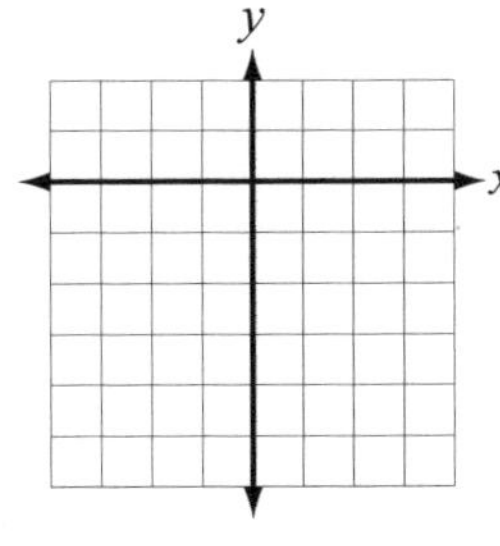

b) $x^2 - y^2 - 2x - 4y - 2 = 0$

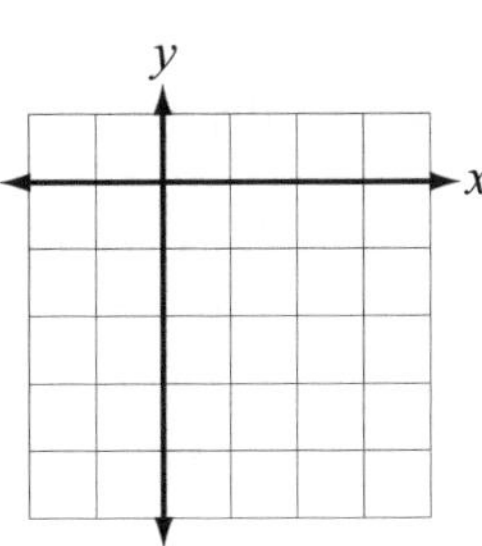

c) $4x^2 - y^2 - 16x - 4y + 8 = 0$

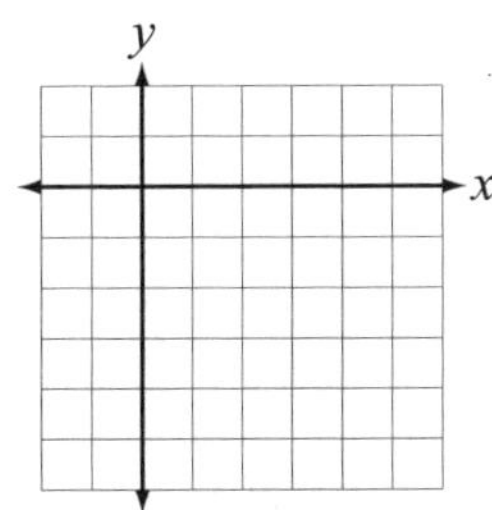

5. Write the standard form equations in general form.

a) $\dfrac{(x+2)^2}{4} - \dfrac{(y-1)^2}{16} = 1$

b) $\dfrac{(y-1)^2}{12} - \dfrac{(x+2)^2}{18} = 1$

6. Find the equation for the hyperbola that passes through $P(x, y)$ and has foci F and F'.

a)

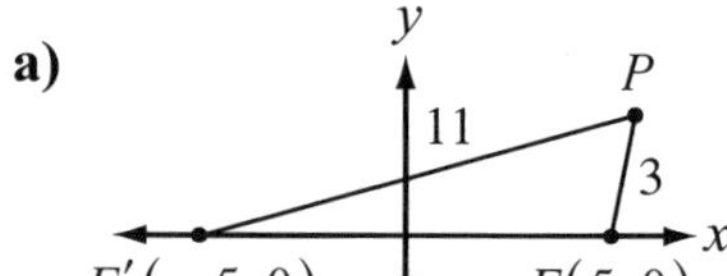

b)

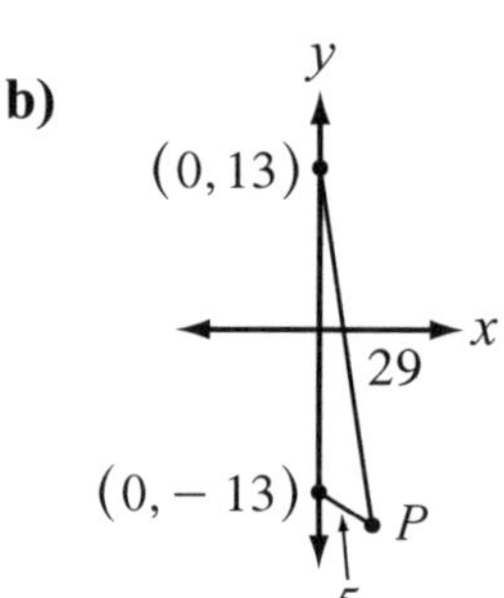

7. Describe the part of the hyperbola given by the equation.

a) $y = \frac{2}{3}\sqrt{x^2 - 36}$

b) $x = -\frac{2}{3}\sqrt{y^2 - 36}$

8. Find the equation of the hyperbola on which point P lies.

a) The difference of the distance between $P(x, y)$ and the points $(1, -2)$ and $(1, 8)$ is 8 units.

b) The distance between $P(x, y)$ and the point $(3, 0)$ is $3/2$ of the distance between P and the line $x = -2$. Leave the equation of the hyperbola in general form.

9. The hyperbolic path of a UFO that starts towards Earth along the line $y = x/4$ and comes within 6000 miles of the Earth's surface. Assume the radius of Earth is 4000 miles. Determine the equation of the path of the UFO.

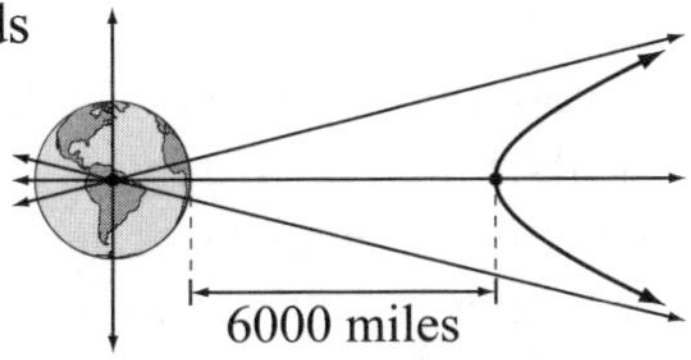

6000 miles

10. The LORAN system has two radio transmitters 52 km apart that send simultaneous signals to a ship. The difference of the distance between the ship and each transmitter is 48 km. Find the equation that describes this curve.

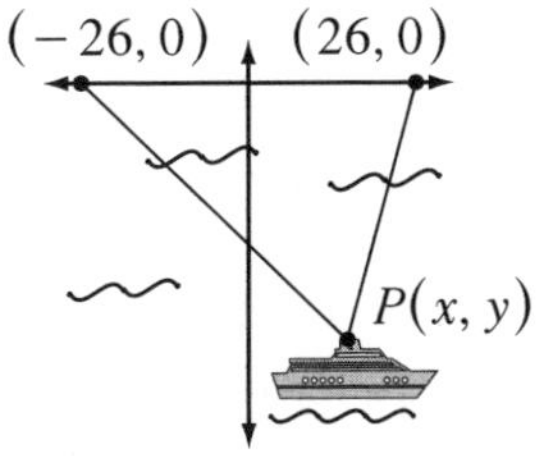

$(-26, 0)$ $(26, 0)$ $P(x, y)$

11. Stones dropped into a calm pond at points A and B create ripples that spread in widening circles. Points A and B are 40 m apart and the radii of the circles differ by 24 m. The point $P(x, y)$ where the circles intersect moves along a curve. Find the equation of the curve.

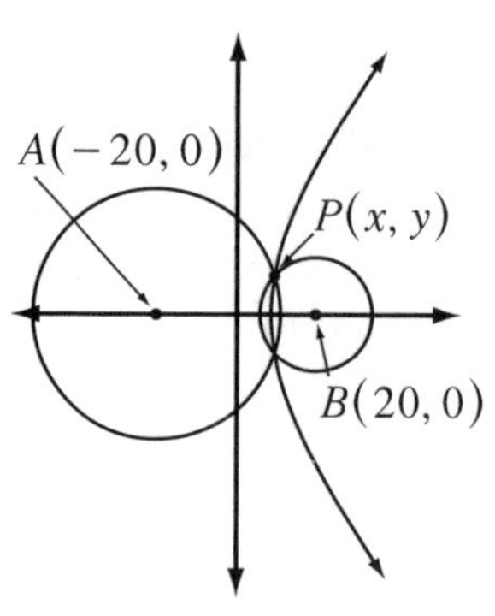

12. A ship 180 km out to sea sends distress signals to two Coast Guard stations at $A(-100, 0)$ and $B(100, 0)$. By measuring the difference in signal reception times, it is determined that the ship is 160 km closer to B than A. What are the coordinates of the ship?

180 km

13. A hyperbolic mirror in a telescope has the property that a light ray directed at a focus will be reflected to the other focus. The focus of the mirror has coordinates $(18, 0)$. Find the vertex of the mirror if the mount at the top edge of the mirror has coordinates $(18, 18)$.

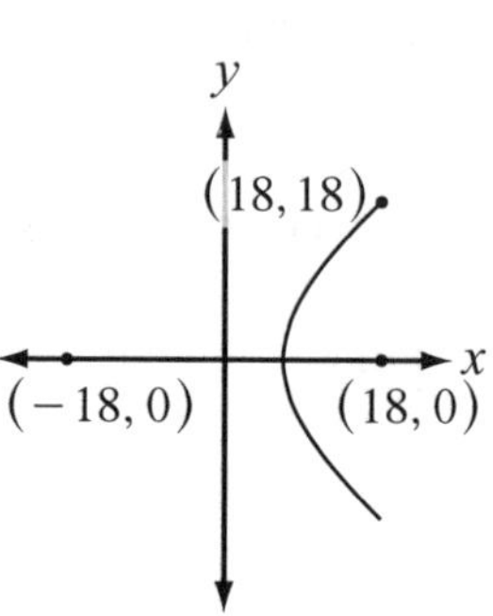

14. A cooling tower has outside walls which form a hyperbolic structure. Suppose its base diameter is 100 metres, and its smallest diameter of 48 meters is 80 metres from the base. If the tower is 120 metres high, calculate its diameter at the top.

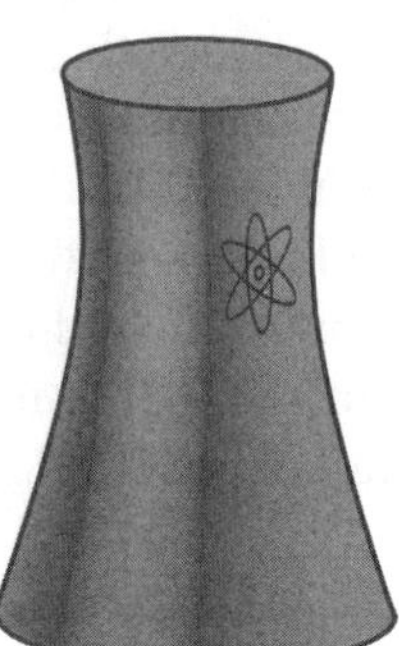

8.6 Chapter Review

The Circle

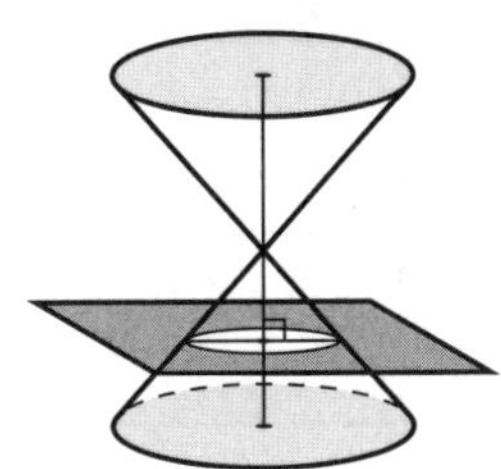

Definition: The set of points at an equal distance from a given point (the centre).

A circle with centre at the origin and a radius of r is: $x^2 + y^2 = r^2$.

A circle with centre at (h, k) and radius r is: $(x - h)^2 + (y - k)^2 = r^2$.

The Parabola

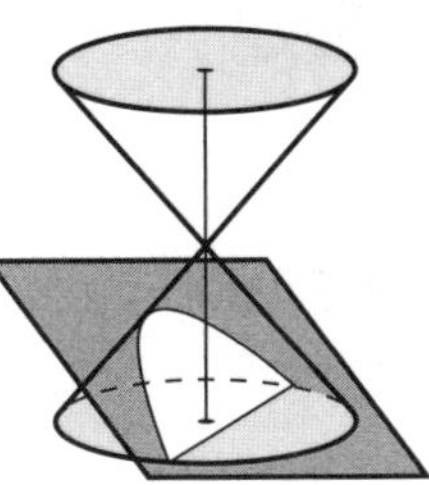

Definition: The set of points at an equal distance from a point (the focus) and a line (the directrix).

A parabola with vertex at the origin is: $4py = x^2$, or $4px = y^2$, where a is a constant $\neq 0$.

A parabola with vertex at (h, k) is: $4p(y - k) = (x - h)^2$ or $4p(x - h) = (y - k)^2$.

The Ellipse

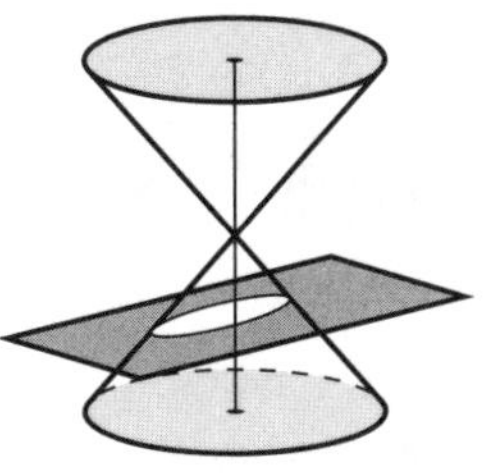

Definition: The sum of the distances from two given points (the foci) is always constant.

An ellipse with centre at the origin is: $\frac{x^2}{a^2} + \frac{y^2}{b^2} = 1$, or $\frac{x^2}{b^2} + \frac{y^2}{a^2} = 1$, $a > b$.

An ellipse with centre at (h, k) is: $\frac{(x - h)^2}{a^2} + \frac{(y - k)^2}{b^2} = 1$, or $\frac{(x - h)^2}{b^2} + \frac{(y - k)^2}{a^2} = 1$, $a > b$.

The length of the major axis is $2a$, and the length of the minor axis is $2b$.

The distance between the two foci is $2c$, with $a^2 = b^2 + c^2$

The Hyperbola

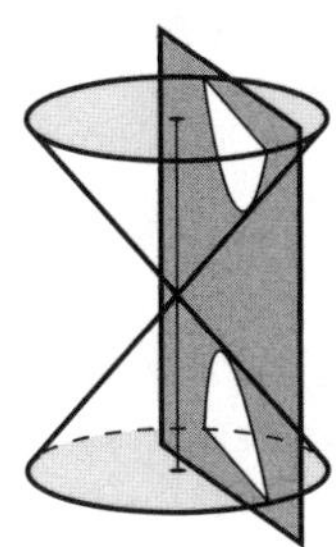

Definition: The absolute value of the difference of the distances from two given points (the foci) is always constant.

A hyperbola with centre at the origin is: $\frac{x^2}{a^2} - \frac{y^2}{b^2} = 1$, or $\frac{y^2}{a^2} - \frac{x^2}{b^2} = 1$.

A hyperbola with centre at (h, k) is: $\frac{(x - h)^2}{a^2} - \frac{(y - k)^2}{b^2} = 1$, with asymptote $y = \pm\frac{b}{a}x + c$ and vertices $(h \pm a, k)$,

or $\frac{(y - k)^2}{a^2} - \frac{(x - h)^2}{b^2} = 1$, with asymptote $y = \pm\frac{a}{b}x + c$ and vertices $(h, k \pm a)$.

The length of the transverse axis is $2a$, and the length of the conjugate axis is $2b$.

The distance between the two foci is $2c$, with $c^2 = a^2 + b^2$.

General Form of Conic Sections

The general form of all conic sections: $Ax^2 + Cy^2 + Dx + Ey + F = 0$, where A and C are not both zero.

Condition on A and C	Conic Section	Example
$AC > 0,\ A = C$	Circle	$4x^2 + 4y^2 + 2x + 3y + 1 = 0$
$AC > 0,\ A \neq C$	Ellipse	$4x^2 + 9y^2 + 2x + 3y + 1 = 0$
$A = 0$ or $C = 0$ (but not both)	Parabola	$5x^2 + 0y^2 + 2x + 3y - 1 = 0$
$AC < 0$ (A and C have opposite signs)	Hyperbola	$2x^2 - 4y^2 - 2x + 3y - 1 = 0$

Example 1 A point P moves so that the product of the slopes of the two line segments that join the points $(-3, 0)$ and $(3, 0)$ is 5. Identify the curve, and write its equation.

► *Solution*: Let the point be (x, y), then use the slope formula for each point $(-3, 0)$ and $(3, 0)$.

$$\frac{y-0}{x+3} \times \frac{y-0}{x-3} = 5 \rightarrow y^2 = 5(x^2 - 9) \rightarrow y^2 = 5x^2 - 45 \rightarrow 5x^2 - y^2 = 45 \rightarrow \frac{x^2}{9} - \frac{y^2}{45} = 1$$

Therefore, the equation is a hyperbola.

Example 2 Determine the restrictions on $Ax^2 + Cy^2 = AC$ such that it represents an ellipse with major axis on the x-axis.

► *Solution*: $Ax^2 + Cy^2 = AC \rightarrow \frac{x^2}{C} + \frac{y^2}{A} = 1$. To have the major axis on the x-axis requires $C > A > 0$.

Example 3 If the equation $x^2 + y^2 + Dx + Ey + F = 0$ represents a circle with centre $(2, -3)$ and radius 5, what value must F be?

► *Solution*: Equation of circle is: $(x-2)^2 + (y+3)^2 = 25 \rightarrow x^2 - 4x + 4 + y^2 + 6y + 9 = 25 \rightarrow$

$x^2 + y^2 - 4x + 6y - 12 = 0$, therefore $F = -12$

Example 4 An ellipse $Ax^2 + Cy^2 + Dx + Ey = 0$, with $A > 0$, has a horizontal major axis with the centre on the positive x-axis.

a) Is $A = C$, $A < C$, or $A > C$?
b) Is $D = 0$, $D < 0$, or $D > 0$?
c) Is $E = 0$, $E < 0$, or $E > 0$?

► *Solution*: **a)** To have a horizontal major axis, $A < C$.
b) To be on the positive x-axis, $D < 0$.
c) To be on the positive x-axis, $E = 0$.

8.6 Exercise Set

1. Classify the graph as a circle, a parabola, an ellipse, a hyperbola, or a non-conic equation.

a) $2y^2 - 4y = x - 2$

b) $4x^2 - 16x - 18y = -9y^2 + 11$

c) $y^2 - 4y = 4x^2 - 8x + 4$

d) $x - 4y^2 - 8y = 0$

e) $2x^2 + 2y^2 = 0$

f) $2x^2 - x = -y^2 + 2y$

g) $x^2 - 2x - 1 = 3y$

h) $2x^2 + 2y^2 - \frac{5}{2} = 0$

i) $4x^2 - 24x - 289 = 25y^2 + 150y$

j) $3x^2 - 3x = -3y^2 + 15$

k) $5x^2 - 4x = 5y^2 - 6y$

l) $2y^2 - 4y = -x^2 + 2$

m) $3x^2 + 12x = -3y^2 - 11$

n) $2x^2 - 2y^2 + 4 = 4$

2. $x^2 + y^2 + Dx + Ey + F = 0$ is the equation of a circle.

a) Find the centre and radius in terms of D, E, and F.

b) State the conditions for D, E, and F that determine whether the equation represents a circle, a point or has no graph.

3. Match each graph with the equation that illustrates that case.

a) Two distinct lines through the origin ________

b) Two distinct parallel lines ________

c) One line through the origin ________

d) A point (the origin) ________

e) No graph ________

i) $x^2 + y^2 = 0$

ii) $x^2 + y^2 = -1$

iii) $x^2 - y^2 = 0$

iv) $x^2 = 1$

v) $x^2 = 0$

4. Which conic could be represented by the equation $Ax^2 + Cy^2 + Dx + Ey + F = 0$ with the given condition.

a) $A = C \neq 0$

b) $A \times C > 0,\ A \neq C$

c) $A = 0,\ C \neq 0$

d) $A < 0,\ C > 0$

e) $A \times C < 0,\ A = -C$

f) $A \times C > 0,\ A = C$

g) A and $C > 0,\ A \neq C$

h) $A = 0$ or $C = 0$, but not both

i) $A \times C = 0,\ A < 0$

j) $A > C > 0$

5. Which type of conic is represented by the equation $(x - 2y)(x + 2y) = 16$.

6. Determine the restrictions on $Ax^2 + Cy^2 + Dx + Ey + F = 0$ for a parabola that opens to the left, and has the x-axis as the axis of symmetry.

7. What conic consists of all points that are twice as far from $(0, 2)$ as from $(3, 2)$? Give the standard form equation of this conic.

8. A high school is 6 km from the ocean with a straight shoreline. If a house is positioned such that it is twice as far from the shoreline as it is from the high school, find the equation of the curve that describes the situation. The x-axis is the shoreline, and the high school is at $(0, 6)$.

8.7 Multiple Choice Questions

1. Determine the vertex of $x - 2 = \frac{1}{3}(y + 4)^2$.

   a) $(-4, 2)$
   b) $(4, -2)$
   c) $(-2, 4)$
   d) $(2, -4)$

2. Find the length of the minor axis of $\frac{x^2}{16} + \frac{y^2}{25} = 1$.

   a) 4
   b) 5
   c) 8
   d) 10

3. Determine the axis of symmetry of the parabola $y = 3(x - 2)^2 + 5$.

   a) $x = -2$
   b) $x = 2$
   c) $y = -5$
   d) $y = 5$

4. What is the equation of the axis of symmetry of the parabola $x = -2(y + 1)^2 + 3$?

   a) $x = 3$
   b) $x = -3$
   c) $y = 1$
   d) $y = -1$

5. Determine the asymptotes of the hyperbola whose equation is $4x^2 - 9y^2 = 36$.

   a) $y = \pm\frac{2}{3}x$
   b) $y = \pm\frac{3}{2}x$
   c) $y = \pm\frac{4}{9}x$
   d) $y = \pm\frac{9}{4}x$

6. Determine the equation of a circle with centre $(0, 2)$ and radius 4.

   a) $x^2 + (y + 2)^2 = 4$
   b) $x^2 + (y + 2)^2 = 16$
   c) $x^2 + (y - 2)^2 = 4$
   d) $x^2 + (y - 2)^2 = 16$

7. Find the domain of $\frac{(x - 2)^2}{9} + \frac{(y + 3)^2}{25} = 1$.

   a) $-3 \le x \le 7$
   b) $-3 \le x \le 3$
   c) $-2 \le x \le 8$
   d) $-1 \le x \le 5$

8. Find the range of $16(x - 2)^2 + 25(y + 3)^2 = 400$.

   a) $-23 \le x \le 27$
   b) $-3 \le x \le 7$
   c) $-7 \le y \le 1$
   d) $-19 \le y \le 13$

9. What are the y-intercepts of the ellipse $16x^2 + 9y^2 = 144$?

a) ± 3
b) ± 4
c) ± 9
d) ± 16

10. What conic is described by the equation $3x^2 + 3y^2 + 5x - 12y = 0$?

a) hyperbola
b) ellipse
c) parabola
d) circle

11. Determine one vertex of the hyperbola $x^2 - y^2 = -4$.

a) $(0, 2)$
b) $(0, 4)$
c) $(2, 0)$
d) $(4, 0)$

12. What are the slopes of the asymptotes of the hyperbola $x^2/4 - y^2/9 = -1$?

a) $\pm\frac{2}{3}$
b) $\pm\frac{3}{2}$
c) $\pm\frac{4}{9}$
d) $\pm\frac{9}{4}$

13. Determine the length of the conjugate axis of the hyperbola $x^2/16 - y^2/9 = -1$?

a) 3
b) 6
c) 8
d) 16

14. Find the equation of the line that contains the vertices of the hyperbola $(y-2)^2/9 - (x+1)^2/16 = 1$.

a) $x = -1$
b) $x = 1$
c) $y = -2$
d) $y = 2$

15. For which value of constant A will the equation $3x^2 + Ay^2 = 24$ represent an ellipse?

a) $A = -3$
b) $A = 0$
c) $A = 3$
d) $A = 6$

16. Which conic is represented by the equation $Ax^2 + Cy^2 + Dx + Cy + F = 0$, if $A = -C, A \neq 0$?

a) circle
b) parabola
c) ellipse
d) hyperbola

17. Determine the radius of the circle $x^2 + y^2 + 4x - 2y = 4$.

a) 2
b) 3
c) 4
d) 9

18. Determine the equation of the parabola with vertex $(2, -1)$ that opens left and contains the point $(0, 1)$.

a) $x = -\frac{1}{2}(y + 1)^2 + 2$
b) $x = -2(y + 1)^2 + 2$
c) $x = \frac{1}{2}(y + 1)^2 + 2$
d) $x = 2(y + 1)^2 + 2$

19. Determine the vertex of the parabola given by the equation $2y^2 + 3x + 4y + 14 = 0$.

a) $(-4, -1)$
b) $(-4, 1)$
c) $(-1, -4)$
d) $(1, -4)$

20. Determine the vertex of the parabola $y = 2x^2 - 12x + 20$.

a) $(-2, 3)$
b) $(-3, 2)$
c) $(2, 3)$
d) $(3, 2)$

21. A rectangular hyperbola with centre $(-3, 1)$ has one vertex at $(-3, 5)$. Determine its equation.

a) $(y - 1)^2 - (x - 3)^2 = 4$
b) $(y - 1)^2 - (x - 3)^2 = 16$
c) $(y - 1)^2 - (x + 3)^2 = 4$
d) $(y - 1)^2 - (x + 3)^2 = 16$

22. Determine the equation of the asymptotes of the hyperbola $x^2/9 - (y + 1)^2/16 = 1$.

a) $y = \pm\frac{3}{4}x - 1$
b) $y = \pm\frac{3}{4}x + 1$
c) $y = \pm\frac{4}{3}x - 1$
d) $y = \pm\frac{4}{3}x + 1$

23. A circle with centre $(3, -1)$, goes through the point $(-1, 2)$. Find the equation of the circle.

a) $(x+3)^2+(y-1)^2=5$
b) $(x+3)^2+(y-1)^2=25$
c) $(x-3)^2+(y+1)^2=5$
d) $(x-3)^2+(y+1)^2=25$

24. If $Ax^2 - By^2 = 9,\ A, B > 0$, determine the length of the transverse axis.

a) $3/\sqrt{A}$
b) $3/A$
c) $6/\sqrt{A}$
d) $6/A$

25. If $4x^2 + 9y^2 = A$, and $A > 0$ represents an ellipse, determine the length of the major axis.

a) $\frac{3}{2}\sqrt{A}$
b) $\sqrt{A}$
c) $\frac{3}{2}A$
d) A

26. What condition must be satisfied if the ellipse $Ax^2 + By^2 + Cy = 1$, with $A, B > 0,\ A \neq B$ has its major axis on the x-axis.

a) $A < B,\ C \neq 0$
b) $A > B,\ C \neq 0$
c) $A < B,\ C = 0$
d) $A > B,\ C = 0$

27. If $Ax^2 + By^2 = 1$ is a hyperbola, determine the values for A and B such that its vertices are on the x-axis.

a) $A > 0,\ B > 0$
b) $A > 0,\ B < 0$
c) $A < 0,\ B > 0$
d) $A < 0,\ B < 0$

28. Determine the value of constants $A, C,$ and D, so the equation $Ax^2 + Cy^2 + Dx + Ey = 0$ is a parabola with a horizontal axis of symmetry on the x-axis.

a) $A = 0,\ C \neq 0,\ D \neq 0$
b) $A = 0,\ C = 0,\ D \neq 0$
c) $A \neq 0,\ C \neq 0,\ D = 0$
d) $A = 0,\ C \neq 0,\ D = 0$

29. Determine restrictions on the constants such that $Ax^2 + By^2 + Dx + Ey + F = 0$ represents a parabola that opens down.

a) $AE < 0,\ B = 0$
b) $AE > 0,\ B = 0$
c) $BD < 0,\ A = 0$
d) $BD > 0,\ A = 0$

30. Determine restrictions on the constants such that $Ax^2 + By^2 + Dx + Ey + F = 0$ represents a parabola that has a vertex on the y-axis and opens down

a) $B = D = 0,\ AE > 0$
b) $B = D = 0,\ AE < 0$
c) $A = E = 0,\ BD > 0$
d) $A = E = 0,\ D < 0$

31. Change the conic $4y^2 - 9x^2 - 54x - 8y - 113 = 0$ to standard form.

a) $\frac{(y-1)^2}{9} - \frac{(x-3)^2}{4} = 1$
b) $\frac{(y+1)^2}{9} - \frac{(x+3)^2}{4} = 1$
c) $\frac{(y-1)^2}{9} - \frac{(x+3)^2}{4} = 1$
d) $\frac{(y+1)^2}{9} - \frac{(x-3)^2}{4} = 1$

32. Change the conic $2y^2 + x + 4y + 5 = 0$ to standard form.

a) $x = -2(y+1)^2 - 3$
b) $x = 2(y+1)^2 - 3$
c) $x = -2(y-1)^2 + 3$
d) $x = 2(y-1)^2 + 3$

33. Change the conic $\frac{(x+2)^2}{16} - \frac{(y-1)^2}{9} = 1$ to general form.

a) $9x^2 - 16y^2 + 36x - 32y - 124 = 0$
b) $9x^2 - 16y^2 + 36x + 32y - 124 = 0$
c) $9x^2 - 16y^2 - 36x + 32y - 124 = 0$
d) $9x^2 - 16y^2 - 36x - 32y - 124 = 0$

34. Change the conic $\frac{(x+3)^2}{25} + \frac{(y-4)^2}{16} = 1$ to general form.

a) $16x^2 + 25y^2 + 96x - 200y + 144 = 0$
b) $16x^2 + 25y^2 - 96x - 200y + 144 = 0$
c) $16x^2 + 25y^2 - 96x + 200y + 144 = 0$
d) $16x^2 + 25y^2 + 96x + 200y + 144 = 0$

35. Given the hyperbola $Ax^2 - By^2 = 1$, determine the values for the constants A and B such that the hyperbola will have vertices on the y-axis.

a) $A < 0,\ B < 0$
b) $A > 0,\ B < 0$
c) $A < 0,\ B > 0$
d) $A > 0,\ B > 0$

36. The vertices of an ellipse are $(2, 2)$ and $(2, -6)$. If the ellipse passes through the point $(0, -2)$, determine the equation of the ellipse.

a) $\frac{(x-2)^2}{4} + \frac{(y+2)^2}{16} = 1$
b) $\frac{(x-2)^2}{16} + \frac{(y-2)^2}{4} = 1$
c) $\frac{(x-2)^2}{16} + \frac{(y+2)^2}{4} = 1$
d) $\frac{(x+2)^2}{4} + \frac{(y-2)^2}{16} = 1$

37. Determine the best answer for F such that $4x^2 + 2y^2 + 8x - 12y + F = 0$ is an ellipse.

a) $F < 10$
b) $F > 10$
c) $F < 22$
d) $F > 22$

38. Determine an equation for one of the asymptotes of the hyperbola $(x+3)^2/9 - (y-1)^2/4 = 1$.

a) $y = \frac{2}{3}x - 1$
b) $y = \frac{2}{3}x + 3$
c) $y = \frac{3}{2}x + 3$
d) $y = \frac{2}{3}x + 1$

39. Determine the coordinates of the highest point on the graph of $x^2 + y^2 - 6x + 4y - 12 = 0$.

a) $(-3, 2)$
b) $(-3, 7)$
c) $(3, -2)$
d) $(3, 3)$

40. A hyperbola $y^2 - x^2 = a^2$ is intersected by all vertical lines. Which point could be a point of intersection?

a) $(-5, 2)$
b) $(4, -3)$
c) $(2, -5)$
d) $(3, 2)$

41. A horizontal line segment is drawn 20 units from the centre of the ellipse $x^2/60^2 + y^2/40^2 = 1$. Determine the length of this line segment.

a) $30\sqrt{2}$
b) $30\sqrt{3}$
c) $60\sqrt{2}$
d) $60\sqrt{3}$

42. A rectangular hyperbola of the form $y^2 - x^2 = a^2$ has points $(3, 6)$ and $(-5, k)$ on the graph. Determine a value of *k*.

a) 7.07
b) 7.21
c) 7.35
d) 7.49

43. The endpoints of the transverse axis of a hyperbola are $(-4, -2)$ and $(8, -2)$. If one of the asymptotes has slope $4/3$, determine the equation of the hyperbola.

a) $\frac{(x-2)^2}{36} - \frac{(y+2)^2}{16} = 1$
b) $\frac{(x+2)^2}{9} - \frac{(y-2)^2}{16} = 1$
c) $\frac{(x-2)^2}{36} - \frac{(y+2)^2}{64} = 1$
d) $\frac{(x+2)^2}{36} - \frac{(y-2)^2}{64} = 1$

44. Determine the value of k, such that the transverse axis of the hyperbola $x^2/k - y^2 = 1$ is 2 units longer than the major axis of the ellipse $x^2/9 + y^2/4 = 1$.

a) 5
b) 8
c) 16
d) 25

45. A parabola has vertex $(8, -2)$, with a horizontal axis of symmetry and passes through the origin. Determine an equation of the parabola.

a) $x = -\frac{1}{2}(y+2)^2 + 8$
b) $x = -2(y+2)^2 + 8$
c) $x = \frac{1}{2}(y-2)^2 - 8$
d) $x = 2(y-2)^2 - 8$

46. A parabola has vertex $(-3, 1)$ and passes through the points $(-7, -6)$ and $(1, -6)$. Determine the equation of this parabola.

a) $y = -\frac{7}{16}(x + 3)^2 + 1$
b) $y = -\frac{5}{16}(x + 3)^2 + 1$
c) $y = -\frac{1}{20}(x + 3)^2 + 1$
d) $y = \frac{1}{20}(x - 3)^2 + 1$

47. A parabola has vertex $(3, -1)$ and passes through the point $(7, 2)$, opening to the right. Determine an equation of this parabola.

a) $y = -\frac{3}{16}(x - 3)^2 - 1$
b) $y = \frac{1}{100}(x + 3)^2 + 1$
c) $x = \frac{4}{9}(y + 1)^2 + 3$
d) $x = 10(y - 1)^2 - 3$

48. The vertices of a hyperbola are $(2, 3)$ and $(2, -5)$. If one of the asymptotes has a slope of $2/3$, determine an equation of the hyperbola.

a) $\frac{(y+1)^2}{4} - \frac{(x-2)^2}{9} = 1$
b) $\frac{(y+1)^2}{16} - \frac{(x-2)^2}{36} = 1$
c) $\frac{(y-1)^2}{4} - \frac{(x+2)^2}{9} = 1$
d) $\frac{(y-1)^2}{16} - \frac{(x+2)^2}{36} = 1$

49. Determine the equation of a circle that intersects the x-axis at $(2, 0)$ and $(8, 0)$, and is tangent to the y-axis at $(0, 4)$.

a) $(x + 5)^2 + (y + 4)^2 = 5$
b) $(x + 5)^2 + (y + 4)^2 = 25$
c) $(x - 5)^2 + (y - 4)^2 = 5$
d) $(x - 5)^2 + (y - 4)^2 = 25$

50. Determine the equation of a rectangular hyperbola with vertices $(-3, -1)$ and $(-3, 5)$.

a) $(x + 3)^2 - (y - 2)^2 = 9$
b) $(x - 3)^2 - (y + 2)^2 = 9$
c) $(y - 2)^2 - (x + 3)^2 = 9$
d) $(y + 2)^2 - (x - 3)^2 = 9$

Sequence and Series - Solutions

1.1 Sequences

1. **a)** natural **b)** finite **c)** infinite **d)** recursive **e)** $t_n = a + (n-1)d$

2. **a)** $-1, 2, 7, 14$ **b)** $\frac{3}{2}, \frac{4}{3}, \frac{5}{4}, \frac{6}{5}$ **c)** $1, -4, 9, -16$ **d)** $1, \frac{9}{5}, 3, \frac{81}{17}$ **e)** $2, 1, \frac{8}{9}, 1$ **f)** $\frac{2}{3}, \frac{4}{9}, \frac{8}{27}, \frac{16}{81}$

3. **a)** $\frac{1}{n}$ **b)** $\frac{1}{2^{n-1}}$ **c)** $\left(\frac{2}{3}\right)^n$ **d)** $(-1)^{n+1} \cdot 2n$

4. **a)** 4, 6, 8, 10 **b)** 3, − 1, 4, 0 **c)** 2, 3, 5, 8 **d)** − 1, 1, 2, 9

5. **a)** 20 **b)** 22 **c)** 50 **d)** 32 **e)** 15 **f)** 194

6. **a)** $\sum_{k=1}^{4}(2k-1)$ **b)** $\sum_{k=1}^{5} k^2$ **c)** $\sum_{k=1}^{n} \frac{k}{k+1}$ **d)** $\sum_{k=1}^{n} \frac{5^k}{k}$

7. **a)** 7, 11, 15, 19, 23 **b)** 15, 12, 9, 6, 3 **c)** 4, 6, 8, 10, 12 **d)** − 1, − 4, − 7, − 10, − 13

e) $-5, -\frac{23}{4}, -\frac{13}{2}, -\frac{29}{4}, -8$ **f)** $-\frac{2}{3}, -\frac{7}{15}, -\frac{4}{15}, -\frac{1}{15}, \frac{2}{15}$

8. **a)** 38 **b)** $-\frac{4}{3}$ **c)** $\frac{15}{4}$ **d)** − 21.25 **e)** 1.2 **f)** − 25.75

9. **a)** 13 **b)** 18 **c)** 44 **d)** 18 **e)** 33 **f)** 42

10. **a)** − 5 **b)** − 4 **c)** 47 **d)** 15 **e)** 21 **f)** $40\frac{1}{3}$

11. **a)** $-\frac{3}{2}$ **b)** 1 **c)** − 4 **d)** − 2 **e)** − 3, 4 **f)** $-3, \frac{1}{2}$

12. $d =$ difference

13. 1, 1, 2, 3, 5, 8, 13

14. $t = a + (n-1)d \rightarrow 50\,000 = 23\,750 + (n-1)(1250) \rightarrow 21 = n - 1 \rightarrow n = 22$ years

15. $t = a + (n-1)d \rightarrow 140 = 8 + (n-1)(4) \rightarrow 33 = n - 1 \rightarrow n = 34$, row 34

16. $t = a + (n-1)d \rightarrow t = 8 + (120-1)(0.75) \rightarrow t = 97.25$; \$97.25

17. $t = a + (n-1)d \rightarrow 24 = 8 + (n-1)\left(\frac{1}{4}\right) \rightarrow 64 = n - 1 \rightarrow n = 65$ days

September has 30 days, October has 31 days, together they have 61 days. Therefore he died November 4th.

18. $\frac{(x-3)+(3x-11)}{2} = \frac{x^2}{25} + 9 \rightarrow x^2 - 50x + 400 = 0 \rightarrow (x-40)(x-10) = 0 \rightarrow x = 10, 40$

$x = 10$: 7, 13, 19, 25; $x = 40$: 37, 73, 109, 145; The fourth term is 25 or 145.

19. $\frac{(2x-1)+(11-x^2)}{2} = x^2 - 3 \rightarrow 3x^2 - 2x - 16 = 0 \rightarrow (3x-8)(x+2) = 0 \rightarrow x = -2, \frac{8}{3}$

$x = -2$: $-5, \_\_\_, 1, \_\_\_, 7$; $x = \frac{8}{3}$: $\frac{39}{9}, \_\_\_, \frac{37}{9}, \_\_\_, \frac{35}{9}$; The second term is -2 or $\frac{38}{9}$.

1.2 Arithmetic Series

1. **a)** $n^2 + 2n$ **b)** $\frac{3n^2 - 5n}{2}$ **c)** 1027 **d)** 1224 **e)** 24 500 **f)** $338\sqrt{5}$ **g)** 120 **h)** − 11 703 **i)** $\frac{531}{8}$ **j)** $-\frac{686}{3}$

k) 101.7 **l)** 1311.04

2. **a)** 730 **b)** 798 **c)** 14 588 **d)** 18 **e)** $\frac{4}{13}$ **f)** 6293 **g)** − 361 **h)** 4940 **i)** − 2040 **j)** 490

3. **a)** 5050 **b)** 15 150 **c)** 7592 **d)** 648 **e)** 636.5 **f)** − 2500

4. **a)** $\frac{20}{3}, \frac{25}{3}$ **b)** $\frac{15}{4}, \frac{9}{2}, \frac{21}{4}$ **c)** $\frac{2a+b}{3}, \frac{a+2b}{3}$ **d)** $\frac{3a+b}{4}, \frac{a+b}{2}, \frac{a+3b}{4}$

5. 8, 14

6. $-5a + 5b + 5$

7. Consider the last term in each row: $1, 3, 6, 10 \rightarrow 1, 1+2, 1+2+3, 1+2+3+4, \ldots, 1+2+\cdots+20$

$S = \frac{n}{2}(2a + (n-1)d) \rightarrow \frac{20}{2}((2)(1) + (20-1)(1)) = 210$

8. $S = \frac{n}{2}(2a + (n-1)d) \rightarrow 0 = \frac{n}{2}((2)(1491) + (n-1)(-7)) \rightarrow 0 = 2982 + (n-1)(-7) \rightarrow 426 = n - 1 \rightarrow n = 427$

9. $t = a + (n-1)d \rightarrow t = 8 + (50-1)(4) \rightarrow t = 204$ seats

10. On the 18th birthday, the child has had 19 birthdays. $S = \frac{n}{2}(2a + (n-1)d) \to \frac{19}{2}((2)(1000) + (19-1)(100)) = \$36\,100$

11. The first multiple of 6 is 54. The last multiple of 6 is 498.

$t = a + (n-1)d \to 498 = 54 + (n-1)(6) \to n = 75;\ S = \frac{n}{2}(a+l) \to S = \frac{75}{2}(54 + 498) = 20\,700$

12. $a + (a+d) + (a+2d) = 3 \to a + d = 1$

$a^2 + (a+d)^2 + (a+2d)^2 = 75 \to (1-d)^2 + 1 + (1+d)^2 = 75 \to d^2 = 36 \to d = \pm 6 \to a = -5, 7$

The first three numbers are $-5, 1, 7$ or $7, 1, -5$.

13. The first person shakes 19 hands, the second person shakes 18 hands, and so on.

$19 + 18 + 17 + \cdots + 1 \to S = \frac{n}{2}(a+l) \to S = \frac{19}{2}(19+1) = 190$ handshakes

14. $S = \frac{n}{2}(a+l) = 234 \to n\left(\frac{a+l}{2}\right) = 234 \to 26n = 234 \to n = 9$ terms

1.3 Geometric Sequences

1. **a)** no **b)** no **c)** yes, $-\frac{1}{2}$ **d)** yes, -1 **e)** no **f)** no **g)** yes, $\frac{2}{3}$ **h)** yes, $-\frac{5}{3}$ **i)** yes, $4x^2y^3$ **j)** yes, $\sqrt{3}$

2. **a)** 1, 4, 16, 64, 256 **b)** 1, 2, 4, 8, 16 or 1, -2, 4, -8, 16 **c)** $\frac{1}{2}, \frac{1}{4}, \frac{1}{8}, \frac{1}{16}, \frac{1}{32}$

d) 4, -6, 9, -13.5, 20.25 **e)** 162, 54, 18, 6, 2 **f)** $1, \sqrt{3}, 3, 3\sqrt{3}, 9$ or $1, -\sqrt{3}, 3, -3\sqrt{3}, 9$

g) $3, 3^{x+1}, 3^{2x+1}, 3^{3x+1}, 3^{4x+1}$ or $3, -3^{x+1}, 3^{2x+1}, -3^{3x+1}, 3^{4x+1}$

h) $1, x^2, x^4, x^6, x^8$ or $1, -x^2, x^4, -x^6, x^8$ **i)** $5, 5^{2x-1}, 5^{4x-3}, 5^{6x-5}, 5^{8x-7}$ **j)** $1, -\frac{x}{3}, \frac{x^2}{9}, -\frac{x^3}{27}, \frac{x^4}{81}$

3. **a)** $-\sqrt{5}$ or $\sqrt{5}$ **b)** $-\frac{1}{2}$ or $\frac{1}{2}$ **c)** $\sqrt{2}$ **d)** $\sqrt[6]{2}$

4. **a)** 8 **b)** $\frac{1}{27}$ **c)** 144 **d)** ± 160 **e)** 9 **f)** 12 **g)** $\frac{1}{3}$ **h)** $\frac{1}{32}$ **i)** ± 3 **j)** $\pm\sqrt{2}$ **k)** 81 **l)** 0.01

5. $t = ar^{n-1} \to b = ar^3 \to r = \sqrt[3]{\frac{b}{a}} \to r = \frac{\sqrt[3]{a^2b}}{a}$; Therefore: $a, \sqrt[3]{a^2b}, \sqrt[3]{ab^2}, b$.

6. $t_n = ar^{n-1} \to t_n = a\left(\frac{1}{b}\right)^{n-1};\ t_{n-1} = a\left(\frac{1}{b}\right)^{n-2};\ t_n - t_{n-1} = a\left(\frac{1}{b}\right)^{n-1} - a\left(\frac{1}{b}\right)^{n-2} \to$

$t_n - t_{n-1} = a\left(\frac{1}{b}\right)^n \cdot b - a\left(\frac{1}{b}\right)^n \cdot b^2 \to ab(1-b)\left(\frac{1}{b}\right)^n$ or $\frac{a(1-b)}{b^{n-1}}$

7. $\frac{x}{x-1} = \frac{x+2}{x} \to x^2 + x - 2 = x^2 \to x = 2$

8. $\frac{5-x}{x-2} = \frac{5x-7}{5-x} \to 5x^2 - 17x + 14 = x^2 - 10x + 25 \to 4x^2 - 7x - 11 = 0 \to (4x-11)(x+1) = 0 \to x = -1, \frac{11}{4}$

$x = -1 \to r = -2,\ x = \frac{11}{4} \to r = 3$

9. $\frac{4+x}{-2+x} = \frac{19+x}{4+x} \to x^2 + 17x - 38 = x^2 + 8x + 16 \to 9x = 54 \to x = 6$

10. $\sqrt{2} \cdot r = \sqrt[3]{2} \to r = \frac{2^{\frac{1}{3}}}{2^{\frac{1}{2}}} \to r = 2^{-\frac{1}{6}};\ t_4 = ar^3 \to t_4 = (2^{\frac{1}{2}})(2^{-\frac{1}{6}})^3 \to t_4 = 1$

11. $a \cdot ar \cdot ar^2 = -8 \to a^3r^3 = -8 \to ar = -2;\ a + ar + ar^2 = \frac{14}{3} \to -\frac{2}{r} + (-2) + (-2r) = \frac{14}{3} \to$

$3r^2 + 10r + 3 = 0 \to (r+3)(3r+1) = 0 \to r = -\frac{1}{3}, -3$

12. $\frac{3+y}{2} = x;\ \frac{y}{x} = \frac{25}{y} \to 25x = y^2 \to 25\left(\frac{3+y}{2}\right) = y^2 \to 2y^2 - 25y - 75 = 0 \to (2y+5)(y-15) = 0 \to y = -\frac{5}{2}, 15$

$x = \frac{1}{4}, y = -\frac{5}{2}$ or $x = 9, y = 15$

13. The number of terms is $2010 - 1973 + 1 = 38$. $t_n = ar^{n-1} \to t_{38} = 400(1.05)^{37} = 2433$ students

14. $t_n = ar^{n-1} \to t_8 = 28\,000(1.06)^7 = \$42\,101.65$

15. $t_n = ar^{n-1} \to t_{11} = 1(0.75)^{10} = 0.056$ left; $1 - 0.056 = 0.944$; 94.4% of the air is removed.

16. $n = 6$ terms in 5 years (0, 1, 2, 3, 4, 5). $t_n = ar^{n-1} \to t_6 = 40\,000(0.84)^5 = \$16\,728.48$

17. $t_n = ar^{n-1} \to t_{13} = 45(0.98)^{12} = 35.3$ cm

18. $t_n = ar^{n-1} \to 0.20 < 10(0.75)^{n-1} \to 0.02 < 0.75^{n-1};\ 0.75^{14-1} = 0.023,\ 0.75^{15-1} = 0.0178$ Therefore 14 bounces are needed.

19. $t_n = ar^{n-1} \to t_8 = 0.75(1.2)^7 = \$2.69$

20. $50, 45, \ldots \to r = \frac{45}{50} = 0.9;\ t_n = ar^{n-1} \to t_6 = 50(0.9)^5 = 29.5$; Pure antifreeze is $50 - 29.5 = 20.5\,l$

1.4 Geometric Series

1. **a)** 15.98 **b)** -3066 **c)** 3 **d)** 33.25 **e)** 23.25 **f)** 3060 or -1020 **g)** 12 **h)** $-4,\ 3$ **i)** 0 **j)** -1

2. **a)** 28 **b)** $b-7$ **c)** $10-a$ **d)** $b-a+1$

3. **a)** 765 **b)** $-265\,720$ **c)** 9.995 **d)** 0.75 **e)** 0.20 **f)** 2.597 **g)** $2\left(1-\left(\frac{2}{3}\right)^n\right)$ **h)** $2(3^n-1)$

4. **a)** $\sum_{k=1}^{5} 3\cdot 2^{k-1}$ **b)** $\sum_{k=1}^{9} 2\cdot(-3)^{k-1}$ **c)** $\sum_{k=1}^{12} 3\cdot(-2)^{k-5}$ **d)** $\sum_{k=1}^{14}\left(\frac{1}{2}\right)^{k-4}$

5. $a^0+a^1+a^2=31 \rightarrow a^2+a-30=0 \rightarrow (a+6)(a-5)=0 \rightarrow a=-6,5$

6. $S_n=\frac{a-rl}{1-r} \rightarrow S_n=\frac{2^0-2(2^{n-1})}{1-2} \rightarrow S_n=\frac{1-2^n}{-1} \rightarrow S_n=2^n-1$; Therefore 2^n is larger by 1 unit.

7. $32+16+8+4+2+1=63$; By proper subsets: $2^n-1=2^6-1=64-1=63$

8. $S_n=\frac{a-rl}{1-r} \rightarrow 101.01=\frac{100-0.01r}{1-r} \rightarrow 101.01-101.01r=100-0.01r \rightarrow 101r=1.01 \rightarrow r=\frac{1}{100}$

$t_n=ar^{n-1} \rightarrow 0.01=100\left(\frac{1}{100}\right)^{n-1} \rightarrow 10^{-4}=10^{-2(n-1)} \rightarrow -4=-2(n-1) \rightarrow n=3$

i) $n=3$ *ii)* $r=\frac{1}{100}$

9. $S_{30}=1000(1.1)+1000(1.1)^2+1000(1.1)^3+\cdots+1000(1.1)^{30}$

$S_{30}=\frac{a-ar^n}{1-r}=\frac{1100-1100(1.1)^{30}}{1-1.1}=\$180\,943.43$; The value of the annuity is \$180 943.43.

Accumulated interest is \$180 943.43 − \$30 000 = \$150 943.43

10.

$$\begin{array}{l} \quad 1+r+r^2+r^3+\cdots+r^{n-1} \\ \hfill 1-r \\ \hline -r-r^2-r^3-\cdots-r^{n-1}-r^n \\ 1+r+r^2+r^3+\cdots+r^{n-1} \\ \hline 1 \hfill -r^n \end{array}$$

Simplifies to $1-r^n$.

11. *i)* $t_6=40\,000(1.05)^5=\$51\,051.26$; $t_6=43\,000(1.03)^5=\$49\,848.79$; The \$40 000 initial pay is better after 5 years by \$1202.47.

ii) $S_5=\frac{a-ar^n}{1-r}=\frac{40\,000-40\,000(1.05)^5}{1-1.05}=\$221\,025.25$ $\quad S_5=\frac{43\,000-43\,000(1.03)^5}{1-1.03}=\$228\,292.84$

The \$43 000 initial pay is better after 5 years by \$7267.59.

12. $S_5=\frac{a-ar^n}{1-r} \rightarrow 155\,680.05=\frac{a-a(1.1)^5}{1-1.1} \rightarrow a-1.61051a=-15\,568.005 \rightarrow -0.61051a=-15\,568.005 \rightarrow a=\$25\,500$

13. *i)* $a=30,\ r=\frac{1}{2};\ t_5=30\left(\frac{1}{2}\right)^{5-1}=\frac{15}{8}$ *ii)* $S_5=\frac{a-ar^n}{1-r} \rightarrow S_5=\frac{30-30\left(\frac{1}{2}\right)^5}{1-\frac{1}{2}}=\frac{465}{8}=58.125$

14. The first day Terry Fox walks $120\times 0.40=48$ km.

$S_n=\frac{a-ar^n}{1-r} \rightarrow S_6=\frac{48-48(0.40)^6}{1-0.40}=79.7$ Terry has $120-79.7=40.3$ km left to walk.

15. A: $S_n=\frac{n}{2}(2a+(n-1)d) \rightarrow S_{1000}=\frac{1000}{2}(2\cdot 1000+999(-1))=500\,500$ $\quad B$: $S_n=\frac{a-ar^n}{1-r} \rightarrow S_{19}=\frac{1-1(2)^{19}}{1-2}=524\,287$

B is larger by 23 787.

16. $a+ar=4 \rightarrow a(1+r)=4 \rightarrow 1+r=\frac{4}{a}$; $\quad ar^2+ar^3=36 \rightarrow ar^2(1+r)=36 \rightarrow ar^2\left(\frac{4}{a}\right)=36 \rightarrow r^2=9 \rightarrow r=\pm 3$

$r=3 \rightarrow a+3a=4 \rightarrow a=1,\quad r=-3 \rightarrow 3-3a=4 \rightarrow a=-2;\ a=1,-2$

17. $ar^2+ar^3=-6 \rightarrow ar^2(1+r)=-6 \rightarrow 1+r=-\frac{6}{ar^2}$; $\quad ar^3+ar^4=-3 \rightarrow ar^3(1+r)=-3 \rightarrow ar^3\left(-\frac{6}{ar^2}\right)=-3 \rightarrow r=\frac{1}{2}$

$ar^2+ar^3=-6 \rightarrow a\left(\frac{1}{4}\right)+a\left(\frac{1}{8}\right)=-6 \rightarrow a=-16$

18. $S_n=2(3^n-1) \rightarrow S_1=a_1=2(3^1-1)=4,\ S_2=2(3^2-1)=16;\ a_2=S_2-S_1=16-4=12$

$r=\frac{a_2}{a_1}=\frac{12}{4}=3;\ t_n=ar^{n-1} \rightarrow t_5=4(3)^4=324$

19. The first motion is downward. The second to fourth motion is upwards and downwards.

$S_n=\frac{a-ar^n}{1-r} \rightarrow S_5=\frac{72-72\left(\frac{3}{4}\right)^4}{1-\frac{3}{4}}-36=160.875$ ft

20. According to the poem, there was only one person, the speaker, definitely going to St. Ives. However if the kits, cats, sacks, and wives and man also decided to go to St. Ives, there would be 2802 traveling to St. Ives.
$1+7+7^2+7^3+7^4=2801$ kits, cats, sacks, wives and man

1.5 Infinite Geometric Series

1. **a)** converge, $r = \frac{1}{4}$ **b)** diverge, $r = 2$ **c)** converge, $r = \frac{1}{1.01}$ **d)** converge, $r = -\frac{1}{2}$

e) converge, $r = \frac{1}{2}$ **f)** diverge, $r = 1$

2. **a)** $\frac{2}{3}$ **b)** $\frac{9}{2}$ **c)** $\frac{40}{33}$ **d)** infinite sum **e)** $\frac{81}{10}$ **f)** -4 **g)** infinite sum **h)** 20

3. **a)** 3 **b)** 3 **c)** 1 **d)** $\frac{5}{2}$ **e)** $-\frac{4}{15}$ **f)** $\frac{9}{4}$ **g)** $\frac{25}{8}$ **h)** 1 **i)** $\frac{40}{7}$ **j)** $\frac{8}{7}$

4. **a)** $\frac{38}{99}$ **b)** $\frac{7}{18}$ **c)** $\frac{53}{37}$ **d)** $\frac{709}{495}$

5. **a)** $\frac{2}{7}$ **b)** $\varnothing$ **c)** $60°,\ 300°$ **d)** $\frac{1}{4}$

6. **a)** $\sum_{j=5}^{\infty} 5^{j-3}\cdot 2^{-j+3}$ **b)** $\sum_{j=4}^{\infty} 2^{3j-13}$ **c)** $\sum_{k=3}^{\infty} 3^{3-k}$ **d)** $\sum_{x=1}^{\infty} 4^{-10-3x}$

7. $r = 1 + x;\ -1 < r < 1 \rightarrow -1 < 1 + x < 1 \rightarrow -2 < x < 0$

8. $r = \frac{1}{3}x;\ -1 < r < 1 \rightarrow -1 < \frac{1}{3}x < 1 \rightarrow -3 < x < 3$

9. If $a = 9$ and $S_\infty = 4$, then $S_\infty = \frac{a}{1-r} \rightarrow 4 = \frac{9}{1-r} \rightarrow 4 - 4r = 9 \rightarrow r = -\frac{5}{4}$.

But an infinite geometric series has a finite sum only if $-1 < r < 1$ and $r = -\frac{5}{4}$ is not in this interval.

10. $S_\infty = \frac{a}{1-r} \rightarrow \frac{3}{1-r} > 4 \rightarrow 3 > 4 - 4r \rightarrow 4r > 1 \rightarrow r > \frac{1}{4}$, therefore $\frac{1}{4} < r < 1$

11. $a = 4(ar + ar^2 + ar^3 + \cdots) = 2 \rightarrow 2 = 4(2r + 2r^2 + 2r^3 + \cdots) = 8(r + r^2 + r^3 + \cdots) \rightarrow \frac{1}{4} = r + r^2 + r^3 + \cdots$

For the series $r + r^2 + r^3 + \cdots$, $a = r$, therefore $S_\infty = \frac{a}{1-r} = \frac{r}{1-r} = \frac{1}{4} \rightarrow 4r = 1 - r \rightarrow r = \frac{1}{5}$

For the original series $2 + 2r + 2r^2 + \cdots$, with $r = \frac{1}{5} < 1$, $S_\infty = \frac{2}{1-\frac{1}{5}} = \frac{2}{\frac{4}{5}} = \frac{5}{2}$

12. $S_\infty = \frac{a}{1-r} = \frac{100}{1-0.96} = 2500$ m

13. $a_1 = 2\cdot 4 = 8,\ a_2 = 1\cdot 2 = 2 \rightarrow r = \frac{1}{4} < 1;\ S_\infty = \frac{a}{1-r} = \frac{8}{1-\frac{1}{4}} = \frac{32}{3}$

14. $S_\infty = \frac{a}{1-r} = \frac{2}{1-\frac{2}{3}} = 6$ cm. Therefore it is impossible to drive the 6.25 cm nail completely into the board.

15. $S_\infty = \frac{a}{1-r} = \frac{30}{1-0.90} = 300$ cm

16. $r = \frac{60}{72} = \frac{5}{6};\ S_\infty = \frac{a}{1-r} = \frac{72}{1-\frac{5}{6}} = 432$ grams

17.

$8\sqrt{2}$ 8

8

The first is perimeter is 64. The second perimeter is $32\sqrt{2}$ by Pythagoras Theorem.

$r = \frac{32\sqrt{2}}{64} = \frac{\sqrt{2}}{2};\ S_\infty = \frac{a}{1-r} = \frac{64}{1-\frac{\sqrt{2}}{2}} = 218.51$ cm

18. The first perimeter is 30. The second perimeter is 15.

$r = \frac{15}{30} = \frac{1}{2};\ S_\infty = \frac{a}{1-r} = \frac{30}{1-\frac{1}{2}} = 60$ cm

19. **a)** $S_\infty = \frac{a}{1-r} = \frac{20}{1-\frac{3}{4}} - 10 = 70$ m **b)** $S_{10} = \frac{a - ar^n}{1-r} = \frac{20 - 20\left(\frac{3}{4}\right)^{10}}{1-\frac{3}{4}} - 10 = 65.495$ m

c) $S_\infty - S_{10} = 70 - 65.495 = 4.505$ m

20. **a)** $S_8 = \frac{a - ar^n}{1-r} = \frac{240 - 240(0.8)^8}{1-0.8} - 120 = 878.67$ m **b)** $t_9 = ar^{n-1} = 120(0.8)^{9-1} = 20.13$ m

c) $S_\infty = \frac{a}{1-r} = \frac{240}{1-0.8} - 120 = 1080$ m

1.6 Chapter Review

Answers

1. d	**8.** c	**15.** b	**22.** d	**29.** a	**36.** b	**43.** a	**50.** b
2. b	**9.** b	**16.** b	**23.** c	**30.** a	**37.** a	**44.** b	**51.** c
3. b	**10.** b	**17.** d	**24.** b	**31.** d	**38.** c	**45.** c	**52.** b
4. c	**11.** a	**18.** b	**25.** d	**32.** b	**39.** d	**46.** c	**53.** a
5. d	**12.** c	**19.** c	**26.** c	**33.** b	**40.** b	**47.** a	
6. d	**13.** c	**20.** a	**27.** b	**34.** c	**41.** d	**48.** a	
7. b	**14.** a	**21.** d	**28.** a	**35.** a	**42.** a	**49.** a	

Solutions

1. $r = \frac{1}{2}$ in d (d)

2. $t_{25} = a + (n-1)d = -2 + 24(-6) = -146$ (b)

3. $2r = -1 \rightarrow r = -\frac{1}{2}$ (b)

4. $x + x = 2x,\ 2x + x = 3x,\ 3x + x = 4x$ (c)

5. $a, \_\_\_, \_\_\_, b\ ;\ t = ar^{n-1} \rightarrow b = ar^3 \rightarrow r^3 = \frac{b}{a} \rightarrow r = \sqrt[3]{\frac{b}{a}}$ (d)

6. $t = a + (n-1)d \rightarrow -111 = 5 + (n-1)(-4) \rightarrow -116 = -4(n-1) \rightarrow n - 1 = 29 \rightarrow n = 30$ (d)

7. $16r = -12 \rightarrow r = -\frac{3}{4};\ S = \frac{a - ar^n}{1 - r} = \frac{16 - 16\left(-\frac{3}{4}\right)^{15}}{1 + \frac{3}{4}} = 9.27$ (b)

8. $\frac{a^3}{b} r = a^2 \rightarrow r = \frac{b}{a},\ t = ar^{n-1} \rightarrow \frac{b^{15}}{a^{13}} = \frac{a^3}{b}\left(\frac{b}{a}\right)^{n-1} \rightarrow \left(\frac{b}{a}\right)^{n-1} = \left(\frac{b}{a}\right)^{16} \rightarrow n - 1 = 16 \rightarrow n = 17$ (c)

9. $t = a + (n-1)d \rightarrow -111 = 5 + (n-1)(-4) \rightarrow -116 = -4(n-1) \rightarrow n - 1 = 29 \rightarrow n = 30$

$S = \frac{n}{2}(a + l) = \frac{30}{2}(5 + (-11)) = -1590$ (b)

10. $S_{n-1} + t_n = S_n$ (b)

11. $S_\infty = \frac{a}{1 - r} = \frac{\frac{2}{100}}{1 - \frac{1}{10}} = \frac{1}{45};\ \frac{1}{45} + \frac{3}{10} = \frac{2}{90} + \frac{27}{90} = \frac{29}{90}$ (a)

12. If $n = 2$ is the first term, then $n = 5$ is the fourth term. $3n - 1 = 3(5) - 1 = 14$ (c)

13. $S = \frac{a - ar^n}{1 - r} \rightarrow 6560 = \frac{a - a(3)^8}{1 - 3} \rightarrow a - 6561a = -13120 \rightarrow -6560a = -13120 \rightarrow a = 2$ (c)

14. $S_\infty = \frac{a}{1 - r} \rightarrow 18 = \frac{a}{1 - \frac{2}{3}} \rightarrow a = 6\ ;\ t = ar^{n-1} \rightarrow t_5 = 6\left(\frac{2}{3}\right)^4 = \frac{32}{27} = 1\frac{5}{27}$ (a)

15. $(5n - 1) - (n + 3) + 1 = 45 \rightarrow 4n - 3 = 45 \rightarrow 4n = 48 \rightarrow n = 12$ (b)

16. $t_n = 16\left(-\frac{3}{2}\right)^{n-1},\ a = 16,\ r = -\frac{3}{2} \rightarrow S = \frac{a - ar^n}{1 - r} = \frac{16 - 16\left(-\frac{3}{2}\right)^{10}}{1 - \left(-\frac{3}{2}\right)} = -362.66$ (b)

17. $x \cdot r = \frac{x + 1}{x} \rightarrow r = \frac{x + 1}{x^2}\ ;\ x,\ \frac{x + 1}{x},\ \frac{(x + 1)^2}{x^3},\ \frac{(x + 1)^3}{x^5}$ (d)

18. $a = f(1) = 2^1 = 2,\ r - 2,\ l = f(9) = 2^9 = 512 \rightarrow S_n = \frac{a - rl}{1 - r} = \frac{2 - 2 \cdot 512}{1 - 2} = 1022$ (b)

19. $S_n = \frac{n}{2}(a + l) = \frac{30}{2}\left(\frac{2}{3} + 20\right) = 310$ (c)

20. $S = \frac{a - ar^n}{1 - r} = \frac{12 - 12(-1.2)^{20}}{1 + 1.2} = -203.66$ (a)

21. $r = 1 - x\ ;\ -1 < r < 1 \rightarrow -1 < 1 - x < 1 \rightarrow -2 < -x < 0 \rightarrow 2 > x > 0 \rightarrow 0 < x < 2$ (d)

22. $r = \frac{1}{3}x\ ;\ -1 < r < 1 \rightarrow -1 < \frac{1}{3}x < 1 \rightarrow -3 < x < 3$ (d)

23. $a = x,\ ar^3 = 2\sqrt{2}x^4 \rightarrow xr^3 = 2\sqrt{2}x^4 \rightarrow r^3 = 2\sqrt{2}x^3 \rightarrow r = \sqrt{2}x;\ t_n = ar^{n-1} \rightarrow t_7 = x(\sqrt{2}x)^6 = 8x^7$ (c)

24. $S = \frac{a - ar^n}{1 - r} \rightarrow 39\,020 = \frac{a - a(1.04)^3}{1 - 1.04} \rightarrow a - 1.124864a = -1560.8 \rightarrow a = 12\,500$ (b)

25. $\frac{y - 3}{y} = \frac{y}{3y + 4} \rightarrow 3y^2 - 5y - 12 = y^2 \rightarrow 2y^2 - 5y - 12 = 0 \rightarrow (2y + 3)(y - 4) = 0 \rightarrow y = -\frac{3}{2}, 4$ (d)

26. $x^0 + x + x^2 = 7 \rightarrow x^2 + x + 1 = 7 \rightarrow x^2 + x - 6 = 0 \rightarrow (x + 3)(x - 2) = 0 \rightarrow x = 2, -3$ (c)

27. $t = a + (n-1)d = 8 + (28 - 1)(4) = 116$ (b)

28. $a = 10\left(-\frac{2}{5}\right)^2 = 10\left(\frac{4}{25}\right) = \frac{8}{5},\ S_\infty = \frac{a}{1-r} = \frac{\frac{8}{5}}{1+\frac{2}{5}} = \frac{8}{7}$ (a)

29. $\frac{11+x}{15+x} = \frac{15+x}{21+x} \rightarrow 231 + 32x + x^2 = 225 + 30x + x^2 \rightarrow 2x = -6 \rightarrow x = -3$ (a)

30. $S_\infty = \frac{a}{1-r} \rightarrow 1 = \frac{a}{1+\frac{2}{3}} \rightarrow a = \frac{5}{3}$; 2nd term is $ar = \frac{5}{3}\left(-\frac{2}{3}\right) = -\frac{10}{9}$ (a)

31. $a = 2(-3)^2 = 18,\ n = 7 - 3 + 1 = 5,\ S = \frac{a - ar^n}{1-r} = \frac{18 - 18(-3)^5}{1+3} = 1098$ (d)

32. From the start (zero years) to the 10th year is 11 terms.
1st year $= 42\,000 \times 0.8 = 33\,600$; 2nd to 10th year: $t = ar^{n-1} \rightarrow t = 33\,600(0.85)^9 = 7782$ (b)

33. $S_n = \frac{n}{2}(a + l) = \frac{n}{2}(3 + 4n - 1) = \frac{n}{2}(4n + 2) = 2n^2 + n$ (b)

34. $t_n = ar^{n-1} \rightarrow 162 = a(-3)^4 \rightarrow 81a = 162 \rightarrow a = 2$ (c)

35. $8x + 7x + 6x = 168 \rightarrow 21x = 168 \rightarrow x = 8$ (a)

36. $10 + 10(1.2) + 10(1.2)^2 + 10(1.2)^3 + 10(1.2)^4 = 74.4$ or $S_n = \frac{a - ar^n}{1-r} = \frac{10 - 10(1.2)^5}{1 - 1.2} = 74.4;\ 100 - 74.4 = 25.6$ km (b)

37. $\frac{-4}{-2x} = \frac{x^2}{-4} \rightarrow -2x^3 = 16 \rightarrow x^3 = -8 \rightarrow x = -2$ (a)

38. $t_1 = a,\ t_4 = ar^3$; $a = 27 \rightarrow ar^3 = 27r^3 = -8 \rightarrow r = -\frac{2}{3}$ (c)

39. $a = 5,\ l = -1215,\ S_n = -910$

$S_n = \frac{a - rl}{1-r} \rightarrow -910 = \frac{5 - r(-1215)}{1-r} \rightarrow -910 + 910r = 5 + 1215r \rightarrow 305r = -915 \rightarrow r = -3$ (d)

40. $(x^2 + 5) - (x + 4) = (x + 30) - (x^2 + 5) \rightarrow x^2 - x + 1 = -x^2 + x + 25 \rightarrow x^2 - x - 12 = 0 \rightarrow$
$(x + 3)(x - 4) = 0 \rightarrow x = -3, 4$ (b)

41. $ar^5 = -160,\ ar^8 = -1280$; $\frac{ar^8}{ar^5} = \frac{1280}{-160} \rightarrow r^3 = -8 \rightarrow r = -2;\ a(-2)^5 = -160 \rightarrow -32a = -160 \rightarrow a = 5$ (d)

42. $ar^3 = 40.5,\ ar^6 = 136.6875$; $\frac{ar^6}{ar^3} = \frac{136.6875}{40.5} \rightarrow r^3 = 3.375 \rightarrow r = 1.5;\ a(1.5)^3 = 40.5 \rightarrow a = 12$ (a)

43. $a = 6(-2)^0 = 6,\ r = -\frac{1}{2}$; $S = \frac{a - ar^n}{1-r} = \frac{6 - 6\left(-\frac{1}{2}\right)^n}{1+\frac{1}{2}} = 4 - 4\left(-\frac{1}{2}\right)^n$ (a)

44. $a = 6(3)^{3-1} = 54,\ r = 3,\ n = 12 - 3 + 1$; $S = \frac{a - ar^n}{1-r} = \frac{54 - 54(3)^{10}}{1-3} = 27(3^{10} - 1)$ (b)

45. $S_n = 2 - 2(-3)^n,\ S_1 = a = 2 - 2(-3)^1 = 8,\ r = -3,\ t_3 = ar^2 = 8(-3)^2 = 72$ (c)

46. $S_n = 2(3^n - 1),\ S_1 = a = 2(3 - 1) = 4,\ r = 3,\ t_5 = ar^4 = 4(3)^4 = 324$ (c)

47. $\sin 0° + \sin 90° + \sin 180° + \sin 270° = 0 + 1 + 0 + (-1) = 0$, every rotation has a sum of zero
$n = 99 - 0 + 1 = 100,\ \frac{100}{4} = 25$ rotations each with sum zero (a)

48. $S_1 = 3(1)^2 - 2(1) = 1,\ S_2 = 3(2)^2 - 2(2) = 8$; $t_1 = 1,\ t_2 = 8 - 1 = 7 \rightarrow d = 6$ (a)

49. fifth term is $ar^4 = 2$, tenth term is $ar^9 = -\frac{1}{16}$; $\frac{ar^9}{ar^4} = \frac{-\frac{1}{16}}{2} \rightarrow r^5 = -\frac{1}{32} \rightarrow r = -\frac{1}{2}$

$ar^4 = 2 \rightarrow a\left(-\frac{1}{2}\right)^4 = 2 \rightarrow a = 32$; $S_n = \frac{a - ar^n}{1-r} = \frac{32 - 32\left(-\frac{1}{2}\right)^8}{1 - \left(-\frac{1}{2}\right)} = 21.25$ (a)

50. $-64, a, b, 27 \rightarrow \frac{a}{-64} = \frac{b}{a} \rightarrow a^2 = -64b$; $\frac{b}{a} = \frac{27}{b} \rightarrow b^2 = 27a \rightarrow a = \frac{b^2}{27}$
$\left(\frac{b^2}{27}\right)^2 = -64b \rightarrow b^4 = 27^2(-64b) \rightarrow b^3 = -27^2 \cdot 64 \rightarrow b = \sqrt[3]{-27^2 \cdot 64} \rightarrow b = -36$ (b)

51. $t_5 = 3x + 2 = ar^4,\ t_7 = 7x - 22 = ar^6$; $\frac{ar^6}{ar^4} = \frac{7x - 22}{3x + 2} \rightarrow r^2 = \frac{7x - 22}{3x + 2}$

$r = -3 \rightarrow \frac{7x - 22}{3x + 2} = (-3)^2 \rightarrow 7x - 22 = 27x + 18 \rightarrow 20x = -40 \rightarrow x = -2$

$a(-3)^4 = 3(-2) + 2 \rightarrow 81a = -4 \rightarrow 81a = -4 \rightarrow a = \frac{-4}{81}$; $t_6 = ar^5 = \left(\frac{-4}{81}\right)(-3)^5 = 12$ (c)

52. $t_4 + t_5 = ar^3 + ar^4 = -3,\ t_3 + t_4 = ar^2 + ar^3 = -6$

$\frac{ar^3(1+r)}{ar^2(1+r)} = \frac{-3}{-6} \rightarrow r = \frac{1}{2},\ a\left(\frac{1}{2}\right)^2 + a\left(\frac{1}{2}\right)^3 = -6 \rightarrow a = -16 \rightarrow t_2 = ar = -16\left(\frac{1}{2}\right) = -8$ (b)

53. $a + ar = 4 \rightarrow a(1 + r),\ ar^2 + ar^3 = 36 \rightarrow ar^2(1 + r) = 36$; $\frac{ar^2(1+r)}{a(1+r)} = \frac{36}{4} \rightarrow r^2 = 9 \rightarrow r = \pm 3$

$a + ar = 4 \rightarrow a + 3a = 4 \rightarrow a = 1$ and $a - 3a = 4 \rightarrow a = -2$ (a)

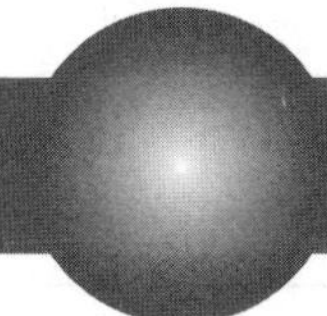

Solutions

Transformation Solutions

2.1 Exercise Set

1. a) domain **b)** range **c)** one-to-one function **d)** function **e)** relation **f)** x-axis **g)** y-axis **h)** vertical, function **i)** vertical, horizontal, one-to-one function

2. a) function **b)** neither **c)** neither **d)** one-to-one function **e)** one-to-one function **f)** function **g)** neither **h)** neither **i)** function **j)** neither

3.

a) D: $-2 \le x \le 4$	**b)** D: $-2 \le x \le 4$	**c)** D: $-4, -2, 0, 2, 4$	**d)** D: $0, 1, 2, 3$	**e)** D: $-4 \le x \le 4$
R: $-1 \le y \le 2$	R: $0 \le y \le 4$	R: $-1, 0, 2$	R: $-3, -2, -1, 0, 1, 2, 3$	R: $-4 \le y \le 4$
F: Yes	F: Yes	F: Yes	F: No	F: No
f) D: $-4 \le x \le 2$	**g)** D: $x \le 2$	**h)** D: $-5 \le x \le 2$	**i)** D: $-3 \le x \le -1,\ 1 \le x \le 3$	**j)** D: $-3 \le x \le 1$
R: $0 \le y \le 1$	R: All real numbers	R: $-3 \le y \le 3$	R: $0 \le y \le 4$	R: $-3 \le y \le 5$
F: Yes	F: No	F: No	F: Yes	F: No

2.2 Exercise Set

1. a) 6 **b)** undefined **c)** 1 **d)** -16 **e)** $\frac{7}{55}$ **f)** $\frac{1}{4}$ **g)** 1 **h)** $\frac{5}{63}$

2. a) $2x^2 + 3x + 4$, all real numbers **b)** $x^2 - 1 + \frac{1}{x},\ x \ne 0$ **c)** $\frac{1}{3x},\ x \ne 0$ **d)** $3x,\ x \ne 0$ **e)** $\frac{2(2x-1)}{x+2},\ x \ne -2$

f) $\frac{2x^2+3x-2}{2},\ x \ne -2$ **g)** $\frac{2x+3}{x-1},\ x \ne \pm 1$ **h)** $2x^3 - x^2 - 2x + 1$, all real numbers

3. a) $\frac{-x^4+6x^2+4x}{(x^2-1)(2x+1)},\ x \ne \pm 1, -\frac{1}{2}$ **b)** 0 **c)** $x^5 + 2x^4$ **d)** $x^5 + 2x^4$ **e)** $-x^5 + x^3 + 3x^2 - 3$ **f)** $-x^5 + x^3 + 3x^2 - 3$ **g)** $4x^2 - 2x + 2$

h) 0 **i)** $6x^2 - 3x - 3$ **j)** -9

4. a)
$(f+g)(x) = x^2 + x - 2$
$(f-g)(x) = x^2 - x - 6$
$(fg)(x) = x^3 + 2x^2 - 4x - 8$
$(ff)(x) = x^4 - 8x^2 + 16$
$\left(\frac{f}{g}\right)(x) = x - 2,\ x \ne -2$
$\left(\frac{g}{f}\right)(x) = \frac{1}{x-2},\ x \ne \pm 2$

b)
$(f+g)(x) = 2x^2 - 2$
$(f-g)(x) = 2x^2 - 2x - 4$
$(fg)(x) = 2x^3 + x^2 - 4x - 3$
$(ff)(x) = 4x^4 - 4x^3 - 11x^2 + 6x + 9$
$\left(\frac{f}{g}\right)(x) = 2x - 3,\ x \ne -1$
$\left(\frac{g}{f}\right)(x) = \frac{1}{2x-3},\ x \ne -1, \frac{3}{2}$

c)
$(f+g)(x) = \sqrt{x} + \frac{1}{x},\ x > 0$
$(f-g)(x) = \sqrt{x} - \frac{1}{x},\ x > 0$
$(fg)(x) = \frac{1}{\sqrt{x}},\ x > 0$
$(ff)(x) = x,\ x \ge 0$
$\left(\frac{f}{g}\right)(x) = x\sqrt{x},\ x > 0$
$\left(\frac{g}{f}\right)(x) = \frac{\sqrt{x}}{x^2},\ x > 0$

d)
$(f+g)(x) = \sqrt{x} + x^2,\ x \ge 0$
$(f-g)(x) = \sqrt{x} - x^2,\ x \ge 0$
$(fg)(x) = x^2\sqrt{x},\ x \ge 0$
$(ff)(x) = x,\ x \ge 0$
$\left(\frac{f}{g}\right)(x) = \frac{\sqrt{x}}{x^2},\ x \ge 0$
$\left(\frac{g}{f}\right)h(x) = x\sqrt{x},\ x > 0$

5. a)

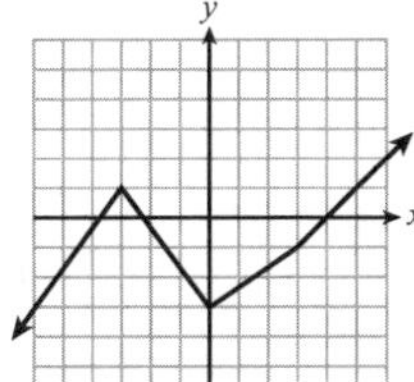

b)

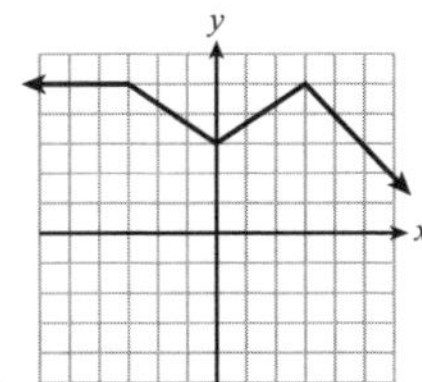

c)

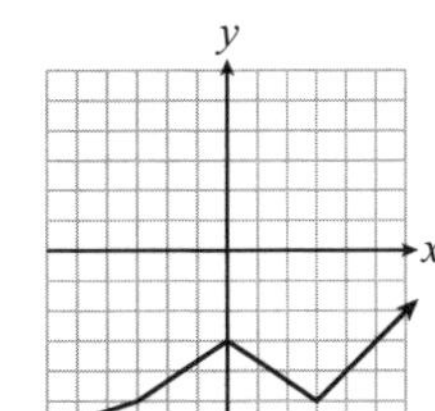

d)

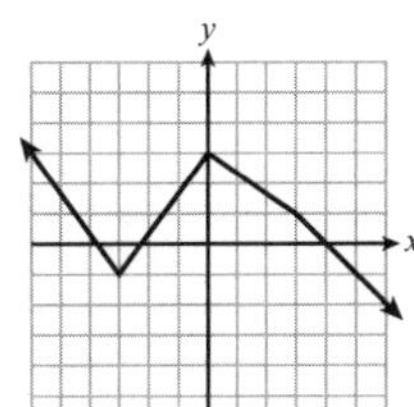

e)

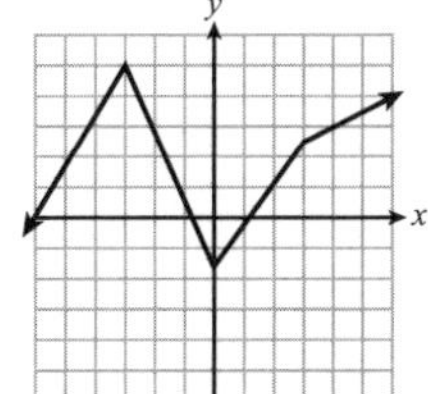

6. a)
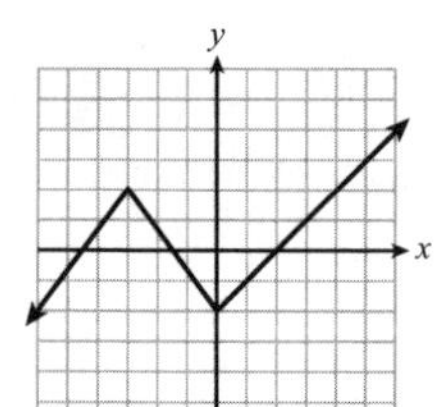
b)
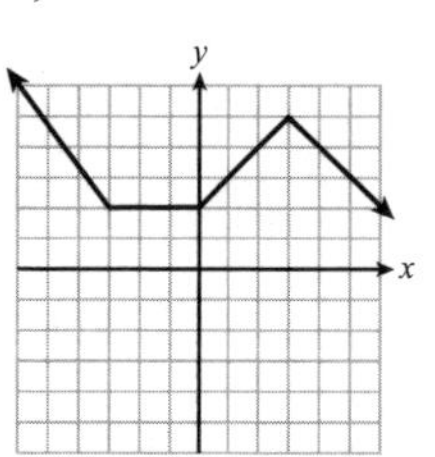
c)
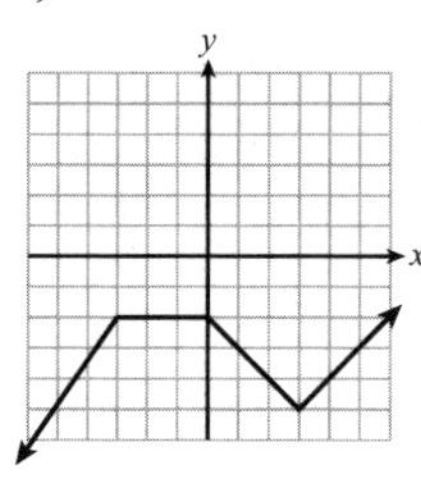
d)
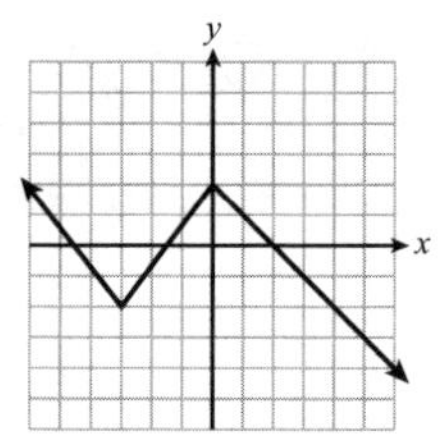
e)
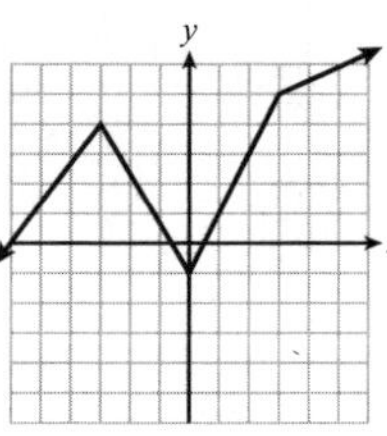

7. a)
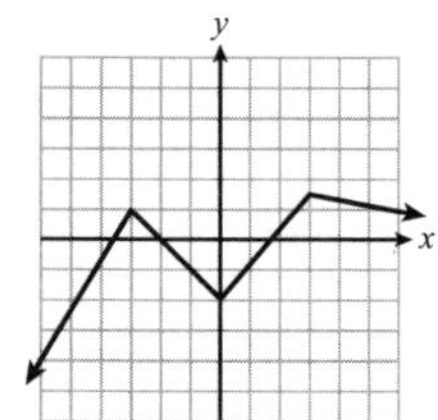
b)
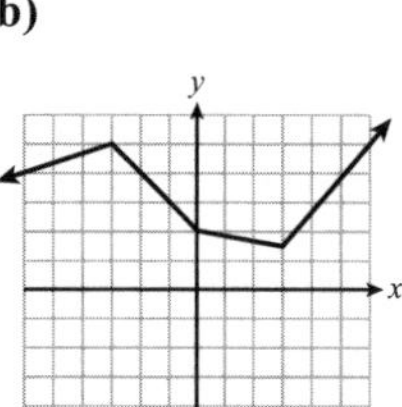
c)
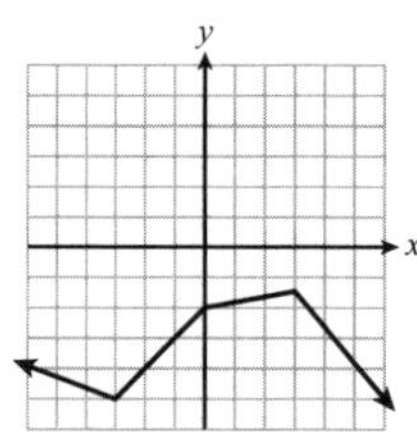
d)
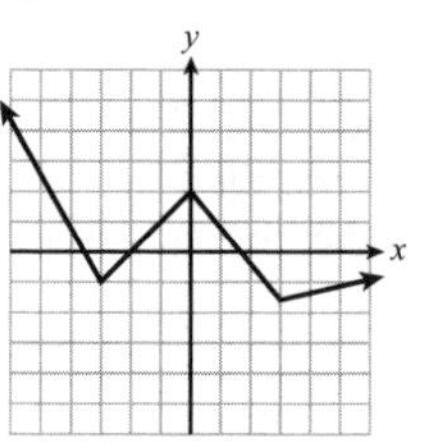
e)
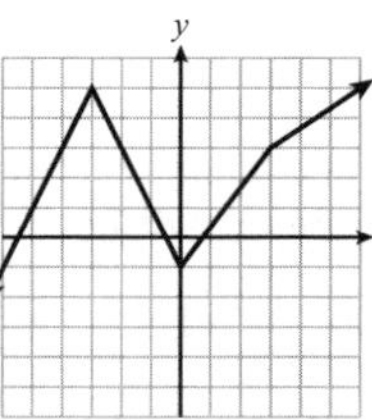

8. a)
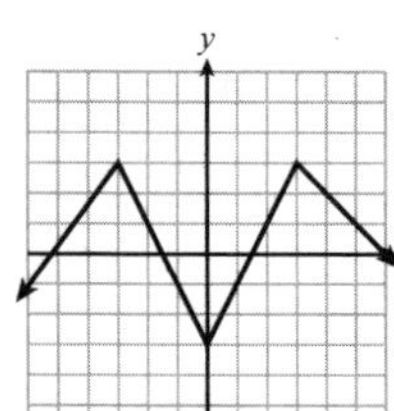
b)
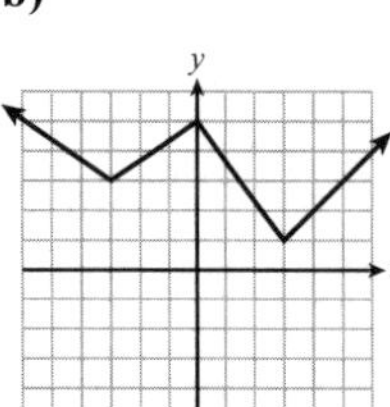
c)
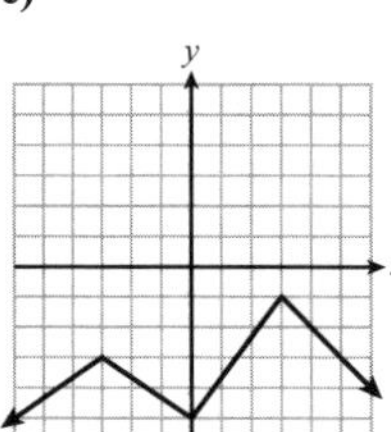
d)
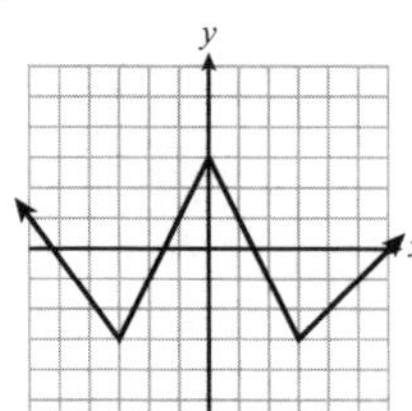
e)
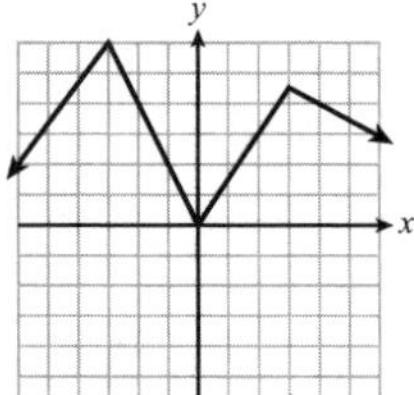

2.3 Exercise Set

1. a) $x \neq 2$ **b)** $x \neq \pm 3$ **c)** $x \geq -2$ **d)** $x \leq 3$ **e)** $x > 0$ **f)** $x \geq 1,\ x \leq -1$ **g)** $-1 \leq x \leq 1$ **h)** $x \geq 2,\ x \leq 0$

2. a)
$$(f \circ g)(2) = f(g(2)) = f(2+1) = f(3) = 2 \cdot 3^2 - 3 \cdot 3 + 1 = 10$$

b)
$$(h \circ j)(-3) = h(j(-3)) = h\left(\frac{-3-1}{-3+1}\right) = h(2) = 5$$

c)
$$(j \circ h)(2) = j(h(2)) = j(5) = \frac{5-1}{5+1} = \frac{2}{3}$$

d)
$$j(g(0)) = j(0+1) = \frac{1-1}{1+1} = 0$$

e)
$$h(j(-1) = h\left(\frac{-1-1}{-1+1}\right) = h\left(\frac{-2}{0}\right)$$
Undefined

f)
$$f(j(3)) = f\left(\frac{3-1}{3+1}\right) = f\left(\frac{1}{2}\right) = 2\left(\frac{1}{2}\right)^2 - 3\left(\frac{1}{2}\right) + 1 = \frac{1}{2} - \frac{3}{2} + 1 = 0$$

g)
$$(h \circ g \circ g)(3) = h(g(g(2))) = h(g(3)) = h(4) = 5$$

h)
$$(f \circ f \circ f)(-1) = f(f(f(-1))) = f(f(6)) = f(55) = 5886$$

i)
$$(j \circ h \circ f)(-3) = j(h(f(-3))) = j(h(25)) = j(5) = \frac{2}{3}$$

j)
$$(g \circ j \circ f)(4) = g(j(f(4))) = g(j(21)) = g\left(\frac{10}{11}\right) = \frac{21}{11}$$

k)
$$(f \circ h \circ j)(2) = f(h(j(2))) = f\left(h\left(\frac{1}{3}\right)\right) = f(5) = 36$$

l)
$$j(j(g(f(-2))))$$
$$j(j(g(15)))$$
$$j(j(16))$$
$$j\left(\frac{15}{17}\right)$$
$$-\frac{1}{16}$$

3. a) 1 **b)** 2 **c)** $f(3) = 4$ **d)** $f(-2) = 0$ **e)** $g(1) = 2$ **f)** $g(6) = -4$ **g)** $f(2)$ is undefined **h)** $g(0)$ is undefined

4. a) $(f\circ g)(x)=\sqrt{2x-1},\ x\geq\frac{1}{2}$

$(g\circ f)(x)=2\sqrt{x+2}-3,\ x\geq -2$

b) $(f\circ g)(x)=\dfrac{2(x-1)}{x},\ x\neq 0,1$

$(g\circ f)(x)=\dfrac{2}{2-x},\ x\neq 0,2$

c) $(f\circ g)(x)=x^2+4x+3,$ all real numbers

$(g\circ f)(x)=x^2-2x+3,$ all real numbers

d) $(f\circ g)(x)=x^2+5x+3,$ all real numbers

$(g\circ f)(x)=x^2+x-1,$ all real numbers

e) $(f\circ g)(x)=\sqrt{3x},\ x\geq 0$

$(g\circ f)(x)=3\sqrt{x-2}+2,\ x\geq 2$

f) $(f\circ g)(x)=|-2x+3|-3,$ all real numbers

$(g\circ f)(x)=-2|x|+9,$ all real numbers

g) $(f\circ g)(x)=3x-12,\ x\neq 4$

$(g\circ f)(x)=\dfrac{x}{3-4x},\ x\neq 0,\dfrac{3}{4}$

h) $(f\circ g)(x)=\left|\dfrac{1-2x}{x}\right|-3,\ x\neq 0$

$(g\circ f)(x)=\dfrac{1}{|x-2|-3},\ x\neq -1,5$

5. a) $f(x)=x^2,\ g(x)=2x-3$

b) $f(x)=\sqrt[3]{x},\ g(x)=3x^2-2$

c) $f(x)=\dfrac{1}{x},\ g(x)=3x-4$

d) $f(x)=\dfrac{2}{x},\ g(x)=x^2+4$

e) $f(x)=\sqrt{x}+3,\ g(x)=x^2+1$

f) $f(x)=\sqrt[3]{x}-1,\ g(x)=3x+4$

g) $f(x)=3x^4-x^7,\ g(x)=2x-3$

h) $f(x)=3x^3+2x^6,\ g(x)=2x+4$

6. a) $(f\circ g)(x)=x+1$

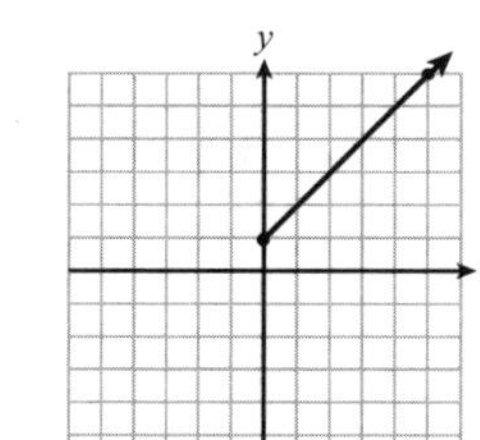

$x\geq 0$

b) $(f\circ g)(x)=x$

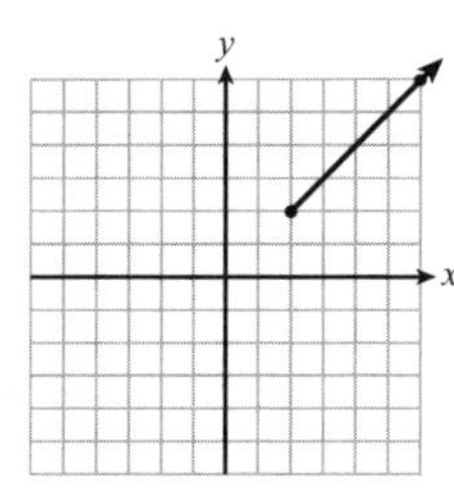

$x\geq 2$

c) $(f\circ g)(x)=x$

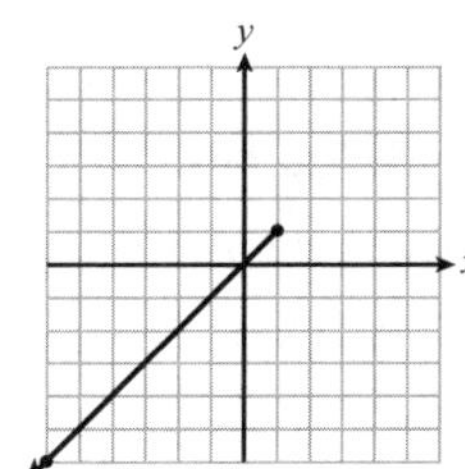

$x\leq 1$

d) $(f\circ g)(x)=-x^2+5$

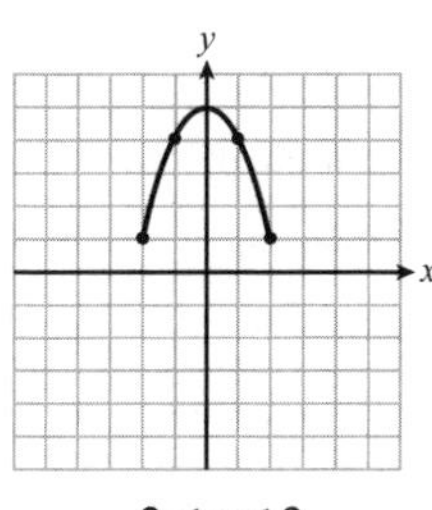

$-2\leq x\leq 2$

7. a) $(g\circ f)(-4)=g(f(-4))=g(0)=-3$

b) $(f\circ g)(3)=f(g(3))=f(0)=2$

c) $(f\circ f)(-2)=f(f(-2))=f(3)=1$

d) $(g\circ g)(3)=g(g(3))=g(0)=-3$

e) $(g\circ f)(-5)=g(f(-5))=g(-3)=-5$

f) $(g\circ f)(-3)=g(f(-3))=g\left(\frac{3}{2}\right)=-\frac{3}{2}$

g) $h(k(0))=h(4)=4$

h) $h(k(-1))=h(3)=3.5$

i) $h(k(2))=h(0)=2$

j) $h(k(-3))=h(-5)=-0.5$

k) $k(h(0))=k(2)=0$

l) $k(h(2))=k(3)=-5$

m) $k(h(-4)=k(0)=4$

n) $k(h(-2))=k(1)=3$

8. a) $g(5)=3\rightarrow f(3)=4$, so (5, 4); $g(7)=-2\rightarrow f(-2)$ is undefined
$g(6)=4\rightarrow f(4)=5$, so (6, 5); $g(8)=0\rightarrow f(0)$ is undefined. Thus, $f\circ g=\{(5,4),(6,5)\}$.

b) $f(3)=4\rightarrow g(4)$ is undefined; $f(5)=6\rightarrow g(6)=4$ so (5, 4)
$f(4)=5\rightarrow g(5)=3$, so (4, 3); $f(6)=7\rightarrow g(7)=-2$ so (6, –2). Thus, $g\circ f=\{(4,3),(5,4),(6,-2)\}$.

9. a) $f(g(x))=f(3x+b)$
$=3(3x+b)-2$

$g(f(x))=g(3x-2)$
$=3(3x-2)+b$

Therefore, $3(3x+b)-2=3(3x-2)+b$
$9x+3b-2=9x-6+b$
$b=-2$

10. a) $$\frac{f(x+h)-f(x)}{h}=\frac{\left[2(x+h)+3\right]-\left[2x+3\right]}{h}=\frac{2x+2h+3-2x-3}{h}=\frac{2h}{h}=2$$

b) $$\frac{f(x+h)-f(x)}{h}=\frac{\left[(x+h)^2+(x+h)\right]-\left[x^2+x\right]}{h}=\frac{x^2+2xh+h^2+x+h-x^2-x}{h}=\frac{2xh+h^2+h}{h}=2x+1+h$$

10. c) $\dfrac{f(x+h)-f(x)}{h}=\dfrac{\left[-3(x+h)^2+2(x+h)\right]-\left[-3x^2+2x\right]}{h}=\dfrac{-3x^2-6xh-3h^2+2x+2h+3x^2-2x}{h}=\dfrac{-6xh-3h^2+2h}{h}=-6x+2-3h$

d) $\dfrac{f(x+h)-f(x)}{h}=\dfrac{\frac{1}{x+h}-\frac{1}{x}}{h}=\dfrac{x-(x+h)}{xh(x+h)}=\dfrac{-h}{xh(x+h)}=\dfrac{-1}{x(x+h)}$

e) $\dfrac{f(x+h)-f(x)}{h}=\dfrac{\left[\frac{4}{2(x+h)-1}\right]-\left[\frac{4}{2x-1}\right]}{h}=\dfrac{4(2x-1)-4\left[2(x+h)-1\right]}{h(2x-1)(2(x+h)-1)}=\dfrac{8x-4-8x-8h+4}{h(2x-1)(2(x+h)-1)}=\dfrac{-8}{(2x-1)(2(x+h)-1)}$

f) $\dfrac{f(x+h)-f(x)}{h}=\dfrac{\frac{1}{\sqrt{x+h}}-\frac{1}{\sqrt{x}}}{h}=\dfrac{\sqrt{x}-\sqrt{x+h}}{h\sqrt{x}\left(\sqrt{x+h}\right)}\cdot\dfrac{\sqrt{x}+\sqrt{x+h}}{\sqrt{x}+\sqrt{x+h}}=\dfrac{x-(x+h)}{h\left[x\sqrt{x+h}+(x+h)\sqrt{x}\right]}=\dfrac{-1}{x\sqrt{x+h}+(x+h)\sqrt{x}}$

11. a) $r(x)=\dfrac{x}{2}$ **b)** $A(r)=\pi r^2$ **c)** $(A\circ r)(x)=\pi\left(\dfrac{x}{2}\right)^2$

12. a) $f(t)=90-27t$ **b)** $g(f)=\sqrt{f^2+90^2}$ **c)** $\sqrt{(90-27t)^2+90^2}$ is the distance the batter is from 2nd base at time t.

2.4 Exercise Set

1. a) $y=(x+4)^2-5$ **b)** $y=-(x-2)^2+3$ **c)** $y=(x-2)^3-3$ **d)** $y=-x^3-1$

e) $y=|x+3|+6$ **f)** $y=-|x+3|$ **g)** $y=-\sqrt{x-7}$ **h)** $y=\sqrt{-x}+4$

2. a) The graph is shifted two units horizontally to the left so the point is $(-5, 1)$ or $(a-2, b)$.

b) The graph is shifted two units up vertically so the point is $(-3, 3)$ or $(a, b+2)$.

c) The graph is shifted two units horizontally to the right and two units vertically down so the point is $(-1,-1)$ or $(a+2, b-2)$.

d) The graph is reflected about the x-axis so the point is $(-3,-1)$ or $(a, -b)$.

e) The graph is reflected about the y-axis so the point is $(3, 1)$ or $(-a, b)$.

f) The graph is reflected about both the x-axis and the y-axis so the point is $(3,-1)$ or $(-a, -b)$.

g) The graph is reflected about the y-axis and then shifted two units vertically down so the point is $(3,-1)$ or $(-a, b-2)$.

h) The graph is reflected about the x-axis and shifted horizontally two units to the left so the point is $(-5,-1)$ or $(a-2, -b)$.

3. a) $y=4x$ **b)** $y=-\dfrac{3}{5}x$ **4. a)** $y=-4x^2$ **b)** $y=\dfrac{1}{8}x^2$ **5. a)** $y=\dfrac{1}{4}x^3$ **b)** $y=-4x^3$

6. a) $y=-2|x|$ **b)** $y=\dfrac{1}{3}|x|$ **7. a)** $y=\dfrac{9}{2}\sqrt{x}$ **b)** $y=-\dfrac{1}{4}\sqrt{-x}$ **8. a)** $y=2x^{\frac{1}{3}}$ **b)** $y=-x^{\frac{1}{3}}$

9. a)

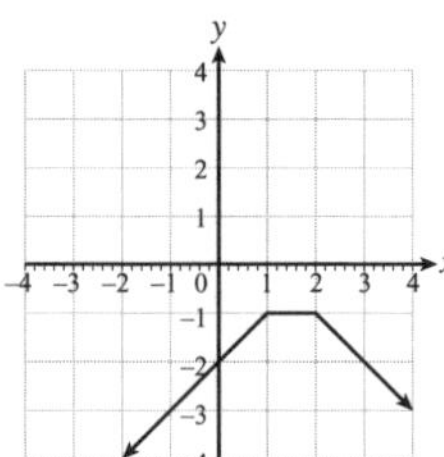

b)

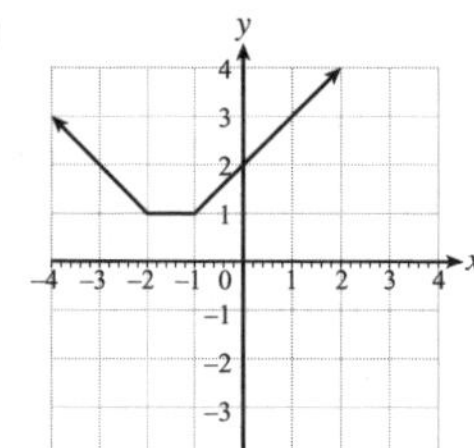

c)

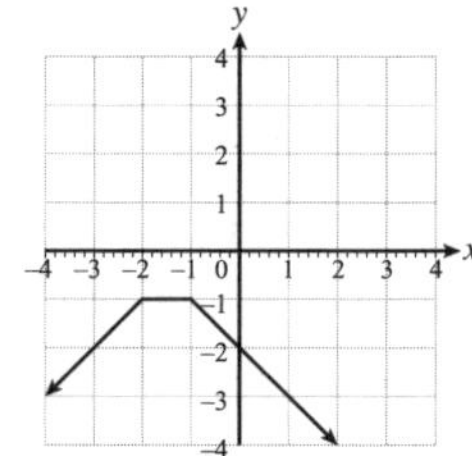

9. d)

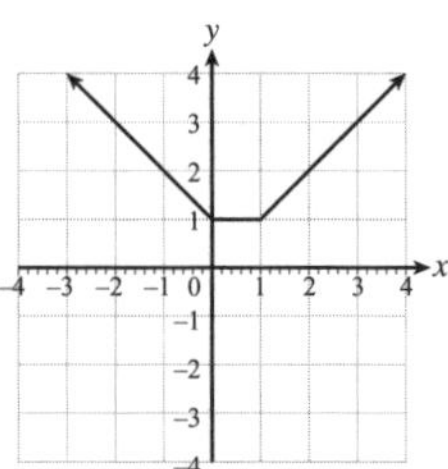

e)

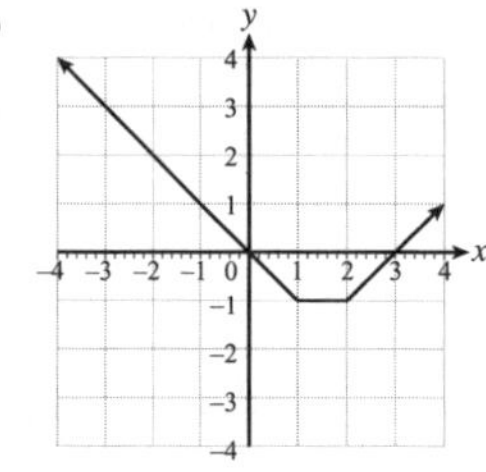

f)

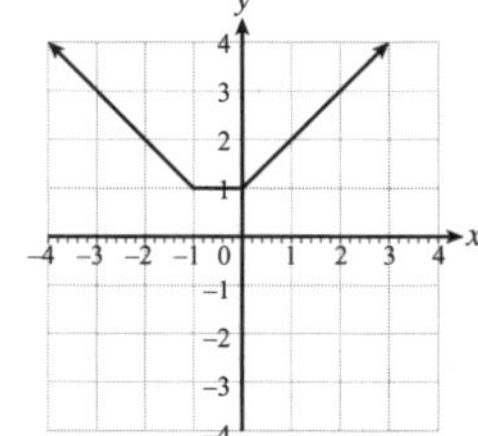

10. a) The graph shifted one unit horizontally to the left, so the point is $(-3, 4)$.
b) The graph is reflected about the x-axis then shifted one unit horizontally to the left, so the point is $(-3,-4)$.
c) The graph is shifted one unit horizontally to the left, then reflected about the y-axis, so the point is $(3, 4)$.
d) The graph is shifted one unit horizontally to the left, and then shifted vertically up 2 units, so the point is $(-3, 6)$.

10. e) The graph is shifted three units horizontally to the left, so the point is (–5, 4).

f) The graph is shifted horizontally one unit to the left, then reflected over both the x-axis and the y-axis, so the point is (3, –4).

11. $0 \le x \le \infty$ **12.** (1, 2) **13.** $0 \le y \le 3$ **14.** (–3, 19)

15. a)

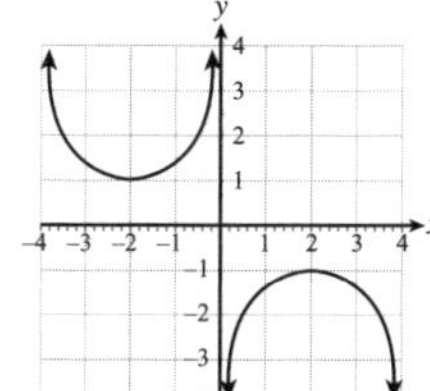

b)

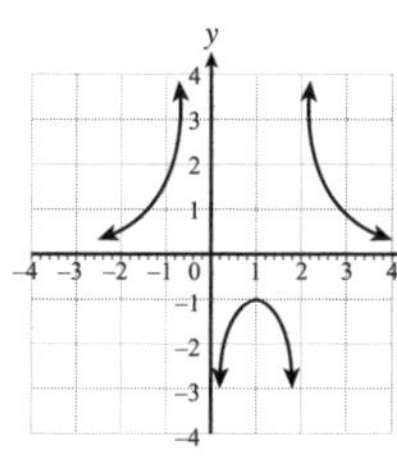

16.

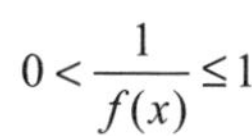

$0 < \dfrac{1}{f(x)} \le 1$

17. $\dfrac{1}{f(x)} \ge 1$

18. a)

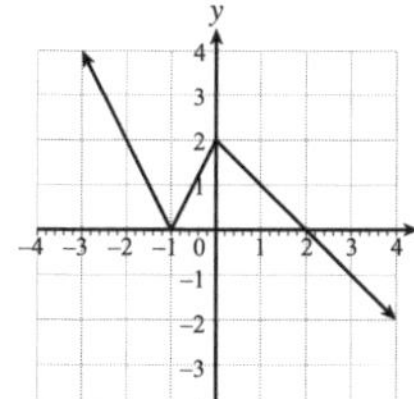

b)

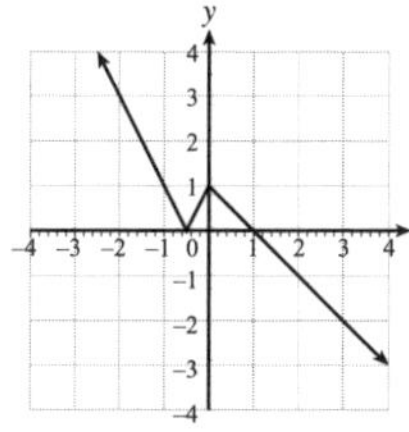

c)

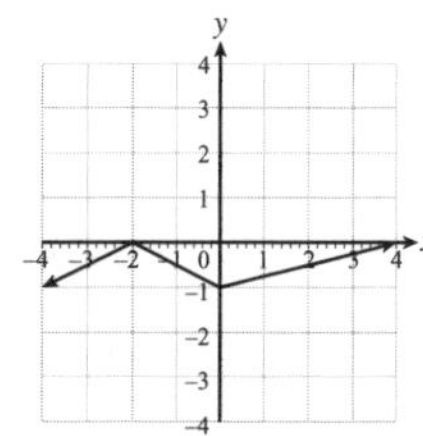

d)

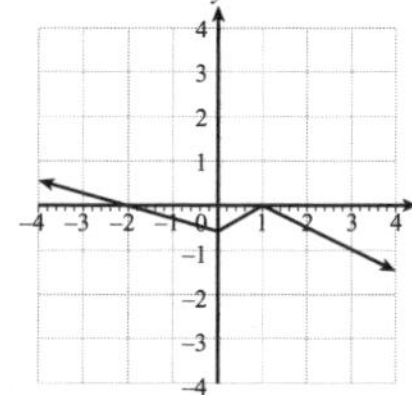

19. a) The graph is compressed vertically by a factor of $\frac{1}{2}$, so $y = \frac{1}{2}f(x)$.

b) The graph is compressed horizontally by a factor of $\frac{1}{2}$, so $y = f(2x)$.

c) The graph is reflected about the x-axis, so $y = -f(x)$.

d) The graph is expanded horizontally by a factor of 2, and compressed vertically by a factor of $\frac{1}{2}$, so $y = \frac{1}{2}f(\frac{1}{2}x)$.

e) The graph is compressed both horizontally and vertically by a factor of $\frac{1}{2}$, and reflected about the x-axis, so $y = -\frac{1}{2}f(2x)$.

f) The graph is retained, and reflected about the x-axis, so $y = \pm f(x)$.

g) The graph is expanded vertically by a factor of 2, and compressed horizontally by a factor of $\frac{1}{2}$, so $y = 2f(2x)$.

h) The graph is expanded both horizontally and vertically by a factor of $\frac{3}{2}$, so $y = \frac{3}{2}f\left(\frac{2}{3}x\right)$.

2.5 Exercise Set

1. a) No **b)** Yes **c)** No **d)** Yes **e)** No **f)** Yes

2. a)

$(f \circ g)(x) = f\left(\frac{5}{3}x\right) = \frac{3}{5}\left(\frac{5}{3}x\right) = x$

$(g \circ f)(x) = g\left(\frac{3}{5}x\right) = \frac{5}{3}\left(\frac{3}{5}x\right) = x$

Yes

b) $(f \circ g)(x) = f(x+3) = x+3-3 = x$

$(g \circ f)(x) = g(x-3) = x-3+3 = x$

Yes

c) $(f \circ g)(x) = f\left(\frac{3-x}{4}\right) = 3-4\left(\frac{3-4x}{4}\right) = x$

$(g \circ f)(x) = g(3-4x) = \dfrac{3-(3-4x)}{4} = x$

Yes

d) $(f \circ g)(x) = f(\sqrt[3]{x+2}) = (\sqrt[3]{x+2})^3 - 2 = x$

$(g \circ f)(x) = g(x^3-2) = \sqrt[3]{(x^3-2)+2} = x$

Yes

e) $(f \circ g)(x) = f(x^2+1) = \sqrt{x^2+1-1} = \sqrt{x^2} = |x|$

$(g \circ f)(x) = g(\sqrt{x-1}) = (\sqrt{x-1})^2 + 1 = x$

No, $(f \circ g)(x)$ not equal to x.

f) $(f \circ g)(x) = f(x^4) = \sqrt[4]{x^4} = |x|$

$(g \circ f)(x) = g(\sqrt[4]{x}) = (\sqrt[4]{x})^4 = x$

No, $(f \circ g)(x)$ equal to x.

g)

$$(f \circ g)(x) = f\left(\frac{x-3}{2x+5}\right) = \frac{5\left(\frac{x-3}{2x+5}\right)+3}{1-2\left(\frac{x-3}{2x+5}\right)} = \frac{\frac{5x-15+6x+15}{2x+5}}{\frac{2x+5-2x+6}{2x+5}} = \frac{11x}{11} = x$$

$$(g \circ f)(x) = g\left(\frac{5x+3}{1-2x}\right) = \frac{\frac{5x+3}{1-2x}-3}{2\left(\frac{5x+3}{1-2x}\right)+5} = \frac{\frac{5x+3-3+6x}{1-2x}}{\frac{10x+6+5-10x}{1-2x}} = \frac{11x}{11} = x$$

Yes

h) $(f \circ g)(x) = f(x^3-1) = \sqrt[3]{(x^3-1)+1} = \sqrt[3]{x^3} = x$

$(g \circ f)(x) = g(\sqrt[3]{x+1}) = (\sqrt[3]{x+1})^3 - 1 = x+1-1 = x$

Yes

3. a) $x \ge 0$ or $x \le 0$ **b)** $x \ge 0$ or $x \le 0$ **c)** $x \ge 2$ or $x \le 2$ **d)** $x \ge -1$ or $x \le -1$

4. a)

$f(x) = 2x-3$

$f: y = 2x-3$

$f^{-1}: x = 2y-3$

$: 2y = x+3 : y = \dfrac{x+3}{2}$

Therefore, $f^{-1}(x) = \dfrac{x+3}{2}$ A one-to-one function.

b)

$f(x) = \sqrt{2x-1},\ x \ge \frac{1}{2}$

$f: y = \sqrt{2x-1}$

$f^{-1}: x = \sqrt{2y-1}$

$: x^2 = 2y-1 : 2y = x^2+1 : y = \dfrac{x^2+1}{2}$

If range of f has $y \ge 0$, the domain of f^{-1} has $x \ge 0$. Therefore, $f^{-1}(x) = \dfrac{x^2+1}{2}, x \ge 0$. A one-to-one function.

c)

$f(x) = x^2+1$

$f: y = x^2+1$

$f^{-1}: x = y^2+1$

$: y^2 = x-1 : y = \pm\sqrt{x-1}$

Because $y = \pm\sqrt{x-1}$ is not a function, we <u>cannot</u> write $f^{-1}(x) = \pm\sqrt{x-1}$. Not a function.

4. d)

$$f(x)=\frac{1}{3x-2},\ x\neq\frac{2}{3},\ f(x)\neq 0$$

$$f: y=\frac{1}{3x-2}$$

$$f^{-1}: x=\frac{1}{3y-2}$$

$$: x(3y-2)=1$$

$$: 3xy-2x=1$$

$$: 3xy=2x+1$$

$$: y=\frac{2x+1}{3x}$$

Therefore,

$f^{-1}(x)=\dfrac{2x+1}{3x},\ x\neq 0,\ f^{-1}(x)\neq\dfrac{2}{3}$.

A one-to-one function.

e)

$$f(x)=\frac{x}{1-x},\ x\neq 1$$

$$f: y=\frac{x}{1-x}$$

$$f^{-1}: x=\frac{y}{1-y}$$

$$: x(1-y)=y$$

$$: x-xy=y$$

$$: xy+y=x$$

$$: y(x+1)=x$$

$$: y=\frac{x}{x+1}$$

Therefore, $f^{-1}(x)=\dfrac{x}{x+1}$, $x\neq -1$.

A one-to-one function.

f)

$$f(x)=\frac{2x-1}{3x+2},\ x\neq-\frac{2}{3}$$

$$f: y=\frac{2x-1}{3x+2}$$

$$f^{-1}: x=\frac{2y-1}{3y+2}$$

$$: x(3y+2)=2y-1$$

$$: 3xy+2x=2y-1$$

$$: 3xy-2y=-2x-1$$

$$: y(3x-2)=-2x-1$$

$$: y=\frac{-2x-1}{3x-2}$$

Therefore, $f^{-1}(x)=\dfrac{-2x-1}{3x-2}$, $x\neq\dfrac{2}{3}$.

A one-to-one function.

5.

$$f(x)=2x-1$$

$$f: y=2x-1$$

$$f^{-1}: x=2y-1$$

$$: 2y=x+1$$

$$: y=\frac{x+1}{2}$$

Therefore, $f^{-1}(x)=\dfrac{x+1}{2}$

$$g(x)=\frac{1}{2}x+3$$

$$g: y=\frac{1}{2}x+3$$

$$g^{-1}: x=\frac{1}{2}y+3$$

$$: \frac{1}{2}y=x-3$$

$$: y=2x-6$$

Therefore, $g^{-1}(x)=2x-6$

a)

$$(f^{-1}\circ g)(x)=f^{-1}(g(x))$$

$$=f^{-1}\left(\frac{1}{2}x+3\right)$$

$$=\frac{\frac{1}{2}x+3+1}{2}$$

$$=\frac{\frac{1}{2}x+4}{2}$$

$$=\frac{1}{4}x+2$$

b)

$$(g^{-1}\circ f^{-1})(x)=g^{-1}(f^{-1}(x))$$

$$=g^{-1}\left(\frac{x+1}{2}\right)$$

$$=2\left(\frac{x+1}{2}\right)-6$$

$$=x+1-6$$

$$=x-5$$

c)

$$(g\circ f^{-1})(x)=g(f^{-1}(x))$$

$$=g\left(\frac{x+1}{2}\right)$$

$$=\frac{1}{2}\left(\frac{x+1}{2}\right)+3$$

$$=\frac{x+1}{4}+3$$

$$=\frac{x+13}{4}$$

d)

$$(f\circ g^{-1})(x)=f(g^{-1}(x))$$

$$=f(2x-6)$$

$$=2(2x-6)-1$$

$$=4x-12-1$$

$$=4x-13$$

e)

$$(f^{-1}\circ g^{-1})(x)=f^{-1}\left(g^{-1}(x)\right)$$

$$=f^{-1}\left(2x-6\right)$$

$$=\frac{2x-6+1}{2}$$

$$=\frac{2x-5}{2}$$

f)

$$y=(f\circ g)^{-1}(x)=\left(f\left(g(x)\right)\right)^{-1}$$

$$=\left(f\left(\frac{1}{2}x+3\right)\right)^{-1}=\left(2\left(\frac{1}{2}x+3\right)-1\right)^{-1}$$

$$=(x+5)^{-1}$$

$$x=y+5$$

$$y=(f\circ g)^{-1}(x)=x-5$$

6. a)

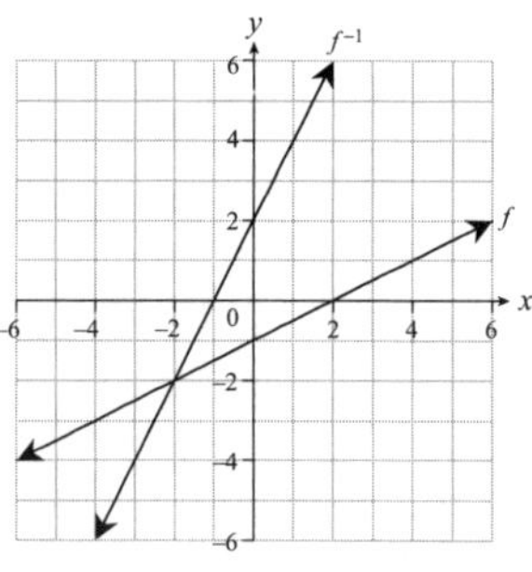

b)

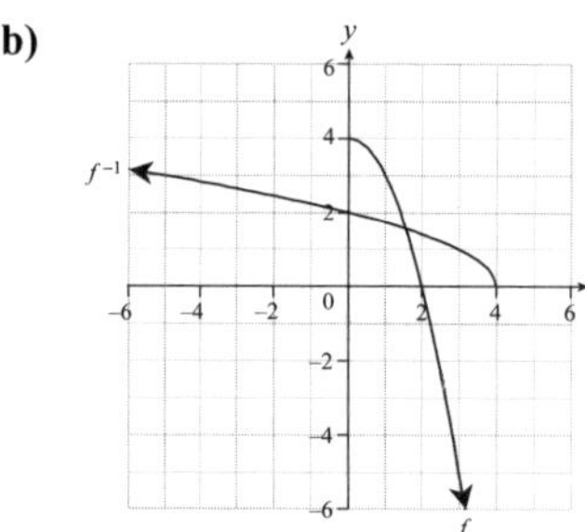

c)

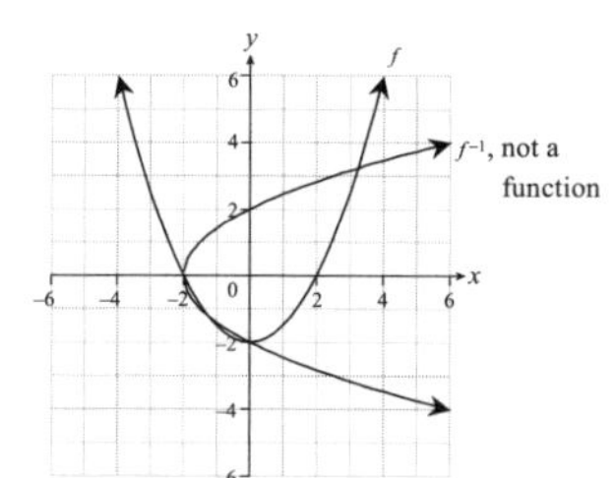

6. d)

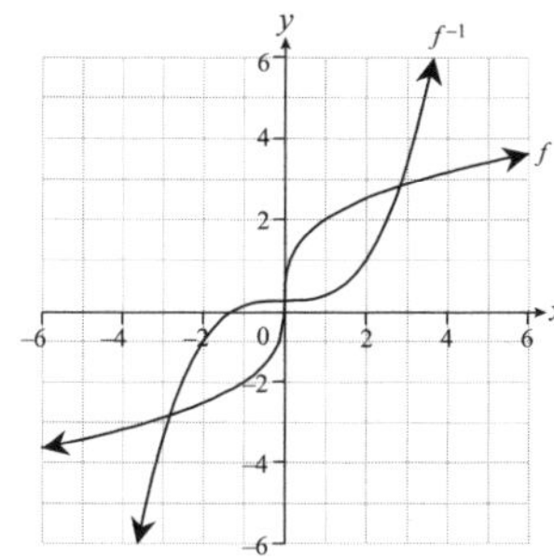

e)

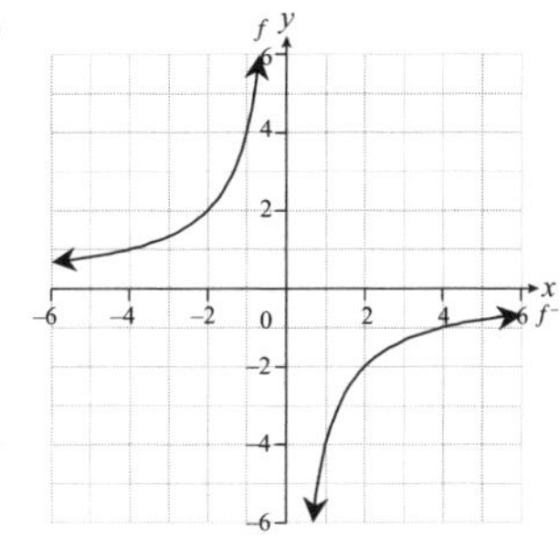

f)

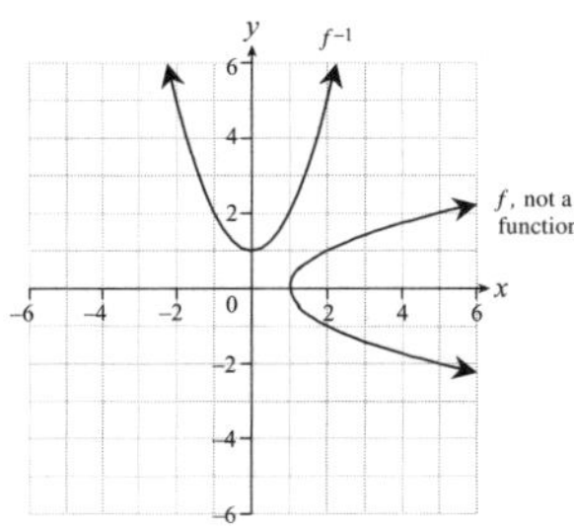

7. a) If $f(a)=b$, then $f^{-1}(b)=a$. Therefore, the point is (2, –1) or (*b, a*).

b) If $f(a-1)=b$, then $f^{-1}(b)=a-1$. Therefore, the point is (2, –2) or (*b, a* – 1).

c) If $f(a)=b-2$, then $f^{-1}(b-2)=a$. Therefore, the point is (0, –1) or (*b* – 2, *a*).

d) If $f(-a)=-b$, then $f^{-1}(-b)=-a$. Therefore, the point is (–2, 1) or (– *b*, – *a*).

e) If $f(-a+1)=-b$, then $f^{-1}(-b)=-a+1$. Therefore, the point is (– 2, 2) or (– *b*, – *a* + 1).

f) If $f(a)=(b-1)$, then $f^{-1}(b-1)=a$. Therefore, the point is (1, – 1) or (*b* – 1, *a*).

8. a) By TI-83 Calculator.
Enter equation, $y=2x-1$, under <Y =>, press <◄><◄> to move the cursor to the left past the equal sign. Press < ENTER > repeatedly until the bold line symbol appears for equation Y_1. (We are doing this to distinguish the function *f* from f^{-1} on the graph). Set appropriate window.
To graph the inverse function, press <2nd> <DRAW>. Press cursor down repeatedly (or press 8) until it reaches 8:DrawInv, then press <ENTER>. Enter equation, 2*x* – 1, then press <ENTER>

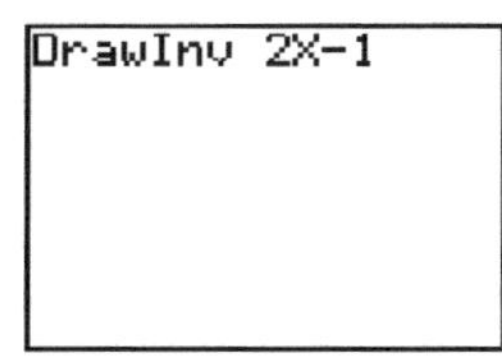

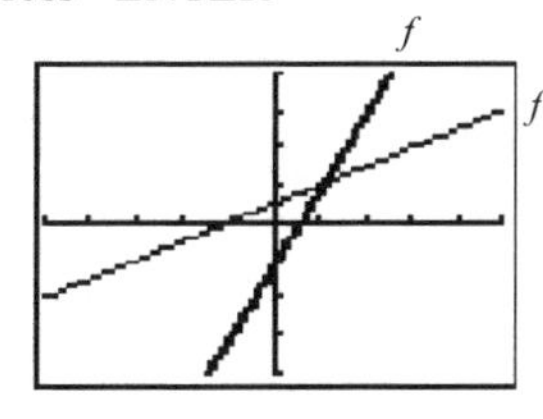

A one-to-one function

x [– 5, 5] *y* [– 4, 4]

Note: When finished drawing inverse for one equation, the next step is very important in order to clear the graph.
Press <2nd><DRAW>. The cursor will highlight 1:ClrDraw, press <ENTER> <ENTER>. This

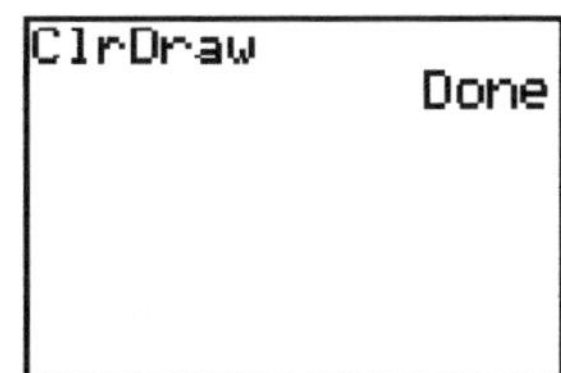

b) Follow same steps as problem **8 a)** for $y=x^2+1$.

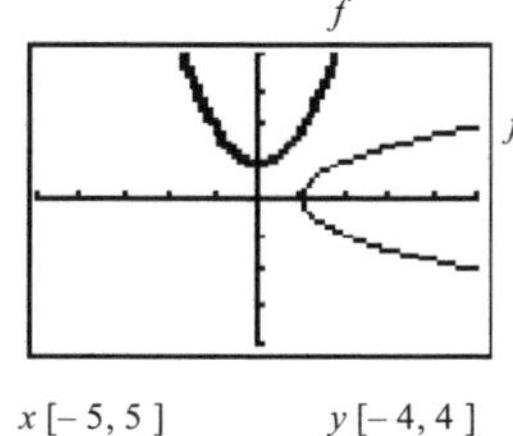

Not a function

x [– 5, 5] *y* [– 4, 4]

c) Follow same steps as problem **8 a)** for $y=x^3-1$.

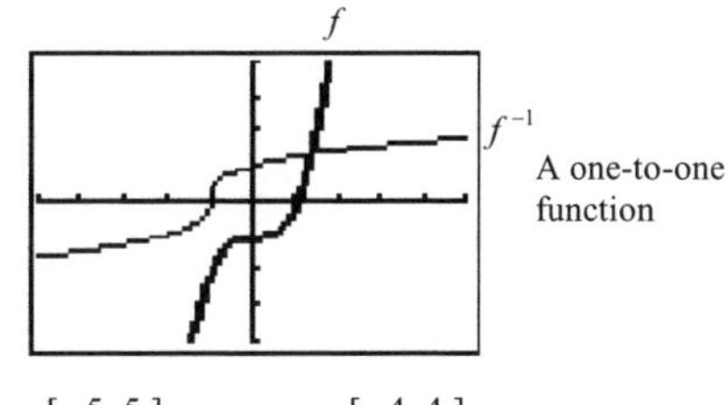

A one-to-one function

x [– 5, 5] *y* [– 4, 4]

d) Follow same steps as problem **8 a)** for $y=\sqrt{x^2-4}$

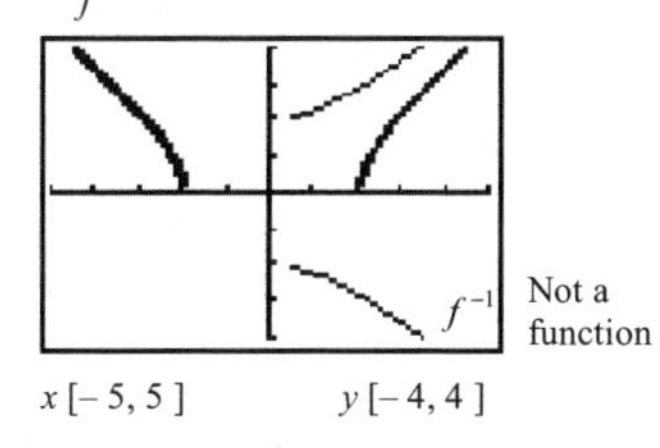

Not a function

x [– 5, 5] *y* [– 4, 4]

9. If $f^{-1}(6)=-2$ then $f(-2)=6$

$$f(x)=a(-x^3-x+2)$$
$$f(-2)=a(-(-2)^3-(-2)+2)=6$$
$$12a=6$$
$$a=\frac{1}{2}$$

10. The inverse of a point in quadrant I must also be a point in quadrant I because an inverse is a reflection over the line $y=x$. The inverse of a point in quadrant II must be in quadrant IV so the inverse must be in quadrants I and IV.

11. $(F\circ C)(x)=F\left(\frac{5}{9}(F-32)\right)=\frac{9}{5}\left(\frac{5}{9}(F-32)\right)+32=F-32+32=F$

$(C\circ F)(x)=C\left(\frac{9}{5}C+32\right)=\frac{5}{9}\left(\frac{9}{5}C+32-32\right)=\frac{5}{9}\left(\frac{9}{5}C\right)=C$

12. $(f\circ g)(x)=f\left(\frac{1}{4}x-3\right)$

$=2\left(\frac{1}{4}x-3\right)+1$

$=\frac{1}{2}x-5$

$(f\circ g)^{-1}(x):x=\frac{1}{2}y-5$

$:\frac{1}{2}y=x+5$

$:y=2x+10$

$g^{-1}(x):x=\frac{1}{4}y-3$

$:\frac{1}{4}y=x+3$

$:y=4x+12$

$f^{-1}(x):x=2y+1$

$:2y=x-1$

$:y=\frac{x-1}{2}$

$(g^{-1}\circ f^{-1})(x):g^{-1}\left(\frac{x+1}{2}\right)=4\left(\frac{x-1}{2}\right)+12$

$=2x-2+12$

$=2x+10$

Yes, it holds for all one-to-one functions.

2.6 Exercise Set

1. a) N **b)** C **c)** H **d)** F **e)** D **f)** L **g)** A **h)** G **i)** K **j)** M **k)** I **l)** E **m)** B **n)** J

2. a) Shift graph horizontally 1 unit to the right, and vertically 3 units down. Points are $(5,-5)$ and $(a+1, b-3)$.

b) Reflect graph about both x and y-axis, and shift graph vertically 1 unit up. Points are $(-4, 3)$ and $(-a, -b+1)$.

c) Reflect graph about x-axis, and shift graph horizontally 2 units to the left, and 1 unit down. Points are $(2, 1)$ and $(a-2, -b-1)$.

d) Graph is compressed horizontally by a factor of $\frac{1}{2}$, and the y-value must be greater than or equal to zero. Points are $(2, 2)$ and $(\frac{1}{2}a, |b|)$.

e) The graph is compressed vertically by a factor of $\frac{1}{2}$, and shifted horizontally 1 unit to the right and vertically 4 units up. Points are $(5, 3)$ and $(a+1, \frac{1}{2}b+4)$.

f) Reflect all parts of graph that are above the x-axis to below the x-axis then shift graph horizontally 2 units to the right. Points are $(6,-2)$ and $(a+2, -|b|)$.

g) Reflect graph about y-axis and expand horizontally by a factor of 2, then shift graph vertically 1 unit up. Points are $(-8,-1)$ and $(-2a, b+1)$.

h) Reflect graph about both x-axis and y-axis and shift graph horizontally 1 unit to the right. Points are $(-3, 2)$ and $(-a+1, -b)$.

i) Reflect graph about the line $y=x$ which interchanges x and y, then shift graph vertically 2 units up. Points are $(-2, 6)$ and $(b, a+2)$.

j) Reflect graph about the line $y=x$ which interchanges x and y, then shift graph horizontally 1 unit to the left. Points are $(-3, 4)$ and $(b-1, a)$.

3. a) $f(x+2)=(x+2)^2-1$

b) $f(\frac{1}{2}x)=(\frac{1}{2}x)^2-1+1=\frac{1}{4}x^2$

c) $-f(x-1)+2=-[(x-1)^2-1]+2$
$=-(x-1)^2+3$

d) $2f(1-x)+3=2[(1-x)^2-1]+3$
$=2(x-1)^2+1$

e) $3f(x)=3(x^2-1)$
$=3x^2-3$

f) $f(\frac{1}{3}x)=(\frac{1}{3}x)^2-1$
$=\frac{1}{9}x^2-1$

4. a) $4\left(\frac{x}{2}\right)^2+y^2=36$
$x^2+y^2=36$

b) $4x^2+\left(\frac{y}{\frac{1}{3}}\right)^2=36$
$4x^2+(3y)^2=36$
$4x^2+9y^2=36$

c) $4\left(\frac{x}{\frac{1}{2}}\right)^2+\left(\frac{y}{\frac{4}{3}}\right)^2=36$
$16x^2+\frac{9}{16}y^2=36$
$256x^2+9y^2=576$

5. a) $f(x)=-\frac{1}{2}x+2$ **b)** $f(x)=-\frac{1}{2}x-2$ **c)** $f(x)=-\frac{1}{2}x$ **d)** $f(x)=-\frac{1}{2}x+6$

6. a)

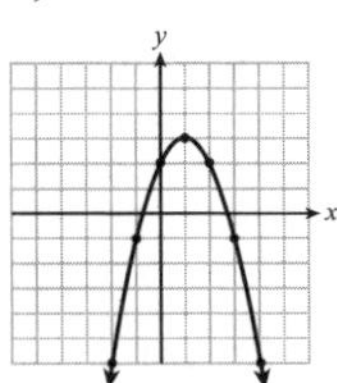

b)

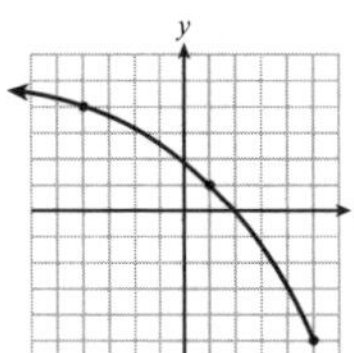

c)

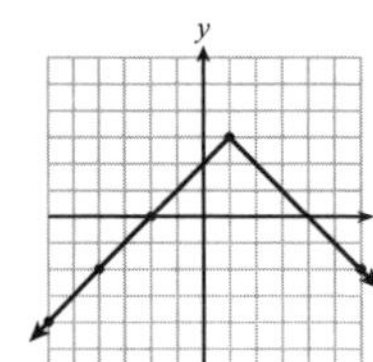

d)

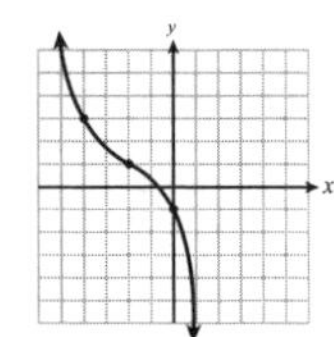

7. a) Method 1: *Note: If using method 1 in all problems of question 7, do only 1 or 2 changes at a time, not all steps at once! Refer to example 2, page 42 of this book.* The graph is stretched horizontally by a factor of 2, and shifted vertically up 1 unit.

Method 2: *Note: If using method 2 review transformation formula on page 13, example 1 of this book and plot key reference points, then draw the transformed graph. My key reference points for all problems of question 7 are (–3, –1), (–1, 1), (0, 0), (1, 1) and (2, 1).*

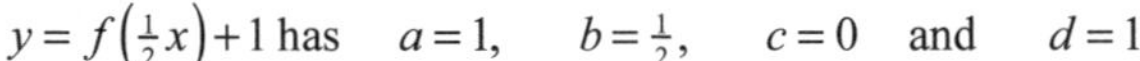

$y=f\left(\frac{1}{2}x\right)+1$ has $a=1,\quad b=\frac{1}{2},\quad c=0$ and $d=1$

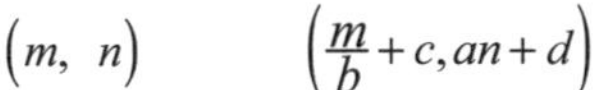

$(m,\ n)$	$\left(\frac{m}{b}+c, an+d\right)$		
$(-3,\ -1)$	$\left(\frac{-3}{\frac{1}{2}}+0,\ 1\cdot-1+1\right)$	=	$(-6,\ 0)$
$(-1,\ 1)$	$\left(\frac{-1}{\frac{1}{2}}+0,\ 1\cdot1+1\right)$	=	$(-2,\ 2)$
$(0,\ 0)$	$\left(\frac{0}{\frac{1}{2}}+0,\ 1\cdot0+1\right)$	=	$(0,\ 1)$
$(1,\ 1)$	$\left(\frac{1}{\frac{1}{2}}+0,\ 1\cdot1+1\right)$	=	$(2,\ 2)$
$(2,\ 1)$	$\left(\frac{2}{\frac{1}{2}}+0,\ 1\cdot1+1\right)$	=	$(4,\ 2)$

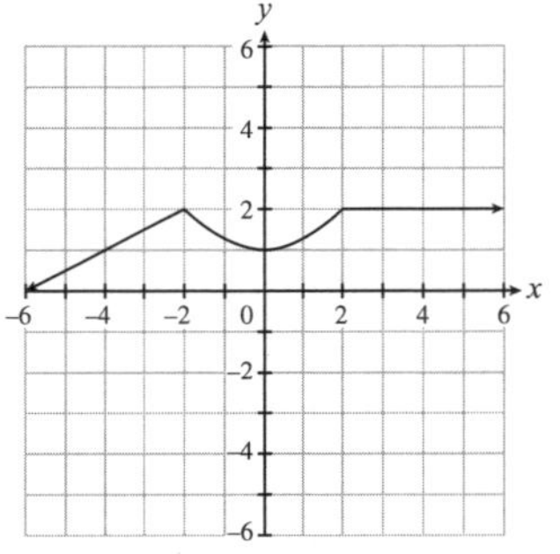

Graph of $y=f(\frac{1}{2}x)+1$

b) Method 1: The graph is reflected about the x-axis, and stretched vertically by a factor of 2, then shifted horizontally 2 units to the left and down vertically 1 unit.

Method 2:

$y=-2f(x+2)-1$ has $a=-2,\quad b=1,\quad c=-2$ and $d=-1$

$(m,\ n)$	$\left(\frac{m}{b}+c, an+d\right)$		
$(-3,\ -1)$	$\left(\frac{-3}{1}-2,\ -2\cdot-1-1\right)$	=	$(-5,\ 1)$
$(-1,\ 1)$	$\left(\frac{-1}{1}-2,\ -2\cdot1-1\right)$	=	$(-3,\ -3)$
$(0,\ 0)$	$\left(\frac{0}{1}-2,\ -2\cdot0-1\right)$	=	$(-2,\ -1)$
$(1,\ 1)$	$\left(\frac{1}{1}-2,\ -2\cdot1-1\right)$	=	$(-1,\ -3)$
$(2,\ 1)$	$\left(\frac{2}{1}-2,\ -2\cdot1-1\right)$	=	$(0,\ -3)$

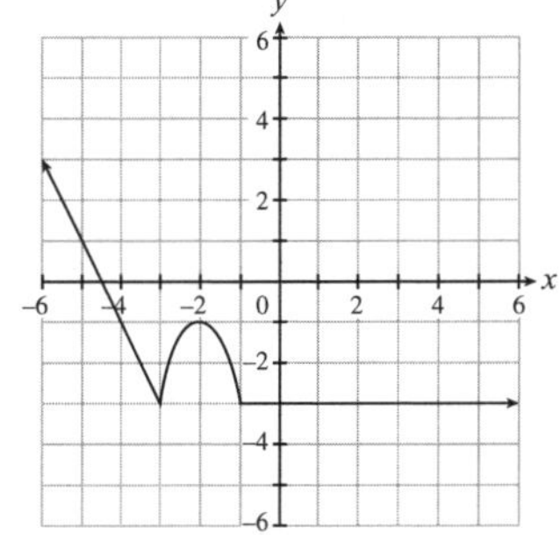

Graph of $y=-2f(x+2)-1$

7. c) Method 1: The graph is expanded horizontally and vertically by a factor of 2, then shifted horizontally 2 units to the right, then shifted up vertically 1 unit.

Method 2:

$y=2f\left(\frac{1}{2}x-1\right)+1 \rightarrow\ y=2f[\frac{1}{2}(x-2)]+1$ has $a=2,\quad b=\frac{1}{2},\quad c=2$ and $d=1$

$(m,\ n)$	$\left(\frac{m}{b}+c, an+d\right)$		
$(-3,\ -1)$	$\left(\frac{-3}{\frac{1}{2}}+2,\ 2\cdot-1+1\right)$	=	$(-4,\ -1)$
$(-1,\ 1)$	$\left(\frac{-1}{\frac{1}{2}}+2,\ 2\cdot1+1\right)$	=	$(0,\ 3)$
$(0,\ 0)$	$\left(\frac{0}{\frac{1}{2}}+2,\ 2\cdot0+1\right)$	=	$(2,\ 1)$
$(1,\ 1)$	$\left(\frac{1}{\frac{1}{2}}+2,\ 2\cdot1+1\right)$	=	$(4,\ 3)$
$(2,\ 1)$	$\left(\frac{2}{\frac{1}{2}}+2,\ 2\cdot1+1\right)$	=	$(6,\ 3)$

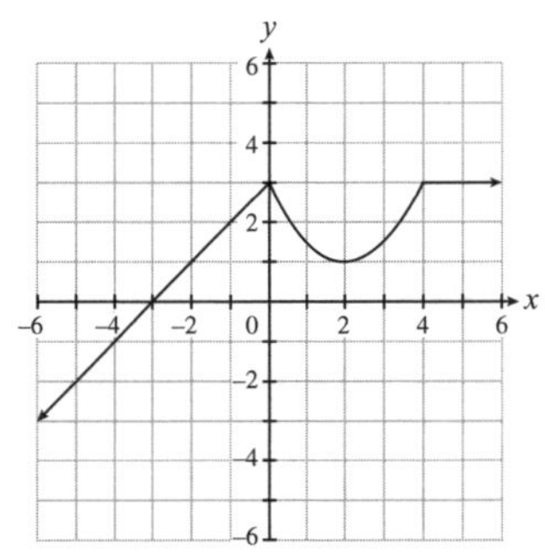

Graph of $y=2f(\frac{1}{2}x-1)+1$

d) Method 1: The graph is reflected about the y-axis, and expanded vertically by a factor of 2, then shifted horizontally 1 units to the right and up vertically 2 units.
Method 2:
$y=2f(1-x)+2 \rightarrow y=2f[-(x-1)]+2$ has $a=2,$ $b=-1,$ $c=1$ and $d=2$

(m, n)	$\left(\frac{m}{b}+c, an+d\right)$		
$(-3, -1)$	$\left(\frac{-3}{-1}+1,\ 2\cdot -1+2\right)$	=	$(4, 0)$
$(-1, 1)$	$\left(\frac{-1}{-1}+1,\ 2\cdot 1+2\right)$	=	$(2, 4)$
$(0, 0)$	$\left(\frac{0}{-1}+1,\ 2\cdot 0+2\right)$	=	$(1, 2)$
$(1, 1)$	$\left(\frac{1}{-1}+1,\ 2\cdot 1+2\right)$	=	$(0, 4)$
$(2, 1)$	$\left(\frac{2}{-1}+1,\ 2\cdot 1+2\right)$	=	$(-1, 4)$

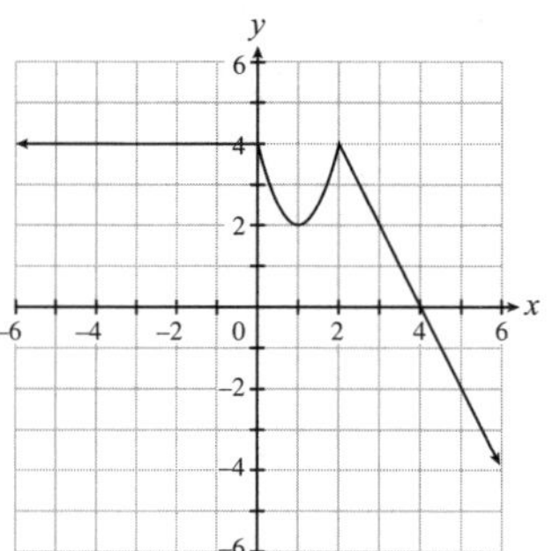
Graph of $y=2f(1-x)+2$

e) Method 1: The graph is reflected over both the x-axis and y-axis, and compressed horizontally by a factor of $\frac{1}{2}$ then shifted 1 unit horizontally to the right and down vertically 2 units.
Method 2:
$y=-f(2-2x)-2 \rightarrow y=-f[-2(x-1)]-2$ has $a=-1,$ $b=-2,$ $c=1$ and $d=-2$

(m, n)	$\left(\frac{m}{b}+c, an+d\right)$		
$(-3, -1)$	$\left(\frac{-3}{-2}+1,\ -1\cdot -1-2\right)$	=	$(2.5, -1)$
$(-1, 1)$	$\left(\frac{-1}{-2}+1,\ -1\cdot 1-2\right)$	=	$(1.5, -3)$
$(0, 0)$	$\left(\frac{0}{-2}+1,\ -1\cdot 0-2\right)$	=	$(1, -2)$
$(1, 1)$	$\left(\frac{1}{-2}+1,\ -1\cdot 1-2\right)$	=	$(0.5, -3)$
$(2, 1)$	$\left(\frac{2}{-2}+1,\ -1\cdot 1-2\right)$	=	$(0, -3)$

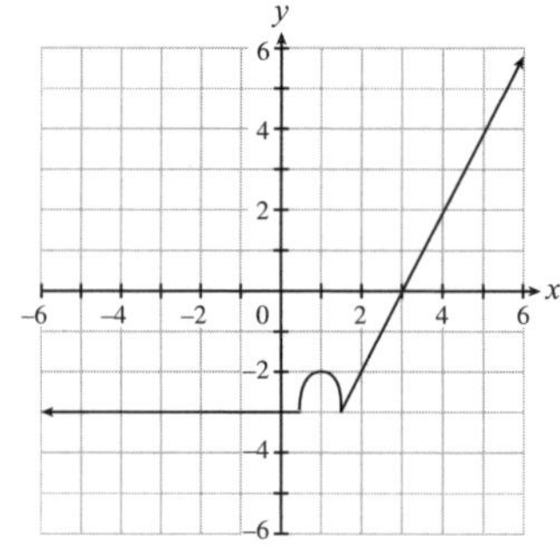
Graph of $y=-f(2-2x)-2$

7. f) $y=-2f(-\frac{1}{2}x-1)+1=-2f[-\frac{1}{2}(x+2)]+1$
The graph is reflected over the x-axis and y-axis, and horizontally and vertically expanded by a factor of 2, then shifted horizontally 2 units left and vertically up 1 unit.

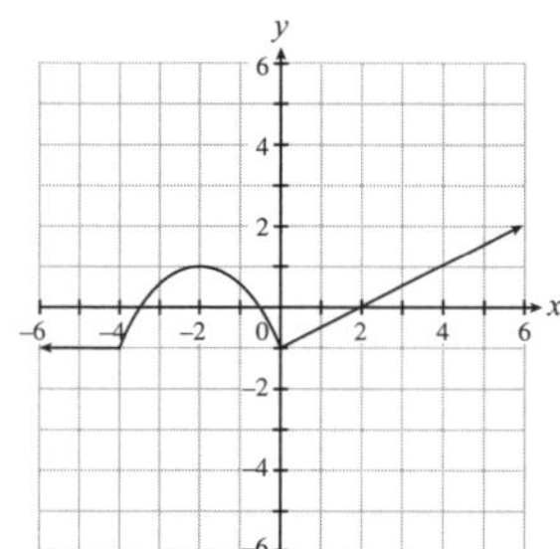

2.7 Chapter Review

Transformations – Multiple-choice Answers

1. a	**8.** b	**15.** d	**22.** c	**29.** d	**36.** b	**43.** b	**50.** b	**57.** d	**64.** a
2. d	**9.** b	**16.** c	**23.** d	**30.** a	**37.** d	**44.** b	**51.** a	**58.** b	**65.** c
3. c	**10.** d	**17.** a	**24.** c	**31.** c	**38.** d	**45.** a	**52.** a	**59.** a	**66.** d
4. b	**11.** c	**18.** b	**25.** a	**32.** a	**39.** b	**46.** c	**53.** d	**60.** c	**67.** a
5. a	**12.** d	**19.** d	**26.** c	**33.** b	**40.** a	**47.** d	**54.** a	**61.** b	
6. b	**13.** c	**20.** a	**27.** d	**34.** a	**41.** d	**48.** c	**55.** a	**62.** d	
7. c	**14.** d	**21.** d	**28.** a	**35.** c	**42.** d	**49.** b	**56.** b	**63.** a	

Transformations – Multiple-choice Solutions

1. $f(-2)-g(-2)=[(-2)^2+3(-2)-1]-[2(-2)+3]=-3-(-1)=-2$. Answer is a.
2. Set $x+1=0 \rightarrow x=-1$, therefore, shift to left 1 unit; +2 shift vertically up 2 units. Answer is d.
3. $y=af(x),\ a>1$ has a vertical expansion factor; $y=-f(x)$ has a reflection on the *x*-axis. Answer is c.
4. Set $x-2=0 \rightarrow x=2$, therefore shift to right 2 units; set $y+3=0 \rightarrow y=-3$, therefore, shift down 3 units. Answer is b.
5. For the graph of $y=f(x)$, the graph of $y=-f(x)$ is a reflection on the *x*-axis. Answer is a.
6. $y=f(ax),\ 0<a<1$ has a horizontal expansion factor. Answer is b.
7. $y=af(bx),\ a>1$ has a vertical expansion; $b>1$ has a horizontal compression. Answer is c.
8. $y=|f(x)|$ will change the range, but not the domain. Answer is b.
9. The absolute value $|-3|=3$ with the range positive up to 3. Answer is b.
10. Reflection on the line $y=x$ is an inverse relation; change every *x* to *y,* and every *y* to *x*. Answer is d.
11. $x=f(y)$ is an inverse of $y=f(x)$, therefore switch *x* and *y*. Answer is c.
12. $y=-f(x)$ is a reflection on the *x*-axis, and vertically down is negative two. Answer is d.
13. $x+1=f(y-1)$ is an inverse relation; switch *x* and *y*, (9, –2), then shift horizontally left ($x=9-1$) and vertically up ($y=-2+1$). Answer is c.
14. $\left(\frac{f}{g}\right)(x)=\frac{f(x)}{g(x)}=\frac{x(x-1)}{x(x^2-1)}=\frac{x(x-1)}{x(x-1)(x+1)}$; restrictions are calculated before simplifying, $x\neq -1, 0, 1$. Answer is d.
15. The inverse is $x=2y-3 \rightarrow 2y=x+3 \rightarrow y=\frac{x+3}{2}$. Answer is d.
16. Reflect in the *x*-axis has $y=-f(x)$, therefore $y=-(x^3-x^2-x+1) \rightarrow y=-x^3+x^2+x-1$. Answer is c.
17. Reflect in the *y*-axis has $y=f(-x)$ therefore $y=(-x)^3-(-x)^2-(-x)+1 \rightarrow y=-x^3-x^2+x+1$. Answer is a.
18. The reciprocal changes the *y*-value. Answer is b.
19. $y=x^3-1 \rightarrow x=y^3-1 \rightarrow y^3=x+1 \rightarrow y=\sqrt[3]{x+1}$, the inverse is a reflection on the line $y=x$. Answer is d.
20. If $f(x)=x^2-4$ then $y=|f(x)|=4-x^2$ when $-2\le x\le 2$, therefore *y*-intercept is 4. Then $y=-2|f(x)|$ reflects in the *x*-axis and expands by a factor of 2, therefore *y*-intercept is –8. Answer is a.
21. The only one not symmetric in the *y*-axis is d. Answer is d.
22. Expand graph horizontally by a factor of 2 and compress graph vertically by a factor of $\frac{1}{3}$. Answer is c.
23. Change $y=\sin\left(\frac{\pi}{2}x+\pi\right)$ to $y=\sin\left[\frac{\pi}{2}(x+2)\right]$, therefore, graph is shifted horizontally 2 units to the left. Answer is d.
24. If $a<0$, then graph is shifted horizontally to the right; if $b<0$ then graph is shifted vertically downward. Answer is c.
25. $y=-af(x)$ is a reflection on the *x*-axis, $0<a<1$ compresses graph vertically. Answer is a.
26. $(f\circ g)(x)=f(g(x))=f(\sqrt{4-x^2})$, thus $\sqrt{4-x^2}=\sqrt{(2-x)(2+x)}\ge 0,\ -2\le x\le 2$. Answer is c.
27. $y=f^{-1}(x)$ reflects values on the line $y=x$, quadrant II reflects to quadrant IV and quadrant III reflects to itself. Answer is d.
28. Change $y=\sin(2x+4)$ to $y=\sin[2(x+2)]$, shifting graph 2 units right is $y=\sin 2x$. Answer is a.
29. Shift graph 2 units left is $y=f[-(x+2)]$, then down 3 units is $y=f[-(x+2)]-3$, then simplify. Answer is d.
30. $y=|f(x)|$ has point $(-2,\ 6)$; $y=-2|f(x)|$ has point $(-2,\ -12)$, then shift point vertically up 3 units to point $(-2,\ -9)$. Answer is a.
31. This graph is a reflection on the line $y=x$, which is an inverse relation. Answer is c.
32. A horizontally expansion by a factor of 2 units is $y=4\left(\frac{x}{2}\right)^2+8$, then simplify. Answer is a.
33. $y=f(-x)$ reflects on the *y*-axis, therefore, point is $(1,\ -2)$, $y=|f(x)|$ of this point is $(1\ ,\ 2)$. Answer is b.
34. $y=f^{-1}(x)$ is an inverse relation, therefore, switch *x* and *y* values to $(4,\ -2)$, then shift graph horizontally to the left 1 unit to $(3,\ -2)$. Answer is a.
35. $y=f^{-1}(x)$ is an inverse, therefore, switch *x* and *y* values to $(4,\ -2)$, then $y=f(-x)$ reflects graph on the *y*-axis to $(-4,\ -2)$. Answer is c.
36. Expand horizontally by a factor of 2 is $y=\sqrt{16-\left(\frac{x}{2}\right)^2}$, then shifted down 2 units is $y=\sqrt{16-\left(\frac{x}{2}\right)^2}-2$, then simplify to

$$y=\sqrt{16-\frac{x^2}{4}}-2=\sqrt{\frac{64-x^2}{4}}-2=\frac{1}{2}\sqrt{64-x^2}-2.$$ Answer is b.

37. $f(-n)=1-\dfrac{1}{(-n)}=\dfrac{n+1}{n}$; $\dfrac{1}{f(n+1)}=\dfrac{1}{1-\dfrac{1}{n+1}}=\dfrac{1}{\dfrac{n+1-1}{n+1}}=\dfrac{n+1}{n}$. Answer is d.

38. Compressed horizontally by a factor of $\dfrac{1}{3}$ is $3x$, and expanded vertically by a factor of 2 is $\dfrac{y}{2}$, then simplify

$9(3x)^2+8\left(\dfrac{y}{2}\right)^2=36\to 81x^2+2y^2=36$. Answer is d.

39. The graph, $y=f(x)$, has been reflected on the x-axis, and compressed vertically by a factor of $\dfrac{1}{2}$ to $y=-\dfrac{1}{2}f(x)$, then reflected on the y-axis, therefore $y=-\dfrac{1}{2}f(-x)$. Answer is b.

40. The graph is reflected on the x-axis, so, $y=-f(x)$, then compressed by a factor of $\dfrac{1}{2}$ to $y=-f(2x)$, then shifted horizontally to the left 2 units, so $y=-f[2(x+2)]$, then simplified to $y=-f(2x+4)$. Answer is a.

41. The graph is expanded vertically by a factor of 2, therefore, $y=2f(x)$, then shifted horizontally 2 units left $y=2f(x-2)$. Answer is d.

42. $f(x)=x^2-9$ then $y=|f(x)|=9-x^2$, $-3\le x\le 3$ therefore $|f(x+2)|=9-(x+2)^2$. The y-intercept has $x=0$, so $9-(0+2)^2=5$. Answer is d.

43. $y=2f(x)\to -4\le y\le 2\to$, $y=-2f(x)\to -2\le y\le 4$, $y=-2f(x)-4\to -6\le y\le 0$. Answer is b.

44. $y=-2f(x)$ will reflect the graph and expanded vertically by a factorial of 2 but the x-intercept will not change since $y=0$. Answer is b.

45. $f(x)=2x^2-3x=x(2x-3)$ has x-intercepts 0 and $\frac{3}{2}$; $f(x)=2x^2+3x=x(2x+3)$ has x-intercepts 0 and $-\frac{3}{2}$. $f(-x)=2(-x)^2-3(-x)=2x^2+3x=g(x)$; $f(-x)$ is $f(x)$ reflected in y-axis which is $x=0$. Answer is a.

46. Step 1 has point $(4,-6)$; Step 2 has point $(4, 6)$; Step 3 has point $(4, 18)$; Step 4 has point $(18, 4)$. Answer is c.

47. Reflect on the x-axis is $f_1(x)=-f(x)=-(x^3-x^2+x-1)=-x^3+x^2-x+1$, reflect on the y-axis is $f_2(x)=f_1(-x)=-(-x)^3+(-x)^2-(-x)+1$, simplify to $y=x^3+x^2+x+1$. Answer is d.

48. Reflect on the y-axis is $y=f(-x)$, then shift horizontally 2 units left is $y=f[-(x+2)]$, then simplify. Answer is c.

49. Change $y=\sqrt{a-x}$ to $y=\sqrt{-(x-a)}$, the graph is reflected on the y-axis, then shifted horizontally to the right. Answer is b.

50. $f^{-1}(x)$ is $x=\dfrac{y}{3y-1}\to x(3y-1)=y\to 3xy-x=y\to 3xy-y=x\to y(3x-1)=x\to y=\dfrac{x}{3x-1}$. Answer is b.

51. $f^{-1}(x)$ is $x=\dfrac{2y}{1-y}\to x(1-y)=2y\to x-xy=2y\to xy+2y=x\to y(x+2)=x\to y=\dfrac{x}{x+2}$. Answer is a.

52. $h(x)=\dfrac{3}{(5x+2)^2}$; $f(x)=\dfrac{3}{x^2}$, $g(x)=5x+2$, check $f(g(x))=f(5x+2)=\dfrac{3}{(5x+2)^2}$. Answer is a.

53. $f(x)=a(x+3)(x)(x-2)$ $\quad f(1-x)=a(1-x+3)(1-x)(1-x-2)=a(4-x)(1-x)(-1-x)$, zeros 4, 1, –1. Answer is d.

54. $(f\circ f)(x)=f(f(x))=f\left(\dfrac{2x-1}{x-2}\right)=\dfrac{2(\frac{2x-1}{x-2})-1}{\frac{2x-1}{x-2}-2}=\dfrac{\frac{4x-2-x+2}{x-2}}{\frac{2x-1-2x+4}{x-2}}=\dfrac{3x}{3}=x$. Answer is a.

55. Change to $y=\dfrac{1}{2}f[-(x-1)]-2$. Reflect on y-axis is $(-3,\ -4)$, vertical compression by a factor of $\dfrac{1}{2}$ is $(-3,\ -2)$ then shift horizontally to the right 1 unit and vertically down 2 units to $(-2, -4)$ or use method used in example 1, page 41 of workbook. Answer is a.

56. $y=f^{-1}(x)$ has point $(4,\ -2)$, then reflect on both x- and y-axis is $(-4,\ 2)$, then shift vertically down 2 units. Answer is b.

57. Graph is reflected on x-axis is $(a,\ -b)$, then shifted horizontally 3 units right and vertically up 1 unit is $(a+3,\ -b+1)$. Answer is d.

58. $y=-f(x)$ reflects graph on x-axis is $(m,\ -n)$, then shifted horizontally to the right 2 units and vertically up 1 unit is $(m+2\ ,\ -n+1)$. Answer is b.

59. Change $y=2f(4-x)-1$ to $y=2f[-(x-4)]-1$. $y=f(-x)$ reflects graph on y-axis is $(-a,\ b)$, $y=2f(x)$ expands graph vertically by a factor 2 is $(-a,\ 2b)$, then shift graph horizontally 4 units to the right and vertically down 1 unit is $(-a+4,\ 2b-1)$. Answer is a.

60. $f(x)=x^3$, $x=y^3\to y=\sqrt[3]{x}$ thus $f^{-1}(x)=\sqrt[3]{x}$ $\quad (f^{-1}\circ f^{-1})(x)=f^{-1}(f^{-1}(x))=f^{-1}(\sqrt[3]{x})=\sqrt[3]{\sqrt[3]{x}}=x^{\frac{1}{9}}=(512)^{\frac{1}{9}}=2$. Answer is c.

61. $f(x)=3x+1$ has intercept of 1 so does $y=\dfrac{1}{f(x)}=\dfrac{1}{3(0)+1}=1$. Answer is b.

62. $f(g(x)) = f(2x+1) = (2x+1)^2$; $f(g(a)) = (2a+1)^2$;

$$\frac{f[g(x)]-f[g(a)]}{x-a} = \frac{(2x+1)^2-(2a+1)^2}{x-a} = \frac{4x^2+4x+1-4a^2-4a-1}{x-a} = \frac{4(x^2-a^2)+4(x-a)}{x-a} =$$

$$\frac{4(x-a)(x+a)+4(x-a)}{x-a} = 4(x+a)+4 = 4x+4a+4.$$ Answer is d.

63. $(g\circ f)(x) = g(f(x)) = g\left(\frac{x^2+1}{x^2-1}\right) = \frac{2\left(\frac{x^2+1}{x^2-1}\right)-5}{3\left(\frac{x^2+1}{x^2-1}\right)+4} = \frac{\frac{2x^2+2-5x^2+5}{x^2-1}}{\frac{3x^2+3+4x^2-4}{x^2-1}} = \frac{-3x^2+7}{7x^2-1}$. Answer is a.

64. A horizontal expansion by a factor of 3 is $\left(\frac{x}{3}\right)^2 + y^2 = 1$.

A vertical compression by a factor of of $\frac{1}{2}$ is $x^2+(2y)^2=1$, together simplified is $\frac{x^2}{9}+4y^2=1$. Answer is a.

65. $y = f(4-2x)-1 \rightarrow y = f\left[-2(x-2)\right]-1$

Method 1: The –2 compresses x-value by a factor of $\frac{1}{2}$, and reflects in the y-axis, (2, 8)

The x – 2 and –1 shifts graph two units right, and one unit down (4, 7). Answer is c.

66 The graph is reflected on the x-axis, therefore, $a = -1$. The graph is compressed horizontally by a factor of $\frac{1}{2}$, therefore, $b = 2$.

Answer is d.

67 The reciprocal of $0 < f(x) \le 2$ is $\frac{1}{f(x)} \ge \frac{1}{2}$, and the reciprocal of $-2 \le f(x) < 0$ is $\frac{1}{f(x)} \le -\frac{1}{2}$. Answer is a.

Polynomial Solutions

3.1 Exercise Set

1. a) continuous **b)** n, 0, n – 1 **c)** n, 1, n – 1 **d)** solution or root; x – a, x-intercept or zero **e)** descending

2.

Equation	Polynomial, Yes / No	Degree	Leading Coefficient	Special Name
a) $-2x^3+x^2-5$	**Yes**	**3**	**–2**	**cubic**
b) $\sqrt{2}x^4-\sqrt{3x}+2$	**No, $\sqrt{x}$ exponent is a fraction**			
c) $-\frac{1}{3}x^2+\sqrt{-2}x+1$	**No, $\sqrt{-2}$ not real**			
d) $3x+2$	**Yes**	**1**	**3**	**linear**
e) 5	**Yes**	**0**	**5**	**constant**

3. Graphs **a)**, **b)**, and **d)** are polynomials.

4. a) A real zero is where the graph crosses or touches the x-axis. Therefore, the real zero is $x = -3$. **b)** Real zeros occur at –2, 1, 3.

5. a) **Maximum** number of solutions is the degree of the polynomial, which is **5**. An odd polynomial must cross the x-axis at least once because an odd polynomial either starts up and ends down, or starts down and ends up. Therefore, **minimum** number of solutions is **one**.

Maximum number of solutions is the degree of the polynomial, which is **6**. An even polynomial either starts up and ends up or starts down and ends down. It doesn't have to cross the x-axis, so the **minimum** number of solutions is **zero**.

b) An odd polynomial must always cross the x-axis. Therefore, ***one*** is the **minimum** number of zeros if n is an **odd** number. The maximum number of zeros is the **degree** of the polynomial. Therefore, "***n***" is the **maximum** number of zeros if n is an **odd** number.

An even polynomial does not have to cross the x-axis. Therefore, ***zero*** is the **minimum** number of zeros if n is an **even** number. The maximum number of zeros is again the **degree** of the polynomial. Therefore, ***n*** is the **maximum** number of zeros if n is an **even** number.

6. a) polynomial, 4 **b)** No, exponent not a whole number **c)** No, exponent not a whole number **d)** polynomial, 0 **e)** polynomial, 3 **f)** No, exponent not a whole number **g)** polynomial, 3 **h)** polynomial, 2 **i)** polynomial, 2 **j)** No, exponent not a whole number

7. a) falls to the left, rises to the right **b)** rises to the left, falls to the right **c)** rises to the left, rises to the right **d)** falls to the left, falls to the right **e)** falls to the left, rises to the right **f)** rises to the left, falls to the right **g)** rises to the left, rises to the right **h)** falls to the left, falls to the right **i)** falls to the left, rises to the right **j)** rises to the left, falls to the right

8. a) $f(x) = -3x^3$ **b)** $g(x) = 2x^3$ **c)** $h(x) = 2.3x^4$ **d)** $k(x) = -2.4x^5$ (Answers may vary.)

9. a) $x = -2, 2$; -2 of multiplicity 1, 2 of multiplicity 1 **b)** $x = 4$; 4 of multiplicity 2 **c)** $x = 0, 2$; 0 of multiplicity 1, 2 of multiplicity 2

d) $x = 0;\ 1\pm\sqrt{2}$ of multiplicity 1 **e)** $x = -4, 0, 5$; -4 of multiplicity 1, 0 of multiplicity 2, 5 of multiplicity 1 **f)** $x = -1, 1$; -1 of multiplicity 1, 1 of multiplicity 1

9. g) $\varnothing$

h) $x=-5, 4, 5; -5$ of multiplicity 1
4 of multiplicity 1
5 of multiplicity 1

i) $x=-3,-2, 2; -3$ of mult. 1
-2 of mult. 1
2 of mult. 1

j) $x=-1, 1, 5; -1$ of multiplicity 1
1 of multiplicity 1
5 of multiplicity 1

k) $x=-1, 1; -1$ of multiplicity 2
1 of multiplicity 2

l) $x=-\sqrt{2}, -1, 1, \sqrt{2};$
$-\sqrt{2}, -1, 1, \sqrt{2}$ of multiplicity 1

m) $x=0, 2; 0$ of multiplicity 2
2 of multiplicity 2

n) $x=-2,-1, 1, 2;$
$-2, -1, 1, 2$ of multiplicity 1

3.2 Exercise Set

1. a) 4 turns, therefore degree 5 **b)** 3 turns, therefore degree 4 **c)** 3 turns, therefore degree 4
d) 4 turns, therefore degree 5 **e)** 4 turns, therefore degree 5 **f)** 6 turns, therefore degree 7

2. a) 3; between $-4<x<-3$, between $3<x<4$, at $x=-2$ **b)** 3; between $-2<x<-1$, at $x=2$, between $-1<x<0$

3. a) $P(x)=a(x+2)(x-1)(x-3)$, with y-intercept -2

$$P(0)=a(0+2)(0-1)(0-3)=-2$$
$$6a=-2$$
$$a=-\tfrac{1}{3}$$

therefore, $P(x)=-\tfrac{1}{3}(x+2)(x-1)(x-3)$

b) $P(x)=a(x+2)(x-1)^2(x-3)$, with y-intercept -3

$$P(0)=a(0+2)(0-1)^2(0-3)=-3$$
$$-6a=-3$$
$$a=\tfrac{1}{2}$$

therefore, $P(x)=\tfrac{1}{2}(x+2)(x-1)^2(x-3)$

c) $P(x)=a(x+1)(x+0)^2(x-3)^3$, with point $(1,-4)$

$$P(1)=a(1+1)(1^2)(1-3)^3=-4$$
$$-16a=-4$$
$$a=\tfrac{1}{4}$$

therefore, $P(x)=\tfrac{1}{4}x^2(x+1)(x-3)^3$

d) $P(x)=a(x+2)^3(x-1)^2(x-3)^2$, with y-intercept 8

$$P(0)=a(0+2)^3(0-1)^2(0-3)^2=8$$
$$72a=8$$
$$a=\tfrac{1}{9}$$

therefore, $P(x)=\tfrac{1}{9}(x+2)^3(x-1)^2(x-3)^2$

4. a) $-\dfrac{1}{3}x^3\ge 0$
$x\le 0$

b) $\dfrac{1}{2}x^3+4\ge 0$
$x^3\ge -8$
$x\ge -2$

c) $-\dfrac{1}{16}x^4+1\ge 0$
$x^4\le 16$
$-2\le x\le 2$

d) $x^5-1\ge 0$
$x^5\ge 1$
$x\ge 1$

e) $x^4-4x^2\ge 0$
$x^2(x-2)(x+2)\ge 0$
$x\le -2,\ x=0,\ x\ge 2$

f) $9x-x^3\ge 0$
$x(3-x)(3+x)\ge 0$
$x\le -3,\ 0\le x\le 3$

g) $-x^3-3x^2+10x\ge 0$
$-x(x+5)(x-2)\ge 0$
$x\le -5,\ 0\le x\le 2$

h) $x^4-3x^3-4x^2\ge 0$
$x^2(x-4)(x+1)\ge 0$
$x\le -1,\ x=0,\ x\ge 4$

i) $x(x+1)^2(x-2)(x-4)\ge 0$
$x=-1,\ 0\le x\le 2,\ x\ge 4$

j) $x^2(x+1)^2(x-1)\ge 0$
$x=-1,\ x=0,\ x\ge 1$

(All of the answers to question 4 can easily be seen by graphing the polynomial function.)

5. a)

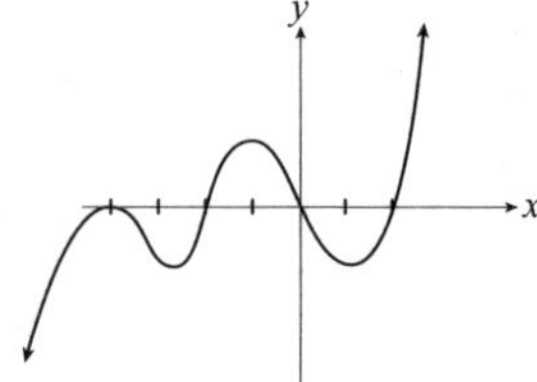

b)

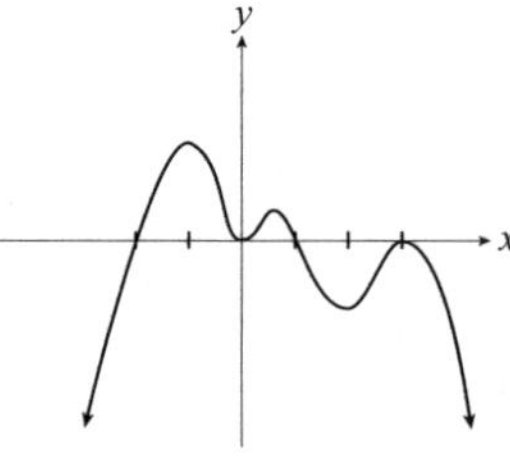

6. a)

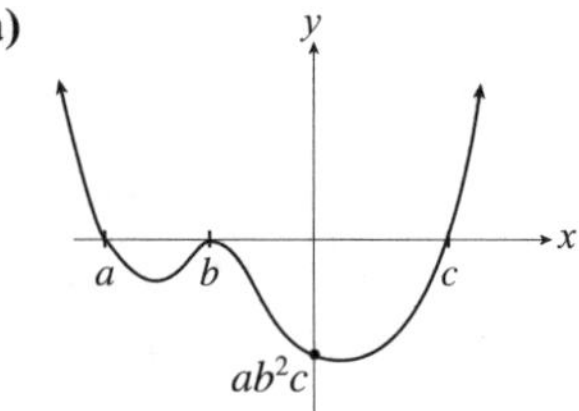

b)

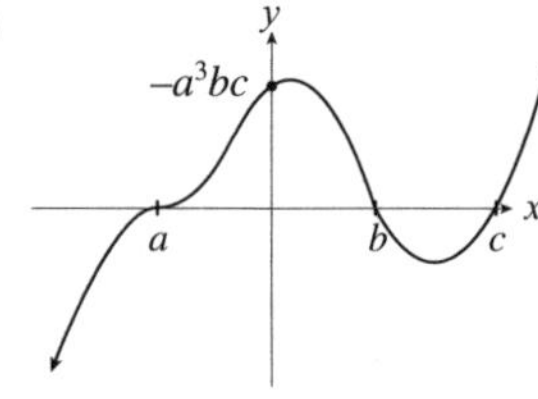

7. a) $P(x) = a(x+1)^2(x-2)$

$P(0) = a(0+1)^2(0-2) = -4$

$-2a = -4$

$a = 2$

therefore, $P(x) = 2(x+1)^2(x-2)$

b) $P(x) = ax^2(x-1)^3(x-2)$

$P(-1) = a(-1)^2(-1-1)^3(-1-2) = 12$

$24a = 12$

$a = \frac{1}{2}$

therefore, $P(x) = \frac{1}{2}x^2(x-1)^3(x-2)$

c) $P(x) = a(2x-1)(3x+2)^2$

$P(0) = a(2\cdot 0-1)(3\cdot 0+2)^2 = -3$

$-4a = -3$

$a = \frac{3}{4}$

therefore, $P(x) = \frac{3}{4}(2x-1)(3x+2)^2$

d) If the root $-\frac{1}{2}$ has multiplicity 3, then it must have $(2x+1)^3$ as a factor.

If $2x^2 - x - 1$ is a factor, then it factors into $(2x+1)(x-1)$.

Find the L.C.M. of these 2 factors $(2x+1)^3$ and $(2x+1)(x-1)$,

therefore, $P(x) = a(2x+1)^3(x-1)$

e) $P(x) = ax(x-2)(x^2-2x-5)$

$P(3) = a\cdot 3(3-2)(3^2 - 2\cdot 3 - 5) = 12$

$-6a = 12$

$a = -2$

therefore, $P(x) = -2x(x-2)(x^2-2x-5)$

f) If the graph is symmetric to the y-axis, it must also be tangent at $(-3, 0)$.

So $P(x) = a(x+3)^2(x-3)^2$

$P(0) = a(0+3)^2(0-3)^2 = 27$

$81a = 27$

$a = \frac{1}{3}$,

therefore, $P(x) = \frac{1}{3}(x+3)^2(x-3)^2$

8. Minimum number of real roots is 2.

3.3 Exercise Set

1. a)

$$\begin{array}{r|l} & x^2 - 5x - 18 \\ x-3 & x^3 - 8x^2 - 3x + 2 \\ & \underline{x^3 - 3x^2} \\ & -5x^2 - 3x \\ & \underline{-5x^2 + 15x} \\ & -18x + 2 \\ & \underline{-18x + 54} \\ & -52 \end{array}$$

$x^3 - 8x^2 - 3x + 2 = (x-3)(x^2 - 5x - 18) - 52$

$$\frac{x^3 - 8x^2 - 3x + 2}{x-3} = x^2 - 5x - 18 - \frac{52}{x-3}$$

b)

$$\begin{array}{r|l} & 4x^2 + 2x + 1 \\ 2x-1 & 8x^3 + 0x^2 + 0x - 1 \\ & \underline{8x^3 - 4x^2} \\ & 4x^2 \\ & \underline{4x^2 - 2x} \\ & 2x - 1 \\ & \underline{2x - 1} \\ & 0 \end{array}$$

$8x^3 - 1 = (2x-1)(4x^2 + 2x + 1)$

$$\frac{8x^3 - 1}{2x-1} = 4x^2 + 2x + 1$$

c)

$$\begin{array}{r|l} & x^3 + 2x^2 - 2x - 1 \\ x^2+1 & x^5 + 2x^4 - x^3 + x^2 - 3x + 4 \\ & \underline{x^5 + \quad x^3} \\ & 2x^4 - 2x^3 + x^2 \\ & \underline{2x^4 + \quad 2x^2} \\ & -2x^3 - x^2 - 3x \\ & \underline{-2x^3 - \quad 2x} \\ & -x^2 - x + 4 \\ & \underline{-x^2 - \quad 1} \\ & -x + 5 \end{array}$$

$x^5 + 2x^4 - x^3 + x^2 - 3x + 4 = (x^2+1)(x^3 + 2x^2 - 2x - 1) - x + 5$

$$\frac{x^5 + 2x^4 - x^3 + x^2 - 3x + 4}{x^2+1} = x^3 + 2x^2 - 2x - 1 + \frac{-x+5}{x^2+1}$$

d)

$$\begin{array}{r|l} & x^2 - 2 \\ x^2-1 & x^4 + 0x^3 - 3x^2 + 0x + 8 \\ & \underline{x^4 - \quad x^2} \\ & -2x^2 + \quad 8 \\ & \underline{-2x^2 + \quad 2} \\ & 6 \end{array}$$

$x^4 - 3x^2 + 8 = (x^2-1)(x^2-2) + 6$

$$\frac{x^4 - 3x^2 + 8}{x^2-1} = x^2 - 2 + \frac{6}{x^2-1}$$

1. e)

$$\begin{array}{r}
x+6 \\
x^2-4x-12\,\overline{)\,x^3+2x^2-13x+10} \\
\underline{x^3-4x^2-12x} \\
6x^2-\quad x+10 \\
\underline{6x^2-24x-72} \\
23x+82
\end{array}$$

$$x^3+2x^2-13x+10=(x^2-4x-12)(x+6)+23x+82$$

$$\frac{x^3+2x^2-13x+10}{x^2-4x-12}=x+6+\frac{23x+82}{x^2-4x-12}$$

f)

$$\begin{array}{r}
x+2 \\
x^2-2x\,\overline{)\,x^3+0x^2-5x+1} \\
\underline{x^3-2x^2} \\
2x^2-5x \\
\underline{2x^2-4x} \\
-x+1
\end{array}$$

$$x^3-5x+1=(x^2-2x)(x+2)-x+1$$

$$\frac{x^3-5x+1}{x^2-2x}=x+2+\frac{-x+1}{x^2-2x}$$

g)

$$\begin{array}{r}
x+6 \\
x^3+3x+2\,\overline{)\,x^4+6x^3+11x^2+6x} \\
\underline{x^4+\qquad 3x^2+2x} \\
6x^3+\ 8x^2+4x \\
\underline{6x^3+\qquad 18x+12} \\
8x^2-14x-12
\end{array}$$

$$x^4+6x^3+11x^2+6x=(x^3+3x+2)(x+6)+8x^2-14x-12$$

$$\frac{x^4+6x^3+11x+6x}{x^3+3x+2}=x+6+\frac{8x^2-14x-12}{x^3+3x+2}$$

h)

$$\begin{array}{r}
x^2+9x-2 \\
x^2-3\,\overline{)\,x^4+9x^3-5x^2-32x+3} \\
\underline{x^4\qquad -3x^2} \\
9x^3-2x^2-32x \\
\underline{9x^3\qquad -27x} \\
-2x^2-5x+3 \\
\underline{-2x^2\qquad +6} \\
-5x-3
\end{array}$$

$$x^4+9x^3-5x^2-32x+3=(x^2-3)(x^2+9x-2)-5x-3$$

$$\frac{x^4+9x^3-5x^2-32x+3}{x^2-3}=x^2+9x-2+\frac{-5x-3}{x^2-3}$$

2. a)

$$\begin{array}{r|rrrr}
2 & 1 & 2 & -3 & 1 \\
 & & 2 & 8 & 10 \\ \hline
 & 1 & 4 & 5 & 11
\end{array}$$

$Q(x)=x^2+4x+5$
$R=11$

b)

$$\begin{array}{r|rrrr}
a & 1 & 0 & 0 & -a^3 \\
 & & a & a^2 & a^3 \\ \hline
 & 1 & a & a^2 & 0
\end{array}$$

$Q(x)=x^2+ax+a^2$
$R=0$

c)

$$\begin{array}{r|rrrr}
-2 & 4 & 0 & 5 & -3 \\
 & & -8 & 16 & -42 \\ \hline
 & 4 & -8 & 21 & -45
\end{array}$$

$Q(x)=4x^2-8x+21$
$R=-45$

d)

$$\begin{array}{r|rrrrrr}
1 & 1 & 0 & -5 & 0 & 0 & 10 \\
 & & 1 & 1 & -4 & -4 & -4 \\ \hline
 & 1 & 1 & -4 & -4 & -4 & 6
\end{array}$$

$Q(x)=x^4+x^3-4x^2-4x-4$
$R=6$

e)

$$\begin{array}{r|rrr}
2.1 & 0.1 & 0 & 0.2 \\
 & & 0.21 & 0.441 \\ \hline
 & 0.1 & 0.21 & 0.641
\end{array}$$

$Q(x)=0.1x+0.21$
$R=0.641$

f)

$$\begin{array}{r|rrrrrr}
-1 & 1 & 0 & 0 & 0 & 0 & 1 \\
 & & -1 & 1 & -1 & 1 & -1 \\ \hline
 & 1 & -1 & 1 & -1 & 1 & 0
\end{array}$$

$Q(x)=x^4-x^3+x^2-x+1$
$R=0$

g)

$$\begin{array}{r|rrrrr}
-\frac{1}{3} & 3 & 1 & 0 & -3 & 1 \\
 & & -1 & 0 & 0 & 1 \\ \hline
 & 3 & 0 & 0 & -3 & 2
\end{array}$$

$Q(x)=x^3-1,\ R=2$

note: multiply divisor by 3, divide quotient by 3

h)

$$\begin{array}{r|rrrrr}
\frac{1}{2} & 2 & -1 & 0 & 2 & -1 \\
 & & 1 & 0 & 0 & 1 \\ \hline
 & 2 & 0 & 0 & 2 & 0
\end{array}$$

$Q(x)=x^3+1,\ R=0$

note: multiply divisor by 2, divide quotient by 2

i)

$$\begin{array}{r|rrrrrr}
-0.8 & 3 & 2 & 5 & 0 & -7 & -3 \\
 & & -2.4 & 0.32 & -4.256 & 3.4048 & 2.87616 \\ \hline
 & 3 & -0.4 & 5.32 & -4.256 & -3.5952 & -0.12384
\end{array}$$

$Q(x)=3x^4-0.4x^3+5.32x^2-4.256x-3.5952$
$R=-0.12384$

j)

$$\begin{array}{r|rrrrr}
0.4 & 3 & -3 & 2 & -3 & 1 \\
 & & 1.2 & -0.72 & 0.512 & -0.9952 \\ \hline
 & 3 & -1.8 & 1.28 & -2.488 & 0.0048
\end{array}$$

$Q(x)=3x^3-1.8x^2+1.28x-2.488$
$R=0.0048$

k) $x^2-1=(x-1)(x+1)$

$$\begin{array}{r|rrrrr}
1 & 1 & -5 & -4 & 5 & 3 \\
 & & 1 & -4 & -8 & -3 \\ \hline
-1 & 1 & -4 & -8 & -3 & 0 \\
 & & -1 & 5 & 3 & \\ \hline
 & 1 & -5 & -3 & 0 &
\end{array}$$

$Q(x)=x^2-5x-3$
$R=0$

l) $x^2-x-6=(x-3)(x+2)$

$$\begin{array}{r|rrrrrr}
-2 & 1 & -1 & -8 & 7 & 7 & -30 \\
 & & -2 & 6 & 4 & -22 & 30 \\ \hline
3 & 1 & -3 & -2 & 11 & -15 & 0 \\
 & & 3 & 0 & -6 & 15 & \\ \hline
 & 1 & 0 & -2 & 5 & 0 &
\end{array}$$

$Q(x)=x^3-2x+5$
$R=0$

3. **a)**
$$\begin{array}{r|rrrr} -2 & 4 & -7 & -11 & 5 \\ & & -8 & 30 & -38 \\ \hline & 4 & -15 & 19 & -33 \end{array}$$
$4x^3-7x^2-11x+5=(x+2)(4x^2-15x+19)-33$

b)
$$\begin{array}{r|rrrr} \frac{2}{3} & 6 & -16 & 17 & -6 \\ & & 4 & -8 & 6 \\ \hline & 6 & -12 & 9 & 0 \end{array}$$
$6x^3-16x^2+17x-6=(x-\frac{2}{3})(6x^2-12x+9)$
$=(3x-2)(2x^2-4x+3)$

c)
$$\begin{array}{r|rrrr} 4 & 1 & 0 & 0 & -64 \\ & & 4 & 16 & 64 \\ \hline & 1 & 4 & 16 & 0 \end{array}$$
$x^3-64=(x-4)(x^2+4x+16)$

d)
$$\begin{array}{r|rrrr} \frac{1}{2} & 4 & 16 & -23 & 15 \\ & & 2 & 9 & -7 \\ \hline & 4 & 18 & -14 & 8 \end{array}$$
$4x^3+16x^2-23x+15=(x-\frac{1}{2})(4x^2+18x-14)+8$
$=(2x-1)(2x^2+9x-7)+8$

e)
$$\begin{array}{r|rrrr} 1-\sqrt{3} & 1 & 0 & -4 & 0 \\ & & 1-\sqrt{3} & 4-2\sqrt{3} & 6-2\sqrt{3} \\ \hline & 1 & 1-\sqrt{3} & -2\sqrt{3} & 6-2\sqrt{3} \end{array}$$
$x^3-4x=(x-1+\sqrt{3})(x^2+(1-\sqrt{3})x-2\sqrt{3})+6-2\sqrt{3}$

f)
$$\begin{array}{r|rrrr} 2+\sqrt{2} & -3 & 8 & 10 & -8 \\ & & -6-3\sqrt{2} & -2-4\sqrt{2} & 8 \\ \hline & -3 & 2-3\sqrt{2} & 8-4\sqrt{2} & 0 \end{array}$$
$(x-2-\sqrt{2})(-3x^2+(2-3\sqrt{2})x+8-4\sqrt{2})$

g)
$$\begin{array}{r|rrrrr} 5 & 1 & -4 & -15 & 58 & -40 \\ & & 5 & 5 & -50 & 40 \\ \hline & 1 & 1 & -10 & 8 & 0 \end{array}$$
$x^4-4x^3-15x^2+58x-40=$
$(x-5)(x^3+x^2-10x+8)$

h)
$$\begin{array}{r|rrrrrr} 2 & 1 & -2 & 1 & 0 & 0 & -5 \\ & & 2 & 0 & 2 & 4 & 8 \\ \hline & 1 & 0 & 1 & 2 & 4 & 3 \end{array}$$
$x^5-2x^4+x^3-5=(x-2)(x^4+x^2+2x+4)+3$

i) $x^2+3x+2=(x+2)(x+1)$
$$\begin{array}{r|rrrr} -2 & 1 & 6 & 11 & 6 \\ & & -2 & -8 & -6 \\ \hline -1 & 1 & 4 & 3 & 0 \\ & & -1 & -3 & \\ \hline & 1 & 3 & 0 & \end{array}$$
$x^4+6x^3+11x^2+6x=x(x^3+6x^2+11x+6)$
$=x(x+3)(x^2+3x+2)$

j) $x^2-4=(x-2)(x+2)$
$$\begin{array}{r|rrrrr} 2 & 1 & 9 & -5 & -36 & 4 \\ & & 2 & 22 & 34 & -4 \\ \hline -2 & 1 & 11 & 17 & -2 & 0 \\ & & -2 & -18 & 2 & \\ \hline & 1 & 9 & -1 & 0 & \end{array}$$
$x^4+9x^3-5x^2-36x+4=(x^2-4)(x^2+9x-1)$

k)
$$\begin{array}{r|rrrr} -4 & 1 & 16 & 64 & 64 \\ & & -4 & -48 & -64 \\ \hline & 1 & 12 & 16 & 0 \end{array}$$
$x^{3n}+16x^{2n}+64x^n+64=(x^n+4)(x^{2n}+12x^n+16)$

l)
$$\begin{array}{r|rrrr} 3 & 1 & -9 & 27 & -27 \\ & & 3 & -18 & 27 \\ \hline & 1 & -6 & 9 & 0 \end{array}$$
$x^{3n}-9x^{2n}+27x^n-27=(x^n-3)(x^{2n}-6x^n+9)$

4. **a)**
$$\begin{array}{r|rrrr} 2 & 1 & 0 & k & 1 \\ & & 2 & 4 & 2k+8 \\ \hline & 1 & 2 & k+4 & -3 \end{array}$$
$1+2k+8=-3$
$k=-6$

b)
$$\begin{array}{r|rrrr} 4 & 1 & -1 & k & -8 \\ & & 4 & 12 & 4k+48 \\ \hline & 1 & 3 & k+12 & 0 \end{array}$$
$-8+4k+48=0$
$k=-10$

c)
$$\begin{array}{r|rrrrr} 2 & 2 & 0 & k & -3 & 5 \\ & & 4 & 8 & 2k+16 & 4k+26 \\ \hline & 2 & 4 & k+8 & 2k+13 & 3 \end{array}$$
$5+4k+26=3$
$k=-7$

d)
$$\begin{array}{r|rrrr} -2 & 1 & 0 & k & 6 \\ & & -2 & 4 & -2k-8 \\ \hline & 1 & -2 & k+4 & 4 \end{array}$$
$6-2k-8=4$
$k=-3$

e)
$$\begin{array}{r|rrrr} -1 & 1 & k & -2 & -7 \\ & & -1 & -k+1 & k+1 \\ \hline & 1 & k-1 & -k-1 & 5 \end{array}$$
$-7+k+1=5$
$k=11$
$$\begin{array}{r|rrrr} 1 & 1 & 11 & -2 & -7 \\ & & 1 & 12 & 10 \\ \hline & 1 & 12 & 10 & \boxed{3} \end{array}$$
Remainder is 3

f)
$$\begin{array}{r|rrrr} 1 & k & m & 1 & -2 \\ & & k & m+k & m+k+1 \\ \hline & k & m+k & m+k+1 & 6 \end{array}$$
$-2+m+k+1=6$
$m+k=7$
$$\begin{array}{r|rrrr} -2 & k & m & 1 & -2 \\ & & -2k & -2m+4k & -2+4m-8k \\ \hline & k & m-2k & 1-2m+4k & 12 \end{array}$$
$-2-2+4m-8k=12$
$4m-8k=16$
$m-2k=4$

Thus $m+k=7$
$m-2k=4$
$3k=3$
$k=1, m+1=7$
$m=6$

4. **g)**

$$\begin{array}{r|rrrrr} 1 & 1 & k & 0 & -m & 15 \\ & & 1 & k+1 & k+1 & -m+k+1 \\ \hline & 1 & k+1 & k+1 & -m+k+1 & 0 \end{array}$$

$15-m+k+1=0$

$-m+k=-16$

$$\begin{array}{r|rrrrr} -3 & 1 & k & 0 & -m & 15 \\ & & -3 & -3k+9 & 9k-27 & 3m-27k+81 \\ \hline & 1 & k-3 & -3k+9 & -m+9k-27 & 0 \end{array}$$

$15+3m-27k+81=0$

$3m-27k=-96$

$m-9k=-32$

Thus $\begin{aligned} -m+k&=-16 \\ m-9k&=-32 \\ \hline -8k&=-48 \\ k=6, -m+6&=-16 \\ m&=22 \end{aligned}$

h)

$$\begin{array}{r|rrrrr} 1 & 3 & 0 & k & 0 & 7 \\ & & 3 & 3 & k+3 & k+3 \\ \hline & 3 & 3 & k+3 & k+3 & k+10 \end{array}$$

$$\begin{array}{r|rrrrr} 2 & 1 & 0 & 0 & k & -4 \\ & & 2 & 4 & 8 & 2k+16 \\ \hline & 1 & 2 & 4 & k+8 & 2k+12 \end{array}$$

Thus $k+10=2k+12$

$k=-2$

3.4 Exercise Set

1. **a)** $P(-2)=(-2)^4+3(-2)^3-7(-2)+2$

$=8$

b) $P(\sqrt{2})=-2(\sqrt{2})^4-3(\sqrt{2})^2-2$

$=-16$

c) $P(1+\sqrt{2})=-2(1+\sqrt{2})^2+4(1+\sqrt{2})+3$

$=-2(1+2\sqrt{2}+2)+4(1+\sqrt{2})+3$

$=-2-4\sqrt{2}-4+4+4\sqrt{2}+3$

$=1$

d) $P(a)=a^5-5a^5+4a^5$

$=0$

2. **a)** $P(2)=2^3+k(2)+1=-3$

$2k=-12$

$k=-6$

b) $P(4)=4^3-4^2+k(4)-8=0$

$4k=-40$

$k=-10$

c) $P(2)=2\cdot 2^4+k\cdot 2^2-3(2)+5=3$

$4k=-28$

$k=-7$

d) $P(-2)=(-2)^3+k(-2)+6=4$

$-2k=6$

$k=-3$

e) $P(-1)=(-1)^3+k(-1)^2-2(-1)-7=5$

$k=11$

$P(1)=1^3+11(1)^2-2(1)-7=3$

Remainder is 3

f) $P(1)=k(1)^3+m(1)^2+1-2=6$

$k+m=7$

$P(-2)=k(-2)^3+m(-2)^2-2-2=12$

$-8k+4m=16$

$2k-m=-4$

$\begin{aligned} k+m&=7 \\ 2k-m&=-4 \\ \hline 3k\quad&=3 \\ k&=1 \end{aligned} \quad \rightarrow \quad \begin{aligned} k+m&=7 \\ 1+m&=7 \\ m&=6 \end{aligned}$

g) $P(1)=1^4+k(1)^3-m(1)+15=0$

$k-m=-16$

$P(-3)=(-3)^4+k(-3)^3-m(-3)+15=0$

$-27k+3m=-96$

$-9k+m=-32$

$\begin{aligned} k-m&=-16 \\ -9k+m&=-32 \\ \hline -8k\quad&=-48 \\ k&=6 \end{aligned} \quad \rightarrow \quad \begin{aligned} k-m&=-16 \\ 6-m&=-16 \\ m&=22 \end{aligned}$

h) $P(1)=3(1)^4+k(1)^2+7=R$

$f(2)=(2)^4+k(2)-4=R$

Therefore, $3+k+7=16+2k-4$

$10+k=12+2k$

$k=-2$

3. a) If a polynomial is divided by $(x-a)$, its remainder is $P(a)$ (*Remainder Theorem*)

b) $P(3)=18$ means the point (3 , 18). Frequently, students get this concept wrong.

$P(x)=x^3-rx^2+3x+r^2$

$P(3)=27-9r+9+r^2=18$

$r^2-9r+18=0 \rightarrow (r-6)(r-3)=0 \rightarrow r=3,6$

c) $f(x)=x^n+x-8$

$f(2)=2^n+2-8=10 \rightarrow 2^n=16 \rightarrow$
$n=4$

d) Remember, if a polynomial is divided by $(x+a)$, its remainder is $f(-a)$.

$P(x)=x^2+5x-2$

$P(-a)=(-a)^2+5(-a)-2=8$

$a^2-5a-10=0$, therefore by quadratic equation, $a=\dfrac{5\pm\sqrt{65}}{2}$

e) Please do not try to do this question by synthetic division!

Remember, if a polynomial is divided by $(x+a)$, its remainder is $P(-a)$.

Therefore,
$P(x)=kx^{50}+2x^{30}+4x+7$

$P(-1)=k(-1)^{50}+2(-1)^{30}+4(-1)+7=23$

$k \quad +2 \quad -4 \quad +7=23$

$k=18$

f) If $P(x)=2x^3+3x^2+kx+m$

$P(1)=2(1)^3+3(1)^2+k(1)+m=8$

$2+3+k+m=8$

$k+m=3$

$P(-2)=2(-2)^3+3(-2)^2+k(-2)+m=-13$

$-16+12-2k+m=-13$

$2k-m=9$

$k+m=3$
$2k-m=9$
$3k=12$
$k=4,$

$4+m=3$
$m=-1$

4. a)

1⌋	2	−7	2	3
		2	−5	−3
	2	−5	−3	0

$(x-1)(2x^2-5x-3)$

$(x-1)(2x+1)(x-3)$

b)

2⌋	1	−3	−10	24
		2	−2	−24
	1	−1	−12	0

$(x-2)(x^2-x-12)$

$(x-2)(x-4)(x+3)$

c)

−1⌋	1	1	−9	−9
		−1	0	9
	1	0	−9	0

$x(x+1)(x^2-9)$

$x(x+1)(x-3)(x+3)$

d)

1⌋	2	−7	9	−5	1
		2	−5	4	−1
1⌋	2	−5	4	−1	0
		2	−3	1	
1⌋	2	−3	1	0	
		2	−1		
	2	−1	0		

therefore, $(x-1)^3(2x-1)$

e)

2⌋	2	5	−11	−20	12
		4	18	14	−12
−2⌋	2	9	7	−6	
		−4	−10	6	
	2	5	−3	0	

$(x^2-4)(2x^2+5x-3)$

$(x^2-4)(2x-1)(x+3)$

f) $x^2-3x+2=(x-2)(x-1)$

2⌋	1	−8	25	−38	28	−8
		2	−12	26	−24	8
1⌋	1	−6	13	−12	4	0
		1	−5	8	−4	
1⌋	1	−5	8	−4	0	
2⌋		1	−4	4		
	1	−4	4	0		
		2	−4			
	1	−2	0			

$\therefore (x-2)^3(x-1)^2$

5. a) Use synthetic division.

2⌋	3	1	−20	12
		6	14	−12
	3	7	−6	0

therefore, the other roots come from
$3x^2+7x-6=0$
$(3x-2)(x+3)=0$
$x=\frac{2}{3}, -3$

b) If $P(x)=-4x^3+2x^2-2kx+k^3$

$P\left(\frac{1}{2}\right)=-4\left(\frac{1}{2}\right)^3+2\left(\frac{1}{2}\right)^2-2k\left(\frac{1}{2}\right)+k^3=0$

$k^3-k=0$

$k(k-1)(k+1)=0$

$k=0,1,-1$

c) This is a very important concept: If $x=c$ is a zero of $P(x)$, then $x-c$ must be a factor of $P(x)$.

d) $P(a)=2a^3-a\cdot a^2+(1-a^2)a+5=0$

$2a^3-a^3+a-a^3+5=0$
$a=-5$

5. e) If $(x+1)$ is a factor, then $f(-1) = 0$, therefore, put -1 into the equation and set it equal to zero.

$$f(x) = 2x^4 + (k+1)x^2 - 6kx + 11,$$

$$f(-1) = 2(-1)^4 + (k+1)(-1)^2 - 6k(-1) + 11 = 0$$

$$2 + k + 1 + 6k + 11 = 0$$

$$7k = -14$$

$$k = -2$$

f) Factor each known factor:

$$\left.\begin{aligned} x^2 - 4 &= (x-2)(x+2) \\ x^2 - 2x &= x(x-2) \\ x^2 + x - 2 &= (x+2)(x-1) \end{aligned}\right\} \text{Find the common denominator.}$$

The lowest degree polynomial

$$P(x) = ax(x-2)(x+2)(x-1) = ax^4 + \cdots\cdots$$

Therefore, the lowest degree is 4.

g)

$$f(k) = 2k^3 - k \cdot k^2 + (3 - k^2) \cdot k - 6 = 0$$

$$2k^3 - k^3 + 3k - k^3 - 6 = 0$$

$$3k = 6$$

$$k = 2$$

h)

-2	1	3	−5	−15	4	12
		−2	−2	14	2	−12
-1	1	1	−7	−1	6	
		−1	0	7	−6	
1	1	0	−7	6	0	
		1	1	−6		
	1	1	−6	0		

therefore, $(x+2)(x+1)(x-1)(x^2+x-6)$

$(x+2)(x+1)(x-1)(x+3)(x-2)$

i)

1	1	−3	0	8	−9	3	
		1	−2	−2	6	−3	
1	1	−2	−2	6	−3	0	→ now guess 2nd $(x-1)$ factor
		1	−1	−3	3		
1	1	−1	−3	3	0		→ now guess 3rd $(x-1)$ factor
		1	0	−3			
	1	0	−3	0			

therefore, $(x-1)^3(x^2-3)$

$(x-1)^3(x-\sqrt{3})(x+\sqrt{3})$

j) $f(x) = x^3 + x^2 + ax + b$, $\quad g(x) = x^3 - x^2 - ax + b$

$x - 1$ is a factor of $f(x)$ →

$f(1) = 1^3 + 1^2 + a(1) + b = 0 \rightarrow a + b = -2$

$x - 1$ is a factor of $g(x)$ →

$g(1) = 1^3 - 1^2 - a(1) + b = 0 \rightarrow -a + b = 0$

$2b = -2$

$b = -1,$

$a + b = -2$

$a - 1 = -2$

$a = -1$

3.5 Exercise Set

1.

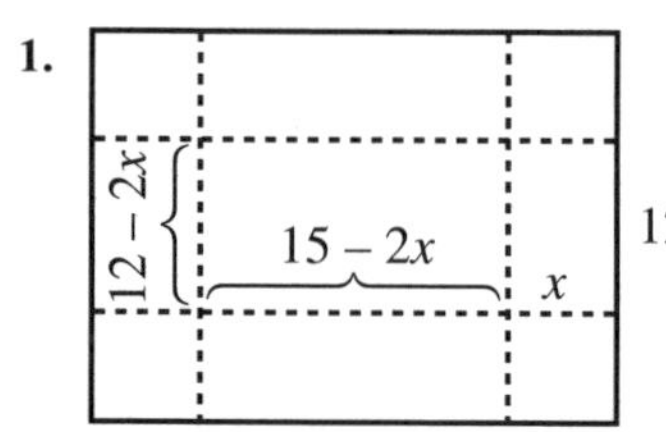

$$V = x(12-2x)(15-2x) = 162$$

$$2x^3 - 27x^2 + 90x - 81 = 0$$

Test 3, 9, 27,...

3	2	−27	90	−81
		6	−63	81
	2	−21	27	0

$$(x-3)(2x^2 - 21x + 27) = 0$$

$$(x-3)(2x-3)(x-9) = 0$$

reject 1.5, less than 2

reject 9, makes length negative

Must cut corner 3 cm wide.

2. $v = x(12-2x)(15-2x) = 150$

$2x^3 - 27x^2 + 90x - 75 = 0$ This does not factor; use graphing calculator.

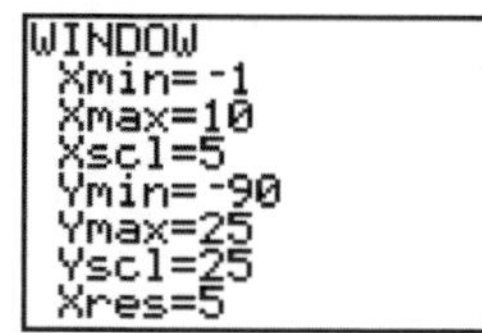

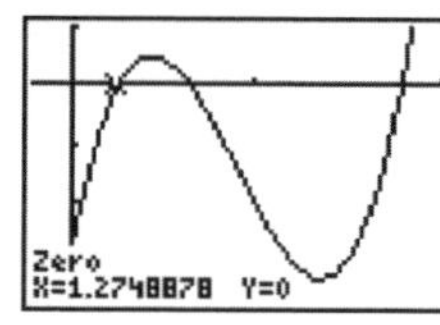

$x = 1.27$ reject, less than 2

$= 3.29$ ok

$= 8.93$ reject

makes length negative

Calculate zero.

Must cut corners 3.29 cm wide.

3. $V_{cylinder} = \pi r^2 h$

$V_{hemisphere} = \dfrac{2}{3}\pi r^3$

Test 2, 3, 4, 6,...

$$V_{total} = \pi r^2 h + \frac{2}{3}\pi r^3$$

$$= \pi r^2 (12 - r) + \frac{2}{3}\pi r^3 = 360\pi$$

$$r^3 - 36r^2 + 1080 = 0$$

r

12 − r

6	1	−36	0	1080
		6	−180	−1080
	1	−30	−180	0

$$(x-6)(x^2 - 30x - 180) = 0$$

$$x = \frac{30 \pm \sqrt{(-30)^2 - 4(1)(-180)}}{2} =$$

−5.12, reject, negative length

35.12, reject, makes height negative

Radius is 6 cm.

4. 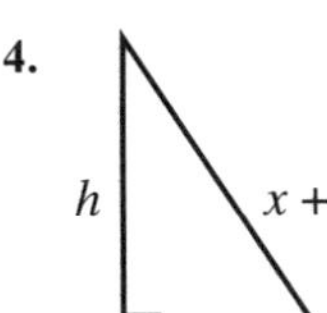

$h^2 + x^2 = (x+1)^2$

$h^2 = 2x+1$

$A = \frac{1}{2}b \cdot h$

$6 = \frac{1}{2}x\sqrt{2x+1}$

$144 = x^2(2x+1)$

$2x^3 + x^2 - 144 = 0$

Test 2, 3, 4

4⌋	2	1	0	−144
		8	36	144
	2	9	36	0

$(x-4)(2x^2+9x+36)=0 \quad x = \frac{-9 \pm \sqrt{81-4(2)(36)}}{4} = \frac{-9 \pm \sqrt{-207}}{4} = \varnothing$ Sides are 3, 4 and 5 cm long.

5. $V = L \cdot W \cdot H$

$= 1 \cdot 2 \cdot 3$

$= 6 \text{ m}^3$

$V = (x+1)(x+2)(x+3) = 6 \times 10$

$x^3 + 6x^2 + 11x - 54 = 0$

$(x-2)(x^2+8x+27)=0$

$x = \frac{-8 \pm \sqrt{8^2 - 4(1)(27)}}{2} = \varnothing$

Test 2, 3, 6

2⌋	1	6	11	−54
		2	16	54
	1	8	27	0

Increase sides by 2 m.

6. $V = L \cdot W \cdot H$

$= 1 \cdot 1 \cdot 2$

$= 2 \text{ m}^3$

$V = (x+1)(x+1)(x+2) = 2 \times 6$

$x^3 + 4x^2 + 5x - 10 = 0$

$(x-1)(x^2+5x+10)=0$

$x = \frac{-5 \pm \sqrt{5^2 - 4(1)(10)}}{2} = \varnothing$

Test 1, 2, 5

1⌋	1	4	5	−10
		1	5	10
	1	5	10	0

Increase sides by 1 m.

7. 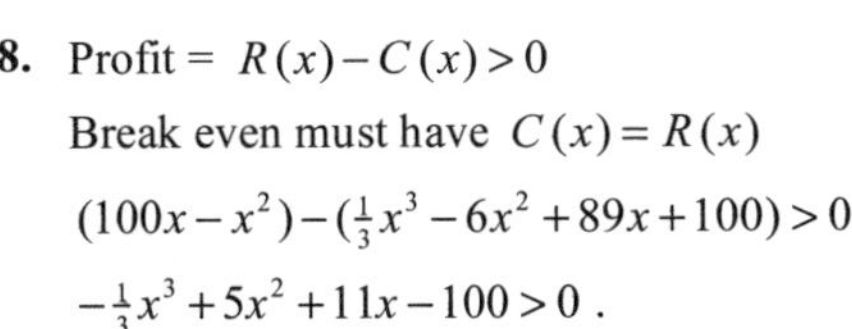

$V = x(5-2x)(8-2x) = 14$

$2x^2 - 13x^2 + 20x - 7 = 0$

$(x - \frac{1}{2})(2x^2 - 12x + 14) = 0$

$(2x-1)(x^2 - 6x + 7) = 0$

$x = \frac{-6 \pm \sqrt{6^2 - 4(1)(7)}}{2} =$

Test $\frac{1}{2}$, 1, ($\frac{7}{2}$, 7) reject, bigger than $\frac{5}{2}$

$\frac{1}{2}$⌋	2	−13	20	−7
		1	−6	7
	2	−12	14	0

1.586 accept
4.414 reject, makes length negative
The cut out squares must have either 0.5-inch sides or 1.586-inch sides.

8. Profit = $R(x) - C(x) > 0$

Break even must have $C(x) = R(x)$

$(100x - x^2) - (\frac{1}{3}x^3 - 6x^2 + 89x + 100) > 0$

$-\frac{1}{3}x^3 + 5x^2 + 11x - 100 > 0$.

Does not factor. Use graphing calculator and find zeros.
Makes a profit from 3.92 to 15.89 units or 4 to 15 units.

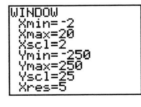

```
WINDOW
 Xmin=-2
 Xmax=20
 Xscl=2
 Ymin=-250
 Ymax=250
 Yscl=25
 Xres=5
```

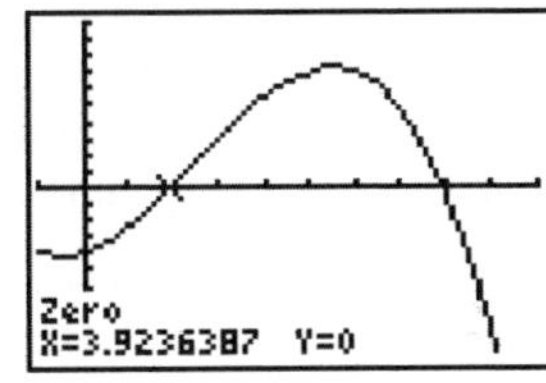

9. 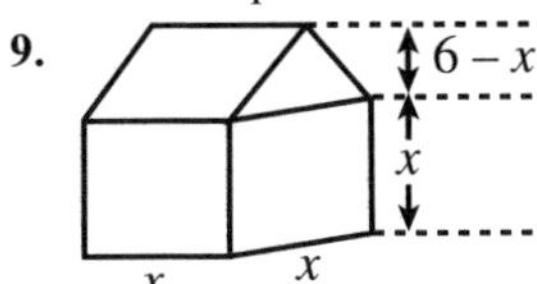

Volume = cube + prism

$= x^3 + \frac{1}{2}(x)(6-x)(x) = 80$

$x^3 + 6x^2 - 160 = 0$

Difficult to factor. Use graphing calculator and find zero. Zero is 4.0. Sides of shed are 4.0 m.

10. To find maximum volume, must use graphing calculator.

$V = x(9-2x)(15-2x)$

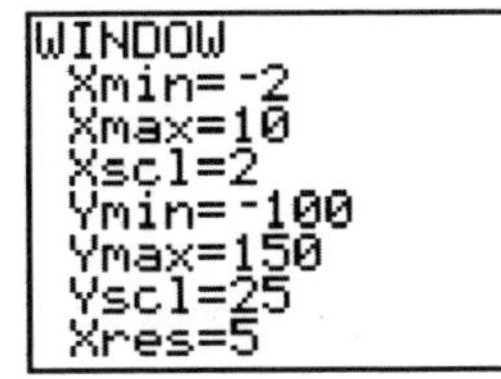

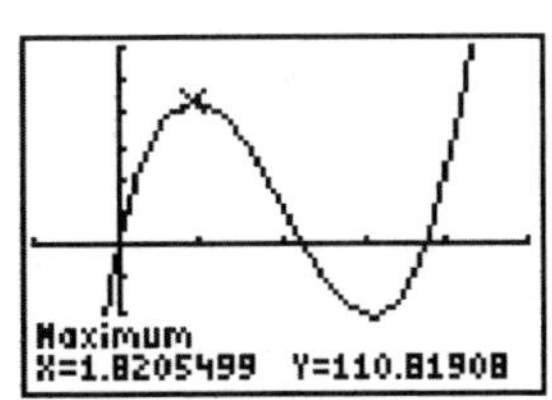

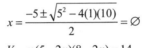

Maximum volume is 110.8 inches^3.

11.

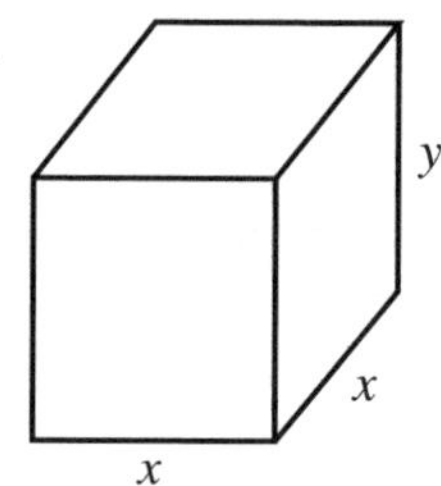

$$V = x^2y,\ 4x + y = 120$$
$$y = 120 - 4x$$
$$V = x^2(120 - 4x) = 13\,500$$
$$x^3 - 30x^2 + 3375 = 0$$
$$(x - 15)(x^2 - 15x - 225) = 0$$

Test 1, 3, 5, 15, …

$$\begin{array}{r|rrrr} 15 & 1 & -30 & 0 & 3375 \\ & & 15 & -225 & -3375 \\ \hline & 1 & -15 & -225 & 0 \end{array}$$

$$x = \frac{15 \pm \sqrt{15^2 - 4(1)(-225)}}{2}$$

$= -9.27$, reject; $= 24.27$, accept

Length of base could be 15 cm or 24.27 cm.

12. To find maximum volume must use graphing calculator.

$$V = x^2y$$
$$= x^2(120 - 4x)$$

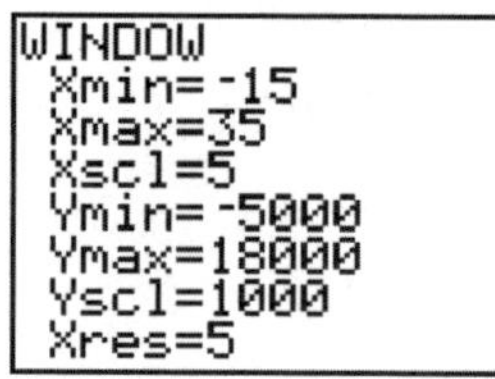

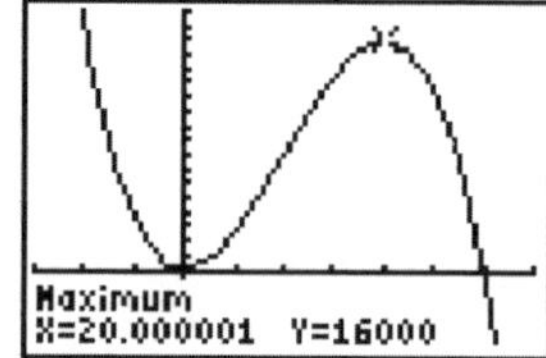

Maximum volume is 16 000 cm^3 when $x = 20$ cm and height $y = 40$ cm.

3.6 Chapter Review

Polynomials – Multiple-choice Answers

1.	b	**6.**	c	**11.**	d	**16.**	b	**21.**	b	**26.**	a	**31.**	b	**36.**	a	**41.**	a	**46.**	a
2.	d	**7.**	d	**12.**	a	**17.**	b	**22.**	c	**27.**	c	**32.**	d	**37.**	c	**42.**	d	**47.**	b
3.	a	**8.**	a	**13.**	c	**18.**	d	**23.**	a	**28.**	b	**33.**	d	**38.**	b	**43.**	a	**48.**	d
4.	c	**9.**	c	**14.**	c	**19.**	a	**24.**	a	**29.**	a	**34.**	c	**39.**	c	**44.**	c	**49.**	c
5.	a	**10.**	a	**15.**	a	**20.**	c	**25.**	c	**30.**	a	**35.**	b	**40.**	b	**45.**	b	**50.**	b

Polynomials – Multiple-choice Solutions

1. The graph is shifted down 2 units.
y-intercept (0, –2) becomes (0, –4)

$$y = a(x + 2)^2(x - 1)$$
$$y = a(0 + 2)^2(0 - 1) = -4$$
$$a = 1$$
$$y = (x + 2)^2(x - 1)$$

Answer is b.

2. Test –1, 1, –2, 2, –3, 3, –6, 6

$$\begin{array}{r|rrrr} -1 & 1 & 0 & -7 & -6 \\ & & -1 & 1 & 6 \\ \hline & 1 & -1 & -6 & 0 \end{array}$$

$$(x + 1)(x^2 - x - 6) = 0$$
$$(x + 1)(x - 3)(x + 2) = 0$$

$x = -1, -2, 3$ Answer is d.

3. By definition, answer is a.
4. $a < 0,\ d \neq 0$. Answer is c.
5. Graph is shifted 2 units to the left. Answer is a.
6. $x^3 + 2x^2 - 5x - 6 = (x - 2)(x^2 + 4x + 3)$. Answer is c.
7. Has 4 turns thus degree 5. Answer is d.
8. $P(x) = x^{23} - 1 \quad P(-1) = (-1)^{23} - 1 = -1 - 1 = -2$. Answer is a.
9. $y = f(x) = -a(x + 2)(x + 1)(x - 1),\ y = x\,f(x) = -ax(x + 2)(x + 1)(x - 1)$. Graph is c.
10. Graph shifts 2 units left and up 1 unit. Answer is a.
11. Graph is above x-axis when $x > 1$. Answer is d.
12. By definition, answer is a.
13. By graphing calculator, answer is c.
14. Graph is shifted 1 unit right, then $P(x)$ is doubled. Answer is c.
15. By definition, point is (–3, 4). Answer is a.
16. Use graphing calculator. Zero is –1.89. Answer is b.
17. $x = 0, x = 3$ are the two real zeros. Answer is b.
18. $f(2) = k(2 - 1)(2 + 2)^2(2 - 3) = 5 \rightarrow -16k = 5 \rightarrow k = -\frac{5}{16}$. Answer is d.
19. $f(x) = a(x + 2)^2(x - 1)(x - 3) \rightarrow f(0) = a(0 + 2)^2(0 - 1)(0 - 3) = 12 \rightarrow 12a = 12 \rightarrow a = 1$. Answer is a.
20. $a > 0$ and $e < 0$. Answer is c.

21.
$$\begin{array}{r} x^2-3x+3 \\ x^2-3\overline{)x^4-3x^3+0x^2+x-3} \\ \underline{x^4 \quad -3x^2} \\ -3x^3+3x^2+x \\ \underline{-3x^3 \quad +9x} \\ 3x^2-8x-3 \\ \underline{3x^2 \quad -9} \\ -8x+6 \end{array}$$
Answer is b.

22. Four turning points, therefore degree 5. Answer is c.

23. $(-2)^3-(-2)^2+k(-2)+5=1 \rightarrow -8-4-2k+5=1 \rightarrow -2k=8 \rightarrow k=-4$. Answer is a.

24. By definition, $P(-3)=0$. Answer is a.

25. By definition, $P(5)$ is the remainder. Answer is c.

26. $P(x)=xf(x)+k \rightarrow P(0)=0f(0)+k \rightarrow a=0+k \rightarrow k=a$. Answer is a.

27. $P(x)=-x^6+\cdots$ with double zero at –4, triple zero at 4. Answer is c.

28. If $P(-3)=5$, then –3 could not be a zero. Answer is b.

29. The zeros will not change, therefore zeros are –2, 2, 4. Answer is a.

30. The zeros are $-2x=0 \rightarrow x=0$ and $x^2-2=0 \rightarrow x^2=2 \rightarrow x=\pm\sqrt{2}$. Answer is a.

31. An odd degree has 1 to n solutions. Answer is b.

32.
$$\begin{array}{r} x-3 \\ x^2+x-1\overline{)x^3-2x^2+0x+6} \\ \underline{x^3+\ x^2-\ x} \\ -3x^2+\ x+6 \\ \underline{-3x^2-3x+3} \\ 4x+3 \end{array}$$
Answer is d.

33. $P(3)=(3-3)q(x)+r=r$. Answer is d.

34. Shift graph 5 right and 4 up and find zeros or an easy way by shift vertical axis 5 left and horizontal axis down 4. Zero is 1. Answer is c.

35. $y=f(x)-3=a(x+2)^2(x-1)$ with $y=f(0)-3=-6 \rightarrow a(0+2)^2(0-1)=-6 \rightarrow a=\frac{3}{2}$ $\quad y=\frac{3}{2}(x+2)^2(x-1)$. Answer is b.

36.
$$\begin{array}{r} x^2+7 \\ x^2+3x-2\overline{)x^4+3x^3+5x^2+21x-13} \\ \underline{x^4+3x^3-2x^2} \qquad\qquad \\ 7x^2+21x-13 \\ \underline{7x^2+21x-14} \\ 1 \end{array}$$
Answer is a.

37. $f(x)=1$ occurs at $x=-5, -1, 5$. Answer is c.

38.
$$\begin{array}{r|rrrr} -4 & 1 & 2 & -11 & -12 \\ & & -4 & 8 & 12 \\ \hline & 1 & -2 & -3 & 0 \end{array}$$
$$x^2-2x-3=0$$
$$(x-3)(x+1)=0$$
Answer is b.

39. $a\times 2=6 \rightarrow a=3 \quad b+3=-1 \rightarrow b=-4$ Answer is c.

40. $k(-1)^{40}+2(-1)^{25}-4(-1)-6=23 \rightarrow k-2+4-6=23 \rightarrow k=27$. Answer is b.

41. $y=-x^4+\cdots-3$, starts down touches x-axis at –1, and goes through at 1 and 3. Answer is a.

42.
$$x^3+\sqrt{2}x^2-4x-4\sqrt{2}=0$$
$$x^2(x+\sqrt{2})-4(x+\sqrt{2})=0$$
$$(x^2-4)(x+\sqrt{2})=0$$
$$(x-2)(x+2)(x+\sqrt{2})=0 \qquad x=-2, 2, -\sqrt{2}$$
Answer is d.

43.

$$\begin{array}{r|rrrr} -1 & 1 & 0 & a & b \\ & & -1 & 1 & -a-1 \\ \hline & 1 & -1 & a+1 & 0 \end{array}$$

$b-a-1=0$

$-a+b=1$

$$\begin{array}{r|rrrr} -2 & 1 & 0 & a & b \\ & & -2 & 4 & -2a-8 \\ \hline & 1 & -2 & a+4 & 0 \end{array}$$

$b-2a-8=0$

$-2a+b=8$

$$\begin{array}{r} -a+b=1 \\ -2a+b=8 \\ \hline a=-7 \end{array}$$

$7+b=1$

$b=-6$

Answer is a.

44. $P(x)=ax^3+x^2-13x+6$

$P(2)=a\cdot 2^3+2^2-13\cdot 2+6=0$

$a=2$

$$\begin{array}{r|rrrr} 2 & 2 & 1 & -13 & 6 \\ & & 4 & 10 & -6 \\ \hline & 2 & 5 & -3 & 0 \end{array}$$

$2x^2+5x-3=0$

$(x+3)(2x-1)=0$

$x=-3, \frac{1}{2}$

Answer is c.

45. $P(x)=x^4+4x^3+ax^2+bx-3$

$P(1)=1+4+a+b-3=-2.5 \to a+b=-4.5 \to$

$P(2)=16+32+4a+2b-3=46 \to 4a+2b=1$

$$\begin{array}{r} -2a-2b=9 \\ 4a+2b=1 \\ \hline 2a \quad =10 \end{array}$$

$a=5,\ b=-9.5$

Answer is b.

46. $8x^3+ax^2+16x+3=(4x-3)(2x^2+bx+1)+6$

$=8x^3+(4b-6)x^2+(4-3b)x+3$

$4-3b=16$

$b=-4$

$a=4b-6$

$=4(-4)-6$

$=-22$

Answer is a.

47. $P(x)=a(x-1)(x-2)(x-c)$

$P(0)=a(0-1)(0-2)(0-c)=10 \to -2ac=10$

$ac=-5$

$P(5)=a(5-1)(5-2)(5-c)=480 \to 12a(5-c)=480$

$5a-ac=40$

$5a+5=40$

$a=7$

$ac=-5$

$7c=-5$

$c=\dfrac{-5}{7}$

Answer is b.

48.

$$\begin{array}{r|rrrr} 1 & 1 & 0 & a & 3 \\ & & 1 & 1 & a+1 \\ \hline & 1 & 1 & a+1 & a+4 \end{array}$$

$$\begin{array}{r|rrrr} -2 & 1 & 0 & a & 3 \\ & & -2 & 4 & -2a-8 \\ \hline & 1 & -2 & a+4 & -2a-5 \end{array}$$

$(a+4)^2=-2a-5$

$a^2+8a+16=-2a-5$

$a^2+10a+21=0$

$(a+3)(a+7)=0 \to a=-3,-7$

Answer is d.

49. $P(x)=x^4+ax^2+bx-5$

$P(2)=16+4a+2b-5=4a+2b+11$

$P(-1)=1+a-b-5=a-b-4$

Thus $4a+2b+11=a-b-4+12$

$3a+3b=-3$

$a+b=-1$

$P(-2)=16+4a-2b-5=31$

$2a-b=10$

$$\begin{array}{r} a+b=-1 \\ 2a-b=10 \\ \hline 3a \quad =9 \end{array}$$

$a=3$

$a+b=-1$

$3+b=-1$

$b=-4$

Answer is c.

50. First slice $V=x^2(x-1)$

Second slice $V=x^2(x-1)-x(x-1)$

$x^3-x^2-x^2+x=36$

$x^3-2x^2+x-36=0$

Test 1, 2, 3, 4

$$\begin{array}{r|rrrr} 4 & 1 & -2 & 1 & -36 \\ & & 4 & 8 & 36 \\ \hline & 1 & 2 & 9 & 0 \end{array}$$

$x^2+2x+9=0 \quad x=\dfrac{-2\pm\sqrt{4-4(1)(9)}}{2}=\varnothing$

Therefore original cube is $4^3=64\text{ cm}^3$. Answer is b.

Radical and Rational Function Solutions

4.1 Exercise Set

1. a) radicand **b)** radical **c)** index **d)** $\sqrt[n]{x}$ **e)** square **f)** cube **g)** even, negative **h)** negative

2. a) ± 3 **b)** $\varnothing$ **c)** 2 **d)** -2 **e)** ± 1 **f)** $\varnothing$ **g)** 2 **h)** -2

3. a) $2x$ **b)** $-2x$ **c)** $3x$ **d)** $-3x$

4. a) all real numbers; all real numbers **b)** $x \geq 0;\ y \geq 0$ **c)** $x \leq 1;\ y \geq 0$ **d)** $x \geq 1;\ y \leq 0$

e) $x \leq 1;\ y \geq -2$ **f)** $x \geq 1;\ y \geq 2$ **g)** $x \geq 2;\ y \geq -3$ **h)** $x \geq -2;\ y \leq 3$ **i)** $x \leq -2;\ y \leq 3$

j) $x \geq 2,\ x \leq -2;\ y \geq 0$ **k)** $-2 \leq x \leq 2;\ y \leq 0$ **l)** $x \geq 2;\ y \leq 0$

5. a) J **b)** E **c)** L **d)** G **e)** M **f)** A **g)** K **h)** D **i)** C **j)** B **k)** N **l)** I **m)** F **n)** H

6. a)

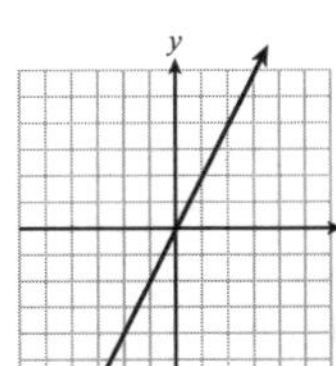

Domain: all real numbers
Range: all real numbers

b)

Domain: $x \geq 0$
Range: $y \geq 0$

c)

Domain: all real numbers
Range: $y \leq 4$

d)

Domain: $-2 \leq x \leq 2$
Range: $0 \leq y \leq 2$

e)

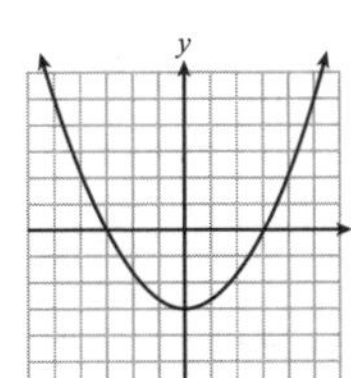

Domain: all real numbers
Range: $y \geq -3$

f)

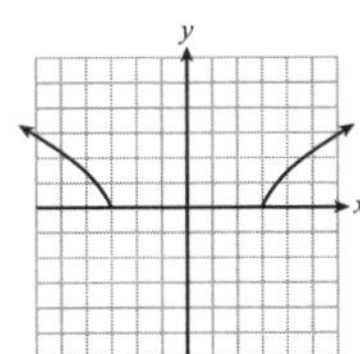

Domain: $x \leq -3,\ x \geq 3$
Range: $y \geq 0$

g)

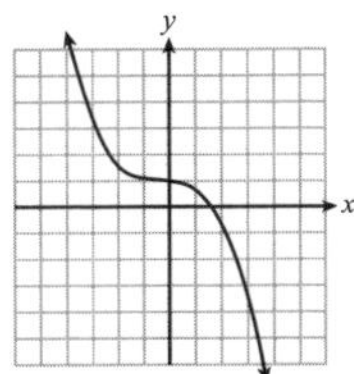

Domain: all real numbers
Range: all real numbers

h)

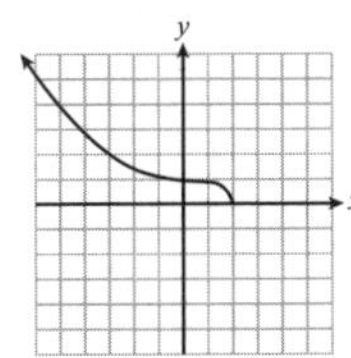

Domain: $x \leq 2$
Range: $y \geq 0$

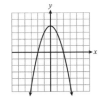

4.2 Exercise Set

1. a) radicand **b)** $x^n = y^n$ **c)** extraneous **2. a)** $x = -2$ **b)** $x = 2$ **c)** $x = -2$

3. a) $\sqrt{2x} - 4 = 0$; $f(0) = \sqrt{2 \cdot 0} - 4$

$\sqrt{2x} = 4$ $\quad = -4$

$2x = 16$

$x = 8$

b) $\sqrt[3]{4x} + 2 = 0$; $f(0) = \sqrt[3]{4 \cdot 0} + 2$

$\sqrt[3]{4x} = -2$ $\quad = 2$

$4x = -8$

$x = -2$

c) $\sqrt{4x-3} - 5 = 0$; $f(0) = \sqrt{4 \cdot 0 - 3} - 5$

$\sqrt{4x-3} = 5$ $\quad f(0) = \varnothing$

$4x - 3 = 25$ $\quad$ no y-intercept

$4x = 28$

$x = 7$

d) $\sqrt[3]{2x-1} - 4 = 0$; $f(0) = \sqrt[3]{2 \cdot 0 - 1} - 4$

$\sqrt[3]{2x-1} = 4$ $\quad = -1 - 4$

$2x - 1 = 64$ $\quad = -5$

$2x = 65$

$x = 32.5$

e) $\sqrt{2x} + 4 = 0$; $f(0) = \sqrt{2 \cdot 0} + 4$

$\sqrt{2x} = -4$ $\quad = 4$

$2x = 16$

$x = 8$

Check

$\sqrt{2 \cdot 8} + 4 \neq 0$ no x-intercept

f) $\sqrt{4-x} - 2 = 0$; $f(0) = \sqrt{4-0} - 2$

$\sqrt{4-x} = 2$ $\quad = 2 - 2$

$4 - x = 4$ $\quad = 0$

$x = 0$

g) $\sqrt{x^2+1} - \sqrt{17} = 0$; $f(0) = \sqrt{0^2+1} - \sqrt{17}$

$\sqrt{x^2+1} = \sqrt{17}$ $\quad = 1 - \sqrt{17}$

$x^2 + 1 = 17$

$x^2 = 16$

$x = \pm 4$

h) $\sqrt{x^2+6x} - 4 = 0$; $f(0) = \sqrt{0^2 + 6 \cdot 0} - 4$

$\sqrt{x^2+6x} = 4$ $\quad = -4$

$x^2 + 6x = 16$

$x^2 + 6x - 16 = 0$

$(x+8)(x-2) = 0$

$x = 2, -8$

i) $\sqrt[4]{x-1} - 2 = 0$; $f(0) = \sqrt[4]{0-1} - 2$

$\sqrt[4]{x-1} = 2$ $\quad = \varnothing$

$x - 1 = 16$ $\quad$ no y-intercept

$x = 17$

3. j)

$\sqrt{x^2-5x}-6=0$; $f(0)=\sqrt{0^2-5\cdot 0}-6$

$\sqrt{x^2-5x}=6$ $\quad = -6$

$x^2-5x=36$

$x^2-5x-36=0$

$(x-9)(x+4)=0$

$x=-4, 9$

4. a)

$\sqrt{13-x}-x+1=0$

$\sqrt{13-x}=x-1$

$13-x=x^2-2x+1$

$x^2-x-12=0$

$(x-4)(x+3)=0$

$x=-3, 4$

Check $\sqrt{13-(-3)}-(-3)+1=0$

$4+3+1=0$

$8\neq 0$ *reject*

$\sqrt{13-4}-4+1=0$

$3-4+1=0$

$0=0$ *accept*

Answer (4, 0)

b)

$\sqrt{2x-3}+x-3=0$

$\sqrt{2x-3}=3-x$

$2x-3=9-6x+x^2$

$x^2-8x+12=0$

$(x-2)(x-6)=0$

$x=2, 6$

Check $\sqrt{2\cdot 2-3}+2-3=0$

$1+2-3=0$

$0=0$ *accept*

$\sqrt{2\cdot 6-3}+6-3=0$

$3+6-3=0$

$6\neq 0$ *reject*

Answer (2, 0)

c)

$\sqrt{5-5x}+x=1$

$\sqrt{5-5x}=1-x$

$\sqrt{(5-5x)^2}=(1-x)^2$

$5-5x=1-2x+x^2$

$x^2+3x-4=0$

$(x+4)(x-1)=0$

$x=-4, 1$

Check $x=-4$

$\sqrt{5-5(-4)}+(-4)=1$

$\sqrt{25}-4=1$

$5-4=1$

$1=1$ *accept*

Check $x=1$

$\sqrt{5-5(1)}+1=1$

$0+1=1$

$1=1$ *accept*

Answers (–4, 0), (1, 0)

4. d)

$2x-8+\sqrt{x+1}=0$

$\sqrt{x+1}=8-2x$

$x+1=64-32x+4x^2$

$4x^2-33x+63=0$

$(4x-21)(x-3)=0$

$x=\frac{21}{4}, 3$

Check $2\left(\frac{21}{4}\right)-8+\sqrt{\frac{21}{4}+1}=0$

$10.5-8+2.5=0$

$5\neq 0$ *reject*

$2(3)-8+\sqrt{3+1}=0$

$6-8+2=0$

$0=0$ *accept*

Answer (3, 0)

e)

$\sqrt{x+3}-x-3=0$

$\sqrt{x+3}=x+3$

$(\sqrt{x+3})^2=(x+3)^2$

$x+3=x^2+6x+9$

$x^2+5x+6=0$

$(x+2)(x+3)=0$

$x=-2, -3$

Check $\sqrt{-2+3}-(-2)-3=0$

$1+2-3=0$

$0=0$ *accept*

$\sqrt{-3+3}-(-3)-3=0$

$0+3-3=0$

$0=0$ *accept*

Answer (–2, 0) and (–3, 0)

f)

$\sqrt{x+5}-x+1=0$

$\sqrt{x+5}=x-1$

$(\sqrt{x+5})^2=(x-1)^2$

$x+5=x^2-2x+1$

$x^2-3x-4=0$

$(x-4)(x+1)=0$

$x=-1, 4$

Check $\sqrt{-1+5}-(-1)+1=0$

$2+1+1=0$

$4\neq 0$ *reject*

$\sqrt{4+5}-4+1=0$

$3-4+1=0$

$0=0$ *accept*

Answer (4, 0)

5. a) $f(x)=\sqrt{x+5}-x$

x	y	
2	$\sqrt{7}-2$	$=0.65$
3	$\sqrt{8}-3$	$=-0.17$

$2<x<3$

b) $f(x)=\sqrt[3]{2x+1}+2$

x	y	
–5	$\sqrt[3]{2(-5)+1}+2$	$=-0.08$
–4	$\sqrt[3]{2(-4)+1}+2$	$=0.09$

$-5<x<-4$

c) $f(x)=\sqrt{2x+6}-x$

x	y	
3	$\sqrt{2\cdot 3+6}-3$	$=0.46$
4	$\sqrt{2\cdot 4+6}-4$	$=-0.26$

$3<x<4$

5. d) $f(x)=\sqrt{x+2}-2x$

x	y	
0	$\sqrt{0+2}-2(0)$	$=1.4$
1	$\sqrt{1+2}-2(1)$	$=-0.3$

$0<x<1$

e) $f(x)=\sqrt{4-x}-x$

x	y	
1	$\sqrt{4-1}-1$	$=0.73$
2	$\sqrt{4-2}-2$	$=-0.59$

$1<x<2$

f) $f(x)=\sqrt{10-x}-x-1$

x	y	
1	$\sqrt{10-1}-1-1$	$=1$
2	$\sqrt{10-2}-2-1$	$=-0.17$

$1<x<2$

6. a)
$$\sqrt{2x-3}-3=0$$
$$\sqrt{2x-3}=3$$
$$2x-3=9$$
$$2x=12$$
$$x=6$$

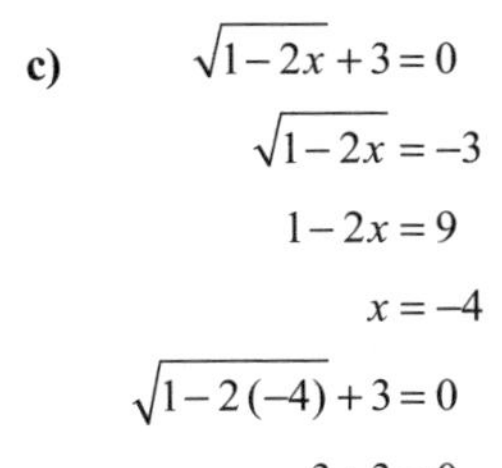

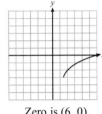

Zero is (6, 0).

b)
$$\sqrt[3]{x+4}+1=0$$
$$\sqrt[3]{x+4}=-1$$
$$x+4=-1$$
$$x=-5$$

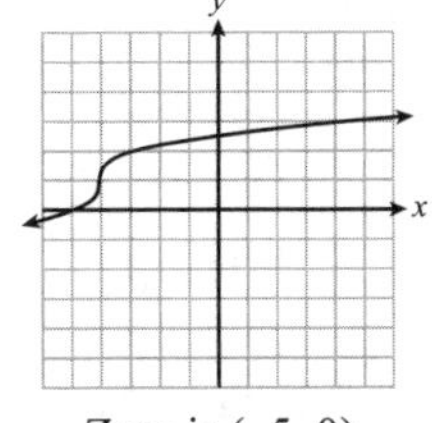

Zero is (–5, 0).

c)
$$\sqrt{1-2x}+3=0$$
$$\sqrt{1-2x}=-3$$
$$1-2x=9$$
$$x=-4$$
$$\sqrt{1-2(-4)}+3=0$$
$$3+3=0$$
$$6\neq 0$$
$\varnothing$, *no zero*

or $\sqrt{1-2x}+3=0$

$\sqrt{1-2x}=-3$ stop; square cannot equal negative number.

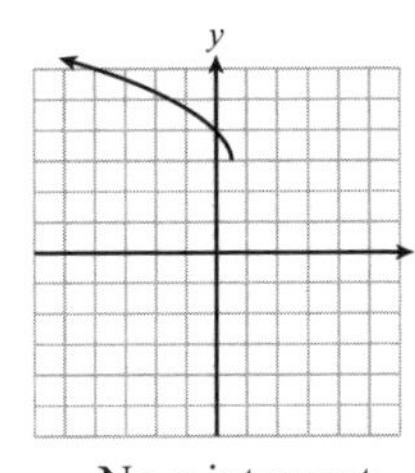

No x-intercept

d)
$$x+8-\sqrt{4-3x}=0$$
$$x+8=\sqrt{4-3x}$$
$$x^2+16x+64=4-3x$$
$$x^2+19x+60=0$$
$$(x+15)(x+4)=0$$
$$x=-4,-15$$

Check $-4+8-\sqrt{4-3(-4)}=0$

$0=0$ *accept*

$-15+8-\sqrt{4-3(-15)}=0$

$-14\neq 0$ *reject*

$x=-4$

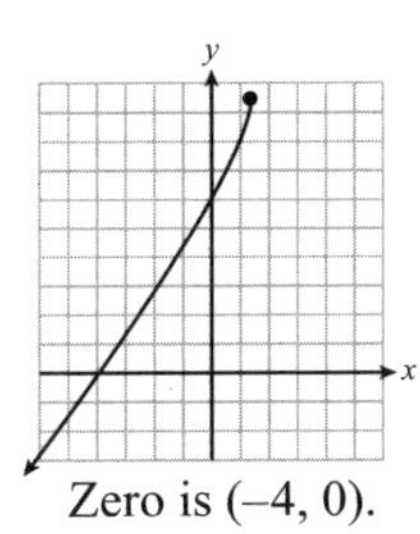

Zero is (–4, 0).

e)
$$\sqrt{x+1}-x-1=0$$
$$\sqrt{x+1}=x+1$$
$$x+1=x^2+2x+1$$
$$x^2+x=0$$
$$x(x+1)=0$$
$$x=0,-1$$

Check $\sqrt{0+1}-0-1=0$

$0=0$ *accept*

$\sqrt{-1+1}+1-1=0$

$0=0$ *accept*

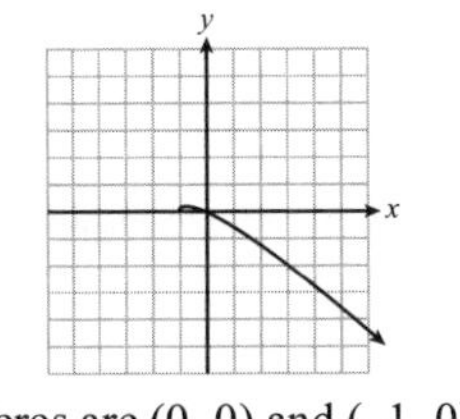

Zeros are (0, 0) and (–1, 0).

4.3 Exercise Set

1. a) ratio, denominator **b)** polynomial, rational **c)** denominator, zero **d)** vertical asymptote **e)** horizontal asymptote **f)** x = 2, y = 0

2. a) Domain: $x\neq -3$
x-intercept (3, 0)
y-intercept $(0,-\frac{3}{4})$

b) Domain: $x\neq 2$
x-intercept (–3, 0), (–6, 0)
y-intercept $(0,\frac{9}{2})$

c) Domain: $x\neq -2, 3$
x-intercept (–1, 0), (9, 0)
y-intercept $(0,\frac{3}{2})$

d) Domain: $x\neq 0$
x-intercept (–1, 0), (1, 0)
y-intercept $\varnothing$

e) Domain: all real numbers
x-intercept (–2, 0)
y-intercept $(0,\frac{1}{2})$

f) Domain: $x\neq -3, 3$
x-intercept (–2, 0), (2, 0)
y-intercept $(0,-\frac{4}{3})$

g) Domain: $x\neq -4$
x-intercept $\varnothing$
y-intercept $(0,\frac{1}{4})$

h) Domain: $x\neq -2, 2$
x-intercept (–3, 0), (3, 0)
y-intercept $(0,\frac{9}{8})$

i) Domain: all real numbers
x-intercept (–2, 0)
y-intercept $(0,\frac{1}{2})$

j) Domain: $x\neq -1, 4$
x-intercept $\varnothing$
y-intercept (0, –1)
hole at (–1, –1), (4, –1)

3.

	a)	b)	c)	d)
horizontal asymptote	$y=0$	$y=0$	$y=1$	$y=2$
vertical asymptote	$x=0$	$x=0$	$x=0$	$x=0$
x-intercept	$\varnothing$	$\varnothing$	(–1, 0)	$(\frac{1}{2}, 0)$
y-intercept	$\varnothing$	$\varnothing$	$\varnothing$	$\varnothing$

	e)	f)	g)	h)
horizontal asymptote	$y=-4$	$y=-1$	$y=0$	$y=0$
vertical asymptote	$x=0$	$x=0$	$x=-1$	$x=-1$
x-intercept	$(-\frac{1}{2}, 0), (\frac{1}{2}, 0)$	$\varnothing$	$\varnothing$	$\varnothing$
y-intercept	$\varnothing$	$\varnothing$	(0, –1)	(0, –2)

	i)	j)
horizontal asymptote	$y=3$	$y=1$
vertical asymptote	$x=1$	$x=-1$
x-intercept	$(\frac{1}{3}, 0)$	$(-1-\sqrt{2}, 0), (-1+\sqrt{2}, 0)$
y-intercept	(0, 1)	(0, –1)

4. a) $f(x)=\dfrac{1}{x}$

vertical asymptote: $x=0$

horizontal asymptote:

$f(x)=0$

b) $f(x)=\dfrac{2x}{x+3}$

vertical asymptote: $x+3=0$

$x=-3$

horizontal asymptote:

$$f(x)=\frac{2x}{x+3}=\frac{\frac{2x}{x}}{\frac{x+3}{x}}=\frac{2}{1+\frac{3}{x}}=\frac{2}{1+\frac{3}{\infty}}=\frac{2}{1+0}=2$$

c) $f(x)=\dfrac{1}{x^2-7x+12}$

vertical asymptotes:

$x^2-7x+12=0$

$(x-3)(x-4)=0$

$x=3\,,4$

horizontal asymptote: $f(x)=0$

d) $g(x)=\dfrac{x^2}{x^2-9}$

vertical asymptotes: $x^2-9=0$

$(x-3)(x+3)=0$

$x=-3\,,3$

horizontal asymptote:

$$f(x)=\frac{x^2}{x^2-9}=\frac{\frac{x^2}{x^2}}{\frac{x^2}{x^2}-\frac{9}{x^2}}=\frac{1}{1-\frac{9}{x^2}}=\frac{1}{1-\frac{9}{\infty^2}}=\frac{1}{1-0}=1$$

e) $h(x)=\dfrac{x}{x^2+1}$

vertical asymptote: $x^2+1=0$

$x^2=-1$

$x=\varnothing$

horizontal asymptote: $h(x)=0$

f) $k(x)=\dfrac{x^3}{x^2-x-20}$

vertical asymptotes: $x^2-x-20=0$

$(x-5)(x+4)=0$

$x=-4\,,5$

horizontal asymptote: power of numerator higher than power of denominator, therefore no horizontal asymptote.

g) $p(x)=\dfrac{x^2+3x-1}{4-x^2}$

vertical asymptotes: $4-x^2=0$

$(2-x)(2+x)=0$

$x=-2\,,2$

horizontal asymptote: $$p(x)=\frac{x^2+3x-1}{4-x^2}=\frac{\frac{x^2}{x^2}+\frac{3x}{x^2}-\frac{1}{x^2}}{\frac{4}{x^2}-\frac{x^2}{x^2}}=\frac{1+\frac{3}{x}-\frac{1}{x^2}}{\frac{4}{x^2}-1}=\frac{1+\frac{3}{\infty}-\frac{1}{\infty^2}}{\frac{4}{\infty^2}-1}=\frac{1+0-0}{0-1}=-1$$

h) $m(x)=\dfrac{2x^3-18x}{x^3-3x^2-4x}$

vertical asymptotes: $x^3-3x^2-4x=0 \rightarrow x(x^2-3x-4)=0 \rightarrow x(x-4)(x+1)=0$

$x=-1\,,0\,,4$

horizontal asymptote: $$m(x)=\frac{2x^3-18x}{x^3-3x^2-4x}=\frac{\frac{2x^3}{x^3}-\frac{18x}{x^3}}{\frac{x^3}{x^3}-\frac{3x^2}{x^3}-\frac{4x}{x^3}}=\frac{2-\frac{18}{x^2}}{1-\frac{3}{x}-\frac{4}{x^2}}=\frac{2-\frac{18}{\infty^2}}{1-\frac{3}{\infty}-\frac{4}{\infty^2}}=\frac{2-0}{1-0-0}=2$$

i) $n(x)=\dfrac{x^2-4}{2x^3+7x^2-4x}$

$=\dfrac{(x-2)(x+2)}{x(2x-1)(x+4)}$

vertical asymptotes: $2x^3+7x^2-4x=0$

$x(2x^2+7x-4)=0$

$x(2x-1)(x+4)=0$

$x=0, \frac{1}{2}, -4$

horizontal asymptote: $$n(x)=\frac{\frac{x^2}{x^3}-\frac{4}{x^3}}{\frac{2x^3}{x^3}+\frac{7x^2}{x^3}-\frac{4x}{x^3}}=\frac{\frac{1}{x}-\frac{4}{x^3}}{2+\frac{7}{x}-\frac{4}{x^2}}=\frac{0\cdot 0}{2+0-4}=0$$

$n(x)=0$

4. j)

$$t(x)=\frac{9-6x}{4x^2-9}=\frac{-3(2x-3)}{(2x-3)(2x+3)}=\frac{-3}{2x+3}$$

vertical asymptote: $2x+3=0$, $2x=-3$, $x=-\frac{3}{2}$

horizontal asymptote: $t(x)=\dfrac{\frac{9}{x^2}-\frac{6x}{x^2}}{\frac{4x^2}{x^2}-\frac{9}{x^2}}=\dfrac{\frac{9}{x^2}-\frac{6}{x}}{4-\frac{9}{x^2}}=\dfrac{0-0}{4-0}=0$

$t(x)=0$

hole in graph: $2x-3=0$, $x=\frac{3}{2}$, $\left(\frac{3}{2},-\frac{1}{2}\right)$

k)

$$r(x)=\frac{16x-x^3}{2x^3+7x^2-4x}=\frac{-x(x-4)(x+4)}{x(2x-1)(x+4)}=\frac{-(x-4)}{2x-1}=\frac{-x+4}{2x-1}$$

vertical asymptote: $2x-1=0$, $x=\frac{1}{2}$

horizontal asymptote: $r(x)=\dfrac{\frac{16x}{x^3}-\frac{x^3}{x^3}}{\frac{2x^3}{x^3}+\frac{7x^2}{x^3}-\frac{4x}{x^3}}=\dfrac{\frac{16}{x^2}-1}{2+\frac{7}{x}-\frac{4}{x^2}}=\dfrac{0-1}{2+0-4}=-\frac{1}{2}$

$r(x)=-\frac{1}{2}$

hole in graph: $x=0, x+4=0$, $x=-4$, $(0,-4),(-4,-\frac{8}{9})$

l)

$$s(x)=1-\frac{3}{x^2-1}=\frac{x^2-1-3}{x^2-1}=\frac{(x-2)(x+2)}{(x-1)(x+1)}$$

vertical asymptotes: $x-1=0, x+1=0$, $x=-1,1$

horizontal asymptote: $s(x)=1-\dfrac{3}{x^2-1}=1-\dfrac{\frac{3}{x^2}}{\frac{x^2}{x^2}-\frac{1}{x^2}}=1-\dfrac{0}{1-0}=1$

$s(x)=1$

4.4 Exercise Set

1.

	a)	b)	c)	d)
Domain	$x\neq 1$	$x\neq -2,2$	$x\neq -3,1$	all real numbers
vertical asymptote	$x=1$	$x=-2,2$	$x=-3,1$	nil
horizontal asymptote	$y=2$	$y=0$	$y=1$	$y=3$
x-intercept	$(-2,0)$	nil	$(-1,0)$, $(2,0)$	$(0,0)$
y-intercept	$(0,-4)$	$(0,-1)$	$\approx(0,0.7)$	$(0,0)$

	e)	f)
Domain	$x\neq -2,3$	$x\neq -3,3$
vertical asymptote	$x=-2,3$	$x=-3,3$
horizontal asymptote	$y=0$	$y=2$
x-intercept	$(1,0)$	$\approx(2.8,0),(-3.3,0)$
y-intercept	$\approx(0,-0.2)$	$(0,2)$

2. a) $y = x + 2$

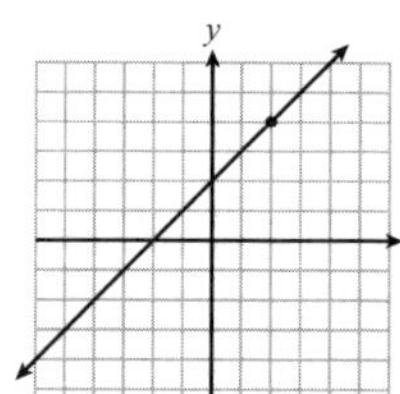

Hole at (2, 4)

b) $y = x - 1$

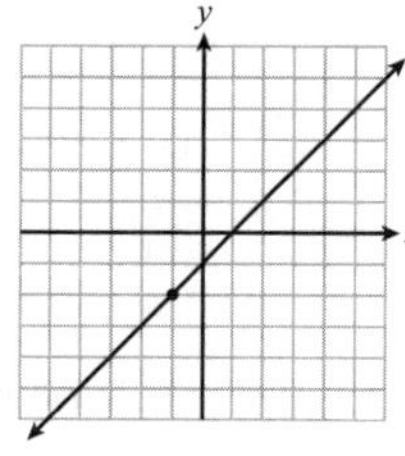

Hole at (–1, –2)

c) $y = -x - 3$

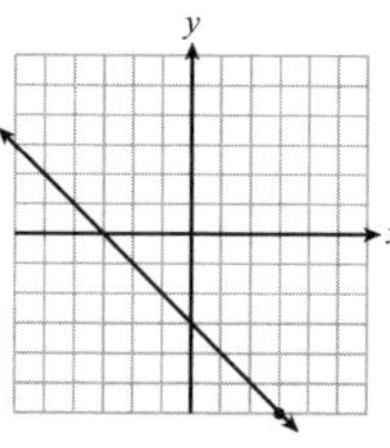

Hole at (3, –6)

d) $y = -x + 2$

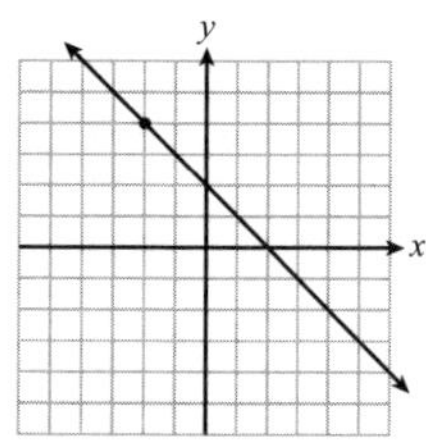

Hole at (–2, 4)

3. a)

x	0.5	1.5	0.9	1.1	0.99	1.01
$f(x)$	**–6**	**6**	**–30**	**30**	**–300**	**300**

As $x \to 1^+$, from right $f(x) \to \infty$
As $x \to 1^-$, from left $f(x) \to -\infty$

x	10	100	1000	–10	–100	–1000
$f(x)$	**$0.\overline{3}$**	**$0.\overline{03}$**	**$0.\overline{003}$**	**$-0.\overline{27}$**	**$-0.\overline{0297}$**	**–0.003**

As $x \to \infty$, $f(x) \to 0^+$
As $x \to -\infty$, $f(x) \to 0^-$

b)

x	–0.5	0.5	–0.1	0.1	–0.01	0.01
$f(x)$	**–1**	**–1**	**–97**	**–97**	**–9997**	**–9997**

As $x \to 0^+$, from right $f(x) \to -\infty$
As $x \to 0^-$, from left $f(x) \to -\infty$

x	10	100	1000	–10	–100	–1000
$f(x)$	**2.99**	**2.9999**	**2.999999**	**2.99**	**2.9999**	**2.999999**

As $x \to \infty$, $f(x) \to 3^-$
As $x \to -\infty$, $f(x) \to 3^-$

c)

x	1.5	2.5	1.9	2.1	1.99	2.01
$f(x)$	**–3**	**5**	**–19**	**21**	**–199**	**201**

As x ! 2^+, from right $f(x)$! ∀
As $x \to 2^-$, from left $f(x) \to -\infty$

x	10	100	1000	–10	–100	–1000
$f(x)$	**1.25**	**1.02**	**1.002**	**0.83**	**0.98**	**0.998**

As x ! ∀, $f(x)$! 1^+
As $x \to -\infty$, $f(x) \to 1^-$

4. a)
$$\frac{x^2-4}{x-2} = 0$$
$$\frac{(x-2)(x+2)}{x+2} = 0$$
$$x - 2 = 0$$
$$x = 2$$
$$(2, 0)$$

b)
$$1 - \frac{3}{x^2+2} = 0$$
$$x^2 + 2 - 3 = 0$$
$$(x-1)(x+1) = 0$$
$$x = -1, 1$$
$$(-1, 0), (1, 0)$$

c)
$$1 - \frac{3}{x-3} = 0$$
$$x - 3 - 3 = 0$$
$$x = 6$$
$$(6, 0)$$

d)
$$-1 + \frac{4}{x^2+1} = 0$$
$$-x^2 - 1 + 4 = 0$$
$$x^2 - 3 = 0$$
$$x = \pm\sqrt{3}$$
$$(-\sqrt{3}, 0), (\sqrt{3}, 0)$$

e)
$$1 + \frac{4}{x^2+1} = 0$$
$$x^2 + 1 + 4 = 0$$
$$x^2 = -5$$
$$x = \varnothing$$
No solution
No zero

f)
$$x^3 + 8 = 0$$
$$x^3 = -8$$
$$x = -2$$
$$(-2, 0)$$

5. a) E **b)** H **c)** J **d)** I **e)** A **f)** C **g)** D **h)** B **i)** G **j)** F

6. a)

x	–1.99	–2.01	0	–1000	1000	–3	–1
$f(x)$	∞	$-\infty$	0	-1^+	-1^-	–3	1

Domain: $x \neq -2$
Vertical asymptote: $x = -2$
Horizontal asymptote: $y = -1$
x- and y-intercepts: (0, 0)

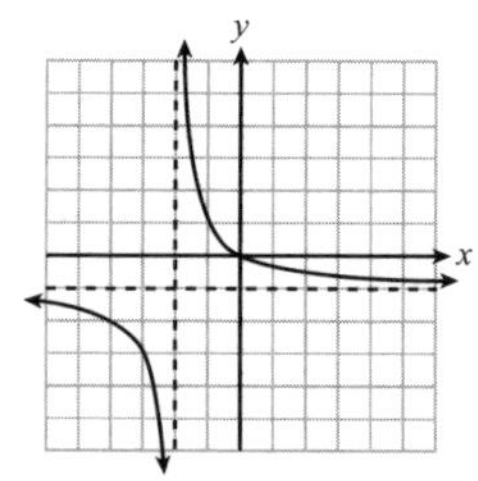

6. b)

x	0.99	1.01	0	–1000	1000	–2	–4
$f(x)$	$-\infty$	∞	–2	1^-	1^+	0	2

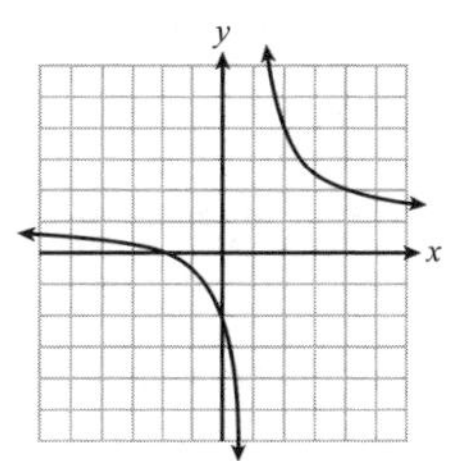

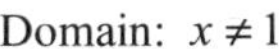

Domain: $x \neq 1$
Vertical asymptote: $x = 1$
Horizontal asymptote: $y = 1$
x-intercept: (–2, 0)
y-intercept: (0, –2)

c)

x	1.99	2.01	0	–1	–1000	1000	5
$f(x)$	$-\infty$	∞	$\frac{1}{2}$	0	1^-	1^+	2

Domain: $x \neq -2, 2$
Vertical asymptote: $x = 2$
Hole at (–2, $\frac{1}{4}$)
Horizontal asymptote: $y = 1$
x-intercept: (–1, 0)
y-intercept: (0, $-\frac{1}{2}$)

d)

x	–3.01	–2.99	2.99	3.01	–1000	1000
$f(x)$	$-\infty$	∞	$-\infty$	∞	0^-	0^+

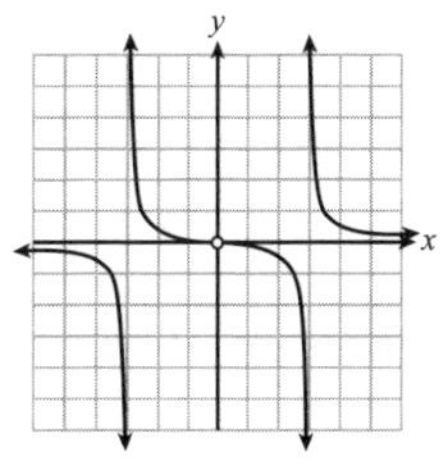

Domain: $x \neq -3, 0, 3$
Vertical asymptote: $x = -3$ and $x = 3$
Hole at (0, 0)
Horizontal asymptote: $y = 0$
x-intercept: no x-intercept
y-intercept: no y-intercept

4.5 Chapter Review

Multiple-choice Answers

1. a	**4.** d	**7.** b	**10.** d	**13.** a	**16.** c	**19.** c	**22.** d	**25.** a	**28.** d
2. c	**5.** b	**8.** d	**11.** b	**14.** d	**17.** d	**20.** c	**23.** a	**26.** b	**29.** b
3. d	**6.** b	**9.** c	**12.** b	**15.** a	**18.** c	**21.** a	**24.** c	**27.** d	**30.** d

Multiple-choice Solutions

1. The domain of a is all real numbers, therefore answer is a.

2. $f(x) = \dfrac{x^2-4}{x+2} = \dfrac{(x-2)(x+2)}{x+2} = x-2$, therefore c has a hole at (–2, –4), not a horizontal asymptote. Answer is c.

3. Domain is all values except 1, –2, –3. Answer is d.

4. An odd root radical always has a solution. Answer is d.

5. In most cases, a radical has 1 solution, but some have two. Look at Section 3.2 question 6e. Answer is b.

6. To make the answer positive, x must be negative. Answer is b.

7. Simplifies to $-2x$. Answer is b.

8. An even power must be greater than or equal to zero. Answer is d.

9. $4-x^2 \geq 0, (2-x)(2+x) \geq 0 \to -2 \leq x \leq 2$. Answer is c.

10. $\sqrt{1-x} \geq 0$, therefore $f(x)-3 \leq 0 \to f(x) \leq 3$. Answer is d.

11. $3x^2-3x-6=0 \to 3(x+1)(x-2) \geq 0 \to x = -1, 2$. Answer is b.

12. $x^2-a^2 \geq 0 \to (x-a)(x+a) \geq 0 \to x \leq -a, x \geq a$. Answer is b.

13. $y = -\sqrt{a-x}-b \to y = -\sqrt{-(x-a)}-b$, $x-a$ is quadrant I, IV, $-b$ is quadrant III, IV, thus quadrant IV. Answer is a.

14. $f(x) = \dfrac{(x-3)(x+3)}{(x-3)(x+1)} = \dfrac{x+3}{x+1}$, therefore hole is $\left(3, \dfrac{3+3}{3+1}\right) = \left(3, \dfrac{3}{2}\right)$. Answer is d.

15. $f(x)=\dfrac{x^2-4}{4-x^2}=-1$ has holes when $x=2,-2$. Answer is a.

16. $f(x)=\dfrac{3x+2}{2x+3}=\dfrac{\frac{3x}{x}+\frac{2}{x}}{\frac{2x}{x}+\frac{3}{x}}=\dfrac{3+\frac{2}{x}}{2+\frac{3}{x}}=\dfrac{3+\frac{2}{\infty}}{2+\frac{3}{\infty}}=1.5^{+}$. Answer is c.

17. To have a horizontal asymptote of $y=0, n<m$. Answer is d.

18. By definition, answer is c.

19. By definition, answer is c.

20. Symmetry about the y-axis requires an even power of x. Answer is c.

21. The only function with a horizontal asymptote of $y=-2$ is a. Answer is a.

22, 23, 24, 25. If $h>0$, graph in quadrant I, IV; if $k>0$, in quadrant I, II. If $a>0$, graph opens up; if $b>0$, graph opens right.

22. Answer is d.

23. Answer is a.

24. Answer is c.

25. Answer is a.

26. By definition, answer is b.

27. Volume $=x^2y=30\rightarrow y=\dfrac{30}{x^2}$, Surface Area $x^2+4xy=x^2+4x\cdot\dfrac{30}{x^2}=x^2+\dfrac{120}{x}$. Answer is d.

28. Cost/km = 0.20 + Rental Cost per x km = $0.20+\dfrac{25}{x}$ Answer is d.

29. x-intercept: $\dfrac{ax+b}{cx+d}=0\rightarrow ax+b=0\rightarrow x=-\dfrac{b}{a}$; y-intercept: $f(0)=\dfrac{a(0)+b}{c(0)+d}=\dfrac{b}{d}$. Answer is b.

30. Horizontal asymptote: $f(x)=\dfrac{ax+b}{cx+d}=\dfrac{\frac{ax}{x}+\frac{b}{x}}{\frac{cx}{x}+\frac{d}{x}}=\dfrac{a+\frac{b}{x}}{c+\frac{d}{x}}=\dfrac{a+\frac{b}{\infty}}{c+\frac{d}{\infty}}=\dfrac{a+0}{c+0}=\dfrac{a}{c}$

Vertical asymptote: $cx+d=0\rightarrow cx=-d\rightarrow x=\dfrac{-d}{c}$. Answer is d.

Logarithms Solutions

5.1 Exercise Set

1. a) $\dfrac{\left(3^{\frac{1}{5}}\right)^{10}\left(3^{-3}\right)}{9}=\dfrac{3^2\cdot 3^{-3}}{3^2}=3^{-3}=\dfrac{1}{3^3}=\dfrac{1}{27}$

b) $\dfrac{\left(-4x^2y^{-2}\right)^{-3}}{x^{-1}y^2}=\dfrac{(-4)^{-3}x^{-6}y^6}{x^{-1}y^2}=\dfrac{-y^4}{64x^5}$

c) $\dfrac{125^{3x-1}\cdot 25^{1-2x}}{\left(\frac{1}{5}\right)^{2x-3}}=\dfrac{5^{3(3x-1)}\cdot 5^{2(1-2x)}}{5^{-1(2x-3)}}=\dfrac{5^{9x-3}\cdot 5^{2-4x}}{5^{-2x+3}}=5^{9x-3+2-4x+2x-3}=5^{7x-4}$

d) $\dfrac{2x^4\cdot 3^{5x}-4x^3\cdot 3^{5x}}{x^3-2x^2}=\dfrac{2x^3\cdot 3^{5x}(x-2)}{x^2(x-2)}=2x\cdot 3^{5x}$

e) $\left(4^{-x}\cdot 8^{x}\right)^2=4^{-2x}\cdot 8^{2x}=\left(2^2\right)^{-2x}\cdot\left(2^3\right)^{2x}=2^{-4x}\cdot 2^{6x}=2^{-4x+6x}=2^{2x}=4^x$

f) $\dfrac{2^x\left(2^x+2^{-x}\right)-2^x\left(2^x-2^{-x}\right)}{2^{-2}}=\dfrac{2^{2x}+2^0-2^{2x}+2^0}{2^{-2}}=\dfrac{1+1}{2^{-2}}=2\cdot 2^2=2^3=8$

2. a) $4^{x^2-x}=1\rightarrow 4^{x^2-x}=4^0\rightarrow x^2-x=0\rightarrow x(x-1)=0\rightarrow x=0, 1$

b) $3^{x^2}=9\cdot 3^{-x}\rightarrow 3^{x^2}=3^2\cdot 3^{-x}\rightarrow 3^{x^2}=3^{-x+2}\rightarrow x^2=-x+2\rightarrow x^2+x-2=0\rightarrow$ $(x+2)(x\,!\,1)=0\,\forall\ x=!\,2,\ 1$

c) $4^{\sqrt{x+1}}=2^{3x-2}\rightarrow 2^{2\sqrt{x+1}}=2^{3x-2}\rightarrow 2\sqrt{x+1}=3x-2\rightarrow\left(2\sqrt{x+1}\right)^2=(3x-2)^2\rightarrow$

$4(x+1)=9x^2-12x+4\rightarrow 9x^2-16x=0\rightarrow x(9x-16)=0\rightarrow x=0,\ \dfrac{16}{9}$ Check, reject 0, $\therefore\ x=\dfrac{16}{9}$

d) $4^{-|x+1|}=\dfrac{1}{16}\rightarrow 4^{-|x+1|}=4^{-2}\rightarrow -|x+1|=-2\rightarrow |x+1|=2\rightarrow x+1=2$ or $x+1=-2\rightarrow x=1,\ -3$

e) $4^{-2x+1}=8^{x-4}\rightarrow 2^{2(-2x+1)}=2^{3(x-4)}\rightarrow 2^{-4x+2}=2^{3x-12}\rightarrow -4x+2=3x-12\rightarrow -7x=-14\rightarrow x=2$

f) $9^{2x-1}=\left(\dfrac{1}{27}\right)^{x+2}\rightarrow 3^{2(2x-1)}=3^{-3(x+2)}\rightarrow 2(2x-1)=-3(x+2)\rightarrow 4x-2=-3x-6\rightarrow 7x=-4\rightarrow x=-\dfrac{4}{7}$

3. a) $y = -ab^x = -f(x)$ will reflect the graph over the x-axis.

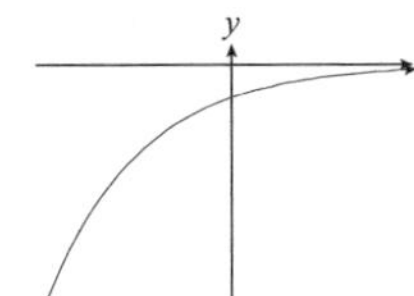

b) 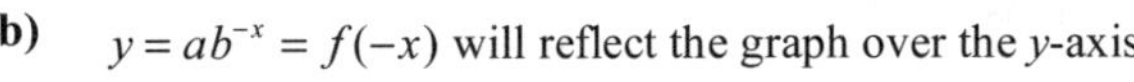 $y = ab^{-x} = f(-x)$ will reflect the graph over the y-axis.

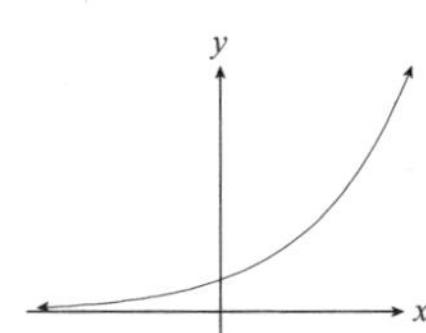

4. a) Graph $y = 3^{x+2} - 3$ is shifted left two units and down three units.

Domain: all real numbers
Range: $y > -3$
x-intercept: -1
y-intercept: 6
Asymptote: $y = -3$

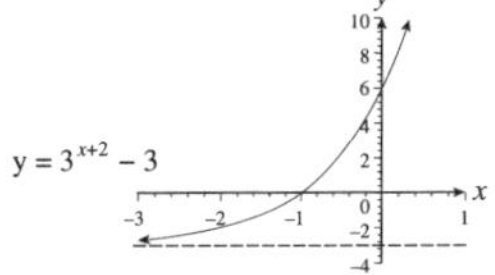

b) Graph $y = 3^{-x} + 2$ is reflected about the y-axis and up two units.

Domain: all real numbers
Range: $y > 2$
x-intercept: no x-intercept
y-intercept: 3
Asymptote: $y = 2$

$y = (\frac{1}{3})^x + 2$

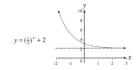

c) Graph of $y = -3^{-x}$ is reflected about both the x-axis and y-axis.

Domain: all real numbers
Range: y < 0
x-intercept: no x-intercept
y-intercept: -1
Asymptote: $y = 0$

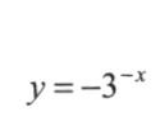

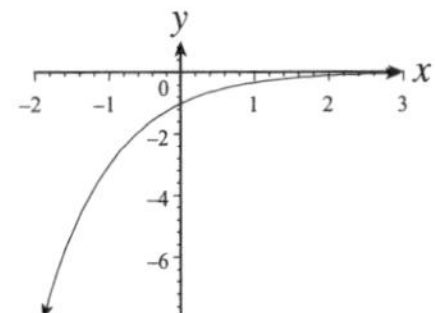

5. a) D **b)** C **c)** F **d)** A **e)** E **f)** B

6. a) $y = b^x \rightarrow 3 = b^{-1} \rightarrow b = \dfrac{1}{3}$

b) $y = b^x \rightarrow 27 = b^{\frac{3}{2}} \rightarrow b = 27^{\frac{2}{3}} \rightarrow b = \left(3^3\right)^{\frac{2}{3}} \rightarrow b = 3^2 \rightarrow b = 9$

c) $y = b^x \rightarrow \dfrac{1}{9} = b^{-\frac{2}{3}} \rightarrow b = \left(\dfrac{1}{9}\right)^{-\frac{3}{2}} \rightarrow b = \left(3^{-2}\right)^{-\frac{3}{2}} \rightarrow b = 3^3 \rightarrow b = 27$

7. $y = c \cdot 2^{kx} \rightarrow 4 = c \cdot 2^{k \cdot 0} \rightarrow c = 4 \rightarrow y = 4 \cdot 2^{kx} \rightarrow 256 = 4 \cdot 2^{12k} \rightarrow 64 = 2^{12k} \rightarrow 2^6 = 2^{12k} \rightarrow 12k = 6 \rightarrow k = \dfrac{1}{2}$,

therefore, $y = 4 \cdot 2^{\frac{1}{2}x}$ or $y = 2^{\frac{1}{2}x+2}$

8. 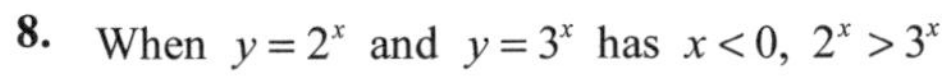 When $y = 2^x$ and $y = 3^x$ has $x < 0$, $2^x > 3^x$
When $y = 2^x$ and $y = 3^x$ has $x > 0$, $3^x > 2^x$

x	-3	-2	-1	0	1	2	3
2^x	$\frac{1}{8}$	$\frac{1}{4}$	$\frac{1}{2}$	1	2	4	8
3^x	$\frac{1}{27}$	$\frac{1}{9}$	$\frac{1}{3}$	1	3	9	27

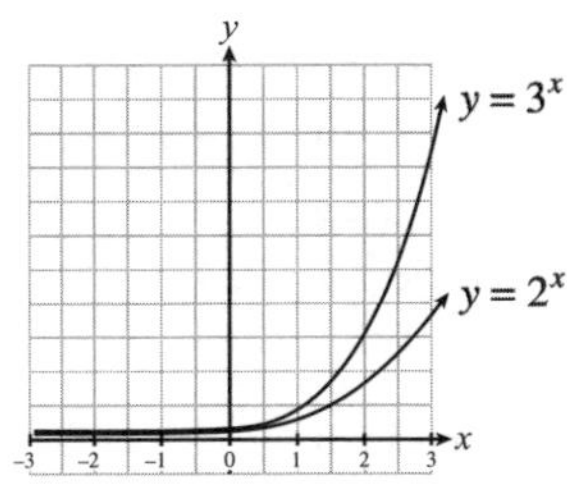

9. a) $\dfrac{10^{8.9}}{10^{6.4}} = 10^{2.5} =$ 316 times as strong

b) $1000 = 10^3$. A 4.9 earthquake is a $10^{4.9}$ measure. So the San Francisco earthquake has a $10^{4.9} \cdot 10^3 = 10^{4.9+3} = 10^{7.9}$ or a Richter scale measure of 7.9

c) $A = P\left(1 + \frac{r}{n}\right)^{nt} \rightarrow A = 1000\left(1 + \frac{0.06}{4}\right)^{4 \times 8} \rightarrow A = 1000\left(1.015\right)^{32} \rightarrow A = \$1610.32$

d) $A = A_0(x)^{\frac{t}{T}} \rightarrow A = 84(\frac{1}{2})^{\frac{23}{4}} \rightarrow A = 1.56$ grams of argon-39 remains

e) $A = P(1 + \frac{r}{n})^{nt} \rightarrow A = 12\,250(1 + \frac{0.096}{12})^{12 \times 10} = \$31\,871.31$

f) $A = P\left(1 + \frac{r}{n}\right)^{nt} \rightarrow A = 30000000\left(1 + \frac{0.019}{1}\right)^{1 \times 32} \rightarrow A = 30000000\left(1.019\right)^{32} = 54\,789\,223 = 55$ million to the nearest million.

5.2 Exercise Set

1. a) $4^2=16$ b) $3^4=81$ c) $6^{-2}=\frac{1}{36}$ d) $10^{-2}=\frac{1}{100}$ e) $32^{\frac{3}{5}}=8$ f) $8^1=8$ g) $5^0=1$ h) $10^3=1000$ i) $8^{\frac{2}{3}}=4$ j) $4^{-\frac{3}{2}}=\frac{1}{8}$

2. a) $\log_2 16=4$ b) $\log_8 64=2$ c) $\log_{16} 2=\frac{1}{4}$ d) $\log_3 \frac{1}{9}=-2$ e) $\log_3 1=0$

f) $\log_{10} 0.01=-2$ g) $\log_5 5=1$ h) $\log_9 27=\frac{3}{2}$ i) $\log_8 16=\frac{4}{3}$ j) $\log_{\frac{2}{3}} \frac{81}{16}=-4$

3. a) $f(x)=\log_2 8$; $2^y=8$; $2^y=2^3$; $y=3$

b) $f(x)=\log_4 16$; $4^y=16$; $4^y=4^2$; $y=2$

c) $f(x)=\log_8 2$; $8^y=2$; $2^{3y}=2$; $3y=1$; $y=\frac{1}{3}$

d) $f(x)=\log_{16} 4$; $16^y=4$; $4^{2y}=4^1$; $2y=1$; $y=\frac{1}{2}$

e) $f(x)=\log_5 1$; $5^y=1$; $5^y=5^0$; $y=0$

f) $f(x)=\log_7 7$; $7^y=7$; $7^y=7^1$; $y=1$

g) $f(x)=\log_a a$; $a^y=a$; $a^y=a^1$; $y=1$

h) $f(x)=\log_a a^3$; $a^y=a^3$; $y=3$

i) $f(x)=\log_b b^{-4}$; $b^y=b^{-4}$; $y=-4$

j) $f(x)=\log_5 0$; $5^y=0$; undefined; log cannot be zero

4. a) $x^3=27$; $x^3=3^3$; $x=3$

b) $x=4^{-3}$; $x=\frac{1}{64}$

c) $10^x=1000$; $10^x=10^3$; $x=3$

d) $x^1=8$; $x=8$

e) $x=7^{-2}$; $x=\frac{1}{49}$

f) $9^x=27$; $3^{2x}=3^3$; $2x=3$; $x=\frac{3}{2}$

g) $x^2=32$; $x=\sqrt{32}$; $x=4\sqrt{2}$; (reject $x=-\sqrt{32}$)

h) $x=4^0$; $x=1$

i) $32^x=8$; $2^{5x}=2^3$; $5x=3$; $x=\frac{3}{5}$

j) $x^4=625$; $x^4=5^4$; $x=5$

k) $x=4^{\frac{3}{2}}$; $=(2^2)^{\frac{3}{2}}$; $=2^3$; $x=8$

l) $4^x=0.25$; $4^x=\frac{1}{4}$; $4^x=4^{-1}$; $x=-1$

m) $x=\sqrt{2}^8$; $=(2^{\frac{1}{2}})^8$; $=2^4$; $x=16$

n) $x=\sqrt{3}^4$; $=(3^{\frac{1}{2}})^4$; $=3^2$; $x=9$

o) $x^{\frac{1}{2}}=\sqrt{3}$; $x^{\frac{1}{2}}=3^{\frac{1}{2}}$; $x=3$

p) $(3x)^2=36$; $9x^2=36$; $x^2=4$; $x=2$; (reject $x=-2$)

q) $\sqrt{2}^x=16$; $2^{\frac{1}{2}x}=2^4$; $\frac{1}{2}x=4$; $x=8$

r) $\sqrt{3}^x=9$; $3^{\frac{1}{2}x}=3^2$; $\frac{1}{2}x=2$; $x=4$

s) $x^2+24=7^2$; $x^2=25$; $x=\pm5$

t) $(x-2)^2=10^{-2}$; $(x-2)^2=\frac{1}{100}$; $x-2=\pm\frac{1}{10}$; $x=2\pm\frac{1}{10}$; $x=1.9$ or 2.1

5. a) $x-1>0$; $x>1$

b) $x>0$

c) $2-x>0$; $2-x\neq1$; $-x>-2$; $-x\neq-1$; $x<2$; $x\neq1$

d) $-x>0$; $x<0$

e) $y=\log_{x+1}(x-2)$ The base $x+1>0$ and $x+1\neq1$ $\therefore$ $x>-1$ and $x\neq0$.
The log term is $(x-2)>0$ so $x>2$.
Take the intersection of $x>-1$, $x\neq0$ with $x>2$ which is $x>2$.
Therefore, the domain of $y=\log_{x+1}(x-2)$ is $x>2$.

f) $y=\log_{x-2}(x+1)$ The base is $x-2>0$ and $x-2\neq1$
$x>2$ and $x\neq3$
The log term is $x+1>0$
$x>-1$
Take the intersection of $x>-1$ with $x>2$ which is $x>2$.
Therefore, the domain of $y=\log_{x-2}(x+1)$ is $x>2, x\neq3$.

6. a) E b) B c) C d) F e) A f) D

7. a) $y = -\log_b a = -f(a)$ will reflect the graph over the x-axis.

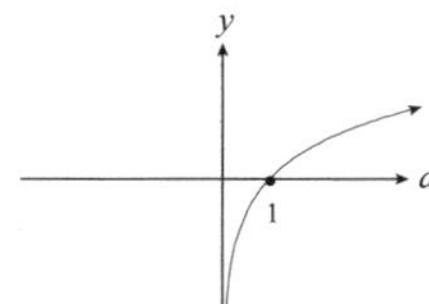

b) $y = \log_b(-a) = f(-a)$ will reflect the graph over the y-axis.

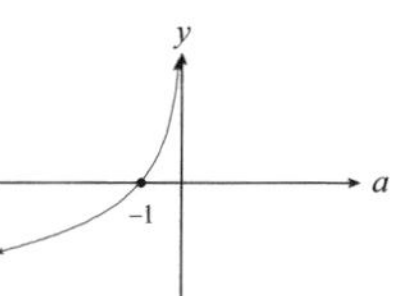

c) $y = \log_{\frac{1}{b}} a = -\log_b a$, which makes the graph the same as **7 a)**, above. (See question 10 as to why $y = \log_{\frac{1}{b}} a = -\log_b a$

8. $y = 5^x$ and $y = \log_5 x$ are the inverse of each other. Therefore, if (a, b) is a point on $y = 5^x$ then (b, a) must be a point on $y = \log_5 x$. Two other points on $y = \log_5 x$ are (5, 1) and (1, 0).

9. $f(x) = \log_2 x \rightarrow -f(x) = -\log_2 x : -f(x)$ is reflected over the x-axis. So putting a negative in front of a logarithmic statement reflects the equation over the x-axis. The point (1, 0) is on the x-axis, so the point will not change, therefore the answer is (1, 0).

10. If $y = \log_{\frac{1}{b}} a$ then $a = \left(\frac{1}{b}\right)^y = b^{-y}$, thus $-y = \log_b a \rightarrow y = -\log_b a$. So if (c, d) is a point on the graph $y = \log_b a$ then $(c, -d)$ must be on the graph $y = \log_{\frac{1}{b}} a$. Two other points on $y = \log_{\frac{1}{b}} a$ are $(\frac{1}{b}, 1)$ and (1, 0).

11. a) $\log 1253$

$\log 1000 = x \rightarrow 10^x = 1000$; $\log 10\,000 = x \rightarrow 10^x = 10\,000$

$10^x = 10^3$ $\qquad$ $10^x = 10^4$

$x = 3$ $\qquad$ $x = 4$

Thus $3 < \log 1253 < 4$

b) $\log 0.025$

$\log 0.01 = x \rightarrow 10^x = 0.01$; $\log 0.1 = x \rightarrow 10^x = 0.1$

$10^x = 10^{-2}$ $\qquad$ $10^x = 10^{-1}$

$x = -2$ $\qquad$ $x = -1$

Thus $-2 < \log 0.025 < -1$

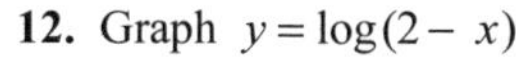

12. Graph $y = \log(2 - x)$

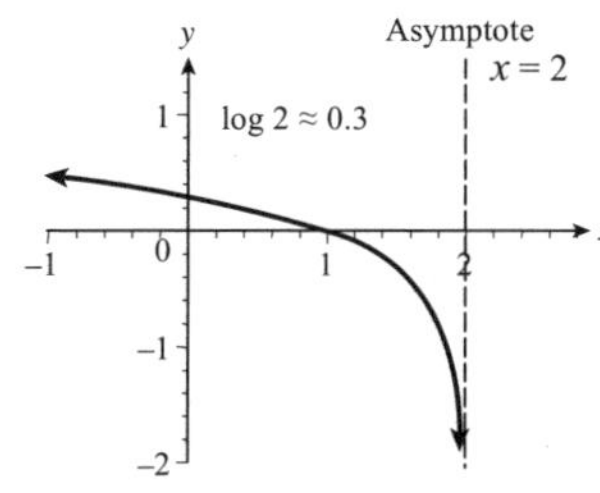

13. a) $y = 8^{x-2} \rightarrow f^{-1} : x = 8^{y-2} \rightarrow \log_8 x = y - 2 \rightarrow y = 2 + \log_8 x \rightarrow f^{-1}(x) = 2 + \log_8 x$

b) $f(x) = 5^{4x-1} + 6 \rightarrow f^{-1} : x = 5^{4y-1} + 6 \rightarrow x - 6 = 5^{4y-1} \rightarrow \log_5 (x-6) = 4y - 1 \rightarrow$

$4y = \log_5 (x-6) + 1 \rightarrow f^{-1}(x) = \frac{1}{4}\log_5 (x-6) + \frac{1}{4}$

c) $f : y + 1 = \log_3(x-2) \rightarrow f^{-1} : x + 1 = \log_3(y-2) \rightarrow y - 2 = 3^{x+1} \rightarrow y = 3^{x+1} + 2 \rightarrow f^{-1}(x) = 3^{x+1} + 2$

d) $f(x) = 2 + \log(5x-3) \rightarrow f^{-1}(x) : x = 2 + \log(5y-3) \rightarrow x - 2 = \log(5y-3) \rightarrow$

$5y - 3 = 10^{x-2} \rightarrow 5y = 10^{x-2} + 3 \rightarrow y = \dfrac{10^{x-2}+3}{5} \rightarrow f^{-1}(x) = \dfrac{10^{x-2}+3}{5}$

5.3 Exercise Set

1. a) $\log 6 = \log(2 \cdot 3) = \log 2 + \log 3$

b) $\log 12 = \log\left(2^2 \cdot 3\right) = 2\log 2 + \log 3$

c) $\log 72 = \log\left(2^3 \cdot 3^2\right) = 3\log 2 + 2\log 3$

d) $\log 3200 = \log\left(2^5 \cdot 100\right) = 5\log 2 + 2$

e) $\log 0.36 = \log\dfrac{36}{100} = \log\left(\dfrac{2^2 \cdot 3^2}{100}\right) = 2\log 2 + 2\log 3 - 2$

f) $\log_2 216 = \log_2\left(2^3 \cdot 3^3\right) = 3\log_2 2 + 3\log_2 3 = 3 + \dfrac{3\log 3}{\log 2}$

g) $\log 5.4 = \log\dfrac{2!3^3}{10} = \log 2 + 3\log 3 \forall 1$

1. h) $\log_6 180 = \frac{\log 180}{\log 6} = \frac{\log(2\cdot 3^2\cdot 10)}{\log(2\cdot 3)} = \frac{\log 2 + 2\log 3 + 1}{\log 2 + \log 3}$

i) $\log_{18} 2160 = \frac{\log\left(2^3\cdot 3^3\cdot 10\right)}{\log\left(2\cdot 3^2\right)} = \frac{3\log 2 + 3\log 3 + 1}{\log 2 + 2\log 3}$

j) $\log_{12} 0.108 = \log_{12}\left(\frac{108}{1000}\right) = \log_{12} 108 - \log_{12} 1000 = \frac{\log 108 - \log 1000}{\log 12} = \frac{\log\left(2^2\cdot 3^3\right) - 3}{\log\left(2^2\cdot 3\right)} = \frac{2\log 2 + 3\log 3 - 3}{2\log 2 + \log 3}$

2. a) $\log_3 81 = \log_3 3^4 = 4\log_3 3 = 4$

b) $\log_2 \frac{1}{32} = \log_2 2^{-5} = -5\log_2 2 = -5$

c) $\log_2 \sqrt[4]{8} = \log_2 2^{\frac{3}{4}} = \frac{3}{4}\log_2 2 = \frac{3}{4}$

d) $\log_5 \sqrt{125} = \log_5 5^{\frac{3}{2}} = \frac{3}{2}\log_5 5 = \frac{3}{2}$

e) $\log_9 27^{2.2} = 2.2\frac{\log 3^3}{\log 3^2} = \frac{6.6\log 3}{2\log 3} = 3.3$

f) $\log_4 \frac{1}{32} = \frac{\log 2^{-5}}{\log 2^2} = \frac{-5\log 2}{2\log 2} = \frac{-5}{2}$

g) $\left(\log_4 8\right)\left(\log_{16} 32\right) = \frac{\log 2^3}{\log 2^2}\cdot\frac{\log 2^5}{\log 2^4} = \frac{(3\log 2)(5\log 2)}{(2\log 2)(4\log 2)} = \frac{15}{8}$

h) $\frac{\log_{27} 81}{\log_{15} 125} = \frac{\log 3^4}{\log 3^3}\cdot\frac{\log 5^2}{\log 5^3} = \left(\frac{4\log 3}{3\log 3}\right)\left(\frac{2\log 5}{3\log 5}\right) = \frac{8}{9}$

i) $\log_4 2 + \log_2 32 = \frac{\log 2}{2\log 2} + \frac{\log 2^5}{\log 2} = \frac{\log 2}{2\log 2} + \frac{5\log 2}{\log 2} = \frac{11}{2}$

j) $\log_9 16 - 2\log_3 2 = \frac{\log 2^4}{\log 3^2} - 2\log_3 2 = \frac{4\log 2}{2\log 3} - 2\log_3 2 = 2\log_3 2 - 2\log_3 2 = 0$

3. a) $\log 100x^2y^3 = \log 100 + \log x^2 + \log y^3 = 2 + 2\log x + 3\log y$

b) $\log\frac{x^3}{1000y^2} = \log x^3 - \log 1000 - \log y^2 = 3\log x - 2\log y - 3$

c) $\log\left(x^2+y^3\right)^4 = 4\log\left(x^2+y^3\right)$

d) $\log^4\left(x^2+y^3\right)$ cannot be expanded

e) $\log_5\frac{25x^2y^3}{z} = \log_5 25 + \log_5 x^2 + \log_5 y^3 - \log_5 z = 2\log_5 x + 3\log_5 y - \log_5 z + 2$

f) $\log\sqrt{x^2(x+2)} = \frac{1}{2}\log\left[x^2(x+2)\right] = \frac{1}{2}\log x^2 + \frac{1}{2}\log(x+2) = \log x + \frac{1}{2}\log(x+2)$

g) $4\log_2(2x)^{12} = 48\log_2 2x = 48\left[\log_2 2 + \log_2 x\right] = 48 + 48\log_2 x$

h) $\log_a\sqrt{\frac{x^2y+1}{a^3}} = \frac{1}{2}\left[\log_a(x^2y+1) - \log_a a^3\right] = \frac{1}{2}\log_a(x^2y+1) - \frac{3}{2}$

i) $\log\frac{(x^3+y)^3}{x^3} = \log(x^3+y)^3 - \log x^3 = 3\log(x^3+y) - 3\log x$

j) $\log\sqrt[3]{\frac{xy^3}{z^6}} = \frac{1}{3}\log\frac{xy^3}{z^6} = \frac{1}{3}\left[\log x + 3\log y - 6\log z\right] = \frac{1}{3}\log x + \log y - 2\log z$

4. a) $\log_5 x - \log_5 25 = \log_5\frac{x}{25}$

b) $\log_3 x - 2\log_3 27 = \log_3 x - \log_3 x - \log_3(3^3)^2 = \log_3\frac{x}{729}$

c) $\log\sqrt{x} + \log x^{\frac{3}{2}} = \log x^{\frac{1}{2}}\cdot x^{\frac{3}{2}} = \log x^2$

d) $\log(x^2-1) - \log(x+1) - \log x = \log\frac{(x^2-1)}{x(x+1)} = \log\frac{(x-1)(x+1)}{x(x+1)} = \log\left(\frac{x-1}{x}\right)$

e) $\log(3x^2-5x-2) - \log(x^2-4) - \log(3x+1) = \log\frac{(3x+1)(x-2)}{(x-2)(x+2)(3x+1)} = \log\left(\frac{1}{x+2}\right) = \log 1 - \log(x+2) = -\log(x+2)$

f) $\log_3(2x-3) - \log_3(2x^2-x-3) + \log_3 3(x+1) = \log_3\left[\frac{3(2x-3)(x+1)}{(2x-3)(x+1)}\right] = \log_3 3 = 1$

g) $2\left[\log(x^2-1) - \log(x+1) - \log(x-1)\right] = 2\log\left[\frac{(x-1)(x+1)}{(x-1)(x+1)}\right] = 2\log 1 = 0$

h) $\frac{3}{2}\log 4x^4 - \frac{1}{2}\log y^6 = \log(4x^4)^{\frac{3}{2}} - \log(y^6)^{\frac{1}{2}} = \log\left(\frac{8x^6}{y^3}\right)$

i) $\frac{1}{4}\left[\log(x^2-4) - \log(x-2)\right] - \log x = \frac{1}{4}\log\frac{(x-2)(x+2)}{x-2} - \log x = \log\frac{\sqrt[4]{x+2}}{x}$

j) $\log(x^2-4) - \left[\log(x-2) + \log(x+2)\right] = \log\frac{(x-2)(x+2)}{(x-2)(x+2)} = \log 1 = 0$

5. a) $\log_b x^{\log_x a} = \log_x a\cdot\log_b x = \frac{\log a}{\log x}\cdot\frac{\log x}{\log b} = \frac{\log a}{\log b} = \log_b a$

b) $x^{\log_x 20 - \log_x 4} = x^{\log_x\frac{20}{4}} = x^{\log_x 5} = 5$ (rule #7, p. 176)

5. c) $(\log_2 10)(\log 48 - \log 3) = \dfrac{\log 10}{\log 2}\cdot \log 16 = \dfrac{1}{\log 2}\cdot \log 2^4 = \dfrac{4\log 2}{\log 2} = 4$

d) Method 1: $\dfrac{\log x^3 + \log x^5}{\log x^6 - \log x^3} = \dfrac{\log x^3\cdot x^5}{\log \dfrac{x^6}{x^3}} = \dfrac{\log x^8}{\log x^3} = \dfrac{8\log x}{3\log x} = \dfrac{8}{3}$ Method 2: $\dfrac{\log x^3 + \log x^5}{\log x^6 - \log x^3} = \dfrac{3\log x + 5\log x}{6\log x - 3\log x} = \dfrac{8\log x}{3\log x} = \dfrac{8}{3}$

e) $\left(\dfrac{a}{b}\right)^{\log 0.5}\cdot\left(\dfrac{a}{b}\right)^{\log 0.2} = \left(\dfrac{a}{b}\right)^{\log 0.5+\log 0.2} = \left(\dfrac{a}{b}\right)^{\log (0.5)(0.2)} = \left(\dfrac{a}{b}\right)^{\log 0.1} = \left(\dfrac{a}{b}\right)^{-1} = \dfrac{b}{a}$

f) Method 1: $4^{-2\log_4 3} = x \rightarrow \log_4 x = -2\log_4 3 \rightarrow \log_4 x = \log_4 3^{-2} \rightarrow x = 3^{-2} \rightarrow x = \frac{1}{9}$

Method 2: $4^{\log_4 3^{-2}} = 3^{-2} \rightarrow x = \frac{1}{9}$. (rule #7, p. 176)

g) $10\log_4 x - 12\log_8 x = \dfrac{10\log x}{\log 4} - \dfrac{12\log x}{\log 8} = \dfrac{10\log x}{\log 2^2} - \dfrac{12\log x}{\log 2^3} = \dfrac{10\log x}{2\log 2} - \dfrac{12\log x}{3\log 2} = 5\log_2 x - 4\log_2 x = \log_2 x$

h) Method 1: $\log \pi + \log \dfrac{\sqrt{2}}{\pi} + \dfrac{1}{2}\log\dfrac{3}{2} - \log\dfrac{\sqrt{3}}{10} = \log\left(\dfrac{\pi\cdot\frac{\sqrt{2}}{\pi}\cdot\left(\frac{3}{2}\right)^{\frac{1}{2}}}{\frac{\sqrt{3}}{10}}\right) \rightarrow \log\left(\dfrac{3^{\frac{1}{2}}}{\frac{\sqrt{3}}{10}}\right) = \log 10 = 1$

Method 2: $\log \pi + \log\sqrt{2} - \log \pi + \log\sqrt{3} - \log\sqrt{2} - \log\sqrt{3} + \log 10 = \log 10 = 1$

i) $\log(1-x^3) - \log(1+x+x^2) - \log(1-x) = \log\dfrac{(1-x^3)}{(1+x+x^2)(1-x)} = \log\dfrac{(1-x^3)}{(1-x^3)} = \log 1 = 0$

j) $\dfrac{\log_a x}{\log_{ab} x} - \dfrac{\log_a x}{\log_b x} = \dfrac{\frac{\log x}{\log a}}{\frac{\log x}{\log ab}} - \dfrac{\frac{\log x}{\log a}}{\frac{\log x}{\log b}} = \dfrac{\log ab}{\log a} - \dfrac{\log b}{\log a} = \dfrac{\log a + \log b - \log b}{\log a} = 1$

k) $\dfrac{1}{\log_a x} + \dfrac{1}{\log_b x} = \log_x a + \log_x b = \log_x a\,b$ (rule #8, p. 176)

l) $\left(\log_5 9\right)\left(\log_3 7\right)\left(\log_7 5\right) = \dfrac{\log 9}{\log 5}\cdot\dfrac{\log 7}{\log 3}\cdot\dfrac{\log 5}{\log 7} = \dfrac{\log 9}{\log 3} = \dfrac{\log 3^2}{\log 3} = \dfrac{2\log 3}{\log 3} = 2$

5.4 Exercise Set

1. a) $\log_5(2x-1) + \log_5(x-2) = 1 \rightarrow \log_5(2x-1)(x-2) = 1 \rightarrow (2x-1)(x-2) = 5^1 \rightarrow$

$2x^2 - 5x + 2 = 5 \rightarrow 2x^2 - 5x - 3 = 0 \rightarrow (2x+1)(x-3) = 0 \rightarrow x = -\dfrac{1}{2}, 3$

Check: $(2x-1) \rightarrow 2\left(-\dfrac{1}{2}\right) - 1 = -2$, logarithm must be positive, therefore, reject $x = -\dfrac{1}{2}$

$(x-2) \rightarrow 3 - 2 = 1$, o.k. $(2x-1) \rightarrow 2\cdot 3 - 1 = 5$, o.k. Therefore, $x = 3$

b) $\log_2(2-2x) + \log_2(1-x) = 5 \rightarrow \log_2(2-2x)(1-x) = 5 \rightarrow (2-2x)(1-x) = 2^5 \rightarrow$

$2 - 4x + 2x^2 = 32 \rightarrow 2x^2 - 4x - 30 = 0 \rightarrow x^2 - 2x - 15 = 0 \rightarrow (x-5)(x+3) = 0 \rightarrow x = 5, -3$

Check: $(1-x) \rightarrow 1 - 5 = -4$ logarithm must be positive, therefore, reject $x = 5$

$(1-x) \rightarrow 1 - (-3) = 4$ o.k., $(2-2x) \rightarrow (2 - 2(-3))$ o.k. Therefore, $x = -3$

c) $\dfrac{1}{2} - \log_{16}(x-3) = \log_{16} x \rightarrow \log_{16} x + \log_{16}(x-3) = \dfrac{1}{2} \rightarrow \log_{16} x(x-3) = \dfrac{1}{2} \rightarrow x(x-3) = 16^{\frac{1}{2}} \rightarrow$

$x^2 - 3x - 4 = 0 \rightarrow (x-4)(x+1) = 0 \rightarrow x = 4, -1$ Check and reject $x = -1$ Therefore, $x = 4$

d) $\log_2(3x+1) + \log_2(x-1) = \log_2(10x+14) \rightarrow \log_2(3x+1)(x-1) = \log_2(10x+14) \rightarrow$

$(3x+1)(x-1) = 10x + 14 \rightarrow 3x^2 - 2x - 1 = 10x + 14 \rightarrow 3x^2 - 12x - 15 = 0 \rightarrow x^2 - 4x - 5 = 0 \rightarrow$

$(x-5)(x+1) = 0 \rightarrow x = -1, 5$ Check and reject $x = -1$ Therefore, $x = 5$

e) $\log_4(3x^2 - 5x - 2) - \log_4(x-2) = 1 \rightarrow \log_4\dfrac{(3x+1)(x-2)}{(x-2)} = 1 \rightarrow \dfrac{(3x+1)(x-2)}{(x-2)} = 4 \rightarrow 3x + 1 = 4 \rightarrow 3x = 3 \rightarrow x = 1$

Check and reject. Therefore, answer is ϕ

f) $\log x + \log(29-x) = 2 \rightarrow \log x(29-x) = 2 \rightarrow x(29-x) = 10^2 \rightarrow\, !\, x^2 + 29x = 100\ \forall\ x^2 - 29x + 100 = 0 \rightarrow (x-25)(x-4) = 0 \rightarrow$

$x = 4$ and 25 Check answers, both work. Therefore, $x = 4, 25$

1. g) $\log_{25}(x-1)+\log_{25}(x+3)=\log_7\sqrt{7} \rightarrow \log_{25}(x-1)(x+3)=\frac{1}{2}\log_7 7=\frac{1}{2} \rightarrow$

$(x-1)(x+3)=25^{\frac{1}{2}} \rightarrow x^2+2x-3=5 \rightarrow x^2+2x-8=0 \rightarrow (x+4)(x-2)=0 \rightarrow$

$x=-4\,,2$ Check and reject -4 Therefore, $x = 2$

h) $2\log(4-x)-\log 3 = \log(10-x) \rightarrow \log\frac{(4-x)^2}{3} = \log(10-x) \rightarrow$

$\frac{(4-x)^2}{3} = 10-x \rightarrow 16-8x+x^2 = 30-3x \rightarrow x^2-5x-14=0 \rightarrow$

$(x-7)(x+2) = 0 \rightarrow x = -2\,,7$ Check and reject 7 Therefore, $x=-2$

i) $2\log_2(x+2)-\log_2(3x-2)=2 \rightarrow \log_2\frac{(x+2)^2}{(3x\,!\,2)}=2\,\forall\, \frac{(x+2)^2}{(3x-2)}=2^2 \rightarrow x^2+4x+4=12x-8 \rightarrow$

$x^2-8x+12=0 \rightarrow (x-6)(x-2)=0,\ x=2,\ 6$ Check answers, both work Therefore, $x=2,\ 6$

j) $2\log_4 x+\log_4(x-2)-\log_4 2x=1 \rightarrow \log_4\frac{x^2(x-2)}{2x}=1 \rightarrow \frac{x(x-2)}{2}=4 \rightarrow x^2-2x-8=0 \rightarrow$

$(x-4)(x+2)=0,\ x=-2,\ 4$ Check and reject -2 Therefore, $x=4$

2. a) $\log\frac{x^3}{y^2} \rightarrow \log x^3-\log y^2 \rightarrow 3\log x-2\log y \rightarrow 3a-2b$

b) $\log_{16}81=\frac{\log 81}{\log 16}=\frac{\log 3^4}{\log 2^4}=\frac{4\log 3}{4\log 2}=\log_2 3=a$ **c)** $\log\frac{9}{5}=\log\frac{3^2}{25^{\frac{1}{2}}}=\log 3^2-\log 25^{\frac{1}{2}}=2\log 3-\frac{1}{2}\log 25=2a-\frac{1}{2}b$

d) $\log\frac{25}{9}=\log 5^2-\log 3^2=2\log 5-2\log 3=2\log\frac{10}{2}-2\log 3 = 2(\log 10-\log 2)-2\log 3 = 2(1-a)-2b = 2-2a-2b$

e) **(*i*)** $\log\frac{A}{B^2}=\log A-2\log B=2-2(3)=2-6=-4$ **(*ii*)** $(\log AB)^2=(\log A+\log B)^2=(2+3)^2=25$

f) $\log_5 12=\frac{\log 12}{\log 5}=\frac{\log 2^2\cdot 3}{\log\frac{10}{2}}=\frac{2\log 2+\log 3}{\log 10-\log 2}=\frac{2a+b}{1-a}$

g) $\log AB=8 \rightarrow \log A+\log B=8\,,\ \log A-4=8 \rightarrow \log A=12$ Therefore, $A=10^{12}$

h) $\log_2\sqrt[3]{12.6}=\log_2\left(\frac{63}{5}\right)^{\frac{1}{3}}=\frac{\frac{1}{3}(\log 63-\log 5)}{\log 2}=\frac{\frac{1}{3}(\log 3^2\,!7\,\forall\log 5)}{\log\left(\frac{10}{5}\right)}=\frac{\frac{1}{3}(2\log 3+\log 7-\log 5)}{\log 10-\log 5}=\frac{\frac{1}{3}(2x+z-y)}{1-y}=\frac{2x-y+z}{3-3y}$

i) $a=\log_8 3 \rightarrow a=\frac{\log 3}{\log 8}\,,\ b=\log_3 5 \rightarrow b=\frac{\log 5}{\log 3}$ Therefore, $ab = \frac{\log 3}{\log 8}\cdot\frac{\log 5}{\log 3}=\frac{\log 5}{\log 8}$

so $\log 5= ab\log 8 = ab\log 2^3 = 3ab\log 2 = 3ab\log\frac{10}{5} = 3ab(\log 10-\log 5)=3ab(1-\log 5)=$

$3ab-3ab\log 5$, so, $3ab\log 5+\log 5 = 3ab \rightarrow \log 5(3ab+1) = 3ab \rightarrow \log 5 = \frac{3ab}{3ab+1}$

3. a) $A=\log 3B-\log C \rightarrow A=\log\frac{3B}{C} \rightarrow 10^A=\frac{3B}{C} \rightarrow B=\frac{C\cdot 10^A}{3}$

b) $1+\log(AB)=\log C \rightarrow \log(AB)-\log C=-1 \rightarrow \log\left(\frac{AB}{C}\right) = -1 \rightarrow 10^{-1}=\frac{AB}{C} \rightarrow A=\frac{C}{10B}$

c) $3\log A+\log B=\log C \rightarrow \log A^3+\log B=\log C \rightarrow \log A^3\cdot B=\log C \rightarrow A^3B=C \rightarrow A=\sqrt[3]{\frac{C}{B}}$

d) $\log A=\log B-C\log x \rightarrow \log A=\log B-\log x^c \rightarrow \log A=\log\frac{B}{x^c} \rightarrow x^c=\frac{B}{A} \rightarrow x=\left(\frac{B}{A}\right)^{\frac{1}{c}}$ or $\sqrt[c]{\frac{B}{A}}$

4. a) $2^{3x}=5^{x-1} \rightarrow \log 2^{3x}=\log 5^{x-1} \rightarrow 3x\log 2=(x-1)\log 5 \rightarrow$

$3x\log 2=x\log 5-\log 5 \rightarrow x\log 5-3x\log 2=\log 5 \rightarrow x(\log 5-3\log 2)=\log 5 \rightarrow$

$x=\frac{\log 5}{\log 5-3\log 2}$ (acceptable answer) $\rightarrow x=\frac{\log 5}{\log\frac{5}{2^3}}=\log_{\frac{5}{8}}5$ (better answer)

b) $7^{2x-1}=17^x \rightarrow \log 7^{2x-1}=\log 17^x \rightarrow (2x-1)\log 7=x\log 17 \rightarrow 2x\log 7-\log 7=x\log 17 \rightarrow$

$2x\log 7-x\log 17=\log 7 \rightarrow x(2\log 7-\log 17)=\log 7 \rightarrow x=\frac{\log 7}{2\log 7-\log 17}$ or $x=\log_{\frac{49}{17}}7$

4. c) $3^{x-1} = 9 \cdot 10^x \rightarrow \dfrac{3^{x-1}}{9} = 10^x \rightarrow \dfrac{3^{x-1}}{3^2} = 10^x \rightarrow 3^{x-3} = 10^x \rightarrow \log 3^{x-3} = \log 10^x \rightarrow$

$(x-3)\log 3 = x \log 10 \rightarrow x \log 3 - 3 \log 3 = x \rightarrow x \log 3 - x = 3 \log 3 \rightarrow$

$x(\log 3 - 1) = \log 3^3 \rightarrow x = \dfrac{\log 27}{\log 3 - 1}$ or $\dfrac{\log 27}{\log 3 - \log 10}$ or $\dfrac{\log 27}{\log \frac{3}{10}}$ or $\log_{\frac{3}{10}} 27$

d) $7^{x-1} = 2 \cdot 5^{1-2x} \rightarrow \log 7^{x-1} = \log 2 \cdot 5^{1-2x} \rightarrow (x-1)\log 7 = \log 2 + (1-2x)\log 5 \rightarrow$

$x \log 7 - \log 7 = \log 2 + \log 5 - 2x \log 5 \rightarrow x \log 7 + 2x \log 5 = \log 2 + \log 5 + \log 7 \rightarrow$

$x(\log 7 + 2\log 5) = \log 2 + \log 5 + \log 7 \rightarrow x = \dfrac{\log 2 + \log 5 + \log 7}{\log 7 + 2\log 5}$ or $\dfrac{\log 70}{\log 175}$ or $\log_{175} 70$

5. a) $\log_2(\log_8 x) = -1 \rightarrow \log_8 x = 2^{-1} \rightarrow \log_8 x = \dfrac{1}{2} \rightarrow x = 8^{\frac{1}{2}} = (2^3)^{\frac{1}{2}} \rightarrow x = 2^{\frac{3}{2}}$ or $2\sqrt{2}$

b) $\log_2(\log_x(\log_3 27)) = -1 \rightarrow \log_x(\log_3 27) = 2^{-1} \rightarrow \log_x(\log_3 3^3) = \dfrac{1}{2} \rightarrow$

$\log_x 3(\log_3 3) = \dfrac{1}{2} \rightarrow \log_x 3 = \dfrac{1}{2} \rightarrow x^{\frac{1}{2}} = 3 \rightarrow x = 3^2 = 9$

c) $\log_{\frac{1}{2}}(\log_4(\log_2 x)) = 1 \rightarrow \log_4(\log_2 x) = \dfrac{1}{2} \rightarrow \log_2 x = 4^{\frac{1}{2}} = 2 \rightarrow x = 2^2 = 4$

d) $\log x = \frac{2}{3}\log 27 + 2\log 2 - \log 3 = \log \dfrac{27^{\frac{2}{3}} \cdot 2^2}{3} \rightarrow x = \dfrac{27^{\frac{2}{3}} \cdot 2^2}{3} = \dfrac{9 \cdot 4}{3} = 12$

e) $\log x = \log 2 + 3\log_{\sqrt{10}} y - \log 2z = \log 2 + \dfrac{\log y^3}{\log\sqrt{10}} - \log 2z \rightarrow \log x = \log 2 + \dfrac{\log y^3}{\frac{1}{2}\log 10} - \log 2z = \log 2 + 2\log y^3 - \log 2z \rightarrow$

$\log x = \log 2 + \log y^6 - \log 2z = \log \dfrac{2y^6}{2z}$! $x = \dfrac{y^6}{z}$

f) $2\log x = -\log a + 3\log b + 4\log \dfrac{1}{c} \rightarrow \log x^2 = \log a^{-1} + \log b^3 + \log\left(\dfrac{1}{c}\right)^4 \rightarrow$

$\log x^2 = \log a^{-1} \cdot b^3 \cdot \left(\dfrac{1}{c}\right)^4 \rightarrow x^2 = \dfrac{b^3}{ac^4} \rightarrow x = \sqrt{\dfrac{b^3}{a \cdot c^4}} \rightarrow x = \sqrt{\dfrac{b^2 \cdot b \cdot a}{a^2 \cdot c^4}} = \dfrac{b\sqrt{ab}}{ac^2}$

6. a) $x = \dfrac{a^2}{b^3 c^{\frac{1}{2}}} \rightarrow \log x = \log \dfrac{a^2}{b^3 c^{\frac{1}{2}}} \rightarrow \log x = 2 \log a - 3 \log b - \frac{1}{2} \log c$

b) $x = \dfrac{a^{-2} b^3}{c^{-\frac{1}{2}}} \rightarrow x = \dfrac{b^3 c^{\frac{1}{2}}}{a^2} \rightarrow \log x = \log \dfrac{b^3 c^{\frac{1}{2}}}{a^2} \rightarrow \log x = 3 \log b + \frac{1}{2} \log c - 2 \log a$

c) $x = \dfrac{\sqrt[3]{a^2} \cdot b^{-\frac{2}{5}}}{c^{\frac{1}{2}}} \rightarrow \log x = \log \dfrac{\sqrt[3]{a^2} \cdot b^{-\frac{2}{5}}}{c^{\frac{1}{2}}} \rightarrow \log x = \frac{2}{3}\log a - \frac{2}{5}\log b - \frac{1}{2}\log c$

d) $x = \dfrac{\sqrt{a^5}\, b^{-\frac{1}{3}}}{c^3 d^{-\frac{2}{3}}} = \dfrac{a^{\frac{5}{2}} d^{\frac{2}{3}}}{b^{\frac{1}{3}} c^3} \rightarrow \log x = \log \dfrac{a^{\frac{5}{2}} d^{\frac{2}{3}}}{b^{\frac{1}{3}} c^3} \rightarrow \log x = \dfrac{5}{2}\log a + \dfrac{2}{3}\log d - \dfrac{1}{3}\log b - 3\log c$

7. a) $\log_2 16^{2x+1} = 8 \rightarrow 2^8 = 16^{2x+1} \rightarrow 2^8 = 2^{4(2x+1)} \rightarrow 2^8 = 2^{8x+4} \rightarrow 8x + 4 = 8 \rightarrow 8x = 4 \rightarrow x = \dfrac{1}{2}$

b) $\log_{16} x + \log_4 x + \log_2 x = 1 \rightarrow \dfrac{\log_2 x}{\log_2 16} + \dfrac{\log_2 x}{\log_2 4} + \log_2 x = 7 \rightarrow \dfrac{\log_2 x}{4} + \dfrac{\log_2 x}{2} + \log_2 x = 7 \rightarrow \dfrac{7}{4}\log_2 x = 7 \rightarrow \log_2 x = 4 \rightarrow x = 2^4 = 16$

c) $\log_9 x + 3\log_3 x = 7 \rightarrow \dfrac{\log_3 x}{\log_3 9} + 3\log_3 x = 7 \rightarrow \dfrac{\log_3 x}{\log_3 3^2} + 3\log_3 x = 7 \rightarrow \dfrac{1}{2}\log_3 x + 3\log_3 x = 7 \rightarrow \dfrac{7}{2}\log_3 x = 7 \rightarrow \log_3 x = 7 \cdot \dfrac{2}{7}$

$= 2 \rightarrow x = 3^2 = 9$

d) $2\log_4 x - 3\log_x 4 = 5 \rightarrow 2\log_4 x - \dfrac{3}{\log_4 x} = 5 \rightarrow 2(\log_4 x)^2 - 3 = 5\log_4 x \rightarrow$

$2(\log_4 x)^2 - 5\log_4 x - 3 = 0 \rightarrow (2\log_4 x + 1)(\log_4 x - 3) = 0 \rightarrow \log_4 x = -\dfrac{1}{2} \rightarrow x = 4^{-\frac{1}{2}} = \dfrac{1}{2}$ and $\log_4 x = 3 \rightarrow x = 4^3 = 64$

Therefore, $x = \dfrac{1}{2}$ or 64

e) $(\log_4 a)(\log_a 2a)(\log_{2a} x) = \log_a a^3 \rightarrow \frac{\log a}{\log 4}\cdot\frac{\log 2a}{\log a}\cdot\frac{\log x}{\log 2a} = 3 \rightarrow \frac{\log x}{\log 4} = 3 \rightarrow \log_4 x = 3 \rightarrow x = 4^3 \rightarrow x = 64$

f) $\sqrt{\log x} = \log\sqrt{x} \rightarrow \sqrt{\log x} - \frac{1}{2}\log x = 0 \rightarrow \sqrt{\log x}\left(1 - \frac{1}{2}\sqrt{\log x}\right) = 0$

$$\sqrt{\log x} = 0 \text{ or } 1 - \frac{1}{2}\sqrt{\log x} = 0$$

$$\log x = 0 \text{ or } \log x = 4$$

$$x = 10^0 \text{ or } x = 10^4\text{, therefore, } x = 1, 10000$$

8. a) In step 6, you are dividing by $\log\frac{1}{2}$ which is a negative number, therefore, the direction of the inequality **must be changed**.

b) When you multiply by $\log\frac{1}{2}$ in step 2, the value of two **positive** numbers is changed to two **negative** numbers, without changing the direction of the inequality.

5.5 Exercise Set

1. $A = A_0(x)^{\frac{t}{T}} \rightarrow 10\,000 = 40\,000\,(0.85)^{\frac{t}{1}} \rightarrow 0.25 = 0.85^t \rightarrow \log_{0.85} 0.25 = t$

$t = \frac{\log\ 0.25}{\log\ 0.85} = 8.53$ It takes 8.53 years to depreciate to \$10 000.

2. a) $A = P\left(1 + \frac{r}{n}\right)^{nt} \rightarrow 1\,000\,000 = 10\,000\left(1 + \frac{0.12}{4}\right)^{4t} \rightarrow 100 = 1.03^{4t} \rightarrow \log_{1.03} 100 = 4t \rightarrow t = \frac{\log 100}{4\log 1.03} = 38.95$ years

b) $A = Pe^{rt} \rightarrow 1\,000\,000 = 10\,000e^{0.12t} \rightarrow 100 = e^{0.12t} \rightarrow \ln 100 = 0.12t \rightarrow t = \frac{\ln 100}{0.12} = 38.38$ years

3. a) $A = P\left(1 + \frac{r}{n}\right)^{nt} \rightarrow 3P = P\left(1 + \frac{r}{2}\right)^{2\cdot 15} \rightarrow 3 = \left(1 + \frac{r}{2}\right)^{30} \rightarrow 1 + \frac{r}{2} = 3^{\frac{1}{30}} \rightarrow \frac{r}{2} = 3^{\frac{1}{30}} - 1 \rightarrow r = 2\,(3^{\frac{1}{30}} - 1) = 7.46\%$

b) $A = Pe^{rt} \rightarrow 3P = Pe^{15r} \rightarrow 3 = e^{15r} \rightarrow \ln 3 = 15r \rightarrow r = \frac{\ln 3}{15} = 7.32\%$

4. Method 1: $A = A_0(x)^{\frac{t}{T}} \rightarrow 0.8 = 1\left(\frac{1}{2}\right)^{\frac{30}{T}}$ (if 20% lost , 80% remains) $\rightarrow \log_{\frac{1}{2}} 0.8 = \frac{30}{T} \rightarrow$

$$T = \frac{30}{\log_{\frac{1}{2}} 0.8} = \frac{30}{\frac{\log 0.8}{\log\frac{1}{2}}} = \frac{30\log\frac{1}{2}}{\log 0.8} = 93.2 \text{ hours}$$

Method 2: $A = A_0e^{kt} \rightarrow 0.8 = 1\cdot e^{k\cdot 30} \rightarrow \ln 0.8 = 30k \rightarrow k = \frac{\ln 0.8}{30}$

$$A = A_0e^{\left(\frac{\ln 0.8}{30}\right)t} \rightarrow \frac{1}{2} = 1\cdot e^{\left(\frac{\ln 0.8}{30}\right)t} \rightarrow \ln 0.5 = \left(\frac{\ln\ 0.8}{30}\right)t \rightarrow t = \frac{30\ln 0.5}{\ln 0.8} = 93.2 \text{ hours}$$

5. Remember, the **smaller** the pH values of an acidic solution, the **stronger** the acidity. The **larger** the pH value of an alkaline solution, the **stronger** the alkalinity.

a) $4.8 - 2.1 = 2.7$, then $10^{2.7} = 501$, therefore, lemon juice is 501 times more acidic than black coffee.

b) $10^x = 75 \rightarrow x = \log 75 \rightarrow x = 1.9$, therefore, $4.2 + 1.9 = 6.1$ is the pH of milk.

6. $A = A_0(x)^{\frac{t}{T}} \rightarrow 400\,000\,(1.02)^t = 300\,000\,(1.03)^t \rightarrow 1.02^t = \frac{3}{4}(1.03)^t \rightarrow \log 1.02^t = \log\frac{3}{4}(1.03)^t = \log\frac{3}{4} + \log 1.03^t \rightarrow$

$t\log 1.02 = \log\frac{3}{4} + t\log 1.03 \rightarrow t\,(\log 1.02 - \log 1.03) = \log\frac{3}{4} \rightarrow t = \frac{\log\frac{3}{4}}{\log\frac{1.02}{1.03}} \approx 29.5$ Surrey catches up in population to Vancouver in 29.5 years.

7. a) $A = P\left(1 + \frac{r}{n}\right)^{nt} \rightarrow 3 = 1\left(1 + \frac{0.08}{365}\right)^{365t} \rightarrow 365t = \frac{\log 3}{\log\left(1 + \frac{0.08}{365}\right)} \rightarrow t = \frac{\log 3}{365\log\left(1 + \frac{0.08}{365}\right)} = 13.73$ years

b) $A = Pe^{rt} \rightarrow 3 = 1e^{0.08t} \rightarrow \ln 3 = 0.08t \rightarrow t = \frac{\ln 3}{0.08} = 13.73$ years

8. $C = 8\,e^{0.3\,t} \rightarrow 100 = 8\,e^{0.3\,t} \rightarrow 12.5 = e^{0.3\,t} \rightarrow 0.3\,t = \ln 12.5 \rightarrow t = \frac{\ln 12.5}{0.3} = 8.42°\,C$ $t = 8.42$ degrees Celsius

9. $P(t) = 4\,000\,000\ e^{0.012\ t} \rightarrow 6\,400\,000 = 4\,000\,000\ e^{0.012\ t} \rightarrow 1.6 = e^{0.012\ t} \rightarrow$

$\ln 1.6 = 0.012\,t \rightarrow t = \dfrac{\ln 1.6}{0.012} = 39.2$ Therefore, in year 2039 the population will reach 6 400 000.

10. Method 1: $A = A_0(x)^{\frac{t}{T}} \rightarrow 100\,000 = 1\,200\,(2)^{\frac{t}{4}} \rightarrow \dfrac{250}{3} = 2^{\frac{t}{4}} \rightarrow \log_2 \dfrac{250}{3} = \dfrac{t}{4} \rightarrow t = \dfrac{4\log\frac{250}{3}}{\log 2} = 25.5$ days

Method 2: $A = A_0 e^{k\,t} \rightarrow 2 = 1 \cdot e^{k \cdot 4} \rightarrow \ln 2 = 4\,k \rightarrow k = \dfrac{\ln 2}{4} \rightarrow A = A_0 e^{\left(\frac{\ln 2}{4}\right)t} \rightarrow$

$100\,000 = 1200\,e^{\left(\frac{\ln 2}{4}\right)t} \rightarrow \dfrac{250}{3} = e^{\left(\frac{\ln 2}{4}\right)t} \rightarrow \ln\left(\dfrac{250}{3}\right) = \left(\dfrac{\ln 2}{4}\right)t \rightarrow t = \dfrac{4\ \ln\left(\frac{250}{3}\right)}{\ln 2} = 25.5$ days

11. $A = A_0 e^{kt} \rightarrow \dfrac{1}{2} = 1 \cdot e^{k \cdot 5570} \rightarrow \ln 0.5 = 5570\,k \rightarrow k = \dfrac{\ln\ 0.5}{5570}$ $A = A_0 e^{\left(\frac{\ln 0.5}{5570}\right)t} = 500\,e^{\left(\frac{\ln 0.5}{5570}\right)2500} = 366.3$ grams

12. *Let* $q = 2^{74207281} - 1$ *with* $2 = 10^x \rightarrow x = \log 2 \rightarrow 2 = 10^{\log 2}$ *Substitute* $q = \left(10^{\log 2}\right)^{74207281}$! 1 $= 10^{22338617.48} - 1$

But 10^n *has n + 1 digits so q has 22 338 618 digits. (By the way, printing this number would take about 3700 pages!)*

5.6 Chapter Review

Logarithms – Multiple-choice Answers

1.	a	**8.**	d	**15.**	b	**22.**	b	**29.**	d	**36.**	b	**43.**	a	**50.**	b	**57.**	a	**64.**	d
2.	d	**9.**	c	**16.**	a	**23.**	a	**30.**	a	**37.**	d	**44.**	b	**51.**	b	**58.**	b	**65.**	a
3.	c	**10.**	c	**17.**	b	**24.**	c	**31.**	a	**38.**	a	**45.**	c	**52.**	d	**59.**	d		
4.	b	**11.**	a	**18.**	c	**25.**	c	**32.**	d	**39.**	c	**46.**	b	**53.**	d	**60.**	d		
5.	b	**12.**	b	**19.**	c	**26.**	c	**33.**	d	**40.**	b	**47.**	d	**54.**	a	**61.**	d		
6.	d	**13.**	a	**20.**	b	**27.**	b	**34.**	d	**41.**	c	**48.**	c	**55.**	b	**62.**	a		
7.	d	**14.**	a	**21.**	c	**28.**	c	**35.**	c	**42.**	b	**49.**	c	**56.**	a	**63.**	a		

Logarithms – Multiple-choice Solutions

1. Basic definition. Answer is a.

2. $\log 5 = \log x - \log 2 \rightarrow \log 5 = \log\dfrac{x}{2} \rightarrow 5 = \dfrac{x}{2} \rightarrow x = 10$. Answer is d.

3. $x - 2 = 0 \rightarrow x = 2$. Answer is c.

4. $\dfrac{\log 10^x}{10^{\log x}} = \dfrac{x \log 10}{x} = \log 10 = 1$. Answer is b.

Note: *If you don't understand that* $10^{\log x} = x$, *review Helpful log rule #7,* p. 220.

5. $y = \log x$ then $y + 2 = \log x + 2 = \log x + \log 100 = \log 100x$. Answer is b.

6. $x = \dfrac{\sqrt{A}}{3B} \rightarrow \log x = \log\dfrac{\sqrt{A}}{3B} \rightarrow \log x = \dfrac{1}{2}\log A - \log 3 - \log B$. Answer is d.

7. If $\log_a 2 = b$ then $a^b = 2$ and if $\log_c 5 = d$ then $c^d = 5$, therefore, $a^b \cdot c^d = 2 \cdot 5 = 10$. Answer is d.

8. $4\log a^2 - 2\log a = \log a^8 - \log a^2 = \log\dfrac{a^8}{a^2} = \log a^6$. Answer is d.

9. Basic definition. Answer is c.

10. $2 - x > 0 \rightarrow -x > -2 \rightarrow x < 2$. Answer is c.

11. $3^{\log x} = \dfrac{1}{27} \rightarrow 3^{\log x} = 3^{-3} \rightarrow \log x = -3 \rightarrow x = 10^{!3} \rightarrow x = \dfrac{1}{1000}$. Answer is a

12. $\left(\dfrac{1}{9}\right)^{2x-1} = 27^{2-x} \rightarrow 3^{-2(2x-1)} = 3^{3(2-x)} \rightarrow -4x + 2 = 6 - 3x \rightarrow -x = 4 \rightarrow x = -4$. Answer is b.

13. $4^{x^2-2x} = 8^{1-x} \rightarrow 2^{2(x^2-2x)} = 2^{3(1-x)} \rightarrow 2x^2 - 4x = 3 - 3x \rightarrow 2x^2 - x - 3 = 0 \rightarrow (2x-3)(x+1) = 0 \rightarrow x = \dfrac{3}{2}, -1$. Answer is a.

14. *x*-intercept has $y = 0 \rightarrow x = \log_3(0+5) - 2 \rightarrow x = \dfrac{\log 5}{\log 3} - 2 \rightarrow x = -0.535$

y-intercept has $x = 0 \rightarrow 0 = \log_3(y+5) - 2 \rightarrow \log_3(y+5) = 2 \rightarrow y + 5 = 3^2 \rightarrow y = 4$. Answer is a.

15. $y = -\log_4(x+8) + \dfrac{1}{2} = 0 \rightarrow \log_4(x+8) = \dfrac{1}{2} \rightarrow x + 8 = 4^{\frac{1}{2}} \rightarrow x + 8 = 2 \rightarrow x = -6$. Answer is b.

16. $y = \log_2(0+8) - 3 \rightarrow y = \log_2 8 - 3 \rightarrow y = \log_2 2^3 - 3 \rightarrow y = 3\log_2 2 - 3 = 0$. Answer is a.

17. $x + 2 > 0 \rightarrow x > -2$. Answer is b.

18. $y = -3 \cdot 2^{x-1} + 4$ has the basic graph $y = 2^x$ reflected in the *x*-axis and shifted up 4, therefore, range is $y < 4$. Answer is c.

19. $2\log_x\left(\frac{1}{\sqrt{x}}\right) = 2\log_x x^{-\frac{1}{2}} = -\log_x x = -1$. Answer is c.

20. $\frac{10^{8.1}}{10^{7.4}} = 10^{0.7} = 5.01$. Answer is b

21. $x = \frac{\sqrt[3]{a}}{bc^2} \to \log x = \log\frac{\sqrt[3]{a}}{bc^2} \to \log x = \frac{1}{3}\log a - \log b - 2\log c$. Answer is c.

22. The inverse of $y = \log\left(\frac{x}{2}\right)$ is $x = \log\left(\frac{y}{2}\right) \to 10^x = \frac{y}{2} \to y = 2\cdot 10^x$. Answer is b.

23. $\log_{\frac{1}{a}}(\sqrt{a})^a = \frac{\log a^{\frac{a}{2}}}{\log\frac{1}{a}} = \frac{\frac{a}{2}\log a}{\log 1 - \log a} = \frac{\frac{a}{2}}{-1} = \frac{-a}{2}$. Answer is a.

24. The restriction on $y = \log_x a$ is $a > 0$, $x > 0$, $x\ !\ 1$, therefore, $y = \log_x(x+2)$ has restriction $x+2>0$ and base $x>0$, $x \neq 1$ $\to$ $x > -2$ and $x > 0$, $x \neq 1$, the intersection is $x > 0$, $x\ !\ 1$. Answer is c.

25. $\log_3(x+5) - \log_3(x-3) = 2 \to \log_3\left(\frac{x+5}{x-3}\right) = 2 \to \frac{x+5}{x\ !\ 3} = 3^2 \to x+5 = 9x-27 \to -8x = -32 \to x = 4$. Answer is c.

26. $3 - 2\log a + \log b \to \log 1000 - \log a^2 + \log b \to \log\frac{1000b}{a^2}$. Answer is c.

27. If $(m,\ n)$ is on $f(x) = \log_a x$, then $(n,\ m)$ is on $h(x) = a^x$, so $h(x) = a^{-x}$ reflects the graph on the y-axis, therefore point is $(-n,\ m)$. Answer is b.

28. $(\log_9 x)(\log_5 3) = 1 \to \frac{\log x}{\log 9}\cdot\frac{\log 3}{\log 5} = 1 \to \frac{\log x}{\log 3^2}\cdot\frac{\log 3}{\log 5} = 1 \to \frac{\log x}{2\log 3}\cdot\frac{\log 3}{\log 5} = 1 \to \frac{\log x}{2\log 5} = 1 \to$

$\log_5 x = 2 \to x = 5^2 \to x = 25$. Answer is c.

29. $f(x) = 2^{-x}$ has inverse $x = 2^{-y} \to \log_2 x = -y \to y = -\log_2 x \to y = \log_2 x^{-1} \to y = \log_2\left(\frac{1}{x}\right)$. Answer is d.

30. $2^{3\log_8 5} = x \to 8^{\log_8 5} = x \to x = 5$. Answer is a.

31. The inverse of $f(x) = 6^{x+1} - 2$ is $x = 6^{y+1} - 2 \to x+2 = 6^{y+1} \to \log_6(x+2) = y+1 \to y = \log_6(x+2) - 1$. Answer is a.

32. The inverse of $f(x) = \log_5(x-1) - 2$ is $x = \log_5(y-1) - 2 \to x+2 = \log_5(y-1) \to y-1 = 5^{x+2} \to y = 5^{x+2} + 1$. Answer is d.

33. $\log_{81} x = a \to x = 81^a = 3^{4a}$ $\log_{27} x = \log_{27}(3^{4a}) = 4a\log_{27} 3 = 4a\log_{27} 27^{\frac{1}{3}} = \frac{4a}{3}$. Answer is d.

34. $A = A_0\left(\frac{1}{2}\right)^{\frac{t}{T}} \to A = 50\left(\frac{1}{2}\right)^{\frac{t}{14}}$. Answer is d.

35. $A = P\left(1+\frac{r}{n}\right)^{nt} \to 1000 = P\left(1+\frac{0.12}{4}\right)^{4\cdot 5} \to 1000 = P(1.03)^{20} \to P = \frac{1000}{1.03^{20}}$. Answer is c.

36. $10^x = 240 \to x = \log 240 \to x = 2.4$, so 7.3 – 2.4 = 4.9. Answer is b.

37. $P = 30e^{0.019t} \to P = 30e^{(0.019)(50)} \to P = 77.57$. Answer is d.

38. $A = A_0(3)^{\frac{t}{T}} \to 200 = A_0(3)^{\frac{t}{5}} \to A_0 = \frac{200}{3^{\frac{t}{5}}}$. Answer is a.

39. 9.8 – 8.2 = 1.6, therefore, $10^{1.6} = 39.8$. Answer is c.

40. $10^x = 160 \to x = \log 160 \to x = 2.2$, therefore 8.7 + 2.2 = 10.9. Answer is b.

41. $\log_3\left(\frac{a}{9b^2}\right) = \log_3 a - \log_3 9 - \log_3 b^2 = \log_3 a - \log_2 3^2 - 2\log_3 b = \log_3 a - 2 - 2\log_3 b$. Answer is c.

42. $\log_2\left(\frac{25}{72}\right) = \log_2\frac{5^2}{2^3\cdot 3^2} = 2\log_2 5 - 3\log_2 2 - 2\log_2 3 = 2a - 3 - 2b$. Answer is b.

43. $1 - \log\frac{3}{b} - \log c = \log 10 - \log\frac{3}{b} - \log c = \log\frac{10}{\frac{3}{b}\cdot c} = \log\frac{10b}{3c}$. Answer is a.

44. $y = ab^x \to \frac{y}{a} = b^x \to x = \log_b\left(\frac{y}{a}\right)$. Answer is b.

45. $\log_2(a-3) = b \to a-3 = 2^b \to a = 2^b + 3$. Answer is c.

46. $\log\left(\frac{2}{9}\right) = \log\left(\frac{\sqrt{4}}{3^2}\right) = \log\left(\frac{4^{\frac{1}{2}}}{3^2}\right) = \frac{1}{2}\log 4 - 2\log 3 = \frac{a}{2} - 2b$. Answer is b.

47. $\log_b a$ has restrictions $a>0$, $b>0$, $b\neq 1$, therefore, $2-x>0\rightarrow\ x<2$; $x+1>0\rightarrow\ x>-1$; $x+1\neq 1\ \rightarrow x\neq 0$, therefore, $-1<x<2$, $x\neq 0$. Answer is d.

48. $2\log(3-x)=\log 2+\log(22-2x)\rightarrow\ \log(3-x)^2=\log 2(22-2x)\ \rightarrow\ (3-x)^2=2(22-2x)\ \rightarrow$ $9-6x+x^2=44-4x\ \rightarrow\ x^2-2x-35=0\ \rightarrow\ (x-7)(x+5)=0\ \rightarrow x=7\,,-5$, reject 7. Answer is c.

49. $\log_x 12-\log_x(x-1)=1\rightarrow\ \log_x\left(\dfrac{12}{x-1}\right)=1\ \rightarrow\ x=\dfrac{12}{x-1}\ \rightarrow\ x^2-x=12\ \rightarrow\ x^2-x-12=0\ \rightarrow$ $(x-4)(x+3)=0\ \rightarrow x=-3\,,4$, reject -3. Answer is c.

50. $\log_5(2x+1)=1-\log_5(x+2)\rightarrow\ \log_5(2x+1)+\log_5(x+2)=1\ \rightarrow\ \log_5(2x+1)(x+2)=1\ \rightarrow$ $(2x+1)(x+2)=5\ \rightarrow\ 2x^2+5x+2=5\ \rightarrow\ 2x^2+5x-3=0\ \rightarrow\ (2x-1)(x+3)=0\ \rightarrow\ x=\dfrac{1}{2}\ ,\ -3$, reject -3. Answer is b.

51. $a=3\log_8 c\rightarrow\ \dfrac{a}{3}=\log_8 c\ \rightarrow\ c=8^{\frac{a}{3}}\ \rightarrow\ c=2^a\quad b=\log_4 d\ \rightarrow\ d=4^b\ \rightarrow d=2^{2b}$, therefore, $\dfrac{c}{d}=\dfrac{2^a}{2^{2b}}=2^{a-2b}$. Answer is b.

52. $x=2^a$, $y=a$, in answer d, $y=\log_2 x\rightarrow\ a=\log_2 2^a\ \rightarrow\ a=a\log_2 2\ \rightarrow a=a$. Answer is d.

53. $\log_3[\log_x(\log_2 8)]=-1\rightarrow\ \log_x(\log_2 8)=3^{-1}=\dfrac{1}{3}\ \rightarrow\ x^{\frac{1}{3}}=\log_2 8\ \rightarrow\ x^{\frac{1}{3}}=\log_2 2^3=3\log_2 2=3\ \rightarrow\ x^{\frac{1}{3}}=3\ \rightarrow x=3^3=27$. Answer is d.

54. $\log 4=x\rightarrow\ \log 2^2=x\ \rightarrow\ 2\log 2=x\ \rightarrow\ \log 2=\dfrac{x}{2}\quad \log\dfrac{1}{3}=y\ \rightarrow\ \log 1-\log 3=y$ $\rightarrow \log 3=-y$, $\log 6=\log(2\cdot 3)=\log 2+\log 3=\dfrac{x}{2}-y$. Answer is a.

55. $2^{x-1}=3^x\rightarrow\ \log 2^{x-1}=\log 3^x\ \rightarrow\ (x-1)\log 2=x\log 3\ \rightarrow\ x\log 2-\log 2=x\log 3\ \rightarrow$ $x\log 2-x\log 3=\log 2\ \rightarrow\ x(\log 2-\log 3)=\log 2\ \rightarrow x=\dfrac{\log 2}{\log 2-\log 3}$. Answer is b.

56. $a=\log 2\rightarrow\ a=\log 4^{\frac{1}{2}}\ \rightarrow\ a=\dfrac{1}{2}\log 4\ \rightarrow\ \log 4=2a\quad b=\log 9\ \rightarrow\ b=\log 3^2\ \rightarrow\ b=2\log 3\ \rightarrow\ \log 3=\dfrac{b}{2}$ $\log 12=\log(3\cdot 4)=\log 3+\log 4=2a+\dfrac{b}{2}$. Answer is a.

57. $\dfrac{1}{\log_3 x}-\log_x 27=2\rightarrow\ \log_x 3-\log_x 27=2\ \rightarrow\ \log_x\dfrac{3}{27}=2\ \rightarrow\ x^2=\dfrac{1}{9}\ \rightarrow x=\dfrac{1}{3}$. Answer is a.

58. $\log_4 3=x\rightarrow\ 4^x=3\ \rightarrow\ 2^{2x}=3$; $\log_8 7=y\rightarrow\ 8^y=7\ \rightarrow\ 2^{3y}=7$
$\log_2 21=\log_2 3\cdot 7=\log_2 2^{2x}\cdot 2^{3y}=\log_2 2^{2x+3y}=(2x+3y)\log_2 2=2x+3y$. Answer is b.

59. $A=A_0(0.99)^{\frac{t}{T}}\rightarrow\ 0.15=1(0.99)^{\frac{t}{100}}\ \rightarrow\ \log_{0.99}0.15=\dfrac{t}{100}\ \rightarrow\ t=100\dfrac{\log 0.15}{\log 0.99}=18\,876$. Answer is d.

60. $A=A_0\left(\dfrac{1}{2}\right)^{\frac{t}{T}}\ \rightarrow\ 0.75=1\left(\dfrac{1}{2}\right)^{\frac{40}{T}}\ \rightarrow\ \log_{\frac{1}{2}}0.75=\dfrac{40}{T}\ \rightarrow T=40\dfrac{\log 0.5}{\log 0.75}=96.38$. Answer is d.

61. $\log_3(2-4x)-\log_3(3-x)=2\rightarrow\ \log_3\left(\dfrac{2-4x}{3-x}\right)=2\rightarrow\ \dfrac{2-4x}{3-x}=3^2\rightarrow\ 2-4x=27-9x\rightarrow\ 5x=25\rightarrow$ $x=5$, check solution, 5 rejected. No solution. Answer is d.

62. $3a^{x-1}=b^x\rightarrow\ \log 3a^{x-1}=\log b^x\rightarrow\ \log 3+(x-1)\log a=x\log b\rightarrow\ \log 3+x\log a-\log a=x\log b\rightarrow$ $x\log a-x\log b=\log a-\log 3\rightarrow\ x(\log a-\log b)=\log a-\log 3\rightarrow\ x=\dfrac{\log a-\log 3}{\log a-\log b}$. Answer is a.

63. $2\log_3(-x)=2-\log_3 4\rightarrow 2\log_3(-x)+\log_3 4=2\rightarrow\ \log_3 4(-x)^2=2\rightarrow\ 4(-x)^2=3^2\rightarrow\ x=\pm\dfrac{3}{2}$ check solution, reject $\dfrac{3}{2}$, accept $-\dfrac{3}{2}$. Answer is a.

64. $A=P\left(1+\dfrac{r}{n}\right)^{nt}\ \rightarrow\ 3P=P\left(1+\dfrac{r}{12}\right)^{12\times 10}\ \rightarrow\ 3=\left(1+\dfrac{r}{12}\right)^{120}\ \rightarrow\ 1+\dfrac{r}{12}=3^{\frac{1}{120}}\rightarrow\ \dfrac{r}{12}=3^{\frac{1}{120}}-1\rightarrow$ $r=12\,(3^{\frac{1}{120}}-1)\rightarrow r=0.11036=11.0\%$. Answer is d.

65. $A=A_0(x)^{\frac{t}{T}}\rightarrow\ 200=600\left(\dfrac{1}{2}\right)^{\frac{10}{t}}\ \rightarrow\ \left(\dfrac{1}{2}\right)^{\frac{10}{t}}=\dfrac{1}{3}\rightarrow\ \log_{\frac{1}{2}}\left(\dfrac{1}{3}\right)=\dfrac{10}{t}\rightarrow\ t=\dfrac{10\log\left(\frac{1}{2}\right)}{\log\left(\frac{1}{3}\right)}=6.3$. Answer is a.

Trigonometry (Part I) Solutions

6.1 Exercise Set

1. **a)** II **b)** III **c)** IV **d)** I **e)** $612^\circ - 360^\circ = 252^\circ$, III **f)** $-537^\circ + 2\times 360^\circ = 183^\circ$, III

g) $1100^\circ - 3\times 360^\circ = 20^\circ$, I **h)** $\dfrac{6325^\circ}{360^\circ} = 17^+$, $6325^\circ - 17\times 360^\circ = 205^\circ$, III **i)** $810^\circ - 2\times 360^\circ = 90^\circ$, not in quadrant **j)** $-900^\circ + 3\times 360^\circ = 180^\circ$, not in quadrant

2. **a)** 45° **b)** 72° **c)** 300° **d)** 405° **e)** 504° **f)** 420°

3. **a)** $\dfrac{\pi}{3}$ **b)** $\dfrac{3\pi}{2}$ **c)** $\dfrac{4\pi}{3}$ **d)** $\dfrac{9\pi}{2}$ **e)** $\dfrac{13\pi}{6}$ **f)** $\dfrac{11\pi}{4}$

4. **a)** $150^\circ + 360^\circ = 510^\circ, 150^\circ - 360^\circ = -210^\circ$ **b)** $-150^\circ + 360^\circ = 210^\circ$, $-150^\circ - 360^\circ = -510^\circ$

c) $314^\circ + 360^\circ = 674^\circ, 314^\circ - 360^\circ = -46^\circ$ **d)** $-314^\circ + 360^\circ = 46^\circ$, $-314^\circ - 360^\circ = -674^\circ$

e) $612^\circ - 360^\circ = 252^\circ, 612^\circ - 2\times 360^\circ = -108^\circ$ **f)** $-537^\circ + 2\times 360^\circ = 183^\circ$, $-537^\circ + 360^\circ = -177^\circ$

g) $1100^\circ - 360^\circ = 740^\circ, 1100^\circ - 4\times 360^\circ = -340^\circ$ **h)** $6325^\circ - 360^\circ = 5965^\circ$, $6325^\circ - 18\times 360^\circ = -155^\circ$

i) $810^\circ - 2\times 360^\circ = 90^\circ, 810^\circ - 3\times 360^\circ = -270^\circ$ **j)** $-900^\circ + 3\times 360^\circ = 180^\circ$, $-900^\circ + 360^\circ = -540^\circ$

Note: *There are an infinite number of possible answers for each question. List above represents just one possible answer for each question.*

5. **a)** $45^\circ \times \dfrac{\pi}{180^\circ} = \dfrac{\pi}{4}$ **b)** $90^\circ \times \dfrac{\pi}{180^\circ} = \dfrac{\pi}{2}$ **c)** $150^\circ \times \dfrac{\pi}{180^\circ} = \dfrac{5\pi}{6}$ **d)** $240^\circ \times \dfrac{\pi}{180^\circ} = \dfrac{4\pi}{3}$

e) $300^\circ \times \dfrac{\pi}{180^\circ} = \dfrac{5\pi}{3}$ **f)** $360^\circ \times \dfrac{\pi}{180^\circ} = 2\pi$ **g)** $405^\circ \times \dfrac{\pi}{180^\circ} = \dfrac{9\pi}{4}$ **h)** $420^\circ \times \dfrac{\pi}{180^\circ} = \dfrac{7\pi}{3}$

i) $450^\circ \times \dfrac{\pi}{180^\circ} = \dfrac{5\pi}{2}$ **j)** $630^\circ \times \dfrac{\pi}{180^\circ} = \dfrac{7\pi}{2}$

6. **a)** $70^\circ \times \dfrac{\pi}{180^\circ} = 1.222$ **b)** $37.5^\circ \times \dfrac{\pi}{180^\circ} = 0.654$ **c)** $130^\circ \times \dfrac{\pi}{180^\circ} = 2.269$ **d)** $\dfrac{90^\circ}{\pi} \times \dfrac{\pi}{180^\circ} = 0.5$

e) $400^\circ \times \dfrac{\pi}{180^\circ} = 6.981$ **f)** $527^\circ \times \dfrac{\pi}{180^\circ} = 9.198$ **g)** $-248^\circ \times \dfrac{\pi}{180^\circ} = -4.328$ **h)** $718^\circ \times \dfrac{\pi}{180^\circ} = 12.531$

i) $1025^\circ \times \dfrac{\pi}{180^\circ} = 17.890$ **j)** $-1349^\circ \times \dfrac{\pi}{180^\circ} = -23.544$

7. **a)** $\dfrac{\pi}{3} \times \dfrac{180^\circ}{\pi} = 60^\circ$ **b)** $\dfrac{5\pi}{6} \times \dfrac{180^\circ}{\pi} = 150^\circ$ **c)** $\dfrac{3\pi}{4} \times \dfrac{180^\circ}{\pi} = 135^\circ$ **d)** $\dfrac{11\pi}{6} \times \dfrac{180^\circ}{\pi} = 330^\circ$

e) $\dfrac{17\pi}{6} \times \dfrac{180^\circ}{\pi} = 510^\circ$ **f)** $\dfrac{21\pi}{4} \times \dfrac{180^\circ}{\pi} = 945^\circ$ **g)** $\dfrac{11\pi}{3} \times \dfrac{180^\circ}{\pi} = 660^\circ$ **h)** $\dfrac{20\pi}{3} \times \dfrac{180^\circ}{\pi} = 1200^\circ$

i) $\dfrac{31\pi}{6} \times \dfrac{180^\circ}{\pi} = 930^\circ$ **j)** $\dfrac{23\pi}{4} \times \dfrac{180^\circ}{\pi} = 1035^\circ$

8. **a)** $3 \times \dfrac{180^\circ}{\pi} = 171.9^\circ$ **b)** $-4 \times \dfrac{180^\circ}{\pi} = -229.2^\circ$ **c)** $2.7 \times \dfrac{180^\circ}{\pi} = 154.7^\circ$

d) $-1.2 \times \dfrac{180^\circ}{\pi} = -68.8^\circ$ **e)** $8.2 \times \dfrac{180^\circ}{\pi} = 469.8^\circ$ **f)** $-12.8 \times \dfrac{180^\circ}{\pi} = -733.4^\circ$

9. $s = r\theta \rightarrow 3 = r\cdot 30^\circ \cdot \dfrac{\pi}{180} \rightarrow 3 = r\cdot\dfrac{\pi}{6} \rightarrow r = \dfrac{18}{\pi} \rightarrow r \approx 5.73$ cm

10. $s = r\theta \rightarrow s = 15\cdot 130^\circ \cdot \dfrac{\pi}{180} \rightarrow s = \dfrac{65\pi}{6} \rightarrow s \approx 34.03$ cm

11. $s = r\theta \rightarrow 5 = 6\cdot\theta\cdot\dfrac{\pi}{180^\circ} \rightarrow 5 = \dfrac{\pi}{30^\circ}\cdot\theta \rightarrow \theta = \dfrac{150^\circ}{\pi} \rightarrow \theta \approx 47.75^\circ$

12. **a)** The minute hand makes one-half of a turn in one half an hour so the radian value is π.

b) The hour hand makes one twenty-fourth of a turn in one half hour so the radian value is $\dfrac{1}{24}\cdot 2\pi = \dfrac{\pi}{12}$.

13. $s = r\theta \rightarrow s = (4\text{ m})(2\pi \times 15) = 120\pi \approx 377\text{ m}$

14. $12\text{ rpm} = \dfrac{12 \times 2\pi}{60}$ radians per second $= \dfrac{2\pi}{5} \times \dfrac{180}{\pi} = 72^\circ$ per second. Thus $\dfrac{216^\circ}{72^\circ}$ per second = 3 seconds

15. $s = r\theta \rightarrow s = 6400 \times 2\pi$ in one day. In 8 hrs $s = 6400 \times 2\pi \times \dfrac{8}{24} = \dfrac{12800\pi}{3} \approx 13\,404\text{ km}$

16. $20^\circ \cdot \dfrac{\pi}{180} = \dfrac{\pi}{9}$ $\quad s = r\theta \rightarrow s = 6400 \cdot \dfrac{\pi}{9} = 2234\text{ km}$

6.2 Exercise Set

1. a) $c^2 = 5^2 + 12^2$, $c = 13$ **b)** $c^2 = 2^2 + 3^2$, $c = \sqrt{13}$ **c)** $b^2 = 17^2 - 15^2$, $b = 8$ **d)** $a^2 = 3^2 - \left(2\sqrt{2}\right)^2$, $a = 1$ **e)** $a^2 = \left(3\sqrt{5}\right)^2 - 6^2$, $a = 3$ **f)** $b^2 = \sqrt{17}^2 - \left(2\sqrt{2}\right)^2$, $b = 3$

2. a) $\sin\theta > 0$ in quadrant I, II, $\sec\theta > 0$ in quadrant I, IV, therefore, answer is quadrant I.
b) $\tan\theta < 0$ in quadrant II, IV, $\cos\theta > 0$ in quadrant I, IV, therefore, answer is quadrant IV.
c) $\csc\theta > 0$ in quadrant I, II, $\cot\theta < 0$ in quadrant II, IV, therefore, answer is quadrant II.
d) $\cos\theta < 0$ in quadrant II, III, $\csc\theta < 0$ in quadrant III, IV, therefore, answer is quadrant III.
e) $\sin\theta < 0$ in quadrant III, IV, $\tan\theta < 0$ in quadrant II, IV, therefore, answer is quadrant IV.
f) $\cot\theta > 0$ in quadrant I, III, $\sec\theta < 0$ in quadrant II, III, therefore, answer is quadrant III.
g) $\tan\theta < 0$ in quadrant II, IV, $\csc\theta > 0$ in quadrant I, II, therefore, answer is quadrant II.
h) $\cos\theta$ and $\sec\theta$ are reciprocals of each other so it is impossible for one to be negative and the other positive
i) $\sin\theta < 0$ in quadrant III, IV, $\cot\theta < 0$ in quadrant II, IV, therefore, answer is quadrant IV.
j) $\tan\theta < 0$ in quadrant II, IV, $\sec\theta > 0$ in quadrant I, IV, therefore, answer is quadrant IV.

3. All trigonometry values are reciprocals of each other.

a) $\dfrac{1}{2}$ **b)** $-\dfrac{3}{2}$ **c)** $-\dfrac{1}{5}$ **d)** $-\dfrac{1}{0.23} = -4.348$ **e)** $\dfrac{1}{2.35} = 0.426$ **f)** $-\dfrac{1}{2.4} = -0.417$

4. All values are $90^\circ - \theta$ or $\dfrac{\pi}{2} - \theta$ of each other.

a) 60° **b)** 25° **c)** 65° **d)** $\dfrac{\pi}{4}$ **e)** $\dfrac{\pi}{3}$ **f)** $\dfrac{\pi}{6}$

5. a) $r = \sqrt{4^2 + 3^2} = 5$, $\sin\theta = \dfrac{3}{5}$, $\cos\theta = \dfrac{4}{5}$, $\tan\theta = \dfrac{3}{4}$, $\cot\theta = \dfrac{4}{3}$, $\sec\theta = \dfrac{5}{4}$, $\csc\theta = \dfrac{5}{3}$

b) $r = \sqrt{\left(-\sqrt{7}\right)^2 + 3^2} = 4$, $\sin\theta = \dfrac{3}{4}$, $\cos\theta = \dfrac{-\sqrt{7}}{4}$, $\tan\theta = \dfrac{-3}{\sqrt{7}}$, $\cot\theta = \dfrac{-\sqrt{7}}{3}$, $\sec\theta = \dfrac{-4}{\sqrt{7}}$, $\csc\theta = \dfrac{4}{3}$

c) $r = \sqrt{\left(-\sqrt{3}\right)^2 + (-1)^2} = 2$, $\sin\theta = \dfrac{-1}{2}$, $\cos\theta = \dfrac{-\sqrt{3}}{2}$, $\tan\theta = \dfrac{1}{\sqrt{3}}$, $\cot\theta = \sqrt{3}$, $\sec\theta = \dfrac{-2}{\sqrt{3}}$, $\csc\theta = -2$

d) $r = \sqrt{\left(\sqrt{5}\right)^2 + (-2)^2} = 3$, $\sin\theta = \dfrac{-2}{3}$, $\cos\theta = \dfrac{\sqrt{5}}{3}$, $\tan\theta = \dfrac{-2}{\sqrt{5}}$, $\cot\theta = \dfrac{-\sqrt{5}}{2}$, $\sec\theta = \dfrac{3}{\sqrt{5}}$, $\csc\theta = \dfrac{-3}{2}$

e) $r = \sqrt{0^2 + (-4)^2} = 4$, $\sin\theta = -1$, $\cos\theta = 0$, $\tan\theta =$ undefined, $\cot\theta = 0$, $\sec\theta =$ undefined, $\csc\theta = -1$

6. a)

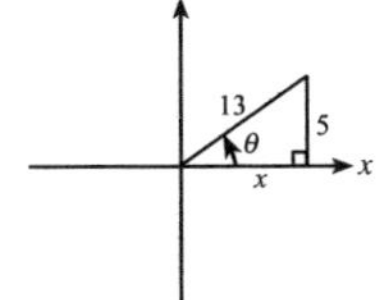

$x^2 + 5^2 = 13^2$

$x = 12$

$\cos\theta = \dfrac{12}{13}$, $\tan\theta = \dfrac{5}{12}$, $\cot\theta = \dfrac{12}{5}$, $\sec\theta = \dfrac{13}{12}$,

$\csc\theta = \dfrac{13}{5}$

b)

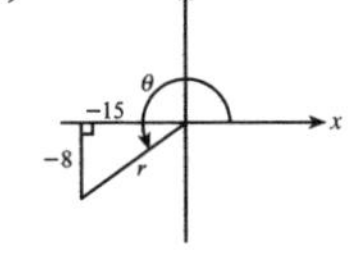

$r^2 = (8)^2 + (-15)^2$

$r = 17$

$\sin\theta = \dfrac{-8}{17}$, $\cos\theta = \dfrac{-15}{17}$, $\cot\theta = \dfrac{15}{8}$,

$\sec\theta = \dfrac{-17}{15}$, $\csc\theta = \dfrac{-17}{8}$

c)

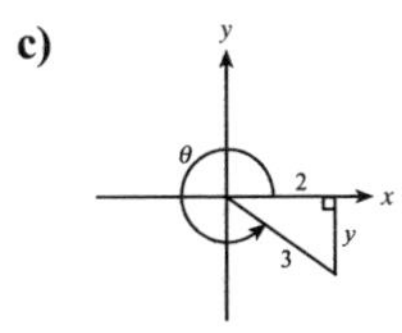

$y^2 + 2^2 = 3^2 \rightarrow y = -\sqrt{5}$ $\quad \sin\theta = \dfrac{-\sqrt{5}}{3}$,

$\cos\theta = \dfrac{2}{3}$

$\tan\theta = \dfrac{-\sqrt{5}}{2}$, $\cot\theta = \dfrac{-2}{\sqrt{5}} = \dfrac{-2\sqrt{5}}{5}$,

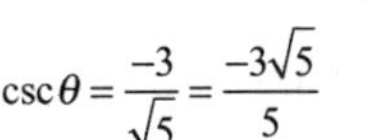

$\csc\theta = \dfrac{-3}{\sqrt{5}} = \dfrac{-3\sqrt{5}}{5}$

d)

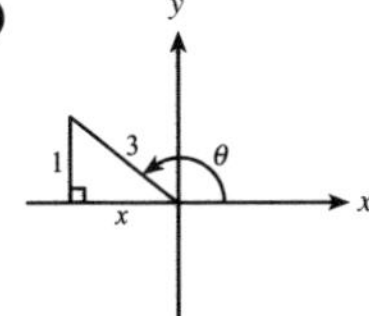

$\csc x > 0$ in quadrant I, II, $\tan x < 0$ in quadrant II, IV, therefore, answer in quadrant II.

$x^2 + 1^2 = 3^2 \rightarrow x = -2\sqrt{2}$ $\quad \sin\theta = \dfrac{1}{3}$,

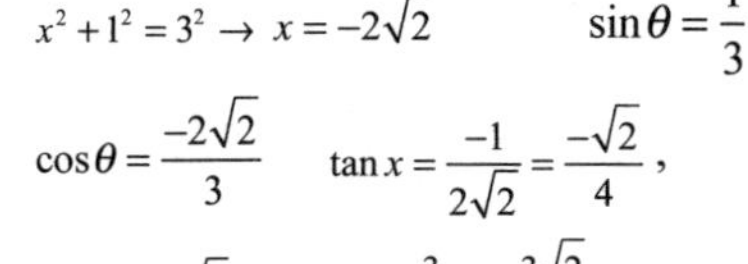

$\cos\theta = \dfrac{-2\sqrt{2}}{3}$ $\quad \tan x = \dfrac{-1}{2\sqrt{2}} = \dfrac{-\sqrt{2}}{4}$,

$\cot x = -2\sqrt{2}$, $\sec\theta = \dfrac{-3}{2\sqrt{2}} = \dfrac{-3\sqrt{2}}{4}$

6. e)

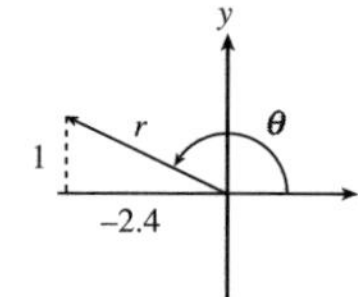

$r^2 = 1^2 + (-2.4)^2$, $r = 2.6$

$\sin\theta = \dfrac{1}{2.6} = \dfrac{5}{13}$, $\cos\theta = \dfrac{-2.4}{2.6} = \dfrac{-12}{13}$,

$\tan\theta = \dfrac{1}{-2.4} = \dfrac{-5}{12}$, $\sec\theta = \dfrac{-13}{12}$, $\csc\theta = \dfrac{13}{5}$

f)

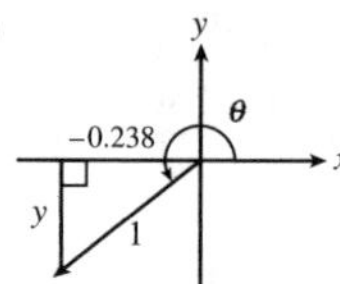

$y^2 + (-0.238)^2 = 1^2$, $y = -0.971$

$\sin\theta = \dfrac{-0.971}{1} = -0.971$,

$\tan\theta = \dfrac{-0.971}{-0.238} = 4.081$, $\cot\theta = \dfrac{-0.238}{-0.971} = 0.245$,

$\sec\theta = \dfrac{1}{-0.238} = -4.201$, $\csc\theta = \dfrac{1}{-0.971} = -1.030$

7. a)

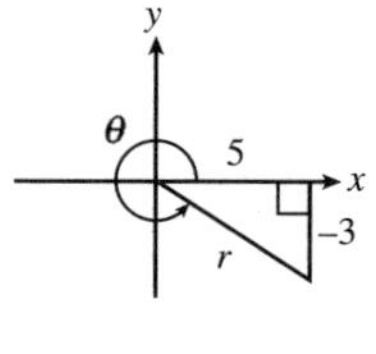

$r^2 = (-3)^2 + 5^2$, $r = \sqrt{34}$

$\sin\theta = \dfrac{-3}{\sqrt{34}}$, $\cos\theta = \dfrac{5}{\sqrt{34}}$

$\tan\theta = -\dfrac{3}{5}$, $\cot\theta = -\dfrac{5}{3}$, $\sec\theta = \dfrac{\sqrt{34}}{5}$,

$\csc\theta = \dfrac{-\sqrt{34}}{3}$

b)

$r^2 = (-2)^2 + (-3)^2$, $r = 13$

$\sin\theta = \dfrac{-2}{\sqrt{13}}$, $\cos\theta = \dfrac{-3}{\sqrt{13}}$

$\tan\theta = \dfrac{-2}{-3} = \dfrac{2}{3}$, $\cot\theta = \dfrac{3}{2}$, $\sec\theta = \dfrac{-\sqrt{13}}{3}$,

$\csc\theta = \dfrac{-\sqrt{13}}{2}$

c)

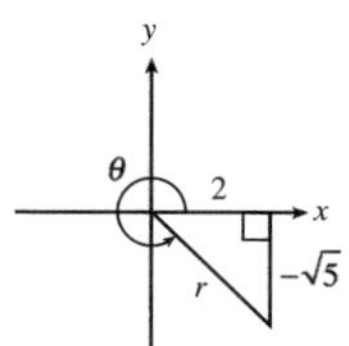

$r^2 - 2^2 + (-\sqrt{5})^2$, $r = 3$

$\sin\theta = \dfrac{\sqrt{5}}{3}$, $\cos\theta = \dfrac{2}{3}$

$\tan\theta = \dfrac{-\sqrt{5}}{2}$, $\cot\theta = \dfrac{-2}{\sqrt{5}}$, $\sec\theta = \dfrac{3}{2}$, $\csc\theta = \dfrac{-3}{\sqrt{5}}$

d)

(0,–1), $r = 1$

$\sin\theta = -1$, $\cos\theta = 0$, $\tan\theta =$ undefined,
$\cot\theta = 0$, $\sec\theta =$ undefined, $\csc\theta = -1$

8. a) If $\sin\theta = \dfrac{3}{5}$ in quadrant II, then $a^2 + b^2 = r^2$,

$a^2 + 3^2 = 5^2$

$a = -4$

therefore point is (–4, 3) with $r = 5$;
if $r = 10$, then point is (–8, 6).

b) If $\tan\theta = 1$ in quadrant III, then $r^2 = (-1)^2 + (-1)^2$,

$r = \sqrt{2}$

therefore point is $(-1, -1)$ with $r = \sqrt{2}$;
if $r = 3$, then point is

c) If $\sec\theta = 2$ in quadrant I, then $1^2 + b^2 = 2^2$,

$b = \sqrt{3}$

therefore point is $(1, \sqrt{3})$ with $r = 2$;
if $r = 8$, then point is $(4, 4\sqrt{3})$.

d) If $\csc\theta = \dfrac{13}{5}$ in quadrant II, then $a^2 + 5^2 = 13^2$,

$a = -12$

therefore point is $(-12, 5)$ with $r = 13$;
if $r = 8$, then point is $\left(\dfrac{-96}{13}, \dfrac{40}{13}\right)$.

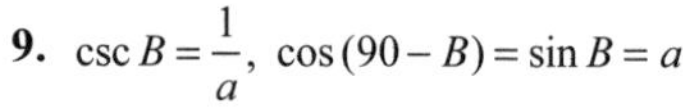

9. $\csc B = \dfrac{1}{a}$, $\cos(90 - B) = \sin B = a$

10. $\sec P = \dfrac{1}{b}$, $\sin\left(\dfrac{\pi}{2} - P\right) = \cos P = b$

11. a)

$2x - y = 10$
$3x + y = 5$
$5x = 15$
$x = 3$

$3(3) + y = 5$
$y = -4$

$r^2 = 3^2 + (-4)^2$
$r = 5$

$\sin\theta = \dfrac{-4}{5}$, $\cos\theta = \dfrac{3}{5}$

b)

$y = x^2 + 4x$
$y = -4x - 16$
$x^2 + 4x = -4x - 16$
$x^2 + 8x + 16 = 0$
$(x + 4)^2 = 0$
$x = -4$

$y = -4(-4) - 16$
$= 0$
$r^2 = (-4)^2 + 0^2$
$r = 4$

$\sin\theta = 0$, $\cos\theta = -1$

12. $\sin\theta = \cos\theta$ where the opposite = adjacent. Sine and cosine are both positive in quadrant I and both negative in quadrant III. Thus $\theta = 45°$ and $225°$.

13. If $1 + \sin\theta = 3\sin\theta$, then $\sin\theta = \dfrac{1}{2}$; $\tan\theta < 0$ is in quadrant II, $a = -\sqrt{2^2 - 1^2} = -\sqrt{3}$, $\cos\theta = \dfrac{-\sqrt{3}}{2}$.

14.

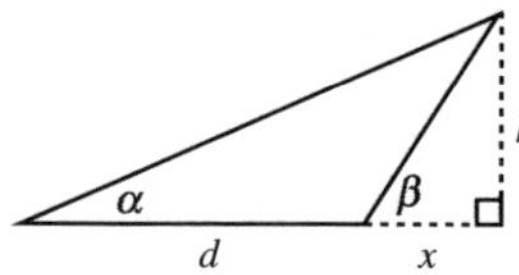

$\cot\alpha = \dfrac{d + x}{h}$ $\quad \cot\beta = \dfrac{x}{h}$

$x = h\cot\alpha - d$ $\quad x = h\cot\beta$

$h\cot\alpha - d = h\cot\beta$

$h(\cot\alpha - \cot\beta) = d$

$h = \dfrac{d}{\cot\alpha - \cot\beta}$

15.

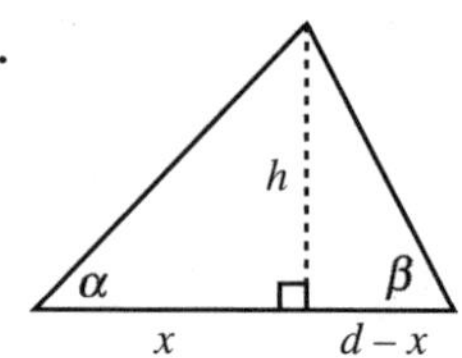

$\cot\alpha = \dfrac{x}{h}$ $\quad \cot\beta = \dfrac{d - x}{h}$

$x = h\cot\alpha$ $\quad x = d - h\cot\beta$

$h\cot\alpha = d - h\cot\beta$

$h(\cot\alpha + \cot\beta) = d$

$h = \dfrac{d}{\cot\alpha + \cot\beta}$

6.3 Exercise Set

1. **a)** 30° **b)** 30° **c)** 46° **d)** 46° **e)** 72° **f)** 3° **g)** 20° **h)** 25° **i)** 90° **j)** 0° **k)** $\frac{\pi}{6}$ **l)** $\frac{\pi}{4}$ **m)** $\frac{\pi}{5}$ **n)** $\frac{3\pi}{7}$ **o)** $\frac{\pi}{3}$ **p)** $\frac{\pi}{5}$

2. **a)** $\sin 120° = \sin 60° = \frac{\sqrt{3}}{2}$

b) $\cot 135° = -\cot 45° = -1$

c) $\cos 330° = \cos 30° = \frac{\sqrt{3}}{2}$

d) $\tan 660° = \tan 300° = -\tan 60° = -\sqrt{3}$

e) $\csc 1125° = \csc 45° = \sqrt{2}$

f) $\sec\frac{\pi}{6} = \frac{2}{\sqrt{3}} = \frac{2\sqrt{3}}{3}$

g) $\sin\frac{5\pi}{4} = -\sin\frac{\pi}{4} = \frac{-1}{\sqrt{2}} = \frac{-\sqrt{2}}{2}$

h) $\tan\frac{11\pi}{6} = -\tan\frac{\pi}{6} = \frac{-1}{\sqrt{3}} = \frac{-\sqrt{3}}{3}$

i) $\csc\frac{19\pi}{6} = \csc\frac{7\pi}{6} = -\csc\frac{\pi}{6} = \frac{2}{-1} = -2$

j) $\cot\frac{13\pi}{3} = \cot\frac{\pi}{3} = \frac{1}{\sqrt{3}} = \frac{\sqrt{3}}{3}$

k) $\cot(-240°) = \cot 120° = -\cot 60° = \frac{-\sqrt{3}}{3}$

l) $\sec(-945°) = \sec 135° = -\sec 45° = \frac{\sqrt{2}}{-1} = -\sqrt{2}$

m) $\cos\left(\frac{-5\pi}{3}\right) = \cos\frac{\pi}{3} = \frac{1}{2}$

n) $\tan\left(\frac{-29\pi}{6}\right) = \tan\frac{7\pi}{6} = \tan\frac{\pi}{6} = \frac{1}{\sqrt{3}} = \frac{\sqrt{3}}{3}$

o) $\sin\left(\frac{-20\pi}{3}\right) = \sin\frac{4\pi}{3} = -\sin\frac{\pi}{3} = \frac{-\sqrt{3}}{2}$

p) $\csc\left(\frac{-27\pi}{4}\right) = \csc\frac{5\pi}{4} = -\csc\frac{\pi}{4} = -\frac{\sqrt{2}}{1} = -\sqrt{2}$

3. **a)** never **b)** never **c)** 90°, 270° **d)** 0°, 180° **e)** 90°, 270° **f)** 0°, 180°

4. **a)** never **b)** never **c)** $\frac{\pi}{2}, \frac{3\pi}{2}$ **d)** $0, \pi$ **e)** $\frac{\pi}{2}, \frac{3\pi}{2}$ **f)** $0, \pi$

5. **a)** 210° **b)** 120° **c)** 240° **d)** 135° **e)** 120° **f)** 150°

6. **a)** $\frac{4\pi}{3}$ **b)** $\frac{5\pi}{6}$ **c)** $\frac{5\pi}{4}$ **d)** $\frac{5\pi}{6}$ **e)** $\frac{3\pi}{4}$ **f)** $\frac{2\pi}{3}$

7. **a)** $\frac{\sqrt{3}}{2}$ **b)** $\frac{\sqrt{3}}{2}$ **c)** 1 **d)** 1 **e)** 1 **f)** 1 **g)** $\frac{1}{2}$ **h)** $\frac{1}{2}$ **i)** $\sqrt{3}$ **j)** $\sqrt{3}$

8. **a)** $\frac{5\pi}{6}$ **b)** $\frac{5\pi}{4}$ **c)** $\frac{7\pi}{6}$ **d)** $\frac{5\pi}{3}$

9. **a)** $\frac{11\pi}{6}$ **b)** $\frac{\pi}{4}$ **c)** $\frac{5\pi}{6}$ **d)** $\frac{2\pi}{3}$

10. **a)** $\frac{7\pi}{6}$ **b)** $\frac{3\pi}{4}$ **c)** $\frac{5\pi}{6}$ **d)** $\frac{\pi}{3}$

11. **a)** $\cos x > 0$ in quadrant I, IV, therefore, by special angles, answers are $\frac{\pi}{6}, \frac{11\pi}{6}$

b) in quadrant III, IV, therefore, by special angles, answers are

c) $\tan x < 0$ in quadrant II, IV, therefore, by special angles, answers are $\frac{3\pi}{4}, \frac{7\pi}{4}$

d) $\csc x > 0$ in quadrant I, II, therefore, by special angles, answers are $\frac{\pi}{6}, \frac{5\pi}{6}$

e) $\sec x < 0$ in quadrant II, III, therefore, by special angles, answers are $\frac{3\pi}{4}, \frac{5\pi}{4}$

f) $\sin x = -1$ by special angle at $\frac{3\pi}{2}$

g) $\cot x =$ undefined by special angles at $0, \pi$

h) $\cos x = 0$ by special angles at $\frac{\pi}{2}, \frac{3\pi}{2}$

i) $\csc x =$ undefined by special angles at $0, \pi$

j) $\sec x = -1$ by special angles at π

k) $\cot x < 0$ in quadrant II, IV, therefore, by special angles, answers are $\frac{2\pi}{3}, \frac{5\pi}{3}$

l) $\csc x < 0$ in quadrant III, IV, therefore, by special angles, answers are $\frac{5\pi}{4}, \frac{7\pi}{4}$

12. **a)** 0, 0 **b)** $-1, \frac{1}{2}$ **c)** $1, -\frac{1}{2}$ **d)** $0, -\frac{\sqrt{3}}{2}$

13. **a)** 1, 1 **b)** $0, \frac{\sqrt{3}}{2}$ **c)** $0, \frac{\sqrt{3}}{2}$ **d)** $-1, \frac{1}{2}$

14. $\sin(-\theta) = -\sin\theta$

15. $\cos(-\theta) = \cos\theta$

6.4 Exercise Set

1. $f(x)=C,\ \ g(x)=D,\ \ h(x)=A,\ \ i(x)=F,\ \ j(x)=B,\ \ k(x)=E$

2. a) C **b)** D **c)** B **d)** A

3. a) $\frac{1}{3},\ \pi,\ -\frac{\pi}{6},\ -1$ **b)** $\frac{1}{2},\ 2,\ -\frac{3}{4},\ 1$ **c)** 4, 6, 1, 2 **d)** $1,\ \pi,\ \frac{\pi}{6},\ 0$ **e)** $3,\ 2,\ \frac{2}{3},\ -2$ **f)** $\frac{3}{2},\ \pi,\ -\frac{\pi}{4},\ 0$

4. a) 3π **b)** 2

5. a) $y=3\sin\frac{\pi}{2}x$ $y=3\cos\frac{\pi}{2}(x-1)$ **b)** $y=2\sin\frac{\pi}{3}(x-5)$ $y=2\cos\frac{\pi}{3}\left(x-\frac{1}{2}\right)$ **c)** $y=4\sin 2\left(x-\frac{3\pi}{4}\right)$ $y=4\cos 2x$ **d)** $y=2\sin\frac{2}{3}(x-\pi)$ $y=2\cos\frac{2}{3}\left(x-\frac{7\pi}{4}\right)$ **e)** $y=\pi\sin\frac{\pi}{6}(x-10)$ $y=\pi\cos\frac{\pi}{6}(x-1)$

f) $y=2\sin\frac{2\pi}{5}\left(x-\frac{3}{2}\right)$ $y=2\cos\frac{2\pi}{5}\left(x-\frac{11}{4}\right)$ **g)** $y=\sin\frac{2}{5}\left(x-\frac{13\pi}{4}\right)$ $y=\cos\frac{2}{5}\left(x-\frac{9\pi}{2}\right)$ **h)** $y=3\sin\frac{12}{17}\left(x-\frac{3\pi}{8}\right)$ $y=3\cos\frac{12}{17}\left(x-\frac{13\pi}{12}\right)$ **i)** $y=\sin\frac{3}{2}\left(x-\frac{5\pi}{6}\right)$ $y=\cos\frac{3}{2}\left(x-\frac{7\pi}{6}\right)$ **j)** $y=2\sin\frac{12}{7}(x-\pi)$ $y=2\cos\frac{12}{7}\left(x-\frac{\pi}{8}\right)$

6. $y=-3\sin\frac{\pi}{3}(x+2)+1$, amplitude $=|-3|=3$, period $=\frac{2\pi}{\frac{\pi}{3}}=6$

phase shift $=\frac{\pi}{3}(x+2)=0\rightarrow x=-2$, vertical displacement = 1

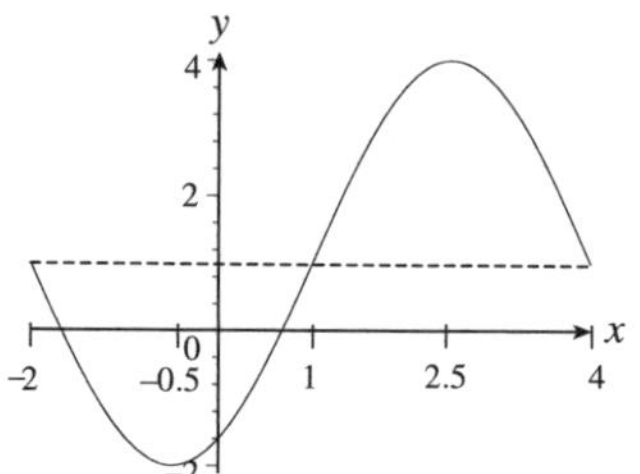

7. $y=2\cos\left(\frac{\pi}{2}x+\pi\right)-1$, amplitude = 2, period = $\frac{2\pi}{\frac{\pi}{2}}=4$,

phase shift $=\frac{\pi}{2}x+\pi=0\rightarrow x=-2$, vertical displacement = –1

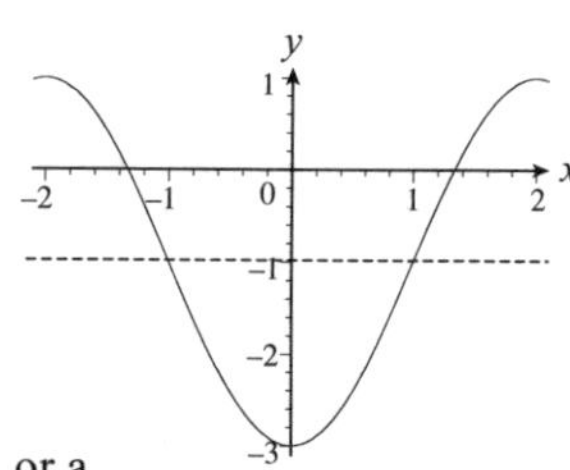

8. If it has a maximum point (2 , 3) and a minimum point of $(6,-7)$, then it has one half period of 4, or a period of 8 ; a vertical displacement of $\frac{-7+3}{2}=-2$; and an amplitude of $\frac{3+7}{2}=5$

So, $p=\frac{2\pi}{b}\rightarrow 8=\frac{2\pi}{b}\rightarrow b=\frac{\pi}{4}$. Therefore, $y=5\sin\frac{\pi}{4}x-2$

9. Same maximum and minimum points as question 8. The period of the sine and cosine equation are both 8 with amplitude 5 and vertical displacement –2. The cosine equation is just a shift of two units to the right.

Therefore, the equation is $y=5\cos\frac{\pi}{4}(x-2)-2$ (*Other possible answers*)

10. a) This graph has a period of 12; an amplitude of 2; a vertical displacement of 1. The phase shift depends on where we start; there are an infinite number of possibilities.

i) Period $=\frac{2\pi}{|b|}\rightarrow 12=\frac{2\pi}{b}\rightarrow b=\frac{\pi}{6}$, vertical displacement = 1, amplitude = 2 .

If $a>0$ then the graph must start at $4\pm 12n$, n being an integer; let's use 4.

Therefore, $y=2\sin\frac{\pi}{6}(x-4)+1$

ii) If $a<0$ then the graph must start at $-2\pm 12n$; use -2, therefore, $y=-2\sin\frac{\pi}{6}(x+2)+1$

b) **i)** If $a>0$ then the graph must start at $7\pm 12n$; use 7, $y=2\cos\frac{\pi}{6}(x-7)+1$

ii) If $a<0$ then the graph must start at $1\pm 12n$; use 1, therefore, $y=-2\cos\frac{\pi}{6}(x-1)+1$

Note: The four graphic equations in **10a** and **10b** above represent the same graph.

6.5 Exercise Set

1. Period $=\frac{2\pi}{b}=\frac{2\pi}{\frac{\pi}{2}}=4$ $0\le x\le 8$ has 2 periods. Cosine equals zero at $\frac{\pi}{2},\frac{3\pi}{2},\frac{5\pi}{2},\ldots$

Thus $\frac{\pi}{2}t=\frac{\pi}{2}$ $\quad \frac{\pi}{2}t=\frac{3\pi}{2}$ $\quad \frac{\pi}{2}t=\frac{5\pi}{2}$ $\quad \frac{\pi}{2}t=\frac{7\pi}{2}$

$t=1$ $\quad t=3$ $\quad t=5$ $\quad t=7$

The spring passes through the origin at 1 sec., 3 sec., 5 sec., and 7 sec.

2. a) Amplitude is 4.

Period: $\frac{2\pi}{b}=60\pi$ $\quad b=\frac{1}{30}$ second

b) 30 cycles/second

3. 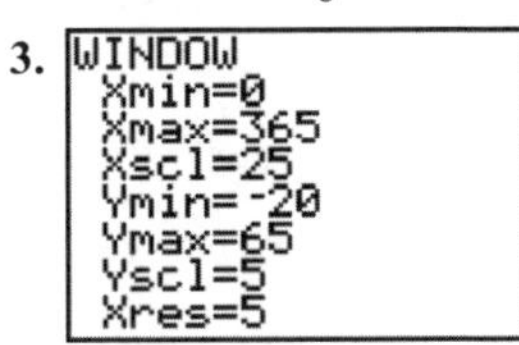

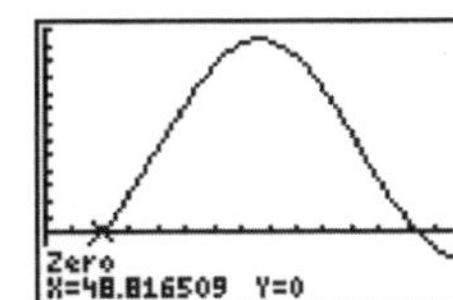

It is below zero on the first 49 days and last 32 days of the year.

Therefore, below zero from November 30th to February 17th.

4. Sales will reach zero when

$S=200+200\cos\left[\frac{\pi}{6}(t+2)\right]=0$ or $\cos\left[\frac{\pi}{6}(t+2)\right]=-1$

Cosines equals –1 at π by special angle

$\frac{\pi}{6}(t+2)=\pi$

$t+2=6$

$t=4$

If January is $t=0$ then May is $t=4$.

5. amplitude: 3; vertical displacement: 12; period: $\frac{2\pi}{b}=365\rightarrow b=\frac{2\pi}{365}$;

phase shift is the days from January 1st to March 21st: 80 days. Therefore, $H(t)=3\sin\left[\frac{2\pi}{365}(t-80)\right]+12$

6. amplitude: $\frac{0.84}{2}=0.42$; vertical displacement: $0.42+0.08=0.50$; period: $\frac{2\pi}{b}=4\rightarrow b=\frac{\pi}{2}$

If the start is breathing in, then $L(t)=-0.42\cos\left(\frac{\pi t}{2}\right)+0.50,\ 0\le t\le 8$ has two periods.

Maximum capacity is when $\cos\left(\frac{\pi t}{2}\right)=-1$; $\frac{\pi t}{2}=\pi\rightarrow t=2$ or $\frac{\pi t}{2}=3\pi\rightarrow t=6$ Air capacity is maximum at 2 sec. and 6 sec.

7. $P=\frac{2\pi}{b}\rightarrow\frac{1}{60}=\frac{2\pi}{b}\rightarrow b=120\pi$ $\qquad E=110\cos(120\pi t)$

8. a) Period $=\frac{60}{20}=3$ seconds

b) $P=\frac{2\pi}{b}\rightarrow 3=\frac{2\pi}{b}\rightarrow b=\frac{2\pi}{3}$

Vertical displacement $=\frac{30\ +\ 8}{2}=19$ cm, Amplitude $=\frac{30-8}{2}=11$ cm

$y=a\cos(bt)+c\rightarrow y=11\cos\left(\frac{2\pi}{3}t\right)+19$

9. a) Vertical displacement = 25 + 1 = 26 m
Maximum height = 51 m
Minimum height = 1 m
Amplitude = radius = 25 m

Period $=\frac{2\pi}{b}\rightarrow 24=\frac{2\pi}{b}\rightarrow b=\frac{\pi}{12}$, phase shift = 0 $\quad H=25\sin\left(\frac{\pi}{12}t\right)+26$

b) $H=25\sin\left(\frac{\pi}{12}\cdot 16\right)+26\rightarrow H=4.35$ m

c) Graph $y=25\sin\left(\frac{\pi}{12}x\right)+26$ and $y=35$. Find the intersect of these two equations.

They are (1.40668 , 35) and (10.59332 , 35). Therefore, the time above 35 m is 10.59332 – 1.40668 = 9.1866 seconds on each rotation.

10. a) Amplitude: $\dfrac{11.8-4.2}{2} = 3.8$ m, Vertical displacement: $\dfrac{11.8+4.2}{2} = 8$ Phase shift: 4.5 hours

Period: $(11.5 - 4.5) \cdot 2 = 14$ hours, $P = \dfrac{2\pi}{b} \rightarrow 14 = \dfrac{2\pi}{b} \rightarrow b = \dfrac{\pi}{7}$

$H = -3.8\cos\left(\dfrac{\pi}{7}(t-4.5)\right) + 8$ or $H = 3.8\sin\left(\dfrac{\pi}{7}(t-8)\right) + 8$

b) 1:15 p.m. = 13.25 hours $H = -3.8\cos\left(\dfrac{\pi}{7}(13.25-4.5)\right) + 8 \rightarrow H = 10.69$ m or $H = 3.8\sin\left(\dfrac{\pi}{7}(13.25-8)\right) + 8 \rightarrow H = 10.69$ m

11. a) Amplitude: 1.1 m Vertical displacement: 1.6 m Period: 1.0 seconds $P = \dfrac{2\pi}{b} \rightarrow 1.0 = \dfrac{2\pi}{b} \rightarrow b = 2\pi$ $H = -1.1\cos(2\pi t) + 1.6$

b) $H = -1.1\cos(2\pi \cdot 2.3) + 1.6 \rightarrow H = 1.94$ m

12. a) Vertical displacement: 6 m; Maximum: $6 + 8 = 14$ m; Minimum: $6 - 8 = -2$, therefore, zero height of water

b) Amplitude: 8 m, Vertical displacement: 6 m, Period: 16 minutes $\rightarrow P = \dfrac{2\pi}{b} \rightarrow 16 = \dfrac{2\pi}{b} \rightarrow b = \dfrac{\pi}{8}$ $S = -8\sin\dfrac{\pi}{8}t + 6$

c) Since the period is so long, a person in a boat would hardly notice the tsunami.

6.6 Chapter Review

Trigonometry (Part I) – Multiple-choice Answers

1. d	**5.** c	**9.** a	**13.** c	**17.** c	**21.** b	**25.** a	**29.** b	**33.** d	**37.** c
2. d	**6.** d	**10.** a	**14.** c	**18.** b	**22.** a	**26.** b	**30.** d	**34.** d	**38.** c
3. c	**7.** c	**11.** c	**15.** a	**19.** c	**23.** a	**27.** a	**31.** c	**35.** d	**39.** c
4. d	**8.** c	**12.** b	**16.** d	**20.** d	**24.** a	**28.** a	**32.** b	**36.** c	**40.** a

Trigonometry (Part I) – Multiple-choice Solutions

1. Amplitude $|-2| = 2$, period $\dfrac{2\pi}{\frac{\pi}{2}} = 4$. Answer is d.

2. Phase shift $\dfrac{\pi}{2}x - \pi = 0 \rightarrow \dfrac{\pi}{2}x = \pi \rightarrow x = 2$, vertical displacement 3. Answer is d.

3. Period $= \dfrac{\pi}{b} = \dfrac{\pi}{\frac{\pi}{3}} = 3$. Answer is c.

4. $a = r\theta$, $a =$ arc length, $r =$ radius, $\theta =$ angle in radians; $12 = 6\theta \rightarrow \theta = 2$ radians, degree angle $2 \cdot \dfrac{180^\circ}{\pi} = 115^\circ$. Answer is d.

5. Cosecant is negative in quadrant III and IV, tangent is negative in quadrant II and IV therefore, solution is in quadrant IV.

$\csc x = \dfrac{hyp}{opp} = \dfrac{2}{-\sqrt{3}}$, by Pythagoras Theorem $\left(-\sqrt{3}\right)^2 + a^2 = 2^2 \rightarrow a^2 = 1 \rightarrow a = \pm 1$, but $a = 1$ in quadrant IV,

therefore, $\cos x = \dfrac{adj}{hyp} = \dfrac{1}{2}$. Answer is c.

6. By Pythagoras Theorem $r^2 = 2^2 + (-3)^2 \rightarrow r = \sqrt{13}$, $\sec\theta = \dfrac{hyp}{adj} = \dfrac{\sqrt{13}}{2}$. Answer is d.

7. The smallest negative angle for cosecant is in quadrant III. Answer is c.

8. $10 \cdot \dfrac{180^\circ}{\pi} = 573^\circ - 360^\circ = 213^\circ$. Answer is c.

9. $\csc\dfrac{5\pi}{3} = \dfrac{2}{-\sqrt{3}} = \dfrac{2}{-\sqrt{3}} \cdot \dfrac{\sqrt{3}}{\sqrt{3}} = \dfrac{-2\sqrt{3}}{3}$. Answer is a.

10. $\cot\dfrac{17\pi}{6} = \cot\left(\dfrac{17\pi}{6} - 2\pi\right) = \cot\dfrac{5\pi}{6}$ in quadrant II cotangent is negative. Therefore, reference angle is $-\cot\dfrac{\pi}{6} = -\dfrac{\sqrt{3}}{1} = -\sqrt{3}$.
Answer is a.

11. $\sec\theta < 0$ in Quadrant II, III, $\tan\theta > 0$ in quadrant I, III, therefore quadrant III. Answer is c.

12. Positive angle is $-\dfrac{7\pi}{6} = 2\pi - \dfrac{7\pi}{6} = \dfrac{5\pi}{6}$, reference angle is $\pi - \dfrac{5\pi}{6} = \dfrac{\pi}{6}$. Answer is b.

13. $\sec\theta = \dfrac{\text{hypotenuse}}{\text{adjacent}} = \dfrac{1}{a}$. Answer is c.

14. Amplitude $|-a| = a$, displacement $= -b$ therefore maximum value $a - b$. Answer is c.

15. Start at vertical displacement value of $-b$ then go down a. Answer is a.

16.

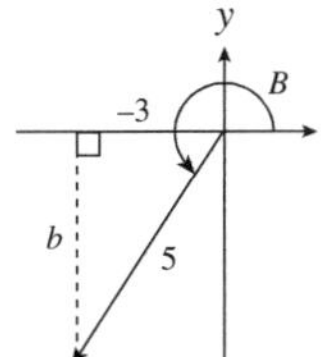

by Pythagoras Theorem, $(-3)^2 + b^2 = 5^2 \rightarrow \; b = -4$, $\tan B = \dfrac{-4}{-3} = \dfrac{4}{3}$. Answer is d.

17. $\sec x < 0$ in quadrants II, III, by special angles, reference angle is $\dfrac{\pi}{6}$, therefore answers are $\dfrac{5\pi}{6}, \dfrac{7\pi}{6}$. Answer is c.

18. Set calculator in radian mode, set window Xmin = 0, Xmax = 60, Ymin = 0, Ymax = 55

Graph $Y_1 = 25\sin\dfrac{\pi}{30}(x-10)+76$ and $Y_2 = 40$ and find intersection points

$(34.32, 40)$ and $(15.68, 40)$, difference $34.32 - 15.68 = 18.64$ sec. Answer is b.

19. Period $= \dfrac{2\pi}{|b|}$, $b > 0 \rightarrow P = \dfrac{2\pi}{b}$ Therefore minimum value occurs $\dfrac{1}{2}$ a period away at $\dfrac{\pi}{b}$. Answer is c.

20. $\csc x = -1.325$, determine reference angle $\sin x = \dfrac{1}{1.325} \rightarrow x = \sin^{-1}\left(\dfrac{1}{1.325}\right) = 0.855$

cosecant is negative in quadrant III, IV therefore $2\pi - 0.855 = 5.43$ and $\pi + 0.855 = 4.00$. Answer is d.

21. Tangent negative in quadrant II and IV, cosine negative in quadrant II and III, therefore, quadrant II

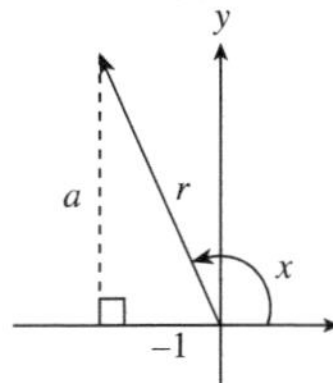

$$r^2 = a^2 + (-1)^2 \qquad \csc x = \frac{\sqrt{a^2+1}}{a}$$
$$r = \sqrt{a^2+1}$$

Answer is b.

22. $\tan\theta < 0$ in quadrant II and IV, $\sec\theta > 0$ in quadrant I and IV, therefore, quadrant IV

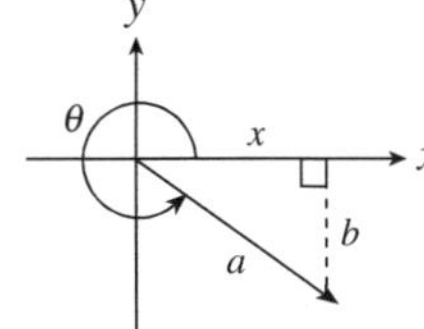

$$a^2 = x^2 + b^2$$
$$x^2 = a^2 - b^2 \qquad \cos\theta = \frac{\sqrt{a^2-b^2}}{a}$$
$$x = \sqrt{a^2-b^2}$$

Answer is a.

23. $\cot\theta = -a$ is quadrant II, IV, $\sin\theta < 0$ in quadrant III, IV, therefore, quadrant IV

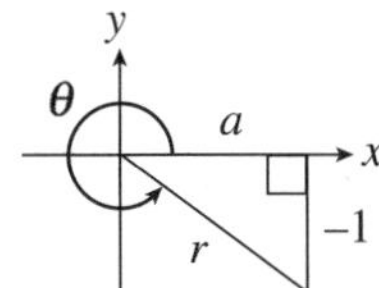

$$r^2 = (-a)^2 + 1^2 \qquad \sec\theta = \frac{\sqrt{a^2+1}}{a}$$
$$r = \sqrt{a^2+1}$$

Answer is a.

24. If the maximum point is $(2, 16)$ and the nearest minimum point is $(7, 4)$, then its half period is $7 - 2 = 5$ and the period is 10;

a vertical displacement of $\dfrac{4+16}{2} = 10$; and an amplitude of $\dfrac{16-4}{2} = 6$, therefore, $P = \dfrac{2\pi}{b} = 10 \rightarrow \; b = \dfrac{\pi}{5}$, phase shift = 2

So $y = a\cos b(x-c)+d \rightarrow y = 6\cos\dfrac{\pi}{5}(x-2)+10$. Answer is a

25. All equations except "a" produce reciprocal graphs of the diagram. Answer is a.

26. $\cot\dfrac{2\pi}{5} = \dfrac{1}{\tan\dfrac{2\pi}{5}} = 0.325$. Answer is b.

27. $\sec\theta = -2.202 \rightarrow \dfrac{1}{\cos\theta} = -2.202 \rightarrow \cos\theta = \dfrac{-1}{2.202} \rightarrow \theta = \cos^{-1}\left(\dfrac{-1}{2.202}\right) = 117°$. Answer is a.

28. 3 units to the left is $f(x) = \cos(x+3)$. Answer is a.

29. area of circle is $\pi r^2 = \pi(10)^2 = 100\pi$, therefore $\frac{2.1}{2\pi} \times 100\pi = 105$. Answer is b.

30. sec > 0 in quadrants I, IV. $\sec x = 3.45 \rightarrow \cos x = \frac{1}{3.45} \rightarrow x = \cos^{-1}\left(\frac{1}{3.45}\right) = 1.28$ and $2\pi - 1.28 = 5.01$. Answer is d.

31. $\csc\theta = \frac{\text{radius}}{\text{opposite}} = \frac{1}{b}$. Answer is c.

32. minimum value is vertical displacement – amplitude = $d - a$. Answer is b.

33. $y = \tan x$ has asymptotes at $x = \frac{\pi}{2} + n\pi$ therefore $y = \tan bx$ has asymptotes $bx = \frac{\pi}{2} + n\pi \rightarrow x = \frac{\pi}{2b} + \frac{n\pi}{b}$. Answer is d.

34. vertical displacement is 25; amplitude is 20; period is $\frac{2\pi}{b} = 10 \rightarrow b = \frac{\pi}{5}$ therefore $h = -20\cos\frac{\pi}{5}t + 25$. Answer is d.

35. Graph $Y_1 = 3.9\sin 0.16\pi(t-3) + 6.5$ and $Y_2 = 8$. Set windows $X(0, 24)$ and $Y(-2, 12)$. Find difference of intersects of two intervals. Answer is d.

36. Amplitude is 25, $p = \frac{2\pi}{b} = 80 \rightarrow\ b = \frac{\pi}{40}$, vertical displacement is 25 + 2 = 27, start upside down from standard cosine,

therefore, $h = -25\cos\left(\frac{\pi}{40}t\right) + 27$. Answer is c.

37. Set calculator in radian mode, set window X(0, 60) and Y(0, 55).

Graph $Y_1 = -25\cos\left(\frac{\pi}{40}x\right) + 27$ and $Y_2 = 35$, and determine the 1st intersection point. Answer is c.

38. If the maximum depth occurred at 4:00, and the minimum depth occurred 6 hours later, then the period is 12 hours.

Therefore $P = \frac{2\pi}{b} \rightarrow 12 = \frac{2\pi}{b} \rightarrow b = \frac{\pi}{6}$. If the maximum depth is 8 meters and minimum depth 2 metres then the displacement

is 5 meters with amplitude 3 meters. The only equation that fits these parameters is $d(t) = 3\sin\frac{\pi}{6}(t-1) + 5$. Answer is c.

39. Graph $Y_1 = 3\sin\frac{\pi}{6}(x-1) + 5$ set windows $X[0, 13]$, $Y[-1, 10]$ On calculator enter $X = 12$, gives $Y = 3.5$

or $y = 3\sin\frac{\pi}{6}(12-1) + 5 = 3\sin\frac{11\pi}{6} + 5 = 3\left(-\frac{1}{2}\right) + 5 = 3.5$. Answer is c.

40. Graph $Y_1 = 3\sin\frac{\pi}{6}(x-1) + 5$ and $Y_2 = 7$; first intersection is at $X = 2.394$ hr $\rightarrow$ 2:24 a.m. Answer is a.

Trigonometry (Part II) Solutions

7.1 Exercise Set

1. **a)** F **b)** C **c)** B **d)** A **e)** E **f)** D **g)** H

2. **a)** $\frac{3\sin x - 8}{2\sin^2 x}$ **b)** $\frac{1}{\sin x(1-\sin x)}$ **c)** $\tan x(1+\tan x)$ **d)** $\cot^2 x$

e) $\csc x$ **f)** $2\csc^2 x$ **g)** $2\sec x$ **h)** $-\cot x$

3. **a)** $(1-\sin x)(1+\sin x)$ **b)** $(\sec x - \tan x)(\sec x + \tan x)$ **c)** $\sin^2 x$ **d)** $\sec^4 x$

e) $\sin^2 x\tan^2 x$ **f)** $\csc x + 1$ **g)** $\csc^4 x$ **h)** $\cos^4 x$

i) $\sin^2 x - \cos^2 x = (\sin x - \cos x)(\sin x + \cos x)$ **j)** $\tan^2 x(\sec x - 1)$

4. **a)** $1 + 2\sin x\cos x$ **b)** $\cos^2 x$ **c)** $\cot^2 x$ **d)** $4\sin^2 x$ **e)** 1 **f)** –1

5. **a)** $2\sin^2 x - 1$ **b)** $\frac{1}{1-\sin^2 x}$ **c)** $\frac{1}{1-\sin x}$ **d)** $\sin x$

6. **a)** $1 - 2\cos^2 x$ **b)** $\frac{1-\cos^2 x}{\cos^2 x}$ **c)** $\cos^2 x$ **d)** $\frac{1}{1-\cos x}$

7. **a)** $\frac{\sin x}{1-\cos x}$ or $\frac{1+\cos x}{\sin x}$ **b)** $\frac{\cos x}{1-\sin x}$ or $\frac{1+\sin x}{\cos x}$ **c)** $\sin x\cos x$ **d)** $\frac{\sin x}{\cos x}$

8. *Note: expression is undefined whenever sin θ or cos θ has a zero value in the denominator.*

a) $\frac{\cot x}{1+\sin x} = \frac{\cos x}{\sin x(1+\sin x)}$, therefore, $\sin x \neq 0,\ -1$; for $0 \le x < 2\pi,\ x \neq 0,\ \pi,\ \frac{3\pi}{2}$

b) $\dfrac{\sec x}{1-\cos x}=\dfrac{1}{\cos x(1-\cos x)}$, therefore, $\cos x\neq 0$, 1; for $0\le x<2\pi$, $x\neq 0$, $\dfrac{\pi}{2}$, $\dfrac{3\pi}{2}$

c) $\dfrac{1}{2\cos^2 x+\cos x-1}=\dfrac{1}{(2\cos x-1)(\cos x+1)}$, therefore, $\cos x\neq\dfrac{1}{2},-1$; for $0\le x<2\pi$, $x\neq\dfrac{\pi}{3}$, π, $\dfrac{5\pi}{3}$

d) $\cot x+\tan x=\dfrac{\cos x}{\sin x}+\dfrac{\sin x}{\cos x}$, therefore, $\sin x\neq 0$, $\cos x\neq 0$ for $0\le x<2\pi$, $x\neq 0$, $\dfrac{\pi}{2}$, π, $\dfrac{3\pi}{2}$

9. a) $(\sec x\cdot\csc x-\cot x)(\sin x-\csc x)=\left(\dfrac{1}{\cos x}\cdot\dfrac{1}{\sin x}-\dfrac{\cos x}{\sin x}\right)\left(\sin x-\dfrac{1}{\sin x}\right)=\left(\dfrac{1}{\cos x}\cdot\dfrac{1}{\sin x}-\dfrac{\cos x}{\sin x}\cdot\dfrac{\cos x}{\cos x}\right)\left(\sin x-\dfrac{1}{\sin x}\right)=$

$\left(\dfrac{1-\cos^2 x}{\sin x\cos x}\right)\left(\dfrac{\sin^2 x-1}{\sin x}\right)=\left(\dfrac{\sin^2 x}{\sin x\cos x}\right)\left(-\dfrac{\cos^2 x}{\sin x}\right)=-\cos x$

b) $\dfrac{\dfrac{\cot x+1}{\cot x}-1}{\dfrac{\cot x-1}{\cot x}-1}=\dfrac{\dfrac{\cot x+1-\cot x}{\cot x}}{\dfrac{\cot x-1-\cot x}{\cot x}}=\dfrac{1}{-1}=-1$

c) $\dfrac{\tan^2 x}{\cos^2 x+\sin^2 x+\tan^2 x}=\dfrac{\tan^2 x}{1+\tan^2 x}=\dfrac{\tan^2 x}{\sec^2 x}=\dfrac{\sin^2 x}{\cos^2 x}\cdot\cos^2 x=\sin^2 x$

d) $\dfrac{\cos x\cdot\tan x+\sin x}{2\tan x}=\dfrac{\cos x}{2\sin x}\left(\cos x\cdot\dfrac{\sin x}{\cos x}+\sin x\right)=\dfrac{\cos x}{2\sin x}\cdot 2\sin x=\cos x$

e) $\dfrac{1-\sec^2 x}{\sec^2 x}-\cos^2 x=\cos^2 x\left(-\tan^2 x\right)-\cos^2 x=\cos^2 x\left(\dfrac{-\sin^2 x}{\cos^2 x}\right)-\cos^2 x=-\sin^2 x-\cos^2 x=-\left(\sin^2 x+\cos^2 x\right)=-1$

f) $\dfrac{\sec x-\cos x}{\csc x-\sin x}=\dfrac{\dfrac{1}{\cos x}-\cos x}{\dfrac{1}{\sin x}-\sin x}=\dfrac{\dfrac{1-\cos^2 x}{\cos x}}{\dfrac{1-\sin^2 x}{\sin x}}=\dfrac{(1-\cos^2 x)\sin x}{(1-\sin^2 x)\cos x}=\dfrac{(\sin^2 x)\sin x}{(\cos^2 x)\cos x}=\dfrac{\sin^3 x}{\cos^3 x}=\tan^3 x$

g) $\dfrac{\cot x(\sin x+\tan x)}{\csc x+\cot x}=\dfrac{\dfrac{\cos x}{\sin x}\left(\sin x+\dfrac{\sin x}{\cos x}\right)}{\dfrac{1}{\sin x}+\dfrac{\cos x}{\sin x}}=\dfrac{\dfrac{\cos x}{\sin x}\left(\dfrac{\sin x\cos x+\sin x}{\cos x}\right)}{\dfrac{1+\cos x}{\sin x}}=\dfrac{\sin x(\cos x+1)}{1+\cos x}=\sin x$

h) $\dfrac{\sec x-\cos x}{\tan x}=\dfrac{\dfrac{1}{\cos x}-\cos x}{\dfrac{\sin x}{\cos x}}=\dfrac{\dfrac{1-\cos^2 x}{\cos x}}{\dfrac{\sin x}{\cos x}}=\dfrac{1-\cos^2 x}{\sin x}=\dfrac{\sin^2 x}{\sin x}=\sin x$

i) $\dfrac{\sec^2 x(1+\csc x)-\tan x(\sec x+\tan x)}{\csc x(1+\sin x)}=\dfrac{\dfrac{1}{\cos^2 x}\left(1+\dfrac{1}{\sin x}\right)-\dfrac{\sin x}{\cos x}\left(\dfrac{1}{\cos x}+\dfrac{\sin x}{\cos x}\right)}{\dfrac{1+\sin x}{\sin x}}=$

$\dfrac{\sin x}{1+\sin x}\left[\dfrac{1}{\cos^2 x}\left(\dfrac{\sin x+1}{\sin x}\right)-\dfrac{\sin x}{\cos x}\left(\dfrac{1+\sin x}{\cos x}\right)\right]=\dfrac{1}{\cos^2 x}-\dfrac{\sin^2 x}{\cos^2 x}=\dfrac{1-\sin^2 x}{\cos^2 x}=\dfrac{\cos^2 x}{\cos^2 x}=1$

j) $\dfrac{\csc^2 x+\sec^2 x}{\csc x\cdot\sec x}=\dfrac{\dfrac{1}{\sin^2 x}+\dfrac{1}{\cos^2 x}}{\dfrac{1}{\sin x}\cdot\dfrac{1}{\cos x}}=\dfrac{\cos^2 x+\sin^2 x}{\sin^2 x\cdot\cos^2 x}\cdot\sin x\cdot\cos x=\dfrac{1}{\sin x\cdot\cos x}=\csc x\cdot\sec x$

k) $\dfrac{\cos x+\cot x}{1+\csc x}=\dfrac{\cos x+\dfrac{\cos x}{\sin x}}{1+\dfrac{1}{\sin x}}=\dfrac{\dfrac{\sin x\cdot\cos x+\cos x}{\sin x}}{\dfrac{\sin x+1}{\sin x}}=\dfrac{\cos x(\sin x+1)}{\sin x+1}=\cos x$

l) $\dfrac{\sec x}{\tan x-\cot x}=\dfrac{\dfrac{1}{\cos x}}{\dfrac{\sin x}{\cos x}+\dfrac{\cos x}{\sin x}}=\dfrac{\dfrac{1}{\cos x}}{\dfrac{\sin^2 x+\cos^2 x}{\sin x\cdot\cos x}}=\dfrac{\dfrac{1}{\cos x}}{\dfrac{1}{\sin x\cdot\cos x}}=\dfrac{\sin x\cdot\cos x}{\cos x}=\sin x$

7.2 Exercise Set

1.
$$\sin^2 x-\cos^2 x=2\sin^2 x-1$$
$$\sin^2 x-(1-\sin^2 x)=$$
$$\sin^2 x-1+\sin^2 x=$$
$$2\sin^2 x-1=$$

2.
$$\sin x+\cos x\cot x=\csc x$$
$$\sin x+\cos x\frac{\cos x}{\sin x}=\frac{1}{\sin x}$$
$$\frac{\sin^2 x+\cos^2 x}{\sin x}=$$
$$\frac{1}{\sin x}=$$

3.
$$\frac{1}{\cos x}-\cos x=\frac{\sin^2 x}{\cos x}$$
$$\frac{1-\cos^2 x}{\cos x}=$$
$$\frac{\sin^2 x}{\cos x}=$$

4.
$$\frac{1}{\sec x\tan x}=\csc x-\sin x$$
$$\cos x\cdot\frac{\cos x}{\sin x}=\frac{1}{\sin x}-\sin x$$
$$\frac{\cos^2 x}{\sin x}=\frac{1-\sin^2 x}{\sin x}$$
$$=\frac{\cos^2 x}{\sin x}$$

5.
$$\frac{\cos^4 x-\sin^4 x}{1-\tan^4 x}=\cos^4 x$$
$$\frac{\cos^4 x-\sin^4 x}{1-\frac{\sin^4 x}{\cos^4 x}}=$$
$$\frac{\cos^4 x-\sin^4 x}{\left(\frac{\cos^4 x-\sin^4 x}{\cos^4 x}\right)}=$$
$$\cos^4 x=$$

6.
$$\frac{\sec^4 x-1}{\tan^2 x}=2+\tan^2 x$$
$$\frac{(\sec^2 x-1)(\sec^2 x+1)}{\tan^2 x}=2+\sec^2 x-1$$
$$\frac{\tan^2 x(\sec^2 x+1)}{\tan^2 x}=\sec^2 x+1$$
$$\sec^2 x+1=$$

7.
$$\frac{\sin x+\cos x}{\csc x+\sec x}=\sin x\cos x$$
$$\frac{\sin x+\cos x}{\left(\frac{1}{\sin x}+\frac{1}{\cos x}\right)}=$$
$$\frac{\sin x+\cos x}{\left(\frac{\cos x+\sin x}{\sin x\cos x}\right)}=$$
$$\sin x\cos x=$$

8.
$$\frac{\cos x+\sin x}{\cos x-\sin x}=\frac{1+\tan x}{1-\tan x}$$
$$=\frac{1+\frac{\sin x}{\cos x}}{1-\frac{\sin x}{\cos x}}$$
$$=\frac{\left(\frac{\cos x+\sin x}{\cos x}\right)}{\left(\frac{\cos x-\sin x}{\cos x}\right)}$$
$$=\frac{\cos x+\sin x}{\cos x-\sin x}$$

9.
$$\frac{\sec x}{1-\cos x}=\frac{\sec x+1}{\sin^2 x}$$
$$\frac{\sec x}{1-\cos x}\cdot\frac{1+\cos x}{1+\cos x}=$$
$$\frac{\sec x+1}{1-\cos^2 x}=$$
$$\frac{\sec x+1}{\sin^2 x}=$$

10.
$$\frac{\sin\theta+\cos\theta\cdot\cot\theta}{\cos\theta\csc\theta}=\sec\theta$$
$$\frac{\sin\theta+\cos\theta\cdot\frac{\cos\theta}{\sin\theta}}{\frac{\cos\theta}{\sin\theta}}=\frac{1}{\cos\theta}$$
$$\frac{\sin^2\theta+\cos^2\theta}{\sin\theta}\cdot\frac{\sin\theta}{\cos\theta}=$$
$$\frac{1}{\cos\theta}=$$

11.
$$\frac{1+\sec\theta}{\sin\theta+\tan\theta}=\csc\theta$$
$$\frac{1+\frac{1}{\cos\theta}}{\sin\theta+\frac{\sin\theta}{\cos\theta}}=$$
$$\frac{\frac{\cos\theta+1}{\cos\theta}}{\frac{\sin\theta\cdot\cos\theta+\sin\theta}{\cos\theta}}=$$
$$\frac{\cos\theta+1}{\sin\theta(\cos\theta+1)}=$$
$$\csc\theta=$$

12.
$$\frac{\sec x}{1-\sin x}=\frac{1+\sin x}{\cos^3 x}$$
$$\frac{\sec x(1+\sin x)}{(1-\sin x)(1+\sin x)}=$$
$$\frac{\sec x(1+\sin x)}{1-\sin^2 x}=$$
$$\frac{\sec x(1+\sin x)}{\cos^2 x}=$$
$$\frac{1+\sin x}{\cos^3 x}=$$

13.
$$\cos^2 x=\frac{1-2\sin^2 x}{1-\tan^2 x}$$
$$=\frac{1-2\sin^2 x}{1-\frac{\sin^2 x}{\cos^2 x}}$$
$$=\frac{1-2\sin^2 x}{\left(\frac{\cos^2 x-\sin^2 x}{\cos^2 x}\right)}$$
$$=\frac{\cos^2 x(1-2\sin^2 x)}{\cos^2 x-\sin^2 x}$$
$$=\frac{\cos^2 x(1-2\sin^2 x)}{1-\sin^2 x-\sin^2 x}$$
$$=\frac{\cos^2 x(1-2\sin^2 x)}{1-2\sin^2 x}$$
$$=\cos^2 x$$

14.
$$\frac{\tan x}{\tan x+\sin x}=\frac{1-\cos x}{\sin^2 x}$$
$$\frac{\frac{\sin x}{\cos x}}{\frac{\sin x}{\cos x}+\sin x}=\frac{1-\cos x}{1-\cos^2 x}$$
$$\frac{\frac{\sin x}{\cos x}}{\frac{\sin x+\sin x\cos x}{\cos x}}=\frac{1-\cos x}{(1-\cos x)(1+\cos x)}$$
$$\frac{\sin x}{\sin x(1+\cos x)}=\frac{1}{1+\cos x}$$
$$\frac{1}{1+\cos x}=$$

15.
$$\frac{1-\cos\theta}{\sin\theta}=\frac{1}{\csc\theta+\cot\theta}$$
$$\frac{1-\cos\theta}{\sin\theta}\cdot\frac{(1+\cos\theta)}{(1+\cos\theta)}=\frac{1}{\frac{1}{\sin\theta}+\frac{\cos\theta}{\sin\theta}}$$
$$\frac{1-\cos^2\theta}{\sin\theta(1+\cos\theta)}=\frac{1}{\frac{1+\cos\theta}{\sin\theta}}$$
$$\frac{\sin^2\theta}{\sin\theta(1+\cos\theta)}=\frac{\sin\theta}{1+\cos\theta}$$
$$\frac{\sin\theta}{1+\cos\theta}=$$

16. $\dfrac{\sec x}{1-\cos x}=\dfrac{\sec x+1}{\sin^2 x}$

$\dfrac{\sec x}{1-\cos x}\cdot\dfrac{1+\cos x}{1+\cos x}=$

$\dfrac{\sec x+1}{1-\cos^2 x}=$

$\dfrac{\sec x+1}{\sin^2 x}=$

17. $\dfrac{\sin^2 x-\tan x}{\cos^2 x-\cot x}=\tan^2 x$

$\dfrac{\sin^2 x-\dfrac{\sin x}{\cos x}}{\cos^2 x-\dfrac{\cos x}{\sin x}}=\dfrac{\sin^2 x}{\cos^2 x}$

$\dfrac{\left(\dfrac{\sin^2 x\cos x-\sin x}{\cos x}\right)}{\left(\dfrac{\sin x\cos^2 x-\cos x}{\sin x}\right)}=$

$\dfrac{\sin x(\sin x\cos x-1)}{\cos x(\sin x\cos x-1)}\cdot\dfrac{\sin x}{\cos x}=$

$\dfrac{\sin^2 x}{\cos^2 x}=$

18. $\cos^2 x-\sin^2 x=\dfrac{\cot x-\tan x}{\cot x+\tan x}$

$=\dfrac{\dfrac{\cos x}{\sin x}-\dfrac{\sin x}{\cos x}}{\dfrac{\cos x}{\sin x}+\dfrac{\sin x}{\cos x}}$

$=\dfrac{\left(\dfrac{\cos^2 x-\sin^2 x}{\sin x\cos x}\right)}{\left(\dfrac{\sin^2 x+\cos^2 x}{\sin x\cos x}\right)}$

$=\dfrac{\cos^2 x-\sin^2 x}{\sin^2 x+\cos^2 x}$

$=\cos^2 x-\sin^2 x$

19. $\csc x-\dfrac{\sin x}{1+\cos x}=\cot x$

$\dfrac{1}{\sin x}-\dfrac{\sin x}{1+\cos x}=\dfrac{\cos x}{\sin x}$

$\dfrac{1+\cos x-\sin^2 x}{\sin x(1+\cos x)}=$

$\dfrac{\cos x+\cos^2 x}{\sin x(1+\cos x)}=$

$\dfrac{\cos x(1+\cos x)}{\sin x(1+\cos x)}=$

$\dfrac{\cos x}{\sin x}=$

20. $\cot x-\tan x=\dfrac{2\cos^2 x-1}{\sin x\cos x}$

$\dfrac{\cos x}{\sin x}-\dfrac{\sin x}{\cos x}=$

$\dfrac{\cos^2 x-\sin^2 x}{\sin x\cos x}=$

$\dfrac{\cos^2 x-(1-\cos^2 x)}{\sin x\cos x}=$

$\dfrac{2\cos^2 x-1}{\sin x\cos x}=$

21. $\dfrac{1-\sin x}{1+\sin x}=(\sec x-\tan x)^2$

$=\left(\dfrac{1}{\cos x}-\dfrac{\sin x}{\cos x}\right)^2$

$=\dfrac{(1-\sin x)^2}{\cos^2 x}$

$=\dfrac{(1-\sin x)^2}{1-\sin^2 x}$

$=\dfrac{(1-\sin x)^2}{(1-\sin x)(1+\sin x)}$

$=\dfrac{1-\sin x}{1+\sin x}$

22. $\dfrac{\cos x}{\csc x+1}+\dfrac{\cos x}{\csc x-1}=2\tan x$

$\dfrac{\cos x(\csc x-1)+\cos x(\csc x+1)}{\csc^2 x-1}=\dfrac{2\sin x}{\cos x}$

$\dfrac{\cos x\ \csc x-\cos x+\cos x\ \csc x+\cos x}{\csc^2 x-1}=$

$\dfrac{2\cos x\csc x}{\cot^2 x}=$

$\dfrac{2\cos x}{\sin x}\cdot\dfrac{\sin^2 x}{\cos^2 x}=$

$\dfrac{2\sin x}{\cos x}=$

23. $\tan x(\csc x+1)=\dfrac{\cot x}{\csc x-1}$

$\dfrac{\csc x+1}{\cot x}=\dfrac{\cot x}{(\csc x-1)}\cdot\dfrac{(\csc x+1)}{(\csc x+1)}$

$=\dfrac{\cot x(\csc x+1)}{\csc^2 x-1}$

$=\dfrac{\cot x(\csc x+1)}{\cot^2 x}$

$=\dfrac{\csc x+1}{\cot x}$

24. $\dfrac{\csc x+\cot x}{\tan x+\sin x}=\cot x\csc x$

$\dfrac{\dfrac{1}{\sin x}+\dfrac{\cos x}{\sin x}}{\dfrac{\sin x}{\cos x}+\sin x}=$

$\dfrac{\dfrac{1+\cos x}{\sin x}}{\left(\dfrac{\sin x+\sin x\cos x}{\cos x}\right)}=$

$\dfrac{1+\cos x}{\sin x}\cdot\dfrac{\cos x}{\sin x(1+\cos x)}=$

$\csc x\cdot\cot x=$

25. $\dfrac{\cos x-\cos y}{\sin x+\sin y}+\dfrac{\sin x-\sin y}{\cos x+\cos y}=0$

$\dfrac{\cos^2 x-\cos^2 y+\sin^2 x-\sin^2 y}{(\sin x+\sin y)(\cos x+\cos y)}=$

$\dfrac{(\sin^2 x+\cos^2 x)-(\sin^2 y+\cos^2 y)}{(\sin x+\sin y)(\cos x+\cos y)}=$

$\dfrac{1-1}{(\sin x+\sin y)(\cos x+\cos y)}=$

$0=$

26. $\csc^2\left(\dfrac{\pi}{2}-x\right)-1=\tan^2 x$

$\sec^2 x-1=$

$\tan^2 x=$

7.3 Exercise Set

1. a) $\frac{\pi}{3}, \frac{2\pi}{3}; \frac{\pi}{3}+2n\pi, \frac{2\pi}{3}+2n\pi$ b) $\frac{\pi}{4}, \frac{7\pi}{4}; \pm\frac{\pi}{4}+2n\pi$ c) $\frac{\pi}{6}, \frac{7\pi}{6}; \frac{\pi}{6}+n\pi$ d) $\frac{\pi}{3}, \frac{4\pi}{3}; \frac{\pi}{3}+n\pi$

e) $\frac{\pi}{6}, \frac{11\pi}{6}; \pm\frac{\pi}{6}+2n\pi$ f) $\frac{\pi}{6}, \frac{5\pi}{6}; \frac{\pi}{6}+2n\pi, \frac{5\pi}{6}+2n\pi$ g) $\frac{7\pi}{6}, \frac{11\pi}{6}; \frac{7\pi}{6}+2n\pi, \frac{11\pi}{6}+2n\pi$ h) $\pi; \pi+2n\pi$

i) $\frac{2\pi}{3}, \frac{5\pi}{3}; \frac{2\pi}{3}+n\pi$ j) $\frac{\pi}{2}, \frac{3\pi}{2}; \frac{\pi}{2}+n\pi$ k) $\frac{3\pi}{4}, \frac{5\pi}{4}; \frac{3\pi}{4}+2n\pi, \frac{5\pi}{4}+2n\pi$ l) $\frac{4\pi}{3}, \frac{5\pi}{3}; \frac{4\pi}{3}+2n\pi, \frac{5\pi}{3}+2n\pi$

2. a) $\sin x>0$ in quadrant I, II, $x=\sin^{-1}(0.6234)=0.673$, $x=\pi-0.673=2.469$. $x=0.673+2\pi n$, $x=2.469+2\pi n$, n an integer

b) $\cos x>0$ in quadrant I, IV, $x=\cos^{-1}(0.4821)=1.068$, $x=2\pi-1.068=5.215$. $x=1.068+2\pi n$, $x=5.215+2\pi n$, n an integer

c) $\tan x>0$ in quadrant I, III, $x=\tan^{-1}(1.7258)=1.046$, $x=\pi+1.046=4.187$. Because of tangent symmetry, $x=1.046+\pi n$, n an integer

d) $\cot x>0$ in quadrant I, III, $x=\tan^{-1}\left(\frac{1}{0.7238}\right)=0.944$, $x=\pi+0.944=4.086$. Because of cotangent symmetry, $x=0.944+\pi n$, n an integer

e) $\sec x>0$ in quadrant I, IV, $x=\cos^{-1}\left(\frac{1}{3.1743}\right)=1.250$, $x=2\pi-1.250=5.033$. $x=1.250+2\pi n$, $x=5.033+2\pi n$, n an integer

f) $\csc x>0$ in quadrant I, II, $x=\sin^{-1}\left(\frac{1}{1.5243}\right)=0.716$, $x=\pi-0.716=2.426$. $x=0.716+2\pi n$, $x=2.426+2\pi n$, n an integer

g) $\sin x<0$ in quadrant III, IV, reference angle is $x=\sin^{-1}(0.4173)=0.430$, therefore, answers are $x=\pi+0.430=3.572$, $x=2\pi-0.430=5.853$. $x=3.572+2\pi n$, $x=5.853+2\pi n$, n an integer

h) $\cos x<0$ in quadrant II, III, reference angle is $x=\cos^{-1}(0.4821)=1.068$, therefore, answers are $x=\pi-1.068=2.074$, $x=\pi+1.068=4.209$. $x=2.074+2\pi n$, $x=4.209+2\pi n$, n an integer

i) $\tan x<0$ in quadrant II, IV, reference angle is $x=\tan^{-1}(0.3124)=0.303$, therefore, answers are $x=\pi-0.303=2.839$, $x=2\pi-0.303=5.980$. Because of tangent symmetry, $x=2.839+\pi n$, n an integer

j) $\cot x<0$ in quadrant II, IV, reference angle is $x=\tan^{-1}\left(\frac{1}{1.1482}\right)=0.717$, therefore, answers are $x=\pi-0.717=2.425$, $x=2\pi-0.717=5.567$. Because of cotangent symmetry, $x=2.425+\pi n$, n an integer

k) $\sec x<0$ in quadrant II, III, reference angle is $x=\cos^{-1}\left(\frac{1}{1.9105}\right)=1.020$, therefore, answers are $x=\pi-1.020=2.122$, $x=\pi+1.020=4.162$. $x=2.122+2\pi n$, $x=4.162+2\pi n$, n an integer

l) $\csc x<0$ in quadrant III, IV, reference angle is $x=\sin^{-1}\left(\frac{1}{2.3124}\right)=0.447$, therefore, answers are $x=\pi+0.447=3.589$, $x=2\pi-0.447=5.836$. $x=3.589+2\pi n$, $x=5.836+2\pi n$, n an integer

3. Remember, every time you go from 0° to 360°, or from 0 to 2π, each trigonometric function is positive in two quadrants and negative in two quadrants. But if the trigonometric function is a maximum or minimum value it can have one or two solutions. *Example*: $\cos\theta=-1$ only at 180°, but $\cos\theta=0$ at both 90° and 270°.

a) $\sin 3x=-\frac{1}{4}$. Sine has a value of $-\frac{1}{4}$ in quadrants III, IV. Since the period is $\frac{2\pi}{3}$, to go to 2π requires multiplying $\frac{2\pi}{3}$ by 3, therefore, $2\times 3=6$ solutions.

b) $\sin 3x=-1$. Sine has a value of -1 only at $\frac{3\pi}{2}$. Since the period is $\frac{2\pi}{3}$, to go to 2π requires multiplying $\frac{2\pi}{3}$ by 3, therefore, $1\times 3=3$ solutions.

c) $\sin\frac{1}{2}x=\frac{1}{3}$. Sine has a value of $\frac{1}{3}$ in quadrants I, II. Since the period is $\frac{2\pi}{\frac{1}{2}}=4\pi$, to go to 2π requires multiplying 4π by $\frac{1}{2}$, therefore $\frac{1}{2}$the period, solutions in quadrants I, II, so 2 solutions.

d) $\cos\frac{1}{2}x=\frac{1}{3}$. Cosine has a value of $\frac{1}{3}$ in quadrants I, IV. Since the period is $\frac{2\pi}{\frac{1}{2}}=4\pi$, to go to 2π requires multiplying 4π by $\frac{1}{2}$, therefore, $\frac{1}{2}$ the period finds a solution in quadrant I, so 1 solution.

3. e) $\tan^2 2x=1\to\tan 2x=\pm 1$. Tangent has a positive or negative value in all 4 quadrants. The period of $\frac{\pi}{2}$ gives a positive and negative value of tangent, $\frac{\pi}{2}\times 4=2\pi$ would give $2\times 4=8$ solutions.

f) $\sin bx=\frac{1}{2}$. Sine has a value of $\frac{1}{2}$ in quadrants I, II. Since the period is $\frac{2\pi}{b}$, to go to 2π requires multiplying $\frac{2\pi}{b}$ by b, therefore, $2\times b=2b$ solutions.

4. a) $\sin 2x=\frac{\sqrt{3}}{2}$. Sine has a positive value of $\frac{\sqrt{3}}{2}$ in quadrants I, II at $\frac{\pi}{3}$ and $\frac{2\pi}{3}$. The period is $\frac{2\pi}{2}=\pi$; since 2π requires multiplying π by 2, therefore $2\times 2=4$ solutions.

Therefore, $2x=\frac{\pi}{3}$, $2x=\frac{2\pi}{3}$, $2x=\frac{\pi}{3}+2\pi=\frac{7\pi}{3}$, $2x=\frac{2\pi}{3}+2\pi=\frac{8\pi}{3}$ The general solution is $2x=\frac{\pi}{3}+2n\pi$, $2x=\frac{2\pi}{3}+2n\pi$

$x=\frac{\pi}{6}$ $x=\frac{\pi}{3}$ $x=\frac{7\pi}{6}$ $x=\frac{4\pi}{3}$ $x=\frac{\pi}{6}+n\pi$ $x=\frac{\pi}{3}+n\pi$, n an integer

b) $\tan 3x = -1$. Tangent has a negative value of -1 in quadrants II, IV at $\frac{3\pi}{4}$ and $\frac{7\pi}{4}$.

The period is $\frac{2\pi}{3}$; since 2π requires multiplying $\frac{2\pi}{3}$ by 3, therefore $2\times 3 = 6$ solutions.

$3x = \frac{3\pi}{4}$, $3x = \frac{7\pi}{4}$, $3x = \frac{3\pi}{4} + 2\pi = \frac{11\pi}{4}$, $3x = \frac{7\pi}{4} + 2\pi = \frac{15\pi}{4}$, $3x = \frac{3\pi}{4} + 4\pi = \frac{19\pi}{4}$, $3x = \frac{7\pi}{4} + 4\pi = \frac{23\pi}{4}$

$x = \frac{\pi}{4}$ $\quad x = \frac{7\pi}{12}$ $\quad x = \frac{11\pi}{12}$ $\quad x = \frac{5\pi}{4}$ $\quad x = \frac{19\pi}{12}$ $\quad x = \frac{23\pi}{12}$

The general solution is $3x = \frac{3\pi}{4} + n\pi$ $\quad x = \frac{\pi}{4} + \frac{\pi}{3}n$, n an integer

c) $\sec\frac{x}{2} = -\frac{2}{\sqrt{3}}$. Secant has a negative value of $-\frac{2}{\sqrt{3}}$ in quadrants II, III at $\frac{5\pi}{6}$ and $\frac{7\pi}{6}$. The period is $\frac{2\pi}{\frac{1}{2}} = 4\pi$; since 4π requires dividing by 2, therefore $2\times\frac{1}{2} = 1$ solution. Therefore, $\frac{x}{2} = \frac{5\pi}{6}$ $\quad x = \frac{5\pi}{3}$ The general solution is $\frac{x}{2} = \frac{5\pi}{6} + 2n\pi$ $\quad x = \frac{5\pi}{3} + 4n\pi$, n an integer

d) $\sin 2x = -0.4173$. Sine has a value of -0.4173 in quadrants III, IV. Radian values are 3.572, 5.853

The period is $\frac{2\pi}{2} = \pi$; since 2π requires multiplying π by 2, therefore, $2\times 2 = 4$ solutions.

Therefore, $2x = 3.572$, $2x = 5.853$, $2x = 3.572 + 2\pi = 9.855$, $\quad 2x = 5.853 + 2\pi = 12.136$

$x = 1.786$, $\quad x = 2.926$, $x = 4.928$, $\quad x = 6.068$

The general solution is $2x = 3.572 + 2\pi n$, $\quad 2x = 5.853 + 2\pi n$

$x = 1.786 + \pi n$, $x = 2.926 + \pi n$, n an integer

e) $\tan 2x = 1.7258$. Tangent has a value of 1.7258 in quadrants I, III. Radian values are 1.046, 4.187

The period is $\frac{2\pi}{2} = \pi$; since 2π requires multiplying π by 2, therefore, $2\times 2 = 4$ solutions.

Therefore, $2x = 1.046$, $2x = 4.187$, $2x = 1.046 + 2\pi = 7.329$, $\quad 2x = 4.187 + 2\pi = 10.470$

$x = 0.523$, $\quad x = 2.094$, $x = 3.664$, $\quad x = 5.235$

The general solution is $2x = 1.046 + \pi n$, $x = 0.523 + \frac{\pi}{2}n$, n an integer

f) $\tan bx = 1.7258$ Tangent has a value of 1.7258 in quadrants I, III. Radian values are 1.046, 4.187

Therefore, $bx = 1.046$, $bx = 4.187$, $bx = 1.046 + 2\pi = 7.329$, $\quad bx = 4.187 + 2\pi = 10.470$

$x = \frac{1.046}{b}$, $\quad x = \frac{4.187}{b}$, $x = \frac{7.329}{b}$, $x = \frac{10.470}{b}$, ... $< 2\pi$

The general solution is $bx = 1.046 + \pi n$, $x = \frac{1.046}{b} + \frac{\pi}{b}n$, n an integer

5. a) $2\cos x + 1 = 0 \rightarrow \cos x = \frac{-1}{2}$, $\cos x < 0$ in quadrant II, III, by special angles at $x = \frac{2\pi}{3}, \frac{4\pi}{3}$. $\quad x = \frac{2\pi}{3} + 2\pi n$,

$x = \frac{4\pi}{3} + 2\pi n$, n an integer

b) $(2\sin x - 1)(\cos x + 1) = 0 \rightarrow \sin x = \frac{1}{2}$ at $\frac{\pi}{6}, \frac{5\pi}{6}$, $\quad \cos x = -1$ at π. Therefore, $x = \frac{\pi}{6}, \frac{5\pi}{6}, \pi$.

$x = \frac{\pi}{6} + 2\pi n$, $x = \frac{5\pi}{6} + 2\pi n$, $x = \pi + 2\pi n$, n an integer

c) $\sqrt{2}\cos^2 x - \cos x = 0 \rightarrow \cos x(\sqrt{2}\cos x - 1) = 0 \rightarrow \cos x = 0$ at $\frac{\pi}{2}, \frac{3\pi}{2}$, $\quad \cos x = \frac{1}{\sqrt{2}}$ at $\frac{\pi}{4}, \frac{7\pi}{4}$

Therefore, $x = \frac{\pi}{4}, \frac{\pi}{2}, \frac{3\pi}{2}, \frac{7\pi}{4}$ $\quad x = \frac{\pi}{2} + \pi n$, $x = \frac{\pi}{4} + 2\pi n$, $x = \frac{7\pi}{4} + 2\pi n$, n an integer

d) $4\sin^2 x = 3 \rightarrow \sin^2 x = \frac{3}{4} \rightarrow \sin x = \frac{\pm\sqrt{3}}{2}$ is found in all 4 quadrants at $\frac{\pi}{3}, \frac{2\pi}{3}, \frac{4\pi}{3}, \frac{5\pi}{3}$. $x = \frac{\pi}{3} + \pi n$, $x = \frac{2\pi}{3} + \pi n$, n an integer

e) $\sin^2 x = \sin x \rightarrow \sin^2 x - \sin x = 0 \rightarrow \sin x(\sin x - 1) = 0 \rightarrow \sin x = 0, \sin x = 1$

$\sin x = 0$ at $0, \pi$, $\quad \sin x = 1$ at $\frac{\pi}{2}$ Therefore, answers are $x = 0, \frac{\pi}{2}, \pi$ $\quad x = \pi n$, $x = \frac{\pi}{2} + 2\pi n$, n an integer

5. f) $6\sin^2 x + 11\sin x - 10 = 0 \rightarrow (3\sin x - 2)(2\sin x + 5) = 0 \rightarrow \sin x = \frac{2}{3},\ -\frac{5}{2}$. $\sin x = -\frac{5}{2} \rightarrow x = \phi$
sine is positive in quadrants I, II. So, $x = 0.730$, $x = \pi - 0.730 = 2.412$; $x = 0.730 + 2\pi n$, $x = 2.412 + 2\pi n$, n an integer

g) $5\cos^2 x + 6\cos x - 8 = 0 \rightarrow (5\cos x - 4)(\cos x + 2) = 0 \rightarrow \cos x = \frac{4}{5},\ -2$, $\cos x = -2 \rightarrow x = \phi$ Cosine is positive in quadrants I, IV. $x = \cos^{-1}\left(\frac{4}{5}\right) = 0.644$, $x = 2\pi - 0.644 = 5.640$ $x = 0.644 + 2\pi n$, $x = 5.640 + 2\pi n$, n an integer

h) $2\cos^2 x - \cos x - 1 = 0 \rightarrow (2\cos x + 1)(\cos x - 1) = 0 \rightarrow \cos x = -\frac{1}{2},\ 1$ $\cos x = -\frac{1}{2}$ at $\frac{2\pi}{3}, \frac{4\pi}{3}$, and $\cos x = 1$ at 0
Because of the symmetry of $0, \frac{2\pi}{3}, \frac{4\pi}{3}$, $x = \frac{2\pi}{3}n$, n an integer

i) $2\cos^2 x - 3\cos x - 2 = 0 \rightarrow (2\cos x + 1)(\cos x - 2) = 0 \rightarrow \cos x = -\frac{1}{2},\ 2$ $\cos x = 2 \rightarrow x = \phi$, cosine has a value of $-\frac{1}{2}$ in quadrant II, III. Radian values are $\frac{2\pi}{3}, \frac{4\pi}{3}$ $x = \frac{2\pi}{3} + 2\pi n$, $x = \frac{4\pi}{3} + 2\pi n$, n an integer

j) $2\tan^2 x + 5\tan x + 2 = 0 \rightarrow (2\tan x + 1)(\tan x + 2) = 0 \rightarrow \tan x = -\frac{1}{2},\ -2$ $\tan x = -\frac{1}{2} \rightarrow x = \tan^{-1}\left(\frac{1}{2}\right) = 0.464 \rightarrow x = \pi - 0.464 = 2.678$, $x = 2\pi - 0.464 = 5.820$ $\tan x = -2 \rightarrow x = \tan^{-1}(2) = 1.107 \rightarrow x = \pi - 1.107 = 2.034$, $x = 2\pi - 1.107 = 5.176$ $x = 2.678 + \pi n$, $x = 2.034 + \pi n$, n an integer

k) $\tan^2 x - 2\tan x - 3 = 0 \rightarrow (\tan x + 1)(\tan x - 3) = 0 \rightarrow \tan x = -1,\ 3$ $\tan x = -1$ in quadrants II, IV. The special angle values are $\frac{3\pi}{4}, \frac{7\pi}{4}$ $\tan x = 3$ in quadrants I, III. $x = \tan^{-1}(3) = 1.249$, $x = \pi + 1.249 = 4.391$ $x = \frac{3\pi}{4} + \pi n$, $x = 1.249 + \pi n$, n an integer

l) $\cot^2 x - \cot x - 6 = 0 \rightarrow (\cot x - 3)(\cot x + 2) = 0 \rightarrow \cot x = 3,\ -2$. $\cot x = -2$ in quadrants II, IV. $x = \cot^{-1}(2) = \tan^{-1}\left(\frac{1}{2}\right) = 0.464$, $x = \pi - 0.464 = 2.678$, $x = 2\pi - 0.464 = 5.820$ $\cot x = 3$ in quadrants I, III. $x = \cot^{-1}(3) = \tan^{-1}\left(\frac{1}{3}\right) = 0.322$, $x = \pi + 0.322 = 3.463$
$x = 2.678 + \pi n$, $x = 0.322 + \pi n$, n an integer

m) $\tan x - 2\tan x \cdot \sin x = 0 \rightarrow \tan x(1 - 2\sin x) = 0$, $\tan x = 0$ at $0, \pi$, $\sin x = \frac{1}{2}$ at $\frac{\pi}{6}, \frac{5\pi}{6}$.
$x = \pi n$, n an integer, $x = \frac{\pi}{6} + 2\pi n$, n an integer, $x = \frac{5\pi}{6} + 2\pi n$, n an integer

n) $3\sin^2 x + 4\sin x - 4 = 0 \rightarrow (3\sin x - 2)(\sin x + 2) = 0 \rightarrow \sin x = \frac{2}{3},\ -2$. $\sin x = -2 \rightarrow x = \phi$
$\sin x = \frac{2}{3}$ in quadrants I, II. $x = \sin^{-1}\left(\frac{2}{3}\right) = 0.730$, $x = \pi - 0.730 = 2.412$; $x = 0.730 + 2\pi n$, $x = 2.412 + 2\pi n$, n an integer

o) $\sec^2 x - 3\sec x + 2 = 0 \rightarrow (\sec x - 1)(\sec x - 2) = 0 \rightarrow \sec x = 1$ at 0, $\sec x = 2$ at $\frac{\pi}{3}, \frac{5\pi}{3}$.
$x = 2\pi n$, $x = \frac{\pi}{3} + 2\pi n$, $x = \frac{5\pi}{3} + 2\pi n$, n an integer

p) $2\cos^2 x - 3\sin x - 3 = 0 \rightarrow 2(1 - \sin^2 x) - 3\sin x - 3 = 0 \rightarrow 2 - 2\sin^2 x - 3\sin x - 3 = 0 \rightarrow$
$2\sin^2 x + 3\sin x + 1 = 0 \rightarrow (2\sin x + 1)(\sin x + 1) = 0 \rightarrow \sin x = -\frac{1}{2},\ -1$; $\sin x = -\frac{1}{2}$ at $\frac{7\pi}{6}, \frac{11\pi}{6}$, $\sin x = -1$ at $\sin x = -1$ *at* $\frac{3\pi}{2}$
$x = \frac{7\pi}{6} + 2\pi n$, $x = \frac{11\pi}{6} + 2\pi n$, $x = \frac{3\pi}{2} + 2\pi n$, n an integer

q) $3\csc x - \sin x - 2 = 0 \rightarrow \left(\frac{3}{\sin x} - \sin x - 2 = 0\right)\sin x \rightarrow 3 - \sin^2 x - 2\sin x = 0 \rightarrow \sin^2 x + 2\sin x - 3 = 0$
$(\sin x - 1)(\sin x + 3) = 0 \rightarrow \sin x = 1,\ -3$. $\sin x = -3 \rightarrow x = \phi$, $\sin x = 1$ *at* $\frac{\pi}{2}$ $x = \frac{\pi}{2} + 2\pi n$, n an integer

r) $3\sin x = \sqrt{3}\cos x \rightarrow \frac{\sin x}{\cos x} = \tan x = \frac{\sqrt{3}}{3}$ at $x = \frac{\pi}{6}, \frac{7\pi}{6}$ $x = \frac{\pi}{6} + \pi n$, n an integer

5. s) $\sin x\tan 2x = \sin x \to \sin x\tan 2x - \sin x = 0 \to \sin x(\tan 2x - 1) = 0 \to \sin x = 0,\ \tan 2x = 1$

Tangent equals 1 at $\frac{\pi}{4}, \frac{5\pi}{4} \to 2x = \frac{\pi}{4},\ 2x = \frac{5\pi}{4},\ 2x = \frac{\pi}{4} + 2\pi = \frac{9\pi}{4},\ 2x = \frac{5\pi}{4} + 2\pi = \frac{13\pi}{4}$

$x = \frac{\pi}{8}\quad x = \frac{5\pi}{8}\quad x = \frac{9\pi}{8}\quad x = \frac{13\pi}{8}$

$\sin x = 0$ at $0, \pi$. Therefore answers are $0, \pi, \frac{\pi}{8}, \frac{5\pi}{8}, \frac{9\pi}{8}, \frac{13\pi}{8}$ $\quad 2x = \frac{\pi}{4} + \pi n \to x = \frac{\pi}{8} + \frac{\pi}{2}n,\ \pi n,\ n$ an integer

t) $3\sin^2 2x - 2\sin 2x - 1 = 0 \to (\sin 2x - 1)(3\sin 2x + 1) = 0 \to \sin 2x = -\frac{1}{3},\ 1$

Sine has a value of $-\frac{1}{3}$ in quadrants III, IV. Radian values are $\pi + 0.340 = 3.481,\ 2\pi - 0.340 = 5.943$

Therefore $2x = 3.481,\quad 2x = 5.954,\quad 2x = 3.481 + 2\pi,\quad 2x = 5.943 + 2\pi$

$x = 1.741\quad x = 2.977\quad x = 4.883\quad x = 6.113$

Sine has a value of 1 at $\frac{\pi}{2}$, therefore $2x = \frac{\pi}{2} \to x = \frac{\pi}{4},\quad 2x = \frac{\pi}{2} + 2\pi = \frac{5\pi}{2} \to x = \frac{5\pi}{4}$. Therefore, answers are 1.741, 2.977, 4.883, 6.113, $\frac{\pi}{4}$, and $\frac{5\pi}{4}$ $\quad 2x = 3.481 + 2\pi n\quad 2x = 5.943 + 2\pi n\quad 2x = \frac{\pi}{2} + 2\pi n\quad x = 1.741 + \pi n,\ x = 2.977 + \pi n,\ x = \frac{\pi}{4} + \pi n$, n an integer

6. a)

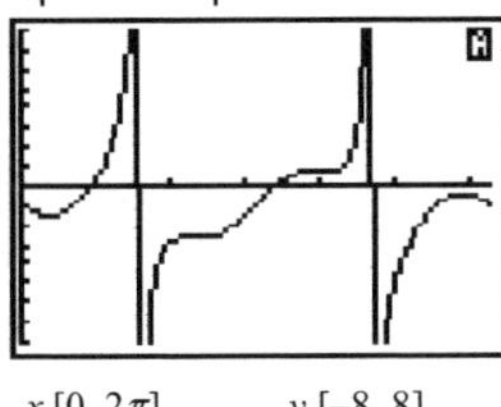

$x\ [0, 2\pi]\qquad y\ [-8, 8]$

$Y_1 = \tan x - \sin 3x - 1$

The solutions are where the graph crosses the x-axis. Therefore, the solutions are $x =$ 0.9306, 3.4113

b)

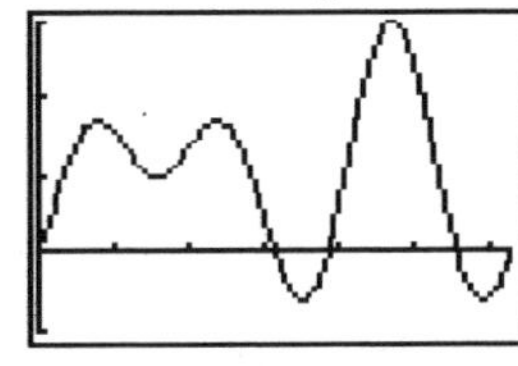

$x\ [0, 2\pi]\qquad y\ [-1, 3]$

$Y_1 = \sin 3x - \cos 2x + 1$

The solutions are where the graph crosses the x-axis. Therefore, the solutions are $x = 0$, 3.1416, 3.8510, 5.5738

c)

$x\ [0, 2\pi]\qquad y\ [-4, 4]$

$Y_1 = \frac{1}{\tan 2x} + \tan 0.5x$

The solutions are where the graph crosses the x-axis. Therefore, the solutions are $x =$ 1.0472, 5.2360

7.4 Exercise Set

1. a) $\sin 15° = \sin(45° - 30°) = \sin 45°\cos 30° - \cos 45°\sin 30° = \frac{\sqrt{2}}{2}\cdot\frac{\sqrt{3}}{2} - \frac{\sqrt{2}}{2}\cdot\frac{1}{2} = \frac{\sqrt{6}}{4} - \frac{\sqrt{2}}{4} = \frac{\sqrt{6}-\sqrt{2}}{4}$

b) $\cos(-75°) = \cos 75° = \cos(45° + 30°) = \cos 45°\cos 30° - \sin 45°\sin 30° = \frac{\sqrt{2}}{2}\cdot\frac{\sqrt{3}}{2} - \frac{\sqrt{2}}{2}\cdot\frac{1}{2} = \frac{\sqrt{6}-\sqrt{2}}{4}$

c) $\tan\frac{5\pi}{12} = \tan\left(\frac{\pi}{4} + \frac{\pi}{6}\right) = \frac{\tan\frac{\pi}{4} + \tan\frac{\pi}{6}}{1 - \tan\frac{\pi}{4}\tan\frac{\pi}{6}} = \frac{1 + \frac{1}{\sqrt{3}}}{1 - 1\cdot\frac{1}{\sqrt{3}}} = \frac{\sqrt{3}+1}{\sqrt{3}-1}\cdot\frac{(\sqrt{3}+1)}{(\sqrt{3}+1)} = \frac{4 + 2\sqrt{3}}{2} = 2 + \sqrt{3}$

d) $\cot\frac{11\pi}{12} = \cot\left(\frac{2\pi}{3} + \frac{\pi}{4}\right) = \frac{1}{\tan\left(\frac{2\pi}{3} + \frac{\pi}{4}\right)} = \frac{1}{\left(\frac{\tan\frac{2\pi}{3} + \tan\frac{\pi}{4}}{1 - \tan\frac{2\pi}{3}\tan\frac{\pi}{4}}\right)} = \frac{1+\sqrt{3}}{1-\sqrt{3}}\cdot\frac{(1+\sqrt{3})}{(1+\sqrt{3})} = \frac{4 + 2\sqrt{3}}{-2} = -2 - \sqrt{3}$

e) $\sec\frac{19\pi}{12} = \sec\left(\frac{4\pi}{3} + \frac{\pi}{4}\right) = \frac{1}{\cos\left(\frac{4\pi}{3} + \frac{\pi}{4}\right)} = \frac{1}{\cos\frac{4\pi}{3}\cos\frac{\pi}{4} - \sin\frac{4\pi}{3}\sin\frac{\pi}{4}} = \frac{1}{\left(-\frac{1}{2}\right)\left(\frac{\sqrt{2}}{2}\right) - \left(\frac{-\sqrt{3}}{2}\right)\left(\frac{\sqrt{2}}{2}\right)} =$

$\frac{1}{-\frac{\sqrt{2}}{4} + \frac{\sqrt{6}}{4}} = \frac{1}{\frac{\sqrt{6}-\sqrt{2}}{4}} = \frac{4}{\sqrt{6}-\sqrt{2}}\cdot\frac{(\sqrt{6}+\sqrt{2})}{(\sqrt{6}+\sqrt{2})} = \frac{4(\sqrt{6}+\sqrt{2})}{4} = \sqrt{6} + \sqrt{2}$ $\quad \frac{1}{-\frac{\sqrt{2}}{4} + \frac{\sqrt{6}}{4}} = \frac{1}{\frac{\sqrt{6}-\sqrt{2}}{4}} = \frac{4}{\sqrt{6}-\sqrt{2}}\cdot\frac{(\sqrt{6}+\sqrt{2})}{(\sqrt{6}+\sqrt{2})} = \frac{4(\sqrt{6}+\sqrt{2})}{4} = \sqrt{6} + \sqrt{2}$

2. a) $\sin 24°\cos 36° + \cos 24°\sin 36° = \sin(24° + 36°) = \sin 60°\ \frac{\sqrt{3}}{2}$

2. b) $\cos 55°\cos 10° + \sin 55°\sin 10° = \cos(55° - 10°) = \cos 45° \frac{\sqrt{2}}{2}$

c) $\dfrac{\tan\frac{\pi}{5} - \tan\frac{\pi}{30}}{1 + \tan\frac{\pi}{5}\tan\frac{\pi}{30}} = \tan\left(\frac{\pi}{5} - \frac{\pi}{30}\right) = \tan\frac{\pi}{6} = \frac{1}{\sqrt{3}}$

d) $\sin\frac{23\pi}{18}\cos\frac{\pi}{9} - \cos\frac{23\pi}{18}\sin\frac{\pi}{9} = \sin\left(\frac{23\pi}{18} - \frac{\pi}{9}\right) = \sin\frac{7\pi}{6} = -\frac{1}{2}$

e) $\cos\frac{\pi}{8}\cos\frac{7\pi}{8} + \sin\frac{\pi}{8}\sin\frac{7\pi}{8} = \cos\left(\frac{7\pi}{8} - \frac{\pi}{8}\right) = \cos\frac{3\pi}{4} = -\frac{\sqrt{2}}{2}$

f) $\dfrac{\tan\frac{2\pi}{9} + \tan\frac{\pi}{9}}{1 - \tan\frac{2\pi}{9}\tan\frac{\pi}{9}} = \tan\left(\frac{2\pi}{9} + \frac{\pi}{9}\right) = \tan\frac{\pi}{3} = \sqrt{3}$

g) $\frac{\sin 3x}{\csc x} - \frac{\cos 3x}{\sec x} = \sin 3x \cdot \sin x - \cos 3x \cdot \cos x = -\left(\cos 3x \cdot \cos x - \sin 3x \cdot \sin x\right) = -\cos\left(3x + x\right) = -\cos 4x$

h) $\cos(A+B) \cdot \cos B + \sin(A+B) \cdot \sin B \rightarrow \cos(A+B-B) \rightarrow \cos A$

i) $\tan^2(\frac{\pi}{2} - x) \cdot \sec^2 x - \sin^2(\frac{\pi}{2} - x) \cdot \csc^2 x = \cot^2 x \sec^2 x - \cos^2 x \csc^2 x =$

$\frac{\cos^2 x}{\sin^2 x} \cdot \frac{1}{\cos^2 x} - \cos^2 x \cdot \frac{1}{\sin^2 x} = \frac{1}{\sin^2 x} - \frac{\cos^2 x}{\sin^2 x} = \frac{1 - \cos^2 x}{\sin^2 x} = \frac{\sin^2 x}{\sin^2 x} = 1$

j) Remember: $\sin\left(A+B\right) = \sin A \cdot \cos B + \cos A \cdot \sin B$

Therefore, $\sin\left(\frac{\pi}{3} - x\right) \cdot \cos\left(\frac{\pi}{3} + x\right) + \cos\left(\frac{\pi}{3} - x\right) \cdot \sin\left(\frac{\pi}{3} + x\right) = \sin\left[\left(\frac{\pi}{3} - x\right) + \left(\frac{\pi}{3} + x\right)\right] = \sin\frac{2\pi}{3} = \frac{\sqrt{3}}{2}$

3. a) $\tan\left(x + \frac{\pi}{4}\right) = \dfrac{\tan x + \tan\frac{\pi}{4}}{1 - \tan x \tan\frac{\pi}{4}} = \frac{\tan x + 1}{1 - \tan x} = \frac{3+1}{1-3} = -2$

b) $\sin x = \frac{4}{5}$ in quadrant I, then $\cos x = \frac{3}{5}$ by Pythagorean Theorem

$\sin\left(x + \frac{\pi}{6}\right) = \sin x \cos\frac{\pi}{6} + \cos x \sin\frac{\pi}{6} = \frac{\sqrt{3}}{2}\sin x + \frac{1}{2}\cos x = \frac{\sqrt{3}}{2} \cdot \frac{4}{5} + \frac{1}{2} \cdot \frac{3}{5} = \frac{4\sqrt{3} + 3}{10}$

c) $\cos x = \frac{12}{13}$ in quadrant I, then $\sin x = \frac{5}{13}$ by Pythagorean Theorem

$\cos\left(x + \frac{2\pi}{3}\right) = \cos x \cos\frac{2\pi}{3} - \sin x \sin\frac{2\pi}{3} = -\frac{1}{2}\cos x - \frac{\sqrt{3}}{2}\sin x = -\frac{1}{2} \cdot \frac{12}{13} - \frac{\sqrt{3}}{2} \cdot \frac{5}{13} = \frac{-12 - 5\sqrt{3}}{26}$

d) If $\sin A = -\frac{3}{5}$ and in quadrant III, then $\cos A = -\frac{4}{5}$ by Pythagorean Theorem. If $\cos B = -\frac{12}{13}$ and in quadrant III, then $\sin B = -\frac{5}{13}$ by Pythagorean Theorem. $\sin(A-B) = \sin A \cos B - \cos A \sin B = (-\frac{3}{5})(-\frac{12}{13}) - (-\frac{4}{5})(-\frac{5}{13}) = \frac{36}{65} - \frac{20}{65} = \frac{16}{65}$

e) If $\sin A = \frac{12}{13}$ in quadrant II , then $\cos A = -\frac{5}{13}$ by Pythagorean Theorem. If $\sec B = \frac{5}{4}$ in quadrant IV, then $\cos B = \frac{4}{5}$ and $\sin B = -\frac{3}{5}$ by Pythagorean Theorem $\cos(A+B) = \cos A \cdot \cos B - \sin A \cdot \sin B = \left(\frac{-5}{13}\right)\left(\frac{4}{5}\right) - \left(\frac{12}{13}\right)\left(\frac{-3}{5}\right) = \frac{-20}{65} + \frac{36}{65} = \frac{16}{65}$

f) If $\tan A = \frac{5}{12}$ in quadrant III, then by Pythagorean Theorem the hypotenuse is 13 and $\sin A = -\frac{5}{13}$, $\cos A = -\frac{12}{13}$. If $\cos B = -\frac{3}{5}$ in quadrant II then by Pythagorean Theorem the third side is 4 and $\sin B = \frac{4}{5}$ So $\sin(A - B) = \sin A \cos B - \cos A \sin B =$ $(-\frac{5}{13})(-\frac{3}{5}) - (-\frac{12}{13})(\frac{4}{5}) = \frac{15}{65} + \frac{48}{65} = \frac{63}{65}$

4. a) $\cos\theta \cos 10° - \sin\theta \sin 10° = \frac{1}{2} \rightarrow \cos(\theta + 10°) = \frac{1}{2}$, therefore, $\theta + 10° = 60° \rightarrow \theta = 50°$ and, $\theta + 10° = 300° \rightarrow \theta = 290°$.

b) $\sin\theta \cdot \cos 12° + \cos\theta \cdot \cos 78° = \frac{\sqrt{3}}{2} \rightarrow \sin\theta \cdot \cos 12° + \cos\theta \cdot \sin 12° = \frac{\sqrt{3}}{2}$ $\sin(\theta + 12°) = \frac{\sqrt{3}}{2}$, therefore, $\theta + 12° = 60° \rightarrow \theta = 48°$ and, $\theta + 12° = 120° \rightarrow \theta = 108°$

4. c) $\cos 3x\cos x+\sin 3x\sin x=0\rightarrow\cos(3x-x)=0\rightarrow\cos 2x=0\quad \cos=0$ at $\frac{\pi}{2}$ and $\frac{3\pi}{2}$

Therefore $2x=\frac{\pi}{2}\quad 2x=\frac{3\pi}{2}\quad 2x=\frac{\pi}{2}+2\pi=\frac{5\pi}{2}\quad 2x=\frac{3\pi}{2}+2\pi=\frac{7\pi}{2}$

$x=\frac{\pi}{4}\quad x=\frac{3\pi}{4}\quad x=\frac{5\pi}{4}\quad x=\frac{7\pi}{4}$

d) $2\tan x+\tan(\pi-x)=\sqrt{3}\rightarrow 2\tan x+\frac{\tan\pi-\tan x}{1+\tan\pi\tan x}=\sqrt{3}\rightarrow 2\tan x-\tan x=\sqrt{3}\rightarrow\ \tan x=\sqrt{3},\ x=\frac{\pi}{3},\ \frac{4\pi}{3}$

e) $\sqrt{2}\sin 3x\cos 2x=1+\sqrt{2}\cos 3x\sin 2x\rightarrow\sin 3x\cos 2x-\cos 3x\sin 2x=\frac{1}{\sqrt{2}}\rightarrow\sin(3x-2x)=\frac{1}{\sqrt{2}}\rightarrow$

$\sin x=\frac{1}{\sqrt{2}}\quad x=\sin^{-1}\left(\frac{1}{\sqrt{2}}\right)\quad x=\frac{\pi}{4},\ \frac{3\pi}{4}$

f) $\cos\left(x+\frac{\pi}{4}\right)+\cos\left(x-\frac{\pi}{4}\right)=1\rightarrow\cos x\cos\frac{\pi}{4}-\sin x\sin\frac{\pi}{4}+\cos x\cos\frac{\pi}{4}+\sin x\sin\frac{\pi}{4}=1\rightarrow$

$2\cos x\cdot\cos\frac{\pi}{4}=1\rightarrow 2\cdot\frac{\sqrt{2}}{2}\cos x=1\rightarrow\cos x=\frac{1}{\sqrt{2}}\quad x=\cos^{-1}\left(\frac{1}{\sqrt{2}}\right),\ x=\frac{\pi}{4},\ \frac{7\pi}{4}$

5. a)

$$\sin(A+B)-\sin(A-B)=2\sin B\cos A$$
$$\sin A\cos B+\cos A\sin B-\sin A\cos B+\cos A\sin B=$$
$$2\sin B\cos A=$$

b)

$$\frac{\sin(A+B)}{\cos(A-B)}=\frac{\cot A+\cot B}{1+\cot A\cot B}$$
$$\frac{\sin A\cos B+\cos A\sin B}{\cos A\cos B+\sin A\sin B}=$$
$$\frac{\left(\frac{\sin A\cos B}{\sin A\sin B}+\frac{\cos A\sin B}{\sin A\sin B}\right)}{\left(\frac{\cos A\cos B}{\sin A\sin B}+\frac{\sin A\sin B}{\sin A\sin B}\right)}=$$
$$\frac{\cot B+\cot A}{\cot A\cot B+1}=$$

c)

$$\frac{\sin(A-B)}{\sin B}+\frac{\cos(A-B)}{\cos B}=\frac{\sin A}{\sin B\cos B}$$
$$\frac{\sin A\cos B-\cos A\sin B}{\sin B}+\frac{\cos A\cos B+\sin A\sin B}{\cos B}=$$
$$\frac{\sin A\cos^2 B-\cos A\cos B\sin B+\sin B\cos A\cos B+\sin A\sin^2 B}{\sin B\cos B}=$$
$$\frac{\sin A\cos^2 B+\sin A\sin^2 B}{\sin B\cos B}=$$
$$\frac{\sin A(\cos^2 B+\sin^2 B)}{\sin B\cos B}=$$
$$\frac{\sin A}{\sin B\cos B}=$$

d)

$$\frac{1+\tan A}{\tan\left(A+\frac{\pi}{4}\right)}=1-\tan A$$
$$\frac{1+\tan A}{\left(\frac{\tan A+\tan\frac{\pi}{4}}{1-\tan A\tan\frac{\pi}{4}}\right)}=$$
$$\frac{1+\tan A}{\left(\frac{\tan A+1}{1-\tan A}\right)}=$$
$$1-\tan A=$$

e)

$$\sin(A+B)\sin(A-B)=\sin^2 A-\sin^2 B$$
$$(\sin A\cos B+\cos A\sin B)(\sin A\cos B-\cos A\sin B)=$$
$$\sin^2 A\cos^2 B-\cos^2 A\sin^2 B=$$
$$\sin^2 A(1-\sin^2 B)-(1-\sin^2 A)\sin^2 B=$$
$$\sin^2 A-\sin^2 A\sin^2 B-\sin^2 B+\sin^2 A\sin B=$$
$$\sin^2 A-\sin^2 B=$$

f)

$$\cos(A+B)\cos(A-B)=\cos^2 A-\sin^2 B$$
$$(\cos A\cos B-\sin A\sin B)(\cos A\cos B+\sin A\sin B)=$$
$$\cos^2 A\cos^2 B-\sin^2 A\sin^2 B=$$
$$\cos^2 A(1-\sin^2 B)-(1-\cos^2 A)\sin^2 B=$$
$$\cos^2 A-\sin^2 B\cos^2 A-\sin^2 B+\sin^2 B\cos^2 A=$$
$$\cos^2 A-\sin^2 B=$$

5. g)

$$\sec(A+B)=\frac{\sec A\sec B}{1-\tan A\tan B}$$

$$\frac{1}{\cos(A+B)}=\frac{\frac{1}{\cos A\cos B}}{1-\frac{\sin A}{\cos A}\cdot\frac{\sin B}{\cos B}}$$

$$\frac{1}{\cos A\cos B-\sin A\sin B}=\frac{\frac{1}{\cos A\cos B}}{\left(\frac{\cos A\cos B-\sin A\sin B}{\cos A\cos B}\right)}$$

$$=\frac{1}{\cos A\cos B-\sin A\sin B}$$

h)

$$\csc(A-B)=\frac{\csc A\csc B}{\cot B-\cot A}$$

$$\frac{1}{\sin(A-B)}=\frac{\frac{1}{\sin A\sin B}}{\frac{\cos B}{\sin B}-\frac{\cos A}{\sin A}}$$

$$\frac{1}{\sin A\cos B-\cos A\sin B}=\frac{\frac{1}{\sin A\sin B}}{\left(\frac{\sin A\cos B-\cos A\sin B}{\sin A\sin B}\right)}$$

$$=\frac{1}{\sin A\cos B-\cos A\sin B}$$

6. a)

$$\cos(90°-A)\sin(180°-B)+\cos(360°-A)\sin(90°-B)$$

$$\sin A(\sin 180°\cos B-\cos 180°\sin B)+(\cos 360°\cos A+\sin 360°\sin A)\cos B$$

$$\sin A(\quad 0 \quad + \quad \sin B \quad)+(\quad 1\cdot\cos A \quad + \quad 0 \quad)\cos B$$

$$\sin A\sin B+\cos A\cos B$$

$$\cos(A-B)$$

b)

$$\cos(A-90°)\sin(90°-B)-\sin(B-270°)\cos(90°-A)$$

$$\cos-(90°-A)\sin(90°-B)-(\sin B\cos 270°-\cos B\sin 270°)\cos(90°-A)$$

$$\sin A\cos B \qquad -(\quad 0 \quad + \quad \cos B \quad)\sin A$$

$$0$$

c)

$$\tan(90°-A)\tan(180°-A)\sec A+\csc B\sin(90°-B)\csc(90°-B$$

$$\cot A\left(\frac{\tan 180°-\tan A}{1+\tan 180°\tan A}\right)\sec A+\csc B\cos B\cdot\sec B$$

$$\frac{\cos A}{\sin A}\left(-\frac{\sin A}{\cos A}\right)\frac{1}{\cos A}+\frac{1}{\sin B}\cdot\cos B\frac{1}{\cos B}$$

$$-\frac{1}{\cos A}+\frac{1}{\sin B}$$

$$-\sec A+\csc B$$

6. d)

$$\sec(180°-A)\csc(270°-A)-\cot(630°+A)\tan(540°-A)$$

$$\left(\frac{1}{\cos 180°\cos A+\sin 180°\sin A}\right)\left(\frac{1}{\sin 270°\cos A-\cos 270°\sin A}\right)-\left(\frac{\cos 630°\cos A-\sin 630°\sin A}{\sin 630°\cos A+\cos 630°\sin A}\right)\left(\frac{\sin 540°\cos A-\cos 540°\sin A}{\cos 540°\cos A+\sin 540°\sin A}\right)$$

$$\left(\frac{1}{-\cos A}\right)\cdot\left(\frac{1}{-\cos A}\right)-\left(\frac{\sin A}{-\cos A}\right)\cdot\left(\frac{\sin A}{-\cos A}\right)$$

$$\frac{1}{\cos^2 A}-\frac{\sin^2 A}{\cos^2 A}$$

$$\frac{1}{\cos^2 A}-\frac{\sin^2 A}{\cos^2 A}$$

$$\frac{1-\sin^2 A}{\cos^2 A}$$

$$\frac{\cos^2 A}{\cos^2 A}$$

$$1$$

7. a)

$$y=\cos 3x\cos x-\sin 3x\sin x$$

$$=\cos(3x+x)$$

$$=\cos 4x$$

Amplitude: 1,

Period: $\frac{2\pi}{4}=\frac{\pi}{2}$,

Phase shift: 0

b)

$$y=-2\sin 2x\cos\frac{\pi}{3}+2\cos 2x\sin\frac{\pi}{3}$$

$$=-2\left(\sin 2x\cos\frac{\pi}{3}-\cos 2x\sin\frac{\pi}{3}\right)$$

$$=-2\sin\left(2x-\frac{\pi}{3}\right)$$

$$=-2\sin 2\left(x-\frac{\pi}{6}\right)$$

Amplitude: $|-2|=2$,

Period: $\frac{2\pi}{2}=\pi$, Phase shift: $2\left(x-\frac{\pi}{6}\right)=0$

$x=\frac{\pi}{6}$

c)

$$y=3\sin\frac{\pi}{6}x\cos\frac{\pi}{3}+3\cos\frac{\pi}{6}x\sin\frac{\pi}{3}$$

$$=3\left(\sin\frac{\pi}{6}x\cos\frac{\pi}{3}+\cos\frac{\pi}{6}x\sin\frac{\pi}{3}\right)$$

$$=3\sin\left(\frac{\pi}{6}x+\frac{\pi}{3}\right)$$

$$=3\sin\frac{\pi}{6}(x+2)$$

Amplitude: 3,

Period: $\frac{2\pi}{\frac{\pi}{6}}=12$,

Phase shift: $\frac{\pi}{6}(x+2)=0$

$x=-2$

d)

$$y=-\sin\frac{\pi}{4}x\sin\frac{\pi}{2}-\cos\frac{\pi}{4}x\cos\frac{\pi}{2}$$

$$=-\left(\cos\frac{\pi}{4}x\cos\frac{\pi}{2}+\sin\frac{\pi}{4}x\sin\frac{\pi}{2}\right)$$

$$=-\cos\left(\frac{\pi}{4}x-\frac{\pi}{2}\right)$$

$$=-\cos\frac{\pi}{4}(x-2)$$

Amplitude: $|-1|=1$, Period: $\frac{2\pi}{\frac{\pi}{4}}=8$,

Phase shift: $\frac{\pi}{4}(x-2)=0 \quad x=2$

8. Cannot use $\tan(A+B)$ since $A=\frac{\pi}{2}$ and $\tan\frac{\pi}{2}$ is undefined.

9. $\tan\left(\frac{\pi}{2}+x\right)=\dfrac{\sin\left(\frac{\pi}{2}+x\right)}{\cos\left(\frac{\pi}{2}+x\right)}=\dfrac{\sin\frac{\pi}{2}\cos x+\cos\frac{\pi}{2}\sin x}{\cos\frac{\pi}{2}\cos x-\sin\frac{\pi}{2}\sin x}=\dfrac{\cos x}{-\sin x}=-\cot x$

7.5 Exercise Set

1. a) $4\sin 10x$ **b)** $2\sin x$ **c)** $-2\cos 4x$ **d)** $4\tan 8x$ **e)** -1 **f)** $\sin 12x$ **g)** $\cot 8x$ **h)** $\frac{\csc 12x}{2}$ **i)** $-2\cos x$ **j)** $\cos 16x$

k) $\cos 3x$ **l)** 0 **m)** -1 **n)** $-\cos 6x$ **o)** $\csc^2 4x$ **p)** $-2\tan 6x$

2. a)
$$\sin 2x+\cos x=0$$
$$2\sin x\cos x+\cos x=0$$
$$\cos x(2\sin x+1)=0$$
$$\cos x=0 \quad \sin x=-\frac{1}{2}$$
$$\frac{\pi}{2},\ \frac{3\pi}{2},\ \frac{7\pi}{6},\ \frac{11\pi}{6}$$

b)
$$\sin x+\cos 2x=1$$
$$\sin x+1-2\sin^2 x=1$$
$$\sin x(1-2\sin x)=0$$
$$\sin x=0 \quad \sin x=\frac{1}{2}$$
$$0,\ \pi,\ \frac{\pi}{6},\ \frac{5\pi}{6}$$

c)
$$3\cos 2x+2\sin^2 x=2$$
$$3(1-2\sin^2 x)+2\sin^2 x=2$$
$$4\sin^2 x=1$$
$$\sin x=\pm\frac{1}{2}$$
$$\frac{\pi}{6},\ \frac{5\pi}{6},\ \frac{7\pi}{6},\ \frac{11\pi}{6}$$

d)
$$\sin 2x=\cot x$$
$$2\sin x\cos x=\frac{\cos x}{\sin x}$$
$$2\sin^2 x\cos x-\cos x=0$$
$$\cos x(2\sin^2 x-1)=0$$
$$\cos x=0 \quad \sin x=\pm\frac{1}{\sqrt{2}}$$
$$\frac{\pi}{2},\ \frac{3\pi}{2},\ \frac{\pi}{4},\ \frac{3\pi}{4},\ \frac{5\pi}{4},\ \frac{7\pi}{4}$$

e)
$$\csc^2 x=2\sec 2x$$
$$\frac{1}{\sin^2 x}=\frac{2}{1-2\sin^2 x}$$
$$4\sin^2 x=1$$
$$\sin x=\pm\frac{1}{2}$$
$$\frac{\pi}{6},\ \frac{5\pi}{6},\ \frac{7\pi}{6},\ \frac{11\pi}{6}$$

f)
$$\tan x-\cot x=2$$
$$\tan x-\frac{1}{\tan x}=2$$
$$\tan^2 x-1=2\tan x$$
$$\frac{2\tan x}{1-\tan^2 x}=-1$$
$$\tan 2x=-1$$
$$\frac{3\pi}{8},\ \frac{7\pi}{8},\ \frac{11\pi}{8},\ \frac{15\pi}{8}$$

g)
$$\tan 2x+\tan x=0$$
$$\frac{2\tan x}{1-\tan^2 x}+\tan x=0$$
$$2\tan x+\tan x-\tan^3 x=0$$
$$\tan x(\tan^2 x-3)=0$$
$$\tan x=0 \quad \tan x=\pm\sqrt{3}$$
$$0,\ \pi,\ \frac{\pi}{3},\ \frac{2\pi}{3},\ \frac{4\pi}{3},\ \frac{5\pi}{3}$$

h)
$$4\sin^2 x=2-\cos^2 2x$$
$$\cos^2 2x=2(1-2\sin^2 x)$$
$$\cos^2 2x=2\cos^2 2x$$
$$\cos 2x=0$$

$$2x=\frac{\pi}{2} \quad , \quad 2x=\frac{3\pi}{2}$$
$$x=\frac{\pi}{4} \qquad x=\frac{3\pi}{4}$$
$$2x=\frac{\pi}{2}+2\pi=\frac{5\pi}{2},\ 2x=\frac{3\pi}{2}+2x=\frac{7\pi}{2}$$
$$x=\frac{5\pi}{4} \qquad x=\frac{7\pi}{4}$$
$$\frac{\pi}{4},\ \frac{3\pi}{4},\ \frac{5\pi}{4},\ \frac{7\pi}{4}$$

i)
$$\cos 4x+2\cos^2 2x=2$$
$$\cos 4x+2\left(\frac{1+\cos 4x}{2}\right)=2$$
$$\cos 4x=\frac{1}{2}$$

$$4x=\frac{\pi}{3}+2\pi n \quad \text{or} \quad 4x=\frac{5\pi}{3}+2\pi n$$
$$4x=\frac{\pi}{3},\ \frac{7\pi}{3},\ \frac{13\pi}{3},\ \frac{19\pi}{3} \qquad 4x=\frac{5\pi}{3},\ \frac{11\pi}{3},\ \frac{17\pi}{3},\ \frac{23\pi}{3}$$
$$x=\frac{\pi}{12},\ \frac{7\pi}{12},\ \frac{13\pi}{12},\ \frac{19\pi}{12} \qquad x=\frac{5\pi}{12},\ \frac{11\pi}{12},\ \frac{17\pi}{12},\ \frac{23\pi}{12}$$

j)
$$\csc^2 x=2\sec 2x$$
$$\frac{2}{1-\cos 2x}=\frac{2}{\cos 2x}$$
$$1-\cos 2x=\cos 2x$$
$$\cos 2x=\frac{1}{2}$$

$$2x=\frac{\pi}{3}+2\pi n \ \text{or} \ 2x=\frac{5\pi}{3}+2\pi n$$
$$2x=\frac{\pi}{3},\ \frac{7\pi}{3} \qquad 2x=\frac{5\pi}{3},\ \frac{11\pi}{3}$$
$$x=\frac{\pi}{6},\ \frac{7\pi}{6} \qquad x=\frac{5\pi}{6},\ \frac{11\pi}{6}$$

3. a)

$$\cot x - \tan x = \frac{4\cos^2 x - 2}{\sin 2x}$$
$$\frac{\cos x}{\sin x} - \frac{\sin x}{\cos x} = \frac{2(2\cos^2 x - 1)}{\sin 2x}$$
$$\frac{\cos^2 x - \sin^2 x}{\sin x \cos x} = \frac{2\cos 2x}{\sin 2x}$$
$$\frac{\cos 2x}{\frac{1}{2}\sin 2x} =$$
$$\frac{2\cos 2x}{\sin 2x} =$$

b)

$$\frac{\sin 4x - \sin 2x}{\cos 4x + \cos 2x} = \tan x$$
$$\frac{2\sin 2x\cos 2x - \sin 2x}{2\cos^2 2x - 1 + \cos 2x} = \frac{\sin x}{\cos x}$$
$$\frac{\sin 2x(2\cos 2x - 1)}{(2\cos 2x - 1)(\cos 2x + 1)} =$$
$$\frac{2\sin x\cos x}{(2\cos^2 x - 1) + 1} =$$
$$\frac{2\sin x\cos x}{2\cos^2 x} =$$
$$\frac{\sin x}{\cos x} =$$

c)

$$\tan 2x = \frac{2}{\cot x - \tan x}$$
$$\frac{\sin 2x}{\cos 2x} = \frac{2}{\frac{\cos x}{\sin x} - \frac{\sin x}{\cos x}}$$
$$= \frac{2}{\frac{\cos^2 x - \sin^2 x}{\sin x \cos x}}$$
$$= \frac{2\sin x\cos x}{\cos^2 x - \sin^2 x}$$
$$= \frac{\sin 2x}{\cos 2x}$$

d)

$$\frac{\cot x - \cos x}{1 - \sin x} = \frac{\sin 2x}{1 - \cos 2x}$$
$$\frac{\frac{\cos x}{\sin x} - \cos x}{1 - \sin x} = \frac{2\sin x \cos x}{1 - (1 - 2\sin^2 x)}$$
$$\frac{\cos x - \sin x \cos x}{\sin x(1 - \sin x)} = \frac{2\sin x \cos x}{2\sin^2 x}$$
$$\frac{\cos x(1 - \sin x)}{\sin x(1 - \sin x)} = \frac{\cos x}{\sin x}$$
$$\cot x = \cot x$$

e)

$$\cot 2x = \frac{\cot^2 x - 1}{2\cot x}$$
$$\frac{\cos 2x}{\sin 2x} = \frac{\tan x}{2}\left(\frac{\cos^2 x}{\sin^2 x} - 1\right)$$
$$= \frac{\sin x}{2\cos x}\left(\frac{\cos^2 x - \sin^2 x}{\sin^2 x}\right)$$
$$= \frac{\cos^2 x - \sin^2 x}{2\sin x\cos x}$$
$$= \frac{\cos 2x}{\sin 2x}$$

f)

$$\frac{\cos 2x}{1 - \sin 2x} = \frac{1 + \tan x}{1 - \tan x}$$
$$= \frac{1 + \frac{\sin x}{\cos x}}{1 - \frac{\sin x}{\cos x}}$$
$$= \frac{\frac{\cos x + \sin x}{\cos x}}{\frac{\cos x - \sin x}{\cos x}}$$
$$= \frac{(\cos x + \sin x)(\cos x - \sin x)}{(\cos x - \sin x)(\cos x - \sin x)}$$
$$= \frac{\cos^2 x - \sin^2 x}{\cos^2 x - 2\sin x \cos x + \sin^2 x}$$
$$= \frac{\cos 2x}{1 - \sin 2x}$$

4.

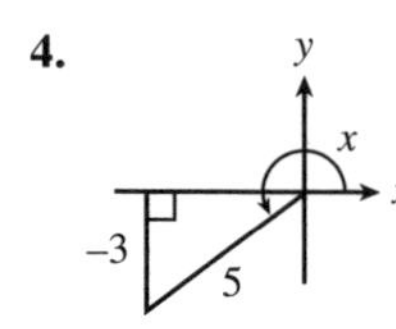

$$a^2 + (-3)^2 = 5^2$$
$$a = -4$$

a) $\sin 2x = 2\sin x\cos x$

$$= 2\left(-\frac{3}{5}\right)\left(-\frac{4}{5}\right) = \frac{24}{25}$$

b) $\cos 2x = 1 - 2\sin^2 x$

$$= 1 - 2\left(-\frac{3}{5}\right)^2 = \frac{7}{25}$$

c) $\tan 2x = \frac{2\tan x}{1 - \tan^2 x}$

$$= \frac{2\left(\frac{3}{4}\right)}{1 - \left(-\frac{3}{4}\right)^2} = \frac{24}{7}$$

5.

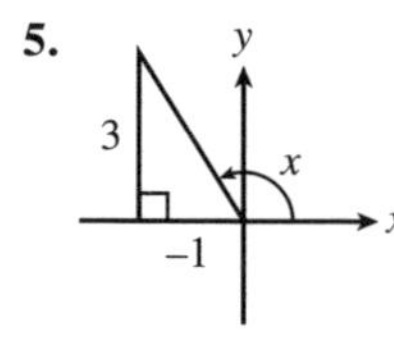

$$r^2 = (-1)^2 + 3^2$$
$$r = \sqrt{10}$$

a) $\sin 2x = 2\sin x\cos x$

$$= 2\left(\frac{3}{\sqrt{10}}\right)\left(-\frac{1}{\sqrt{10}}\right) = -\frac{3}{5}$$

b) $\cos 2x = 2\cos^2 x - 1$

$$= 2\left(-\frac{1}{\sqrt{10}}\right)^2 - 1 = -\frac{4}{5}$$

c) $\sec 2x = \frac{1}{\cos 2x}$

$$= \frac{1}{-\frac{4}{5}} = -\frac{5}{4}$$

6.

$$\cos 3x = \cos(2x + x)$$
$$= \cos 2x\cos x - \sin 2x\sin x$$
$$= (2\cos^2 x - 1)\cos x - 2\sin^2 x\cos x$$
$$= \cos x(2\cos^2 x - 1) - 2\cos x(1 - \cos^2 x)$$
$$= 2\cos^3 x - \cos x - 2\cos x + 2\cos^3 x$$
$$= 4\cos^3 x - 3\cos x$$

7.

$$\cos 4x = \cos(2x + 2x)$$
$$= \cos 2x\cos 2x - \sin 2x\sin 2x$$
$$= (2\cos^2 x - 1)^2 - (2\sin x\cos x)^2$$
$$= 4\cos^4 x - 4\cos^2 x + 1 - 4\sin^2 x\cos^2 x$$
$$= 4\cos^4 x - 4\cos^2 x + 1 - 4\cos^2 x(1 - \cos^2 x)$$
$$= 4\cos^4 x - 4\cos^2 x + 1 - 4\cos^2 x + 4\cos^4 x$$
$$= 8\cos^4 x - 8\cos^2 x + 1$$

8. $\sin 5x = \sin(x+4x)$

$= \sin x\cos 4x + \cos x \sin 4x$

$= \sin x(1-2\sin^2 2x) + \cos x(2\sin 2x\cos 2x)$

$= \sin x - 2\sin x\sin^2 2x + 2\cos x\sin 2x\cos 2x$

$= \sin x - 2\sin x(2\sin x\cos x)^2 + 2\cos x(2\sin x\cos x)(1-2\sin^2 x)$

$= \sin x - 8\sin^3 x(1-\sin^2 x) + 4\sin x(1-\sin^2 x)(1-2\sin^2 x)$

$= \sin x - 8\sin^3 x + 8\sin^5 x + 4\sin x - 12\sin^3 x + 8\sin^5 x$

$= 16\sin^5 x - 20\sin^3 x + 5\sin x$

9. $\tan^4 x = \tan^2 x \cdot \tan^2 x$

$= \left(\dfrac{1-\cos 2x}{1+\cos 2x}\right)^2$

$= \dfrac{1-2\cos 2x+\cos^2 2x}{1+2\cos 2x+\cos^2 2x}$

$= \dfrac{1-2\cos 2x+\left(\dfrac{1+\cos 4x}{2}\right)}{1+2\cos 2x+\left(\dfrac{1+\cos 4x}{2}\right)}$

$= \dfrac{3-4\cos 2x+\cos 4x}{3+4\cos 2x+\cos 4x}$

10. $\sin^2 x\cos^4 x$

$(1-\cos^2 x)\left(\dfrac{1+\cos 2x}{2}\right)^2$

$\dfrac{(1-\cos x)(1+\cos x)(1+2\cos 2x+\cos^2 2x)}{4}$

$\dfrac{(1-\cos x)(1+\cos x)\left(1+2\cos 2x+\dfrac{1+\cos 4x}{2}\right)}{4}$

$\dfrac{1}{8}(1-\cos x)(1+\cos x)(3+4\cos 2x+\cos 4x)$

11. $\sin^4 x+\cos^4 x = \left(\dfrac{1-\cos 2x}{2}\right)^2 + \left(\dfrac{1+\cos 2x}{2}\right)^2 =$

$\dfrac{1-2\cos 2x+\cos^2 2x+1+2\cos 2x+\cos^2 2x}{4} =$

$\dfrac{2+2\cos^2 2x}{4} = \dfrac{1}{4}\left[2+2\left(\dfrac{1+\cos 4x}{2}\right)\right] = \dfrac{1}{4}(3+\cos 4x)$

12. $\tan 30° = \dfrac{x+y}{12}$, $\quad \tan 15° = \dfrac{x}{12}$

$x = -y + 12\tan 30°$, $\quad x = 12\tan 15°$

$-y + 12\tan 30° = 12\tan 15°$

$y = 12\tan 30° - 12\tan 15°$

$= 3.71$

13. $\tan 2\theta = \dfrac{9}{3} = 3$ $\quad \tan\theta = \dfrac{x}{3}$

$2\theta = \tan^{-1}(3)$ $\quad x = 3\tan\theta$

$= 71.56°$ $\quad = 3\tan 35.78°$

$\theta = 35.78°$ $\quad = 2.16$

14. $\tan 2\theta = \dfrac{h}{4}$ $\quad \tan\theta = \dfrac{h}{12}$

$h = 4\tan 2\theta$ $\quad h = 12\tan\theta$

$4\tan 2\theta = 12\tan\theta$

$\dfrac{2\tan\theta}{1-\tan^2\theta} = 3\tan\theta$

$3\tan^3\theta - \tan\theta = 0$

$\tan\theta(3\tan^2\theta - 1) = 0$, reject $\tan\theta = 0$

$\tan\theta = \pm\dfrac{1}{\sqrt{3}}$, reject $\tan\theta = -\dfrac{1}{\sqrt{3}}$

$h = 12\tan\theta = 12\left(\dfrac{1}{\sqrt{3}}\right) = \dfrac{12}{\sqrt{3}}\cdot\dfrac{\sqrt{3}}{\sqrt{3}} = 4\sqrt{3} \approx 6.93$

15. $\tan 2\theta = \dfrac{40}{x}$, $\quad \tan\theta = \dfrac{15}{x}$

$x = \dfrac{40}{\tan 2\theta}$, $\quad x = \dfrac{15}{\tan\theta}$

Thus $\dfrac{40}{\tan 2\theta} = \dfrac{15}{\tan\theta}$

$\dfrac{40}{\left(\dfrac{2\tan\theta}{1-\tan^2\theta}\right)} = \dfrac{15}{\tan\theta}$

Solve for $\tan\theta$

$\dfrac{40-40\tan^2\theta}{2\tan\theta} = \dfrac{15}{\tan\theta}$

$40 - 40\tan^2\theta = 30$

$40\tan^2\theta = 10$

$\tan^2\theta = \dfrac{1}{4}$

$\tan\theta = \dfrac{1}{2}$, reject $-\dfrac{1}{2}$

Thus $x = \dfrac{15}{\tan\theta} = \dfrac{15}{\frac{1}{2}} = 30$

7.6 Chapter Review

Trigonometry (Part II) – Multiple-choice Answers

1.	**d**	6.	**a**	11.	**b**	16.	**b**	21.	**d**	26.	**a**	31.	**d**	36.	**b**	41.	**c**	46.	**b**
2.	**b**	7.	**b**	12.	**c**	17.	**c**	22.	**d**	27.	**a**	32.	**d**	37.	**a**	42.	**a**	47.	**c**
3.	**a**	8.	**a**	13.	**d**	18.	**a**	23.	**d**	28.	**c**	33.	**b**	38.	**a**	43.	**c**	48.	**d**
4.	**b**	9.	**a**	14.	**b**	19.	**b**	24.	**b**	29.	**a**	34.	**c**	39.	**d**	44.	**a**	49.	**b**
5.	**c**	10.	**d**	15.	**a**	20.	**b**	25.	**c**	30.	**a**	35.	**c**	40.	**b**	45.	**b**	50.	**b**

Trigonometry (Part II) – Multiple-choice Solutions

1. $1-\cos 2x = 1-(1-2\sin^2 x) = 1-1+2\sin^2 x = 2\sin^2 x$. Answer is d.

2. $\sin^4\theta - \cos^4\theta = (\sin^2\theta+\cos^2\theta)(\sin^2\theta-\cos^2\theta) = 1(\sin^2\theta-\cos^2\theta) = -(\cos^2\theta-\sin^2\theta) = -\cos 2\theta$. Answer is b.

3. $\cos(90°+\alpha) = \cos 90°\cos\alpha - \sin 90°\sin\alpha = 0\cdot\cos\alpha - 1\cdot\sin\alpha = -\sin\alpha$. Answer is a.

4. $4\cos\frac{1}{2}x = 1 \to \cos\frac{1}{2}x = \frac{1}{4}$. The period is $\frac{2\pi}{\frac{1}{2}} = 4\pi$, therefore, 4π requires dividing by 2, therefore $2\cdot\frac{1}{2} = 1$ solution. Answer is b.

5. $\tan(x+y) - \tan x\tan y\tan(x+y) = \tan(x+y)(1-\tan x\tan y) = \frac{(\tan x+\tan y)}{1-\tan x\tan y}(1-\tan x\tan y) = \tan x+\tan y$. Answer is c.

6. $\frac{\sin 2x}{1+\cos 2x} = \frac{2\sin x\cos x}{1+(2\cos^2 x-1)} = \frac{2\sin x\cos x}{2\cos^2 x} = \frac{\sin x}{\cos x} = \tan x$. Answer is a.

7. $\frac{\sin 6x}{\sin 3x} = \frac{2\sin 3x\cos 3x}{\sin 3x} = 2\cos 3x$. Answer is b.

8. $\sin 2A = 2\sin A\cos A$, therefore, $\cos\frac{x}{3}\sin\frac{x}{3} = \frac{1}{2}\sin\frac{2x}{3}$. Answer is a.

9. $\sin^2 x+\cos^2 x+\cot^2 x = 1+\cot^2 x = \csc^2 x$. Answer is a.

10. $-1-\cos^2 x+\sin^2 x = -\cos^2 x-\cos^2 x = -2\cos^2 x$. Answer is d.

11. $\cos(2x+\pi) = \cos 2x\cos\pi - \sin 2x\sin\pi = \cos 2x(-1) - \sin 2x(0) = -\cos 2x$

$2\sin^2 x-1 = -\cos 2x,\ \cos^2 x-\sin^2 x = \cos 2x,\ 1-2\cos^2 x = -\cos 2x,\ \sin^2 x-\cos^2 x = -\cos 2x$ Answer is b.

12. $\tan x$ is undefined at $\frac{\pi}{2}$ and $\frac{3\pi}{2}$, $0 \le x < 2\pi$, at these terminal values $\sin x \ne 0$, $\cos x = 0$ Answer is c.

13. $\cos 5x\sin 3x + \sin 5x\cos 3x = \sin(5x+3x) = \sin 8x$ Answer is d.

14. $f(x) = -3\sin(\pi+x) = -3\sin(\pi+0) = -3\sin\pi = -3(0) = 0$. Answer is b.

15. Graph $y = 2^x - \frac{1}{\tan x}$ on calculator and find zeros (mode radian $X(0, 2\pi)$, $Y(-10, 10)$). Answer is a.

16. Graph $y = \frac{1}{\tan x} - \sin 3x$, find crossings of x-axis (zeroes) (mode radian $X(0, 2\pi)$, $Y(-10, 10)$). Answer is b.

17. Amplitude $|-a| = a$, displacement $= -b$ therefore maximum value $a-b$. Answer is c.

18. Start at vertical displacement value of $-b$ then go down a. Answer is a.

19. $\frac{\cos^3 A-\cos A}{\sin^3 A} = \frac{\cos A(\cos^2 A-1)}{\sin^3 A} = \frac{-\cos A\cdot\sin^2 A}{\sin^3 A} = \frac{-\cos A}{\sin A} = -\cot A$. Answer is b.

20. $\frac{\sin\left(x-\frac{\pi}{2}\right)+\sin\left(\frac{\pi}{2}-x\right)}{\tan^2 x-\cot^2 x} = \frac{\sin\left[-\left(\frac{\pi}{2}-x\right)\right]+\sin\left(\frac{\pi}{2}-x\right)}{-1} = \frac{-\cos x+\cos x}{-1} = \frac{0}{-1} = 0$. Answer is b.

21. $\frac{\csc x}{\cos x} = \frac{1}{\sin x\cdot\cos x}$, denominator must not be zero. Answer is d.

22. $\cos(A+B) = \cos A\cos B - \sin A\sin B$, therefore, $\cos\frac{x}{4}\cos\frac{x}{3} - \sin\frac{x}{4}\sin\frac{x}{3} = \cos\left(\frac{x}{4}+\frac{x}{3}\right) = \cos\frac{7x}{12}$. Answer is d.

23. $\cos^2 x = \frac{1}{a} \to \cos x = \pm\frac{1}{\sqrt{a}}$; Each trig. function is positive in 2 quadrants and negative in 2 quadrants. Answer is d.

24. $(a\sin\theta - a)(\tan^3\theta - b) = 0 \to \sin\theta = 1$ or $\tan\theta = \sqrt[3]{b}$, $\sin\theta = 1$ at $\frac{\pi}{2}$, one solution, tangent is positive in quadrants I and III, therefore, 3 total solutions. Answer is b.

25. $(2\sin 3x-1)(\cos 2x+1)=0 \rightarrow \sin 3x=\frac{1}{2}$ or $\cos 2x=-1$ $\sin 3x=\frac{1}{2}$. Sine has a value of $\frac{1}{2}$ in quadrants I, II. Since the period is $\frac{2\pi}{3}$, to go to 2π requires multiplying $\frac{2\pi}{3}$ by 3, therefore, $2\times 3=6$ solutions. $\cos 2x=-1$. Cosine has a value of -1 only at π. Since the period is $\frac{2\pi}{2}=\pi$, to go to 2π requires multiplying π by 2, therefore, $1\times 2=2$ solutions. Total of 8 solutions. Answer is c.

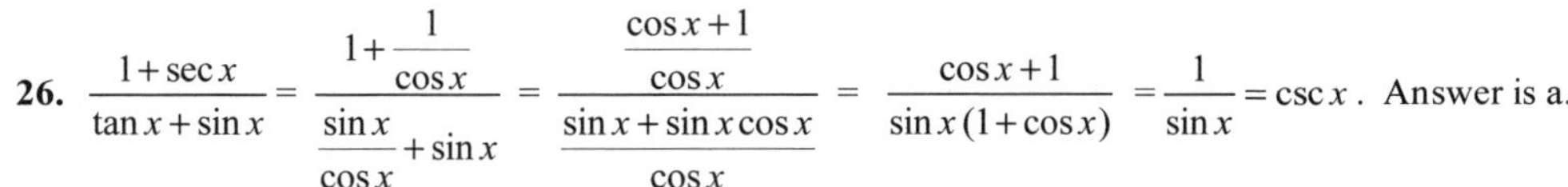

26. $\frac{1+\sec x}{\tan x+\sin x}=\frac{1+\frac{1}{\cos x}}{\frac{\sin x}{\cos x}+\sin x}=\frac{\frac{\cos x+1}{\cos x}}{\frac{\sin x+\sin x\cos x}{\cos x}}=\frac{\cos x+1}{\sin x(1+\cos x)}=\frac{1}{\sin x}=\csc x$. Answer is a.

27. $\frac{\cos x}{1-\sin x}-\frac{1}{\cos x}=\frac{\cos^2 x-1+\sin x}{\cos x(1-\sin x)}=\frac{-\sin^2 x+\sin x}{\cos x(1-\sin x)}=\frac{\sin x(1-\sin x)}{\cos x(1-\sin x)}=\tan x$. Answer is a.

28. A cosecant graph is a reciprocal of the sine graph, therefore, where sine equals zero, cosecant is undefined.

For $y=-2\csc\frac{\pi}{4}x+1$, $Period=\frac{2\pi}{\frac{\pi}{4}}=8$, *Amplitude of sine*: $|-2|=2$, *Vertical displacement* $=1$.

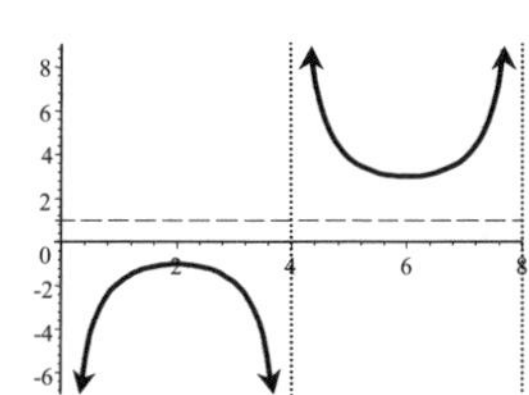

- Graph is undefined when $x=0$, 4, 8.
- Graph has a maximum of -1 when $x=2$, and a minimum of 3 when $x=6$, but $x\neq 6$
- Therefore, the range for $4\leq x<6$ is $y>3$.

Answer is c

29. $\sin 2x=1$, sine equals 1 at $\frac{\pi}{2}$, therefore, $2x=\frac{\pi}{2}+2n\pi \rightarrow x=\frac{\pi}{4}+n\pi$, n an integer. Answer is a.

30. By the double angle identity, $y=1-2\sin^2 6x=\cos 12x$, $P=\frac{2\pi}{12}=\frac{\pi}{6}$. Answer is a.

31. $\frac{\csc^2 x-1}{\sec^2 x-1}=\frac{\frac{1}{\sin^2 x}-1}{\frac{1}{\cos^2 x}-1}=\frac{\frac{1-\sin^2 x}{\sin^2 x}}{\frac{1-\cos^2 x}{\cos^2 x}}=\frac{\cos^2 x}{\sin^2 x}\cdot\frac{\cos^2 x}{\sin^2 x}=\frac{\cos^4 x}{\sin^4 x}=\cot^4 x$. Answer is d.

32. $\frac{\cot x}{2+3\cos x}=\frac{\cos x}{\sin x(2+3\cos x)}$, therefore, restrictions are $\sin x\neq 0$, $\cos x\neq -\frac{2}{3}$. Answer is d.

33. $a\sin x+b=0 \rightarrow \sin x=-\frac{b}{a}$, since $0<a<b$, $\frac{b}{a}>1$, therefore no solutions $a\tan x+a=0\rightarrow \tan x=-1$, therefore 2 solutions

$a\sec x-b=0\rightarrow \sec x=\frac{b}{a}$ since $0<a<b$, $\frac{b}{a}>1$, therefore 2 solutions for a total of 4 solutions. Answer is b.

34. $8\sin^2 6x-4=-4(1-2\sin^2 6x)=-4\cos 2(6x)=-4\cos 12x$. Answer is c.

35. Period $=\frac{2\pi}{|b|}$, $b>0 \rightarrow P=\frac{2\pi}{b}$ Therefore minimum value occurs $\frac{1}{2}$ a period away at $\frac{\pi}{b}$. Answer is c.

36. $\sin A\cos B+\cos A\sin B=\sin(A+B)=\sin(90^\circ-B+B)=\sin 90^\circ=1$. Answer is b.

37. $\sec(\pi-x)=\frac{1}{\cos(\pi-x)}=\frac{1}{\cos\pi\cos x+\sin\pi\sin x}=\frac{1}{-\cos x}=-\sec x$. Answer is a.

38. $y=-4\sin 6x\cos 6x=-2\sin 2(6x)=-2\sin 12x$, amplitude $|-2|=2$ therefore range is $-2\leq y\leq 2$. Answer is a.

39. $\frac{\csc^2 x+\sec^2 x}{\csc^2 x-\sec^2 x}=\frac{\frac{1}{\sin^2 x}+\frac{1}{\cos^2 x}}{\frac{1}{\sin^2 x}-\frac{1}{\cos^2 x}}=\frac{\frac{\cos^2 x+\sin^2 x}{\sin^2 x\cos^2 x}}{\frac{\cos^2 x-\sin^2 x}{\sin^2 x\cos^2 x}}=\frac{\cos^2 x+\sin^2 x}{\cos^2 x-\sin^2 x}=\frac{1}{\cos 2x}=\sec 2x$. Answer is d.

40. $\cos(A+B)=\cos A\cdot\cos B-\sin A\cdot\sin B$

Therefore, $\cos\left(\frac{\pi}{6}+x\right)\cdot\cos\left(\frac{\pi}{6}-x\right)-\sin\left(\frac{\pi}{6}+x\right)\cdot\sin\left(\frac{\pi}{6}-x\right)=\cos\left[\left(\frac{\pi}{6}+x\right)+\left(\frac{\pi}{6}-x\right)\right]=\cos\frac{\pi}{3}=\frac{1}{2}$, Answer is b.

41. $y=6\sin x\cos^3 x+6\sin^3 x\cos x=6\sin x\cos x(\cos^2+\sin^2 x)=6\sin x\cos x=3\sin 2x$ $A=3$, $B=2$. Answer is c.

42. $\frac{\sin A}{1+\cos A}-\frac{1-\cos A}{\sin A}=\frac{\sin^2 A-1+\cos^2 A}{\sin A(1+\cos A)}=\frac{1-1}{\sin A(1+\cos A)}=0$. Answer is a.

43. 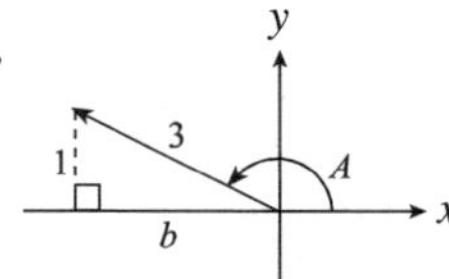

$b^2+1^2=3^2$ $b=-\sqrt{8}=-2\sqrt{2}$, then $\cos A=\dfrac{-2\sqrt{2}}{3}$

Therefore, $\sin 2A=2\sin A\cos A=2\left(\dfrac{1}{3}\right)\left(\dfrac{-2\sqrt{2}}{3}\right)=\dfrac{-4\sqrt{2}}{9}$. Answer is c.

44. $\sin A=\dfrac{-3}{5}$, therefore, by Pythagoras Theorem, $\cos A=\dfrac{4}{5}$ in quadrant IV $\cos B=\dfrac{3}{5}$, therefore, by Pythagoras Theorem, $\sin B=\dfrac{-4}{5}$ in quadrant IV $\sin(A+B)=\sin A\cdot\cos B+\cos A\cdot\sin B=\left(\dfrac{-3}{5}\right)\left(\dfrac{3}{5}\right)+\left(\dfrac{4}{5}\right)\left(\dfrac{-4}{5}\right)=\dfrac{-9}{25}-\dfrac{16}{25}=-1$. Answer is a.

45. Tangent has a value of $-\sqrt{3}$ at $\dfrac{2\pi}{3}$ and $\dfrac{5\pi}{3}$ which is π distance apart. Therefore, $bx=\dfrac{2\pi}{3}+n\pi\rightarrow x=\dfrac{2\pi}{3b}+\dfrac{n\pi}{b}$. Answer is b.

46. $\cos\left(x+\dfrac{\pi}{2}\right)-\cos\left(x-\dfrac{\pi}{2}\right)=\left(\cos x\cos\dfrac{\pi}{2}-\sin x\sin\dfrac{\pi}{2}\right)-\left(\cos x\cos\dfrac{\pi}{2}+\sin x\sin\dfrac{\pi}{2}\right)=(0-\sin x)-(0+\sin x)=-2\sin x$. Answer is b.

47. $8\sin^4 x+2\sin^2 x-1=0\rightarrow(4\sin^2 x-1)(2\sin^2 x+1)=0\rightarrow\sin x=\pm\dfrac{1}{2}$, $\sin x=\pm\sqrt{\dfrac{-1}{2}}$ (reject)

$\sin x=\pm\dfrac{1}{2}$ at 30°, 150°, 210°, 330°, $\sin x=\pm\sqrt{\dfrac{-1}{2}}$, ϕ. Answer is c.

48. $(\sin x-\cos x)^2-(\sin x+\cos x)^2=(\sin^2 x-2\sin x\cos x+\cos^2 x)-(\sin x^2+2\sin x\cos x+\cos^2 x)$

$=1-2\sin x\cos x-1-2\sin x\cos x=-4\sin x\cos x=-2\sin 2x$. Answer is d.

49. cosine has value $-\dfrac{1}{2}$ at $\dfrac{2\pi}{3}$ and $\dfrac{4\pi}{3}$, therefore, $2x=\dfrac{2\pi}{3}+2n\pi$, $2x=\dfrac{4\pi}{3}+2n\pi$ $x=\dfrac{\pi}{3}+n\pi$, $x=\dfrac{2\pi}{3}+n\pi$ Answer is b.

50. $\cos x+2\cos^2 x=0\rightarrow\cos x(1+2\cos x)=0\rightarrow\cos x=0,\ -\dfrac{1}{2}$ $\cos x=0$ at $\dfrac{\pi}{2}+n\pi$, $\cos x=-\dfrac{1}{2}$ at $\dfrac{2\pi}{3}+2n\pi$ and $\dfrac{4\pi}{3}+2n\pi$. Answer is b.

Conics - Solutions

8.1 Plane Geometry Formulas

1. a) $d=\sqrt{(-3-6)^2+(5+2)^2}=\sqrt{130}\approx 11.40$ **b)** $d=\sqrt{(1.3+4.5)^2+(4.7+2.8)^2}=\sqrt{33.64+56.25}=\sqrt{89.89}\approx 9.48$

c) $d=\sqrt{\left(\frac{1}{4}+3\right)^2+\left(-2+\frac{1}{3}\right)^2}=\sqrt{10.5625+2.7778}=\sqrt{13.3403}\approx 3.65$

d) $d=\sqrt{(4\sqrt{2}-\sqrt{2})^2+(-3\sqrt{3}+\sqrt{3})^2}=\sqrt{18+12}=\sqrt{30}\approx 5.48$

2. a) $M=\left(\frac{5-5}{2},\frac{-2-2}{2}\right)=(0,-2)$ **b)** $M=\left(\frac{\frac{3}{5}+\frac{1}{2}}{2},\frac{\frac{2}{3}-3}{2}\right)=\left(\frac{11}{20},\frac{-7}{6}\right)$ **c)** $M=\left(\frac{-7+7}{2},\frac{4-4}{2}\right)=(0,0)$ **d)** $M=\left(\frac{a+c}{2},\frac{-b+d}{2}\right)$

3. a) $4=\frac{x+2}{2}\to x=6,\ 6=\frac{y+5}{2}\to y=7,\ B(6,7)$ **b)** $-4=\frac{x+1}{2}\to x=-9,\ 5=\frac{y-6}{2}\to y=16,\ B(-9,16)$

c) $4=\frac{x+4}{2}\to x=4,\ 4=\frac{y-4}{2}\to y=12,\ B(4,12)$ **d)** $0=\frac{x-6}{2}\to x=6,\ 0=\frac{y+3}{2}\to y=-3,\ B(6,-3)$

4. a) $m=\frac{5-(-5)}{-3-1}=\frac{10}{-4}=-\frac{5}{2};\ y=mx+b\to 5=-\frac{5}{2}(-3)+b\to b=-\frac{5}{2};\ y=-\frac{5}{2}x-\frac{5}{2}$ or $5x+2y=-5$

b) $m=\frac{-\sqrt{2}+5\sqrt{2}}{\sqrt{2}+3\sqrt{2}}=\frac{4\sqrt{2}}{4\sqrt{2}}=1$

$y-y_1=m(x-x_1)\to y+\sqrt{2}=1\cdot(x-\sqrt{2})\to y+\sqrt{2}=x-\sqrt{2}\to x-y=2\sqrt{2}$ or $y=x-2\sqrt{2}$

5. a) Method 1: Using the distance formula

Call a point on the line (x,y)
Let the distance from $(-5,3)$ to (x,y) be d_1
Let the distance from $(7,2)$ to (x,y) be d_2

$$\begin{aligned}d_1&=d_2\\d_1^2&=d_2^2\\(x+5)^2+(y-3)^2&=(x-7)^2+(y-2)^2\\x^2+10x+25+y^2-6y+9&=x^2-14x+49+y^2-4y+4\\10x-6y+34&=-14x-4y+53\\24x-2y=19 &\text{ or } y=12x-\frac{19}{2}\end{aligned}$$

Method 2: Using midpoint, slope of perpendicular, and equation of a line
Find the perpendicular bisector of the line that connects the points
Midpoint $=\left(\frac{-5+7}{2},\frac{3+2}{2}\right)=\left(1,\frac{5}{2}\right)$; Slope $m=\frac{3-2}{-5-7}=-\frac{1}{12},\ m_\perp=12$
$y-\frac{5}{2}=12(x-1)\to 2y-5=24x-24\to 24x-2y=19$ or $y=12x-\frac{19}{2}$

b) Method 1: Using the distance formula

Call a point on the line (x,y)
Let the distance from $(2,-6)$ to (x,y) be d_1
Let the distance from $(-8,-2)$ to (x,y) be d_2

$$\begin{aligned}d_1&=d_2\\d_1^2&=d_2^2\\(x-2)^2+(y+6)^2&=(x+8)^2+(y+2)^2\\x^2-4x+4+y^2+12y+36&=x^2+16x+64+y^2+4y+4\\-4x+12y+40&=16x+4y+68\\20x-8y&=-28\\5x-2y=-7 &\text{ or } y=\frac{5}{2}x+\frac{7}{2}\end{aligned}$$

Method 2: Using midpoint, slope of perpendicular, and equation of a line
Find the perpendicular bisector of the line that connects the points
Midpoint $=\left(\frac{2-8}{2},\frac{-6-2}{2}\right)=(-3,-4)$; Slope $m=\frac{-6+2}{2+8}=-\frac{2}{5},\ m_\perp=\frac{5}{2}$
$y+4=\frac{5}{2}(x+3)\to 2y+8=5x+15\to 5x-2y=-7$ or $y=\frac{5}{2}x+\frac{7}{2}$

6. a) $AC=\sqrt{(14-6)^2+(-1+1)^2}=8,\ AB=\sqrt{(14-10)^2+(-1+7)^2}=\sqrt{52},\ BC=\sqrt{(10-6)^2+(-7+1)^2}=\sqrt{52}$
$AB=BC$, therefore triangle ABC is isosceles.

b) $m_{DE}=\frac{5-2}{-1+3}=\frac{3}{2},\ m_{DF}=\frac{2-4}{-3+6}=-\frac{2}{3},\ m_{EF}=\frac{5-4}{-1+6}=\frac{1}{5}$
m_{DE} and m_{DF} are negative reciprocals of each other, therefore triangle DEF is a right triangle, with $\angle D=90°$.

7. Midpoint $\left(\frac{2+0}{2},\frac{6+0}{2}\right)=(1,3)$ $d=\sqrt{(1+0)^2+(3-0)^2}=\sqrt{10}$
Midpoint $\left(\frac{9+0}{2},\frac{-3+0}{2}\right)=\left(\frac{9}{2},-\frac{3}{2}\right)$ $d=\sqrt{\left(\frac{9}{2}-0\right)^2+\left(-\frac{3}{2}-0\right)^2}=\sqrt{\frac{81}{4}+\frac{9}{4}}=\sqrt{\frac{90}{4}}=\frac{\sqrt{90}}{2}$
Area $=DB\times DE=\sqrt{10}\times\frac{\sqrt{90}}{2}=\frac{\sqrt{900}}{2}=\frac{30}{2}=15$

8. Method 1: $M_{AC}=\left(\frac{7+3}{2},\frac{5+11}{2}\right)=(5,8),\ M_{BC}=\left(\frac{7+5}{2},\frac{11+7}{2}\right)=(6,9);\ MN=\sqrt{(5-6)^2+(8-9)^2}=\sqrt{2}$
Method 2: recognize $MN=\frac{1}{2}AB$ $AB=\sqrt{(3-5)^2+(5-7)^2}=\sqrt{4+4}=\sqrt{8}=2\sqrt{2}\to MN=\frac{1}{2}(2\sqrt{2})=\sqrt{2}$

8.2 Circles

1. **a)** $C(0,0); r = 5$ **b)** $C(0,0); r = \sqrt{7}$ **c)** $C(-2,3); r = 4$ **d)** $C(-3,0); r = 3$

2. **a)** $x^2 + y^2 = 9$ **b)** $(x+3)^2 + (y-4)^2 = 25$ **c)** $(x+4)^2 + (y+2)^2 = 7$ **d)** $x^2 + (y+3)^2 = 5$

3. **a)**

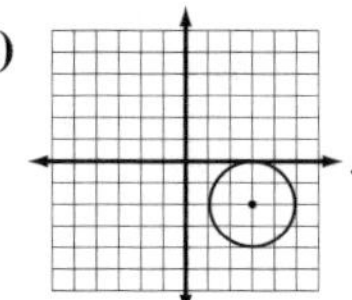

Centre: $(3, -2)$

Radius: 2

b)

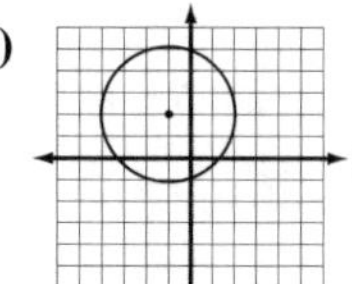

Centre: $(-1, 2)$

Radius: $\sqrt{10}$

4. **a)** $x^2 + y^2 - 2y + 6x + 1 = 0$

$(x^2 + 6x + \_\_) + (y^2 - 2y + \_\_) = -1$

$(x^2 + 6x + 9) + (y^2 - 2y + 1) = -1 + 9 + 1$

$(x+3)^2 + (y-1)^2 = 9$

Therefore $C(-3,1)$, $r = 3$

b) $2x^2 + 2y^2 + 4x - 8y + 2 = 0$

$x^2 + y^2 + 2x - 4y + 1 = 0$

$(x^2 + 2x + \_\_) + (y^2 - 4y + \_\_) = -1$

$(x^2 + 2x + 1) + (y^2 - 4y + 4) = -1 + 1 + 4$

$(x+1)^2 + (y-2)^2 = 4$

Therefore $C(-1,2)$, $r = 2$

c) $9x^2 + 9y^2 + 6x - 6y - 142 = 0$

$x^2 + y^2 + \frac{2}{3}x - \frac{2}{3}y - \frac{142}{9} = 0$

$\left(x^2 + \frac{2}{3}x + \_\_\right) + \left(y^2 - \frac{2}{3}y + \_\_\right) = \frac{142}{9}$

$\left(x^2 + \frac{2}{3}x + \frac{1}{9}\right) + \left(y^2 - \frac{2}{3}y + \frac{1}{9}\right) = \frac{142}{9} + \frac{1}{9} + \frac{1}{9}$

$\left(x + \frac{1}{3}\right)^2 + \left(y - \frac{1}{3}\right)^2 = 16$

Therefore $C\left(-\frac{1}{3}, \frac{1}{3}\right)$, $r = 4$

d) $4x^2 - 12x + 4y^2 - 30 = 0$

$x^2 - 3x + y^2 - \frac{15}{2} = 0$

$(x^2 - 3x + \_\_) + y^2 = \frac{15}{2}$

$\left(x^2 - 3x + \frac{9}{4}\right) + y^2 = \frac{15}{2} + \frac{9}{4}$

$\left(x - \frac{3}{2}\right)^2 + y^2 = \frac{39}{4}$

Therefore $C\left(\frac{3}{2}, 0\right)$, $r = \frac{\sqrt{39}}{2}$

5. **a)** $(x-1)^2 + (y+3)^2 = 9$

$x^2 - 2x + 1 + y^2 + 6y + 9 = 9$

$x^2 + y^2 - 2x + 6y + 1 = 0$

b) $(x+2)^2 + (y-4)^2 = 7$

$x^2 + 4x + 4 + y^2 - 8y + 16 = 7$

$x^2 + y^2 + 4x - 8y + 13 = 0$

6. New centre is $(-4, 1)$ and new radius is 5. Therefore $(x+4)^2 + (y-1)^2 = 25$.

7. Centre = midpoint of the diameter $\left(\frac{2-4}{2}, \frac{-7+1}{2}\right) = (-1, -3)$; radius $r = \sqrt{(2-(-1))^2 + (-7-(-3))^2} = \sqrt{9+16} = 5$
Therefore $(x+1)^2 + (y+3)^2 = 25$

8. $x^2 + y^2 - 2x + 4y + k = 0$

$(x^2 - 2x + \_\_) + (y^2 + 4y + \_\_) = -k$

$(x^2 - 2x + 1) + (y^2 + 4y + 4) = -k + 1 + 4$

$(x-1)^2 + (y+2)^2 = -k + 5$

Therefore $-k + 5 = 16 \rightarrow k = -11$

9. $(m+4)^2 = 9^2 \rightarrow m + 4 = \pm 9 \rightarrow m = 5$ or -13

10. $\begin{aligned} 3x + y &= 1 \\ 2x + 3y &= -4 \end{aligned} \rightarrow \begin{aligned} -3(3x + y &= 1) \\ 2x + 3y &= -4 \end{aligned} \rightarrow \begin{aligned} -9x - 3y &= -3 \\ 2x + 3y &= -4 \\ \hline -7x \quad &= -7 \end{aligned} \rightarrow x = 1 \rightarrow \begin{aligned} 3x + y &= 1 \\ 3(1) + y &= 1 \\ y &= -2 \end{aligned}$ $C(1, -2)$, $r = 5$ $(x-1)^2 + (y+2)^2 = 25$

11. The distance from the centre of the circle $(0, y)$ to $(1, 5)$ = the distance from $(0, y)$ to $(7, 4)$. Both are radii.
$r_1 = r_2 \rightarrow r_1^2 = r_2^2 \rightarrow (0-1)^2 + (y-5)^2 = (0-7)^2 + (y-4)^2 \rightarrow 1 + y^2 - 10y + 25 = 49 + y^2 - 8y + 16 \rightarrow$
$-10y + 26 = 65 - 8y \rightarrow y = -\frac{39}{2}$ Therefore $C\left(0, -\frac{39}{2}\right)$

12. The centre is $(2, 6)$ so $(x-2)^2 + (y-6)^2 = r^2$. The tangent is $y = x + 2$, which has slope 1; the radius, perpendicular to the tangent has slope -1. Therefore $y - 6 = -1(x-2)$ is the equation of the radius, which simplifies to $y = -x + 8$. This intersects $y = x + 2$ at $-x + 8 = x + 2 \rightarrow x = 3$, so the tangent point is $(3, 5)$. The distance to the centre $(2, 6)$ is $r = \sqrt{(3-2)^2 + (5-6)^2} = \sqrt{2}$. Therefore the equation of the circle is $(x-2)^2 + (y-6)^2 = 2$.

13. Take the midpoint of $(-12, 0)$ and $(2, 0)$ which is $x = -5$. Take the midpoint of $(0, -2)$ and $(0, 12)$ which is $y = 5$. $(-5, 5)$ is the centre of the circle. The distance from $(-5, 5)$ to any of the four points will give the radius.. Using $(2, 0) \rightarrow r = \sqrt{(2-(-5))^2 + (0-5)^2} = \sqrt{74}$. Therefore the equation of the circle is $(x+5)^2 + (y-5)^2 = 74$

8.3 Parabolas

1. **a)** $(0,0),\ (0,4),\ y=-4,\ x=0$ **b)** $(0,0),\ (-4,0),\ x=4,\ y=0$ **c)** $(0,-2),\ (4,-2),\ x=-4,\ y=-2$

d) $(0,-3),\ (0,-5),\ y=-1,\ x=0$ **e)** $(2,-1),\ (2,-4),\ y=2,\ x=2$ **f)** $(-2,1),\ (-5,1),\ x=1,\ y=1$

2. **a)** $4p(y-0)=(x-0)^2 \rightarrow 4py=x^2,\ p=-4 \rightarrow -16y=x^2$ **b)** $4p(y+5)=(x-3)^2,\ p=-4 \rightarrow -16(y+5)=(x-3)^2$

c) Vertex $(2,3),\ p=3 \rightarrow 4p(x-2)=(y-3)^2 \rightarrow 12(x-2)=(y-3)^2$

d) Vertex $(-2,-1),\ p=2 \rightarrow 4p(y+1)=(x+2)^2 \rightarrow 8(y+1)=(x+2)^2$

e) $4p(y-1)=(x-3)^2$; Using point $(2,3)$ (also okay to use $(4,3)$): $4p(3-1)=(2-3)^2 \rightarrow 8p=1 \rightarrow p=\frac{1}{8}$

$4(\frac{1}{8})(y-1)=(x-3)^2 \rightarrow \frac{1}{2}(y-1)=(x-3)^2$

f) $4p(x-3)=(y+2)^2$; Using point $(5,2)$ (also okay to use $(5,-6)$): $4p(5-3)=(2+2)^2 \rightarrow 8p=16 \rightarrow p=2$

$8(x-3)=(y+2)^2$

3. **a)** $y=x^2+4x+9 \rightarrow y-9=x^2+4x+\_\_ \rightarrow y-9+4=x^2+4x+4 \rightarrow y-5=(x+2)^2,\ p=\frac{1}{4}$

Vertex: $(-2,5)$; Focus: $(-2,5\frac{1}{4})$; Directrix: $y=4\frac{3}{4}$; Axis of Symmetry: $x=-2$

b) $y=-\frac{1}{8}x^2-x-3 \rightarrow y+3=-\frac{1}{8}(x^2+8x+\_\_) \rightarrow y+3-2=-\frac{1}{8}(x^2+8x+16) \rightarrow y+1=-\frac{1}{8}(x+4)^2,\ p=-2$

Vertex: $(-4,1)$; Focus: $(-4,-3)$; Directrix: $y=1$; Axis of Symmetry: $x=-4$

c) $4y=x^2+6x+5 \rightarrow 4y-5=x^2+6x+\_\_ \rightarrow 4y-5+9=x^2+6x+9 \rightarrow 4(y+1)=(x+3)^2,\ p=1$

Vertex: $(-3,-1)$; Focus: $(-3,0)$; Directrix: $y=-2$; Axis of Symmetry: $x=-3$

d) $y^2+16x-6y=7 \rightarrow y^2-6y+\_\_=-16x+7 \rightarrow y^2-6y+9=-16x+7+9 \rightarrow (y-3)^2=-16x+16 \rightarrow$

$-16(x-1)=(y-3)^2,\ p=-4$; Vertex: $(1,3)$; Focus: $(-3,3)$; Directrix: $x=5$; Axis of Symmetry: $y=3$

e) $x^2+2x+8y-15=0 \rightarrow x^2+2x+\_\_=-8y+15 \rightarrow x^2+2x+1=-8y+15+1 \rightarrow (x+1)^2=-8(y-2) \rightarrow$

$-8(y-2)=(x+1)^2,\ p=-2$; Vertex: $(-1,2)$; Focus: $(-1,0)$; Directrix: $y=4$; Axis of Symmetry: $x=-1$

f) $y^2-4y=12x+8 \rightarrow y^2-4y+\_\_=12x+8 \rightarrow y^2-4y+4=12x+8+4 \rightarrow (y-2)^2=12(x+1) \rightarrow$

$12(x+1)=(y-2)^2,\ p=3$; Vertex: $(-1,2)$; Focus: $(2,2)$; Directrix: $x=-4$; Axis of Symmetry: $y=2$

4. $-(y-4)=(x-3)^2$ flipped over $y=4$ is $y-4=(x-3)^2$; then moved down 2 units is $y-2=(x-3)^2$

5. $y-1=x^2$ has vertex $(0,1)$, $y-1=(x+4c)^2$ has vertex $(-4c,1)$; Therefore $-4c=-3 \rightarrow c=\frac{3}{4}$

6. $4p(y-k)=(x-h)^2$ because of a vertical axis of symmetry

With the vertex point $(-2,-3)$: $4p(y+3)=(x+2)^2 \rightarrow$ Using point $(1,1)$: $4p(1+3)=(1+2)^2 \rightarrow 16p=9 \rightarrow p=\frac{9}{16}$

Therefore the equation is $\frac{9}{4}(y+3)=(x+2)^2$

7. $4py=x^2$ with points $\left(-1,\frac{1}{3}\right)$ and $\left(1,\frac{1}{3}\right)$. Using point $\left(-1,\frac{1}{3}\right)$ (also okay to use $\left(1,\frac{1}{3}\right)$): $4p\left(\frac{1}{3}\right)=(-1)^2 \rightarrow \frac{4}{3}p=1 \rightarrow p=\frac{3}{4}$

Focus point is $\left(0,\frac{3}{4}\right)$

8.

$4p(y-15)=x^2$ Use either point $(-450,120)$ or $(450,120)$

$4p(120-15)=450^2 \rightarrow 420p=202\,500 \rightarrow p=\frac{202500}{420}=\frac{3375}{7}$

The equation of the parabola is $\frac{13500}{7}(y-15)=x^2$

9.

$4py=x^2 \rightarrow 4p(-192)=96^2 \rightarrow p=-12$

$-48y=x^2 \rightarrow$ 60 m above ground is at $(x,-132) \rightarrow -48(-132)=x^2 \rightarrow x\approx 79.6$

The width is $2x \rightarrow 159.2$ m

10.

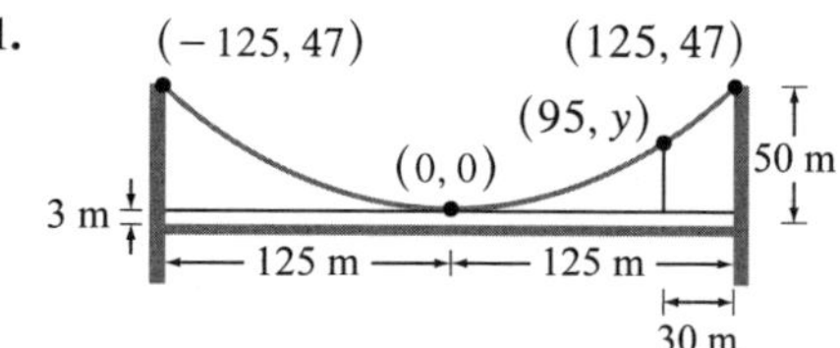

$$y = ax^2 \qquad -h = a \cdot 5^2 \qquad a = -\frac{h}{25}$$

$$y = -\frac{h}{25}x^2$$
$$-h + 5 = -\frac{h}{25} \cdot 4^2$$
$$-25h + 125 = -16h$$
$$9h = 125$$
$$h = \frac{125}{9} = 13.9 \text{ m}$$

11.

(− 125, 47) (125, 47) (95, y) (0, 0) 3 m 50 m 125 m 125 m 30 m

Let the vertex be $(0,0)$, then a point on $y = ax^2$ must be $(125, 47)$ or $(-125, 47)$.
Therefore $y = ax^2 \rightarrow 47 = a(125)^2 \rightarrow a = 0.003008 \rightarrow y = 0.003008x^2$
30 metres from the end of the parabola is 95 metres horizontally from the vertex, $(95, y)$
Therefore $y = 0.003008(95)^2 = 27.1472$ metres above the vertex.
The height of the cable 30 m from the tower is $27.1472 + 3 = 30.15$ m above the road.

8.4 Ellipses

1. **a)** $a = 6,\ c = 4,\ b^2 = a^2 - c^2 \rightarrow b^2 = 36 - 16 = 20$, therefore $\frac{x^2}{20} + \frac{y^2}{36} = 1$ **b)** $a = 5,\ b = 4$, therefore $\frac{x^2}{25} + \frac{y^2}{16} = 1$

c) $c = 4,\ a = 5,\ b^2 = a^2 - c^2 \rightarrow b^2 = 25 - 16 = 9$, therefore $\frac{x^2}{25} + \frac{y^2}{9} = 1$

d) $c = 2,\ b = 4,\ a^2 = b^2 + c^2 \rightarrow a^2 = 16 + 4 = 20$, therefore $\frac{x^2}{20} + \frac{y^2}{16} = 1$

e) $c = 4,\ \frac{2}{5} = \frac{4}{a} \rightarrow 2a = 20 \rightarrow a = 10;\ b^2 = a^2 - c^2 \rightarrow b^2 = 100 - 16 = 84$, therefore $\frac{x^2}{100} + \frac{y^2}{84} = 1$

f) $a = 6,\ \frac{2b^2}{a} = 4 \rightarrow \frac{b^2}{6} = 2 \rightarrow b^2 = 12$, therefore $\frac{x^2}{12} + \frac{y^2}{36} = 1$

2. **a)**
$$4x^2 + 9y^2 - 16x + 18y - 11 = 0$$
$$4(x^2 - 4x + \_\_) + 9(y^2 + 2y + \_\_) = 11$$
$$4(x^2 - 4x + 4) + 9(y^2 + 2y + 1) = 11 + 16 + 9$$
$$4(x-2)^2 + 9(y+1)^2 = 36$$
$$\frac{(x-2)^2}{9} + \frac{(y+1)^2}{4} = 1$$
C: $(2, -1)$ V: $(-1, -1), (5, -1)$
M: $(2, 1), (2, -3)$ F: $(2 + \sqrt{5}, -1), (2 - \sqrt{5}, -1)$

b)
$$x^2 + 2y^2 - 10x + 8y + 29 = 0$$
$$(x^2 - 10x + \_\_) + 2(y^2 + 4y + \_\_) = -29$$
$$(x^2 - 10x + 25) + 2(y^2 + 4y + 4) = -29 + 25 + 8$$
$$(x-5)^2 + 2(y+2)^2 = 4$$
$$\frac{(x-5)^2}{4} + \frac{(y+2)^2}{2} = 1$$
C: $(5, -2)$ V: $(3, -2), (7, -2)$
M: $(5, -2 + \sqrt{2}), (5, -2 - \sqrt{2})$ F: $(5 + \sqrt{2}, -2), (5 - \sqrt{2}, -2)$

c)
$$9x^2 + 4y^2 + 54x - 8y + 49 = 0$$
$$9(x^2 + 6x + \_\_) + 4(y^2 - 2y + \_\_) = -49$$
$$9(x^2 + 6x + 9) + 4(y^2 - 2y + 1) = -49 + 81 + 4$$
$$9(x+3)^2 + 4(y+1)^2 = 36$$
$$\frac{(x+3)^2}{4} + \frac{(y-1)^2}{9} = 1$$
C: $(-3, 1)$ V: $(-3, 4), (-3, -2)$
M: $(-5, 1), (-1, 1)$ F: $(-3, 1 + \sqrt{5}), (-3, 1 - \sqrt{5})$

d)
$$36x^2 + 64y^2 + 108x - 128y - 431 = 0$$
$$36(x^2 + 3x + \_\_) + 64(y^2 - 2y + \_\_) = 431$$
$$36\left(x^2 + 3x + \tfrac{9}{4}\right) + 64(y^2 - 2y + 1) = 431 + 81 + 64$$
$$\frac{36\left(x + \frac{3}{2}\right)^2}{576} + \frac{64(y-1)^2}{576} = \frac{576}{576}$$
$$\frac{\left(x + \frac{3}{2}\right)^2}{16} + \frac{(y-1)^2}{9} = 1$$
C: $\left(-\frac{3}{2}, 1\right)$ V: $\left(-\frac{11}{2}, 1\right), \left(\frac{5}{2}, 1\right)$
M: $\left(-\frac{3}{2}, 4\right), \left(-\frac{3}{2}, -2\right)$ F: $\left(-\frac{3}{2} + \sqrt{7}, 1\right), \left(-\frac{3}{2} - \sqrt{7}, 1\right)$

3. **a)**
$$\frac{(x+2)^2}{4} + \frac{(y-1)^2}{16} = 1$$
$$16\left(\frac{(x+2)^2}{4} + \frac{(y-1)^2}{16} = 1\right)$$
$$4(x+2)^2 + (y-1)^2 = 16$$
$$4(x^2 + 4x + 4) + (y^2 - 2y + 1) = 16$$
$$4x^2 + 16x + 16 + y^2 - 2y + 1 = 16$$
$$4x^2 + y^2 + 16x - 2y + 1 = 0$$

b)
$$\frac{(x-3)^2}{64} + \frac{(y+1)^2}{32} = 1$$
$$64\left(\frac{(x-3)^2}{64} + \frac{(y+1)^2}{32} = 1\right)$$
$$(x-3)^2 + 2(y+1)^2 = 64$$
$$(x^2 - 6x + 9) + 2(y^2 + 2y + 1) = 64$$
$$x^2 - 6x + 9 + 2y^2 + 4y + 2 = 64$$
$$x^2 + 2y^2 - 6x + 4y - 53 = 0$$

4. $4x^2 + 9y^2 = 36 \rightarrow \frac{x^2}{9} + \frac{y^2}{4} = 1;\ a = 3,\ b = 2;\ A = \pi ab = \pi(3)(2) = 6\pi$ square units

5. (units are million km) Major axis $= 146 + 152 = 298;\ a = \frac{298}{2} = 149,\ c = 152 - 149 = 3,\ b^2 = a^2 - c^2 = 149^2 - 3^3 = 22\,192$

Therefore $\frac{x^2}{149^2} + \frac{y^2}{22\,192} = 1 \rightarrow \frac{x^2}{22\,201} + \frac{y^2}{22\,192} = 1$ million km

6. $\frac{x^2}{25}+\frac{y^2}{9}=1$: $c^2=25-9=16 \rightarrow c=4 \rightarrow \frac{c}{a}=\frac{4}{5}=0.8$

$\frac{x^2}{36}+\frac{y^2}{16}=1$: $c^2=36-16=20 \rightarrow c=\sqrt{20} \rightarrow \frac{c}{a}=\frac{\sqrt{20}}{6}=0.745$

Since $0.745<0.8$, $\frac{x^2}{36}+\frac{y^2}{16}=1$ is closer to being a circle

7. $a=\frac{608\,000}{2}=304\,000$, $\frac{c}{a}=\frac{11}{200} \rightarrow \frac{11}{200}=\frac{c}{304\,000} \rightarrow c=16\,720$, Greatest distance $=304\,000+16\,720=320\,720$ km

8. $c=12,\ b=5,\ a^2=b^2+c^2=5^2+12^2=169 \rightarrow a=\sqrt{169}=13$; The distance travelled is $2a$, therefore $2\times 13=26$ metres

9. $a=25,\ c=20,\ b^2=a^2-c^2=25^2-20^2=225 \rightarrow b=\sqrt{225}=15$ metres

10. 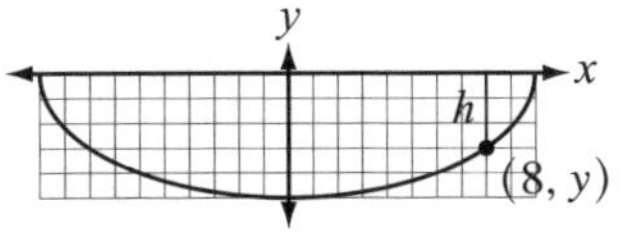

$\frac{x^2}{100}+\frac{y^2}{25}=1 \rightarrow \frac{64}{100}+\frac{y^2}{25}=1 \rightarrow \frac{y^2}{25}=\frac{36}{100} \rightarrow y^2=\frac{25\cdot 36}{100} \rightarrow y=\pm\frac{5\cdot 6}{10}=\pm 3$

Therefore $h=3$ metres

11. $a=30,\ b=20,\ \frac{x^2}{30^2}+\frac{y^2}{20^2}=1$; $x=\pm 10$ ft from centre, $\frac{10^2}{30^2}+\frac{y^2}{20^2}=1 \rightarrow y^2=\frac{3200}{9}$, $y=18.9$ feet high

$x=\pm 20$ ft from centre, $\frac{20^2}{30^2}+\frac{y^2}{20^2}=1 \rightarrow y^2=\frac{2000}{9}$, $y=14.9$ feet high

The heights every 10 feet are: 14.9 feet, 18.9 feet, 20 feet, 18.9 feet, 14.9 feet, 0 feet

12. If the endpoints are $(8,4)$ and $(-4,4)$, the centre is $\left(\frac{8-4}{2},4\right)=(2,4)$

The ellipse is $\frac{(x-2)^2}{a^2}+\frac{(y-4)^2}{b^2}=1$ and the semi major axis is $8-2=6$, therefore, $\frac{(x-2)^2}{36}+\frac{(y-4)^2}{b^2}=1$

But the graph goes through the origin, so $\frac{(0-2)^2}{36}+\frac{(0-4)^2}{b^2}=1 \rightarrow \frac{16}{b^2}=1-\frac{4}{36} \rightarrow b^2=18$, therefore $\frac{(x-2)^2}{36}+\frac{(y-4)^2}{18}=1$

13. 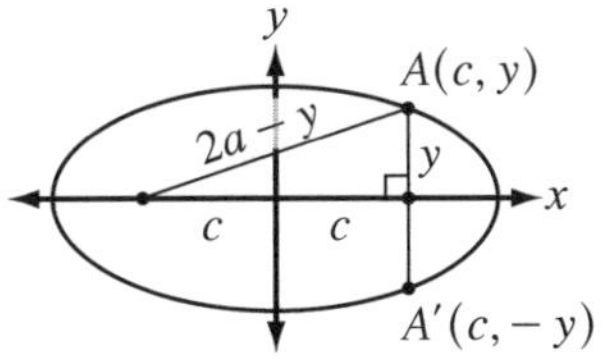

By definition of an ellipse, $y^2+(2c)^2=(2a-y)^2$

$\cancel{y^2}+4c^2=4a^2-4ay+\cancel{y^2}$

$4(a^2-b^2)=4a^2-4ay$

$\cancel{4a^2}-4b^2=\cancel{4a^2}-4ay$

$b^2=ay$

$y=\frac{b^2}{a}$

$AA'=2y$

$=2\left(\frac{b^2}{a}\right)$

$=\frac{2b^2}{a}$

8.5 Hyperbolas

1. **a)** $2a=12 \rightarrow a=6,\ 2b=20 \rightarrow b=10$, therefore $\frac{x^2}{36}-\frac{y^2}{100}=1$

b) $2a=6 \rightarrow a=3,\ c=5,\ b^2=c^2-a^2=5^2-3^2=16$, therefore $\frac{y^2}{9}-\frac{x^2}{16}=1$

c) $2b=10 \rightarrow b=5,\ c=\sqrt{70},\ a^2=c^2-b^2=70-25=45$, therefore $\frac{y^2}{45}-\frac{x^2}{25}=1$

d) $2b=14 \rightarrow b=7,\ c=\sqrt{200},\ a^2=c^2-b^2=200-49=151$, therefore $\frac{x^2}{151}-\frac{y^2}{49}=1$

2. **a)** $y=\pm\frac{b}{a}x,\ y=\frac{3}{5}x$ and $y=-\frac{3}{5}x$ **b)** $y=\pm\frac{a}{b}x,\ y=\frac{5}{3}x$ and $y=-\frac{5}{3}x$

c) $y=\frac{3}{5}x+c \rightarrow -1=\frac{3}{5}(5)+c \rightarrow c=-4 \rightarrow y=\frac{3}{5}x-4$; $y=-\frac{3}{5}x+c \rightarrow -1=-\frac{3}{5}(5)+c \rightarrow c=2 \rightarrow y=-\frac{3}{5}x+2$

d) $y=\frac{5}{3}x+c \rightarrow -1=\frac{5}{3}(3)+c \rightarrow c=-6 \rightarrow y=\frac{5}{3}x-6$; $y=-\frac{5}{3}x+c \rightarrow -1=-\frac{5}{3}(3)+c \rightarrow c=4 \rightarrow y=-\frac{5}{3}x+4$

3. **a)** $a=4,\ c=6,\ b^2=c^2-a^2=36-16=20 \rightarrow \frac{x^2}{16}-\frac{y^2}{20}=1$

b) $\frac{(y-4)^2}{a^2}-\frac{(x+2)^2}{b^2}=1,\ a=2,\ c=4,\ b^2=c^2-a^2=16-4=12 \rightarrow \frac{(y-4)^2}{4}-\frac{(x+2)^2}{12}=1,$

c) $C(0,2),\ a=2,\ \frac{(y-2)^2}{4}-\frac{x^2}{b^2}=1$, point$(\sqrt{5},-1)$, $\frac{(-1-2)^2}{4}-\frac{\sqrt{5}^2}{b^2}=1 \rightarrow b^2=4 \rightarrow \frac{(y-2)^2}{4}-\frac{x^2}{4}=1$

d) $2c=16 \rightarrow c=8$, Centre $\left(-2,\frac{12-4}{2}\right)=(-2,4)$, $\frac{8}{a}=\frac{4}{3} \rightarrow a=6,\ b^2=c^2-a^2=64-36=28 \rightarrow \frac{(y-4)^2}{36}-\frac{(x+2)^2}{28}=1$

e) $\frac{(x+1)^2}{4}-\frac{(y-3)^2}{16}=1$ or $\frac{(y-3)^2}{4}-\frac{(x+1)^2}{16}=1$

f) $\frac{(x-3)^2}{a^2}-\frac{(y+1)^2}{b^2}=1$ y-intercept $=-1$, $(0,-1)$, $\frac{(0-3)^2}{a^2}-\frac{(-1+1)^2}{b^2}=1 \rightarrow a^2=9$

x-intercept $=3+\frac{3\sqrt{5}}{2}$, $\left(3+\frac{3\sqrt{5}}{2},0\right)$, $\frac{\left(3+\frac{3\sqrt{5}}{2}-3\right)^2}{9}-\frac{(0+1)^2}{b^2}=1 \rightarrow b^2=4$; $\frac{(x-3)^2}{9}-\frac{(y+1)^2}{4}=1$

4. **a)** $4x^2 - y^2 + 8x - 4y - 4 = 0$

$4(x^2 + 2x + __) - (y^2 + 4y + __) = 4$

$4(x^2 + 2x + 1) - (y^2 + 4y + 4) = 4 + 4 - 4$

$4(x + 1)^2 - (y + 2)^2 = 4$

$(x + 1)^2 - \dfrac{(y + 2)^2}{4} = 1$

C: $(-1, -2)$, $a = 1, b = 2$

V: $(-1 \pm \sqrt{1}, -2) = (-2, -2), (0, -2)$

A: $y = \pm 2x + b$, through centre $(-1, -2)$

$-2 = 2(-1) + b \rightarrow b = 0 \rightarrow y = 2x$

$-2 = -2(-1) + b \rightarrow b = -4 \rightarrow y = -2x - 4$

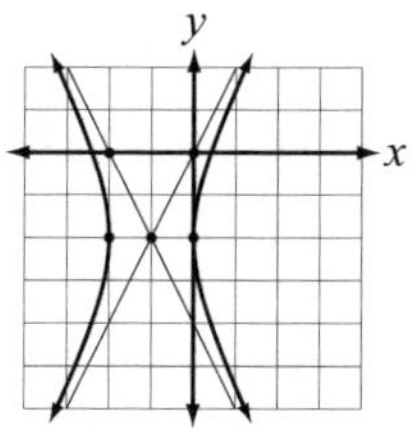
y
x

b) $x^2 - y^2 - 2x - 4y - 2 = 0$

$(x^2 - 2x + __) - (y^2 + 4y + __) = 2$

$(x^2 - 2x + 1) - (y^2 + 4y + 4) = 2 + 1 - 4$

$(x - 1)^2 - (y + 2)^2 = -1$

$(y + 2)^2 - (x - 1)^2 = 1$

C: $(1, -2)$, $a = 1, b = 1$

V: $(1, -2 \pm \sqrt{1}) = (1, -1), (1, -3)$

A: $y = \pm x + b$, through centre $(1, -2)$

$-2 = 1 + b \rightarrow b = -3 \rightarrow y = x - 3$

$-2 = -1 + b \rightarrow b = -1 \rightarrow y = -x - 1$

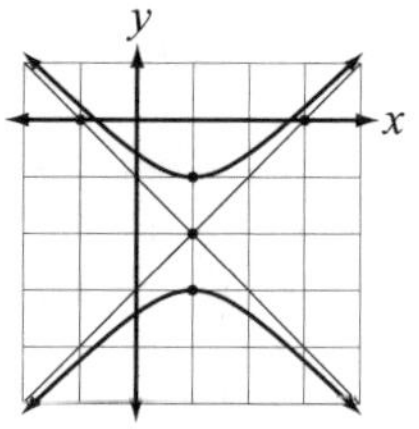
y
x

c) $4x^2 - y^2 - 16x - 4y + 8 = 0$

$4(x^2 - 4x + __) - (y^2 + 4y + __) = -8$

$4(x^2 - 4x + 4) - (y^2 + 4y + 4) = -8 + 16 - 4$

$4(x - 2)^2 - (y + 2)^2 = 4$

$(x - 2)^2 - \dfrac{(y + 2)^2}{4} = 1$

C: $(2, -2)$, $a = 1, b = 2$

V: $(2 \pm \sqrt{1}, -2) = (1, -2), (3, -2)$

A: $y = \pm 2x + b$, through centre $(2, -2)$

$-2 = 2(2) + b \rightarrow b = -6 \rightarrow y = 2x - 6$

$-2 = -2(2) + b \rightarrow b = 2 \rightarrow y = -2x + 2$

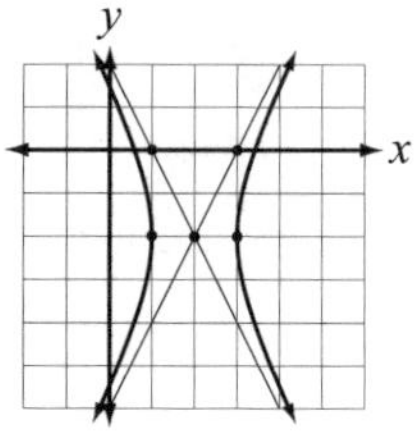
y
x

5. **a)** $\dfrac{(x + 2)^2}{4} - \dfrac{(y - 1)^2}{16} = 1 \rightarrow 16\left(\dfrac{(x + 2)^2}{4} - \dfrac{(y - 1)^2}{16} = 1\right) \rightarrow 4(x + 2)^2 - (y - 1)^2 = 16 \rightarrow$

$4(x^2 + 4x + 4) - (y^2 - 2y + 1) = 16 \rightarrow 4x^2 + 16x + 16 - y^2 + 2y - 1 = 16 \rightarrow 4x^2 - y^2 + 16x + 2y - 1 = 0$

b) $\dfrac{(y - 1)^2}{12} - \dfrac{(x + 2)^2}{18} = 1 \rightarrow 36\left(\dfrac{(y - 1)^2}{12} - \dfrac{(x + 2)^2}{18} = 1\right) \rightarrow 3(y - 1)^2 - 2(x + 2)^2 = 36 \rightarrow$

$3(y^2 - 2y + 1) - 2(x^2 + 4x + 4) = 36 \rightarrow 3y^2 - 6y + 3 - 2x^2 - 8x - 8 = 36 \rightarrow 2x^2 - 3y^2 + 8x + 6y + 41 = 0$

6. **a)** centre $(0, 0)$, $2a = 8 \rightarrow a = 4$, $c = 5$, $b^2 = c^2 - a^2 = 25 - 16 = 9 \rightarrow \dfrac{x^2}{16} - \dfrac{y^2}{9} = 1$

b) centre $(0, 0)$, $2a = 24 \rightarrow a = 12$, $c = 13$, $b^2 = c^2 - a^2 = 13^2 - 12^2 = 169 - 144 = 25 \rightarrow \dfrac{y^2}{144} - \dfrac{x^2}{25} = 1$

7. **a)** $y = \frac{2}{3}\sqrt{x^2 - 36} \rightarrow \frac{3}{2}y = \sqrt{x^2 - 36} \rightarrow \frac{9}{4}y^2 = x^2 - 36 \rightarrow 9y^2 = 4x^2 - 144 \rightarrow 4x^2 - 9y^2 = 144 \rightarrow \dfrac{x^2}{36} - \dfrac{y^2}{16} = 1$

Upper half of $\dfrac{x^2}{36} - \dfrac{y^2}{16} = 1$, $y \geq 0$

b) $x = -\frac{2}{3}\sqrt{y^2 - 36} \rightarrow \frac{3}{2}x = \sqrt{y^2 - 36} \rightarrow \frac{9}{4}x^2 = y^2 - 36 \rightarrow 9x^2 = 4y^2 - 144 \rightarrow 4y^2 - 9x^2 = 144 \rightarrow \dfrac{y^2}{36} - \dfrac{x^2}{16} = 1$

Left half of $\dfrac{y^2}{36} - \dfrac{x^2}{16} = 1$, $x \leq 0$

8. **a)** Centre $\left(1, \dfrac{8 - 2}{2}\right) = (1, 3)$, $2a = 8 \rightarrow a = 4$

$\dfrac{(y - 3)^2}{16} - \dfrac{(x - 1)^2}{b^2} = 1$, $2c = 10 \rightarrow c = 5$

$b^2 = c^2 - a^2 = 25 - 16 = 9 \rightarrow \dfrac{(y - 3)^2}{16} - \dfrac{(x - 1)^2}{9} = 1$

b)

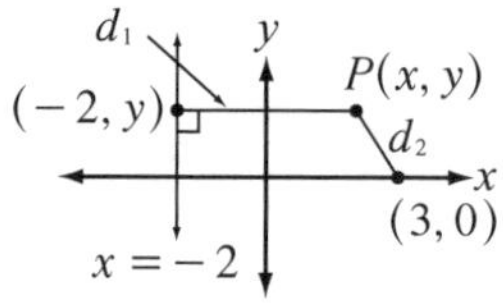
d1
y
(−2, y)
P(x, y)
d2
x
(3, 0)
x = −2

$d_2 = \frac{3}{2}d_1$

$\frac{3}{2}\sqrt{(x + 2)^2 + (y - y)^2} = \sqrt{(x - 3)^2 + y^2}$

$\frac{9}{4}(x + 2)^2 = (x - 3)^2 + y^2$

$9x^2 + 36x + \cancel{36} = 4x^2 - 24x + \cancel{36} + 4y^2$

$5x^2 - 4y^2 + 60x = 0$

9. Centre of Earth to vertex: $4000 + 6000 = 10\,000$ miles, asymptote $y = \dfrac{b}{a}x = \dfrac{x}{4} \rightarrow b = \dfrac{a}{4} = \dfrac{10\,000}{4} = 2500$

$\dfrac{x^2}{10\,000^2} - \dfrac{y^2}{2500^2} = 1$

10. $2c = 52 \rightarrow c = 26$, $2a = 48 \rightarrow a = 24$, $b^2 = c^2 - a^2 = 26^2 - 24^2 = 100$, therefore $\dfrac{x^2}{24^2} - \dfrac{y^2}{100} = 1 \rightarrow \dfrac{x^2}{576} - \dfrac{y^2}{100} = 1$

11. $2a = 24 \rightarrow a = 12$, $c = 20$, $b^2 = c^2 - a^2 = 20^2 - 12^2 = 256$ The equation is $\dfrac{x^2}{144} - \dfrac{y^2}{256} = 1$

12. $c = 100$, $2a = 160 \rightarrow a = 80$, $b^2 = c^2 - a^2 = 100^2 - 80^2 = 3600 \rightarrow \dfrac{x^2}{6400} - \dfrac{y^2}{3600} = 1$, with $y = 180$

$\dfrac{x^2}{6400} - \dfrac{180^2}{3600} = 1 \rightarrow \dfrac{x^2}{6400} = \dfrac{9}{1} \rightarrow x^2 = 6400 \times 9 \rightarrow x = 240 \rightarrow (240, 180)$ km

13.

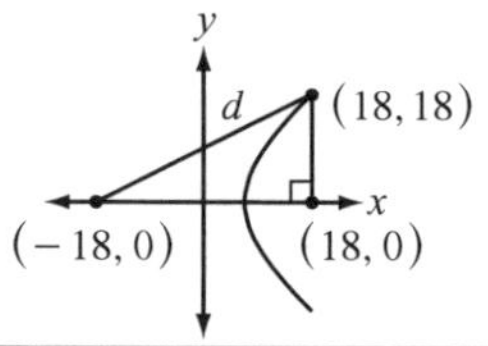
y
d
(18, 18)
x
(−18, 0)
(18, 0)

By Pythagorean theorem $d = \sqrt{36^2 + 18^2} = \sqrt{1620} = 18\sqrt{5}$

$2a = 18\sqrt{5} - 18 \rightarrow a = 9\sqrt{5} - 9$

Vertex is $(9\sqrt{5} - 9, 0) \approx (11.1, 0)$

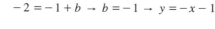

14. y; $(-x, 40)$; $(x, 40)$; x; $(-24, 0)$; $(24, 0)$; $(-50, -80)$; $(50, -80)$

$\frac{x^2}{24^2} - \frac{y^2}{b^2} = 1$, use either point $(-50, -80)$ or $(-50, 80)$ and solve for b^2.

$\frac{(-50)^2}{24^2} - \frac{(-80)^2}{b^2} = 1 \rightarrow b^2 = 1916.01$

$\frac{x^2}{576} - \frac{y^2}{1916.01} = 1 \rightarrow$ at top $(x, 40)$: $\frac{x^2}{576} - \frac{40^2}{1916.01} = 1 \rightarrow x = 32.51$

Diameter $= 2x = 2 \times 32.51 = 65.02$ m

8.6 Chapter Review

1. **a)** parabola **b)** ellipse **c)** hyperbola **d)** parabola **e)** a point (circle radius zero) **f)** ellipse **g)** parabola **h)** circle **i)** hyperbola **j)** circle **k)** hyperbola **l)** ellipse **m)** circle **n)** two intersecting lines, $y = \pm x$

2. **a)** $x^2 + Dx + \_\_\_ + y^2 + Ey + \_\_\_ = -F$

$x^2 + Dx + \frac{D^2}{4} + y^2 + Ey + \frac{E^2}{4} = -F + \frac{D^2}{4} + \frac{E^2}{4}$

$\left(x + \frac{D}{2}\right)^2 + \left(y + \frac{E}{2}\right)^2 = \frac{D^2 + E^2}{4} - F$

$C\left(-\frac{D}{2}, -\frac{E}{2}\right)$, $r = \sqrt{\frac{D^2 + E^2}{4} - F}$

b) Circle: $\frac{D^2 + E^2}{4} - F > 0$

Point: $\frac{D^2 + E^2}{4} - F = 0$

No Graph: $\frac{D^2 + E^2}{4} - F < 0$

3. **a)** *iii* **b)** *iv* **c)** *v* **d)** *i* **e)** *ii*

4. **a)** circle **b)** ellipse **c)** parabola **d)** hyperbola **e)** hyperbola **f)** circle **g)** ellipse **h)** parabola **i)** parabola **j)** ellipse

5. $(x - 2y)(x + 2y) = 16 \rightarrow x^2 - 4y^2 = 16 \rightarrow \frac{x^2}{16} - \frac{y^2}{4} = 1$, therefore the equation is a hyperbola

6. A parabola that opens left or right must have $A = 0$, $C \neq 0$, and $D \neq 0$. To open to the left, $C \times D > 0$. Axis of symmetry on x-axis must have $E = 0$, the value of F could have any value (no restrictions).

7. $d_1 = 2d_2$ (If d_1 is twice as far away as d_2, multiply d_2 by 2, not d_1)

$\sqrt{x^2 + (y-2)^2} = 2\sqrt{(x-3)^2 + (y-2)^2}$ (square both sides)

$x^2 + y^2 - 4y + 4 = 4(x^2 - 6x + 9 + y^2 - 4y + 4)$

$3x^2 - 24x + 3y^2 - 12y = -48$

$(x^2 - 8x + \_\_\_) + (y^2 - 4y + \_\_\_) = -16$

$(x^2 - 8x + 16) + (y^2 - 4y + 4) = -16 + 16 + 4$

$(x-4)^2 + (y-2)^2 = 4$ is a circle with centre $(4, 2)$, radius $= 2$

8.

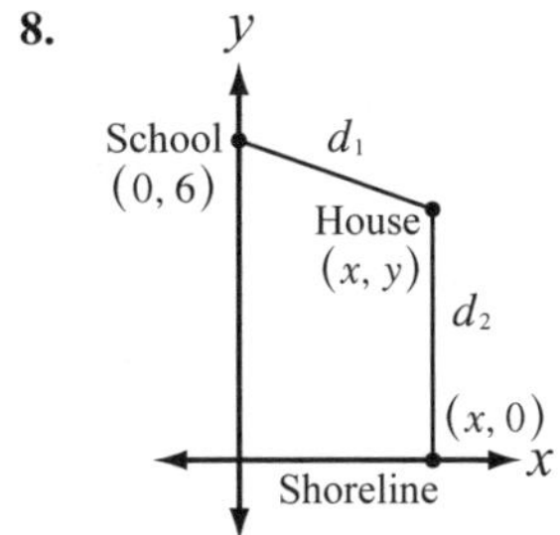

$2d_1 = d_2$

$2\sqrt{(x-0)^2 + (y-6)^2} = \sqrt{(x-x)^2 + (y-0)^2}$

$4(x^2 + y^2 - 12y + 36) = y^2$

$4x^2 + 4y^2 - 48y + 144 = y^2$

$4x^2 + 3(y^2 - 16y + 64) = -144 + 192$

$4x^2 + 3(y-8)^2 = 48$

$\frac{x^2}{12} + \frac{(y-8)^2}{16} = 1$ Therefore the conic is an ellipse, with centre $(0, 8)$.

8.7 Multiple Choice Questions

Answers

1. d	**5.** a	**9.** b	**13.** c	**17.** b	**21.** d	**25.** b	**29.** b	**33.** b	**37.** c	**41.** d	**45.** b	**49.** d
2. c	**6.** d	**10.** d	**14.** a	**18.** a	**22.** c	**26.** c	**30.** a	**34.** a	**38.** b	**42.** b	**46.** a	**50.** c
3. b	**7.** d	**11.** a	**15.** d	**19.** a	**23.** d	**27.** b	**31.** c	**35.** a	**39.** d	**43.** c	**47.** c	
4. d	**8.** c	**12.** b	**16.** d	**20.** d	**24.** c	**28.** a	**32.** a	**36.** a	**40.** c	**44.** c	**48.** b	

Solutions to Multiple Choice Questions

1. $x - 2 = 0 \rightarrow x = 2$, $y + 4 = 0 \rightarrow y = -4$, answer is d.

2. $b^2 = 16 \rightarrow b = 4$, then multiply by $2 \rightarrow 8$, answer is c.

3. $x - 2 = 0 \rightarrow x = 2$, answer is b.

4. $y + 1 = 0 \rightarrow y = -1$, answer is d.

5. $4x^2 - 9y^2 = 36 \rightarrow \frac{x^2}{9} - \frac{y^2}{4} = 1$, asymptote $y = \pm\frac{b}{a}x \rightarrow y = \pm\frac{\sqrt{4}}{\sqrt{9}}x \rightarrow y = \pm\frac{2}{3}x$, answer is a.

6. Circle $(x - h)^2 + (y - k)^2 = r^2 \rightarrow (x - 0)^2 + (y - 2)^2 = 4^2 \rightarrow x^2 + (y - 2)^2 = 16$, answer is d.

7. $\frac{(x-2)^2}{9} + \frac{(y+3)^2}{25} = 1$, centre $(2, -3)$, $b^2 = 9 \rightarrow b = \pm 3$, therefore $2 - 3 = -1$ and $2 + 3 = 5$, domain: $-1 \le x \le 5$, answer is d.

8. $16(x-2)^2 + 25(y+3)^2 = 400 \rightarrow \frac{(x-2)^2}{25} + \frac{(y+3)^2}{16} = 1$, centre is $(2, -3)$, $b^2 = 16 \rightarrow b = \pm 4$

therefore $-3 - 4 = -7$ and $-3 + 4 = 1$, range is $-7 \le y \le 1$, answer is c.

9. The y-intercepts have $x = 0$, therefore $16(0)^2 + 9y^2 = 144 \rightarrow y^2 = \frac{144}{9} \rightarrow y = \pm\frac{12}{3} = \pm 4$, answer is b.

10. If both squared terms are positive and the coefficients are equal, the equation is a circle, answer is d.

11. This is a hyperbola going up and down, therefore the vertices are $(0, \pm 2)$, answer is a.

12. Equation of asymptote is $y = \pm\frac{a}{b}x \rightarrow y = \pm\frac{\sqrt{9}}{\sqrt{4}} \rightarrow y = \pm\frac{3}{2}x$, therefore the slope is $\pm\frac{3}{2}$, answer is b.

13. Conjugate axis is perpendicular to the transverse axis, therefore $b^2 = 16 \rightarrow b = \pm 4$, length is $4 \times 2 = 8$.

14. Centre $(-1, 2)$ with vertices $\pm\sqrt{9} = \pm 3$ units from centre, or $(-1, -1), (-1, 5)$, therefore the line is $x = -1$, answer is a.

15. A must be a positive value not equal to 3, answer is d.

16. If $A = -C$, $A \neq 0$, then this is a rectangular hyperbola, answer is d.

17. $x^2 + y^2 + 4x - 2y = 4 \rightarrow (x^2 + 4x + \_\_) + (y^2 - 2y + \_\_) = 4 \rightarrow (x^2 + 4x + 4) + (y^2 - 2y + 1) = 4 + 4 + 1 \rightarrow$

$(x+2)^2 + (y-1)^2 = 9$, $r = 3$, answer is b.

18. $x = a(y+1)^2 + 2$, with $(0, 1) \rightarrow 0 = a(1+1)^2 + 2 \rightarrow 4a = -2 \rightarrow a = -\frac{1}{2}$, therefore $x = -\frac{1}{2}(y+1)^2 + 2$, answer is a.

19. $2y^2 + 3x + 4y + 14 = 0 \rightarrow 3x + 14 = -2y^2 - 4y \rightarrow 3x + 14 = -2(y^2 + 2y + \_\_) \rightarrow 3x + 14 - 2 = -2(y^2 + 2y + 1) \rightarrow$

$3x = -2(y+1)^2 - 12 \rightarrow x = -\frac{2}{3}(y+1)^2 - 4$, vertex is $(-4, -1)$, answer is a.

20. $y = 2x^2 - 12x + 20 \rightarrow y - 20 = 2(x^2 - 6x + \_\_) \rightarrow y - 20 + 18 = 2(x^2 - 6x + 9) \rightarrow y = 2(x-3)^2 + 2$, vertex $(3, 2)$, answer is d

21. $(y-1)^2 - (x+3)^2 = a^2$, $a = 4 \rightarrow (y-1)^2 - (x+3)^2 = 16$, answer is d.

22. $y = \pm\frac{b}{a}x + c \rightarrow y = \pm\frac{4}{3}x + c$, centre $(0, -1)$, $-1 = \pm\frac{4}{3}(0) + c \rightarrow c = -1 \rightarrow y = \pm\frac{4}{3}x - 1$, answer is c.

23. Distance from $(3, -1)$ to $(-1, 2)$ is $d = \sqrt{(3+1)^2 + (-1-2)^2} = \sqrt{25} = 5$, therefore $(x-3)^2 + (y+1)^2 = 5^2$, answer is d.

24. $Ax^2 - By^2 = 9 \rightarrow \frac{x^2}{\frac{9}{A}} - \frac{y^2}{\frac{9}{B}} = 1$, transverse axis length is $2\sqrt{\frac{9}{A}} = \frac{6}{A}$, answer is c.

25. $4x^2 + 9y^2 = A \rightarrow \frac{x^2}{\frac{A}{4}} - \frac{y^2}{\frac{A}{9}} = 1$, $\frac{A}{4}$ is larger, therefore the major axis is $2\sqrt{\frac{A}{4}} = \sqrt{A}$, answer is b.

26. If the major axis is horizontal, then $A < B$; to be on the x-axis, $C = 0$, answer is c.

27. To be a hyperbola, $A > 0$, $B < 0$ or $A < 0$, $B > 0$. To be on the x-axis, $A > 0$, answer is b.

28. To have a horizontal axis of symmetry, $A = 0$, $C \neq 0$, $D \neq 0$, answer is a.

29. To be a parabola opening up or down, $A \neq 0$, $B = 0$, $E \neq 0$. To open down, $AE > 0$, answer is b.

30. To be a parabola opening up or down, $A \neq 0$, $B = 0$, $E \neq 0$, vertex on the y-axis $D = 0$, opens down $AE > 0$, answer is a.

31. $4y^2 - 9x^2 - 54x - 8y - 113 = 0 \rightarrow 4(y^2 - 2y + \_\_) - 9(x^2 + 6x + \_\_) = 113 \rightarrow$

$4(y^2 - 2y + 1) - 9(x^2 + 6x + 9) = 113 + 4 - 81 \rightarrow 4(y-1)^2 - 9(x+3)^2 = 36 \rightarrow \frac{(y-1)^2}{9} - \frac{(x+3)^2}{4} = 1$, answer is c.

32. $2y^2 + x + 4y + 5 = 0 \rightarrow x + 5 = -2y^2 - 4y \rightarrow x + 5 = -2(y^2 + 2y + \_\_) \rightarrow x + 5 - 2 = -2(y^2 + 2y + 1) \rightarrow$

$x = -2(y+1)^2 - 3$, answer is a.

33. $144\left(\frac{(x+2)^2}{16} - \frac{(y-1)^2}{9} = 1\right) \rightarrow 9(x^2 + 4x + 4) - 16(y^2 - 2y + 1) = 144 \rightarrow 9x^2 + 36x + 36 - 16y^2 + 32y - 16 = 144 \rightarrow$

$9x^2 - 16y^2 + 36x + 32y - 124 = 0$, answer is b.

34. $400\left(\frac{(x+3)^2}{25}+\frac{(y-4)^2}{16}=1\right) \to 16(x^2+6x+9)+25(y^2-8y+16)=400 \to 16x^2+96x+144+25y^2-200y+400=400 \to$ $16x^2+25y^2+96x-200y+144=0$, answer is a.

35. $\frac{1}{B}$ must be greater than $\frac{1}{A}$, and B must be less than 0, therefore $A<0$, answer is c.

36. If $(2,2)$ and $(2,-6)$ are vertices, then $(2,-2)$ is the centre with $a=4$, therefore $\frac{(x-2)^2}{b^2}+\frac{(y+2)^2}{16}=1$, substitute $\frac{(0-2)^2}{b^2}+\frac{(-2+2)^2}{16}=1 \to b^2=4$, answer is a.

37. $4x^2+2y^2+8x-12y+F=0 \to 4(x^2+2x+\_\_)+2(y^2-6y+\_\_)+F=0 \to 4(x^2+2x+1)+2(y^2-6y+9)+F=4+18 \to$ $4(x+1)^2+2(y-3)^2+F=22$. The right side must have a positive value to be an ellipse, therefore $F<22$, answer is c.

38. $y=\pm\frac{\sqrt{4}}{\sqrt{9}}x+b \to y=\pm\frac{2}{3}x+b$, centre $(-3,1) \to 1=\frac{2}{3}(-3)+b \to b=3,\ y=\frac{2}{3}x+3$, answer is b.

39. $x^2+y^2-6x+4y-12=0 \to (x^2-6x+\_\_)+(y^2+4y+\_\_)=12 \to (x^2-6x+9)+(y^2+4y+4)=12+9+4 \to$ $(x-3)^2+(y+2)^2=25$, centre $(3,-2)$, with radius 5, 5 units up for $(3,-2)$ is $(3,3)$, answer is d.

40. In a rectangular hyperbola going up and down, the only asymptotes are $y=\pm x$, therefore the point must be between $45°$ and $135°$ or $225°$ and $315°$. The only point that fits is $(2,-5)$, answer is c.

41. $\frac{x^2}{60^2}+\frac{20^2}{40^2}=1 \to x^2=2700 \to x=30\sqrt{3}$, length is $2x=60\sqrt{3}$, answer is d.

42. If $y^2-x^2=a^2$ has point $(3,6)$, then $36-9=a^2 \to a^2=27 \to y^2-x^2=27$, with point $(-5,k) \to k^2-(-5)^2=27 \to$ $k^2=52 \to k=\sqrt{52}=7.21$, answer is b.

43. If endpoints are $(-4,-2)$ and $(8,-2)$, then the centre is $(2,-2)$ with $a=6$, therefore $\frac{(x-2)^2}{36}-\frac{(y+2)^2}{b^2}=1$ Asymptote is $y=\frac{b}{6}x+c$, but slope is $\frac{4}{3}$, therefore $\frac{b}{6}=\frac{4}{3} \to b=8$, so $\frac{(x-2)^2}{36}-\frac{(y+2)^2}{64}=1$, answer is c.

44. The length of the major axis of $\frac{x^2}{9}+\frac{y^2}{4}=1$ is $2\sqrt{9}=6$, so $\frac{x^2}{k}-y^2=1$ must have a transverse axis length of 8, therefore $2\sqrt{k}=8 \to k=16$, answer is c.

45. $x=a(y+2)^2+8 \to 0=-a(0+2)^2+8 \to 4a=-8 \to a=-2,\ x=-2(y+2)^2+8$, answer is b.

46. If the parabola has a vertex $(-3,1)$ and passes through points $(-7,-6)$ and $(1,-6)$, then the parabola must open down. $y=a(x+3)^2+1$, use either point to solve for a, $-6=a(1+3)^2+1 \to 16a=-7 \to a=-\frac{7}{16}$, answer is a.

47. Open to the right gives $x=a(y+1)^2+3$, substitute $7=a(2+1)^2+3 \to 9a=4 \to a=\frac{4}{9}$, answer is c.

48. If the vertices are $(2,3)$ and $(2,-5)$, then the centre is $(2,-1)$ with $a=4$, therefore $\frac{(y+1)^2}{16}-\frac{(x-2)^2}{b^2}=1$, with asymptote slope $\frac{4}{b}$ but given slope is $\frac{2}{3}$, therefore $\frac{4}{b}=\frac{2}{3} \to b=6$, $\frac{(y+1)^2}{16}-\frac{(x-2)^2}{36}=1$, answer is b.

49. The perpendicular bisector line from $(2,0)$ and $(8,0)$ is the line $x=5$. The perpendicular to the tangent at $(0,4)$ is the line $y=4$. Therefore, the centre of the circle is $(5,4)$, with radius 5, so $(x-5)^2+(y-4)^2=25$, answer is d.

50. If the vertices are $(-3,-1)$ and $(-3,5)$, then the centre is $(-3,2)$, with $a=3$, therefore $(y-2)^2-(x+3)^2=9$, answer is c.